Communications
in Computer and Information Science   157

T0074226

K. R. Venugopal   L. M. Patnaik (Eds.)

Computer Networks and Intelligent Computing

5th International Conference
on Information Processing, ICIP 2011
Bangalore, India, August 5-7, 2011
Proceedings

 Springer

Volume Editors

K. R. Venugopal
University Visvesvaraya
College of Engineering
Bangalore, India
E-mail: venugopalkr@gmail.com

L. M. Patnaik
Defence Institute of Advanced Technology
Pune, India
E-mail: lalitblr@gmail.com

ISSN 1865-0929   e-ISSN 1865-0937
ISBN 978-3-642-22785-1   e-ISBN 978-3-642-22786-8
DOI 10.1007/978-3-642-22786-8
Springer Heidelberg Dordrecht London New York

Library of Congress Control Number: 2011932983

CR Subject Classification (1998): I.2, C.2, H.4, H.3, I.4, I.5

Typesetting: Camera-ready by author, data conversion by Scientific Publishing Services, Chennai, India

Printed on acid-free paper

Springer is part of Springer Science+Business Media (www.springer.com)

Preface

This volume of *Communications in Computer Information Science* contains the proceedings of the 5th International Conference on Information Processing (ICIP 2011) held in Bangalore, India, August 5-7, 2011. ICIP 2011 was fortunate to have some of the world's leading researchers as plenary and invited speakers in the theme areas of the conference. This gave an opportunity to the delegates and participants to interact with the best minds for inspiration and guidance to address some of the challenging interdisciplinary problems.

ICIP 2011 successfully attracted over 514 submissions. Through rigorous peer reviews, 86 high-quality papers were recommended by the international Program Committee to be accepted and included in CCIS 157. ICIP conferences are one of the first series of international conferences on information processing that aptly focus on the tools and techniques for the development of information systems.

Following the success of the past four ICIP events, ICIP 2011 made good progress in the analysis and design of newly developed methods in the fields of pattern recognition, artificial intelligence and image processing, bio-computing, distributed systems, software engineering, wireless networks, security aspects in computer networks, signal processing and hardware synthesis, optimization techniques, data mining and information processing. The conference featured several keynote addresses in the areas of advanced information processing tools. These areas have been recognized as one of the key technologies poised to shape modern society in the next decade.

On behalf of the Organizing Committee, we would like to acknowledge the support from sponsors who helped in one way or another to achieve our goals for the conference. We wish to express our appreciation to Springer for publishing the proceedings of ICIP 2011. We also wish to acknowledge the dedication and commitment of the CCIS editorial staff. We would like to thank the authors for submitting their work, as well as the Technical Program Committee members and reviewers for their enthusiasm, time, and expertise. The invaluable help of members from the Organizing Committee and volunteers in setting up and maintaining the online submission systems, assigning the papers to the reviewers, and preparing the camera-ready version of the proceedings is highly appreciated. We would like to thank them personally for making ICIP 2011 a success.

August 2011

Venugopal K.R.
L.M. Patnaik

Organization

The 5th International Conference on Information Processing (ICIP 2011) was held in Bangalore, India and was organized by, the Society of Information Processing, Bangalore, India.

General Chair

L.M. Patnaik — Defence Institute of Advanced Technology (Deemed University), Girinagar, Pune, India

Program Chair

Venugopal K.R. — University Visvesvaraya College of Engineering, Bangalore University, Bangalore, India

General Co-chairs

S.S. Iyengar — Lousiana State University, USA
M. Palaniswami — University of Melbourne, Australia
Erol Gelenbee — Imperial College, UK

Advisory Committee

R.L. Kashyap — Purdue University, USA
Dharma P. Aggarwal — University of Cincinnati, USA
M. Vidya Sagar — University of Texas, Dallas, USA

Program Committee

David Kahaner — Association of Independent Information Professionals, Japan
P. Sreenivasa Kumar — Indian Institute of Technology, Madras, India
Sajal K. Das — University of Texas, Arlington, USA
Sharad Purohit — Center for Development of Advanced Copmuting, India
K. Sivarajan — Tejas Networks, India
Kentaro Toyama — Microsoft, India
Vittal S. Rao — National Science Foundation, USA
Rajkumar Buyya — University of Melbourne, Australia
B.P. Sinha — Indian Statistical Institute, Kolkata, India

Ram Mohan Rao Kotagiri   University of Melbourne, Australia
Rajeev Shorey   General Motors, India
Asok K. Talukdar   Indian Institute of International Business,
   India
Dinesh K. Anvekar   Honeywell, Bangalore, India
Bhanu Prasad   Florida Agricultural and Mechanical
   University, USA
M. Srinivas   Mentor Graphics, India
Rajib Mall   Indian Institute of Technology, Kharagpur,
   India
Bharat Jayaraman   University of Buffalo, USA
J. Mohan Kumar   University of Texas, Arlington, USA
Tomio Hirata   Nagoya University, Japan
Takao Nishizeki   Tohoku University, Japan
G. Shivakumar   Indian Institute of Technology, Mumbai,
   India
P. Raveendran   University of Malaysia, Malaysia
K. Chandrasekaran   National Institute of Technology,
   Karnataka, India
Sneha Kasera   University of Utah, USA
Bhabani P. Sinha   Indian Statistical Institute, Kolkata, India
Francis Lau   University of Hong Kong, Hong Kong
P. Ramaswamy   University of Essex, UK
Nalini Venkatasubramanian   University of Illinois, USA
Suresh M.   University of York, UK
Teo Yong M.   National University of Singapore, Singapore

Organizing Committee

P. Deepa Shenoy   University Visvesvaraya College of Engineering
K.B. Raja   University Visvesvaraya College of Engineering
K. Suresh Babu   University Visvesvaraya College of Engineering
Vibha L.   B.N.M. Institute of Technology
S.H. Manjula   University Visvesvaraya College of Engineering
Sujatha D.N.   B.M. Sreenivasaiah College of Engineering
Thriveni J.   University Visvesvaraya College of Engineering
K.G. Srinivasa   M.S. Ramaiah Institute of Technology
Prashanth C.R.   Vemana Institute of Technology
Ramachandra A.C.   Alpha College of Engineering
Shaila K.   Vivekananda Institute of Technology
Srikantaiah K.C.   S.J.B. Institute of Technology
Kiran K.   University Visvesvaraya College of Engineering
Sivasankari H.   A.M.C. College of Engineering and
   Management
ShivaPrakash T.   Vijaya Vittala Institute of Technology
Pushpa C.N.   University Visvesvaraya College of Engineering

Thippeswamy B.M.	Sambraham Institute of Technology
Viswanath Hullipad	Sambraham Institute of Technology
Vidya A.	Vivekananda Institute of Technology
Girish K.	B.M. Sreenivasaiah College of Engineering
Nalini L.	University Visvesvaraya College of Engineering

Sponsoring Institutions

Technically Sponsored   Defence Institute of Advanced Studies (DIAT), Pune, India

Technically Co-sponsored   University Visvesvaraya College of Engineering, Bangalore University, Bangalore, India

IEEE-UVCE, India

Alpha College of Engineering, Bangalore, India

Vijaya Vittala Institute of Technology, Bangalore, India

Table of Contents

Section I: Data Mining

Section II: Web Mining

Section III: Artificial Intelligence

Section IV: Soft Computing

Section V: Software Engineering

Section VI: Computer Communication Networks

Section VII: Wireless Networks

Section VIII: Distributed Systems and Storage Networks

Section IX: Signal Processing

Section X: Image Processing and Pattern Recognition

Interestingness Analysis of Semantic Association Mining in Medical Images

Saritha S. and Santhosh Kumar G.

Department of Computer Science, Cochin University of Science and Technology,
Kochi.
{sarithas.sarithas,sancochin}@gmail.com

Abstract. Medical images provide rich information and are repositories of implicit knowledge, which can be mined effectively. Diagnosis rules, new and established ones can be revealed and verified from the patterns existing in a medical image. In this paper, the spatial patterns existing in medical images are mined to obtain association rules of the diagnosis rules' category. The semantics of the association rules obtained are highly improved by introducing the concept of fuzziness into the spatial relationships existing between the anatomical structures. The utility of the association rules extracted is analyzed through the interestingness measures computed, and it is thereby concluded that the rules mined are highly relevant.

Keywords: Association Rule mining, Image Mining, Interestingness Measures, Semantic Mining, Spatial Pattern, Spatial Relationship.

1 Introduction

The incredible increase in the amount of image collection has led to the evolvement of image mining as a major field of data mining. Image mining deals with the extraction of implicit knowledge, image data relationship or other patterns not explicitly stored in the image databases. It is an interdisciplinary endeavor that essentially draws upon proficiency in computer vision, image processing, image retrieval, data mining, machine learning, database and artificial intelligence[1]. The glory of image mining lies in the fact that it explores image meanings, as per human insight and detects relevant patterns in images or relations between numerous images in the archive. The various types of image archive consist of satellite images, medical images and photographs. Among these, the medical images are of numerous types like CT images, ECT images, MR images and so on.

Concepts gained from medical images are very much powerful as they have copious interpretations associated with them. This is inherent on the features of the medical images. Features constitute the visual properties of an image as well as its semantics. The competence of image mining is deeply rooted in the extracted features of the images. The features range from the syntatic features like color, shape and texture in the pixel level, spatial relationship features in

K.R. Venugopal and L.M. Patnaik (Eds.): ICIP 2011, CCIS 157, pp. 1–10, 2011.

the object level and semantic features described using ontology, depending on the domain under consideration.

The different paradigms of image mining are image classification, image clustering and image association mining. Image classification and clustering [2] are the supervised and unsupervised classification of images into appropriate groups respectively. Association mining of images involves extraction of features from images as relationships between the objects/scenes in the images, identifying the interesting/frequent pattern existing in the image set and generating knowledge.

Spatial association mining was first introduced in architectural images by Hsu and Lee through Viewpoint Miner [3]. Also a different approach to perform the same task on simple images is given by [4],[5]. Recently there has been efficient association rule based methods to support medical image diagnosis of mammograms [6]. Association rule based mining of medical images is used to validate the diagnosis in [7]. However, there has been no attempt to perform a spatial association mining in medical images to the best of our knowledge up till date. Implicit spatial information in medical images is highly critical for interpretation of the image, and association rules mined from medical images will aid us in concluding to an interesting spatial relationship existing between the structures existing in images.

The remaining of the paper is organized as follows. Section 2 introduces the architecture of the proposed system and also describes the different steps involved in the process. Section 3 outlines the implementation details and interprets the significance of the diagnosis rules mined. In Section 4 the paper is concluded.

2   System Description

The proposed system here is based on the relationship existing between the objects in an image. This type of feature which describes each object in the scene/image with respect to each other is termed the spatial relationship feature. Spatial relationship features are devised based on how humans differentiate one spatial situation from another or identify the spatial situations as same.

Medical imagery contains images of human anatomical structures. It is evident that there exists a defined spatial relationship between the anatomical structures for normal situations. Of course, the spatial relationships deviate when there is an anomaly. The medical advisors or the expert systems read the spatial deviation exhibited by anatomical structures for diagnostic purposes. The readability of spatial relationships between certain objects is highly prominent, where as the readability of spatial relationships between some other objects is ambiguous and if missed out will result in erroneous diagnosis. Therefore it is highly necessary to form spatial association rules of the form antecedent $\rightarrow$ consequent, where (i) antecedent contains spatial patterns of anatomical structures and consequent contains the anomaly description or diagnosis result or (ii) antecedent contains spatial patterns between prominent structures and consequent contains spatial patterns between ambiguous structures. This can be achieved by mining the relevant spatial relationship pattern existing in the medical image archive.

In the proposed system, the spatial relationships existing between the anatomical structures in medical images are defined by means of fuzzy set theory [8], so that the knowledge mined is more realistic and adaptable. Fuzzy set approach provides a measure for imprecise spatial representation, and also the computational representation associated with it is relatively simple. The fuzzy spatial relationship features of the structures are then mined to identify the significant pattern and thus generate characteristic rules which also exhibit fuzziness.

The medical images considered here are MRI scans of the brain. The overall design of the proposed scheme can be depicted using the block diagram as shown in Fig. 1.

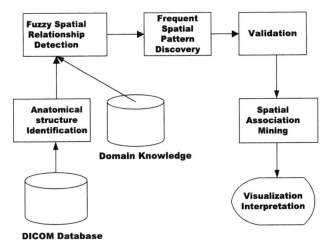

Fig. 1. Design of the proposed system

2.1   Anatomical Structure Identification

MRI scan consists of sagittal renderings, coronal and axial slices. The structures identified in each category of slices are different. The axial slices of the MRI scan are considered here for experiments. A sample of the MRI axial scan is shown in Fig. 2. A few anatomical structures like Caudate Nucleus (CN), Thalamus (TH), Lateral Ventricle (LV) and Putamen (PU) are marked in the figure. The right hemisphere of the brain is normal, whereas the left hemisphere shows and anomaly. It is evident from the figure that the spatial relationship existing between the anatomical structures in normal and pathological situations is different. Spatial patterns that deviate from the normal situation point towards an anomaly.

The MRI slice has to be segmented to identify the anatomical structures. The step involved in segmenting the images is as in Fig. 3.

We can identify different anatomical structures in the MRI images. Some of the anatomical structures identified after the segmentation process is RPU, RLV, RTH, RCN, LPU, LLV, LTH, LCN etc. The following Table 1 summarizes the MRI images after anatomical structure identification. The Col. I of the table

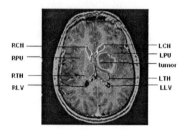

Fig. 2. Axial slice of a MRI brain image

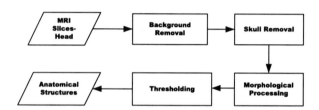

Fig. 3. Anatomical Structure Identification Process

Table 1. MRI image expression with anatomical structures identified

Col I	Col II	Col III		Col IV
Image Id	*Structure Id*	*Disp.(X)*	*Disp.(Y)*	*Image Attribute*
I1	RTH	X_{RTH_1}	Y_{RTH_1}	Normal(N)
I1	RCN	X_{RCN_1}	Y_{RCN_1}	Normal(N)
I1	RPU	X_{RPU_1}	Y_{RPU_1}	Normal(N)
....	......		......	....
I2	LLV	X_{LLV_2}	Y_{LLV_2}	DiseaseI(D1)
I2	LPU	X_{LPU_2}	Y_{LPU_2}	DiseaseI(D1)
.....	......	.....	.....	....
I3	RTH	X_{RTH_3}	Y_{RTH_3}	DiseaseII(D2)

contain MRI image ID's. The structure ID's are in Col. II. Col. III describes the
position of each structure identified in terms of spatial displacement and Col. IV
is the description of the diagnosis regarding the image under consideration.

2.2 Fuzzy Spatial Relationship Detection

Once the anatomical structures are identified, the spatial relationship between
the structures is detected. The spatial relationships existing between the structures in the normal and abnormal situations are different as evident from Fig. 2.
Also it is obvious that the spatial relationships existing between the structures
vary with respect to different abnormalities of the brain. The spatial relationships between structures are here modeled in terms of fuzzy set theory.

Fuzzy spatial relationships are computed in four primitive directions, left, right, above or below, and the corresponding mathematical representation is given by [8]. There is a degree of membership associated in the four directions for every structure in the image. There are a number of fuzzy model evaluation methods in existence, which is used extensively depending upon the application under consideration. Here we are considering the centroid method as it has linear complexity.

If 'k' anatomical structures are identified from a medical image, we are considering only $k(k-1)/2$ spatial patterns existing between them. It is to be noted that the rest of the spatial relationships are redundant from these.

The following Table 2 gives the image expression in terms of fuzzy spatial relationship existing between samples of four structures identified in the medical image as in Col. II. For example, image I1 has four structures identified as LCN, LLV, LPU and LTH. The fuzzy spatial relationship existing between these structures are given in Col. III of the table. F_{12} gives the spatial relationship existing between structures 1 and 2 with 1 as reference. Col. IV gives the description of the image. Table 3 gives the membership degree of each structure with respect to another in terms of the primitive directions.

Table 2. Fuzzy spatial relationship in image data for four structures

Col I	Col II				Col III						Col IV
Img Id	Str1	Str2	Str3	Srt4	F_{12}	F_{13}	F_{14}	F_{23}	F_{24}	F_{34}	Img Attr.
I1	LCN	LLV	LPU	LTH	μ_{12}	μ_{13}	μ_{14}	μ_{23}	μ_{24}	μ_{34}	N
I2	LCN	LLV	LPU	LTH	μ_{12}	μ_{13}	μ_{14}	μ_{23}	μ_{24}	μ_{34}	D1
I3	RCN	RLV	RPU	RTH	μ_{12}	μ_{13}	μ_{14}	μ_{23}	μ_{24}	μ_{34}	D2
...	....	.....	.....	....	....	....	.....	....	.....	....	.....

Table 3. Membership degree in four primitive directions right, left, above and below

Col I	Col II	Col III			
Image Id	Fuzzy Spatial Pointer	μ_{right}	μ_{left}	μ_{above}	μ_{below}
I1	μ_{12}	0.01	0	0	0.99
I1	μ_{13}	0.27	0	0	0.73
I1	μ_{14}	0	0.02	0	0.98

2.3   Frequent Spatial Pattern Discovery

A spatial pattern consists of two or more anatomical structures and the spatial relationships among the structures. As an example, a spatial pattern for four structures can be of the form $(S_1, S_2, S_3, S_4, S_{r12}, S_{r13}, S_{r14}, S_{r23}, S_{r24}, S_{r34})$, where S_i indicates an anatomical structure and S_{rij} denotes spatial relationship between the structures S_i and S_j. The length of a spatial pattern is the number of spatial relationships existing between structures in the pattern.

Quantitative Analysis of the Data. Two k-patterns is joinable if the first $(k-1)$ items and the corresponding spatial relations between them are identical in both k-patterns. For fuzzy spatial relationships, the patterns are joinable if the weighted fuzzy membership values are above a threshold value, in any of the four directions, as per the guidance of domain knowledge.

Medically Meaningful Patterns. Brain is composed of left and right hemispheres, and meaningful relations are easily recognizable inside the hemispheres separately, rather than together. So a group constraint function $(group(S_i)=L$ or $group(S_i)=R)$ is assigned to each structure, with the aid of priori knowledge.

Frequent Pattern Length. The number of structures and corresponding spatial relations in a frequent pattern should be restricted in size, so that the patterns are easy to interpret and thus help in generation of simple association rules in the next phase. Let S_{max} be the maximum number of spatial relationships existing between structures appearing in a pattern. The concepts of the Apriori algorithm is borrowed and modified as in Table 4 by taking into consideration the above challenges.

Table 4. Modified Apriori Algorithm

Modified Apriori Algorithm
Input: (i) Image expression data in Tabular format (Refer Table 2 and 3) (ii) Support count, sup
Output: Frequent spatial pattern - L
1. C2 ←candidate 2 length pattern set
2. L2 ← frequent 2 length pattern set from sup
3. k = 2;
4. while $(k < S_{max})$
5. $L_{k+1} = \Phi$
6. For each pattern $\alpha=(P_1, P_2, P_3, P_k, P_{r12}, P_{r13}, , P_{rk(k-1)/2})$ in L_k
7. For each pattern $\beta=(Q_1, Q_2, Q_3, Q_k, Q_{r12}, Q_{r13}, , Q_{rk(k-1)/2})$ in L_k
8. Joining α to β, to form C_{k+1}
8.1 The weighted threshold spatial relation in α is in alignment with that in β in the desired direction (as per domain knowledge)
8.2 group(P_1, P_2, P_3, P_k)=group(Q_1, Q_2, Q_3, Q_k)
9. Check the support for each candidate, say c, in C_{k+1} to be above sup to be added to form L_{k+1}
10. k=k+1;
11. end while
12. L=∪ L_i

2.4   Spatial Association Mining

A spatial association rule in medical images is a rule that associates spatial relations among anatomical structures to themselves or to the image characteristics. Some examples of such rules are (P_1, P_2, P_{r12}) and $(P_1, P_3, P_{r13}) \rightarrow$ Disease1,$(P_1, P_2, P_3, P_{r12}, P_{r13}, P_{r23}) \rightarrow$ Disease 2 ,$(P_1, P_2, P_{r12}) \rightarrow (P_3, P_4, P_{r34})$ and Normal, with necessary confidence. To strengthen association rule generation phase, in addition to the confidence, we are introducing a constraint function, such that $cons(S_i) = a$, if the structure S_i should appear in the antecedent of the rule and $cons(S_i) = c$, if it should appear in the consequent. An association rule of the form $\alpha \rightarrow \beta$ is valid if and only if it has minimum confidence and also $cons(S_\alpha) = a$ and $cons(S_\beta) = c$.

3   Results and Discussions

The objective of the experiment was to find association rules resembling diagnosis rules. The rules describe fuzzy relationship between spatial patterns of the anatomical structures in MRI slices of brain tumor patients. Here the intention is to confirm the validity of established diagnosis and also to find new rules. The dataset was MRI images which for simplicity was categorized as Normal (N) or Abnormal (A) as per diagnosis records and was obtained from [9-10]. The experiments were run with $S_{max} = 4$, i.e., length of a spatial pattern existing in an association/diagnosis rule is restricted to a maximum of four.

The threshold value for support was fixed by experimenting with different values, for which sets of association rules containing different length spatial patterns were obtained. Fig. 4 shows a plot of the number of association rules obtained for different support values. It is evident from the graph that that association rules were obtained significantly in the range 60%-50%. Also a frequency graph for different length spatial patterns against support values was plotted as in the Fig. 5. The graph shows a close examination of support values ranging from 49% to 59%. It is observed that the number of single length spatial pattern (SL=1) rules remain almost constant from 49% to 59% support values. The number of two length and three length spatial pattern rules (SL=2 and SL=3) kept on decreasing as the support values increased. At 59% number of two length and three length spatial pattern rules were practically *nil*. Hence a threshold value of 57% support is chosen in the scenario.

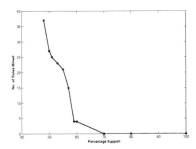
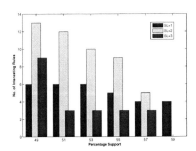

Fig. 4. Comparison of support Values   **Fig. 5.** Frequency of single, two and three length spatial pattern rules

The objective analysis of the extracted association rule is done with the aid of objective measures given in Table 5. The table presents the numerical measures like support, confidence, conviction, lift and leverage for an association rule X → Y and its corresponding formula.

Table 5. Objective measures and formula

Sl No	Numerical Measure	Formula
1	Support	$P(X \cap Y)$
2	Confidence	$P(X \cap Y) / P(X)$
3	Lift	$P(X \cap Y) / P(X)P(Y)$
4	Conviction	$P(X)P(\neg Y) / P(X \cap \neg Y)$
5	Leverage	$P(X \cap Y) - P(X)P(Y)$

Table 6 presents a subset of extracted association rules containing spatial patterns of length one two and three with threshold values of support as 57% and confidence as 60%. The objective measures are highly useful in identifying the interestingness of the rules. Of the interestingness measures computed, 'confidence' measure can give misleading results, as it is an asymmetric measure. Therefore to overcome this problem, 'lift', a symmetric measure is used, in addition to support and confidence measures. A lift value greater than one, implies that the spatial patterns on both sides of the rules are positively correlated and are interesting.

'Leverage' is also a symmetric measure which can be considered as equivalent to lift for interestingness measures. Values greater than zero for 'leverage' is desirable for quality association rules. 'Conviction' is also a symmetric measure which can be considered in place of 'leverage'. The minimum values possible for the symmetric measure conviction is 0.5. The Table 6 gives conviction values ranging from 2.47 to infinity. As the value of conviction moves farther from one, the rules are of the interesting type category. The value of conviction reaches infinity when rules are primarily logical implications.

Table 6. Interestingness measures of rules mined

Rules	Support%	Confidence%	Lift	Conviction	Leverage
1	59.26	86.48	1.29	2.47	70.05
2	62.96	91.89	1.45	4.56	78.81
3	62.96	91.89	1.45	4.56	78.81
4	55.55	88.23	1.40	3.15	75.67
5	55.55	88.23	1.40	3.15	75.67
6	68.52	100	1.10	Inf.	36.37
7	66.67	100	1.10	Inf.	35.40
8	62.96	100	1.10	Inf.	33.43

Some sample rules obtained are as follows in Table. 7.

Table 7. Sample diagnosis Rules

Rule 1	LCN is not totally above LLV→LPU is not totally left LCN
Rule 2	LCN is not totally above LLV→LCN is not totally above LTH
Rule 3	LCN is not totally above LLV→ LTH is not totally above LLV
Rule 4	LTH is not totally below LCN→ LTH is not totally above LLV
Rule 5	LTH is not totally below LCN→LPU is not totally left and above LLV
Rule 6	LCN is not totally above LLV→Abnormal
Rule 7	LTH is not totally below LCN→Abnormal
Rule 8	LTH is not totally above LLV→Abnormal

4   Conclusions

In this paper, the concept of fuzzy spatial relationship and association rule mining is extended to medical images. As per the design of the system, the medical image is segmented to identify the anatomical structures and its spatial location. Once the structures are identified, their spatial relationship is estimated in terms of fuzzy set theory, which brings the situation more close to real scenarios. These spatial relationships are then mined to obtain relevant spatial patterns between the structures. From this, simple and interesting association rules relating the spatial relationships with image attributes are derived. Future work includes obtaining new diagnosis rule for MRI images. The objective analysis was done with the aid of interestingness measures, whereas subjective analysis of the rules obtained was verified in consultation with a domain expert. The entire system can also be viewed from the perspective of an application. It can be used to compute the success rates of vast number of tumor removal surgery in brain performed by an expert. The spatial displacement of the anatomical structures 'before' and 'after' the surgery, along with domain knowledge guidance, will give us an implication of how far the surgery was a success.

References

1. Burl, M.C.: Mining for Image Content. Systemics, Cybernetics, and Informatics / Information Systems: Analysis and Synthesis (1999)
2. Jain, A.K., Murt, M.N., Flynn, P.J.: Data Clustering: A Review. ACM Computing Survey 31(3) (1999)
3. Hsu, W., Dai, J., Lee, M.: Mining Viewpoint patterns in Image Databases. In: 9th ACM SIGKDD International Conference on Knowledge Discovery and Data Mining, Washington DC (2003)
4. Lee, A.J.T., Hong, R.W., Ko, W.M., Tsao, W.K., Lin, H.H.: Mining Spatial Association Rules in Image Databases. J. Information Sciences 177(7), 1593–1608 (2007)
5. Lee, A.J.T., Liu, Y.H., Tsai, H.M., Lin, H.H., Wu, H.W.: Mining frequent Patterns in Image Databases with 9D-SPA Representation. J. Systems and Software 82, 603–618 (2009)

6. Megalooikonomou, V., Barnathan, M., Zhang, J., Kontos, D., Bakic, P., Maidment, A.: Analyzing Tree-Like Structures in Biomedical Images Based on Texture and Branching: An Application to Breast Imaging. In: Krupinski, E.A. (ed.) IWDM 2008. LNCS, vol. 5116, pp. 25–32. Springer, Heidelberg (2008)
7. Pan, H., Han, Q., Yin, G.: A ROI-Based Mining Method with Medical Domain Knowledge Guidance. In: IEEE International Conference on Internet Computing in Science and Engineering (2008)
8. Bloch, I., Hudelot, C., Jamal, A.: Fuzzy Spatial Relation Ontology for Image interpretation. J. Fuzzy Sets and Systems 159, 1929–1951 (2008)
9. BrainWeb Project, http://mouldy.bic.mni.mcgill.ca/brainweb/
10. Harvard Medical School, http://www.med.harvard.edu/AANLIB/

On Improving the Generalization of
SVM Classifier

Seetha H.[1], Narasimha Murty M.[2], and Saravanan R.[3]

[1] School of Computing Science and Engineering,
VIT University, Vellore-632014, India
hariseetha@gmail.com
[2] Department of Computer Science and Automation,
Indian Institute of Science, Bangalore, India
[3] School of Information Technology and Engineering,
VIT University, Vellore-632014, India

Abstract. The generalization performance of the SVM classifier depends mainly on the VC dimension and the dimensionality of the data. By reducing the VC dimension of the SVM classifier, its generalization performance is expected to increase. In the present paper, we argue that the VC dimension of SVM classifier can be reduced by applying bootstrapping and dimensionality reduction techniques. Experimental results showed that bootstrapping the original data and bootstrapping the projected (dimensionally reduced) data improved the performance of the SVM classifier.

Keywords: Bootstrapping, LDA, Outlier Removal, PCA, Random Projection, VC Dimension.

1 Introduction

Support Vector Machines (SVMs) were found to be one of the most successful classifiers that have their origin in statistical learning theory. SVM training always finds a global minimum when compared to neural networks [1],[2]. However, it has been found in the literature that this method can be sensitive to overfitting [3] which may be either due to noise or due to more parameters (dimensions) in the training data [4]. There exists no evidence which shows that good generalization performance is guaranteed for SVMs [1]. Yu et al., [5] improved its performance by generating best SVM boundary using clustering based techniques in case of large data sets.

Bartlett et al.,[6] have argued that the margin and the number of support vectors are both the estimators of the degree to which the distribution generating the inputs assists in the identification of the target hyper plane. It was however open that which distributions and kernels guarantee this assumption. Later, Steinwart [7] showed that soft margin algorithms with universal kernels are consistent for a large class of classification problems and also proved that even for noise free classification problems SVM's with polynomial kernels can behave arbitrarily badly. Dwight Kuo et al.,[8] showed that, removal of outliers

K.R. Venugopal and L.M. Patnaik (Eds.): ICIP 2011, CCIS 157, pp. 11–20, 2011.
© Springer-Verlag Berlin Heidelberg 2011

when training SVMs improves its generalization performance. Victoria et al., [9] discussed that due to increasing dimensionality, the convex hull becomes harder to discern and is known as the *Curse of Dimensionality* and suggested that feature extraction techniques can be used to compact the convex hull.

The generalization performance of a classifier depends on two parameters: the VC dimension and the number of feature vectors used for training. Keeping the VC dimension minimum suggests that we can expect support vector machines to exhibit good generalization performance [10]. So far, there was no investigation to improve the generalization of SVM classifier by reducing its VC dimension. This was the main motivation that led us to prove that the VC dimension of SVM classifier can be reduced by bootstrapping as well as by dimensionality reduction techniques. It is interesting to note that, the experimental results have also shown that bootstrapping the original and the projected data has improved the performance of the SVM classifier.

This paper is organized as follows: The proof of minimizing the VC dimension of SVM classifier is given in Section 2. Section 3 describes dimensionality reduction techniques. Bootstrapping is explained in Section 4. Section 5 comprises of experimental evaluation along with experimental results and analysis. The concluding remarks are summarized in Section 6.

2   Reducing the VC Dimension of SVM Classifier

According to Burges [1], a gap tolerant classifier is a special kind of SVM classifier. He proved that for data in R^d, the VC dimension of gap tolerant classifiers of margin M and diameter D is bounded above by $min\left\{\lceil\frac{D}{M}\rceil^2, d\right\} + 1$. Thus,

$$VC(dim) \leq min\left\{\left\lceil\frac{D}{M}\right\rceil^2, d\right\} + 1. \tag{1}$$

Hence the VC dimension of the gap tolerant classifier can be reduced by appropriately transforming the data in terms of one or more of these parameters i.e., diameter, margin and dimensionality. Further, these parameters affect the data distribution. So, VC dimension is affected by the data distribution.

Theorem 1. *The bootstrapping and the dimensionality reduction techniques reduce the VC dimension of the SVM classifier and hence improve its generalization performance.*

Proof. Let X^+ and X^- be the set of training samples of C^+ and C^- class given by $X^+ = (x_1, x_2, ...x_i)$ and $X^- = (x_{i+1}, x_{i+2}, ...x_n)$ respectively. Let X_s^+ and X_s^- be the set of support vectors that belong to class C^+ and C^- class respectively. Let $\left(x_1^1, x_1^2, ...x_1^k\right)$ be the k nearest neighbors of the training pattern x_1 where $x_1 \in X^+$. Then, the bootstrapped vector of x_1 is given by $x_1^b = \frac{1}{k}\sum_{m=1}^k x_1^m$. Each training pattern is replaced by its bootstrapped sample only once and the new training set consists of such bootstrapped samples for each class respectively.

Let X_b^+ and X_b^- be the set of bootstrapped training samples of C^+ class and C^- class respectively, given by $X^{b+} = \left(x_1^b, x_2^b, ...x_i^b\right)$ and $X^{b-} = \left(x_{i+1}^b, x_{i+2}^b, ...x_n^b\right)$. Let X_s^{b+} and X_s^{b-} be the set of bootstrapped support vectors that belong to C^+ class and C^- class respectively. Let M_b be the margin of bootstrapped vectors and M be the margin of original vectors. Let D_b be the diameter of enclosing sphere of bootstrapped vectors and D be the diameter of enclosing sphere of original vectors. Then (i) $M_b \geq M$ and (ii) $D_b \leq D$.

Let us prove (i) by contradiction. Let us assume that the margin of the support vector plane decreases by bootstrapping. This happens only if any of the bootstrapped support vectors belonging to X_s^{b+} or X_s^{b-} fall into marginal area. But, this never happens because the bootstrapped training samples are not in the marginal area. Hence, $M_b > M$.

The margin of bootstrapped vectors will be equal to the margin of original vectors i.e., $M_b = M$ if $\exists x_p \in X^{b+}$ such that $x_p^b \in X_s^{b+}$ and $\exists x_q \in X^{b-}$ such that $x_q^b \in X_s^{b-}$ and x_p^b, x_q^b lie on the support vector plane of X_s^+ and X_s^- respectively. Thus, $M_b \geq M$ is proved.

(ii). The centroid of any subset of samples has to lie within the sphere and hence the diameter can never increase. Therefore, $D_b \leq D$ is proved. Thus, in the inequality (1) the right hand side can decrease further because of bootstrapping.

Now if the dimensionality reduction techniques are applied to the original data and the number of feature vectors used for training is reduced then d decreases and the VC dimension of the SVM classifier gets reduced. On further bootstrapping the projected data, the diameter decreases and the margin of the bootstrapped support vector plane increases when compared to that of support vector plane of only projected data.

Thus by applying bootstrapping and dimensionality reduction techniques the VC dimension of the SVM classifier can be reduced and thereby its generalization performance can increase. The effect of bootstrapping on the margin of the support vector plane and the diameter of the enclosing sphere is shown in the Fig. 1. Bootstrapping, helps in reducing the noise in training data, while, the dimensionality

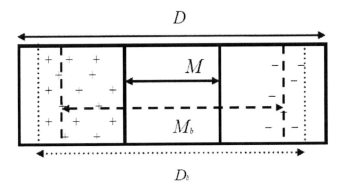

Fig. 1. Effect of bootstrapping on the margin M of the support vector plane and diameter D of the enclosing sphere

reduction techniques help in reducing the overfitting due to several parameters and thus improve the generalization performance and training time of the SVM classifier.

3   Dimensionality Reduction

In the present work, the dimensionality reduction (DR) techniques viz., Random Projection (RP), Principal Component Analysis (PCA) and Linear Discriminant analysis (LDA) are applied.

RP: RP is a powerful dimensionality reduction technique based on Johnson-Lindenstrauss (JL) Lemma [11]. Dasgupta et al., [12] have indicated that projection matrix R, whose entries are independently drawn from a normal distribution, represents such a mapping that satisfies JL lemma. It is computationally simple: forming the random matrix and projecting the data matrix $X_{d \times n}$ into $k1$ dimensions is of order $O\,(dk1n)$[13]. In random projection, the original d-dimensional data is projected to a $k1$-dimensional ($k1 << d$) subspace through the origin, using a random matrix $R_{k1 \times d}$ whose columns have unit lengths. Using matrix notation $X_{d \times n}$ is the original set of n observations each of dimension d. $X_{k1 \times n}^{RP}$ is the projection of the data onto a lower $k1$-dimensional subspace[14] defined by

$$X_{k1 \times n}^{RP} = \frac{1}{\sqrt{k1}} \left[R_{k1 \times d} X_{d \times n} \right]. \tag{2}$$

PCA: PCA is a linear transformation technique that transforms the high dimensional data to a low dimensional space. Let the original data set consist of n observations each of dimension d. Firstly, it is transformed to a mean centered matrix $X_{d \times n}$. Then the Eigen value decomposition of covariance matrix XX^T is computed as $E\left(XX^T\right) = ESE^T$ where the columns of matrix E are the Eigen vectors of the data covariance matrix $E\left(XX^T\right)$ and S is a diagonal matrix containing the respective Eigen values [13]. The dimensionality reduction of the data set is achieved by projecting the data onto a subspace spanned by the most important Eigen vectors

$$X^{PCA} = E_{k1}^T X. \tag{3}$$

where the $d \times k1$ matrix E_{k1} contains $k1$ Eigen vectors corresponding to the largest $k1$ Eigen values. But the computation complexity of estimating PCA is $O\left(d^2 n\right) + O\left(d^3\right)$.

LDA: LDA is a supervised dimensionality reduction technique. The multi class LDA has been used in a number of applications including pattern recognition, bioinformatics etc., where the original large number of features has to be reduced. The major goal of LDA is to compute an optimal transformation by minimizing the within-class distance and maximizing the between-class distance simultaneously, thus achieving maximum class discrimination [15]. If the set of samples $y_1, y_2, \ldots, y_n$ are divided into subsets Y_1, Y_2 and so on, and if the mean vector of n_i number of samples belonging to class i is μ_i and the total mean vector is μ, where c is the number of classes, then the within class scatter matrix S_W and between class scatter matrix S_B are given as follows:

$$S_W = \sum_c^{i=1} \sum_{y \in Y_i} (y - \mu_i)(y - \mu_i)^t \text{ and } S_B = \sum_c^{i=1} n_i (\mu_i - \mu)(\mu_i - \mu)^t. \quad (4)$$

Thus, the goal of LDA is to maximize the ratio $\dfrac{|S_B|}{|S_W|}$. The computational complexity of LDA is $O\left(dnt + t^3\right)$ where d is the number of features, n is the number of samples and $t = min(n, d)$.

4   Bootstrap Technique

The bootstrap technique is a process of generating artificial training set from the original training set. The artificial samples are called bootstrap samples. Conventional bootstrapping techniques sample the training tuples uniformly with replacement. They have been successfully applied for accuracy estimation of classifiers. We used the bootstrap technique given by Hamamoto et al., [16] to generate an artificial training set. The bootstrapping method is as follows: Let X be a training pattern and $X_1, X_2 \ldots X_r$ be its r nearest neighbors in its class. Then $X' = \frac{1}{r} \sum_{h=1}^{r} X_h$ is the artificial pattern generated for X [20]. This process is repeated for each training pattern without selecting it more than once. The purpose of using this bootstrapping technique lies in its ability to remove outliers which therefore reduces the variability in the data as well as removes noise. Note that bootstrapping makes sense even in the case of parity problems when there is sufficient data around each point.

5   Experimental Evaluation

The proposed work is carried out in the following way:

*Case*1: Bootstrapping the training set of original data and performing classification using SVM classifier.

*Case*2: Bootstrapping training set of the projected data (obtained by applying RP, PCA and LDA to the original data) and then performing classification using SVM classifier.

5.1   Dataset Details and Experimental Setup

The experiments are performed with three of the benchmark datasets namely, Thyroid, PenDigits and Breast Cancer data sets from UCI machine learning repository [17]. The number of classes, features, training patterns and testing patterns are respectively shown in brackets under the name of each dataset in Table 1.

Table 1. CA% vs nsv of original data using Polynomial,RBF and Linear kernels

Operation Performed	Dataset (Properties)	CA%(nsv) Polynomial kernel	CA%(nsv) RBF kernel	CA%(nsv) Linear kernel
SVM classification without bootstrapping	Thyroid (3,21,3772,3333)	93.9032(566) C=0.125	97.1704(432) C=16	97.112(276) C=4
	PenDigits (10,16,7498,3428)	97.6844(983) C=2	97.9417(1198) C=1	95.426(1047) C=0.25
	Breast Cancer (2,30,342,227)	96.4758(93) C=4	97.3568(69) C=4	96.9163(39) C=0.125
SVM classification with bootstrapping	Thyroid	93.9615(486) r_m=30,C=0.125	97.7830(326) r_m=2,C=16	97.9288(112) r_m=3,C=4
	PenDigits	97.7130(609) r_m=8,C=2	97.9703(966) r_m=3,C=1	95.5975(455) r_m=23,C=0.25
	Breast Cancer	96.9163(90) r_m=16,C=4	98.2379(46) r_m=2,C=4	98.2379(5) r_m=58,C=0.125

For Thyroid and PenDigits, the training set and testing set are separately available. For Breast Cancer, approximately the first 60% of the data of each class was used for training and the remaining was used for testing. These datasets have continuous valued features. These datasets are normalized to have zero mean and unit variance.

In case 1, the original training set is bootstrapped and the classification is performed using polynomial, RBF and linear kernels separately. In case 2, firstly the dimensionality reduction techniques (RP, PCA and LDA) are separately applied on combining both training set and testing set. Then the training and testing set are separated. The projected training set is then bootstrapped and classification is performed using polynomial, RBF and linear kernels separately. By varying the parameter C (in case of polynomial, RBF and linear kernels) the classification accuracy (CA %) is observed in both the cases. The value of C (in case of polynomial, RBF and linear kernels), for which the CA% of bootstrapped data is maximum is chosen. For RBF and polynomial kernels, except C, all other parameters are chosen to have default values. Varying r (the number of nearest neighbors), the CA% is observed. In Table 1 and Table 3 the number of nearest neighbors r_m for which the CA% of bootstrapped data was maximum is shown along with the number of support vectors (nsv) obtained in each of the above mentioned cases in brackets next to CA%. The experiments are implemented in Matlab. For LDA, *compute_mapping* routine of Matlab drttoolbox [18] was used. Matlab routine *princomp* was used for PCA and *normrnd*$(0, 1, d, k1)$ is used to generate random matrix [14] respectively. The value of $k1$ is chosen by

$$k1 \geq \epsilon^{-2} \log(n). \tag{5}$$

Finally, the classification is performed using LIBSVM [19].

5.2 Experimental Results and Analysis

The experimental results for case 1 are shown in Table 1 and the results for case 2 are shown in Table 2 and Table 3. From Table 1, it can be noted that mostly the CA% obtained using RBF kernel was more than the CA% obtained using linear and polynomial kernels. From Table 2, the CA% of Thyroid data obtained with RP using RBF kernel is slightly more than that obtained using PCA. From Table 2 and Table 3, the CA% using linear kernel for Breast Cancer was more on applying RP and PCA whereas for Thyroid CA% using RBF was more on applying RP and PCA. For PenDigits the CA% using polynomial and RBF were better than that using linear kernel. It can also be noted that the LDA still yields better CA% though there is a drastic reduction in the dimensionality.

It can also be observed that CA% is increased and nsv is decreased on bootstrapping the original data as well as projected data using polynomial, RBF and linear kernels. This shows that the generalization of SVM is improved on bootstrapping as it could remove noise in the training data and reduce the VC dimension.

Fig. 2(a), Fig. 2(b) and Fig. 2(c) show the variation in CA% w.r.t the number of nearest neighbors on bootstrapping the original data of PenDigits. In almost all these figures, it can be noticed that the CA% increases with increasing number of nearest neighbors, reaches maximum and then decreases. A similar observation is also made on bootstrapping the projected data(due to space limitation they are not shown here). This is because, if smoothing is less or not done at all, noise will not be eliminated and leads to overfitting. Smoothing is good to some extent, but excessive smoothing of the data leads to underfitting of the data.

Table 2. CA% vs nsv of projected data using Polynomial, RBF and Linear kernels

Dataset	DR Technique	CA%(nsv) Polynomial kernel	CA%(nsv) RBF kernel	CA%(nsv) Linear kernel
Thyroid	PCA ($k1=12$)	93.7865(489) C=1	95.245(510) C=16	94.0782(520) C=4
	RP ($k1=12$)	93.7281(531) C=0.5	96.7911(517) C=16	93.9323(548) C=1
	LDA ($k1=2$)	93.9907(430) C=0.03125	94.1074(489) C=0.25	94.0198(428) C=0.25
PenDigits	PCA ($k1=10$)	97.1698(1041) C=0.5	97.1412(1888) C=0.25	93.4248(1528) C=0.125
	RP ($k1=10$)	93.825(1627) C=2	93.8822(2419) C=0.5	86.1063(3733) C=0.03125
	LDA ($k1=9$)	94.8256(735) C=1	95.3402(1366) C=1	92.2241(1212) C=0.125
BreastCancer	PCA ($k1=12$)	96.9163(70) C=1	96.4758(122) C=2	96.9163(26) C=1
	RP ($k1=12$)	93.3921(103) C=2	92.511(125) C=2	95.5947(74) C=0.125
	LDA ($k1=1$)	96.4758(36) C=1	97.3568(36) C=2	96.9163(28) C=1

Table 3. CA% vs nsv on bootstrapping the projected data using Polynomial, RBF and Linear kernels

Dataset	DR Technique	CA%(nsv) Polynomial kernel	CA%(nsv) RBF kernel	CA%(nsv) Linear kernel
Thyroid	PCA ($k1=12$)	93.8448(405) $r_m=86,C=1$	96.4702(314) $r_m=8,C=16$	94.9533(356) $r_m=11,C=4$
	RP ($k1=12$)	93.8448(487) $r_m=4,C=0.5$	97.3746(425) $r_m=2,C=16$	94.049(509) $r_m=2,C=1$
	LDA ($k1=2$)	94.3116(403) $r_m=19,C=0.03125$	94.1365(481) $r_m=3, C=0.25$	94.224(411) $r_m=9,C=0.25$
PenDigits	PCA ($k1=10$)	97.3128(636) $r_m=10,C=0.5$	97.2842(1341) $r_m=14,C=0.25$	93.7107(1044) $r_m=8,C=0.125$
	RP ($k1=10$)	94.1109(1405) $r_m=2,C=2$	94.0537(2145) $r_m=3,C=0.5$	86.2207(3604) $r_m=2,C=0.03125$
	LDA ($k1=9$)	94.8542(576) $r_m=2,C=1$	95.3688(1144) $r_m=2,C=1$	92.3957(1054) $r_m=2,C=0.125$
Breast Cancer	PCA ($k1=12$)	97.3568(62) $r_m=10,C=1$	96.9163(77) $r_m=2,C=2$	97.7974(6) $r_m=58,C=1$
	RP ($k1=12$)	93.8326(88) $r_m=18,C=2$	94.7137(23) $r_m=24,C=2$	96.4758(41) $r_m=7,C=0.125$
	LDA ($k1=1$)	96.9163(30) $r_m=16,C=1$	97.7974(23) $r_m=10,C=2$	97.7974(18) $r_m=16,C=1$

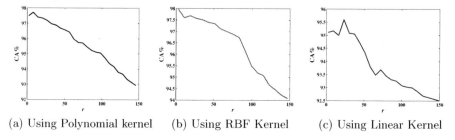

(a) Using Polynomial kernel   (b) Using RBF Kernel   (c) Using Linear Kernel

Fig. 2. CA% vs r of PenDigits data

6   Conclusions

In the present investigation, the effect of bootstrapping and dimensionality reduction on the generalization performance of the SVM classifier is studied on three of the benchmark data sets. The main findings are summarized below:

– The CA% of the SVM classifier is increased and the nsv is decreased on bootstrapping both the original training data and the projected training data due to the removal of outliers.
– The classification performance in case of PCA is mostly better than that of RP. But for real time data the time taken by RP for dimensionality reduction would be lesser than that of PCA which may be due to their respective

computational complexities. Though there is a significant decrease in the dimensionality by LDA, the classification performance of the SVM classifier (using polynomial, RBF and linear kernels) was comparable to that of other two dimensionality reduction methods. On the original data with and without bootstrapping RBF kernel showed better performance. On applying dimensionality reduction, no single kernel was superior.
– These experimental results were in good agreement with those obtained by Viswanath et al., [20] on the application of bootstrapping for nearest neighbor classification.

References

1. Christopher, J., Burges, C.: A Tutorial on Support Vector Machines for Pattern Recognition. Data Mining and Knowledge Discovery 2, 121–167 (1998)
2. Han, J., Kamber, M.: Data Mining Concepts and Techniques. Morgan Kauffmann, San Francisco (2006)
3. Cristianini, N., ShaweTaylor, J.: An Introduction to Support Vector Machines and other Kernel based Learning Methods. Cambridge University Press, Cambridge (2000)
4. Witten, I.H., Frank, E.: Data Mining. Morgan Kauffmann, Academic Press (2000)
5. Yu, H., Yang, J., Han, J.: Classifying Large Datasets using SVMS with Hierarcical Clusters. In: Proc. of 9th SIGKDD, Washington DC, USA (2003)
6. Bartlett, P., Shawe-Taylor, J.: Generalization Performance of Support Vector Machines and other Pattern Classifiers. In: Advances in Kernel Methods-Support Vector Learning, pp. 43–54. MIT press, Cambridge (1999)
7. Steinwart, I.: On the Influence of the Kernel on the Consistency of Support Vector Machines. J. Machine Learning Research 2, 67–93 (2001)
8. Dwight Kuo, P., Banzah, W.: Setting a good Example: Improving the Generalization Performance in Support Vector Machines through Outlier Exclusion (2004), http://www.neuro.bstu.by/ai/Wisconsin/SVMOutlier3.pdf
9. Victoria, J., Hodge, J.A.: A Survey of Outlier Detection Methodologies. Artificial Intelligence Review 22(2), 85–126 (2004)
10. Theodridis, S., Koutroumbas, K.: Pattern Recognition, 4th edn. Academic Press, London (2008)
11. Achiloptas, D.: Database-friendly Random Projection. In: Int. Proc ACM Symposium on the Principles of Database Systems, pp. 274–281 (2001)
12. Dasgupta, S., Gupta, A.: An Elementary Proof of the Johnson Lindenstrauss Lemma. J. Random Structures and Algorithms 22(1), 60–65 (2002)
13. Bingham, E., Mannila, H.: Random Projections in Dimensionality Reduction: Applications to Image and Text Data. In: 7th ACM KDD International Conference on Knowledge Discovery and Data Mining (KDD 2001), pp. 245–250 (2001)
14. Pal, B., Adithan, G., Narasimha Murthy, M.: Speeding up AdaBoost Classifier with Random Projection. In: 7th International Conference on Advances in Pattern Recognition (ICAPR 2009), pp. 251–254 (2009)
15. Richard, O., Duda, P.E.H., Stork, D.G.: Pattern Classifcation. John Wiley & Sons Inc., Chichester (2005)
16. Hamamoto, Y., Uchimura, S., Tomita, S.: A Bootstrap Technique for Nearest Neighbor Classifier Design. IEEE Trans. on Pattern Analysis and Machine Intelligence 19(1), 73–79 (1997)

17. UCI Machine learning repository, `http://archive.ics.uci.edu/ml/datasets.html`
18. Maaten,   L.V.:   Matlab   Toolbox   for   Dimensionality   Reduction, `http://homepage.tudelft.nl/19j49/Software.html`
19. Chang, C.-C., Lin, C.-J.: LIBSVM: A library for Support Vector Machines (2001) Software, `http://www.csie.ntu.edu.tw/~cjlin/libsvm`
20. Viswanath, P., Narasimha Murty, M., Bhatnagar, S.: Partition based Pattern Synthesis Technique with Efficient Algorithms for Nearest Neighbor Classification. Pattern Recognition Letters 27, 1714–1724 (2006)

A Practical Rough Sets Analysis in Real-World Examination Timetabling Problem Instances

Joshua Thomas J.[1], Ahamad Tajudin Khader[2], and Bahari Belaton[2]

[1] Department of Information and Technology, KDU College (PG) Sdn Bhd
Penang, Malaysia 10400
[2] School of Computer Sciences University Sains Malaysia
Penang, Malaysia 11800
`joshopever@yahoo.com`, {`tajudin`,`bahari`}`@cs.usm.my`

Abstract. The examination timetabling problem is widely studied and a major activity for academic institutions. In real world cases, an increasing number of student enrolments, variety of courses throw in the growing challenge in the research with a wider range of constraints. Many optimization problems are concerned with the best feasible solution with minimum execution time of algorithms. The aim of this paper is to propose rough sets methods to investigate the Carter datasets. Two rough sets (RS) approaches are used for the data analysis. Firstly, the discretization process (DP) returns a partition of the value sets into intervals. Secondly the rough sets Boolean reasoning (RSBR) achieves the best decision table on the large data instances. The rough sets classified datasets are experimented with an examination scheduler. The improvements of the solutions on Car-s-91 and Car-f-91 datasets are reported.

Keywords: Datasets, Discretization, Examination Timetabling, Rough Sets.

1 Introduction

Examination timetabling is a problem of allocating a timeslot for all exams in the problem instances within a limited number of permitted timeslots, in such a way that none of the specified hard constraints are violated. In most cases, the problem is highly constrained and, moreover, the set of constraints which are required to be satisfied is different from one institution to another as reported by Burke et al. [1]. In general, the most common hard constraint is to avoid any student being scheduled for two different exams at the same time. In practice, each institution usually has a different way of evaluating the quality of the developed timetable. In many cases, the quality is calculated based on a penalty function which represents the degree to which the constraints are satisfied. Over the years, numerous approaches have been investigated and developed for exam timetabling. Such approaches include constraint programming, graph colouring, and various metaheuristic approaches including genetic algorithms, tabu search, simulated annealing, the great deluge algorithm, and hybridized methods which draw on two or more of these techniques. Some recent important papers which reflect this broad range of activity are [2–5]. The earlier work by authors focus on interaction on the scheduling data and, this is a continuous research on the data analysis on the same problem. These approaches can be found in paper [6], [7]. In examination timetabling

K.R. Venugopal and L.M. Patnaik (Eds.): ICIP 2011, CCIS 157, pp. 21–30, 2011.
© Springer-Verlag Berlin Heidelberg 2011

problem the exams are ordered prior to assignment to a timeslot, have been discussed by several authors including Boizulmault et al. [8], Brailsford et al. [9], Burke et al. [10], Burke and Newall [11], Burke and Petrovic [12] and Carter et al. [13]. Carter et al. [13] reports the use of four ordering criteria to rank the exams in decreasing order to estimate how difficult it is to schedule each of the exams. Each one of these techniques has its own properties and features including their ability of finding important rules and information that could be useful for the examination timetabling domain. However, no literature is discussed on the rough sets based methodology to address the problem instances. Rough set theory [14–16] is a comparatively innovative intelligent technique that has been applied to the real-world cases, and is used for the discovery of data dependencies, discovers the patterns of data, and seeks the minimum subset of values. One advantage of the rough set is the creation of readable if-then rules. Such rules have a potential to reveal new patterns in the data material. More advanced and intelligent techniques have been used in data analysis such as neural network, Bayesian classifier, genetic algorithms, decision trees, fuzzy theory, and rough set however rough set methods are not popular yet used for scheduling datasets. It offers a problem-solving tool between the precision of classical mathematics and the natural vagueness of the real world. Other approaches like case-based reasoning and decision trees [17], [18] are also widely used to solve data analysis problems. The objective of the investigation has been to develop intervals that could rank the dataset on the basis of rough set discretization process and make decision. The newly created rough sets based dataset will then inject to the examination evaluator to generate quality feasible solution. The structure of the paper is as follows. Section 2 discusses the rough sets data analysis method in detail. The characteristics of the benchmark dataset are presented in section 3. The modeling process based on rough sets is briefly described in section 4. Experimental analysis and Results are in Section 5. Finally, the conclusion is presented in Section 6.

2   Rough Sets Methods

Rough sets methods is to analyze datasets of the Carter, Laporte and Lee [13], [19] with a set of 12 real-world exam timetabling problems from 3 Canadian highs schools, 5 Canadian, 1 American, 1 UK and 1 mid-east universities. The methods used in this study consist of two main stages: Discretization process (DP) and Rough sets Boolean reasoning (RSBR) data processing. Preprocessing stage (DP) includes discretization. Data Processing (RSBR) includes the generation of preliminary knowledge, such as computation of object ranking from data, and the classification processes. The final goal is of generating rules from the information or decision system for the benchmark datasets. Fig. 1 shows the overall steps in the proposed rough sets data analysis methods.

3   Dataset

Many researchers are using the benchmarking Carter dataset [13] to applying the methods and test the results with quality feasible solution. There are two standard dataset used by the examination timetabling community Carter dataset and the ITC(International Timetabling Competition) dataset [20]. Everybody in the scientific community uses in order to test any proposed algorithms. The Carter dataset were introduced in 1996 by

Carter, Laporte and Lee in a paper published in the Journal of the Operational Research Society. One of the major drawbacks of most articles in the timetabling literature is that testing is limited to randomly generated problems and perhaps to one practical example.

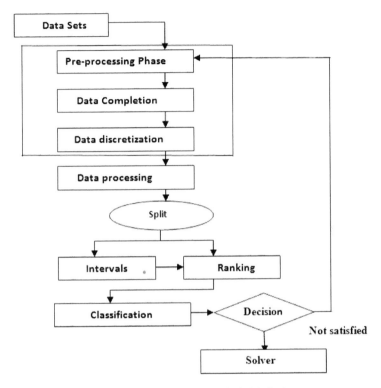

Fig. 1. Rough Set Data Analysis Method

The formulation for the Carter dataset as follows:

1. The room capacities for the examination rooms (which is why is it considered an uncapacitated problem).
2. The fact that two consecutive examinations, which are on different days, is better than two consecutive examinations on the same day.

Both of these scenarios would give the same penalty cost using the usual objective function used in the Carter dataset, even though the student would have the evening (indeed, all night) to revise, as opposed to no time at all if the examinations were truly consecutive. Indeed, each instance in the dataset just has a number of timeslots. There is concept of different days.

The recent examination timetabling review paper [21] has explained the two versions of the datasets and the modifications. However, the contributions of the works are not with the data values, but on the problem instances. Few works were done on modifying with respective of real-world scenario provided by the institutions. Table 1. shows Carter dataset with the problem instances.

Table 1. Carter Examination Timetabling Problem Instances

	Exams	Students	Slots
car-f-92	543	18,419	32
car-s-91	682	16,925	35
ear-f-83	190	1,125	24
hec-s-92	81	2,823	18
kfu-s-93	461	5,349	20
ise-f-91	381	2,726	18
pur-s-93	2,419	30,032	43
rye-f-92	486	11,483	23
sta-f-83	139	611	13
tre-s-92	261	4,360	23
uta-s-92	622	2,126	35
ute-s-92	184	2,750	10
yor-f-83	181	941	21

4   Pre - processing

In real world examination timetabling, many decisions are required to take into account several factors simultaneously under various sets of constraints (soft constraints). Usually it is not known which parameter(s) need to be emphasized more in order to generate a better solution or decision. In many cases, a tradeoff between the various potentially conflicts on assignment of exams into timeslots. Rough sets usually employ a dataset is represented as a table, where each row represents an object. Every column represents a variable, an observation that can be evaluated for each object.

Table 2. Sample Information Syatem

	Course	Enrollment
X1	0001	280
X2	0002	100
X3	0003	64
X4	004	73
X5	0005	73
X6	0006	68
X7	0007	67
X8	0008	45
X9	0009	42
X10	0026	61
X11	0027	60
X12	0028	61

This table is called an information system. The following ordering criteria were considered when selecting which exam should be scheduled first:
   1. Number of conflict exams, largest degree (LD)
   2. Number of student enrolled, largest enrollment (LE)

3. Number of available slot, saturation degree (SD)

In each case, two out of the three criteria above were selected as input variables. More formally, a pair $V = (U, A)$, where U is a non-empty finite set of objects called the universe and A is a non-empty finite set of attributes such that $a : U \rightarrow V_a$ for every $a \epsilon A$. The set V_a is called the value set of a. An example of simple information system is shown in Table 2. There are 12 cases or variable objects, and two conditions (Course and Enrollment). The cases of variable objects x_4 and x_5 as well as x_{10} and x_{12} have exactly the same values of conditions. A decision system is any information system of the form $V = (U, A \bigcup d)$, where $d \epsilon A$ is the decision conditions or criteria. A

Table 3. Decision Table on the car-s-91 Data Instances

	Course	Enrollment	No of Students Enrolled(LE)
X1	0001	280	Large
X2	0002	100	Large
X3	0003	64	Average
X4	004	73	Medium
X5	0005	73	Medium
X6	0006	68	Average
X7	0007	67	Average
X8	0008	45	Low
X9	0009	42	Low
X10	0026	61	Average
X11	0027	60	Average
X12	0028	61	Average

small example decision table can be found in Table 3. The table has the same 12 cases or variable objects as in the previous example, but one decision attribute number of student enrollment (LE) with two three possible outcomes has been added. The reader may again notice that cases x_4 and x_5 as well as x_{10} and x_{12} still have exactly same values of conditions, but the second pair has a different outcome. The definition to be synthesized from the decision tables is in of the rule form:

IF Course = 0004 and Enrollment = 73 then LE = Medium

It is assumed that a decision table expresses all the knowledge about the model. Same objects may be represented several times or objects overflows. The notion of equivalence must be considered first. A binary relation (R_B) which is reflexive, a value is in relation with itself $(x \ R_B \ x)$, symmetric (if $x \ R_B \ y$ then $y \ R_B \ x$) and transitive if $(x \ R_B \ x$ and $y \ R_B \ z$ then $x \ R_B \ z)$ is called an equivalence relation.

Let $V = (U, A)$ be an information system, then with any $B \subseteq A$ there is associated an equivalence relation $IND_A \ (R_B)$

$$IND_A(R_B) = \{(x, x^{'}) \epsilon U^2 | \forall_a \epsilon R_B a(x) = a(x^{'})\} . \tag{1}$$

$IND_A \ (R_B)$ is called the indiscernibility relation. For instance define an indiscernibility relation. The subsets of the conditional attributes are $[Course], [Enrollment]$. If for instance, $[No. \ of students Enrollment(LE)]$only, objects x_4 and x_5 belongs to the same equivalence class and indiscernible. We look at the relation $IND_A (R_B)$ defines three equivalence class identified below.

$$IND_A ((R_B\{\text{Course}\})\quad = \{\{ x_1, \}, \{ x_2, \}, \{ x_3, \}, \{ x_4, \}, \{ x_5, \}, \{ x_6, \}, \{ x_7, \},$$
$$\{ x_8, \}, \{ x_9, \}, \{ x_{10}, \}, \{ x_{11}, \}, \{ x_2, \}\}$$
$$IND_A ((R_B\{\text{Enrollment}\}) = \{\{ x_4, x_5 \}, \{ x_{10}, x_{12} \}\}$$
$$IND_A ((R_B\{\text{LE}\})\qquad = \{\{ x_1, x_2 \}, \{ x_3, x_6, x_7, x_{10}, x_{11}, x_{12} \}, \{ x_4, x_5 \},$$
$$\{ x_8, x_9 \}\}$$

4.1   Data Completion and Discretization of Data Value

The rough set approach requires only indiscernibility it is not necessary to define an order or distance when the values of different kinds are combined (e.g., courses, enrollment). The discretization step determines how roughly the data to be processed. We called this as pre-processing. For instance, course or enrollment values have to establish cut-off points. The intervals might be refined based on good domain knowledge. Setting the cut-off points are computationally expensive for the large datasets and that domain expert to prepare discretization manually. Let M be an information system with n objects. The discernibility matrix of M is symmetric nxn matrix with entries c_{ij} as given below. Each entry thus consists of the set of values upon which objects x_i and x_j differ.

$$c_{ij} = \{a \epsilon V | a(x_i) \neq a(x_j)\} \; for \; i, j = 1, ..., n \; . \tag{2}$$

The *discrenibility function* F_V for an information system V is a Boolean function m Boolean variables $(a_1..a_m)$.

$$F_V (a_1..a_m) = \wedge \{ \vee c_{ij} \, | 1 \leq j \leq i \leq n, c_{ij} \neq 0\}$$

The discernibility function is

$$F_V (c, e, d) = (c, d)(c, e, d)(c, e)(e, d)$$

$$= (d,c,e) \, (d,c) \, (d,e)$$

$$= (d) \, (r) \, (c,e)$$

$$= (d,e,r)$$

Where "," stands for disjunction in the Boolean expression, after simplification, the function is $F_V (c, e, d) = (e, r)$ where (e denotes enrollment and r denotes rank the data values).

4.2   Data Processing

Processing stage includes generating knowledge, such as computation of object from data, split intervals, ranking and classification. These stages lead towards the final goal of generating rules from information or decision system of the Carter dataset. Let $V = (U, A \bigcup \{d\})$ be given. The cardinality of data $d(U) = \{ k | d(x) = k, x \in U \}$ is called the rank of d and is denoted by $r(d)$. Assume the setV_d of values of decision d is equal to $\{ v_d^1 ... v_d^{r(d)} \}$. Quite often the rank is of two Boolean values ($e.g.$, Y, N) or it can be an arbitrary number, in the above example, we could have four ranks if the decision had values in the set $\{rank\ 3, rank\ 2, rank\ 1, rank\ 0\}$. The decision d determines a partition $INTERVAL_v(d) = \{ D_v^1 ... D_v^{r(d)} \}$.

$$D_v^k = \{x \in U | d(x) = v_d^k, for\ 1 \le k \le r(d)\} . \tag{3}$$

$INTERVAL_v(d)$ is called the classification of objects in V determinded by the decision d. The set D_v^i is called the$i^t h$ decision class of V. Table 4. explains the RSBR discretization algorithm applied on the dataset. Table 4. shows the intervals and ranking of the dataset.

Table 4. Rough Set Boolean Reasoning Discretization

Input:Information table(T) created from the dataset value coloum cij and n is the no.of intervals for each column value **Output**: Information table(DT) with discretization real value column. 1.For $c_{ij} \in$ do 2.Define Boolean variable B = $\sum_i \{ D_v^1 ... D_v^{r(d)} \}$ 3.End For where $\sum_i = INTERVAL_v$(d) correcponding to a set of partition defined on the variable 4.Create a new Information table(DT) by using the set of partition. 5.Fine objects that discerns in the decision class.

For instance, the Table 4. shows the interval and cut-off points used in the Carter dataset problem instances. The column count explains the large, average, medium and low intervals a set on the standard dataset where the number of student enrolled largest enrollment (LE). Searching the reducts form a decision table is NP-complete. Fortunately, Carter dataset has no reducts, and the work directions with setting intervals, ranking with classification on the dataset.

5   Experiments and Results

The algorithm was developed using java based object oriented programming. The experiments were run on a PC with a 2.8 GHz Core(2) Duo and 2GB of RAM. Carters (1996) publicly available exam timetabling datasets were used in the experiments as shown in Table 1. In this work, we evaluate the performance of our approach on twelve instances. In order to test our work modification to the sequential construction method previously developed by Carter et al. [13], the algorithm was initially run with implementing rough set discretization. The experiment works on the exams in the problem instances are in single interval criteria. ($e.g.$, LE) From Table 6. it can be seen that the initial rough sets methods produced comparable results to the single interval criteria.

Table 5. Interval & Ranking of Carter Datasets

Interval	Attribute	Count	Ranking
	car-f-92	2,6,58,476	L,A,M,Low
	car-s-91	1,3,49,628	L,A,M,Low
	ear-f-83	0,0,4,186,	L,A,M,Low
	hec-s-92	0,3,7,9	L,A,M,Low
	kfu-s-92	4,2,28,424	L,A,M,Low
	ise-f-92	0,0,5,373	L,A,M,Low
[2500,950],[950,500],[500,200],[200,1]	pur-s-93	5,18,68,2325	L,A,M,Low
	rye-f-92	0,9,25,499	L,A,M,Low
	sfa-f-83	6,10,37,567	L,A,M,Low
	sfa-f-83	6,10,37,567	L,A,M,Low
	sfa-f-83	6,10,37,567	L,A,M,Low
	sfa-f-83	6,10,37,567	L,A,M,Low
	sfa-f-83	6,10,37,567	L,A,M,Low

Table 6. Rough Set Data Analysis Method

Dataset	Rough Sets discretization method (LE)	Burke et al [11]	Caramia et al [4]	Carter et al [16]	Casey and Thompson [8]
car-f-92	4.0	4.2	6	6.2	4.4
car-s-91	4.42	4.8	6.6	7.1	5.4
ear-f-83	35.9	35.4	29.3	36.4	34.8
hec-s-92	9.1	10.8	9.2	10.8	10.8
kfu-s-93	12.44	13.7	13.8	14	14.1
Ise-f-91	11.83	10.4	9.6	10.5	14.7
pur-s-93	10.81	8.9	6.8	7.3	-
rye-f-92	155.01	159.1	158.2	161.5	134.9
sta-f-83	10.38	8.3	9.4	9.6	8.7
tre-s-92	5.89	3.4	3.5	3.5	-
uta-s-92	25.5	25.7	24.4	25.8	25.4
yor-f-83	38.3	36.7	36.2	41.7	37.5

Slightly modified problem instance of Car-f-91 and Car-f-92 are tested with the algorithm.The algorithm produced similar but better results for the Car-f-91 and Car-f-92 dataset, hec-s-92 and kfu-s-93 other datasets were compared with the standard results.

6   Conclusions

In this paper, we have presented an intelligent data analysis approach based on rough sets theory for generating classification rules from a set of observed 12- real world problem instances as a benchmarking dataset for the examination timetabling community. The main objective is to investigate the problem instances/dataset and with minor modification to obtained better timetables. To increase the classification process rough sets with Boolean reasoning (RSBR) discretization algorithm is used to discretize the data. Further work will be done to minimize the experiment duration in order to get better results with the rough set data analysis.

References

1. Burke, E.K., Elliman, D.G., Ford, P.H., Weare, R.F.: Examination Timetabling in British Universities. In: Burke, E., Ross, P. (eds.) PATAT 1995. LNCS, vol. 1153, pp. 76–90. Springer, Heidelberg (1996)

2. Burke, E.K., Elliman, D.G., Weare, R.F.: A Hybrid Genetic Algorithm for Highly Constrained Timetabling Problems. In: Proceedings of the 6th International Conference on Genetic Algorithms, pp. 605–610. Morgan Kaufmann, San Francisco (1995)

3. Burke, E.K., Bykov, Y., Newall, J., Petrovic, S.: A Time-predefined Local Search Approach to Exam Timetabling Problems. IIE Transactions on Operations Engineering, 509–528 (2004)

4. Caramia, M., DellOlmo, P., Italiano, G.F.: New Algorithms for Examination Timetabling. In: Naher, S., Wagner, D. (eds.) WAE 2000. LNCS, vol. 1982, pp. 230–241. Springer, Heidelberg (2001)

5. Carter, M.W., Laporte, G., Lee, S.Y.: Examination Timetabling: Algorithmic Strategies and Applications. Journal of the Operational Research Society, 373–383 (1996)

6. Joshua, J.: The Perception of Interaction on the University Examination Timetabling Problem. In: McCollum, B., Burke, E., George, W. (eds.) Practice and Theory of Automated Timetabling, ISBN 08-538-9973-3

7. Al-Betar, M.: A Combination of Metaheuristic Components based on Harmony Search for The Uncapacitated Examination Timetabling. In: McCollum, B., Burke, E., George, W. (eds.) Practice and Theory of Automated Timetabling, ISBN 08-538-9973-3 for Annals of Operational Research

8. Boizumault, P., Delon, Y., Peridy, L.: Constraint Logic Programming for Examination Timetabling. The Journal of Logic Programming 26(2), 217–233 (1996)

9. Brailsford, S.C., Potts, C.N., Smith, B.M.: Constraint Satisfaction Problems: Algorithms and Applications. European Journal of Operational Research 119, 557–581 (1999)

10. Burke, E.K., de Werra, D., Kingston, J.: Applications in Timetabling. In: Yellen, J., Gross, J.L. (eds.) Handbook of Graph Theory, pp. 445–474. Chapman Hall, CRC Press (2003)

11. Burke, E.K., Newall, J.P.: Solving Examination Timetabling Problems through Adaption of Heuristic Orderings. Annals of Operations Research 129, 107–134 (2004)

12. Burke, E.K., Petrovic, S.: Recent Research Directions in Automated Timetabling. European Journal of Operational Research 140, 266–280 (2002)

13. Pawlak, Z., Grzymala-Busse, J., Slowinski, R., Ziarko, W.: Rough Sets Communications of the ACM 38(11), 89–95 (1995)

14. IzakVarious, D.: Approaches to Reasoning with Frequency-Based Decision Reducts: A Survey. In: Polkowski, L., Tsumoto, S., Lin, T.Y. (eds.) Rough Sets in Soft Computing and Knowledge Discovery: New Developments. Physica, Heidelberg (2000)

15. Pal, S.K., Polkowski, L., Skowron, A.: Rough-Neuro Computing: Techniques for Computing with Words. Springer, Berlin (2004)

16. Qu, R., Burke, E.K., McCollum, B., Merlot, L.T.G., Lee, S.Y.: A Survey of Search Methodologies and Automated System Development for Examination Timetabling. Journal of Scheduling 12(1), 55–89 (2009), doi:10.1007/s10951-008-0077-5

17. McCollum, B., Schaerf, A., Paechter, B., McMullan, P., Lewis, R., Parkes, A., Di Gaspero, L., Qu, R., Burke, E.: Setting The Research Agenda in Automated Timetabling: The Second International Timetabling Competition. INFORMS Journal on Computing 22(1), 120–130 (2010)

18. Carter, M.W.: A Survey of Practical Applications of Examination Timetabling Algorithms. Operation Research 34(2), 193–202 (1986)
19. Pawlak, Z.: Rough Sets Theoretical Aspect of Reasoning about Data. Kluwer Academic, Boston (1991)
20. Pawlak, Z.: Rough sets. International Journal of Computer and Information Science 11, 341–356 (1982)
21. Carter, M.W., Laporte, G., Lee, S.Y.: Examination Timetabling: Algorithmic Strategies and Applications. Journal of the Operational Research Society 47, 373–383 (1996)

Mining Association Rules Using Non-Negative Matrix Factorization and Formal Concept Analysis

Aswani Kumar Ch

School of Information Technology and Engineering
VIT University, Vellore, India
cherukuri@acm.org

Abstract. Based upon the partial ordering relations, Formal Concept Analysis (FCA) offers effective Association Rules Mining (ARM). However size of the formal context is a major research concern for FCA based ARM. The objective of this paper is to propose Non-Negative Matrix Factorization (NMF) based FCA for the task of ARM. We demonstrate the proposed method on real world healthcare data.

Keywords: Association Rules Mining, Concept Lattice, Dimensionality Reduction, Formal Concept Analysis, Non-Negative Matrix Factorization, Singular Value Decomposition.

1 Introduction

Formal Concept Analysis (FCA) is a theory of human centered data analysis with a basic setting of triplet of set of objects, set of attributes and a crisp relation between objects and attributes, in the form of object-attribute table known as formal context. The goal of FCA is to discover the formal concepts, data dependencies in the form of attribute implications and visualize them by a concept lattice. The attribute implications are closely related to functional dependencies in the database field. Since the past three decades, with a higher intensity, FCA has been studied and successfully applied in many diverse fields [1]. However with the size of the formal context, number of nodes in the concept lattice and attribute implications from FCA grows exponentially. Hence it is required to reduce the dimensionality of the input data before applying FCA [2]. For the reasons of efficiency, it is suggested in the literature to apply Dimensionality reduction (DR) techniques [3] directly on the formal context [4]. In the literature, matrix approximation DR techniques like Singular Value Decomposition (SVD), Non-Negative Matrix Factorization (NMF) and Fuzzy K-Means are available for concept lattice reduction [5], [6], [7]. SVD is known in the literature for its high computational complexity [8,9]. However to the best of our knowledge, mining the attribute associations from the NMF based reduced context is not discussed so far. The motivation behind the current paper is to make such an attempt by applying NMF to reduce dimensionality of the formal context and FCA to mine the associations.

K.R. Venugopal and L.M. Patnaik (Eds.): ICIP 2011, CCIS 157, pp. 31–39, 2011.

2   FCA and NMF

FCA starts with a formal context (G, M, I) where G is a set of objects, M is a set of attributes and I is a binary relation between G and M. A formal concept of the context (G, M, I) can be defined as an ordered pair (A, B) where A⊆G and B⊆M. A, B are known as extent and intent of the concept. The set of all concepts forms a concept lattice. The process of concept formation in FCA is considered as a knowledge discovery task from the data and constructing the concept set constitutes the mining phase. For mathematical foundations, extensive introductory information on FCA algorithms and applications, readers can refer few authoritative references [10,11,12].

Non-negative Matrix Factorization (NMF) is another development in the field of DR and clustering. It differs with other DR methods with constraints that produce nonnegative basis vectors which allows the additive combinations of the vectors to reproduce the original [13]. For the data matrix A of size $t \times d$ with each column of t dimensional non-negative vector of original database (d vectors), NMF factorizes A as

$$A = W.H \qquad (1)$$

where W is $t \times k$ and H is $k \times d$ and $k \le d$. Each column of W contains a basis vector and each column of H contains the weights needed to approximate the corresponding columns in A using the basis from W [14].

3   Proposed Method

In this section we propose a method for mining association rules using NMF and FCA. The idea is to derive equivalence relations between the nodes of the concept lattice using NMF and mine the associations using FCA [6]. Following is the proposed method.

(i) From the given formal context, construct the binary object-attribute incidence matrix.

(ii) Choose the reduced rank value, k, and apply NMF to obtain the reduced rank matrix.

(iii) Choose a threshold value $t, 0 \le t \le 1$, for discriminating purpose. Construct the reduced rank binary matrix.

(iv) Construct the formal context from the reduced rank binary matrix obtained in the above step.

(v) Apply FCA on the formal context to mine the association rules.

Thus with the proposed method, formal context reduces to lower dimension which can lead to minimize the input data to handle the scalability and computational tractability of FCA. Calculating SVD of the data matrix is a computationally complex task. A dense matrix of size $m \times n$ the complexity of computing SVD is $O(mn^2)$ and for sparse matrix with average c non-zero entries per data item the complexity is $O(mnc)$. The complexity of NMF is $O(mk)$, where m is the number of rows of the matrix and k is the number of basis vectors generated.

4   Experimental Results

In this section we demonstrate the implementation of the proposed method on healthcare dataset [15]. However we restrict our analysis to only TB disease due to the page constraints. Tuberculosis (TB) dataset contains details of 21 patients for 12 symptoms related to TB. Table 1 lists various TB symptoms. Table 2 lists domain expert's knowledge, in the form of rules. Table 3 shows the formal context. FCA has produced 33 implications in DG basis. However implications which describe TB are of interest in this study. Table 4 lists all such implications. If the antecedent of an implication which has the target attribute in its consequent is a subset of antecedent of an experts rule then we can consider that the expert rule is subsumed by the implication.

Table 1. TB symptoms

No.	Symptons	Abbreviation
1	Persistent Cough	PC
2	Sputum Production	SP
3	Sputum produced is Muco-Purulent	MC
4	Sputum Bloody	BS
5	Clear Sputum	CS
6	Weight Loss	WL
7	Extreme Night Sweats	NS
8	No Appetite	NA
9	Chest Pain	CP
10	Shortness of Breath	SB
11	Tuberculosis Contact	TC
12	Tiredness	TN

Table 2. Experts rules for TB

No.	Experts rules for TB
1	PC SP BS WL→ TB
2	PC SP BS NS→TB
3	PC WL NS→TB
4	PC SP BS TC→TB
5	PC SP BS CP NA→TB
6	PC SP BS SB→TB
7	PC WL CP SB→TB
8	PC SP BS CP TN→TB

Next we have applied the proposed NMF based FCA on the TB training incidence matrix which is of size 21 x 13 with rank 12. NMF with $k=6$ and binary threshold $t=0.5$ is applied over the incidence matrix. An entry in the reduced matrix is considered as 1 if it is higher than the chosen t value and 0 otherwise.

Table 3. Incidence matrix of TB training dataset

	PC	SP	MC	BS	CS	WL	NS	NA	CP	SB	TC	TN	TB
Obj 1	X	X	X	-	-	X	-	-	X	X	-	-	X
Obj 2	X	X	X	-	-	X	X	X	X	-	-	-	X
Obj 3	X	X	X	-	-	X	X	X	X	-	X	X	X
Obj 4	X	-	-	-	-	X	-	X	-	X	-	X	X
Obj 5	-	-	-	-	-	X	X	X	X	X	-	X	X
Obj 6	X	-	-	-	-	X	X	X	X	X	X	X	X
Obj 7	X	X	-	-	X	X	-	X	X	X	-	X	X
Obj 8	-	-	-	-	-	X	X	-	-	-	-	X	X
Obj 9	-	-	-	-	-	-	X	-	-	-	-	-	X
Obj 10	X	X	X	-	-	X	X	X	X	-	-	X	X
Obj 11	X	X	X	-	-	X	-	X	-	X	-	-	-
Obj 12	X	X	X	-	-	X	-	X	-	-	-	-	-
Obj 13	X	X	-	-	X	-	-	-	X	-	-	X	-
Obj 14	X	X	-	X	-	X	X	X	X	-	-	X	X
Obj 15	-	-	-	-	-	-	-	-	X	-	-	-	-
Obj 16	X	X	X	-	-	X	X	X	X	-	X	X	X
Obj 17	X	-	-	-	-	X	X	X	X	X	-	X	X
Obj 18	X	X	-	-	X	X	X	-	-	-	-	X	X
Obj 19	X	-	-	-	-	-	X	X	-	-	-	X	-
Obj 20	X	X	X	-	-	-	-	-	X	-	-	X	-
Obj 21	-	-	-	-	-	-	-	-	X	-	-	X	-

Table 4. Implications obtained from TB training data using FCA

SI. No.	Implications	No. of objects implication holds
	Implications NOT part of expert rules	-
1	NS CP→ TB	8
2	WL TN→ TB	11
3	PC SP MC CS CP TN→ TB	0
	Implications part of expert rules	-
4	NA CP→ TB	9
5	BS→ TB	1
6	PC SP NS→ TB	6
7	WL NS→ TB	10
8	WL CP→ TB	10
9	TC→ TB	3

We have applied FCA over the reduced context. Fig. 1 shows the concept lattice containing a concept count of 93 with 226 edges and height of 11. NMF-FCA with $k=6$ and $t=0.5$ has produced 20 implications in the DG basis. Implications that are concluding TB are shown in Table 5. We have also studied the influence of discretization parameter t by choosing $t=0.8$. New implications obtained from this analysis are shown in Table 6.

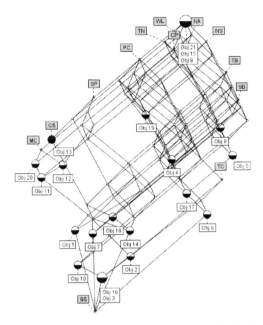

Fig. 1. Concept lattice of TB training data with NMF $k=6$, $t=0.5$

Table 5. Implications obtained using NMF-FCA $k=6$ and $t=0.5$

Sl. No.	Implications	No. objects implication holds
	Implications NOT part of expert rules	-
1	WL TN→ TB	11
	Implications part of expert rules	-
2	BS→ TB	0
3	PC SP NS→ TB	6
4	WL NS→TB	10
5	TC→ TB	4
6	SB→ TB	6

For further analysis we have conducted experiments using different values of k and t. FCA on the reduced context with $k=3$ and $t=0.5$ has produced 25 implications in DG basis. Table 7 lists the 6 implications that are inferring TB. FCA on the NMF based reduced context with $k=3$ and $t=0.8$ has produced 15 implications in the DG basis among which 5 implications are inferring TB as shown in Table 8. In order to compare the performance of NMF reduction we have conducted experiments using SVD with different values of k (6 and 3) and t (0.5 and 0.8). From this summary in Table 9 we can understand that even with less number of concepts and implications NMF-FCA is able to subsume all the experts rules and produce new implications similar to SVD-FCA.

Table 6. Implications obtained using NMF-FCA $k=6$ and $t=0.8$

No.	Implications	No. Objects implication holds
	Implications NOT part of expert rules	-
1	WL TN→ TB	8
2	PC SP WL NA SB → TB	1
3	PC SP MC TN → TB	3
4	PC SP NS TN → TB	4
	Implications part of expert rules	-
5	BS→ TB	0
6	TC→ TB	3
7	WL CP SB→ TB	2

Table 7. Implications obtained using NMF-FCA $k=3$ and $t=0.5$

No.	Implications	No. objects implicat-ion holds
	Implications NOT part of expert rules	-
1	WL TN→ TB	13
2	CS→TB	0
	Implications part of expert rules	-
3	BS→TB	1
4	TC→TB	0
5	SB→ TB	7
6	PC CP TN → TB	12

Table 8. Implications obtained using NMF-FCA $k=3$ and $t=0.8$

No.	Implications	No. objects implication holds
	Implications NOT part of expert rules	-
1	CS→ TB	0
	Implications part of expert rules	-
2	BC→TB	0
3	TC→ TB	0
4	SB→ TB	1
5	NS→ TB	5

Next step of our analysis is to verify quality of the new implications obtained in the analysis using NMF and compare them with that of SVD. Table 10 shows the test dataset Expert's rules, implications produced from FCA, NMF based FCA and SVD based FCA with different values of t and k are compared on the test dataset and their performance results are summarized in Table 11.

From Table 11 we can understand that FCA, NMF-FCA ($k=6$ $t=0.5$; $k=3$ $t=0.8$), SVD FCA (excluding $k=3$ $t=0.8$) have correctly identified the presence or absence of TB for 9 patients. Interestingly NMF-FCA ($k=3$ $t=0.5$) has correctly concluded TB only for 7 patients. Implications from NMF-FCA ($k=3$

Table 9. Summary of the implications from TB data

	Concepts	Edges	No. impli-cations in DG basis	Height of Concept lattice	No. new impli-cations	No. Expert rules subsumed
FCA	101	253	33	11	9	8
NMF-FCA $k=6$ $t=0.5$	93	226	20	11	6	8
NMF-FCA $k=6$ $t=0.8$	57	125	27	9	7	7
NMF-FCA $k=3$ $t=0.5$	25	39	17	9	6	7
NMF-FCA $k=3$ $t=0.8$	33	58	15	8	5	8
SVD-FCA $k=6$ $t=0.5$	98	247	31	11	9	8
SVD-FCA $k=6$ $t=0.8$	74	177	28	8	8	8
SVD-FCA $k=3$ $t=0.5$	44	89	18	9	6	8
SVD-FCA $k=3$ $t=0.8$	32	62	19	7	9	7

Table 10. Incidence matrix of TB test dataset

	PC	SP	MC	BS	CS	WL	NS	NA	CP	SB	TC	TN	TB
Obj 22	X	-	-	-	-	-	-	-	X	-	-	X	-
Obj 23	X	X	X	-	-	X	X	-	X	X	X	X	X
Obj 24	X	X	X	-	-	X	X	X	X	-	X	X	X
Obj 25	X	X	X	-	-	X	-	X	X	X	X	X	X
Obj 26	X	X	X	-	-	X	X	X	-	-	X	X	X
Obj 27	X	X	X	-	-	X	X	-	X	X	-	X	X
Obj 28	X	X	-	-	X	X	X	X	-	-	-	X	X
Obj 29	X	-	-	-	-	X	X	-	X	-	-	X	X
Obj 30	-	-	-	-	-	X	-	-	-	-	-	-	X
Obj 31	-	-	-	-	-	X	X	X	-	-	-	-	X

Table 11. Performance comparisons of FCA, NMFFCA and SVD-FCA on TB test data

Patient	Doctors' review	Experts' rules	FCA	NMF-FCA $k=6$ $t=0.5$	NMF-FCA $k=6$ $t=0.8$	NMF-FCA $k=3$ $t=0.5$	NMF-FCA $k=3$ $t=0.8$	SVD-FCA $k=6$ $t=0.5$	SVD-FCA $k=6$ $t=0.8$	SVD-FCA $k=3$ $t=0.5$	SVD-FCA $k=3$ $t=0.8$
Obj 22	–	–	–	–	–	TB	–	–	–	–	–
Obj 23	TB	TB	TB	TB	TB	TB	TB	TB	TB	TB	TB
Obj 24	TB	TB	TB	TB	TB	TB	TB	TB	TB	TB	TB
Obj 25	TB	TB	TB	TB	TB	TB	TB	TB	TB	TB	TB
Obj 26	TB	TB	TB	TB	TB	TB	TB	TB	TB	TB	TB
Obj 27	TB	TB	TB	TB	TB	TB	TB	TB	TB	TB	TB
Obj 28	TB	TB	TB	TB	TB	TB	TB	TB	TB	TB	TB
Obj 29	TB	TB	TB	TB	TB	TB	TB	TB	TB	TB	TB
Obj 30	TB	–	–	–	–	–	–	–	–	–	–
Obj 31	TB	–	TB	TB	–	–	TB	TB	TB	TB	–
Results	–	80%	90%	90%	80%	70%	90%	90%	90%	90%	80%

t=0.5) have wrongly confirmed the TB for patient 22. Patient 30 is having only one symptomWeight Loss (WL). However for this patient, doctors diagnosis has confirmed TB. Rules from FCA, NMF-FCA and SVD-FCA have failed to confirm the disease for this patient. Implications obtained by FCA, NMF-FCA (k=6 t=0.5; k=3 t=0.8) and SVD-FCA (excluding k=3 t=0.8) have subsumed all the experts rules. From this analysis we can understand that with the reduced context, implications from NMF-FCA (k=6 t=0.5; k=3 t=0.8) are able to subsume all the experts rules, able to diagnose the TB in similar to FCA and SVD-FCA (excluding k=3 t=0.8) but better than the experts rules and SVD-FCA (k=3 t=0.8).

Future work on a larger data from different domains may add further refinements to the current study. Another interesting direction would be reducing the concept lattices using the Junction based on objects similarity (JBOS) [16] for the ARM task. Also the results of this analysis can be compared with that of recently proposed random projections [17].

5   Conclusions

Focus of this paper is on mining the association rules using FCA, after reducing the context size with NMF. Experiments are conducted on healthcare data and the knowledge derived in the form of attribute implications from the FCA on the NMF based reduced context are compared with that of SVD based FCA. Implications from NMF-FCA (k=6 t=0.5; k=3 t=0.8) have subsumed all the experts rules, diagnose in similar to FCA, SVD-FCA and better than the experts rules indicating the effectiveness of the proposed method.

Acknowledgments. Author sincerely acknowledges the financial support from National Board of Higher Mathematics, Dept. of Atomic Energy, Govt. of India under the grant number 2/48(11)/2010-R & D II/10806.

References

1. Priss, U.: Formal Concept Analysis in Information Science. Annual Review of Information Science and Technology 40(1), 521–543 (2007)
2. Snasel, V., Polovincak, M., Dahwa, H.M., Horak, Z.: On Concept Lattices and Implication Bases from Reduced Contexts. In: Proc. of ICCS Supplement, pp. 83–90 (2008)
3. Aswani Kumar, C.: Analysis of Unsupervised Dimensionality Reduction Techniques. Computer Science and Information Systems 6(2), 217–227 (2009)
4. Wu, W.Z., Leung, Y., Mi, J.S.: Granular Computing and Knowledge Reduction in Formal Contexts. IEEE Transactions on Knowledge and Data Engineering 21, 1461–1474 (2009)
5. Snasel, V., Gajdos, P., Abdulla, H.M.D., Polovincak, M.: Using matrix decompositions in formal concept analysis. In: Proc. of the 10th International Conference on Information Systems Implementation and Modeling (2007)

6. Snasel, V., Abdulla, H.M.D., Polovincak, M.: Behavior of the Concept Lattice Reduction to Visualizing Data after using Matrix decomposition. In: Proc. of 4th International Conference on Innovations in Information Technology, pp. 392–396 (2008)

7. Aswani Kumar, C., Srinivas, S.: Concept Lattice Reduction using Fuzzy k means Clustering. Expert Systems with Applications 37(3), 2696–2704 (2010)

8. Aswani Kumar, C., Srinivas, S.: Mining Associations in Health Care Data using Formal Concept Analysis and Singular Value Decomposition. Journal of Biological Systems 18(4), 787–807 (2010)

9. Aswani Kumar, C., Srinivas, S.: Latent Semantic Indexing using Eigenvalue Analysis for Efficient Information Retrieval. International Journal of Applied Mathematics and Computer Science 16(4), 551–558 (2006)

10. Stumme, G.: Formal Concept Analysis, Handbook of Ontologies, pp. 177–199. Springer, Heidelberg (2009)

11. Ganter, B., Wille, R.: Formal Concept Analysis: Mathematical foundations. Springer, Heidelberg (1999)

12. Krotzsch, M., Ganter, B.: A Brief Introduction to Formal Concept Analysis. In: Hitzler, P., Scharfe, H. (eds.) Conceptual Structures in Practice, pp. 3–16. CRC Press, Boca Raton (2009)

13. Lee, D.D., Seung, H.S.: Algorithms for Non-Negative Matrix Factorization. Advances in Neural Information Processing 13, 556–562 (2001)

14. Divya, R., Aswani Kumar, C., Saijanani, S., Priyadarshini, M.: Deceiving Communication Links on an Organization Email Corpus. Malaysian Journal of Computer Science 24(1), 17–33 (2011)

15. Horner, V.: Developing a Consumer Health Informatics Decision Support System using Formal Concept Analysis, Masters Thesis, University of Pretoria (2007)

16. Dias, S.M., Vicira, N.J.: Reducing the Size of Concept Lattices: The JBOS approach. In: Kryszkiewicz, M., Obiedkov, S. (eds.) Proc. CLA 2010, pp. 60–69 (2010)

17. Aswani Kumar, C.: Knowledge Discovery in Data using Formal Concept Analysis and Random Projections. International Journal of Applied Mathematics and Computer Science (accepted 2011)

Study of Diversity and Similarity of Large Chemical Databases Using Tanimoto Measure

Sankara Rao A.[1], Durga Bhavani S.[1], Sobha Rani T.[1], Raju S. Bapi[1], and Narahari Sastry G.[2]

[1] Computational Intelligence Lab, Department of Computer and Information Sciences,
University of Hyderabad, Hyderabad, India
[2] Molecular Modeling Group, Indian Institute of Chemical Technology,
Hyderabad, India
tsrcs@uohyd.ernet.in

Abstract. ZINC is a freely available chemical database which contains 27 million compounds including Drug-like, Natural Products, FDA etc., along with 9 molecular features. In this paper firstly we compute an additional number of 49 molecular features and represent the entire chemical space in the 58-length finger print space. Tanimoto metric, a popular similarity measure is used to mine the chemical space for extracting similar and diverse fingerprints. One of the important issues is that of choosing a proper reference string. Experiments with different reference strings are carried out to assess the appropriateness of a reference string. A finger print which is constituted by mandating non-trivial presence of each feature is found to be the best. Further a method which is independent of reference string is proposed using pairwise distribution but this raises the time complexity from linear to quadratic. A subgoal of this paper is also to propose a scheme that extracts a small sample data set that reflects the similarity and diversity of the population. Towards this, we conduct stratified sampling of Natural Products Database(NPD) which has 90,000 chemical compounds by dividing the space along strata representing distinct structures (rings) and then compute pairwise similarity profile. This scheme can be extended to other data bases that reside in ZINC.

Keywords: Chemical Space, Functional Groups, Molecular Finger Print, Representative Set, Stratified Sampling.

1   Introduction

Chemoinformatics is a new emerging area at the interface of chemistry and computer science in the context of drug discovery. The chemical space of drug like molecules is a huge space and computational tools are required to interpret the information available, for example, to look for molecules having interesting substructures.

K.R. Venugopal and L.M. Patnaik (Eds.): ICIP 2011, CCIS 157, pp. 40–50, 2011.

Chemical space is a collection of theoretically available chemical compounds. It is unbounded and still growing. ZINC is a free database of commercially available chemical compounds for virtual screening [1], containing Druglike as well as other databases like Natural products, FDA, Leadlike, Fragmentlike etc. Since the chemical space is very huge, there is a need to extract a representative data set of the chemical space without losing the original diversity and similarity. But the space of drug-like molecules is bounded by some constraints such as Lipinski rules of five where a set of empirically derived rules is used to define molecules that are more likely to be orally consumable as drugs. However, even this reduced druglike chemistry space is estimated to contain anything from 10^{12} - to 10^{180} molecules.

The literature on study of chemical data mainly deals with similarity searching of the databases. Willet et al. [2], analyze different measures of similarity on chemical spaces and compare the fingerprint based approach to structural based representations. Baldi et al. [3], explore the chemical data base ChemDB represented using fingerprint approach applying the tanimoto similarity measure. The authors model the chemical data using correlated Gaussians approach and further calculate significance scores which in turn enable them to propose a BLAST-like tool to search for similar molecules in the chemical space. Work of Karwath et al. [4], relates to extracting interesting substructures using Tanimoto measure for classification purposes. Nathan Brown gives a comprehensive suvey of the entire area of chemoinformatics and in particular writes about the work related to similarity and diversity of the chemical space [5]. Early studies into molecular diversity attempted to select subsets of a dataset that bound the dataset by covering the extremities of the space. But this would unbalance the selection with the centers of the distribution omitted. It is clear that maintaining diversity of the space would entail choosing a representative data set which 'covers' the whole of chemical space. We basically explore the hypothesis of Nathan Brown if similarity and diversity can be retained by doing random sampling of the data base. This certainly would work if the random sample is large enough. Suppose a small representative sample is required, then one needs to look inside the data set and choose from each of the different molecular clusters that make up the data set.

1.1   ZINC Database

Molecular data in ZINC [1], is available in different formats out of which SMILES (Simplified Molecular Input Line Entry System) is an exciting representation from algorithms perspective (Fig. 1). The 3D chemical compounds are represented as linear sequences which can be searched very fast for substructures. String algorithms starting from a simple regular expression search yields many interesting insights into the structures of 'drug-like' chemical compounds.

SMILES [6], gives a string representation for a 2D or 3D molecule. There exist many tools to convert a 2D molecular structure into SMILES format. The

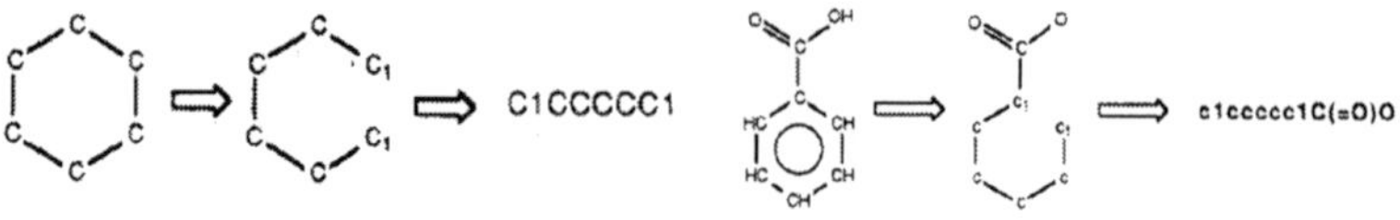

(a) Cyclic structures Conversion

(b) Cyclic Structure with Branches Conversion

Fig. 1. SMILES Representation

alphabet of the string includes atoms, symbols corresponding to chemical bonds and branches. Branches are specified by enclosures in parentheses. Branches can be nested or stacked. Cyclic structures are represented by breaking one single (or aromatic) bond in each ring. Clearly, SMILES notation need not be unique for a chemical compound. Aromatic structures may be distinguished by writing the atoms in the aromatic ring in lower case letters.

2   Molecular Fingerprint

A chemical compound is represented as a fingerprint which is a bit string encoding of structural features using calculated molecular properties of the molecule. Each bit position in a fingerprint corresponds to one molecular feature and it monitors the presence or absence of a particular molecular property [4]. The different types of fingerprints introduced in the literature are the key-type fingerprints [7], hashed fingerprints, MACCAS keys and MDL fingerprints [8], etc.

2.1   Fingerprint Representation

Many different molecular descriptors are available and come from a range of distinct descriptor classes such as physical, structural and functional groups. In the current work we have calculated 49 features in addition to the available 9 physical properties from ZINC to build a 58-length fingerprint.

- ZINC provides 9 physico-chemical properties such as molecular weight(MW), logP, and so on. These properties provide values that are intuitive to chemists and thereby permit informed decisions to be made.
- Since each molecule in ZINC is formed by using the organic subset of atoms $\{Br, C, Cl, F, H, I, N, Na, O, P, S\}$, we counted these individual atoms in each molecule (Features numbering from 10 to 19 in Table 1). These features capture the atomic content of a chemical molecule.
- Structural features identified by domain experts in each molecule are number of chiral centers, cyclic or acyclic, nature of cycles and cycles with hetero atoms. (Features from 20 to 28 in Table 1).
- We evaluated nearly 30 Functional Groups like -C, furon, -COOH, -COOCl. These features are suggested by domain experts (Features from 29 to 58 in Table 1).

Table 1. Features

Physical(9)	Atom Count(10)	Structural(9)
1. Mol. Weight	10. Br Count	20. Cyclic
2. logP	11. C Count	21. Acyclic
3. De_apolar	12. Cl Count	22. Mono Cyclic
4. De_polar	13. F Count	23. Bi Cyclic
5. HBD 14.	I Count	24. Tri Cyclic
6. HBA	15. N Count	25. Tetra Cyclic
7. tPSA	16. Na Count	26. Hi cyclic(>5 cycles)
8. Charge	17. O Count	27. Hetero cyclic
9. NRB	18. P Count	28. Chiral Centers
	19. S Count	
Functional Groups(30)		
29. -Cl	39. -COOH	49. -CHO
30. -Br	40. -COOR	50. Ketone
31. -F	41. -COOCl	51. Thiketone
32. -O	42. Cyano	52. Peptide
33. -S	43. Isocynate	53. Nitroso
34. -N	44. −C=N-R	54. Nitro
35. Alkylamino	45. Acetyne	55. Furon
36. Dialkylamino	46. Ethylene	56. Pynol
37. Amide	47. Azo N#N	57. Aromatic S
38. Amide2	48. Phenol	58. Phenyl

An example of a finger print is shown in Fig. 2.

3 Similarity and Diversity

Similarity measures like Tanimoto, Dice and Cosine coefficients are used to compute similarity. We use the popular Tanimoto coefficient (TC) [2], to measure similarity of molecules. For any two molecular fingerprints A and B we have

$$TC(A, B) = \frac{\sum_{i=0}^{n} A_i B_i}{\sum_{i=0}^{n} A_i^2 + \sum_{i=0}^{n} B_i^2 - \sum_{i=0}^{n} A_i B_i}. \tag{1}$$

If $TC(A, B) \equiv 1$ then A, B are similar and if $TC(A, B) \equiv 0$ then A, B are dissimilar.

In Fig. 3 we show the effectiveness of Tanimoto coefficient by querying the data base with a molecule and obtaining similar molecules that is, having Tanimoto coefficient value equal to 1 from the first molecule in the Fig. 3(a) and molecules with Tanimoto coefficient less than 0.5 (Fig. 3(b)) from the first molecule.

If we see in Fig. 3(a), the molecules having Tanimoto coefficient 1 seem to exhibit common substructures with the query molecule, and those having Tanimoto value less than 0.5 to be structurally different from the first molecule. To our knowledge, molecules in Fig. 3(a) are similar, and those are in Fig. 3(b) are dissimilar.

ZINCID	SMILES	MWT	logP	De_apolar	De_polar	HBD	HBA
ZINC00000053	CC(=O)Oc1ccccc1C(=O)[O-]	1	1	1	1	0	1
ZINC00000076	c1ccc(cc1)[C@@H](C(=O)c2ccccc2)O	0	1	1	1	1	1
ZINC00000204	Cc1cc(c(c(=O)o1)C(=O)C)O	1	1	1	1	0	1
ZINC00000226	CC(=O)Nc1ccc(cc1)C(=O)[O-]	1	1	1	1	1	1

tPSA	Charge	NRB	Br	C	Cl	F	I	N	Na	O	P	S	Cyclic	Acyclic	Mono	BiCy	TriCy	Chi
1	1	1	0	1	0	0	0	0	1	0	0	1	0	1	0	0	0	0
1	0	1	0	1	0	0	0	0	0	1	0	0	1	0	0	1	0	1
1	0	1	0	1	0	0	0	0	0	1	0	0	1	0	1	0	0	0
1	-1	1	0	1	0	0	1	0	1	0	0	1	0	1	0	0	0	0

Fig. 2. Example Fingerprint Representation

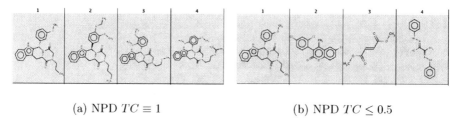

(a) NPD $TC \equiv 1$ (b) NPD $TC \leq 0.5$

Fig. 3. Similar and Dissimiliar Molecules Obtained for a query given in 1

In the next section we explore the chemical fingerprint space using Tanimoto measure. Any distance measure needs a reference from which the distance is computed and hence extracting an appropriate reference molecule forms the study of the next section.

4   Distribution of Fingerprints with Respect to Different Reference Strings

Here we have performed many experiments on resultant fingerprints by using Tanimoto similarity coefficient. All these experiments reflect the profile of distributions of the database to some extent. For experimental purpose, we selected 3 datasets Druglike, Natural Products, FDA approved Drugs from ZINC database.

In order to compare the fingerprint overlap between a reference fingerprint and a database molecular fingerprint, it is important to choose a proper reference molecule from the database based on some criteria. Here we have taken various types of reference fingerprints and calculated Tanimoto coefficient between a reference and each database molecule. Every reference has its own significance. One of reference strings that can be considered is a string having all 1's which is based on the assumption that the reference molecule has all the 58 features. Of course it is practically impossible to find such a molecule because our set of descriptors contains some complimentary features.

4.1   Reference Fingerprint with all Positions Set to On

Initially we constructed a reference fingerprint with all of its positions set equal
to 1. We calculated Tanimoto coefficient values from this reference fingerprint
to other database molecule fingerprints.The distribution of the profiles obtained
for all the three data sets of Drug-like, NPD and FDA are shown in the Fig. 4.

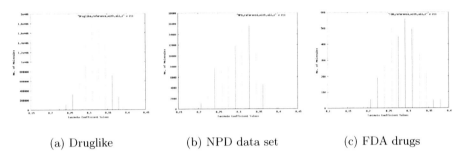

| (a) Druglike | (b) NPD data set | (c) FDA drugs |

Fig. 4. Tanimoto similarity distribution using reference fingerprint with all 1's

If we observe the Fig. 4, we can see that the TC values are confined to the
range of 0.137 to 0.414 only and are grouped into a few classes. There are no
molecules with TC value greater than 0.5 or near to 1. Clearly complimentary
features like cyclic and acyclic features cannot be present in any molecule simultaneously. On the other hand, some features haven't contributed at all to
a finger print and as shown in Table 2, approximately only half of the features
participate in any given molecule. Hence this query distribution may not reflect
the distribution of the population so well.

Table 2. Minimum and maximum number of features present in each database

	Druglike	NPD	FDA drugs
Minimum no. of features	9	10	8
Maximum no. of features	26	24	23

4.2   Reference with Maximum Number of Features Present

In this experiment we select a molecule which contains the highest number of
features as a reference molecule. Since such a molecule is not unique in either
of the data sets, we select randomly one among such molecules. For example,
there are about 35 molecules with 26 features in Druglike data set, we select one
molecule from these 35 molecules as a reference molecule. It is to be noted that
all these 35 molecules have same number of features but may not have same
features. Fig. 5 shows the distribution of Tanimoto values obtained for all the
three data sets from the corresponding reference molecule.

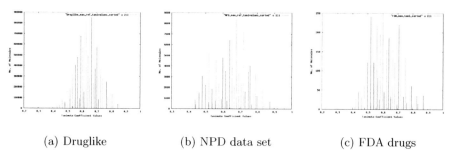

| (a) Druglike | (b) NPD data set | (c) FDA drugs |

Fig. 5. TC distribution with reference fingerprint having maximum number of bits on

If we compare the Fig. 4 and the Fig. 5, it can be seen that Tanimoto values are more dense in Fig. 5 varying from 0.35 to 0.9. So both similarity and diversity paradigms are going to be achieved in this direction.

Varying this experiment a little, we consider only features that actually contribute to tanimoto measure upto a certain threshold.

4.3   Reference Based on the Percentage of Contribution of Features

We calculated the average contribution of each feature in the three chemical data sets of NPD, Drug-like and FDA. It is observed that some of the features are present in all molecules and a few are not present in any molecule. For example, 100% of molecules have carbon and no molecule has sodium. And the molecular weight feature (MW) which relates to the Lipinski bound for drug like molecules is satisfied by 88.67% of molecules in FDA and 95.12% of molecules in NPD. Some features like bromine and pynol are present in very few molecules. While constructing the reference fingerprint, the threshold is chosen such that such low contibution features are ignored.

It is not always a good idea to avoid a feature which is absent only in a few molecules. Hence reference fingerprint is constructed in such a way that if there are T% or more molecules having a particular feature then we set the corresponding bit position to 1, otherwise it is set to 0. Here we have chosen the threshold T to be 10%. The experiments could be repeated by changing the threshold value. The distribution shown in the Fig. 6 corresponds to a threshold of 10%.

So far we have only concentrated on different reference fingerprints selection with different srategies. The reference strings discussed may not belong to the data set. The problem of picking a reference string is an issue. One way of avoiding this issue is to compute distances between all pairs of molecules and plotting the distribution.

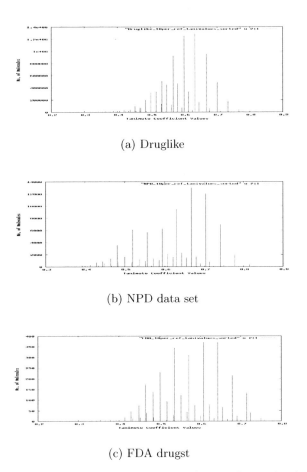

(a) Druglike

(b) NPD data set

(c) FDA drugst

Fig. 6. Tanimoto distribution with respect to reference fingerprint having features present in at least 10% of the data set

5   Study of Fingerprint Distribution Independent of Reference String

We suggest that we calculate all the pair-wise Tanimoto distances between every pair of fingerprints and plot the distribution. It can be seen that it is an $O(n^2)$ operation on n molecules. Even though this computation involves many calculations, we prefer this approach because of its effectiveness. In this section all the experiments are carried out on NPD which is the smaller of the data sets present in ZINC. The Fig. 7 shows the plot of Tanimoto coefficient values, carried out pairwise, of 1000 randomly generated molecules from NPD. It can be seen in the Fig. 7 that many pairs of molecules have Tanimoto values between 0.5 and 0.9. Also, it was verified that all molecules having values close to 1 contain the same number of cycles.

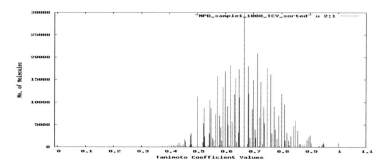

Fig. 7. Tanimoto Distribution profile of a sample of 1000 molecules taken randomly from NPD

On the other hand, as said before, this strategy involves many calculations. For instance, 76,287,297 million calculations are required in case of Druglike and it involves 3960.5 million calculations for NPD. So it is a tough job to handle. It would then be better to divide the data set and conquer the distribution calculation.

5.1 Stratified Sampling of Population

It is clear from the Fig. 3(a) that if we take a cyclic molecule as a reference, all the molecules having TC value near to 1 with this reference have same number of cycles. So it is worthwhile to classify the whole database into small number of subsets based on the number of cycles in a molecule. Of course there is a possibility for two similar molecules having different number of cycles. In order to conduct stratified sampling, we study the dataset for frequency and percentage of density of each cycle and it is found that the subsets bi-cyclic, tri cyclic and tetra cyclic molecules are very dense in each database.

NPD is split into eight subsets in order to form a sample set with 5000 molecules by taking the union of random samples from each of the eight subsets. This union is constructed using stratified sampling approach, that is the sample contains same percentage of each of the categories of molecules as the original database. For example, if we want to find a stratified sample set with 5000 NPD molecules, then it must contain 36 (0.71% of 5000) acyclic molecules, 264 (5.28% of 5000) monocyclic molecules, 735 (14.7% of 5000) bicyclic molecules, 1229 (24.57% of 5000) tricyclic molecules, 1451 (29.03% of 5000) tetracyclic molecules and so on.

A result of extracting a sample of one category is shown here. We consider acyclic population, generate random samples and plot the distribution for each sample. Then compare the distribution profile and statistical values of each sample with that of the population. Select one sample that gives the best approximation to the population. The selected sample could be treated as a representative set of the original dataset. We generated five random samples from each population and calculated the statistical values- mean, variance, median, and mode.

Table 3. Statistical Values - Acyclic molecules in NPD

DATASET	MEAN	VARIANCE	MODE	MEDIAN
Population	0.709	0.011	0.667	0.706
Sample1	0.714	0.012	0.667	0.706
Sample2	0.706	0.011	0.667	0.688
sample3	0.715	0.010	0.667	0.706
Sample4	0.720	0.010	0.706	0.706
Sample5	0.691	0.011	0.667	0.688

6 Conclusions

ZINC is a huge database containing Druglike as well as other databases like Natural products, FDA, Leadlike, Fragmentlike compounds. Since the chemical space is very huge, there is a need to formalize an approach for studying the underlying distribution in order to get an idea of the similarity and diversity present in the data set. In the first part of the paper, with the help of domain experts, a 58-length finger print is defined and the whole data set is represented in this feature space. Tanimoto coefficient which is a popular similarity measure is utilized to study the fingerprints of the molecules for similarity and diversity. In order to plot a distribution of Tanimoto values, we need a reference string from which the distances have to be computed. The paper discusses many kinds of reference strings and plots the distributions so obtained and further analyzes their strengths and weaknesses. We conclude that one of the objective methods for obtaining Tanimoto distribution is to plot all the pair-wise distances of the molecules present in the data set. But this operation blows up the time and space complexity. It is not possible to plot the distribution of pair-wise distances for the entire data set, so we choose a small random sample for which the distribution is plotted. In order to reduce the time and space complexity, a stratified sampling approach is proposed to obtain a 'representative' sample of the whole population. It is shown in a preliminary statistical verification this distribution is close to the distribution parameters of the whole population. A thorough investigation is necessary to verify if stratified sample actually selects a 'representative' sample of the whole data set or not. This is part of the ongoing study.

References

1. Irwin, J.J., Shoichet, B.K.: ZINC - A Free Database of Commercially Available Compounds for Virtual Screening. Journal on Chemical Information Model 45(1), 177–182 (2005)
2. Willett, P., Barnard, J.M., Downs, G.M.: Chemical Similarity Searching. J. Chemical Information Computer Science 38, 983–996 (1998)
3. Baldi, P., Benz, R.W.: BLASTing Small Molecules Statistics and Extreme Statistics of Chemical Similarity Scores. J. Chem. Inf. Model 24, i357-i365 (2008)
4. Karwath, A., Raedt, L.D.: SMIREP. Journal of Chemical Information Model 46, 2432–2444 (2006)

5. Brown, N.: Chemoinformatics-An Introduction for Computer Scientists. ACM Computer Survey 41(2), 1–38 (2009)
6. Weininger, D.: SMILES, A Chemical Language and Information System. Journal of Chemical Information Computer Science 28, 31–36 (1988)
7. Wang, Y., Bajorath, J.: Bit Silencing in Fingerprints Enables the Derivation of Compound Class-Directed Similarity Metrics. Journal of Chemical Information Model 48, 1754–1759 (2008)
8. Durant, J.L., Leland, B.A., Henry, D.R., Nourse, J.G.: Reoptimization of MDL Keys for use in Drug Discovery. Journal of Chemical Information Computer Science 42, 1273–1280 (2002)

Byte Level n–Gram Analysis for Malware Detection

Sachin Jain and Yogesh Kumar Meena

Malaviya National Institute of Technology, Jaipur, Rajasthan, India
sachin.mnit.internship@gmail.com, yogimnit@yahoo.co.in

Abstract. Advent of Internet and all legal transactions through it has made computer systems vulnerable. Malicious code writers launch illicit programs to the compromised systems to gain access to the resources, and confidential/intellectual information of the users. The primary reason for systems becoming vulnerable for attack is because of the ignorance of the Naïve users using the system over Internet without worrying about the extent of threats. Hence, malware detection is of prime importance for protecting systems and its resources. Most malware scanners employ signature based detection methods. These scanners fail to detect unseen and obfuscated malware samples. In this paper we propose a non–signature based approach for detecting malicious code. n–grams are extracted from Portable Executable (PE) of benign and malware samples which is considered as feature. n–grams ranging from 1 to 8 is extracted from raw byte patterns. Since the number of unique n–grams extracted from the sample are very large hence, *Classwise document frequency* is used for reducing feature space. Experiments have been conducted on 2138 Portable Executables (PE) samples and classification is performed using classifiers like *Naïve Bayes, Instance Based Learner (IBK), J48* and *AdaBoost1* supported by WEKA(a data mining tool). Experimental results are promising and shows that our proposed approach can be used to effectively classify executables (Malware and Benign) minimizing false alarms.

Keywords: Classifiers, Class-Wise Document Frequency, Malware, n–Gram, Portable Executables.

1 Introduction

Malware is any computer program with malicious intentions. Malware is general term used for viruses, worms, Trojan horse and Backdoors etc., Malicious code recursively replicates to generate copies of itself by infecting a host file, system area of the computer system etc., to take control and then multiply again to form new variants [1].

In today's scenario most of the antivirus products rely on Signature based methods to detect new suspicious sample. The classic signature based detection algorithm uses signatures of known malicious samples to generate detection models. Signatures create a unique fingerprint for each malicious sample so that

K.R. Venugopal and L.M. Patnaik (Eds.): ICIP 2011, CCIS 157, pp. 51–59, 2011.
© Springer-Verlag Berlin Heidelberg 2011

it can be correctly classified with a less false rate. The methods do not generalize well to detect new malicious samples as they would easily escape from the detection using code obfuscation and packing techniques [2]. Increase in number of samples increases the size of signature database and thus the time for scanning a sample relatively increases.

To circumvent these disadvantages, data mining approaches [3] are proposed recently for detection of computer malware. The main idea is to promote supervised classification schemes where the known instances of malware and benign programs are considered as a training set and features extracted from the training set are used to build a classification model to profile benign and malware classes.

Normally n–grams of byte sequences of the programs are considered as the basic features and several classifiers such as *decision trees, Naïve Bayes* are used for classification. In our proposed methodology, we make use of a method to extract features from known malicious sample which could assist in classification of unknown executables. We make use of classwise document frequency to extract prominent features which can distinguish a malware from a benign program. In general, the number of feature space is very large hence, attributes are condensed to minimize the overheads in order to reduce the time required by classifiers during training and testing phase. Different n–gram models are developed using classifiers like *Naïve Bayes, Instance Based Learner (IBK), J48* and *AdaBoost1* which are available in WEKA [4]. Our results show that the proposed method performs better and can be used to assist malware scanners for detection and analysis of sample.

Experiments are performed using collected malware samples from VX Heaven [5] repository. In total malware programs consists of 1018 Portable Executables (PE). Benign program (1120 executables) are gathered mainly from `system32` folder of fresh installation of genuine Windows XP operating system, Cygwin executables and many others utilities (games, media players, browsers etc.). Then hex code of executables (malware and benign) are extracted using 010Editor [6]. Our n–gram module generates n–grams of varying size ($n = 1, 2, \ldots, 8$). In our proposed method, we consider histograms of each n–grams. The entire dataset is divided in two parts for (a) training and (b) testing. Split percentage value of 65 is selected from the WEKA tool for the data set.

2   Related Work

In general, there are two kinds of approaches for malicious code detection: static analysis and dynamic analysis. Static analysis utilizes the information in suspected executable programs without executing them. Dynamic detection method gives detailed analysis of the samples by monitoring the complete execution paths of the sample making it slow detection method.

Theoretically, the detection of malicious executables in general is known to be hard problem [7]. Several techniques have been proposed in literature for the detection of malicious codes. These methods could be classified as (a) signature based and (b) non-signature based. Non–signature based techniques [8] are normally based on data mining and machine learning principles where the detection system models based on behavior of the process or the user based on previous facts.

Lately, the problem of detecting unknown malicious code has been addressed by using machine learning and data mining techniques [9]. In their research they propose to use different data mining methods for detection of new malware. To the best of our knowledge, *n*–grams were used first for malware analysis by an IBM research group [10]. They proposed a method to automatically extract signature for the malware.

We used statistical behavior–based analysis with data mining method to find out most appropriate features which can distinguish a malware from a benign program. To find out most prominent features *Classwise document frequency* is used. Different *n*–gram models are prepared using the classifiers like *Naïve Bayes*, *Instance Based Learner (IBK)*, *J48* and *AdaBoost1(J48* as base classifier).

3   Malware Features

Feature is synonym for input variables or attributes. The key idea is to select relevant attributes or patterns existing with higher frequency in order to classify a sample as malware or benign. In our proposed work we have extracted raw *n*–grams from PE file. Features are processed using *Classwise Document Frequency* to eliminate redundant features to avoid classifier overheads during training and testing phase. In the proposed methodology *n*–gram from code section of the samples are extracted.

3.1   *n*–Gram

n–grams are overlapping sub-strings collected in sliding window fashion. Basically, these are sequences with length of *n*. The main advantage of using *n*–gram is that it captures the frequencies of words of length *n*, also represents the frequencies of longer substrings. We have extracted *n*–gram by targeting executable sections of PE samples (Malware and Benign). Table 1 shows *n*–gram for *n* = 1, 2, 3, 4 for the pattern `C3908D7426005589`.

Table 1. *n*–grams for different values of *n* = 1, 2, 3, 4, · · · , 8

1gram	text2gram	text3gram	text4gram
C3	C390	C3908D	C3908D74
90	908D	908D74	908D7426
8D	8D74	8D7426	8D742600

Motivated by the text categorization, we arrived at the conclusion that malicious programs (of same functionality) share commonalities in form of opcode patterns, API calling sequence, system calls, byte patterns, mnemonic patterns etc., Therefore in malware, we think that there may be some n–grams that might with high frequencies which can be used for classification of samples.

4   Classwise Document Frequency

Classwise document frequency is a method to select prominent features from the feature space. It is a method of reducing the dimensionality of feature by appropriately selecting subset of the features. Discriminant attributes extracted is used for classification using the expression given below.

$$\sum_{val\epsilon(0,1)} \sum_{C\epsilon(M,B)} P(val,C)\frac{P(val,C)}{P(val)P(C)}. \tag{1}$$

Where C is one of two classes benign or malware, parameter V_{Ng} can either be 0 or 1, where 0 represents absence of n–gram N_g in a class C and 1 represents presence of n–gram. $P(V_{Ng},C)$ is the proportion of samples belonging to class C with presence of n–gram N_g. $P(V_{Ng})$ is the proportion of samples in entire data set consisting of n–gram N_g with the value V_{Ng}. $P(C)$ is the prior probability of classes which in our case is 0.5.

Each n–gram is sorted in descending order by $F(M_{Ng})$ value and top features are extracted. Using these features a feature vector table for the entire data–set is prepared. Finally, different n–gram models ($n = 1, 2, \ldots\ldots\ldots, 8$) is prepared using various classifiers like *Naïve Bayes, Instance Based Learner (IBK), J48, AdaBoost1 (J48* as base classifier).

Table 2. Some prominent attributes selected for different n–grams (for different values of $n = 1, 2, 3, 4$)

1gram	text2gram	text3gram	text4gram
C9	555B	85C074	85C08945
15	58EC	85C075	85C07410
DB	45EC	8B4508	83F8FF74
85	8D45	85C00F	83F8FF89

5   Brief Outline of Proposed Work

In this section we discuss our methodology for classifying malware and benign samples. Following are the steps adopted in our approach Fig. 1.

- Collect malware and benign sample in PE file formats.
- Extract raw byte patterns targeting the code section of the executables.
- Generate n–grams for n = 1, 2, $\ldots\ldots$, 8 for malware and benign sample
- Extract subset of features according to *Classwise Document frequency*.

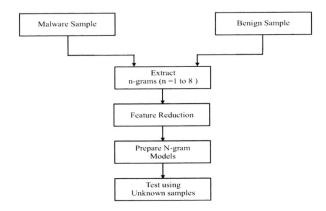

Fig. 1. Outline of the steps involved for analyzing the samples as suspicious or benign

- Generate different n–gram model using the classifier supported by WEKA (e.g. *Naïve Bayes, J48, RF* etc.,).
- Test samples are validated using each n–gram model. The evaluation metrics like TPR, FNR, TNR, FPR is used to find the sensitivity and accuracy of classification. Best n–gram and classifier are selected by analyzing results of evaluation metrics.

6   Classification Algorithm

In our proposed method malware and benign samples are trained and tested using classification algorithms supported by a data mining tool WEKA largely used by researchers. Brief introduction of some of the classifiers used for classification is described below.

(i)   *Naïve Bayes(NB):* The *Naïve Bayes* [3] Classifier is based on the Bayesian theorem and is particularly suited when the dimensionality of the inputs is high. *Naïve Bayes* classifier assumes that the presence (or absence) of a particular feature of a class is unrelated to the presence (or absence) of any other feature. Depending on the precise nature of the probability model, Naïve Bayes classifiers can be trained very efficiently in a supervised learning manner. An advantage of the *Naïve Bayes* classifier is that it requires a small amount of training data to estimate the parameters (means and variances of the variables) necessary for classification. Because independent variables are assumed, only the variances of the variables for each class need to be determined and not the entire covariance matrix.

(ii)   *Instance Based learner (IBK):* In the *Instance Based learner* [3] each instance in the total set of instance space is represented as a set of attribute. One of the attributes is a predictor attribute, based on this attribute the instances are classified. Instance Based Learning algorithm (IBL) produces concepts or concept descriptor as output. The concept descriptor represents the category (predicted value) to which a particular instance belongs. IBL makes use of a similarity, classification function, and a updater for concept descriptor. The similarity function estimates the similarities between the training instances and the instances in the concept descriptor. The classification estimates the instances and generates the classification using the information available in the concept descriptor. The Updater decides instances should be maintained in the concept descriptor. In IBK the classification is performed on the basis on majority of votes received from k Neighbours.

(iii)   *Decision Trees (J48):* The decision tree [3] is a form of prediction model constituting a root node with two child nodes known as (a) decision and (b) class. The input is a labelled training data and the output is a hierarchical structure of the input. The tree partitions complete data set such that the difference between the dependent variables are maximized there by reducing the dimensionality. Each node basically contains two information (a) an purity index which gives the information that all instances belong to the same class (b) and the total size of data under consideration. The *J48* algorithm constructs the decision tree based on the attributes obtained from the training set. The classifier extracts the attributes which can classify the instances such attributes are called discriminant attributes. A decision tree model is build using the training instances and the attribute selection is done using information gain.

(iv)   *AdaBoost1: AdaBoost1 (J48* as base classifier) [3]is a meta classifier designed for boosting the performance of existing classifier or the base classifier. In our proposed work we have considered *J48* as the base classifier. In boosting the training samples are initially assigned equal weights. Individual classifiers are learned iteratively. Finally, a boosted classifier is built based on the votes gathered from individual classifiers. Boosting assigns a weight to individual classifier based on its performance which is measured by classifier error rate. Lower the error rate better the accuracy of the classifier selected for predicting the unknown tuples.

(v)   *Random Forest:* A *Random Forest* [3] is a collection of many decision trees. It is usually used when the data set is very large. The decision tree is constructed by randomly selecting subset of the training data and attributes which can primarily partition the available data set. The final decision tree is an ensemble (i.e., a collection) of forest such that each decision tree contributes for generating the result.

7   Evaluation Metrics

Experiments are evaluated using evaluation metrics like TPR, TNR, FPR, FNR. True positive (TP) is the number of samples classified as malware, where as True negative (TN) total samples classified as benign. The performance of classifier can be measured by primarily checking the TPR and TNR which are also called as the sensitivity and specificity.

- *textTruePositiveRate(TPR)* : Is the ratio of actual positives correctly classified as positives. TPR=(TP/(TP+FN))
- *textFalsePositiveRate(FPR)* : The proportion of benign samples being incorrectly classified as malicious. This is also called as false alarm rate or fall out. FPR=(FP/(FP+TN))
- *textTrueNegativeRate(TNR)* : The ratio of negatives (benign sample) correctly identified as negatives. TNR=(TN/(TN+FP))
- *textFalseNegativeRate(FNR)* : The proportions of cases in which a test produces negative outcome for a malicious sample. FNR=(FN/(FN+TP))
  In case of a protection system high value of TPR and TNR along with low FPR and FNR is required. This would ascertain that the scanner is capable of identifying samples correctly as malware or benign.

8 Experimental Setup and Result Analysis

The experiments have been performed on malicious samples collected from VX Heavens. We have gathered 1018 malware executables (viruses, worms, Trojan, Backdoors etc.,) and 1120 benign samples. The benign samples include executables from `system32` folder of fresh installation of genuine Windows XP operating system, games, media players, browsers etc. The data sets are trained and tested using classifiers supported by WEKA. The experimental results suggests that the *3*–gram models is better compared to other *n*–gram models ($n = 1, 2, 4, 5, 6, 7, 8$). This can be verified by average values of TPR $= 1.0$, TNR $= 0.92$ and lower values of FNR $= 0$, FPR $= 0.08$ refer Table 3.

Table 3. Average Values for various evaluation parameters for different *n*–grams

n–gram	textTPR	textFNR	textTNR	textFPR
1gram	0.89	0.11	0.73	0.27
2gram	0.92	0.08	0.98	0.02
3gram	**1.0**	**0.0**	**0.92**	**0.08**
4gram	0.94	0.06	0.83	0.17
5gram	0.93	0.07	0.81	0.19
6gram	0.94	0.06	0.81	0.19
7gram	0.94	0.06	0.8	0.2
8gram	0.94	0.06	0.78	0.22

The performance of *n*–gram ($n = 4, 5, 6, 7, 8$) are approximately similar this can be argued by monitoring the TPR, FNR, TNR, FPR values. Looking at the average classification accuracies of *n*–gram produced classifiers we feel that the performance of *IBK* is better. The classification accuracies and detection rates of classifiers for different *n*–grams are illustrated in Tables 5 to 9.

Table 4. Mean values of evaluation parameters obtained for different classifiers

classifier	TPR	FNR	TNR	TPR
NB	0.93	0.07	0.55	0.45
IBK	0.94	0.06	0.90	0.10
J48	0.94	0.06	0.89	0.11
ADABOOSTI	0.94	0.06	0.91	0.09
RF	**0.96**	**0.04**	**0.92**	**0.08**

Table 5. Evaluation Metrics using Naïve Bayes Classifier for n–grams

Ngram	textTPR	textFNR	textTNR	textFNR
1gram	0.92	0.08	0.07	0.93
2gram	0.63	0.37	0.99	0.01
3gram	**1.0**	**0.0**	**0.77**	**0.23**
4gram	0.95	0.05	0.52	0.48
5gram	0.96	0.04	0.46	0.54
6gram	0.98	0.02	0.55	0.45
7gram	0.98	0.02	0.54	0.46
8gram	0.98	0.02	0.51	0.49

Table 6. Evaluation Metrics using IBK Classifier for n–grams

Ngram	TPR	FNR	TNR	FNR
1gram	0.89	0.11	0.90	0.10
2gram	0.97	0.03	0.98	0.02
3gram	**0.99**	**0.01**	**0.96**	**0.04**
4gram	0.94	0.06	0.90	0.10
5gram	0.92	0.08	0.88	0.12
6gram	0.93	0.07	0.87	0.13
7gram	0.94	0.06	0.85	0.15
8gram	0.93	0.07	0.84	0.16

Table 7. Evaluation Metrics using J48 Classifier for n–grams

Ngram	TPR	FNR	TNR	NR
1gram	0.87	0.13	0.85	0.15
2gram	0.98	0.02	0.98	0.02
3gram	**0.99**	**0.01**	**0.96**	**0.04**
4gram	0.93	0.07	0.91	0.09
5gram	0.93	0.07	0.88	0.12
6gram	0.93	0.07	0.86	0.14
7gram	0.93	0.07	0.84	0.16
8gram	0.94	0.06	0.83	0.17

Table 8. Evaluation Metrics using AdaBoost1 Classifier for n–grams

Ngram	TPR	FNR	TNR	FNR
1gram	0.88	0.12	0.90	0.10
2gram	0.99	0.01	0.98	0.02
3gram	**0.99**	**0.01**	**0.96**	**0.04**
4gram	0.93	0.07	0.92	0.08
5gram	0.92	0.08	0.89	0.11
6gram	0.93	0.07	0.88	0.12
7gram	0.92	0.08	0.88	0.12
8gram	0.92	0.08	0.86	0.14

Table 9. Evaluation Metrics using Random Forest Classifier for n–grams

Ngram	TPR	FNR	TNR	FNR
1gram	0.89	0.11	0.87	0.13
2gram	0.98	0.02	0.98	0.02
3gram	**1.00**	**0.00**	**0.96**	**0.04**
4gram	0.93	0.07	0.92	0.08
5gram	0.93	0.07	0.90	0.10
6gram	0.94	0.06	0.88	0.12
7gram	0.92	0.08	0.84	0.16
8gram	0.92	0.08	0.87	0.13

9   Conclusions and Future Work

In our proposed work, we have outlined nonsignature based method for malware analysis. Features in the form of Table 9 TPR, FNR, TNR, FPR are obtained using *RANDOM FOREST* classifier for different values of n–grams (FOR $n = 1, 2, 3, 4, 5, 6, 7, 8$). n–grams of length $n = 1, 2, .., 8$ have been extracted and redundant features are eliminated using classwise document frequency. Following are the key outcome from the proposed methodology.

- The detection accuracy of our proposed method is approximately 99 percent with a low NR value of 0.01.
- It has been observed that all classifiers performs better for *3*–gram because as the size of n–gram increases the frequency of the relevant n–gram decreases.
- The performance of *Naïve Bayes* classifier is not better as it assumes attribute independency and also suffers from zero frequency error.
- *Random Forest* outperforms other classifiers due to its properties like bagging and boosting.

In our future work, we would like to experiment on larger dataset primarily consisting of packed malicious codes. We would like to investigate different features of a Portable Executable (PE) samples and evaluate best features for identifying malicious code.

References

1. Peter, S.: The Art of Computer Virus Research and Defense. Addison-Wesley Professional, Reading (2005)
2. Christodorescu, M., Jha, S., Seshia, S. A., Song, D. Bryant, R.E.: Semantics-Aware Malware Detection. In: Proceedings of the 2005 IEEE Symposium on Security and Privacy, pp. 32–46 (2005)
3. Witten, I.H., Frank, E., Morgan, K.: Data Mining: Practical Machine Learning Tools and Techniques (2005)
4. The Weka Data Mining Software: an update, http://www.cs.waikato.ac.nz/ml/weka/
5. Malware Repository: Vx Heavens, http://vx.netlux.org/lib
6. Professional Hex Editor with Binary Templates, http://www.sweetscape.com/010editor/
7. Cohen, F.: Computer Viruses: theory and experiments. Computer Security 6, 22–35 (1987)
8. Yoo, I.S., Nitsche, U.U.: Non-Signature Based Virus Detection: Towards Establishing Unknown Virus Detection Technique Using Som. Computer Virology 2, 163–186 (2006)
9. Schultz, M.G., Eskin, E., Zadok, E., Stolfo, S.J.: Data Mining Methods for Detection of New Malicious Executables. In: Proceedings of the IEEE Symposium on Security and Privacy, pp. 38–49 (2003)
10. Kephart, J.O.: A Biologically Inspired Immune System for Computers. In: Proceedings of the Fourth International Workshop on the Synthesis and Simulation of Living Systems, Artificial Life IV, pp. 130–139. MIT Press, Cambridge (1994)

Integrating ILM, E-Discovery and DPA 1998 for Effective Information Processing

Anshul Kesarwani, Chandani Gupta, Manas Mani Tripathi, Vishnu Gupta, Rahul Gupta, and Vijay K Chaurasiya

Indian Institute of Information Technology, Allahabad, UP, India
anshulkesarwani@gmail.com

Abstract. We know the importance of information retrieval associated with the modern world organizations. Two concepts which play a crucial role in saving the organization from losing superfluous time and cost are the well managed Information Lifecycle Management (ILM) process and the E-discovery process. The paper proposes a relationship between the Information Lifecycle Management and the E-discovery. Today organizations keep on encountering legal issues which require information retrieval. Technologies related to information retrieval play a critical role in the process. The cost and time are of utmost importance to the organizations. Therefore, there is a need to integrate ILM and E-discovery to reduce the overall cost of information maintenance in an organization. This paper aims at optimizing the E-discovery process to make it more productive and rewarding. The paper also proposes a mapping of the principles of the Data Protection Act 1998 (DPA) associated with ILM and E-discovery. It also states the importance of rights and duties which are necessary to be considered in the process of information flow.

Keywords: Data Mining, Data Processing, Data Protection Act, E-discovery, Information Retrieval, Lifecycle Management.

1 Introduction

A successful organization is equipped with a well defined information lifecycle management. In the case of legal issues the organization takes the help of the E-discovery process. The initiation of the E-discovery process incurs a lot of cost to the organizations. The cost of E-discovery–probably the largest single cost in litigation today–poses an economic threat to any company facing litigation [1]. Gone are the days when organizations used to rely on paper documentation. Organizations are trying to create more electronic documents than the paper documents because of high acceptability of the electronic documents in the modern world. Today most of the work is digitalized. More than 90 percent of the information is handled digitally [1]. Hence in case of litigations, the cost rises due to heavy amount of searching among the humungous amount of unstructured digital data. Adding to this, a large volume of data is redundant in the form of shared or duplicates. The E-discovery process is very much similar

K.R. Venugopal and L.M. Patnaik (Eds.): ICIP 2011, CCIS 157, pp. 60–68, 2011.

to the information lifecycle management process. Organization repeatedly faces the legal challenges commencing within or outside. The management of information will surely be of immense help to the organization in handling these issues. Instead of handling the information lifecycle management process and the legal issues independently, a more proficient approach can be optimization of both the processes and combining ILM with E-discovery.

Viewing the whole scenario from a diverse perspective, regulatory requirements, such as Sarbanes-Oxley, HIPAA, and DOD5015.2-STD in the US and the European Data Privacy Directive in the European Union are changing how organizations manage their data[2]. If providing a dynamic approach during the processing of data with respect to the DPA principles while in the midst of the E-discovery process can help in slackening the process, then why not change the fashion. Hence we have tried to map the data protection act 1998 and have tried to come up with a comprehensive framework.

This paper explains the three important concepts that can be involved and used for effective management of information in the organizations i.e., the E-discovery [3], the information lifecycle management [4] process and the data protection act 1998 [5] section 2. Section 3 elaborates the proposed framework and its significance to the organization.

2   Related Work

Before we advance into the complexities of the proposed framework with collective ILM and E-discovery, concurrently mapped with DPA principles, we need to know a bit about the involved actors for better understanding [1–17].

2.1   E-discovery Process

Whenever there is any legal issue before an organization, the E-discovery process is of great help to the organization. Commercial expenditures on Electronic Data Discovery (EDD) topped $2.7 billion in 2007 according to the George Socha and Tom Gelbmann report in the 2008 Socha-Gelbmann Survey [6] Organizations are now relying on the effective E-discovery process which saves a lot of time and cost. Today organization cannot function in the absence of digital data. Hence whenever some legal matter arises, the need of digital information retrieval is required. Fast and effective retrieval of such information is of utmost importance for the successful stand against the legal matter. Hence an effective information retrieval mechanism is a must for the organization. Such information retrieval sometimes can be stated as digital forensics because digital evidences are collected to support the case. This is done by various forensic tools and methodologies. Statistics, extrapolations and counting by Radicati Group[7] from April 2010 estimate the number of emails sent per day (in 2010) to be around 294 billion[8]. Since the process in the subject is all about identifying, collecting and analyzing the digital evidences, there should a way out to do it in a manner which is dynamic and can handle information on the fly. This would definitely save both time and cost.

2.2 Information Lifecycle Management Process

The ILM process is a need of every organization related with digital information collection, storage and retrieval. Physical foundation is laid for the strength
in the physical structure of a building. Similarly ILM is required to strengthen
logical representation of data in the organization. The logical data representation is responsible for secure and efficient information handling, management
and easy retrieval as and when needed. The ILM process involves application of
certain policies and rules which can categorize the information effectively and
efficiently and hence makes it useful and easy to handle throughout its lifecycle.

The lifecycle includes the creation of information which starts from the point
of its origin, followed up by the distribution and its use. Information hence
generated in the initial phase needs to be updated regularly and maintained
according to the organization's need. At the last, the information has to be
destroyed according to its usefulness. The information is categorized on a scale
of active, less active and historical. After this categorization, which is an internal
cycle of its own, the information is destroyed accordingly.

2.3 Data Protection Act 1998 (DPA)

The data protection act basically talks about the protection of personal information and the sensitive personal information. It is a United Kingdom Act of
Parliament defining the processing of data of the living identifiable individuals. It involves UK laws for the processing of personal and sensitive personal
information. Personal information means the information which can directly indentify an individual on the basis of name and address, phone number, email
address etc. Sensitive personal information is that which can be related with
the ethnic/racial origin of the individual, his/ her political views, caste and re-
ligion, physical or mental health condition, sexual life or membership of a trade
union.

A lot of personal data is processed in today's organizations. One example of
such kind of processing can be seen in the BPO industry. It is very important for
the organization to keep a track on the amount and type of data processed and
if any irregularities involved are found, they should be eradicated as and then.

Data protection act involves eight compliance principles (Fig. 1) which are
applicable on all types of information including the information which the organization holds in its databases. Hence the organizations come under the data
protection act. Being a UK based act, it is not necessary that our proposed
framework's DPA mapping is a necessity to the organizations which lies outside
the European boundaries.

In the proposed framework, the DPA compliance principles are mapped with
the integrated E-discovery process and the information lifecycle management
process. This will give a better understanding of the compliance of the DPA
with the organization's stored information and its retrieval and processing.

3   Proposed Framework

This section describes the proposed framework. If we closely study ILM and E-discovery, we find a lot of resemblance between the two. Both the processes are talking about the information processing and management. Whenever there is a call for a legal matter, generation of a new E-discovery cycle occurs. Whenever there is a need of information management, the ILM process is deployed. Consequently, why not to have a single process which can provide both the utilities, providing some dynamicity to the ILM process with every E-discovery cycle.

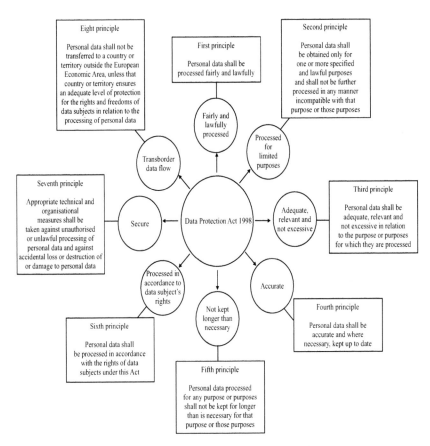

Fig. 1. Principles of Data Protection Act

The proposed framework is represented in Fig. 2. The processes are shown by rectangular solid boxes. The dotted boxes state that the process may or may not occur. The hexagonal box in the beginning and the termination box at the end show the external entities involved. The diamonds show the policies and the parallel lines signify the storage. The solid rectangle shows the involvement of sub activities. Solid and the dotted lines represent mandatory and non mandatory

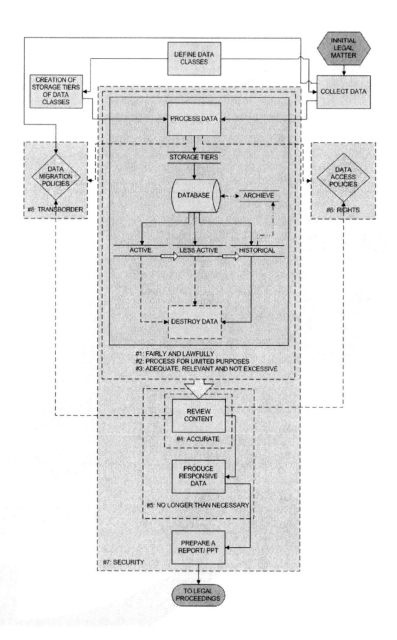

Fig. 2. Proposed Framework

information flow. All the DPA principles are mapped on the proposed framework which can be clearly identified by the dotted rectangles around the processes and the policies.

Our proposed framework is an amalgamation of three singular but related areas. Here the cause of concern is the initial legal matter which can be thought of as a formal court case or any specific legal implement undertaken by the organization. This action triggers the whole process of information retrieval.

The most important entity is the organization's data. Every process in the retrieval and management of data will start with a course of action pointing data collection. Classifying the data according to its usability is a tricky task. Preservation of data plays an important role else recovering the concerned data would become complicated. We feel the need of better data classification which should be done when the information was being collected. The ILM says that we need to classify all the data and then embark on the process of data collection, as indicated in our proposed model. But defining the data classes alone won't help.

We need to create storage tiers which can formally segregate the useful data from the not so useful ones. Storage tiers segment the data physically as well as logically and help various process owners and implementers to work accordingly. After the data collection process is done, the most important section of our proposed framework, the data processing comes into picture. A lot of data and a lot of technicalities get involved with this process. Being more of an ILM step, the data processing starts with the birth of an organization itself. While going through our day to day life we come across many instances where we consciously or subconsciously choose among what to retain and what not. Somewhat similar situations are faced by organizations too, where the problem is immense. Actually we just want to find the answer to this simple question, how to decide that a particular data will be needed, say after 20 years? Apart from contractual data there is a lot of information which get wasted, dumped or deleted and we end up looking for it as and when the need arises. Here our proposed framework can come to rescue.

The data processing starts with bringing into use the storage tier policy which we proposed earlier. As soon as data enters an organization, it is stacked in accordance with the tiers where it belongs. Let us suppose that we have four predefined data classes i.e., top secret, secret, public and unclassified. These four classes can be thought of as storage tiers. Now, as in our daily life, we prioritize things on the basis of its degree of activeness that is it needed immediately or in near future, a driving license has highest degree of activeness for a cab driver. But to that same cab driver the information about the latest fashion may not be of that relevance. So here we propose a further classification of information or the next stage in the information processing which comprises of temporary classifying the data on the basis of its activeness and usefulness. The reason we are emphasizing on temporary classification is because unlike the data tiers this stage is more of a passing out phase in an information's lifecycle as a particular piece of information which is active and useful today may be less active tomorrow and become historical the day after, eventually leading to one of the inevitable and important activities of data destruction.

Having a look at the proposed framework, one could realize that the data destruction activity is triggered once the data exits the historical data phase. But the dotted lines from active and less active data classifiers show that the concept is not hardwired and that the model is flexible to the needs of the concerned organization. Data processing is a step which is not complete without the fulfillment of two more and imperative stages namely the data migration and data access policies. The data migration policies consist of the policies framed by the top management for the flow of data in a secure and legitimate manner. For example, the migration of sensitive user data from a call center in Brazil to the parent firm in UK. A secure mechanism should be in place to facilitate the trans-border data flow. Data migration policies will also be followed when the E-discovery process is initiated, i.e., at the time of starting of the data collection process. The data access policies talk about the "who" factor related to the processing of personal and sensitive personal data, i.e. who should be accessing the data, who should be accountable in case of a failure, who will be accessing it and in what capacity. If we closely look at the proposed framework, the data processing can be stated complete only when the storage tiers and the database, the archive data and the data destruction sub activities get involved in the process. The data processing can be of dynamic nature, which will help concurrently in the ILM process of the organization.

The next part consists of the reviewing of the data which has been collected and processed. Reviewing can be thought of as a filtering technique which is applied to the processed data in order to come up with the meaningful conclusion. A kind of scrutiny of the information gathered so as to make the evidence more strong and self explanatory. We need to follow certain rules and regulations which get involved in this phase, the data migration policies and the data access policies. Every step in E-discovery and ILM is a complicated process, so while refining the data a need may arise of transferring the data across the borders or to granting access to entities which were never expected during the initial phases. The dynamic nature of our framework adds value to it. The dotted lines which are connecting the review content process to the data transfer policy and the data migration policy. The exhaustive exercise of production of responsive data which can now be termed as information is the next process. In this phase the refined data is formatted and produced in the form of a formal evidence report which is ready to be submitted to the court of law.

The penultimate stage of our model is the preparation of a report/presentation. After all it is presentation only that matters at the end of the day. We may have done an excellent job in coming up with solid evidence, but it won't be of any use if it fails to impress the judge, the jury or the concerned authorities.

All this which we have discussed so far is a mapping of two contrasting yet similar activities of information lifecycle management and E-discovery. But everything in this world is governed by some law or the other, our model being no exception. The Data Protection Act of 1998 is applicable within the boundaries of UK but all the eight principles which has been put forward by the Lindop commission completely defines the ways and means to protect data. And since our center piece here is data/information, DPA becomes an easy and natural choice for us. We put forward a unified model which maps the three entities in discussion i.e., ILM, E-discovery and DPA. The data in question is sensitive in nature (that's the reason why it is being discussed here anyway) so the first and foremost thing is its security. So we propose that at every step adequate security measures should be taken both at the time of E-discovery and ILM. And not only this there is a separate provision in DPA for the data which is flowing across the borders, hence the eighth principle which talks about the trans-border data flow can very well be applied at the data migration policies. Having said that we also know that an organization is in existence because of the people, so they must also be given certain rights as to who all will be allowed to view their data, and process it. So the accurate place for the access rights is the data access policies.

Now let's talk about the data processing section, what all principles will cover them. After a lot of heated discussions we came to the conclusion that the first three principles namely "Fairly and lawfully", "Adequate relevant and not excessive" and "Processed for limited purpose" will be better suited for this, reason being they have all the ingredients to cater the needs and demands of data processing and to adequately facilitate it. Principle five, "No longer than necessary" emphasizes on data not being kept for longer period of time than stated. Hence this principle directly maps with the production of responsive data and the review of contents. Principle four, "Accurate" talks about the data in possession should be accurate, which will involve the process of review content. We are trying to map it here as to state the dynamic nature of the framework. If any discrepancies are found during the review content process, the accuracy of the data can be checked then and there, without beginning a whole new cycle of data review. This can save a lot of time and cost to the organization, which as a result is getting done on the fly during the E-discovery process.

4   Conclusions

The proposed framework will be a departure from the traditional way of doing things. It will be more of a process centric approach towards Information life cycle management and E-discovery with the Data Protection Act being the backbone. After the implementation of this framework large organizations with a rigid tall structure will be able to better process, retrieve, use and archive there data after its classification. In this paper, we have tried to come up with a new concept which looks at the processes of Information Life Cycle Management and E-discovery in a totally different light with an additional concept of the Data Protection Act supporting the scheme of things and making it a comprehensive and fulfilling activity. That's not all; the future scope of our work is also tremendous as it's just the beginning. Our next step will be to address the unified compliance issues and how they may be carried out in tune with our proposed framework.

References

1. A Revolution in E-discovery The Persuasive Economics of the Document Analytic Approach: Kpmg Forensic
2. Data Protection Act (1998), http://www.legislation.gov.uk/ukpga/1998/29/contents
3. Preparing for E-discovery: your Roadmap to Compliance, White paper, Hewlett-Packard Development Company, L.P (2008)
4. Information Lifecycle Management: Efficiently Manage Information from Creation Through Disposal, Solutions for Leveraging IT Investments, IBM Corporation (2006)
5. The Data Protection Act 1998 When and How to Complain. Information Commissioner's Office, http://www.ico.gov.uk/
6. Socha, G., Gelbmann, T.: Report in the 2008 Socha-Gelbmann Survey, http://www.law.com/jsp/lawtechnologynews/index.jsp?id=1202423646479
7. Radicati Group, http://www.radicati.com/
8. Email Survey, http://email.about.com/od/emailtrivia/f/emails_per_day.htm
9. Compliance Information Lifecycle Management for Financial Services, IBM Sales and Distribution, IBM Corporation (2010)
10. Hobbs, L.: Information LifeCycle Management for Business Data, An Oracle White Paper (2007)
11. Information Lifecycle Management/Hitachi, Hitachi (2009)
12. Information Lifecycle Management (ILM) The Challenge in the Conflict Zone of IT Optimization and Business Demands, IBM Global Technology Services, IBM Corporation (2008)
13. Stried-Reich, K.B., Nunn, S.: The Fundamentals of E-discovery (2008)
14. Schaufenbuel, B.J.: E-Discovery: Implications of FRCP Changes on IT Risk Management. ISSA Journal (2007)
15. Silverthorn, A.: EMC Adds E-Discovery Services (2006)
16. Yue, Z., He, D.: School of Information Sciences University of Pittsburgh, A Model for Understanding Collaborative Information Behavior in E-discovery
17. The E-discovery paradigm shift, http://ediscoveryconsulting.blogspot.com/2008/09/cost-of-ediscovery.html

A Novel Ensemble Method for Time Series Classification

Sami M. Halawani[1], Ibrahim A. Albidewi[2], and Amir Ahmad[1]

[1] Faculty of Computing and Information Technology,
King Abdulaziz University, Rabigh, Saudi Arabia
[2] Faculty of Computing and Information Technology,
King Abdulaziz University, Jeddah, Saudi Arabia
amirahmad01@gmail.com

Abstract. This paper explores the issue of input randomization in decision tree ensembles for time series classification. We suggest an unsupervised discretization method to create diverse discretized datasets. We introduce a novel ensemble method, in which each decision tree is trained on one dataset from the pool of different discretized datasets created by the proposed discretization method. As the discretized data has a small number of boundaries the decision tree trained on it is forced to learn on these boundaries. Different decision trees trained on datasets having different discretization boundaries are diverse. The proposed ensembles are simple but quite accurate. We study the performance of the proposed ensembles against the other popular ensemble techniques. The proposed ensemble method matches or outperforms Bagging, and is competitive with Adaboost.M1 and Random Forests.

Keywords: Classification, Decision Trees, Ensembles, Time Series.

1 Introduction

Ensembles are a combination of multiple base models [1] the final classification depends on the combined outputs of individual models. Classifier ensembles have shown to produce better results than single models, provided the classifiers are *accurate* and *diverse* [1]. Several different methods have been proposed to build diverse decision trees. Randomization is introduced to build diverse decision trees. *Bagging* [2] and *Boosting* [3] introduce randomization by manipulating the training data supplied to each classifier. Ho [4] proposed *Random Subspaces* that selects random subsets of input features for training an ensemble. Breiman [5] combined Random Subspaces technique with Bagging to create *Random Forests*. To build a tree, it uses a bootstrap replica of the training sample, then during the tree growing phase, at each node the optimal split is selected from a random subset of size K of candidate features.

Generally a time series is defined as a sequence of data points, measured typically at successive time intervals. These data points may be real, binary or categorical valued. A large number of time series are real valued. In this paper, we are concentrating of real valued time series. Times series have large dimensions, many representational techniques [6], [7] have been proposed for analysis of time series. In recent years, the classification of time series data has become a topic of great interest. There are two popular approachs to classify time series, In the first approach, time series classification is two steps process. In first step, time series is transformed into new attributes and these

K.R. Venugopal and L.M. Patnaik (Eds.): ICIP 2011, CCIS 157, pp. 69–74, 2011.

attributes are used by the classification methods [8], [9]. Another popular approach is k nearest neighbours [10] however it suffers from poor efficiency.

In this work, we concentrate on classification of time series which have real data points by using decision trees. Time series classification is different from normal classification problem as time series have high dimensionality, using the raw data may lead to busy tree with poor accuracy. Times series datasets are transformed into low dimensional datasets to overcome this problem [7], [8].

Discretization is a process that divides continuous values into a set of intervals [11] that can be considered as categorical (also called symbolic) values. Discretization is one of the representational technique that is used to convert continuous data points of time series into symbolic data [9], [12]. In this work, we develop a novel discretization method that creates diverse discretized datasets. These diverse datasets are used to create diverse decision trees, hence ensembles of decision trees are created. This method in principle applies to any classifier (the learning process of which is perturbed with different discretization processes) though in this work we evaluate only decision trees.

In Section 2, we introduce the proposed ensemble method. Section 3 discusses experiments and performance evaluation. Section 4 describes conclusion and future work.

2   Random Symbolic Aggregate Approximation (Random SAX) Ensembles

In this section, we discuss the proposed ensemble method for the time series classification. This method uses a popular time series representational technique: Symbolic Aggregate Approximation (SAX) [9].

Discretization divides features values into different categories depending upon intervals they fall into, to create s categories, we need $s - 1$ points. There are different discretization methods [11] to create these points. However, all these methods produce a single and unique discretized dataset. For creating ensembles, we need diverse datasets so that the learning on these datasets creates diverse classifiers.

There are various representational technique[6], [7] available in time series domains, however Symbolic Aggregate Approximation (SAX) [9] technique is quite popular. Lin et al., [9] showed that most of the time series have Gaussian distribution and they proposed Symbolic Aggregate Approximation (SAX) method for time series that uses this distribution information. In SAX, discretization is an online method, *it does not need access of all the data points, for creating discretized dataset.* SAX has following two steps:

1. Dimensionality reduction via Piecewise Aggregate Approximation (PAA) [7]- Time series is divided into equal sized windows, the mean value of data points falling in the window is calculated. The vector of these values becomes the data-reduced representation. A time series C of length n can be represented in a $\frac{n}{w}$ dimensional space by a vector $\overline{C} = \overline{C_1}, \overline{C_2}, .., \overline{C_{\frac{n}{w}}}$, where w is the width of the window. The ith element of $\overline{C}$ is calculated by the following equation:

$$\overline{C_i} = \frac{1}{w} \sum_{k=w \times (i-1)+1}^{w \times i} C_k. \tag{1}$$

Every time series is normalized to have mean 0 and standard deviation 1 before converting it to PAA.

2. Discretization. Lin et al. showed that most of the time series have Gaussian distribution. As it is desirable to have a discretization technique that produces symbols with equiprobability, breakpoints (β_i) are determined that will produce a equal-sized areas under Gaussian curve. For s categories, $s-1$ breakpoints are needed, such that area under Gaussian curve between breakpoints (β_i) and $(\beta_i + 1)$ is equal to $\frac{1}{s}$. For example to get three categories, two points are 0.43 and -0.43, we get three categories by following rules:

$$\text{if } \overline{C_i} < \text{-0.43, the category is 1,}$$
$$\text{if } (\overline{C_i} \geq -0.43) \text{ and } (\overline{C_i} < 0.43)\text{, the category is 2,}$$
$$\text{if } \overline{C_i} \geq 0.43\text{, the category is 3, where } i \text{ is 1 to } n/w.$$

Excellent classification results have been achieved using the discretized data created by SAX process as an input for decision trees [9].

2.1   Random SAX

In the present work, a novel Random SAX method is developed that maintains the online property of SAX. However, in this paper, the study is carried out by using C4.5 decision trees [13] (batch learning). Random SAX method produces diverse integer datasets. Decision trees learnt on these diverse datasets are diverse. In SAX, breakpoints are calculated such that they produce equal-sized areas under Gaussian curve. We propose the following method (instead of the second step of the SAX method) to create diverse data sets.

To get the s breakpoints (β_i), create s points randomly from a Gaussian distribution. These points are not the same as suggested in SAX, however by this method, we get different breakpoints that will generate diverse discretized datasets. Decision trees learning on these diverse datasets will be diverse. We can have ensembles of these diverse decision trees. The advantage of this method is that it maintains the property of SAX that *the discretization process does not need access of all the data points, for creating discretized data* so it could be useful for online learning. However, in this work we have concentrated on batch learning.

Each decision tree in an ensemble learns on one discretized dataset from a pool of different datasets created by Random SAX. If the order of categories is maintained, a discretized dataset is an ordinal dataset. It can be treated as a continuous/integer dataset or a categorical dataset. We treat them as a continous data. In contrast of other popular ensemble methods like Bagging and Random Forests, each classifier in the proposed ensemble method is trained by using the complete training dataset that helps improve the accuracy of a member tree. During prediction of a data point x, we convert it into discretized data points by using the same break points that are used in creating decision trees, and take the prediction result of the corresponding decision trees. For example, if we use a set of break points S_i for creating a decision tree D_i, we will first convert data point x into a discretized data point by using S_i and then take the prediction result of D_i for the discretized x. The prediction results of all decision trees are combined by majority voting to get the final decision. The proposed method is presented in Fig. 1.

Input- Timeseries Dataset T. Each time series is represented by m continuous
features and L is the size of the ensemble. A user defined parameters s, the number
of bins for discretization. The size of the window, A user defined.

Training Phase
for i=1...L do
  Data Generation
  Dimensionality reduction via Piecewise Aggregate Approximation as suggested
  in the SAX method [9].
  To get the s breakpoints (β_i) for discretization, create a set of $s-1$ points, S_i,
  randomly from a Gaussian distribution. Use these points to discretize the dataset.
  The categories are ordered, in other words the generated dataset T_i is integer
  valued.
  Learning Phase
  Treat dataset T_i as continuous and learn D_i decision tree on it.
end for
Classification Phase
For a given data point x
for i=1...L do
  Convert x into a discretized data point x_i by using the same process used in the
  training process by using S_i. Get the prediction for x_i by the decision tree D_i.
end for
Combine the results of L decision trees by the chosen combination rule to get the
final classification result (We use majority voting to combine the results
of classifiers).

Fig. 1. Algorithm for Random SAX Ensembles

The success of ensemble methods depends on the creation of uncorrelated classifiers [14]. The proposed tree has limited tree growing options as it has to follow bin
boundaries. In other words, diverse decision trees are produced as different options are
provided (different bin boundaries) at tree growing phase. These diverse trees help in
creating an accurate ensemble. In the next section, we will study the performance of
Random SAX ensembles.

3 Experiments

We carried out experiments on 16 pure continuous datasets, these datasets were taken
from UCR time series repository ($http://www.cs.ucr.edu/\ eamonn/time\_series$
$\_data$). We used the J48 tree (C4.5 decision tree [13] implementation) of Weka software
[15], with the unpruned option for our experiments. The size of classifier ensembles
was set to 50. Bagging [2], AdaBoost.M1 [3] modules of Weka with J48 decision tree
were used for comparison. We also did experiments with Random Forests [5] module.
Default parameters other than the size of the ensembles were used in all cases.

Following the methodology proposed by Dietterich [16], we performed five replica-
tions of a two-fold cross-validation. 5×2 cross-validation F test proposed by Alpaydin
[17] is used for comparison. The confidence level of 95% was considered for that test.

Table 1. Classification error (in %) for different ensembles methods for different time series datasets. Bold numbers show the best performance. "+/-" shows that the performance of Random SAX ensembles is statistically [17] better/worse than that algorithm for that dataset.

Data	Random SAX Ensembles	Bagging	AdaBoost.M1	Random Forests	Single Tree
50words	35.51	39.45(+)	**33.86**	36.36	59.08(+)
Adiac	46.2	41.05	38.93(-)	**38.52**(-)	53.83(+)
CBF	0.37	2.19(+)	1.23(+)	**0.31**	3.25(+)
Synthetic Control	**3.07**	9.41(+)	4.36(+)	4.03(+)	13.06(+)
ECG	**15.09**	17.99	16.21	16.36	23.89(+)
Faceall	7.82	13.27(+)	**5.96**(-)	7.74	29.19(+)
Fish	23.45	27.55	22.06	**23.15**	40.92(+)
Gun-Point	6.22	7.79	7.14	**4.36**(-)	9.56(+)
OSU Leaf	44.62	47.01	44.34	**41.86**	62.76(+)
Swedish Leaf	**15.13**	20.36(+)	15.59	15.97	38.13(+)
Trace	**11.69**	13.41	12.99	12.69	15.22(+)
Two-Patterns	**3.06**	6.48(+)	3.61(+)	3.93(+)	19.12(+)
Wafer	**0.12**	0.62(+)	0.16(+)	0.17(+)	1.01(+)
Yoga	0.14	0.65(+)	**0.12**	0.15	0.96(+)
Win/draw/Loss		8/6/0	4/8/2	3/9/2	14/0/0

Discretized datasets were created by using SAX. The size of the window was fixed to 5 for PAA process for all the datasets (for the first step of SAX). 5 breakpoints were created for discretization process (for the second step of SAX) . All experiments with all other ensemble methods (Bagging, AdaBoost.M1 and Random Forests) were done on these discretized datasets. The dicretized data was treated as continuous data for the learning process to reduce the data fragmentation problem. In a Random SAX ensemble, 50 different discretized datasets were created using Random SAX method. The size of the window was fixed to 5 for PAA process for all the datasets (for the first step of SAX). However, to increase diversity different datasets were allowed to have different number of break points (2-10) (for the second step of SAX). For each tree, a random integer I between 2 to 10 is generated, and I breakpoints were created by using the proposed discretization method. Results are presented in Table 1. Results show that ensembles using Random SAX are quite competitive to other popular ensemble methods (8 wins against Bagging, 4 wins and 2 losses against AdaBoost.M1, and 3 wins and 2 losses against Random Forests).

4   Conclusions

In this paper, we proposed a novel ensemble method, Random SAX ensembles, for time series classification. We use a novel discretization method that creates random discretization boundaries to create ensembles. This discretization method uses the philosophy of a popular time series representation method, SAX. Experiment results suggest that the proposed ensemble method is quite competitive to the other popular ensemble methods. As Random SAX preserves the online property of SAX, the proposed ensemble method can be used with online classifiers [18]. Hence, The study of online time series classification with the proposed ensemble method is another interesting application area of the proposed ensemble method.

References

1. Hansen, L.K., Salamon, P.: Neural Network Ensembles. IEEE Transactions on Pattern Analysis and Machine Intelligence 12, 993–1001 (1990)
2. Brieman, L.: Bagging Predictiors. Machine Learning 2, 123–140 (1996)
3. Freund, Y., Schapire, R.E.: A Decision Theoretic Generalization of On-Line Learning and an Application to Boosting. Journal of Computer and System Sciences 55, 119–139 (1997)
4. Ho, T.K.: The Random Subspace Method for Constructing Decision Forests. IEEE Transactions on Pattern Analysis and Machine Intelligence 20, 832–844 (1998)
5. Random Forest. Machine Learning 1, 5-32 (2001)
6. Chan, K., Fu, A.W.: Efficient time Series Matching by wavelets. In: The Proceedings of the 15th IEEE International Conference on Data Engineering, sydney, Australia, pp. 126–133 (1999)
7. Keogh, E., Chakrabarthi, K., Pazzani, M., Mehrotra, S.: Locally Adaptive Dimensionality Reduction for Indexing Large Time Seriece Database. In: The Proceedings of ACM SIGMOD Conference on Management of Data, Santa Bardara, CA, pp. 151–162 (2001)
8. Gerurt, P.: Pattern Extraction for Time Series Classification. In: Siebes, A., De Raedt, L. (eds.) PKDD 2001. LNCS (LNAI), vol. 2168, pp. 115–127. Springer, Heidelberg (2001)
9. Lin, J., Keogh, E., Lonardi, S., Chiu, B.: Asymbolic Representaion of Time Series with Implication Demonstration. In: The Proceedings of the 8th ACM SIGMODI Worshop on Research Issues in Data Mining and Knowledge Discovery, San Diego, pp. 2–11 (2002)
10. Keogh, E., Kasetty, S.: On the Need for Time Series Data Mining Benchmarck: A Survey and Emprical Demostration. In: Proceedings of the 8th ACM SIGKDD Internation Conference on Knowledge Discovery and Data Mining, pp. 102–111 (2002)
11. Dougherty, J., Kahavi, R., Sahami, M.: Supervised Discretization of Continuous Features. In: Proceeding of the 12th International Conference on Machine Learning (1995)
12. Daw, C.S., Finney, E.A., Tracy, E.R.: A Review of Symbolic Anaysis of Experimental Data. Review of Scientific Instruments 2, 915–930 (2003)
13. Quinlan, J.R.: Programs for Machine Learning. Morgan Kaufmann Publishers Inc., San Fancisco (1993)
14. Tumer, K., Ghosh, J.: Error Correlation and Error Reduction in Ensemble Classifiers, vol. 3, pp. 385–404 (1996)
15. Witten, I.H., Frank, E.: Data Mining, Practical Machine Learning Tools and Techniques, 2nd edn. Morgan Kaufmann, San Francisco (2005)
16. Dietterich, T.G.: Approximation Statistical Test for Comparing Supervised Classification Learning Algorithms. Neural Computation, 1895–1923 (1998)
17. Alpaydin, E.: Combined $5 \times 2 \, c \, v \, f$ Test Comparing Supervised Classification Learning Algorithms. Neural Computation 8, 1885–1892 (1999)
18. Utgoff, P.E.: Incremental Induction of Desicion Trees. Machine Learning 2, 161–186 (1989)

Apriori-based Research Community Discovery in Bibliographic Database

Baby Manjusha and Sumam Mary Idicula

Department of Computer Science,
Cochin University of Science and Technology, Kochi, India
manjusha1211@gmail.com, sumam@cusat.ac.in

Abstract. Bibliographic Databases are repositories of academic publications in all categories. For a new researcher initiating his research, the Bibliographic Database serves as a tool for exploring the academic social network for gaining the knowledge about the research community and recommending the research collaborators. However, Bibliographic Database contains a huge number of sequential data that exhibit emergent patterns of behavior. Finding inherent regularities in data is still a very challenging task. This paper proposes a novel method to discover research community through association mining.

Keywords: Apriori, Association Mining, Bibliography Databases, Research Community, Potential Collaborators.

1 Introduction

The knowledge on research trends is extremely significant for researchers. Bibliographic databases are repositories of academic publications in all categories. The Bibliographic database provide affluent information regarding the publications like authors, title, pages, year, book title/conference name, abstract, publication, and so on. Bibliographic databases can be thought of as an interface/tool for young researchers to identify active research areas as well as to grasp the evolution of the research disciplines. The academic collaboration and knowledge domain of researchers can be identified through repetitive co-published works in a past period. Also realization of research communities aid in identifying probable/potential collaborators for the researchers. This paper proposes a novel scheme for discovering research community through methods of data mining and this scheme is one of the first in this direction to the best of our knowledge.

A community can be defined as a group of entities that share similar properties or connect to each other *via* certain relations [1]. Mostly graph based mining approaches are used to extract relevant knowledge from bibliographic databases. The entities are modeled as graphs and discover the frequent patterns of graph data. In graph-based community mining, various measures are used to mine substructures of graphs. The selection of the measures depends on the objective and the constraints of the mining approach. The approaches to graph-based data

K.R. Venugopal and L.M. Patnaik (Eds.): ICIP 2011, CCIS 157, pp. 75–80, 2011.

mining are mainly categorized into 5 groups. They are greedy search based approach, inductive logic programming (ILP) based approach, inductive database based approach, mathematical graph theory based approach and kernel function based approach [2].

Of the bibliographic database entries, the most relevant attributes are topics/titles of publications and their corresponding authors. A topic/title is the semantic element [3] that serves the purpose of a basic building block of identifying research area in the concerned field.

The research area is the important constituent to differentiate among research communities. Authors who attend the same conferences might work on various research areas. The metadata of publications can be used for extracting keywords and terms, which can be the starting point towards building taxonomy of topics. The process of building a complete taxonomy of topics in Computer Science is a difficult task. There are Computer Science classification systems readily available that is re-used in our approach. ACM Computing Classification System is one of the well known subject classification system for computer science devised by the Association for Computing Machinery.

The paper is organized as follows. In Section 2, the new system is proposed and entire scheme is explained in three different modules. Section 3 analyses the result obtained and also summarizes the findings. The paper is concluded in Section 4.

2   System Description

In this section, the proposed method is outlined and each phase is explained in detail in terms of the database used here. The proposed method is described in three units, namely, DBLP-XML Parser, Research Topic Identification and Research Community Discovery. Before detailing the method, a close look at the Bibliographic database is portrayed. The database used here is DBLP.

2.1   DBLP Database

DBLP is one of the largest Computer Sciences Bibliographic data source available on the Internet. It provides information on major computing journals and conference proceedings. DBLP bibliographic information is maintained via massive human effort with special attention paid to the author name consistency issue. The DBLP data set is available as *xml* file and can be downloaded from the location *http://dblp.uni-trier.de/xml/*. The file *dblp.xml* contains all bibliographic records which make DBLP. It is accompanied by the data type definition file *dblp.dtd* [4].

2.2   DBLP-XML Parser

The DBLP XML records are parsed using an XML parser to extract all information from it. The information such as authors, title, conference/journal name, year of publication, location of electronic edition if available, are extracted and is stored as like a transaction database. Each entry in the database is considered as a transaction and the extracted information is considered as the items of the transaction.

A mapper function was employed to perform mapping of Computer Science areas with related keywords. This function is highly necessary for relating publications (either conference publications or journal publications) present in DBLP database to parent Computer Science areas. A sample of the mapper function is given in Table 1. The ACM CCS system is taken as a base for building the research topic in the mapper function. Of course, ACM CCS taxonomy is lacking nodes for recent popular topics like peer-to-peer systems. Keywords were built up with the aid of keyword generator tools [5].

Table 1. Sample of Mapper function

Research Topic	Keywords
Compilers	semantic,optimize, ...
Cryptography	authenticate, key, ...
Computer Communication Networks	route, protocol, ...
... ...	... ...

2.3   Research Topic Identification

In this section a method is devised to identify the research topic of each author. This is done with the help of the titles of publications. The following procedure outlines in detail the method adopted.

1. Tokenize the title and remove stop words.
2. Reduce the remaining words to its root form. They are considered as keywords.
3. Also extract keywords using "ee" URL. The URLs are crawled to retrieve "keywords" and "abstracts" for the purpose of identifying a surplus of terms that are related to computer science. The extraction of terms from abstracts can be done using term extractor.
4. Find similarity score between the keywords in the mapper function and the extracted keywords in the transaction. The similarity measure computed here is Jaccard's similarity. The transaction is mapped to the Computer Science research area where the similarity score is high.
5. A correspondence between authors and research area is obtained.

A split of Author-Research Area table is given in Table 2.

2.4   Research Community Discovery

Performing association mining on Author-Research Area table obtained in Section 2.3 will yield associations of authors and related research areas. The association mining is performed using traditional Apriori algorithm. To mine using

Table 2. Author-Research Area

Author	Research Area
Werner Amann	Compilers
Bart Preneel	Cryptography
Sven J. Dickinson	Theory of C.S.
...	...

Apriori algorithm, the support count is given based on the number of transactions containing the authors. The frequent authors and their corresponding research area are formulated as a frequent two pattern. Frequent two patterns, where the last item (Research Area) is same are merged to obtain authors working in the same Research Area. Therefore these patterns constitute a research community.

From this perspective, it is also possible to identify potential collaborators. Frequent collaborators can be identified by applying the same association rule mining algorithm to the co-author data. The algorithm used is again Apriori algorithm with necessary support. However a frequent two pattern of authors (A1,A2) is considered same as that of (A2, A1) to obtain the next three pattern and so on.

Thus authors who co-exist in the same research community but are not frequent collaborators can be identified as potential collaborators.

3   Results and Discussion

The objective of the proposed system was to mine research communities and recommended collaborators from DBLP database. The system was implemented in three units as explained in Section 2. A subset of DBLP database has taken to perform the experiment. Specifically, 1905 entries of DBLP was chosen to perform the experiment.

In discovering research community by means of association rule mining, the threshold value for support is fixed by experimenting with different values, for which different number of research communities was obtained. Fig. 1 shows the plot of the no. of research communities obtained for different support values. We practically obtained no community for large support values. With 0.1% support, the number of research communities mined was 17. It is evident from the graph that number of communities obtained significantly was in the range of 0.15% to 0.25% support value. Hence a support value between these ranges should be chosen. The threshold support chosen here is 0.15%. With this support value, a sample of the research community called "Compiler Construction" is obtained as below.

COMPILERS: [Werner Amann, Mary Lou Soffa, Josef Grosch, R. Nigel Horspool, Bernhard Steffen , Rajiv Gupta, Mikael Pettersson, Reinhard Wilhelm, Laurie J. Hendren, William M. Waite, Henk Corporaal, Peter Fritzson, Thomas

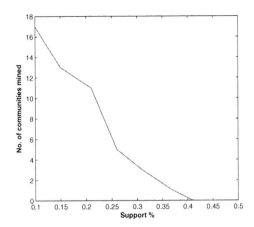

Fig. 1. Comparison of support values

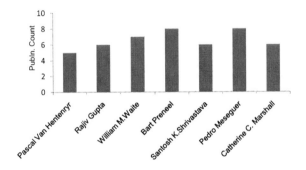

Fig. 2. Publication count of sample authors

W. Reps, James J. Horning, Frank DeRemer, William M. McKeeman, M. Griffiths Jan Hoogerbrugge, John Aycock].

Of this community mined the frequent collaborators and potential collaborators are as follows. Some of the frequent collaborators in this community are ['Mary Lou Soffa', 'Rajiv Gupta'], ['Mikael Pettersson', 'Peter Fritzson'], such that the recommended potential collaborators can also be obtained from the same.

Also a frequency graph for the authors and their corresponding publications is given for a particular support value, say, 0.25%. This is illustrated in Fig. 2. A sample of seven authors and their corresponding number of publications is plotted in the figure.

As the entire DBLP database is modeled as a transaction database, more associations like Author-Conference/journal associations, Author-Period of publication associations, Conference-Conference associations can be efficiently computed from this database effectively.

4   Conclusions

This paper proposed a novel approach that explores the applicability of association rule mining to identify the research communities in bibliographic databases. The entire system was implemented in three units, namely, DBLP-XML Parser, Research Topic Identification and Research Community Discovery. In the first phase, the DBLP database is modeled as a transaction database by means of parsing the XML dtd file of the same. Also a mapper function is necessary to relate Computer Science areas to the corresponding keywords. In the second phase, Research Topic is identified from the title of the publication through steps mentioned in Section 2.3. In the third phase, association rule mining is applied to the output of second phase with necessary support value to obtain research community, frequent collaborators and recommended potential collaborators. A sample of research community, frequent collaborators and recommended potential collaborators is given in the result analysis. In addition to these, subgoals such as publication count of authors, Author-Conference/journal association, Author-Period of publication, conference-conference association can also be achieved by the use of association rule mining algorithm effectively. As an extension, we can also incorporate citation information for identifying high impact authors who have low frequency of publications.

References

1. Zaiane, O.R., Chen, J., Goebel, R.: DBconnect: Mining Research Community on DBLP Data. In: Proceedings of the 9th Web KDD and 1st SNA-KDD 2007 Workshop on Web Mining and Social Network Analysis, pp. 74–81 (2007)
2. Washio, T., Motoda, H.: State of the Art of Graph-based Data Mining. In: Proceedings of the Ninth ACM SIGKDD International Conference on Knowledge Discovery and Data Mining, SIGKDD Explore, vol. 5, p. 5968 (2003)
3. Asur, S., Parthasarathi, S., Ucar, D.: An Event based Framework for Characterizing Evolutionary Behavior of Interaction Graphs. J. ACM Transactions on Knowledge Discovery from Data 3, 16–36 (2009)
4. Ley, M.: DBLP - Some Lessons Learned. In: Proceedings of the VLDB Endowment, vol. 2, pp. 24–28 (2009)
5. WordStream, http://www.wordstream.com/keywords

An Improved *l*-Diversity Anonymisation Algorithm

Tripathy B.K., Kumaran K., and Panda G.K.

School of Computer Science and Engineering, VIT University, Vellore
Tamil Nadu, India
`tripathybk@rediffmail.com, kumarankpl@gmail.com, gkpmail@sify.com`

Abstract. Use of published organizational data for a variety of purposes has the chance of violation of leakage of individual secret information. Preliminary efforts in this direction are susceptible to leakage of valuable information through quasi identifiers. Over the past few years, several algorithms based upon the concept of *k*-anonymity [1-2] have been developed, to handle such problems. A better privacy model, called *l*-diversity [3] was proposed to handle some of the problems in *k*-anonymity. Our main contribution in this paper is to improve the clustering phase of the OKA algorithm [4] so that it takes care of *k*-anonymity and *l*-diversity to a considerable extent and in combination with the improved second and third phases of the algorithm in [5] leads to an efficient *l*-diversity algorithm. We also show that all the three stages of the algorithm are necessary in order to cover different situations.

Keywords: Anonymisation, Clustering, Data Privacy, *k*-anonymity.

1 Introduction

There is a constant demand on organizations to publish micro data (i.e., data published in its raw, non-aggregated form) in their electronic form for a variety of purposes including demographic and public health research. To protect the anonymity of the entities, called the respondents, data holders often remove or encrypt explicit identifiers. However, de-identifying data provides no guarantee of anonymity as released information often contains other data called quasi identifiers, which can be linked to publicly available information for re-identifying data respondents, thus leaking information that was not intended for disclosure. The large amount of information easily accessible today, together with the increased computational power available to the attackers, makes linking attacks a serious problem [2]. To avoid such attacks while preserving the integrity of the released data, Samarati and Sweeney proposed the concept of *k*-anonymity [4].In order to obtain *k*-anonymity, several algorithms have been introduced in recent times [1-7]. Background knowledge and homogeneity attacks are the two attacks where a *k* anonymous table may disclose the sensitive information. Also, *k*-anonymity does not protect against attacks based on prior knowledge of the adversary which results in background knowledge attack. As a solution to these

K.R. Venugopal and L.M. Patnaik (Eds.): ICIP 2011, CCIS 157, pp. 81–86, 2011.
© Springer-Verlag Berlin Heidelberg 2011

problems and provide greater privacy the notion of l-diversity [3] was proposed. The main idea behind l-diversity is the requirement that the values of the k sensitive attributes are well represented in each group. In the present article, the clustering phase of OKA have been modified and improved so that there is less pressure on the other two phases. In section 2 we introduce the basic concepts to be used in the paper. We discuss on the methodology to be used in section 3. we present only the improved clustering and adjustment algorithm n section 4. In section 5, we make an analysis of the algorithm and show that in some cases we have to use all the three phases of the algorithm in order to achieve l-diversity.

2   Basic Concepts

In this section we introduce the basic definitions and notations to be used in the paper. We define a table T as a set of tuples $\{t_1, t_2...t_n\}$ having a set of attributes $\{A_1, A_2...A_n\}$. By $t[A]$, we denote the value of a tuple t for the attribute A_i . The set of attributes can be categorized into three main categories; the identifiers, the quasi-identifiers and the sensitive attributes. The identifiers individually find out tuples uniquely. It is assumed to be removed from the tables before any kind of publication.

2.1   Distinct l-Diversity

The simplest understanding of "well represented" would be to ensure that there are at least l distinct values for the sensitive attribute in each equivalence class.

2.2   Distance Metric

The notion of information loss is used to quantify the amount of information that is lost due to k-anonymisation. Let T denote a set of records, which is described by m numeric quasi-identifiers $\{N_1, N_2...N_m\}$ and q categorical quasi-identifiers $\{C_1, C_2...C_q\}$. Let $\{P_1, P_2...P_q\}$ be a partition of T. Each categorical attribute C_i is associated with a taxonomy tree Tc_i that is used to generalize the values of this attribute.

Consider a set $P \subseteq T$ of records. Let $\underline{N_i}(P)$ and $\overline{N_i}(P)$ denote the minimum and maximum values of the records in P with respect to the numeric attribute N_i . Also, let $C_i(P)$ denote the set of values of records in P with respect to the categorical attribute C_i , and let $H(Tc_i)$ denote the maximal sub tree of Tc_i rooted at the lowest common ancestor of the values of $C_i(P)$. Then, the diversity of P, denoted by $D(P)$, is defined as,

$$D(P) = \sum_{i \in [1,m]} \frac{\overline{N_i}(P) - \underline{N_i}(P)}{\overline{N_i}(T) - \underline{N_i}(T)} + \sum_{i \in [1,q]} \frac{H(Tc_i(P))}{H(Tc_i)}. \qquad (1)$$

where $H(T)$ represents the height of the tree T. The centroid of P is a record whose value of attributes is at minimum distance from all other attribute values in P. To anonymise the records in P means to generalize these records to the same values with respect to each quasi-identifier. The amount of information loss occurred by such a process, denoted as $L(P)$, is defined as

$$L(P) = |P| \times D(P). \tag{2}$$

3   Methodology

In [5] some improvements were made at the clustering stage of the OKA algorithm so that calculation of distances of excess records from the clusters to put them into different clusters can be avoided. With some additional book keeping, this additional effort could be avoided. In this paper we modify the algorithm further.

(i)In the clustering stage seed records are taken for the clusters arbitrarily and the other records are added to these clusters iteratively depending upon their proximity from the centroids of the clusters. However, by doing so we are making the clusters lop-sided in their size. This leads to additional computations at the adjustment stage due to the generation of very small size or highly oversize clusters.

(ii)Also, while adding elements we are considering only the non-sensitive attributes so that the sensitive attribute gets unattended. This leads to make the clusters lacking enough diversity. In this paper we put forth an improved version of the clustering phase algorithm, which tackles the problems mentioned in (i) and (ii) above. We allow records to be added into the clusters till the size 'k' is reached. When a cluster reaches the size 'k', while adding a record into it, we check the dissimilarity of the record from the existing records in the cluster. That is, we find if it is not matching with any of the values of the records already existing in the cluster. If there is no matching occurs we add it. Otherwise, we go for the next cluster according to the distance from centroids of the clusters is considered. This process is continued. Since the maximum diversity 'l' that can be achieved in a k-anonymity algorithm satisfies, $l \leq \{k,$Domain of the sensitive attribute$\}$, we shall arrive at more balanced clusters, in terms of size and diversity.

(iii)We also make some improvement in the *l*-diversity stage of the algorithm. When all the clusters with additional diversity are finished, in the earlier version, we were merging the clusters having less diversity with any cluster such that the distance between the two centroids is the minimum. But, it has been observed that this may unnecessarily minimize the number of clusters. So, we shall now try the same procedure within the clusters having less diversity, so that some new clusters with required diversity can be generated. If some clusters are still there with less diversity even after this stage, we merge them with clusters having minimum diversity required applying the same technique as earlier.

4   The Algorithms

4.1   The Clustering Algorithm

Algorithm *The Clustering Algorithm*
Input: A set T of n records; the value k for k-anonymity and the value l for
l-diversity
Output: A Partition $P = \{P_1, P_2...P_k\}$
1.   Sort all records in T by their quasi-identifiers;
2.   Let $K := \lfloor n/k \rfloor$;
3.   Select K distinct records based on their frequency in sensitive attribute
values;
4.   Let $P_i := \{r_i\}$ for $i = 1$ to K;
5.   Let $T := T \mathbin{/} \{r_1, r_2...r_k\}$;
6.   While ($T \neq \phi$) do
7.   Let r be the first record in T;
8.   Order $\{P_i\}$ according to their distances from r;
9.   Let $i = 1$;
10. $Flag = 0$;
11.   While $((i < K)$ and $(Flag = 0))$
12.   Let $s(P_i)$ be the set of distinct sensitive attribute values of P_i;
13.   Let $s(r)$ be the sensitive attribute value of r;
14. $if(((|P_i| < K)$ or $((s(r) \in s(P_i))$ and $(|s(P_i| < l))$ then add r to P_i;
15.   Update centroid of P_i;
16. $Flag = 1$;
17.   Else $i := i + 1$;
18.   If $(Flag = 0)$ add r to the nearest cluster;
19.   Let $T := T/\{r\}$;
20.   End of while

4.2   The Adjustment Algorithm

We modified the adjustment stage of the algorithm[5] so that the return of excess
elements if any is done to their parent clusters. We present the slightly modified
algorithm as follow.

Algorithm *The Adjustment Algorithm*
Input: a partitioning $P = \{P_1, P_2...P_k\}$ of T
Output: an adjusted partitioning $P = \{P_1, P_2...P_k\}$ of T
1.   Let $S := \phi$;
2.   For each cluster $p \in P$ with $|P| < k/2$ do
3.   Do $S = S \cup P$;
4.   While ($S \neq \phi$) do
5.   Randomly select a record r from S
6.   If P contains cluster P_i with $k/2 < |P_i| < k$ do
7.   Add r to the closest such cluster.
8.   Else add r to the closest cluster in P

9.   End of While
10.   Let $R := \phi$
11.   For each cluster $p \in P$ with $|P| > k$ do
12.   Sort records in P by distance to centroid of P;
13.   While $(|P| > k)$ do;
14. $r \in P$ is the record farthest from centroid of P ;
15.   Let $P := P \: / \: r$; $R := R \cup \{r\}$and $c = Index(P)$;
16.   End of while
17.   End of For
18.   While $(R \neq \phi)$
19.   Randomly select a record r from R;
20.   Let $R := R \: / \: \{r\}$;
21.   If P contains cluster P_i such that $|p| < k$ then
22.   Add r to its closest cluster P satisfying ;
23.   Else
24.   Add r to its cluster P_c;
25.   End if
26.   End While

4.3 Algorithm for l-Diversity

We avoid repeating the l-diversity phase of an algorithm in [5] due to shortage of space.

5 Analysis

If we consider the worst case, as detailed below, we find that all the three stages of the algorithm may be necessary in certain cases. Let us consider that there are K clusters to begin with, each containing only one element. Then we are left with $n - K$ elements at this stage. Adding next $k - 1$ elements as per the algorithm does not create any problem. At this stage we may have one cluster containing k elements. If this cluster does not have l-diversity, we may need at best $l-1$ elements to it (worst case being that when we have all the k tuples having the same sensitive value). Out of $n - K - k$ elements at best $(l - 1)$ elements can go to this cluster. We continue with the rest $(n - K - k)$-$(l - 1)$ elements. If another case like this occurs again with the rest of the clusters then we will be left with $(n - K - k)$-$(l - 1)$-$(k - 1)$-$(l - 1)$ elements. Continuing like this we shall have I clusters with both k-anonymity as well as l-diversity if $n - K - k - (k - 1)...(k - i) - i * (l - 1) \geq 0$. Rest $(K - i)$ clusters may not have either of the properties. So, we cannot do away with the other stage algorithms.

Note 5.1: l-diversity is heavily dependent upon the distribution of the sensitive attribute values. If there are some values which are repeated more often and the cardinality of certain sensitive attribute values are $< K$ then l-diversity cannot be obtained with K clusters in such a case. In such cases we have to merge certain clusters to have l-diversity. Of course, to achieve k-anonymity we do not have any restriction that the number of clusters should be K. So, l-diversity is always a possibility along with k-anonymity so long as $l \leq minimum$ $\{k, \text{Dom}(S)\}$, where S denotes the sensitive attribute. Obviously, for values of 'l' beyond the above value is impossible.

Note 5.2: Also, there is another restriction on l-diversity. Let K be the number of clusters to be formed and S be the sensitive attribute. Let t_i denote the ith tuple in the database and $S(t_i)$ be the value for the sensitive attribute of t_i.

Then $K \leq minimum$ $\{t_i : S(t_i) = s\}$ This obviously is a sacrifice to achieve l-diversity in terms of number of clusters and leads to more information loss.

6   Conclusions

In this paper we introduced an algorithm by modifying the clustering stage algorithm in [5], so that it works faster towards anonymisation of data tables along with k-anonymity and l-diversity. The adjustment phase may be nullified in certain cases. Also, the l-diversity stage becomes simpler. The algorithms have been implemented using JAVA and are tested against standard databases to verify the validity.

References

1. Agrawal, R., Bayardo, R.: Data Privacy through Optimal k-Anonymization. In: Proc. of the 21st International Conference on Data Engineering, pp. 217–218 (2005)
2. Chiu, C.C., Tsai, C.Y.: A k-Anonymity Clustering Method for Effective Data Privacy Preservation. In: Third International Conference on Advanced Data Mining and Applications, ADMA (2007)
3. Machanavajjhala, A., Gehrke, J., Kifer, D., Venkitasubramaniam, M.: l-Diversity: Privacy beyond k-Anonymity. In: Proc. 22nd International Conference Data Engineering (ICDE), vol. 24 (2006)
4. Byun, J.W., Kamra, A., Bertino, E., Li, N.: Efficient k-Anonymization using Clustering Techniques. In: Kotagiri, R., Radha Krishna, P., Mohania, M., Nantajeewarawat, E. (eds.) DASFAA 2007. LNCS, vol. 4443, pp. 188–200. Springer, Heidelberg (2007)
5. Tripathy, B.K., Panda, G.K., Kumaran, K.: A Fast l - Diversity Anonymisation Algorithm. In: Proc. of the Third International Conference on Computer Modeling and Simulation (ICCMS 2011), Mumbai, January 7-9, vol. 2, pp. 648–652 (2011)
6. Samarati, P., Foresti, S., Vimercati, S.D.C.D., Ciriani, V.: k-Anonymity. In: Advances in Information Security, Springer, Heidelberg (2007)
7. Tan, P.N., Steinbach, M., Kumar, V.: Introduction to Data Mining, pp. 487–559. Addison-Wesley, Boston (2005)

Comparison of Performance for Intrusion Detection System Using Different Rules of Classification

Nandita Sengupta[1] and Jaya Sil[2]

[1] University College of Bahrain, Manama, Bahrain
[2] Bengal Engineering and Science University Shibpur, Howrah, WB, India
ngupta@ucb.edu.bh, js@cs.becs.ac.in

Abstract. Classification is very important for designing intrusion detection system that classifies network traffic data. Broadly traffic data is classified as normal or anomaly. In the work classification performance using rules obtained by different methods are applied on network traffic and compared. Classifier is built based on rules of decision table, conjunctive rule, OneR, PART, JRip, NNge, ZeroR, BayesNet, Ridor from WEKA and using rough set theory. Classification performance is compared applying on KDD data set where the whole data set is divided into training and test data set. Rules are formed using training data set by different rule generation methods and later applied on test data set to calculate accuracy of classifiers.

Keywords: Classification, Intrusion Detection System, Rough Set Theory, Rules.

1 Introduction

Online classification of network traffic data is very important to develop intrusion detection system (IDS) that automatically monitors the flow of network packets. Existing works on intrusion detection have been carried out to classify the network traffic as anomaly or normal. A majority of current IDS follow signature based approach [1] in which similar to virus scanners, events are detected that match specific predefined patterns known as "signatures". The limitation of these signature based IDS is their failure to identify novel attacks and even minor variation of patterns are not detected accurately. In addition, sometimes IDS generate false alarm for alerting network administrator due to failure of handling imprecise data which has high possibility to appear in network traffic data. Therefore, accuracy, computation time and system learning are the key issues to be addressed properly for classifying such data.

Classification is an important task in data mining research that facilitates analysis of huge amount of data. Rough Set Theory (RST) [2] is based on mathematical concept can handle vagueness in classification of data. However, prior to applying RST, the data is discretized and selection of discretization procedure

K.R. Venugopal and L.M. Patnaik (Eds.): ICIP 2011, CCIS 157, pp. 87–92, 2011.

has great impact on classification accuracy. In the paper, network traffic data [3] of KDD has been considered for generating training and testing patterns. In order to apply RST, the datasets are discretized and then a minimum subset of attributes of the data set is selected, called reducts by applying genetic algorithm [4]. Rules are generated from the reducts and classifiers are built using rule set classifier [5]. Finally, classification accuracy has been expressed in terms of correctly classified and incorrectly classified instances.

Other classifier rules, like decision table, conjunctive rule, OneR, PART, JRip, NNge, ZeroR, BayesNet, Ridor are applied on the same data set to find out correctly and incorrectly classified instances. These classifier rules are used by WEKA software [6] to measure corresponding classification accuracy and then compared based on the results achieved.

Section 2 describes about rough set theory, Section 3 mentions about other classifier rules, Section 4 depicts experimental results and Section 5 concludes the paper and mentions future work.

2   Rough Set Theory

Rough Set Theory (RST) is used for efficient classification because RST can handle missing value, ambiguous values. Information system is reduced to make the computation easy.

2.1   Information System

Information system [7] is nothing but Data table. Here we consider U as an nonempty set of objects, a data table is a tuple (U, A, V_a) $a \in A$, where A is a set of attributes $a : U \rightarrow V_a$ and V_a is a set of values for the attribute a. The set of attributes can be divided into two subsets, conditional set of attributes, C and decision set of attributes, D. C and D both are subsets of A, $C \subset A$ and $D = A - C$, Conditional set of attributes represent all the features or attributes of objects and decision set of attributes represent the classification of objects.

2.2   Set Approximation

Equivalence classes are called indiscernible [7]. If the values of conditional attributes of some objects are same, those objects are declared as indiscernible. In a data table where indiscernibiliy relations are found, table can be defined in two ways, consistent and inconsistent. If all the objects in indiscernibility relations are classified in the same class, the table is called as consistent on the other hand, if all the objects in indiscernibility relations are not classified as the same class, the table is said as inconsistent. In that case some features/attributes may have not been reflected precisely in the data table. Rough set is defined (see, Fig. 1.) as a pair of crisp sets, lower approximation $\underline{C}X$ and upper approximation $\overline{C}X$ where X is the target set. Lower approximation set is known as positive region because X is characterized by a particular decision value. There are also indiscernibility classes which contain only some tuples in X, which cannot be classified exactly. These are the objects in boundary region and mathematically,

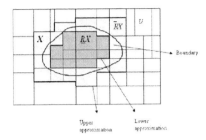

Fig. 1. Rough Set with Lower and Upper Approximation

represented as $\overline{C}X - \underline{C}X$. The elements which are in $U - \overline{C}X$, belongs to the negative region. X is crisp or precise when $\underline{C}X = \overline{C}X$, means boundary region is empty.

2.3 Reducts and Rule Generation

In order to reduce redundant and insignificant attributes, concept of reducts is emerged in RST, a subset of conditional attributes representing the whole data table. Finding reduct is NP hard problem and many researchers [8] are working on fixing up algorithm for finding reduct. Decision rules [9] are generated from reducts and used for classification of objects.

3 Other Classifier Rules on WEKA

In data mining technology, for classification, different rules are applied in training data set to train the system. Classifier rules, like decision table, conjunctive rule, OneR, PART, JRip, NNge, ZeroR, BayesNet, Ridor are applied on the same data to find out correctly and incorrectly classified instances. Decision table [10] of data set D with n attributes A_1, A_2, ..., A_n is a table with schema R (A_1, A_2, ..., A_n, $Class, Sup, Conf$). A row $R_i = (\,a_{1i},\,a_{2i},\,...,\,a_{ni},\,c_i)$ in table R represents a classification rule, where a_{ij} $(1 \leq j \leq n)$ can be either from $DOM(A_i)$ or a special value ANY, c_i belongs to $(c_1,c_2,...,c_m)$, $(minsup \leq sup_i \leq 1)$, and $(minconf \leq conf_i \leq 1)$ and $minsup, minconf$ are predetermined thresholds. The interpretation of the rule is if $(A_1 = a_1)$ and $(A_2 = a_2)$ and ... and $(A_n = a_n)$ then $class = c_i$ with probability $conf_i$ and having support sup_i. In conjunctive rule formation, rule consists of antecedents "AND" ed together and consequent (class value) for the classification. If the rules cannot determine the class for any test data, same can be predicted using the default class value. The OneR algorithm implemented in WEKA is very effective in deducing a "One Rule" based on a single attribute. In PART algorithm, rules are formed with a few attributes "AND"ed on the basis of training data. JRip is a propositional rule learner, Repeated Incremental Pruning to Produce Error Reduction (RIPPER), which is proposed by William W. Cohen. NNge is Instance-Based learning: Nearest Neighbor With Generalization. The simplest of the rule based classifiers is the majority class classifier, called 0-R or ZeroR in Weka. The 0-R (zero rule) classifier takes a look at the target attribute and its possible values. It always provides the output value most commonly found for the target attribute in the given dataset. 0-R as its names suggests; it does not include any rule that works on the non target attributes. All Bayes network algorithms implemented in Weka assume the following for the data set: all variables are discrete finite variables and no instances have missing values. Ridor is the implementation of a RIpple-DOwn Rule learner. It generates the default rule first and then the exceptions for the default rule with the least (weighted) error rate. Then it generates the "best" exceptions for each exception and iterates until pure. Thus it performs a tree-like expansion of exceptions and the leaf has only default rule but no exceptions. The exceptions are a set of rules that predict the class which is different than the class generated using default rules.

4   Experimental Results

KDD data set is considered for our experiment. Total 11850 objects have been considered for the whole information system. Each object has 42 attributes. 34 are continuous attributes and 8 are discrete attributes. 34% of total objects (4029) are considered as test data and 66% of total objects (7821) are considered as training data. WEKA software has been used to apply classifier rule as decision table, conjunctive rule, OneR, PART, JRip, NNge, ZeroR, BayesNet, Ridor and RSES software is used to analyze data for rough set theory (RST). 42 attributes are shown in Table 1.

Different rules are formed with some of these attributes depending on training data set. Subsequently, these rules are applied on test data to determine decision attribute "class". Some of these rules are given here as an example for different rule generation algorithm. In PART decision list 90 rules are generated, out of that 5 rules are shown here as example.

*Rule*1 : srv_count $\leq$ 111 AND protocol_type = tcp AND dst_bytes $\leq$ 715 AND src_bytes $\leq$ 170 AND dst_host_same_src_port_rate $\leq$ 0.01 AND service = telnet AND dst_host_srv_count > 5: anomaly (1369.0).

*Rule*2 : srv_count $\leq$ 111 AND dst_host_srv_rerror_rate > 0.03 AND duration $\leq$ 2078 AND dst_host_same_src_port_rate $\leq$ 0.22 AND count > 6: anomaly (2214.0).

*Rule*3 : srv_count $\leq$ 104 AND dst_host_srv_serror_rate $\leq$ 0.97 AND duration > 0 AND duration $\leq$ 2224 AND hot $\leq$ 2 AND count $\leq$ 6 AND dst_bytes $\leq$ 715 AND protocol_type = tcp AND duration > 2 AND service = pop_3: anomaly (736.0).

*Rule*4 : src_bytes > 568 AND dst_host_srv_count $\leq$ 230 AND num_root $\leq$ 0 AND dst_host_srv_count > 3 AND service = ftp_data AND dst_host_serror_rate $\leq$ 0.15 AND dst_host_same_src_port_rate $\leq$ 0.49: normal (81.0).

Table 1. Attributes of Network Traffic

Sl. No.	Attributes	Sl. No.	Attributes
1	Duration	22	is_guest_login
2	protocol_type	23	count
3	service	24	srv_count
4	flag	25	serror_rate
5	source_bytes	26	srv_serror_rate
6	destination_bytes	27	rerror_rate
7	land	28	srv_rerror_rate
8	wrong_fragment	29	same_srv_rate
9	urgent	30	diff_srv_rate
10	hot	31	srv_diff_host
11	failed_logins	32	dst_host_count
12	logged_in	33	dst_host_srv_count
13	num_compromised	34	dst_host_same_srv_rate
14	root_shell	35	dst_host_diff_srv_rate
15	su_attempted	36	dst_host_same_srv_rate
16	num_root	37	dst_host_srv_diff_host_rate
17	num_file_creations	38	dst_host_serror_rate
18	num_shells	39	dst_host_srv_serror_rate
19	num_access_files	40	dst_host_rerror_rate
20	num_outbound_cmds	41	dst_host_srv_rerror_rate
21	is_host_login	42	class

Table 2. Comparison of Classification Performance

Classifiers	Correctly Classified Instances(%)	Incorrectly Classified Instances(%)
Decision Table	95.3	4.7
Conjunctive Rule	85.8	14.2
OneR	92.1	7.9
PART	97.0	3.0
JRip	97.1	2.9
NNge	95.9	4.1
ZeroR	81.8	18.2
BayesNet	90.6	9.4
Ridor	95.5	4.5
RST	98.5	1.5

*Rule*5 : flag = SF AND service = ftp_data AND dst_host_serror_rate $\leq$ 0.1 AND src_bytes $\leq$ 7280 AND dst_host_same_srv_rate $\leq$ 0.44: normal (6.0).

In JRip, 26 number of rules are generated, out of that 3 rules are shown.

*Rule*1 : (protocol_type = udp) and (srv_count $\geq$ 7) => class = normal (1117.0/18.0).

*Rule*2 : (flag = SF) and (duration $\leq$ 0) and (dst_host_same_srv_rate $\leq$ 0.94) and (srv_count $\geq$ 2) and (protocol_type = udp) => class = normal (109.0/7.0).

Rule3 : (src_bytes $\geq$ 52) and (src_bytes $\leq$ 942) and (src_bytes $\geq$ 167) and (protocol_type = tcp) => class = normal (383.0/47.0). Classification result for these classifiers is compared in Table 2.

5   Conclusions and Future Work

It is clear from Table 2 that RST gives optimum classification result compared to other classifier rules. Rough Set theory has been successfully utilized for data reduction, hidden pattern discovery and decision rule generation was introduced by Pawlak in 1982 and is being expanded every day. Our future work is to explore various features of RST for intrusion detection system, like optimized reduct generation, rules generation so that time efficiency can be improved for classification.

References

1. Neelakantan, S., Rao, S.: A Threat-aware Signature Based Intrusion-detection Approach for Obtaining Network-specific Useful Alarms. In: Proc. The Third International Conference on Internet Monitoring and Protection (2008)
2. Beaubouef, T., Petry, F.E.: Uncertainty Modeling for Database Design Using Intuitionistic and Rough Set Theory. Journal of Intelligent and Fuzzy Systems: Applications in Engineering and Technology 20(3) (August 2009)
3. Nsl-kdd Data Set for Network-based Intrusion Detection Systems
4. Shankar, R.N., Srikanth, T., Ravi, K.B., Rao, A.G.: Genetic Algorithm for Object Oriented Reducts Using Rough Set Theory. International Journal of Algebra 4(17), 827–842 (2010)
5. Kumar, S., Atri, S., Mandoria, L.H.: A Combined Classifier to Detect Landmines Using Rough Set Theory and Hebb Net Learning and Fuzzy Filter as Neural Networks. In: Proc. ICSPS (2009)
6. WEKA software classifier rules,
   http://weka.sourceforge.net/doc/weka/classifiers/rules/
   package-summary.html
7. Sengupta, N., Sil, J.: An Integrated Approach to Information Retrieval Using RST, FS and SOM. In: Proc. ICIS, Bahrain (2008)
8. Zhang, J., Wang, J., Li, D., He, H., Sun, J.: A New Heuristic Reduct Algorithm Based on Rough Sets Theory. In: Dong, G., Tang, C., Wang, W. (eds.) WAIM 2003. LNCS, vol. 2762, pp. 247–253. Springer, Heidelberg (2003)
9. Dembczynski, K., Pindur, R., Susmaga, R.: Generation of Exhaustive Set of Rules within Dominance-based Rough Set Approach. In: Proc. International Workshop on Rough Sets in Knowledge Discovery and Soft Computing (March 2003)
10. Lu, H., Liu, H.: Decision Tables: Scalable Classification Exploring RDBMS Capabilities. In: 26th International Conference on Very Large Databases, Cairo, Egypt (2000)

SR-Match: A Novel Schema Matcher Based on Semantic Relationship

Sonia Khetarpaul[1], Gupta S.K.[1], and Rashmi Chauhan[2]

[1] Department of Computer Science and Engineering, IIT, Delhi, India
[2] Banasthali University, Banasthali, India.
{kpaul.sonia,gupta.shyamkumar,chauhan.rashmiarya}@gmail.com

Abstract. In data integration, schema matching plays an important role. Present schema matching tools combine various match algorithms, each employing a particular technique to improve matching accuracy. However there is still no fully automatic tool is available and also there is lack of accuracy. As a step in this direction, we have proposed a new and efficient Semantic-Relationship schema matching (SR-Match) approach which considers the semantic relationships as one of the parameters for matching. Here in SR-Match, the initial mappings performed by the basic schema mapping techniques, acts as input to the relationship matcher. Relationship matcher compares the remaining unmapped elements based on their semantic relationship with their parents. It is observed that, if both semantics and relationships are taken into account, the degree of accuracy in matching results is improved.

Keywords: Data Integration, Ontology, Schema Mapping, Semantic Relationship.

1 Introduction

Continued high interest in information integration has led to a large body of research work on schema matching (*e.g.*, [1-3]). Schema matching work focuses on taking as input two or more data sources (*e.g.*, XML, OWL, Schemas) and some auxiliary information like a dictionary (*e.g.*, WordNet) to produce a mapping between the similar elements of input data sources [1].

The numerous research efforts have been done on schema matching. But still automatically generating semantic mappings is a task not accomplished till date. However, semi-automatic semantic mappings has gained tremendous interest in the field of databases (schema matching) [1], [2], [4-10].

Schema-based match algorithms take account of schema information and ignore instance data. We briefly examine three of important systems designed for schema matching: COMA++, Similarity Flooding, and Cupid.

The Similarity Flooding (SF) approach, as implemented in Rondo [8], utilizes a hybrid matching algorithm based on the ideas of similarity propagation. It transforms the input schemas into directed labeled graphs, then it discovers the

K.R. Venugopal and L.M. Patnaik (Eds.): ICIP 2011, CCIS 157, pp. 93–102, 2011.
© Springer-Verlag Berlin Heidelberg 2011

matched mappings between the elements of the individual graphs. The algorithm exploits only syntactic techniques at the element and structure level.

Cupid [2] implements a hybrid matching algorithm comprising syntactic techniques at the element (*e.g.*, common prefixes, suffixes tests) and structure level (*e.g.*, tree matching weighted by leaves). It also exploits external resources, in particular, a precompiled thesaurus.

COMA [1] is a composite schema matching system which exploits syntactic and external techniques. It provides a library of matching algorithms; a framework for combining obtained results, and a platform for the evaluation of the effectiveness of the different matchers.

Distinct features of COMA++ with respect to Cupid is a more flexible architecture and keeps less space of performing iterations in the matching process. Present systems are using various element level and/or structure level or instance based schema matching approaches.

So far, to the best of our knowledge, except *seMap* [10] present systems may not consider semantic relationship of elements (*e.g.*, has-a, belongs-to, is-a, teaches etc) as parameter for schema matching. Relationship of element with its parent carries semantic information about the element. This semantic information is important for matching the element with others. This leads us to work on Semantic-Relationship schema matcher (SR-Match).

The approach proposed in SR-Match focuses on semantic relationship of elements with their parents as one of the parameter for schema matching. In this we are using basic element level matcher followed by semantic relationship matcher to produce mapping between elements of two different data sources. SR-Match is proposed to be based on the following characteristics:

1. Syntactic and semantic similarity between elements.
2. Semantic relationship similarity of elements with their parents.

Working and efficacy of SR-Match is organized in this paper as follows: Section 2 gives an overview of SR match architecture, Section 3 describes the working of SR Matcher construct in detail, Section 4 presents the example case to Validate SR matcher, Section 5 gives the comparative analysis of our approach with S-Match and Rondo, Section 6 gives the conclusions and future work's of different data sources. Its components are pre-existing set of element level matchers: Constraints Matcher and Linguistic matcher defined by COMA [6] and iMAP [5]. Here we briefly define these matchers:

2   Semantic-Relationship Schema Matcher Architecture (SR-match)

Schema based Matcher takes as input two schemas of different data sources. Its components are pre-existing set of element level matchers -Constraints Matcher and Linguistic matcher defined by COMA [6] and iMAP [5]. Here we briefly define these matchers in Fig. 1.

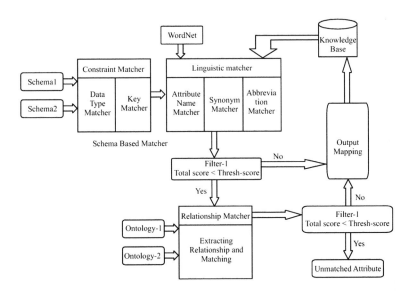

Fig. 1. Architecture of SR-Matcher

Constraints Matcher. The Constraints Matcher determines the similarity of schema elements based on semantic information. It consists of:

- *Data Type Matcher.* The type of schema elements carries the information of data type (*e.g.*, string), value domains (*e.g.*, range of [1-12]). Data type matcher checks whether two elements have identical or compatible types. Compatible types are (integer, number), (real, float), (string, varchar) and so on.
- *Key Matcher.* Key matcher is based upon matching key characteristics like unique, Not Null, referential integrity etc. It checks whether two elements have identical key characteristics or not.

Linguistic Matcher. The linguistic matcher finds semantically and syntactically similar elements. It consists of:

- *Attribute Name Matcher.* Attribute name Matcher checks for syntactic similarity between two elements by comparing their names. Standard set of techniques are used to improve attribute name matching, which include normalization, lemmatization elimination, tokenization, and stop-word elimination.
- *Abbreviation Matcher (AM).* The Abbreviation matcher equates two terms by abbreviating them. Abbreviations are often used to represent items in real life as a shorthand *e.g.*, HOD is equivalent to Head of Department.
- *Synonym Matcher.* The synonym matcher checks whether two elements are synonym of each other. It uses *WordNet* for synonym and their senses. *e.g.*, student and educatee are synonym of each other.

2.1   Ontology Based Matcher

Ontology based Matcher taking inputs as ontology (OWL) of two different data sources. It includes:

Relationship matcher. Relationship Matcher checks whether two elements have same type of relationship with their parent. It takes the output of schema based matcher as another input. It finds the relationship of each unmapped element (marked by schema based matcher) in both data sources with their parent. It matches elements from two different data sources based on their relationships similarity.

2.2   Other Components

- *Filter1.*Filter 1 checks the score of each mapping resulting from schema based matcher. If the score is below the threshold value then it is input to the relationship matcher otherwise it is considered as successful matching.
- *Filter2.* Filter 2 checks the score of each mapping resulted from ontology based matcher. If the score is below the threshold value then it is considered as unmatched otherwise it results as successful matching.
- *Output Mapping and User Validation.*It is the final mapping result generated by matcher. If it requires user validate the mapping for correctness.
- *Knowledge Base.*It stores the input schema, useful output mapping results, matched elements results for future reference

3   Working of Semantic-Relationship Schema Matcher

Step 1: Schema based Matcher. Two schemas ($S_1(n)$ and $S_2(m)$, where n, m represents degree of S_1, S_2) of different data sources are given as Input to schema Based Matcher. Schema based matcher take into the consideration every two attribute ($S_1(A_i)$ and $S_2(B_k)$)and find the score for (A_i, B_k) using algorithm1 given below. Algorithm results the best possible mapping or the scores that crosses the threshold value (defined by user).

Step 2: Ontology based Matcher. The output of the Algorithm 1 and two ontologies (O_1, O_2) are given as input to ontology based matcher. The matcher defined in Algorithm 2 extract relationships specified by ontologies between each unmapped elements and its parents. Then it finds the best mapping for each unmapped element u_i in S_1 with unmapped attribute v_k in S_2 based on their relationships and previous scored returned by Algorithm 1 as shown in Fig. 2.

Algorithm1: for Schema Based matcher

Input : Two attributes A_i , B_k of sources S1 and S2 respectively.
Set of Matchers:
 CM – Constraints Matcher
 LM – Linguistic Matcher
Output: Returns best possible Mapping M' between elements of two schemas and a list of unmapped elements.
Method: This algorithm takes two different attributes as input .apply CM and LM. Generate the aggregated mapping score and return. If score is greater than threshold value (set by the user) then return score else mark A_i and B_k as unmapped.
Find the best match B_k for A_i with highest score greater than threshold. Map A_i with that B_k.

SchemaBasedMatcher(A_i, B_k)
        Score[A_i, B_k]=0
        /* Get score by applying CM and LM*/
        Score[A_i, B_k]= CMScore[A_i, B_k]+LMScore[A_i, B_k]
        If Score[A_i, B_k]>= τ then   /* τ is threshold value set */
                Return Score([A_i, B_k])
        Else
                Mark A_i and B_k as Unmapped
                Return (Score[A_i, B_k])
        End if
          SchemaBasedMatcher(A_i, B_{k-1})
          Find   MAXSCORE[A_i]= max(Score[A_i, B_1],   Score[A_i, B_2],................., Score[A_i, B_m])

 Return Mapping between Ai, Bk (where   Score[Ai, Bk] is maximum)

Fig. 2. Algorithm1: for Schema Based matcher

Algorithm 2: for ontology based matcher

Input : Two Ontology O1 and O2, mapping returned from algorithm1 M' and unmarked element and their scores.

Output: Final Mapping M among attributes of two different schemas.

Method: In this algorithm the output of the algorithm1 and two ontology are taken as input. First algorithm extract relationships specified by ontology (using function extractRelation()) between each unmarked attribute and its parents. Then we find the best mapping for each unmapped attribute u_i in S_1 with unmapped attribute v_k in S_2 based on their relationships and previous scored returned by algorithm1.

OntologyBasedMatcher()

```
/* Extract Relationship of unmarked attributes (ui of S1, vk of S2)with their
parent*/
Rui = extractRelation( ui Pui)  ∀ ui∈ S1

Rvk = extractRelation( vk Pvk)  ∀ vi∈ S2

Maxscore[ui]=0
bestMatch[ui]=NULL
for each rui ∈ Rui do
        for each rvk ∈ Rvk do
                score[ui, vk]= compare(rui, rvk) + Prevscore(ui, vk)
                maxscore[ui]= max(score[ui, vk], maxscore[ui])
                if (maxscore[ui]== score[ui, vk])
                        bestmatch= Vk
                end if
        end for
end for
Output the mapping of ui with bestmatch
Return(M)
/* M is output mapping */
- - - - - - - - - - - - - - - - - - - - - - - - - - - - - - - - - - - - - - - - - -
/*ExtractRelation (u , P) function returns the parent child relationship between u
and P in ontological hierarchical tree */
```

Fig. 3. Algorithm 2: for ontology based matcher

4   Experiment

To validate Schema Relationship Matcher we have taken an example case of two databases ABC and XYZ. Each matcher assign some score D to each ordered pair of attributes. Let (a_1 , x_1) be a ordered pair of attributes from ABC and XYZ such that $a_1 \in ABC$ and $x_1 \in XYZ$.

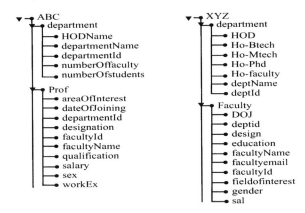

Fig. 4. Attributes of two Databases before applying SR-matcher

Key Matcher Assigns Score D based on Following Criteria.

- $D = 2$: if both attribute are primary key in their respective database relation schema.
- $D = 1$: if one is primary key or other on foreign key in their respective database relation schema.
- $D = 0.5$: if both of the attribute are foreign key in their respective database relation schema.
- $D = 0$: if any of the attribute does not match.

Data Type Matcher Assigns Score based on Following Criteria.

- $D = 2$: if both attribute have same data type otherwise $D = 0$.

Linguistic Matcher Assigns Score based on Following Criteria.

- $D = 2$: if both attribute names are matched otherwise $D = 0$.

Relationship Matcher Assigns Score based on Following Criteria.

- $D = 2$: if both attributes have same parent child relationship otherwise $D = 0$.

A threshold score value is set to four. If sum of D values for any mapping is greater than the threshold value than the mapping it is successful mapping otherwise unsuccessful.

Let the two database relation schemas ABC and XYZ are defined is shown in Fig. 4. After applying schema based matcher (Algorithm 1), we can get mapping among elements of given data sources along with list of unmapped elements. Fig. 5 shows the matched attributes after applying Algorithm 1.

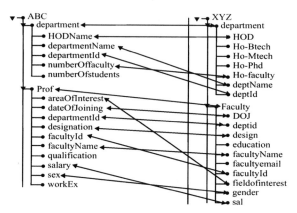

Fig. 5. matched attribute after applying Algorithm 1

After applying ontology based matcher (Algorithm 2) as shown in Fig. 3. We get mapping among lists of unmapped elements (returned by Algorithm 1). Mapping is shown in Fig. 6.

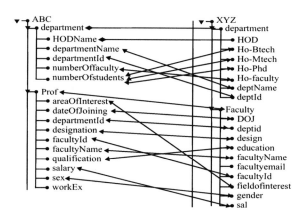

Fig. 6. matched attribute after applying algorithm 2

These manual results shows that by applying relationship matcher we can further map the unmapped elements left by the schema based matcher. It further enhances the efficiency as well, because we are not applying relationship matcher on all attributes. We are applying it on the attributes left unmatched by schema based matcher.

5   Comparative Analysis

We have executed the same example on $S - Match$ [11] and $rondo$ [8]. Result of our analysis is depicted in the following graph. Total number of correct mappings between attributes is 20. We observed that if we compare the relationships of

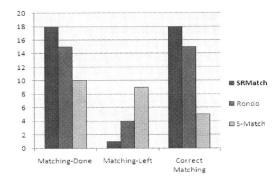

Fig. 7. Comparative Analysis of SR-Matcher, Rondo, S-Match for given example

element with its parent along with syntax and the semantics, then accuracy of correct matching can be increased.

6   Conclusions

In this paper we proposed a schema matcher $(SR - Match)$ which uses semantic relationships of elements as an additional parameter for schema matching. An example is simulated using $SR - Match$ and result are analyzed and compared that shows improvement in accuracy of matching. Our main contributions include (1) we have designed an architecture and algorithms that gives a way for semi-automatic schema mappings based on semantic relationships of elements with their parents, (2) we have ordered schema based matchers in way to improve mapping results, (3) we have improved the efficiency of matcher by applying relationship matcher only on partial unmapped elements. Currently we are implementing $SR - Match$.

References

1. Do, H.H., Rahm, E.: COMA - A System for Flexible Combination of Schema Matching Approach. In: VLDB (2002)
2. Madhavan, J., Bernstein, P., Rahm, E.: Generic Schema Matching with Cupid. In: Proceedings of VLDB, pp. 49–58 (2001)
3. Dhamankar, R., Lee, Y., Doan, A., Halevy, A., Domingos, P.: iMAP: Discovering Complex Semantic Matches Between Database Schemas. In: Proceedings of SIGMOD, pp. 383–394 (2004)

4. Aumller, D., Do, H.H., Massmann, S., Rahm, E.: Schema and Ontology Matching with COMA++ (Software Demonstration). In: Proc. 24. ACM SIGMOD Intl. Conf. Management of Data (2005)
5. Euzenat, J., Valtchev, P.: Similarity-based Ontology Alignment in OWL-lite. In: Proceedings of ECAI, pp. 333–337 (2004)
6. Melnik, S., Garcia-Molina, H., Rahm, E.: Similarity Flooding: A Versatile Graph Matching Algorithm. In: Proceedings of ICDE, pp. 117–128 (2002)
7. Smith, M.K., Welty, C., McGuiness, D.L.: OWL Web Ontology Language Guide. Technical report, World Wide Web Consortium (2004)
8. Melnik, S., Rahm, E., Bernstein, P.: Rondo: A Programming Platform for Generic Model Management. In: Proceedings of SIGMOD, pp. 193–204 (2003)
9. Shvaiko, P., Euzenat, J.: A Survey of Schema-based Matching Approaches. J. Data Semantics IV, 146–171 (2005)
10. Wang, T., Pottinger, R.: SeMap: A Generic Mapping Construction System, College of Computing, University of British Columbia
11. Yu, S., Han, Z., Le, J.: A Flexible and Composite Schema Matching Algorithm, College of Information Science and Technology, Donghua University
12. Giunchiglia, F., Shvaiko, P., Yatskevich, M.: Semantic Schema Matching. Technical Report, DIT-05-014, University of Trento, Povo, Trento, Italy (2005)

Detection and Prevention of SQL Injection Attacks Using Semantic Equivalence

Sandeep Nair Narayanan, Alwyn Roshan Pais, and Radhesh Mohandas

Department of Computer Science & Engineering,
National Institute of Technology Karnataka,
Surathkal, India
{sandeepnairnarayanan,alwyn.pais,radhesh}@gmail.com

Abstract. SQL injection vulnerability is a kind of injection vulnerability in which the database server is forced to execute some illicit operations by crafting specific inputs to the web server. Even though this vulnerability has had it's presence for several years now, most of its popular mitigation techniques are based on safe coding practices, which are neither applicable to the existing applications, nor are application independent. Here we propose a new application logic independent solution to prevent SQL injection attacks which can be applicable to any dynamic web technology. The new solution detects SQL injection by considering the semantic variance between the queries generated by the query function with safe inputs and injection inputs. We have implemented the complete solution in ASP.NET with C# web applications using a custom written tool, SIAP, which patches the SQL Injection vulnerabilities in an existing web application by instrumenting the binaries.

Keywords: Injection Attacks, Injection Vulnerability, SIA, SQL Injection, Web Technology.

1 Introduction

SQL Injection attack is a type of code injection exploit in which the attacker gets unauthorized access to data or bypasses authentication by injecting crafted strings through web inputs. In web applications, some of the data from the web forms are used for constructing Structured Query Language (SQL) statements and are then executed on the database server. In a SQL Injection Attack(SIA), the attacker injects data into the web application, in such a way that the resultant SQL statement will produce malicious outcomes. In advanced SQL injection techniques, the queries are crafted to produce syntax errors on execution. The information disclosed in the error messages are used further for crafting more specific SQL statements which eventually leads to the finger printing of the complete database schema of the application. Injection vulnerability has been listed as the top vulnerability by OWASP [1]. Due to the high impact of the attack and the low cost and skill required to launch the attack, the net risk associated with

K.R. Venugopal and L.M. Patnaik (Eds.): ICIP 2011, CCIS 157, pp. 103–112, 2011.
© Springer-Verlag Berlin Heidelberg 2011

SQL injection vulnerabilities are very high. Even after the attack being well known, there are many enterprise web sites in the Internet which are still vulnerable to such attacks.

The popular solutions for the prevention of SQL injection attacks include coding best practices, input filtering, escaping user input, usage of parameterized queries, implementation of least privilege, white list input validation etc., These solutions should be employed usually during the development of an application. This is the major limitation of such solutions as they do not cover the millions of Web applications already deployed with this vulnerability. Manual patching of the vulnerability at each possible point is quite expensive with regard to the incurred cost and time consumption. This signifies the need for an automated tool to patch this vulnerability.

2   Related Work

We broadly classify the solutions for the prevention of SQL injection attacks as Developer centric solutions and Maintenance centric solutions. In the developer centric solution, the developer tries to prevent the attacks. Following safe coding practices [2], randomized query based methods and using Plug-in's which detect spots of possible vulnerabilities during the development phase are examples of such kind of solutions. SQLrand [3] is a technique in which the developer uses some randomized instructions instead of normal keywords. SAFELI [4] is a framework which uses a symbolic execution engine, a library of attack patterns and a constraint solver to detect the vulnerabilities in a web application. The drawbacks with the Developer centric approach are the need for individual attention for every project to be patched, the cost associated and the inability to handle the existing applications without modifying the code.

In Maintenance centric solutions we patch the deployed application using a third party tool or add new components to the existing system to prevent the attacks. Solutions in this category include Data tainting based solutions [5], Intrusion Detection System (IDS) based solutions, Black box testing solutions, Machine learning based techniques etc., Waves [6] is a black box testing tool which uses machine learning techniques to test for SQL injection vulnerabilities. Some techniques like SQL Guard [7] and SQL Check [8] check the queries for SQLI vulnerabilities based on some models. Another solution is using AMNESIA [9] [10] which uses a hybrid approach having both static analysis for building the model and dynamic analysis for preventing the injection. Yet another solution is CANDID [11] in which the intended query is created by running the application on candidate inputs. Our solution is a Maintenance centric solution, which is applicable to existing applications and can also be used during the development of new applications.

3   Proposed Solution

The process of generation of queries in a dynamic web application can be represented as a function of user's inputs. In this context, SQL injection is any situation in which the user's input is inducing an unexpected change in the output generated by the function. We define two parameters

$$SQL\_Statement = SQL(Arg_i) \quad {\scriptstyle (i=1 \ to \ n)}$$

$$Arg_i \leftarrow Input \ from \ user$$

$$SQL() \leftarrow function \ represented \ by \ web \ application$$

$$SQL\_Statement\_Safe = SQL(Arg\_Safe\_i) \quad {\scriptstyle (i=1 \ to \ n)}$$

$$Arg\_Safe\_i \leftarrow \text{``}qqq\text{''} \ or \ any \ single \ token$$

We require that the application will not allow the user to enter any part of SQL query directly. We define that two statements are semantically equivalent, if they perform similar activities, once they are executed on the database server. So, if we determine that both $SQL\_Statement$ and $SQL\_Statement\_Safe$ are semantically equivalent, then by definition the $SQL\_Statement$ is bound to have an expected behavior and there is no possibility for a SQL Injection. Here semantic action implies a particular activity like comparison, retrieval etc., and not the lexical equality. We use this semantic comparison to detect SQL Injection. The semantic comparison is done by parsing each of the statements and comparing the syntax tree structure. If the syntax trees of both the queries are equivalent, then the queries are inducing equivalent semantic actions on the database server, since the semantic actions are determined by the structure of the SQL statement.

3.1   An Example

Let,
$Arg \quad = \{\alpha, \beta\}$
$Arg\_Safe = \{\text{``}qqq\text{''}, \text{``}qqq\text{''}\}$
Now,

$$SQL\_Statement = SQL(Arg)$$
$$= SELECT \ * \ FROM \ 'User\_Table'$$
$$WHERE \ user\_name =' \alpha' \ AND \ password =' \beta'$$
$$SQL\_Statement\_Safe = SQL(Arg\_Safe)$$
$$= SELECT \ * \ FROM \ 'User\_Table'$$
$$WHERE \ user\_name =' qqq' \ AND \ password =' qqq'.$$

The $SQL\_Statement\_Safe$ is parsed to produce a syntax tree as shown in Fig. 1. We can consider two cases of user inputs, first case without any injection and second with injection.

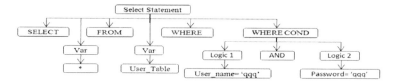

Fig. 1. SQL_Statement_Safe

Case 1: Let,
$Arg\_Normal = \{\alpha, \beta\} = \{admin, admin\_pwd\}$
Now,

$$
\begin{aligned}
SQL\_Statement\_Normal &= SQL(Arg\_Normal) \\
&= SELECT \; * \; FROM \; 'User\_Table' \; WHERE \\
&\quad user\_name =' admin' AND \\
&\quad password =' admin\_pwd'
\end{aligned}
$$

The *SQL_Statement_Normal* can be parsed as shown in Fig. 2. On comparing

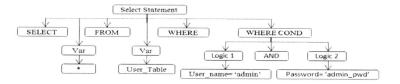

Fig. 2. SQL_Statement_Normal

the semantic structure of *SQL_Statement_Safe* and *SQL_Statement_Normal*, we can see that both of them have similar semantics. Both statements are extracting all values from a table after checking for two logic equalities combined with an AND operator. This implies that there is no possible SQL injection and hence we can safely execute the query.

Case 2: Let,
$Arg\_Injection = \{\alpha, \beta\} = \{admin' \; OR \; '1' =' 1, hacker\_pwd\}$.
Now,

$$
\begin{aligned}
SQL\_Statement\_Injection &= SQL(Arg\_Injection) \\
&= SELECT \; * \; FROM 'User\_Table' \\
&\quad WHERE \; user\_name =' admin' OR \; '1' =' 1' \\
&\quad AND \; password =' hacker\_pwd'
\end{aligned}
$$

In this case, on comparison of *SQL_Statement_Injection* which is represented in Fig. 3 with *SQL_Statement_Safe*, we can see that the semantic structures of

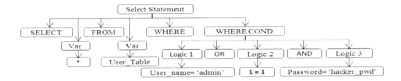

Fig. 3. SQL_Statement_Injection

the two statements are not similar. This is because *SQL_Statement_Injection* is
doing the additional action of "OR '1' = '1' ". This implies that on application of
the input, the semantics of the output has been modified. This detects a possible
SQL injection and the execution of the query should be stopped.

3.2   Algorithm

In a web application, the extraction of the function SQL() is tedious and error
prone. The easily available parameters are the inputs from the users and the
SQL_Statement. So we use a dynamic method to generate *SQL_Statement_Safe*
from *SQL_Statement* and the inputs from the user. The Solution is described in
the Algorithm 1.

The first step in the algorithm checks the *SQL_Statement* for syntax. If the
syntax is incorrect, it detects the SQL Injection straight away and the query
execution is prevented. The rest of the algorithm is split into two main parts

1. *SQL_Statement_Safe* Generation
2. Checking for Equivalence in Semantic Actions

SQL_Statement_Safe Generation: The steps from 4 to 23 encapsulate the
SQL_Statement_Safe Generation process. The usage of sorted inputs with length
facilitates the replacement of the longest input first with the safe sequence. But
the problem here is that, in case, if the web application uses $Modify(Arg\_i)_{i=1\ to\ n}$
instead of Arg_i directly in SQL(), the presence of Arg_i will go undetected. Here
Modify() is any function which modifies the Arg_i, the input from the users.
We divide this problem into two situations. *Modify()* function producing minor
changes in the user's inputs and *Modify()* function producing major changes
in the user's inputs. In the latter case as the intruder/hacker cannot predict
Modify() function, the inputs will result in a probable bad SQL syntax which
will be caught in the step 1.

In order to cope to the former case we added steps from 12 to 22. Here first we
find all the common subsequences of the query and each of the inputs. Then the
substrings from the start of each common sequence to its end are extracted from
the *SQL_Statement*. While finding the common subsequence we will consider two
threshold values to determine, if the common subsequence obtained is actually a
modification of user's inputs. The two thresholds used are the length threshold
and continuity threshold. The length threshold determines if the sequence contains enough parts from the User and the continuity threshold determines if the
detected parts together can form some modification of Arg_i. Once the calculated

Algorithm 1. SIA Detection

Inputs: SQL_Statement is the SQL Statement generated by the web application
Arg_i is the ith input from User, sorted in the descending order of their lengths
n is the number of inputs from the user
Output: Injection = True / False

Is_SyntaxValid($Stmt$): Checks if $Stmt$ has a valid SQL syntax and returns boolean
Replace($SrcStr, PresentStr, ReplaceStr$): Replaces $PresentStr$ with $ReplaceStr$ in $SrcStr$
Get_CommonSubsequence($SrcStmt, SearchStr$): Retruns all common subsequences of $SrcStmt$
and $SearchStr$ satisfying Length and Continuity Threshold
Get_SubString($SrcStr, Str$): Returns the sub string of $SrcStr$ containing the common subsequence Str
Get_StackedQueries(SQL_Stmt): Returns the multiple SQL statements in SQL_stmt
Get_Count(Arr):Returns the number of elements in Arr
Get_QueryTree(SQL_Stmt): Returns the parse tree for SQL_Stmt
Is_Equivalent(SQL_Tree1, SQL_Tree2): Checks if SQL_Tree1 and SQL_Tree2 are sematically
equivalent

```
 1: if (Is_SyntaxValid(SQL_Statement) == False) then
 2:     return true
 3: end if
 4: SQL_Statement_Safe ← SQL_Statement
 5: for i = 0 TO n do
 6:     repeat
 7:         Temp_Query ← Replace(SQL_Statement_Safe, Arg_i, "qqq")
 8:         if Is_SyntaxValid(Temp_Query) == True ) then
 9:             SQL_Statement_Safe ← Temp_Query
10:         end if
11:     until All Occurrences of Arg_i are replaced
12:     Css[] ← Get_CommonSubsequence(SQL_Statement_Safe, Arg_i)
13:     ln ← Get_Count(Css[])
14:     for j = 0 TO ln do
15:         Seq ← Get_SubString(SQL_Statement_Safe, Css[j])
16:         repeat
17:             Temp_Query ← Replace(SQL_Statement_Safe, Seq, "qqq")
18:             if Is_SyntaxValid(Temp_Query) == True ) then
19:                 SQL_Statement_Safe ← Temp_Query
20:             end if
21:         until All Occurrences of Seq are replaced
22:     end for
23: end for
24: Query[] ← Get_StackedQueries(SQL_Statement)
25: Query_Safe[] ← Get_StackedQueries(SQL_Statement_Safe)
26: if Get_Count(Query[])! = Get_Count(Query_Safe[]) then
27:     return True
28: end if
29: for j = 0 TO Get_Count(Query[]) do
30:     QT ← Get_QueryTree(Query[j])
31:     QT_Safe ← Get_QueryTree(Query_Safe[j])
32:     if Is_Equivalent(QT, QT_Safe) == False then
33:         return True
34:     end if
35: end for
36: return False
```

thresholds for an extracted subsequence goes over the specified threshold values, the corresponding substring will be replaced with the safe expression, "qqq". Before replacement of each of the user's input or the extracted substring in the *SQL_Statement*, the syntax of the resultant query is checked to ensure that no part of the query other than the inputs from the user, is accidentally replaced, even in case the user's input contains some parts of the query.

Checking for Equivalence in Semantic Actions. The SQL Injection is detected in this part. Most of the database servers allow stacking of queries, in which multiple queries are stacked back to back. So here, if the *SQL_Statement* contains multiple stacked queries, first we check if the *SQL_Statement_Safe* also contains an equal number of stacked SQL statements. If not, we declare a possible SQL Injection as the application of user's input caused a new semantic action in the form of a new query. In case if the total number of queries are the same, we parse the cannonicalized *SQL_Statement* and *SQL_Statement_Safe* to identify different semantic actions done by each query. This is done by parsing each of the statements to produce syntax trees and by checking each of the syntax trees are equivalent. If they are, then it ensures that each of the statements perform the same semantic action. In case of stacked queries, each of the corresponding queries need to be parsed and are required to be compared for semantic equivalence with its corresponding counterpart, such that the entire stack of queries makes equivalent semantic actions in the database. If both statements are semantically equivalent, then there is no possible injection and hence it is allowed to be executed in the database server. Else the execution of the query is blocked.

4   Implementation in ASP.NET with C# Applications

We implemented the proposed solution to prevent SQL Injection Attacks in ASP.NET with C#. The implementation includes a tool, SIAP which takes an ASP.NET web application as input and generates an instrumented ASP.NET application as output. SIAP patches the application at the binary level to prevent any kind of SQL injection possibility.

4.1   Sql Injection Attack Patcher (SIAP)

Input: ASP.NET with C Sharp Web Application including the deployed DLL. Configuration files - Hotspot configuration, Instrumentation configuration, Main configuration.
Output: Instrumented DLL and Back up of the existing DLL.

SIAP is a configuration driven tool which is developed based on the proposed solution. The specification of the tool is mention above. The overall architecture of the tool is represented in the Fig. 4. The main modules in the tool include Configuration File Manager(CFM), Back Up Module(BUM) and Instrumentation Engine(IE). The CFM reads the configuration files and decides the different actions to be performed by the IE. The different configuration files include Hotspot

Identifiers and Instrumentation Identifiers which describes the different points of instrumentation and the type of instrumentation to be done respectively. A hotspot is a point in the web application where a particular query is sent to the database server for execution. The main configuration file describes the general options of the tool like the action to be done on detection of SQL Injection, the parser to be used etc., The BUM backs up the existing web application safely to allow the user to revert back to the original state.

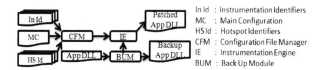

Fig. 4. Tool Architecture

The IE reads the web application and extracts the MSIL (Microsoft Intermediate Language) from the application DLL. Then according the information from the CFM, IE patches the extracted MSIL code such that all the inputs from the user and the query to be executed in the database server is directed to a Monitor Module which checks for injection. To do this, it searches for the different hotspots in the extracted code and a call will be added to the Monitor Module at each spot. It also inserts the Monitor Module into the application MSIL code. Finally the modified MSIL code will be compiled back to the DLL and is replaced in the deployment server.

4.2   Online Monitoring by Patched Application

The patched web application will have two more modules added to it. One is the Input Capturing Module (ICM) and the other is the Monitoring Module (MM). In the existing web application the flow of data is as shown by the thick lines in Fig. 5. The inputs will come in to the web application, the SQL query will be generated and is sent to the database server for execution. But in the instrumented application, all the inputs from the user will be captured by the Input Capturing Module and is sent to the Monitoring Module. The Monitoring Module also receives the final *SQL_Statement* from the web application. Now the Monitoring Module will check for SQL Injection in the *SQL_Statement* using the proposed solution. Once the *SQL_Statement* passes the test, it is sent to the database server for execution. Else its execution is prevented. The modified flow of data is represented by discontinuous lines in Fig. 5.

Fig. 5. Online Monitoring

5   Results

Our test bed for SIAP consists of Microsoft XP operating system, IIS v 6.0 Web Server and MSSQL Server database server. We ran 3 sample web applications, developed by third parties. We collected a set of SQL Injection attack vectors for attacking the deployed web applications. The Injection strings accumulated included tautology based strings, obfuscated strings, piggy backed strings etc. An injection vector in the test case comprises of an injection string and a particular input field to which the injection string is applied.

Table 1. Results SIAP

Web App	Hotspots Instrumented	Normal Working	Injection Vectors Tried	True Positives	True Negatives
BookStore	76	√	1525	549	976
Classifieds	46	√	1281	427	854
Portal	68	√	2013	732	1281

True Negative is a condition in which there is no SQL injection even in case of application of an injection vector. For example, if the developer filters integer type values in to an integer type field, then application of injection string will not produce any SQL injection. Hence it will be a True Negative if the instrumented application does not alarm SQL injection. True positive is a condition if the injection vector produces successful injection and the patched application alarms SQL injection. The observations obtained when the patched applications are applied with collected SQL injection vectors are presented in the Table 1. Unlike some other solutions to prevent SQL injection, the applications instrumented with SIAP, detected True Negatives also successfully. As the instrumented applications are working properly for normal inputs, there are no False Positives or False Negatives.

6   Conclusions and Future Work

Our solution is a novel approach to patch enterprise ASP.NET based web applications against the SQL injection attacks. Unlike the developer centric solutions, our solution is readily applicable to either existing or newly developed web applications and the application as such does not require any design modifications. As we are using easily available parameters in the web application, this solution is less prone to failures. Since our method does not take any rule set to detect the injection, it is capable of handling some unforeseen methods of SQL injection that may evolve in the future. We have implemented the solution for the ASP.NET with C# based web applications including a configuration driven tool, SIAP which automates the addition of the solution to any such application.

Our solution can be extended to other dynamic web technologies like Java Server Pages(JSP), PHP etc. The usage of the proposed solution for the stored procedures is straight forward and it could be implemented directly. Further the safe query generation technique could be further optimized for the performance of the patched application.

Acknowledgments. We acknowledge the financial support provided by MCIT-NewDelhi, GOI, by the sanction Order No: 12(10)/09ESD dated 08.01.2010.

References

1. Owasp, O.W.: Top Ten Most Critical Web Application Vulnerabilities (2010), http://owasptop10.googlecode.com/files/OWASPTop10-2010.pdf
2. Microsoft Developers Site, http://msdn.microsoft.com/en-us/magazine/cc163917.aspx
3. Boyd, S.W., Keromytis, A.D.: SQLrand: Preventing SQL Injection Attacks. In: Jakobsson, M., Yung, M., Zhou, J. (eds.) ACNS 2004. LNCS, vol. 3089, pp. 292–302. Springer, Heidelberg (2004)
4. Xiang, F., Kai, Q.: SAFELI-SQL Injection Scanner Using Symbolic Execution. In: Proceedings of the 2008 Workshop on Testing, Analysis and Verification of Web Services and Applications, pp. 34–39. ACM, New York (2008)
5. Halfond, W., Orso, A., Manolios, P.: WASP: Protecting Web Applications Using Positive Tainting and Syntax Aware Evaluation. IEEE Transactions on Software Engineering, 65–81 (2008)
6. Huang, Y., Huang, S., Lin, T., Tsai, C.: Web Application Security Assessment by Fault Injection and Behavior Monitoring. In: Proceedings of the 11th International World Wide Web Conference (May 2003)
7. Buehrer, G.T., Weide, B.W., Sivilotti, P.A.G.: Using Parse Tree Validation to Prevent SQL Injection Attacks. In: International Workshop on Software Engineering and Middleware (2005)
8. Su, Z., Wassermann, G.: The Essence of Command Injection Attacks in Web Applications. In: The 33rd Annual Symposium on Principles of Programming Languages (January 2006)
9. Halfond, W., Orso, A.: AMNESIA: Analysis and Monitoring for Neutralizing SQL Injection Attacks. In: Proc. 20th IEEE and ACM Intl. Conf. Automated Software Eng., pp. 174–183 (2005)
10. Halfond, W.G., Orso, A.: Combining Static Analysis and Runtime Monitoring to Counter SQL-Injection Attacks. In: Proceedings of the 3rd International ICSE Workshop on Dynamic Analysis, St. Louis, MO, USA, pp. 22–28 (May 2005)
11. Sruthi, B., Prithvi, B., Madhusudan, P., Venkatakrishnan, V.N.: CANDID: Preventing SQL Injection Attacks using Dynamic Candidate Evaluations. In: Proceedings of the 14th ACM Conf. on Computer and Communications Security (2007)

PCF-Engine: A Fact Based Search Engine

Srikantaiah K.C.[1], Srikanth P.L.[1], Tejaswi V.[1], Shaila K.[1],
Venugopal K.R.[1], Iyengar S.S.[2], and Patnaik L.M.[3]

[1] Department of Computer Science and Engineering, University Visvesvaraya College
of Engineering, Bangalore University, Bangalore 560 001
[2] Head of Wireless Sensor Networks and Robotics Research Laboratory,
Department of Computer Science,
Lousiana State University, USA
[3] Vice Chancellor, Defence Institute of Advanced Technology, Pune, India
srikantaiahkc@yahoo.com

Abstract. The World Wide Web (WWW) is the repository of large number of web pages which can be accessed *via* Internet by multiple users at the same time and therefore it is *Ubiquitous* in nature. The search engine is a key application used to search the web pages from this huge repository, which uses the link analysis for ranking the web pages without considering the facts provided by them. A new application called *Probability of Correctness of Facts(PCF)-Engine* is proposed to find the accuracy of the facts provided by the web pages. It uses the Probability based similarity (SIM) function which performs the string matching between the true facts and the facts of web pages to find their probability of correctness. The existing semantic search engines, may give the relevant result to the user query but may not be 100% accurate. Our algorithm probes for the accuracy among the facts to rank the web pages. Simulation results show that our approach is efficient when compared with existing Voting [1] and Truthfinder [1] algorithms with respect to the trustworthiness of the websites.

Keywords: Data mining, Page Rank, Search Engine, Trustworthiness, Web Content Mining.

1 Introduction

World Wide Web (WWW) is a collection of interconnected web pages accessed *via* internet offers information and data from all over the world. When searching for a topic in the WWW, it returns many links or web sites related on the browser to a given topic. The important issue is to determine the website that gives the accurate information. There are many related web sites that give unauthoritative information. While the information in other repositories like books, library and journals is evaluated by scholars, publishers, and subject experts. We have no mechanism to evaluate the information on WWW. Hence, it is necessary to consider some criteria [2] to evaluate the information hosted on WWW. Web search engines are programs used to search information on the WWW and FTP servers and to check the accuracy of the data automatically. It operates in the following order: *Web Crawling, Indexing, Searching* and *Ranking*. Ranking is

K.R. Venugopal and L.M. Patnaik (Eds.): ICIP 2011, CCIS 157, pp. 113–122, 2011.
© Springer-Verlag Berlin Heidelberg 2011

a process of arranging the retrieved WebPages of the Search Engine Result Page (SERP) based on the relevance of the query entered. Relevance of a webpage is calculated based on the contents of the web page, including title, Meta data, popularity, authority, facts, location and frequency of a term in a web page.

Motivation: The existing page rank algorithms such as *Authoritative − Hub* analysis and *PageRank* uses the statistical analysis i.e., the rank for the page is calculated based on the number of links referring to the page and on the importance of the referring pages. The facts provided by the web pages are not considered while assigning the ranks to the pages.

Contribution: A new approach called PCF-Engine is proposed in this paper to find the probability of correctness of the conflicting facts by applying Probability based similarity (SIM) function between conflicting facts and true facts available in the knowlegde base and it is referred as trustworthiness of the website.

Organization: The rest of this paper is organized as follows: Section 2 describes Related Work. Section 3 descibes Background of our work, Section 4 defines problem, describes Mathematical Model and algorithm of PCF-Engine, Section 5 comprises of experimental evaluation along with experimental results and analysis. The concluding remarks are summarized in Section 6.

2   Related Work

Several algorithms have been proposed to rank the webpages retrieved by search engine and they are categorized into Authority Based and Fact Based. PageRank [3] and HITS [4] are authority based rank algorithms. PageRank Algorithm has been developed by Larry Page, ranks the webpages based on the indegree of a node in the web graph and it is a query independent algorithm. Further the original pageRank algorithm has been improved by considering weights to links [5], Cluster Prediction, Subgraphs [6], Timestamp, Extrapolation method, Index [7], and Machine Learning [8]. HITS and its variants [9, 10], rank the webpage based on both indegree and outdegree of a node in the web graph, and it is a query dependent algorithm. But most authority pages do not contain accurate information [11]. Truthfinder [1] is a fact based search engine; it ranks websites by computing trustworthiness score of each website using the confidence of facts provided by websites.

3   Background

Xiaoxin Y et al., [1] have proposed an algorithm Truthfinder to find true facts from conflicting information from different infomation providers on the web. This approach is applied on certain domain such as, book authors and Movie run time. For the books domain, the Truthfinder uses author name as the facts which assigns the weights for first, middle and last name of the authors to find the confidence of the facts and this is repeated for every fact to find trustworthiness of the website. It assigns the weight ratio of 2:1:3 for first, midddle and last name respectively.

Example: True fact says, the author of some book is Graeme C. Simsion, where weight 2 is assigned for Graeme, 1 for C and 3 for Simsion and if the fact obtained from book seller website is Grame Simsio, where it does not contain middle name C and the charater 'n' is missing in the last name, it is only partially correct. Truthfinder assigns the half of the weight allocated for last name, i.e., 3/2 and full weght of 2 to first name and zero to middle name, therefore confidence of the fact is (2+1.5)/6 which is 58.33%.

PCF-Engine performs string matching between author names provided by the book sellers with author names of the corresponding book in the knowledge base and hence, it searches for exactness of the fact. Therefore confidence of the above example is 93.75%. Hence it is more accurate than Truthfinder.

4   Proposed Model

4.1   Problem Definition

Given a set of objects, a set of websites providing conflicting facts for an object and a set of true facts for a specific domain, the main goal is to find the Probability of Correctness of the conflicting facts with respect to the true facts to rank the webpages providing the facts.

Assumption: The facts available in Knowledge base are 100% accurate and it is obtained from the trustworthy resource.

4.2   Mathematical Model

Basic Definitions:

(i)*Probability of Correctness of Fact (PCF)*- is defined as the probability by which the fact is similar to that of the true fact or in other words by the factor that the fact has minimal deviation from the true fact.

(ii)*Implication between the facts* - is defined as the extent by the facts has influence other facts of the same object, i.e., the deviation between the PCFs of the facts from the threshold (maximum allowable deviation between the PCFs of the facts).

Trustworthiness of website is directly proportional to confidence of all the facts provided by that website and implication between the facts [1]. The basic notations used in the model are shown in Table 1.

Table 1. Basic Notations

ε	: is the threshold, i.e., allowable deviation of PCFs between any two facts.
$p(f)$	: is the probability of correctness of the fact about an object in some
$Ob\{\}$	: Set of objects in certain domain.
$TF\{\}$	: Set of true facts indexed by objects.
$F'\{\}$	: Set of facts provided by different websites indexed by objects.
$Web\{\}$	: Set of websites URLS indexed by objects.

Probability of Correctness of Facts (PCF): If $\exists f \in TF\{\}$, such that $f \leftarrow TF\{o\}$, provided by $Web\{o\}$, where, $\forall o \in Ob\{\}$ then,

$$p(F_i'\{o\}) \leftarrow SIM(f, F_i'\{o\}). \tag{1}$$

where, $1 \leq i \leq |F'\{o\}|$, $SIM(f, F') \leftarrow$ is defined as the factor by which F' is true with respect to f and it is based on the domain or context where it is used. If F' is completely true with respect to f, then the probability of F' is correct when f is considered as true fact is 1 $i.e.$, F' is 100% correct about an object, where $F_i'\{o\}$ is a ith fact for an object o provided by some website as shown in Eq. (1).

It implies that facts obtained from the website about an object is exactly similar to that of the true fact of an object and therefore the $SIM(f, F')$ is also used to find the initial trustworthiness of the website by applying this function between all the facts provided by the website and the corresponding objects true facts available in the knowledgebase.

Implication Between Facts: Let Δ represents the difference between the probability of two facts f_1 and f_2, i.e., $\Delta = p(f_1) - p(f_2)$ and based on the value of Δ, there are three cases.

Case 1: If $(0 < \Delta < \varepsilon)$ or $(\Delta > 0$ and $\Delta > \varepsilon$ then, f_1 has low impact on f_2 by $|\varepsilon - \Delta|$.
Example: if $p(f_1)=0.7$ and $p(f_2)=0.2$ then $\Delta=0.5$ which is greater than ε, i.e., 0.4, this implies f_1 is 70% correct and f_2 is 20% correct, the difference is 50% which is greater than 40%(threshold) which is preferably allowed deviation between any two facts, therefore f_1 is having low impact on f_2 by 10% (50-40)%.

Case 2: If $(\Delta > 0)$ and $(\Delta = \varepsilon)$; then, f_1 has impact of ε on f_2.
The difference between the probabilities of correctness of the facts is equivalent to the value of threshold and hence f_1 has the impact ε on f_2.

Case 3: If $(\Delta < 0)$ then, f_1 has high impact on f_2.

Example: if $p(f_1)=0.2$ and $p(f_2)=0.7$, then $\Delta = -0.5$ which is negative and less than ε, i.e., 0.4, this implies f_1 is 20% correct and f_2 is 70% correct, the difference is -50% which is less than 40%(preferably allowed deviation between any two facts), therefore f_1 is having high impact on f_2 by 90% (40-(-50))%. In otherwords, by adding 50% to f_1 gives f_2 correctness, therefore f_2 is having low impact on f_1. Hence impact or influence between any two facts f_1 and f_2 on the same object can be defined as,

$$Inf(f_1, f_2) = \begin{cases} |\varepsilon - \Delta| * s(f_2), & \text{for case 1 and case 3} \\ \varepsilon & \text{for case 2.} \end{cases} \tag{2}$$

Therefore adjusted confidence of a fact is defined as,

$$s'(f_1) = s(f_1) + \sum_{o(f_1)=o(f_2)} Inf(f_1, f_2). \tag{3}$$

where, $s(f)$ is a confidence of a fact f defined in [1]

$$s(f) = 1 - \pi(1 - t(w)).\qquad(4)$$

$$s'(f) = min \left\{ \begin{array}{l} s'(f) * 10^{-\alpha} : s'(f) * 10^{-\alpha} > 1, \\ 1 \leq \alpha \leq \infty \end{array} \right\} * 10^{-1}\qquad(5)$$

and adjusted confidence score is defined in [1]

$$\sigma^*(f) = -ln(s'(f)).\qquad(6)$$

In Eq. (5) dumping factor $i.e.$, $10^{-\alpha}$ is multiplied to the adjusted confidence $s'(f)$ to get the probability value less than or equal to 1.

SIM(TF,F') for Books Domain: Let $Ob = \{ob_1, ob_2, ob_3, \ldots, ob_n\}$, $TF = \{ TF_{11}, TF_{22}, TF_{33}, \ldots, TF_{nn}\}$ and $F = \{F'_{11}, F'_{22}, F'_{33}, \ldots, F'_{nn}\}$. where,

$$F'_{ij} = \{y_{ik} : 1 \leq k \leq n_b\}.\qquad(7)$$

where, n_b is the number of authors in the ith fact about the jth object and $i=j$. F'_{ij} is again the set of authors for j^{th} object (book). For example : $F'_{22} = \{y_{21}, y_{22}, y_{23}, \ldots, y_{2n_b}\}$ is the set of authors of the second book(second object). The true fact can also contain only one author or a set of authors for a book as defined according to Eq. 8,

$$TF_{ij} = \{x_{ik} : 1 \leq k \leq n_a\}.\qquad(8)$$

where, n_a is the number of authors in the ith true fact about the jth object and $i=j$ and $x_{ik} = TF_i - X$, $X = x_l : 1 \leq l \leq n_a$ and $l! = k$. Therefore, the similarity function between i^{th} true fact and corresponding i^{th} fact provided for any object $o \in Ob$ is defined according to the Eq. (9),

$$SIM(TF_i, F'_{io}) = \sum_{j=1}^{|F'_{io}|} \sum_{k=1}^{|TF_{io}|} LEN(F'_{ioj})/LEN(TF_{iok}), if f F'_{ioj} \subseteq TF_{iok}.\qquad(9)$$

Repeat the process for all object $o \in Ob$, therefore

$$SIM(TF, F') = \sum_{i,o=1}^{|F'|} \sum_{j=1}^{|F'_{io}|} \sum_{k=1}^{|TF_{io}|} LEN(F'_{ioj})/LEN(TF_{iok}).\qquad(10)$$

$LEN(f)$: Gives the number of characters found in the author name F' in Eq. 9 and Eq. 10. Here, the probability of correctness is calculated depending on the number of characters matched in the first, last and middle of the author name of obtained facts from different website to the first, last and middle name of the author names taken in that order of the true fact about the object(book) available in the knowledge base.

Example: if $TF=\{\{\text{Cay S Horstmenn,Gary Cornell}\}, TF_{22}, \ldots, TF_{nn}\}$ is a true fact about the book Core java Volume 1 with ISBN 8131701621 and $TF_{11}=\{\text{Cay S Horstmenn,Gary Cornell}\}$, $F'=\{\{\text{Cay S Horstmenn,Gary''},$ ''Horstmenn'',''Corne''$\}, F'_{22}, \ldots, F'_{nn}\}$ where, $F'_{11}=\{\text{Cay S Horstmenn, Gary, Horstmenn, Corne}\}$.

Consider first author F'_{111} *i.e.*, Cay S Horstmenn provided by w_1 which is same as the author name provided in true fact Cay S Horstmenn therefore $p(F'_{111})=1$. Similarly, consider the second author F'_{112} *i.e.*, Gary which is a subpart of true fact Gary Cornell therefore, $p(F'_{112})= \text{LEN(Gary)/LEN(Gary Cornell)}$ which is 0.33 similarly $p(F'_{113})= 0.6$ and $p(F'_{114})=0.416$.

Therefore, initial trustworthiness of w_1, $t(w_1)= (1+0.33)/2$ *i.e.*, 0.625 on ISBN 8131701621; if w_1 provides F'_{111} and F'_{112}. Similarly, initial trustworthiness of w_2 on ISBN 8131701621 is $t(w_2)=1.016/2$, *i.e.*, 0.508 where, 2 indicates number of facts provided by websites on the object(ISBN 8131701621) if it provides F'_{113} and F'_{114}. This process is repeated for every object(every book) provided by the corresponding websites to get their respective initial trustworthiness and they are ranked accordingly.

Initially, it is assumed that none of the websites are trustworthy, therefore initial trustworthiness of all websites are assigned to zero. Therefore the trustworthiness of website $t(w)$ is redefined as,

$$t(w) = \begin{cases} SIM(TF, F'), \; if \; t(w) = 0 \\ \sum_{f \in F(w)} s(f)/|F(w)| : otherwise[1]. \end{cases} \tag{11}$$

where, F' is a set of facts provided by website w and $F' \subseteq F$. If trustworthiness is zero, then the website is added with the new data to the database whose trustworthiness is calculated using $SIM(TF, F')$, otherwise, trustworthiness is calculated by taking the average of confidence of all the facts provided by the website w in Eq. 11.

The proposed *Probability of Correctness of Fact*(PCF) engine ranks the page depending on the accuracy of the facts provided by the websites. The facts which are assumed as true about any object are stored in knowledge base. For example the true facts about the different books are taken from the respective coversheets of the books. Following properties are some of the facts taken for the book, ISBN: Uniquely identifies the fact, Author Names: Authors for the corresponding book, Publisher: publisher for the book, Price: cost of the book. Once knowledge base is constructed, the dataset containing conflicting facts for the various objects are populated using the website *www.abebooks.com*.

The $\in$ is set to 0.4 which indicates that 40% deviation in PCF between the facts are allowed. The algorithm behavior can be rendered by changing the value of threshold. The algorithm includes three important stages:(i) calculation of trustworthiness of all the websites, (ii) calculation of confidence of all the facts available in database and (iii) finding the influence between the facts. Since the algorithm operates on real dataset it is scheduled to run on every day to update the contents of the database.

Table 2. Algorithm: PCF-Engine

Input

$TF\{\}$: Set of true facts indexed by objects.

$F'\{\}$: Set of facts providedby different websites indexed by objects

$Ob\{\}$: Set of objects.

$Web\{\}$: Set of Websites URL'S providing the facts.

ε : Equal to 0.4, allowable deviation between any two facts on the
        same domain.

Output

    Trustworthiness of the websites and confidence of the facts.

Process

begin

for each $w \in Web$; *Compute Trustworthiness for every Website*

    do

        if $t(w)$=0

            then

                $t(w)= SIM(TF, F')$; where F' is the set of facts provided
                                ; by website w

        else

            $t(w)= \sum_{f \in F(w)} s(f)/|F(w)|$

        end if

end for

for each $f \in F$; *Compute the Confidence of the facts*

    do

        $s(f)$=1-π(1-$t(w)$) ; for every website w providing a fact f
        where, $w \in Web\{\}$

        $\sigma(f)$=-$ln(1-s(f))$; confidence score of a fact f

end for

for each $f \in F$; *Compute the Implication between the facts*

    do

        for each $f' \varepsilon F$ and $f' \neq f$

            do

                Δ=$p(f)$ - $p(f')$

                if Δ=ε

                    then

                        $inf(f, f')$+= ε

                else

                        $inf(f, f')$+= $\mid \varepsilon - \Delta \mid$ * s(f')

                end if

        end for

        $s(f)$ ← get the confidence of f from database

        $s'(f)$=s(f)+$\sum_{o(f')=o(f)} inf(f, f')$

end for

end

The Initial trustworthiness is calculated depending on the PCF of all the facts provided by the website where the PCF for every fact is determined by using Probability based similarity (SIM) function. The facts provided by the different websites may be similar to the true fact and hence the PCF for those facts is 1. Which indicates the fact is 100% true and this is calculated on a fly in a single iteration. If PCF of all the facts provided by website is 1 and the deviations in the implications between the facts are low, then the trustworthiness closely approaches to 1 and hence the PCF engine always probes for exactness of the facts about an object.

The algorithm calculates trustworthiness for every websites by finding the PCF for the facts and it also computes the confidence of the facts by taking the trustworthiness of the corresponding websites providing the facts and hence *trustworthiness* and *confidence* are totally depending on each other. The algorithm stops after computing the trustworthiness of all the websites and confidence for all the facts found in the database. It recomputes the trustworthiness and confidence values when it is scheduled for next execution by considering the new facts arrived after the previous Execution. The algorithm is presented in Table 2.

5   Experimental Results

The data set consists of facts for the books domain, where domain in this context corresponds to values of certain attributes of the book such as ISBN, Author Names, Publisher, Price, URL of Book seller website and quantity (availability). The data set consists of the above specified information for 26 websites with 47 facts. The initial trustworthiness of websites, confidence and confidence scores of all the facts are initialized to zero. The Author Name of the book is considered as the important fact for Probability based similarity (SIM) function to perform the relevance analysis. The result of the Probability based similarity (SIM) function for all the facts provided by a website is used to calculate the trustworthiness of the website and this is performed on all the websites to rank them accordingly.

The PCF-Engine is developed using ASP.NET with C# as the underlying language. The Visual Studio 2005 (IDE), Windows XP(OS) and the MySQL 4.0 for database forms the complete development environment. The initial implementation is done with the ε set to 0.4. As shown in Fig. 1, the search is made for the ISBN 8183330088 of the book titled with Web Enabled Commercial Applications Development using HTML DHTML Javascript Perl CGI , the webIds providing the facts about this book are 5, 7, 3, 10, 8, 9 . . . *etc.*, of which the most trustworthy websites with value 1 are 5 and 7 and hence they are occupying the first two positions in the searched result.

The graph is plotted for the websites providing the facts for the book Web Enabled Commercial Application devlopment using HTML, DHTML, Java Scrift, Perl, CGI" by Ivan Bayross. As it is observed from the Fig. 2, the trustworthiness of websites fall in the range 18%-25% for Voting, 26%-33% for Truthfinder

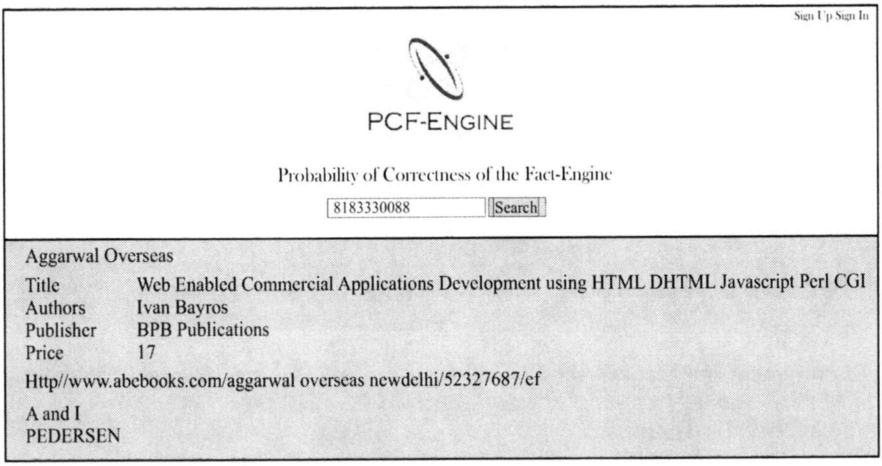

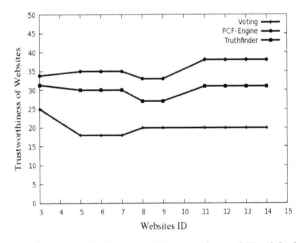

Fig. 1. Snapshot of the PCF-Engine

Fig. 2. Comparison between the Trustworthiness values of Truthfinder, Voting and PCF-Engine

and 33%-38% for PCF-Engine and the deviation between PCF Engine and Truthfinder with trustworthiness calculations is 0.058 and hence PCF-Engine is 5.8% more accurate than the Truthfinder. The probability values are normalized to two digits numbers in Y-axis. Since the Voting uses the facts count without considering the truthness of the facts provided by the websites, its accuracy is low compared to PCF-Engine and Truthfinder algorithms.

6   Conclusions

In this paper a new approach called PCF-Engine which uses Probability based similarity (SIM) function is proposed for resolving the conflicts between the facts provided by the different information providers in web. The Probability based similarity (SIM) function finds the implication between the facts. If the websites provides the fact which is exactly similar to that of true fact in the knowledgebase the PCF-Engine computes its trustworthiness value as 1 on a fly in a single iteration. The work can be extended by dynamically fetching the true facts to the knowledge base and removing the domain specific dependency of true facts.

References

1. Xiaoxin, Y., Jiawei, H., Philip, S.Y.: Truth Discovery with Multiple Conflicting Information Providers on the Web. Journal of IEEE Transactions on TKDE 20(6), 796–808 (2008)
2. Johns Hopkins University,
   http://www.library.jhu.edu/researchhelp/general/evaluating/
3. Brin, S., Page, L.: The Anatomy of a Large-Scale Hypertextual Web Search Engine. Journal of Computer Networks 30(7), 107–117 (1998)
4. Kleinberg, J.M.: Authoratative Sources in a Hyperlinked Environment. Journal of ACM 46(5), 604–632 (1999)
5. Xing, W., AliGhorbani: Weighted PageRank Algorithm. In: 2nd Annual Conference on Communication Networks and Services Research, pp. 305–314. IEEE Press, Los Alamitos (2004)
6. Heasoo, H., Andrey, B., Berthold, R., Erik, N.: BinRank: Scaling Dynamic Authority-Based Search using Materialized Subgraph. Journal of IEEE Transactions on TKDE 22(8), 1176–1190 (2010)
7. Amit, P., Chakrabarti, S., Manish, G.: Index Design for Dynamic Personalized PageRank. In: IEEE 24th International Conference on Data Engineering, pp. 1489–1491. IEEE Press, Los Alamitos (2008)
8. Sweah, L.Y., Markus, H., Ah Chung, T.: Ranking Web Pages using Machine learning Approaches. In: IEEE International Conference on Web Inteligence and Intelligent Agent Technology, pp. 677–680. IEEE Press, Los Alamitos (2008)
9. Matthew, H., Julie, S., Chaoyang, Z.: A Scalable Parallel HITS Algorithm for Page Ranking. In: First International Multi-Symposiums on Computer and Computational Sciences (IMSCCS 2006), pp. 437–442. IEEE Press, Los Alamitos (2006)
10. Allan, B., Gareth, O.R., Jeffrey, S.R., Panayiotis, T.: Link Analysis Ranking Algorithms, Theory and Experiments. Journal of ACM Transactions on Internet Technology 5(1), 231–297 (2005)
11. Brian, A., Loren, T., Hill, W.: Does Authority Mean Quality? Predicting Expert Ratings of Web Documents. In: ACM SIGIR 2000, pp. 296–303 (July 2000)

Online Identification of Illegitimate
Web Server Requests

Asish Kumar Dalai and Sanjay Kumar Jena

Department of Computer Science and Engineering,
National Institute of Technology Rourkela, Odisha, India
dalai.asish@gmail.com, skjena@nitrkl.ac.in

Abstract. Online identification attempts to filter the illegitimate requests based on browsing behavior. The proposed model is designed to implement in web applications. The automated systems like Botnet, Offline browsers, spammers etc., mimic like human users and generate a large number of unnecessary traffic over the web server which in turn results the unavailability of service to the legitimate users. Hence for online identification of such illegitimate request this model has been proposed. Botnet and Offline browsers are used to test the trustworthy of the model. The model has undergone a training phase with the web server log datasets of our test server. The web server features are used to detect the suspicious sessions. A CAPTCHA (acronym for "Completely Automated Public Turing test to tell Computers and Humans Apart") test is done for the suspicious session to restrict from sending further request to the web server.

Keywords: CAPTCHA, Clustering, DOS, IIS Server Log, Web server.

1 Introduction

Application that is deployed in a web server and is meant to access over the network is called as web application. The simplicity of web application is that one can access it using a web browser. Web applications are cross platform compatible. From the developers viewpoint it is easy to update and maintain the web application without disturbing the client. The increasing popularity of web application has brought some critical security risks. Developers are trying their best to reduce the vulnerability in the application. In spite of this, some major organizations has already became the victim of web attacks. Hence the challenge is to make the application attack proof.

The application is said to be secure if it fulfills all basic services of security including "Availability". Intruders are using automated systems to generate large number of request at the web server, which in turn results DOS (Denial of Service) attack. Web applications depend on third party service providers or use a white listing approach based upon the IP address which is not so efficient. This model aims at filtering the illegitimate requests. When developing such intrusion detection system we have to consider accuracy of the system along with timeliness of detection. Hence the goal of this proposed model is online identification

K.R. Venugopal and L.M. Patnaik (Eds.): ICIP 2011, CCIS 157, pp. 123–131, 2011.
© Springer-Verlag Berlin Heidelberg 2011

of the illegitimate requests and restricting them from sending further requests to the web server.

In this paper, the related works in identifying the unlawful request has been studied and a model for online identification of the illegitimate request has been proposed. This paper is structured as follows: Section 2 describes the importance of online identification of intruder. Section 3 contains the proposed model. In Section 4 the results has been discussed. Finally the concluding remarks are given in the last section.

2   Literature Survey

For classifying and then filtering the legitimate requests from unlawful requests, several models has been proposed.

– Jung et al., [1] have used source IP address to distinguish denial of service attack from flash crowd behavior using a topological clustering heuristics for a web server but IP addresses are subject to spoofing and using a white-list of source addresses of legitimate client is difficult, since many host may have dynamic IP addresses due to the use of NAT, DHCP and mobile-IP.
– Juan et al., [2] used Web Content Mining, Web Structure Mining and Web Usage Mining to capture a web users' usage pattern. Which may not very suitable for online detection as it needs intensive computation for page content processing and data mining.
– Dhyani et al.,[3] taken the navigation logs based on previous state to model the URL access patterns using Markov chains. The page dwell time has not been considered. Also, for large websites, the algorithm is too complex for online detection.
– Kandula et al.,[4] used a probabilistic authentication mechanism using "Completely Automated Public Turing test to tell Computers and Humans Apart" (CAPTCHA). It might annoy the users and introduce delays for legitimate user.
– Susanne et al.,[5] analyzed the sequence of user requests models the page jump probability using User Centric Walk algorithm.
– Ranjan et al.,[6] used a suspicion assignment mechanism and a scheduler to schedule the session requests. Flash crowds has not considered also the rate limiting mechanism can monitor the anomaly but can not filter.
– Yi Xie et al.,[7] used HsMM (acronym for "Hidden Semi-Markov Model") to describe the browsing behaviors of web surfers and apply HsMM to detect app-DDoS.
– Wang et al.,[8] click ratio of the web object and use the cluster method to extract the click ratio features. With the click ratio features of the learning stage, they have used the relative entropy to detect the suspicious sessions.

3   Importance of Online Identification

Due to the open access nature of web, any one can access the service including legitimate users and also the spurious users with wrong intention. The spurious user, generally use automated systems like:

- *Botnet*: To generate denial of service attack in application layer.
- *OfflineBrowser*: To download all the links and contents to the local directory for offline browsing.
- *Spammer*: Spider through web pages and collect the email address and send unwanted mails.

These automated systems generally cause harm and needs to be prevented. Organizations has to develop their own protection system in the server or depend up on some third party service providers, which is costly. The problem is to differentiate the unlawful requests and the legitimate request. These issues have been studied and online identification of intruder appears to be a viable solution to the above posed problem. This is a understudied problem and needs careful consideration. Thus motivates to explore online identification processes.

4   Implementation Details

Online identification of the unlawful request which consumes the server resources is intended. A model has been proposed for identifying the user from the users browsing behavior. The proposed model contains several modules like: Log File Preprocessing, Clustering, Feature Selection, Online Identification and finally Decision Fig. 1.

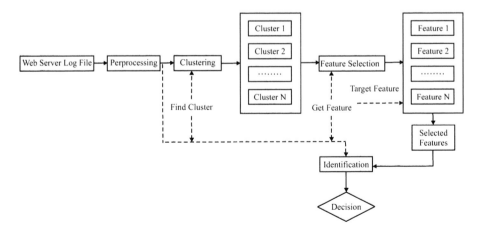

Fig. 1. Model for online identification of unlawful requests

4.1 Log File Preprocessing

The web server log file has been taken from the IIS (Internet Information Services) web server. The IIS log file is in World Wide Web Consortium (W3C) ASCII text format. The log file needs to be pre processed so that it can be entered into the SQL server. Form the log file the lines that start with "#" (these are the header lines in Web logs) has been removed. Out of various fields the fields of our interest "$time$", "$c - ip$", "$css - methods$", "$cs - uri - stem$", "$sc - status$", "$time - taken$", "$cs(Cookies)$" are taken. A table with required fields in SQL-server has been created. Now the query analyzer is used to bulk insert the pre processed file into the table. The "$cs - uri - stem$" column has updated to remove the path to keep only the file names. Then the cookie column has updated by selecting the substring "$Sessionid$" (the unique id created for each user when the user first accessed the application). The Fig. 2 shows the resulting table of the above steps.

date	time	cip	csmethod	csuristem	scstatus	time-taken	Cookie
2010-12-24	17:41:34	127.0.0.1	GET	login.aspx	200	3188	jldov1k0o0b0fcbuaewee4xs
2010-12-24	17:41:34	127.0.0.1	GET	simplelogo.JPG	200	46	jldov1k0o0b0fcbuaewee4xs
2010-12-24	17:41:34	127.0.0.1	GET	WebResource.axd	200	218	jldov1k0o0b0fcbuaewee4xs
2010-12-24	17:41:34	127.0.0.1	GET	WebResource.axd	200	218	jldov1k0o0b0fcbuaewee4xs
2010-12-24	17:41:42	127.0.0.1	POST	login.aspx	302	1281	jldov1k0o0b0fcbuaewee4xs
2010-12-24	17:41:42	127.0.0.1	GET	projectdetails.aspx	200	516	jldov1k0o0b0fcbuaewee4xs
2010-12-24	17:41:42	127.0.0.1	GET	WebResource.axd	200	15	jldov1k0o0b0fcbuaewee4xs
2010-12-24	17:41:42	127.0.0.1	GET	WebResource.axd	200	15	jldov1k0o0b0fcbuaewee4xs
2010-12-24	17:41:51	127.0.0.1	GET	changepassword.aspx	200	31	jldov1k0o0b0fcbuaewee4xs
2010-12-24	17:41:53	127.0.0.1	POST	projectdetails.aspx	200	47	jldov1k0o0b0fcbuaewee4xs
2010-12-24	17:41:55	127.0.0.1	GET	login.aspx	200	0	jldov1k0o0b0fcbuaewee4xs
2010-12-24	17:42:07	127.0.0.1	POST	login.aspx	500	422	jldov1k0o0b0fcbuaewee4xs
2010-12-26	08:34:27	192.168.40.110	GET	login.aspx	200	94	1a35posvhnzopwudghqevxom
2010-12-26	08:34:27	192.168.40.110	GET	simplelogo.JPG	200	78	1a35posvhnzopwudghqevxom
2010-12-26	08:34:27	192.168.40.110	GET	WebResource.axd	200	328	1a35posvhnzopwudghqevxom
2010-12-26	08:34:27	192.168.40.110	GET	WebResource.axd	200	328	1a35posvhnzopwudghqevxom
2010-12-26	08:34:27	192.168.40.110	GET	favicon.ico	404	63	1a35posvhnzopwudghqevxom
2010-12-26	08:34:30	192.168.40.110	GET	favicon.ico	404	0	1a35posvhnzopwudghqevxom
2010-12-26	08:34:35	192.168.40.110	POST	login.aspx	200	140	1a35posvhnzopwudghqevxom
2010-12-26	08:34:42	192.168.40.110	POST	login.aspx	302	31	1a35posvhnzopwudghqevxom
2010-12-26	08:34:42	192.168.40.110	GET	projectdetails.aspx	200	47	1a35posvhnzopwudghqevxom
2010-12-26	08:34:42	192.168.40.110	GET	WebResource.axd	200	15	1a35posvhnzopwudghqevxom
2010-12-26	08:35:00	192.168.40.110	GET	login.aspx	200	0	1a35posvhnzopwudghqevxom

Fig. 2. Processed log data in the database table

4.2 Clustering

Clustering is method of separating the users basing on content of interest. The purpose of visit is analyzed by considering their browsing behavior. The table below contains the cluster and their corresponding pages of our test web site.

From the database the session where no of pages visited n is less then threshold n_{th} are removed. For each session the page viewing time for each page is

Cluster	Pages
Student	1,2, ..., 20
Research	1,21, ..., 43
Alumni	1,43, ..., 59
Industry	1,60, ..., 77
Visitor	1,77, ...,83

calculated using:

$$P(t) = T(t) * 1000 - T(p). \tag{1}$$

The session–id (S_i) and their corresponding page viewing–times (P_j) are stored in a dataset SP.

$$SP = \begin{bmatrix} S_1P_1(t) & S_1P_2(t) & ... & S_1P_N(t) \\ S_2P_1(t) & S_2P_2(t) & ... & S_2P_N(t) \\ ... & ... & ... & ... \\ S_MP_1(t) & S_MP_2(t) & ... & S_MP_N(t) \end{bmatrix}. \tag{2}$$

$S_iP_j = 0$ if the session i has not visited the page j

The Algorithm in Table. 1 is applied to cluster the sessions. After clustering has over the sessions are put into different clusters. The result of which is cluster wise datasets (C_k). Within these dataset the entries for the pages which does not belong to the cluster and for those pages which has not been visited more than the threshold value are removed.

Table 1. Clustering Algorithm

Data: Dataset
Result: Grouping of the sessions into the cluster
Initialize the clusters $(C_1, C_2,...,C_n)$ and corresponding pages $(P_1, P_2,...,P_n)$
for each session S_i in the Dataset do
   for each page P_j do
      for each cluster C_k do
         if P_j is in C_k $then$
            $C_k(t)+=P_j(t)$ // time spend in a cluster
            $C_k(n)+=1$ // no of visit in a cluster
         end
      end
   end
   Find $C_k = max(C(t))$
   if two or more clusters have same time spend $then$
      Find $C_k= $ max-no-visit$(max(C(t)))$
      Put S_i into C_k Dataset end
end

$$C_k = \begin{bmatrix} S_1 P_1(t) & S_1 P_2(t) & ... & S_1 P_R(t) \\ S_2 P_1(t) & S_2 P_2(t) & ... & S_2 P_R(t) \\ ... & ... & ... & ... \\ S_L P_1(t) & S_L P_2(t) & ... & S_L P_R(t) \end{bmatrix}. \tag{3}$$

From the cluster wise dataset the required feature is selected. For each cluster, average page visiting time $P_j(avt)$ for each page calculated.

$$C_k P(avt) = [P_1(avt), P_2(avt), ..., P_R(avt)]. \tag{4}$$

The distance between equation (3) and (4)are calculated.

$$C_k D = \begin{bmatrix} S_1 d_1(t) & S_1 d_2(t) & ... & S_1 d_R(t) \\ S_2 d_1(t) & S_2 d_2(t) & ... & S_2 d_R(t) \\ ... & ... & ... & ... \\ S_L d_1(t) & S_L d_2(t) & ... & S_L d_R(t) \end{bmatrix}. \tag{5}$$

4.3 Feature Selection

On each page visit number of page visit n has incremented. When n becomes $n = n_{th}$ (min no. of pages are visited by all sessions) for each page, the page viewing time $P(t) = T(t) * 1000 - T(p)$ are calculated which produces the following resultant vector QP:

$$QP = [QP_1(t), QP_2(t), ..., QP_n(t)]. \tag{6}$$

The Algorithm mentioned is applied to find in which cluster the current session belongs. The entries for the pages from Eq. 6 which are not present in the cluster are removed.

$$QP_{(1-r)} = [QP_1(t), QP_2(t), ..., QP_r(t)]. \tag{7}$$

4.4 Identification

The distance vector of the current sessions' page visiting time found in Eq. 7 and the corresponding average page visiting time of the cluster as found is calculated in Eq. 4.

$$QD_{(1-r)} = [Qd_1(t), Qd_2(t), ..., Qd_r(t)]. \tag{8}$$

From Eq. 5 only those distances for which the current sessions' distances are present are selected.

$$C_k D_{(1-r)} = \begin{bmatrix} S_1 d_1(t) & S_1 d_2(t) & ... & S_1 d_r(t) \\ S_2 d_1(t) & S_2 d_2(t) & ... & S_2 d_r(t) \\ ... & ... & ... & ... \\ S_L d_1(t) & S_L d_2(t) & ... & S_L d_r(t) \end{bmatrix}. \tag{9}$$

The Euclidean distance between Eq. 8 and Eq. 9 are calculated.

$$D_j = \sqrt{\sum_{i=1}^{r} \left(S_j d_i - Q d_i \right)^2}.$$ (10)

where
$j = 1, 2, ..., L$
L = Number of sessions in the cluster dataset.
r = Number of pages.
M = Minimum(D) is found out.

4.5   Decision

If $M < \tau$ then the session is considered as suspicious.

$$D = \begin{cases} 1 & \text{if } M > \tau \\ 0 & \text{otherwise} \end{cases}$$ (11)

Where τ is threshold value. For further rechecking the user redirected to a CAPTCHA page. If the user is unable to solve the CAPTCHA then user is restricted from further accessing the page. The suspicious sessions data pattern is stored in a suspicious cluster dataset. The suspicious cluster dataset is used for checking it with the current sessions before applying the identification process. If the current session features matches with the suspicious session then session is redirected to the CAPTCHA page for checking its authenticity.

5   Results

The test web server log data has been pre processed and stored in SQL server. The algorithm has been run in the test data set to put the sessions in to the clusters. The model has been trained with all the clusters and entries has been made for respective clusters.

< Cluster, Index>	<Pages, Average Time>
<Student,1>	<1,12276.5 >,<2, 15556.3 > ..., <20, 5888.5 >
<Research, 2>	<1,12345.3 >,<21, 7664.4 > ..., <43, 37451>
<Alumni, 3>	<1, 12543.4 >,<43, 4079.6 > ..., <59, 9847>
<Industry, 4>	<1,12792.2 >,<60, 4678 > ..., <77, 2967>
<Visitor, 5>	<1, 12412.9 >,<77, 13451.7 > ..., <83, 6643>

The offline browser $WinHtTrack$ and $Botnet$ are used to request the test web site and found to be identified and stopped from accessing. The Fig. 3 describes the comparison of time taken by test dataset, offline browser and botnet for randomly selected webpages from the site.

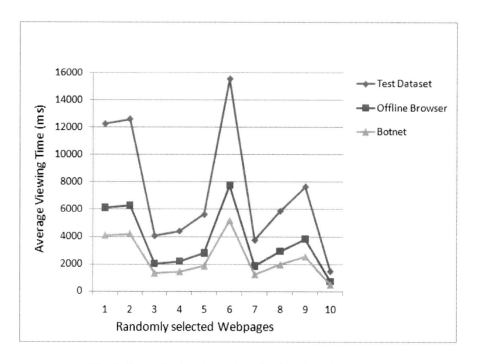

Fig. 3. Page viewing time of randomly selected webpages

6   Conclusions

Web applications are prone to attack due to their open access nature. Hence Security in the web application is highly necessary. The Proposed model may help the web servers for identifying and restricting the suspicious user from accessing the web server and its resources. The model can be used by the web application developers to implement in the web application server.

Acknowledgment

The authors are indebted to Information Security Education and Awareness (ISEA) Project, Ministry of Communication and Information Technology, Department of Information Technology, Govt. of India, for sponsoring this research and development activity.

References

1. Jung, J., Krishnamurthy, B., Rabinovich, M.: Flash Crowds and Denial of Service Attacks: Characterization and Implications for CDNS and Websites. In: WWW, pp. 293–304 (2002),
   http://dblp.uni-trier.de/db/conf/www/www2002.html#JungKR02

2. Velsquez, J.D., Yasuda, H., Aoki, T.: Combining the Web Content and Usage Mining to Understand the Visitor Behavior in a Website. In: ICDM, pp. 669–672. IEEE Computer Society, Los Alamitos (2003),
http://dblp.uni-trier.de/db/conf/icdm/icdm2003.html#VelasquezYA03

3. Dhyani, D., Bhowmick, S.S., Ng, W.K.: Modelling and Predicting Web Page Accesses Using Markov Processes. In: DEXA Workshops, pp. 332–336. IEEE Computer Society, Los Alamitos (2003),
http://dblp.uni-trier.de/db/conf/dexaw/dexaw2003.html#DhyaniBN03

4. Kandula, S., Katabi, D., Jacob, M., Berger, A.: Botz-4-sale: Surviving Organized Ddos Attacks that Mimic Flash Crowds (awarded best student paper). In: NSDI. USENIX (2005),
http://dblp.uni-trier.de/db/conf/nsdi/nsdi2005.html#KandulaKJB05

5. Burklen, S., Marron, P.J., Fritsch, S., Rothermel, K.: User Centric Walk: An Integrated Approach for Modeling the Browsing Behavior of Users on the Web. In: Annual Simulation Symposium, pp. 149–159. IEEE Computer Society, Los Alamitos (2005),
http://dblp.uni-trier.de/db/conf/anss/anss2005.html#BurklenMFR05

6. Ranjan, S.: Ddosresilient Scheduling to Counter Application Layer Attacks Under Imperfect Detection. In: Proceedings of IEEE INFOCOM, pp. 23–29 (2006)

7. Xie, Y., Yu, S.Z.: A Large-Scale Hidden Semi-Markov Model for Anomaly Detection on User Browsing Behaviors. In: IEEE/ACM Transactions in Networking, vol. 17, pp. 54–65 (2009),
http://dblp.uni-trier.de/db/journals/ton/ton17.html#XieY09a

8. Wang, J., Yang, X., K.L.: A New Relative Entropy Based App-Ddos Detection Method. IEEE Journal (2010)

Dynamic Generation of Semantic Documents for Web Resources

Saxena Ashish and Gore M.M.

Department of Computer Science and Engineering,
Motilal Nehru National Institute of Technology,
Allahabad, India
`ashish.saxena.1234@gmail.com, gore@mnnit.ac.in`

Abstract. Web has several resources like request or session objects, HTML, XML and images which do not have semantic information like RDF or ontologies with them. To convert Web into the Semantic Web it is required to add semantic information to Web resources. Previous approaches generate the semantic document statically. This paper provides a model for developers to generate semantic document (RDF) for the request and session data dynamically. It also provides a model which adds semantic information to the Web resources at runtime. Both these proposed models process new threads which use proposed algorithms and invoked by a Web server or a Web entity like servlet.

Keywords: Jena, RDF, Semantic Web, Session, Tomcat.

1 Introduction

The World Wide Web has changed the way people communicate. The Semantic Web communicates with keywords as well as meaning associated with them. Most of todays Web content is suitable for human consumption i.e., people can understand their semantics but computer programs or automatic tools are unable to interpret it.

Development of Semantic Web occurred in a decentralized manner and its growth was chaotic, which led to its current state as an immense repository of semantically unstructured documents. Web pages have text, images as well as links to other Web pages or documents, which do not have structure [1-8]. There are various Web resources which have semantic information. Some of them are,

1. request and session data
2. HTML and XML pages
3. images (JPG, PNG, GIF etc.,)
4. documents (PDF, DOC, RIF, etc.,)

This paper proposes two models to develop RDF(Resource Document Framework) for these types of resources. This paper concentrates only on the first two resource types as mentioned above.

K.R. Venugopal and L.M. Patnaik (Eds.): ICIP 2011, CCIS 157, pp. 132–140, 2011.

The first model is based on request and session data, which generates RDF documents according to the domain of request or session and Web developer's choice. In order to generate it the developers must provide a mapping document according to appropriate domain. This model parses this mapping document and generates RDF document for the request or session variables and their values.

The second model is for the Web server developers. It converts HTML or XML document to RDF document and adds semantic information to all other resources in terms of RDF document. There is an approach to convert HTML to XML in [1] and an approach to convert XML to HTML describe in [2], [3] and [4].

The approaches [1-4] are static. The document conversion takes place with the help of tools or APIs. The problem is with static approaches is that if any document is modified then it is also required to update corresponding semantic document explicitly. Both of the approaches implemented in this paper generate RDF documents dynamically. In the first approach document is updated with the creation or destruction of request or session objects. In second approach we check if the requested document is updated then also update corresponding RDF document at run time with request.

This paper is structured as follows. Section 2 discusses related work. Section 3 introducess our first model which generates RDF documents for request and session. Section 4 introduces second model which convert HTML documents into RDF documents. Finally we conclude in Section 5.

2   Related Work

There are various rules which convert HTML tags into XML tags [1]. These rules are categorized as following:

- Capturing Inter-block Nested structure
- Capturing Intra-block Nested structure

  - converting text-level elements and paragraph elements
  - converting lists
  - capturing the attribute-value pairs of HTML tables
  - recognized Heading of HTML tables

Above approach automatically captures the nested structure in an HTML document and converts it into the XML Document.

In [2], a model is used to convert XML document into RDF document with the help of OWL ontologies. The approach used in this paper is generic which does not depend on domain. Conversion of XML tags into RDF tags in an ontology dependent process. This process uses the links present in the mapping document to make the conversion. Fig. 1 illustrates the approach used in this paper.

Gloze [3] is a set of tools that may be used with jena RDF framework. The Gloze mapping allows us to directly interpret an XML document as an RDF model without passing through RDF/XML. It explores simple Bi-directional translation between XML based on the XML schema.

A generic transformation for XML data into RDF/XML is presented in [4]. This paper uses XSLT to transform XML document into RDF document. A transformation to RDF has to create the URIs of its resources and connect them through the RDF triple structure consisting of subject, predicate and object.

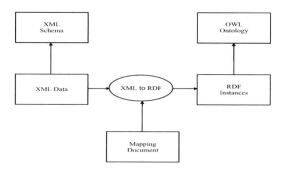

Fig. 1. RDF to XML conversion

3   RDF Generation Form Request and Session Data

Concept and Model. A request or session object has information which is dependent on its domain. Our model generates RDF document by using these objects. Our approach is generic. Fig. 2 illustrates the request flow of Apache Tomcat server and Fig. 3 explains the approach used in this paper.

In J2EE environment this model when Web browser sends a request to the Web Server, Servlet container invokes *service*() method of Servlet Class. The *service*() method invokes *doGet*() or *doPost*() method of HTTPServlet class. web developer can invoke appropriate methods of proposed APIs to generate RDF documents with in definition of *doGet*() or *doPost*() for request objects. To generate RDF document corresponding session object developer can invoke appropriate methods with in any method and before destruction of session objects.

3.1   XML Schema for Mapping Document

Web developers must provide a mapping document to use approach provide in this paper. The Mapping Document is an XML file which has direct mapping of RFD tags to their values and attributes. Schema for mapping document is describe below.

```
1.  <xsd:schema xmlns:xsd="http://www.w3.org/1999/XMLSchema"
    xmlns:md="http://www.mnnit.ac.in/namespace">
2.   <xsd:element name="mapping-document" type="mappingDocType"/>

3.   <xsd:complexType name="mappingDocType">
4.     <xsd:element name="description" type="xsd:string"/>
5.     <xsd:element name="for-request" type="xsd:boolean"/>
6.     <xsd:element name="for-session" type="xsd:boolean"/>
7.     <xsd:element name="resource" type="md:resourceType"/>
8.     <xsd:attribute name="id" type="xsd:string"/>
9.     <xsd:attribute name="type" type="xsd:md:requestType"/>
10.  </xsd:complexType>

11.  <xsd:complexType name="resourceType">
12.    <xsd:element name="var-name" type="xsd:string"/>
13.    <xsd:element name="property" type="md:propertyType"/>
14.    <xsd:element name="bag-items" type="md:bagType"/>
15.    <xsd:attribute name="id" type="xsd:string"/>
16.    <xsd:attribute name="name" type="xsd:string"/>
17.  </xsd:complexType>

18.  <xsd:complexType name="propertyType">
19.    <xsd:element name="var-name" type="xsd:string"/>
20.    <xsd:element name="resource" type="md:resourceType"/>
21.    <xsd:element name="bag-items" type="md:bagType"/>
22.    <xsd:attribute name="id" type="xsd:string"/>
23.  </xsd:complexType>

24.  <xsd:complexType name="bagType">
25.    <xsd:element name="resource" type="md:resourceType"/>
26.    <xsd:element name="property" type="md:propertyType"/>
27.    <xsd:attribute name="id" type="xsd:string"/>
28.  </xsd:complexType>

29.  <xsd:simpleType name="requestType" base="xsd:string">
30.    <xsd:enumeration value="request"/>
31.    <xsd:enumeration value="session"/>
32.  </xsd:simpleType>
33. </xsd:schema>
```

Web programmers have to provide a mapping document which must verify with the above schema. This process is described by following algorithm.

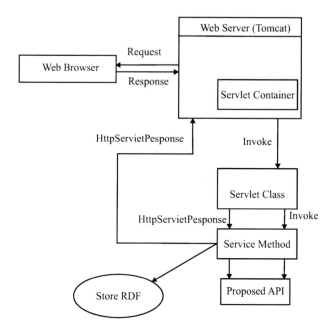

Fig. 2. Apache Request Flow

Table 1. Algorithm: Generation of RDF for request object

GenerateRequestToRDF()
Input :   HTTPServletRequest, Mapping document
Output :   RDF document
read the mapping document.
verify for valid document.
if (mapping document is valid)
parse using standard parsers.
make a tree of resources and properties.
write RDF for that request with Jena.
else
give message Not valid mapping-document

3.2 Guideline for Web Developers

- Web developers must provide mapping document according to the proposed schema.
- Web developers should use the API proposed in this paper after database commit.
- Web developers implement synchronization by two ways.

- • synchronized method
- • synchronized block
- – Web developer must use proper Exception Handling.

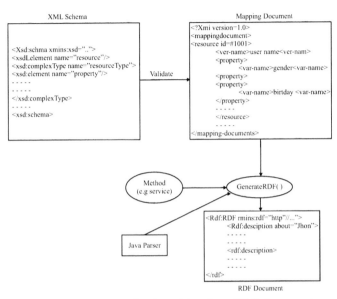

Fig. 3. Request or Session object into RDF document

3.3   Mapping-Document Structure

This is an example of the mapping document. This mapping is for Profile-Update-Request of a user of a social networking site. Developers provide mapping between variables and resources or between variables and properties.

```
1.  <?xml version="1.0"?>
2.  <mapping-document id="102345" type="single">
3.   <description>For User Details update </description>
4.   <for-request>True</for-request>
5.   <for-session>False</for-session>

6.   <resource id="1" name="User">
7.    <var-name>userId</var-name>
8.    <property>
9.      <var-name>firstName</var-name>
10.   </property>
11.   <property>
12.     <var-name>lastName</var-name>
13.   </property>
14.   <property>
15.     <var-name>birthDate</var-name>
```

```
16.    </property>
17.    <property>
18.  </resource>b
18.  <resource id="11" name="EducationalSchool">
19.    <bag-items>
20.      <property>
21.        <var-name>highSchool</var-name>
22.      </property>
23.      <property>
24.        <var-name>InterSchool</var-name>
25.      </property>
26.      <property>
27.        <var-name>graduation</var-name>
28.      </property>
29.      <property>
30.        <var-name>postGraduation</var-name>
31.      </property>
32.    </bag-items>
33.  </resource>
34. </mapping-document>
```

In this scenario the firstname, lastname and the bithday variables are mapped as property with the resource User similarly the EducationalSchool is mapped to its properties.

4   RDF Generation from HTML and XML Resource

This model we are capturing HTTP Requests for static resources (e.g. HTML, XML, image etc.,). Fig. 4 describes request model of Apache Tomcat Web server. The request is captured here when Process() method is invoked at the same time a thread is automatically invoked to generate RDF for that corresponding document. The mapping-document used here is domain specific. The algorithms for above mention process is as following:

Table 2. Algorithm: Generation of RDF for HTML or XML

GenerateRDF()
Input: *HTTP Request for HTML or XML document, mapping-document.* *Output:*   *RDF document.* get request form web browser. get requested document. invoke ConvertRDFThread Thread to convert document into RDF. end

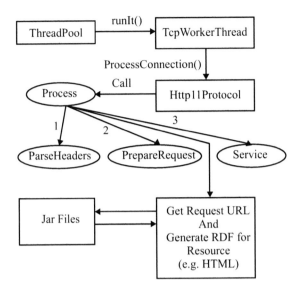

Fig. 4. Apache Request Model

Table 3. Algorithm: Convert HTML or XML into RDF

ConvertRDFThread()
Input: *HTML or XML document, mapping document*
Output: *RDF document*
if (document is HTML)
convert into XML using [4].
if (mapping document [5] is valid)
parse mapping-document
convert XML according to that mapping document.
end

5   Conclusions and Future Work

This paper presents a generic approach to generate RDF documents for HTTP request and HTTP session objects. We also present an approach to convert Static documents (HTML, XML) into RDF document. Generation or conversion is dynamic with the HTTP request. The current work is based on HTML and XML conversion. One can extend this concept to generate annotations for pdf files or add semantic to image files and other web resources. As this work is based on J2EE environment and Apache Tomcat Web server, it can be extended for other environments also.

References

1. Shijun, L., Mengchi, L., Wang, L.T., Zhiyong, P.: Automatic HTML to XML Conversion. In: Li, Q., Wang, G., Feng, L. (eds.) WAIM 2004. LNCS, vol. 3129, pp. 714–719. Springer, Heidelberg (2004)
2. Van Deursen, D., Poppe, C., Martens, G., Mannens, E., Van de Walle, R.: XML to RDF Conversion: A Generic Approach. In: Proceedings of the Fourth International Conference on Automated Solutions for Cross Media Content and Multi-Channel Distribution (2008)
3. Battle, S.: Gloze: XML to RDF and Back Again. In: Jena User Conference (May 2006)
4. Breitling, F.: A standard transformation from XML to RDF via XSLT. Astronomische Nachrichten. J. 330, 755–761 (2009)
5. Antoniou, G., Harmelen, F.V.: A Semantic Web Primer, 2nd edn (Cooperative Information Systems). The MIT Press, Cambridge (2008)
6. Fernando, C., Carvalho, D., Cedric, Luiz, da Silva, Carlos, J.: Semantic Web Support Applications. In: Proceedings of the Euro American Conference on Telematics and Information Systems (EATIS 2008), Article 27 p. 4. ACM, New York (2008)
7. RDF-Semantic Web Standards, http://www.w3.org/RDF/
8. Semantic Web Central, Open source tools for the semantic web, http://www.semwebcentral.org/

Information Propagation on Novel Social Network Model

Sreedhar Bhukya

Department of Computer and Information Sciences,
University of Hyderabad, Hyderabad- 500046, India
sr2naik@gmail.com

Abstract. Recently many researches on social networks are based on a characteristic which includes assortative mixing, high clustering, short average path lengths, broad degree distributions and the existence of community structure. Here, an application has been developed in the domain of information propagation which satisfies all the above characteristics, based on some existing social network models. In addition, this model facilitates interaction between various communities (professional/academic/research and Business groups). This model gives very high clustering coefficient by retaining the asymptotically scale-free degree distribution. Here the community structure is raised from a mixture of random attachment and implicit preferential attachment. In addition to earlier works which only considered Neighbor of Initial Contact (NIC) as implicit preferential contact, we have considered Neighbor of Neighbor of Initial Contact (NNIC) also. This model supports the occurrence of a contact between two Initial contacts if the new vertex chooses more than one initial contacts. Compared to earlier model thus leading a faster application to propagate information over social networks, this ultimately will develop a complex social network rather than the one that was taken as basic reference.

Keywords: Information Propagation, Neighbor of Neighbor Initial Contact, Random Initial Contact, Social Networks, Tertiary Contact

1   Introduction

Recent days professional/academic/research and Business groups are in collaboration becoming domain independent. For example stock market analyst is taking the help of computer simulator for future predictions. Thus there is a necessity of collaboration between people in different domains (different communities, in the language of social networking.) Here we develop a application for collaborations in professional/academic/research and Business communities which gives a possibility of interacting with a person in a different community, yet retaining the community structure. Social networks are made of nodes that are tied by one or more specific types of relationships. The vertex represents individuals or organizations. Social networks have been intensively studied by Social

K.R. Venugopal and L.M. Patnaik (Eds.): ICIP 2011, CCIS 157, pp. 141–148, 2011.
© Springer-Verlag Berlin Heidelberg 2011

scientists [1–3], for several decades in order to understand local phenomena such as local formation and their dynamics, as well as network wide process, like transmission of information, spreading disease, spreading rumor, sharing ideas etc. Various types of social networks, such as those related to professional collaboration [4–6], Internet dating [7], and opinion formation among people have been studied. Social networks involve Financial, Cultural, Educational, Families, Relations and so on. Social networks create relationship between vertices; Social networks include Sociology, basic Mathematics and graph theory. The basic mathematics structure for a social network is a graph. The main social network properties includes hierarchical community structure [8], small world property [9], power law distribution of nodes degree [10] and the most basic is Barabasi Albert model of scale free networks [11]. The more online social network gains popularity, the more scientific community is attracted by the research opportunities that these new fields give. Most popular online social networks is Facebook, where user can add friends, send them messages, and update their personal profiles to notify friends about themselves. Essential characteristics for social networks are believed to include assortative mixing [12], [13], high clustering, short average path lengths, broad degree distributions[14], [15], and the existence of community structure. Growing community can be roughly speaking set of vertices with dense internal connection, such that the inter community connection are relatively sparse.

Here we have considered an existing model [16] of social networks and developed it in way which is suitable for collaborations in academic communities. The model is as follows:

The algorithm consists of two growth processes: (i) random attachment (ii) implicit preferential attachment resulting from following edges from the randomly chosen initial contacts.

The existing model lacks in the following two aspects:

1. There is no connection between initial to initial contacts, if more than one initial contact is chosen.
2. There is no connection between initial contact and its neighbor of neighbor vertices.

These two aspects we have considered in earlier model [17] and from the earlier model we applied application for information propagation in the professional/academic/research and Business community. The advantage of our application can understand from the fallowing example and our application can be applicable to the real-world applications. The advantage of our application can be understood from the following example. Let us consider a person contacting a person in a group for spreading information and the initial person also speeding the information to his neighbor. The same thing will happen in our day to day life also. If a person contacts us for some purpose and we are unable to help him, we will try to help him by some contacts of our friends. The extreme case of this nature is that we may try to contact our friend of friend for this purpose. We have implemented the same thing in our new application. In the old model [16], information about friends only used to be updated, where as in our application information about friend of friend also has been updated for fast spreading of any information in the network community. Of course this application creates a complex social network application but, spreading of information very fast or data will be spread very fast. This fulfills the actual purpose of social networking in an efficient way with a faster growth rate by keeping the community structure as it is.

2   Network Growth Algorithm

The algorithm includes three processes: (1) Random attachment (2) Implicit preferential contact with the neighbors of initial contact (3) In addition to the above we are proposing a contact between the initial contact to its Neighbor of Neighbor contact (tertiary). The algorithm of the model is as follows [1] in this paper we consider vertices as a person.

1) Start with a seed network of N vertices.
2) Pick on average $m_r \geq 1$ random vertex as initial contacts.
3) Pick on average $m_s \geq 0$ neighbors of each initial contact as secondary contact.
4) Pick on average $m_t \geq 1$ neighbors of each secondary contact as tertiary contact.
5) Connect the new vertex to the initial, secondary and tertiary contacts.
6) Repeat the steps 2-5 until the network has grown to desired size.

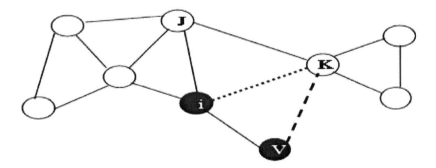

Fig. 1. Growing Process of Community Network

Fig. 1. shows the Growing process of community network. The new vertex V initially connects through some one as initial contact (say i). Now i, updates its neighbor of neighbor contact list and hence connects to k. V connects to m_s number of neighbors (say k) and m_t number of neighbor of neighbors of i (say k). In this model we tried 45 sample vertices and prepared a growing network. The Fig. 2. showing social network graph.

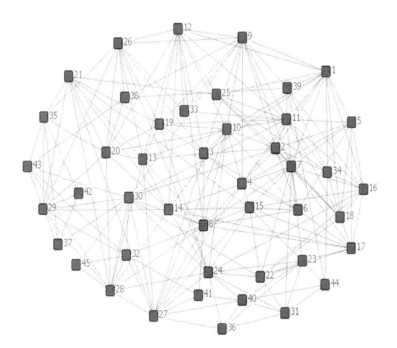

Fig. 2. Showing Social Network Community Graph with 45 vertices

3   Vertex Degree Distribution

We derive approximate value for the vertex degree distribution for growing network model mixing random initial contact, neighbor of neighbor initial contact and neighbor of initial contacts. Power law degree distribution with $p(k) \sim k^{\gamma}$ with exponent $2 < \gamma < \infty$ have derived [10], [18]. In this model also the lower bound to the degree exponent γ is found to be 3, which is same as in the earlier model.

The rate equation which describes how the degree of a vertex changes on average during one time step of the network growth is constructed. The degree of vertex v_i grows in 3 processes:

1. When a new vertex directly links to v_i at any time t, there will be on average $\sim t$ vertices. Here we are selecting m_r out of them with a probability m_r /t.
2. When a vertex links to v_i as secondary contact, the selection will give rise to preferential attachment. These will be $m_r . m_s$ in number.
3. When a vertex links to v_i as tertiary contact, this will also be a random preferential attachment. These will be $2 m_r m_s m_t$ in number.

These three processes lead to following rate equation for the degree of vertex v_i [17]

$$\frac{\partial k_i}{\partial t} = \frac{1}{t}\left(m_r + \frac{m_r m_s + 2m_r m_s m_t}{2(m_r + m_r m_s + 2m_r m_s m_t)}k_i\right) . \tag{1}$$

For this equation detail explanations refer on ref. [17]. From this we got the probability density distribution for degree k_i as

$$P(k) = AB^A(k + C)^{-2}/m_s + 2m_s m_t^{-3} . \tag{2}$$

Here A, B and C are as above. In the limit of large k, the distribution becomes a power law $p(k) \sim k^{-\gamma}$ with $\gamma = 3 + 2/m_s$, $m_s > 0$, leading to $3 < \gamma < \infty$. Hence the lower bound to the degree exponent is 3. Although the lower bound for degree exponent is same as earlier model. The probability density distribution is larger compared to earlier model, where the denominator of the first term of degree exponent is larger compared to the earlier model.

4   Clustering

The clustering coefficient on vertex degree can also be found by the rate equation method [19]. Let us examine how the number of triangles E_i changes with time. The triangle around v_i are mainly generated by three processes:

1. Vertex v_i is chosen as one of the initial contact with probability m_r/t and new vertex links to some of its neighbors as secondary contact, giving raise to a triangle.
2. The vertex v_i is chosen as secondary contact and the new vertex links to it as its primary or tertiary contact giving raise to a triangles.
3. The vertex v_i is chosen as tertiary contact and the new vertex links to it as its primary or secondary contact, giving raise to a triangles.

These three process are described by the rate Eq. [17]

$$\frac{\partial E_i}{\partial t} = \frac{k_i}{t} - \frac{1}{t}\left(m_r - m_r m_s - 3m_r m_s m_t - \frac{5m_r m_s m_t}{2(m_r + m_r m_s + 2m_r m_s m_t)t}k_i\right) . \tag{3}$$

we arrive at the clustering the coefficient

$$c_i(k_i) = \frac{2E_i(k_i)}{k_i(k_i - 1)} . \tag{4}$$

For this equation detail explanation on refer ref. [17] For large values of degree k, the clustering coefficient thus depend on k as $c(k) \sim lnk/k$. This has very large clustering coefficient compared to the earlier work where it was $c(k) \sim 1/k$.

5   Results

Simulation results have been projected for a network of 45 vertices where edge to vertex ratio and triangle to vertex ratio for 45 vertices has been projected. Hence one can see an increase in number of contacts due to the introduction of secondary and neighbor of neighbor contacts.

Table 1. Results of Growing Network Community

Data on our proposed model	Initial Contact (IC)	Secondary Contacts (SC)	Neighbor of Neighbor IC (NNIC)
Vertices	2.73	6.30	3.83
Triangless	0.3	6.4	6.14

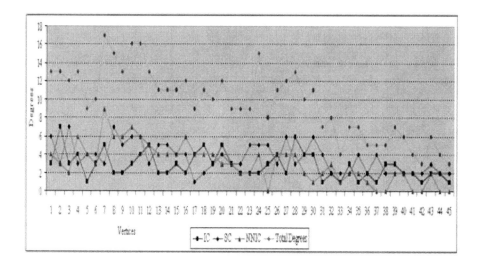

Fig. 3. Comparison Results of Growing Network Community

5.1   Simulation Results

The below results have been represented graphically by calculating the degree (number of contacts) of a node. This also is shows an enormous growth in degree of nodes (Fig. 3.)

Fig. 3. shows the comparison results of growing network community: initial contacts are growing very slow rate compared to secondary contact *i.e.*, ■ indicates initial contact, ◆ indicates secondary contacts, and ▲ indicates neighbor of neighbor of initial contact connects to the vertex v_i, Finally • indicates degree of each vertices, when initial, secondary and tertiary contact connect to a vertex v_i. Our network community is growing very fast and complex when compared to existing model, vertices simulation results based on Table 1.

6   Conclusions

In this paper, an application which reproduces very efficient networks compared to real social networks has been developed. And also here, the lower bound to the degree exponent is the same. The probability distribution for the degree k is in agreement with the earlier result for $m_t = 0$. The clustering coefficient got an enormous raise in growth rate of $ln(k_i)/k_i$ compared to the earlier result $1/k_i$ for large values of the degree k. This is very useful in the case of professional/research/ Business groups, which helps in faster spreading information flow for network community. Thus here an efficient but complex application of social network has been developed which gives an enormous growth in probability distribution and clustering coefficient and edge to vertex ratio by retaining the community structure. This application can be used to develop a new kind of social networking among various professional/ academic/research and Business groups which helps in faster propagation of information which is essential for faster development in the real world.

Tool

We have used C language, UciNet, NetDraw and Excel for creating graph and simulation.

References

1. Milgram, S.: Psychology Today, vol. 2, pp. 60–67 (1967)
2. Granovetter, M.: The Strength of Weak Ties. Am. J. Soc. 78, 1360–1380 (1973)
3. Wasserman, S., Faust, K.: Social Network Analysis. Cambridge University Press, Cambridge (1994)
4. Watts, D.J., Strogatz, S.H.: Collective Dynamics of Small-World Networks. Nature, 393–440 (1998)
5. Newman, M.: The Structure of Scientific Collaboration Networks. PNAS 98, 404–409 (2001)
6. Newman, M.: Coauthorship Networks and Patterns of Scientific Collaboration. PNAS 101, 5200–5205 (2004)
7. Holme, P., Edling, C.R., Liljeros, F.: Structure and Time-Evolution of an Internet Dating Community. Soc. Networks 26, 155–174 (2004)
8. Girvan, M., Newman, M.E.J.: Community Structure in Social and Biological Networks. Proc. Natl. Acad. Sci. USA 99, 7821–7826 (2002)
9. Newman, M.E.J.: The Structure and Function of Complex Networks. SIAM Review. 45, 167–256 (2003)
10. Krapivsky, P.L., Redner, S.: Organization of Growing Random Networks. phys. Rev. E 63, 066–123 (2001)
11. Barabsi, A.L., Albert, R.: Emergence of Scaling in Random Networks. Science 286, 509–512 (1999)
12. Newman, M.E.J.: Assortative Mixing in Networks. Phys. Rev. Lett. 89, 208701 (2002)
13. Newman, M.E.J., Park, J.: Why Social Networks are Different From other Types of Networks. Phys. Rev. E 68, 036122 (2003)

14. Amaral, L.A.N., Scala, A., Barth, M., Stanley, H.E.: Classes of Small-World Networks. PNAS 97, 11149–11152 (2000)
15. Boguna, M., Pastor-Satorras, R., Daz-Guilera, A., Arenas, A.: Models of Social Networks Based on Social Distance Attachment. Phys. Rev. E 70, 056122 (2004)
16. Toivonen, R., Onnela, J.-P., Saramaki, J., Hyvonen, J., Kaski, K.: A Model for Social Networks. Physica A 371, 851–860 (2006)
17. Bhukya, S.: A Novel Model for Social Networks. In: BCFIC, pp. 21–24. IEEE, Los Alamitos (2011)
18. Evans, T., Saramaki, J.: Scale-Free Networks from Self-Organization. Phys. Rev. E 72, 026138 (2005)
19. Szabo, G., Alava, M., Phys, J.K.: Structural Transitions in Scale-Free Networks. Phys. Rev. E 67, 056102 (2003)

Deontic Based Ontology Matching for Conflict Resolution between Text Documents

Jegatha Deborah L., Karthika V., Baskaran R., and Kannan A.

Department of Computer Science, College of Engineering, Guindy,
Anna University, India
blessedjeny@gmail.com

Abstract. Construction of Ontology plays a very crucial role in interpreting and inferring information from text documents. Effective ontology creation has involved many methods including distance measures,
similarity measures and semantic measures. Ontology matching is the
process of discovering similarities between ontology and determines the
relationships holding two sets of entities that belong to different discrete ontology. The traditional methodologies of Ontology matching used
the intersection of Natural Language Processing techniques and ordinary propositional-logic based approaches, mainly focusing on presence
of dominant words in the documents. In this paper a positive attempt
has been taken to analyze the presence of some of the non-dominant
categorization of words like determiners, time clauses and modal verbs
occurring very often in the text documents. The proposed work concentrates on creation of several numbers of ontology for text documents and
performing ontology matching by scripting special form of *Description
Logics (Standard Deontic Rules)*, so that the conflicts among the documents can be found. The framework developed provides better matching
performance and usefulness on applying to software engineering domain,
where in the conflict resolution helps to find the contradictory requirements posed by different stakeholders. The experimental data sets taken
from the requirement text corpus have been found to produce promising
results for the precision and recall performance metrics.

Keywords: Deontic Rules, Description Logics, Natural Language Processing, Ontology, Ontology Matching.

1 Introduction

Ontology matching is the process of discovering similarities between two types of
ontology and determines the relationships holding two sets of entities that belong
to two types of discrete ontology [1],[2]. Several categories of Ontology Matching
techniques exist which includes String-based, Language-based, Constraint-based,
Semantic-based. Our work had the main motivation from the Semantic based
techniques [3] which attempt to align the elements in the ontologys according
to their semantic interpretation. Ontology matching has been carried out using

K.R. Venugopal and L.M. Patnaik (Eds.): ICIP 2011, CCIS 157, pp. 149–154, 2011.

different tools and techniques. Ontology matching was performed through Natural Language Processing techniques and rule-based approaches in the past [4], [5]. Enormous expressivity should be provided for refined ontology construction and ontology matching where the earlier matching tools described above usually failed. The proposal of providing enormous expressivity in the form of identifying relationships between the entities came from the concept Description Logics which had the ability to provide the necessary expressivity and greater flexibility. On further analysis on the relationships defined by Namfon [6] involved identification of 7 implicit relationships on dominant keywords in the requirements text or document which are mainly between the nouns in the document, it was identified that only dominant keyword based relations are handled in most of the earlier literatures [7]. On further analysis, the proposed work deals with special Deontic relationships which could be deduced from the text by including the non dominant keywords such as modal verbs, time clauses and determiners. These non-dominant words are categorized as to identify modal, timeline and quantifier relationships. In the proposed description logic-based framework, we have introduced the notion of writing standard Deontic Rules which are considered to be special type of rules that can specify the above described types of relationships. This work can also be extended in semantic web documents [8]. Deontic logics are framed by analysing the non dominant words such as modal verbs, determiners and time clauses.

The paper organization is as follows: Section 2 presents the complete proposed framework explanation. Section 3 provides the results screenshots and the discussions handled. Section 4 concludes with the future enhancement. The paper finally provides the list of some the refereed journal and conference papers.

2   DEontical Ontology Matching Technique (DEOMT - Proposed Work)

Ontology matching is done to identify the commonalities between the requirements statements given by various stakeholders [9]. The contradictions occur when the software requirements given by one stake holder contradicts with another. These are difficult to identify especially when the documents are of large size. An NLP based method is proposed to identify the conflicts among the requirements statements specified by the user. Usually the ontology matching techniques takes only the dominant keywords into the relationship between the documents. The non dominant keywords are rejected as they are referred to be of insignificant, and has no impact on the document. But when it comes to identifying the conflicts the non dominant keywords play a major role. Those non dominant keywords such as modal verbs, determiner words and adjectival time clauses are taken into account to create deontic rules. The deontic rules created in *ontologyA* is then matched with the rules of *ontologyB*. The matchings shows the rules that conflict with each other. The steps in creation of deontic rules and matching them is described in Fig. 1

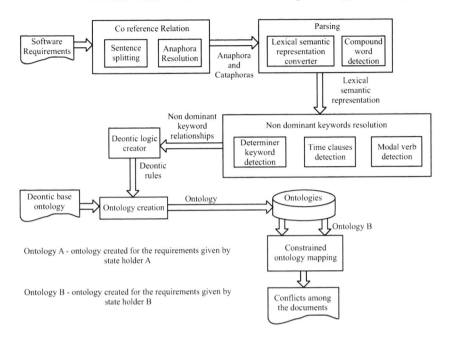

Fig. 1. Architecture of DEOMT framework

Algorithm 1. ALGORITHM - DEONTIC RULES CREATOR

Input: The POS tagged text from text document
Output: The deontic rules from the document

Step 1: Non dominant keyword resolution by using Stanford Part of Speech(POS) tagger.
Step 2: Filtering of useless tags from POS tags obtained.
Step 3: Identifying MUPRET framework dominant words relationships
       e.g., attributeOf, part of, isA, sameAs, propertyOf.
Step 4: Resolution of deontic relationships from the POS tags and
       the MUPRET relationships by using the rules shown in section 2.1
Step 5: Detection of transitive relationshipsby using rules shown in section 2.2
Step 6: Removal of redundant relationships by precedence
       (obligatory-high, forbidden-high, permisibility-low)

2.1   Rules for Detecting Deontic Relations

Rule 1 - If x is a noun and x is related to y by attribute or part of relationship
       and there exists a determiner relationship between X and Y then OBLIG
       ATORY (X HAS Y).
Rule 2 - If x is a noun and x is related to y by attribute or part of relationship
       and there is a modal relationship between X and Y then
Rule 2.1 - If the modal relationship is MUST or SHOULD then OBLIGATORY
       (X HAS Y).

Rule 2.2 - If the modal relationship is CAN then PERMITTED (X HAS Y).

Rule 3 - If X is a noun and X is related to Y by part of or attribute relationship and consists of negative modal relationship

Rule 3.1 - If the modal relationship is MUST NOT or SHOULD NOT then FORBIDDEN (X HAS Y)

Rule 3.2 - If the modal relationship is CAN NOT then PERMITTED (X HAS Y)

Rule 4 - If X and Y are noun and are related with propertyOf relationship OBLIGATORY(X is NOT NULL)

Rule 5 - If X and Y are noun and are related by isA relationship OBLIGA TORY(X has attribute TYPE)

2.2 Transitivity Rules Generation

Rule 6 - If X and Y are related with isA relationship and X is related to another Z with some deontic
relationship then Y is related to Z with deontic relationship

Rule 7 - If X and Y are related with sameAs relationship and X is related to another Z with some deontic relationship then Y is related to Z with deontic relationship

Rule 8 - If X and Y are related by a deontic relationship R and Y and Z are related by deontic relationship R then Y and Z are also related with relationship R

3 Evaluation Results and Discussions

In the proposed algorithm the input text is taken from the web corpus. The sample input data set considered for our approach is Hospital Information System, Doctor Information System and Patient Information System [10].

3.1 Evaluation Procedure

When evaluation and testing had to be performed, we obtained the help of some of the domain experts in identifying the ontological conflicts between any two types of ontology [10]. They worked out manually with the help of a paper and pen. Later, the same web document input was given to the several algorithms present in the system. The number of ontological conflicts uncovered by implementing the different algorithms in the system was stored for analyzing the performance metrics. DEOMT framework is evaluated using a number of web document abstracts. The framework is tested against the traditional performance metrics, precision and recall. It was found that good results were obtained in comparison to the other algorithms explained in the literature survey. The precision(PRE), Specification(SPECI) and the recall(REC) is obtained by analyzing the Positives(P), Negatives(N), True Positives(TP), True Negatives(TN) and False positives(FP) identified from the ontological relatioships.

Table 1. Comparitive study of DEOMT with other frameworks

P	N	DEOMT						MUPRET						S-MATCH						C-MATCH					
		A	B	C	D	E	F	A	B	C	D	E	F	A	B	C	D	E	F	A	B	C	D	E	F
5	3	1	5	2	0.6	0.1	1	1	5	3	0.6	0.1	1	3	3	3	0.5	0.4	0.6	3	2	3	0.8	0.5	0.4
7	4	1	7	4	0.6	0.2	1	2	6	5	0.5	0.2	0.8	3	3	4	0.4	0.5	0.4	4	1	2	0.9	0.6	0.1
12	6	2	12	9	0.6	0.1	1	3	4	11	0.5	0.2	0.9	4	6	7	0.5	0.4	0.5	5	5	7	0.9	0.6	0.1
23	9	3	22	19	0.7	0.1	0.9	20	21	0.4	0.1	0.8	7	8	2	0.5	0.3	0.7	8	15	2	0.9	0.4	0.6	0.4
72	18	7	70	67	0.8	0.1	0.9	10	70	70	0.5	0.1	0.9	3	6	66	0.5	0.1	0.9	16	6	65	0.9	0.2	0.8
99	25	10	99	92	0.8	0.1	0.9	15	99	98	0.5	0.13	0.9	2	9	91	0.5	0.1	0.8	22	7	82	0.9	0.2	0.6

The text domain is the Doctor Information System. The number of Positive, Negative relationships is obtained. Table 1 shows the input and the output values for Precision, Recall performance metrics and the results of the Specificity performance metric.

3.2 Results Analysis

The values of the performance metrics Precision, Recall and Specificity achieve better results when the size of the dataset is less. As the size of the data set increases the values also tend to be low. However, the main limitation of our framework is that the algorithm sometimes fails to achieve scalability. In connection to this, the current ongoing work aims at solving the problem of scalability.

The results are shown for the evaluation of conflicts between any two type of ontology found for the text domain Doctor Information System in comparison to the other ontology matching algorithms MUPRET, S-Match, Content-match

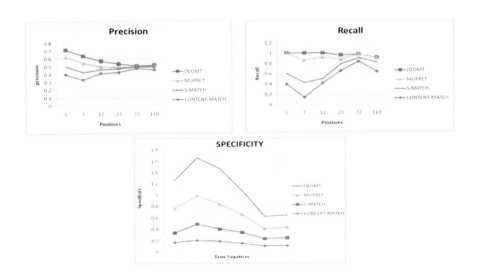

Fig. 2. Comparison graphs for precision, recall and specificity - DEOMT, Content-Match, MUPRET,SMATCH

[5]. The results as visualized in Fig. 2 indicate that our framework DEOMT works better compared to the other algorithms.

4   Conclusions

Ontology plays a vital role in clustering the web documents semantically to enhance the performance of many information extraction and information retrieval systems. As a next step of enhancement, ontology matching could be done which is used in a number of applications. The future work of the authors is to administer the design decisions of a database by constrained based ontology matching. The determiner clauses detection will help to decide on the attribute for the database table. The modal verb detection is used to determine the primary key, the fields that must have values and the fields that can have null values. These kinds of design decisions can be identified. By using the time clause detection, the implementation and the data requirement constraints can be found. Hence, it is concluded that a wide research gap exist in the area of ontology matching.

References

1. Buitelaar, P., Declerck, T.: Linguistic Annotation for the Semantic Web. In: Handschuh, S., Staab, S. (eds.) Annotation for the Semantic Web. IOS Press, Amsterdam (2003)
2. Noll, R.P., Ribeiro, M.B.: Enhancing Traceability using Ontologies. In: Proceedings of the ACM Symposium on Applied Computing (SAC 2007), Seoul, Korea, pp. 1496–1497 (2007)
3. John, A.B.: A Linguistic Ontology of Space for Natural Language Processing. Elsevier journal of Artificial Intelligence 174(14), 1027–1071 (2010)
4. The Stanford Parser: A Statistical Parser (version 1.6) Stanford University (2007), http://nlp.stanford.edu/software/lex-parser.shtml
5. Jrme, E., Pavel, S.: Ontology Matching. Springer-Verlag New York, Inc., Heidelberg (2007)
6. Marcos, Martnez, Romero.:Ontology Alignment Techniques, Online document (2009), http://sabia.tic.udc.es/sabia/articulos/2009/180.pdf
7. David, L., Mohamed, T., Petko, V.: Ontology Alignment with OLA. In: Proceedings of the 3rd EON Workshop, 3rd Intl. Semantic Web Conference, Hiroshima (2004)
8. Jayant, M., Philip, A.B., Erhard, R.: Generic Schema Matching with Cupid, Microsoft Research Technical Report (2001)
9. Marc, E., Steffen, S.: Efficiency of Ontology Mapping Approaches. In: International Workshop on Semantic Intelligent Middleware for the Web and the Grid at ECAI 2004. Valencia, Spain (2004)
10. Namfon, A., Thanwadee, S., Charnyote, P.: Ontology based Multiperspective Requirements Traceability Framework. Knowledge and Information Systems Journal (2009) (Online Publication)

Improving the Precision and Recall of Web People Search Using Hash Table Clustering

Pushpa C.N.[1], Vinay Kumar N.K.[1], Shivaprakash T.[1], Thriveni J.[1],
Manjula S.H.[1], Venugopal K.R.[1], and Patnaik L.M.[2]

[1] Department of Computer Science and Engineering,
University Visvesvaraya College of Engineering, Bangalore
[2] Vice Chancellor, Defence Institute of Advanced Technology, Pune, India
pushpacn@gmail.com

Abstract. Searching the people names on the web is a challenging query types to the web search engines today on the web. When a person name is queried, the returned result often contains web pages related to several distinct keywords that have the queried name. In this paper we have proposed a new approach to improve the precision, recall and F-measure metrics of the web search engine by removing the unwanted resulting web pages and the proposed method outperforms by 15.9 percent of F-measure improvement as compared to WWW2005 algorithm.

Keywords: F-measure, Precision, Recall, Search Engine, Web People Search.

1   Introduction

Search engines are the most helpful tool for obtaining useful information from the Internet. Search engines return a lot of web page links that have nothing to do with the users need. *Zoominfo.com*, *ArnetMiner*, *Spock.com* and *123people.com* are examples of sites which perform web people search, although with limited disambiguation capabilities. The search for entity related to person name with some additional terms such as location, organization accounts to more than 10-18% of current search engines.

A person name may appear in many web pages. If the user wants all his web pages then clustered person search may be very useful as it clusters all the web pages to a single cluster with description, rather than user collecting web pages by searching manually. The search engine extracts the named entities and different people on the Web are identified using machine learning and data mining algorithms. Search engines has the ability to provide refined and more precise results. Search engines aid in organizing the vast amount of information that can sometimes be scattered in various places on the same web page into an organized list that can be used more easily.

Motivation: The growing sophistication of search engine software enables us to precisely describe the information that we seek. Many well thought-out search phrases produces list, after the list of irrelevant web pages. The web pages of

K.R. Venugopal and L.M. Patnaik (Eds.): ICIP 2011, CCIS 157, pp. 155–160, 2011.

the less famous person will be overshadowed in todays search engines and will appear far in the search. A lot of time is wasted on searching, thus there is a need for more efficient person search engine.

Contribution: The proposed approach aims to remove the unwanted resulting web pages and the resultant web pages are clustered based on oraganization name using Hashing Technique.

Organization: The remainder of the paper is organized as follows: Section 2 reviews the related work of the people search engine, Section 3 explains the architecture of the Web People Search system, and Section 4 gives the problem definition and the proposed algorithm. The implementation and the results of the Web People Search system is described in Section 5 and Conclusion are presented in Section 6.

2   Related Work

Extraction of information about any particular person name is not so easy, as the web search engines today provide a number of web pages for a query specified. The First name disambiguation with a single name was proposed around 1998 by Bagga and Baldwin [1]. Later, many researchers focused on automatic methods on large datasets rather than searching a single name. So, limitations in the automatic methods were identified by the Fleischman [2] and his work was related to the pairs sharing the exact person name.

Kalashinokov. et. al, have developed several disambiguation approaches. The approaches in [3], [4] and [5] solve a disambiguation challenge known as Fuzzy Lookup. To address the web page clustering problem studied in this paper, one needs to address a different type of disambiguation known as Fuzzy Grouping. Al-Kamha and Embley [6] used a combination of attributes (like zip codes, state, etc.), links, and page similarity to derive the name clusters while Wan et. al, [7] used lexical features and named entities. Kalashinokov et. al, [8] have developed a Web People Search approach that clusters web pages based on their association to different people. The literature surveys proved the fact that search engines today used to show famous person names on the top of results than the specific person required. Thus there is need for more efficient person search system.

3   System Architecture

The steps of the overall Web People Search approach, in the context of architecture, are illustrated in Fig. 1. They include:

(i) *User Input* : The user issues a query via the input interface.
(ii) *Retrieval* : The system (middleware) sends a query consisting of a person name to a search engine, the stop words like *is, in, on, was, then, that, the, if, for, as, the* etc., are removed from the query which is entered by the user and extract only the keywords. Once all the files from different

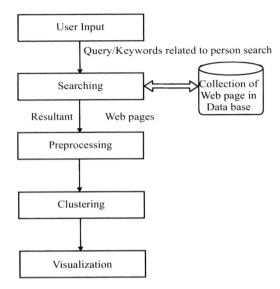

Fig. 1. Architecture of the Web People Search system

folders are retrieved into the list, only the *.html* and *.txt* are selected and stored into the TempList folder. File in Templist folder is checked for the occurrence of all the keywords, if present, the file is included in the Resulting Files List Folder else deleted.

(iii) *Pre − processing* : These web pages are then preprocessed. The main pre-processing step is : *Extraction*: Named Entities, specifically people, locations, organizations are extracted using a third party named entity extraction software (i.e., Stanfords Named Entity Recognizer1). We are using this software to extract only the organization details of the given person. Some auxiliary data structures are built on this data.

(iv) *Clustering* : The resultant web pages are then clustered usig hashing technique.

(v) *Visualization* : The resulting clusters are presented to the user, that can be interactively explored.

4   Problem Defintion and Algorithm

Given a query to extract the person information from the large number of web pages that are stored in the database, our objectives are :

(i) To retrieve only the relevant web pages of a person.
(ii) To improve the Precision, Recall and the F-measure metrics of the web people search engine.

4.1   Algorithm

We proposed an algorithm for web people search system. The Table 1 gives the Hash Table Clustering Algorithm, used to grouping the results based on the Organization name of a person. In Hash Table Clustering Algorithm (HTCA)

Table 1. Hash Table Clustering Algorithm (HTCA)

```
begin
    Step1: Collect the Organization names from Extraction tool.
    Step2: Define a Hash Table variable which holds integer and a string
    Step3: for (all the files)
            while (! EOF )
                if (the organization as prefix in the word)
                    Add that string to the HashTable with the counter variable.
                endif
            endwhile
            endfor
    Step4: while (Process contents of the Hash Table)
            if (the counter variable value is in the order)
            if (Hᵢ - Hᵢ₋₁ = 1)
                Combine the iᵗʰ and (i-1)ᵗʰ words stored in the Hash table
                to make the meaningful organization Name.
                Add the combined value and the related file name into the vector
                delimited with $ for further processing.
            else
                Add the HashTable String directly to vector variable along with the
                related file name for further processing.
            endif
            endif
        endwhile
end
```

we define the hash table which holds the organization name. Adding the organization name and the related file into the vector delimited with the $ symbol for further processing. For example, the organization name is like University Visvesvaraya College of Engineering, then the words *University*, *Visvesvaraya*, *College*, *of* and *Engineering* all are stored in a hash table separately. Then we process contents of the Hash table, if the counter variable value is in order and the difference between H_i and H_{i-1} is 1 then Combine the ith and $(i-1)^{th}$ words stored in the Hash table to make the meaningful Organization Name and add the combined value and the related file name into the vector delimited with $ for further processing else add the Hash Table String directly to vector variable along with the related file name for further processing.

5   Implementation and Results

The Web People Search engine is implemented using Java programming language. Eclipse is an extensible, open source IDE (integrated development environment). The success of a search engine algorithm lies in its ability to retrieve information for a given query. In information retrieval contexts, precision and recall are defined in terms of a set of retrieved documents and a set of relevant documents.

In order to test our system, we selected a set of 12 instance names from the WWW 2005 dataset, 10 of which referred to multiple individuals and 2 of which had only a single referent. The Table 2 shows the result comparison of proposed algorithm with the two existing algorithms. The field #W is the number of the web pages related to the name of the person. The field #C is the number of web pages found correctly and the field #I is the number of pages found incorrectly in the resulting groups.

Table 2. Result Comparison of HTCA algorithm with existing algorithms

Name	#W	WWW'05 Algo. #C	#I	F-measure	WEPS Algo. #C	#I	F-measure	HTCA Algo. #C	#I	F-measure
Adam Cheyer	96	62	0	78.5	94	0	98.9(+20.4)	96	0	100.0(+21.5)
William Cohen	6	6	4	75	4	0	80.0(+5.0)	6	0	100.0(+25.0)
Steve Hardt	64	16	2	39	51	2	87.2(+48.2)	63	0	99.2(+60.2)
David Israel	20	19	4	88.4	17	2	87.2(-1.2)	18	1	92.3(+3.9)
Leslie Kaelbling	88	84	1	97.1	88	1	99.4(+2.3)	88	1	99.4(+2.3)
Bill Mark	11	6	9	46.2	8	1	80.0(+33.8)	9	0	90.0(+43.8)
Andrew MaCllum	54	54	2	98.2	54	1	99.1(+0.9)	54	1	99.1(+0.9)
Tom Mitchell	15	14	5	2.4	12	5	75.0(-7.4)	13	2	86.6(+4.2)
David Mulford	1	1	0	100	1	0	100.0(+0.0)	1	0	100.0(+0.0)
Andrew Ng	32	30	6	88.2	25	1	86.2(-2.0)	29	1	93.5(+5.3)
Fernando Pereira	32	21	14	62.7	25	11	73.5(+10.8)	28	4	87.5(+24.8)
Lynn Voss	1	0	1	0	0	0	0.0(+0.0)	1	0	100.0(+0.0)
Overall	455	313	47	80.3	379	24	92.1(+11.8)	406	10	95.6(+15.9)

The proposed algorithm outperforms by 15.9 percent of F-measure. The results are better than the existing algorithms, in proposed method there is no negative values found in brackets, because, here we trying to extract only the related web pages of a person by checking all keywords entered by the user. The values mentioned in bracket shows that the percentage of F-measure improvement of the WWW'05 Algorithm.

6   Conclusion

People Search is one of the most common query types to the web search engines today on the web. In this paper we have proposed a new approach to improve the precision and recall metrics of the web search engine. When user gives keywords such as a person name, summary description of the keyword is displayed. The user can get the required web pages of interest by reading description provided with each cluster. As compared to WWW'05 algorithm and WEPS algorithm, the proposed method outperforms by 15.9 percent of F-measure improvement.

References

1. Bagga, A., Baldwin, B.: Entity-based Crossdocument Coreferencing using the Vector Space Model. In: 17th International Conference on Computational Linguistics (CoLing- CL), Montreal, Canada, pp. 79–85 (1998)
2. Fleischman, M., Hovy, E., Echihabi, A.: Offline Strategies for Online Question Answering: Answering Questions Before They Asked. In: 41st Annual Meeting of the Association for Computational Linguistics, Sapporo, Japan (2003)
3. Kalashnikov, D.V., Mehrotra, S.: Domain-Independent Data Cleaning via Analysis of Entity-Relationship Graph. ACM Transactions on Database Systems 31(2), 716–767 (2006)
4. Kalashnikov, D.V., Mehrotra, S., Chen, Z.: Exploiting Relationships for Domain-Independent Data Cleaning. In: SIAM International Conference on Data Mining (SDM 2005) (April 2005)
5. Nuray-Turan, R., Kalashnikov, D.V., Mehrotra, S.: Self-Tuning in Graph-Based Reference Disambiguation. In: Kotagiri, R., Radha Krishna, P., Mohania, M., Nantajeewarawat, E. (eds.) DASFAA 2007. LNCS, vol. 4443, pp. 325–336. Springer, Heidelberg (2007)
6. Al-Kamha, R., Embley, D.W.: Grouping Search-Engine returned Citations for Person-Name Queries. In: 6th Annual ACM International workshop on Web Information and Data Management, pp. 96–103 (2004)
7. Wan, X., Gao, J., Li, M., Ding, B.: Person resolution in Person Search Results: Webhawk. In: 14th ACM International Conference on Information and knowledge management, pp. 163–170 (2005)
8. Kalashnikov, D.V., Chen, Z., Mehrotra, S.: Web People Search via Connection Analysis. IEEE Transactions on Knowledge and Data Engineering 20(11) (November 2008)

Video Shot Cut Detection Using Least Square Approximation Method

Lakshmi Priya G.G. and Domnic S.

Department of Computer Applications, National Institute of Technology,
Tiruchirappalli, Tamilnadu, India-620015
gg_lakshmipriya@yahoo.co.in, domnic@nitt.edu

Abstract. Video shot boundary detection is the basic step in the area of content based video analysis and retrieval. Various automatic shot boundary detection techniques have been proposed and their performances are reliable, especially for video cut detection. However most of the proposed methods are sensitive to camera, object motion and lighting changes. In this paper, we have focused mainly on the improvement of the existing traditional shot detection methods. In our technique, approximation of the discontinuity values obtained from the various existing methods has been done using the Least Square polynomial approximation method to diminish the sensitivity to motion. An automatic threshold calculation algorithm is also used in our method. Experimental results demonstrate that our method can detect maximum shot breaks and reduces the occurrence of false hit that are difficult with the previous approaches when motion occurs in the video.

Keywords: Feature Extraction, Least Square Approximation, Shot Cut Boundary Detection, Threshold.

1 Introduction

Indexing and retrieval of digital video is an active research area. Video shot detection is the primary step for video indexing and content based video retrieval. The initial step towards this direction is to partition the video contents into smaller units called the shot in order to proceed with indexing and browsing. A shot is defined as an unbroken sequence of frames captured from one camera. The video shots are the basic structural building blocks of a video sequence. They are assembled during the editing phases using varieties of techniques like fade, dissolve, and wipe. A sudden transition from one video shot to another is simply referred to as hard cuts or cuts. A soft cut represents a gradual transition between two shots which means a sequence of video frames that belongs to both the first and the second video shot. In this paper we focus on the hard cut detection in the video sequences. Various shot boundary detection methods: pixel wise differences [1], [2], RGB color histogram differences [3], HSV histogram differences [4], statistics based method [5], Edge based method [6], [7] and Exclusive OR method [8] are discussed in section 2. The major drawback of these methods

K.R. Venugopal and L.M. Patnaik (Eds.): ICIP 2011, CCIS 157, pp. 161–170, 2011.
© Springer-Verlag Berlin Heidelberg 2011

is they are sensitivity to object and camera motion. In order to improve the performance of the existing methods, a new algorithm which reduces the sensitivity to object and camera motion is proposed in this paper. In the proposed algorithm, the least square approximation method and the automatic threshold calculation algorithms are used to reduce the rate of false hits and missed hits. This paper is structured as follows: In Section 2, the detailed summary of previous works on shot boundary detection is presented. The proposed method is presented in section 3. Experimental results are presented and commented in section 4. Conclusions are drawn in section 5.

2   Previous Works on Shot Cut Boundary Detection

Different methods exist for extracting features from the video sequence. For each selected feature, a number of suitable distance metrics can be applied for computing the discontinuity values. The different types of features and metrics used for shot-boundary detection with respect to the quality of the obtained discontinuity values can be found in [1-3]. Cut detection methods are grouped in to several classes, which are discussed in the next subsections.

2.1   Pixel Differences Method

The simplest way of measuring the dissimilarity between two frames is to compute the mean absolute change of intensity $I(x, y)$ between the frames k and $k + 1$ for all frame pixels [9] . An alteration of this technique is only counting the pixels that change considerably from one frame to another [10]. Here, the absolute intensity change is compared with the pre-specified threshold T, and is only considerable if it exceeds that specified threshold value, that is

$$Z(k, k + 1) = \frac{1}{XY} \sum_{x=1}^{X} \sum_{y=1}^{Y} D_{k,k+1}(x, y). \tag{1}$$

with

$$D_{k,k+1}(x, y) = \begin{cases} 1, & \text{if} |_k(x, y) - I_k + I(x, y)| > T. \\ 0, & \text{else} \end{cases} \tag{2}$$

With the major advantage of this method is simplicity of their implementation. The drawback of this method is that they are sensitive to camera and scene object motion.

2.2   Block Based Method

Zhang et al. [3] presented a technique which expands the idea of pixel differences by breaking the images into regions and comparing statistical measures of the pixels in those regions. The statistical features based on the mean and standard deviation of the image gray levels are used as the features to detect the shot boundary. One of the statistical feature based techniques [5] uses the block likelihood ration as the metric to obtain better results. The ratio L_b for corresponding block regions (b) of i and $i+1$ frame is calculated as follows:

$$L_b = \frac{\left[\frac{\sigma_i + \sigma_{i+1}}{2} + \left(\frac{\mu_i - \mu_{i+1}}{2}\right)^2\right]}{\sigma_i \sigma_{i+1}}. \qquad (3)$$

Where μ_i and σ_i denote, respectively, the mean and variance of intensity of a given region in frame i. The difference metric is calculated by averaging the sum of L_b over the total number of blocks. If the average distance value is greater than a certain threshold T, a shot change is declared.

2.3   RGB Color Histogram Difference Method

Histograms [2] are the most common method used to detect shot boundary. It computes gray level or color histogram of two images. The color histogram difference CHD_i between two color frames I_{i-1} and I_i is given by

$$CHD_i = \frac{1}{N} \sum_{r=0}^{2^B-1} \sum_{g=0}^{2^B-1} \sum_{b=0}^{2^B-1} |p_i(r, g, b) - p_{i-1}(r, g, b)|. \qquad (4)$$

Here is the number of pixels of color $p_i(r, g, b)$ in frame I_i of N pixels. If the bin wise difference between the two histograms is above a threshold, a shot boundary is detected. The drawback of this method is that if two images have quite same histogram while their contents are dissimilar extremely, they may result in missed hit.

2.4   HSV Color Histogram Difference Method

Another histogram based method [4] has been proposed in HSV color space. The HSV histogram difference D_i is computed as follows:

$$D_i = max(H_i, S_i, V_i). \qquad (5)$$

where H_i, S_i and V_i are the histogram differences of H, S, and V component, respectively. The obtained D_i is compared against a Threshold T. If the D_i value is greater than the T, a cut is detected. The main disadvantage of this method is that it fails if two successive shots have same histogram and it cannot distinguish fast object or camera motion.

2.5   Edge Oriented Method

Zabih, Miller and Mai [6] have proposed an algorithm using edge information using [11]. In this paper, the metric, Edge Change Ratio (ECR) is used to detect boundary. The ECR is defined as follows

$$ECR_n = max(X_i^{in}/\sigma_n, X_{n-1}^{out}/\sigma_{n-1}). \qquad (6)$$

Here σ_n, the number of edge pixels in frame n, X_n^{in} and X_{n-1}^{out} the number of entering and exiting edge pixels in frames n and $n-1$ respectively. The obtained ECR is compared against a Threshold T. If the ECR value is greater than the T, a cut is detected. The main disadvantage is when high speed motion occurs in the video scenes this method produces relatively high number of false hits.

2.6   SBD Using Exclusive OR

To measure the amount of discontinuity at a pixel level between two consecutive frames Siripinyo et al. [8] captured the exclusive or of two frames in the grey scale:

$$BWX_i = \sum_{j=i...J} P_{i-1}(j) \oplus P_i(j). \tag{7}$$

where $\oplus$ implies the 'exclusive or ' operation, J is the total number of pixels per frame, and $P_{i-1}(j)$ and $P_i(j)$ are the black/white value of pixel j in frames i_1 and i respectively. If the value for BWX_i is greater than a predefined threshold, 'cut ' is assigned between frames i_1 and i. The main drawbacks of the most existing methods are that they are sensitive to Camera/object movements and are threshold dependent. The rate of false hits can be reduced by using appropriate threshold values. But if there is no prior knowledge about the visual content of a video it is difficult to select an appropriate threshold. Kolekar [12] in his paper, calculated the threshold using the following formula

$$\text{Threshold T} = \mu + k\sigma. \tag{8}$$

Where, k is a pre-specified constant, mean μ and the standard deviation σ of the feature vector distances. The constant k varies according to the input video sequence. In papers [1,2] predefined values are set as threshold T. This paper is proposed to overcome the above mentioned two drawbacks using the least square approximation method over the features extracted and the threshold values are calculated using the standard deviation of the deviation of the approximated discontinuity values.

3   The Proposed Shot Boundary Detection Method

The Proposed Shot Boundary detection method In this paper, we have proposed a new algorithm to improve the performance of the existing methods [1,8] by reducing the sensitivity to object and camera motion. The initial step in shot boundary detection is feature extraction. Here features are extracted using the existing traditional methods discussed in section 2. In the proposed algorithm we have used the least square approximation method for reducing the rate of false hits due to motion influences and a threshold calculation algorithm is also used in order to reduce the number of missed hits obtained by the existing threshold calculation method [12].

3.1   Approximation of Discontinuity Values

The sensitivity to object and camera motion can be diminished by approximating the discontinuity values obtained from the existing methods discussed in section 2 using the least square polynomial approximation method [13]. The resultant discontinuity values are considered to be a polynomial function $f(x)$. The least square polynomial approximation problem leads to a system of linear equations of the form

$$b = Ha. \tag{9}$$

where b is a $(1 \times n)$ vector with components:

$$b_j = \int_0^1 x^{j-1} f(x) dx, j = 1, ...n. \tag{10}$$

$f(x)$ is the function to be approximated, a is the $(n \times 1)$ vector of coefficients of the polynomial of order $n-1$, and H is a Hessian matrix of the form G the gram matrix $(n \times n)$, M the matrix of size $(m \times n)$, M^T is the transpose of the matrix M and zero matrix of $(m \times m)$. Order n of the matrix is considered to depend on the degree of the polynomial, and hence for our work we have considered the order of n as 4 and m as 2. The Hessian matrix takes the form $(n+m, n+m)$ is taken as The solution of linear equation (10) is given by

$$a = H^{-1}b. \tag{11}$$

The equation (11) can be represented as

$$a_i = \sum_{j=1}^{m+n} b_j h_{i,j}.i = 1, ...m + n. \tag{12}$$

$h_{i,j}$ is inverse of the hessian matrix, b_{m+1} is equal to $f(0)$ and b_{m+2} is equal to $f(1)$. This assignment is done to perform matrix multiplication in Eq. (9). Then error value can be calculated as follows

$$g(x) = f(x) - \sum_{i=1}^{n} a_i x^{j-1}, j = 1, ..., n. \tag{13}$$

To obtain the approximated discontinuity value $L(x)$, the linear interpolation is performed in $g(x)$ to model a set of discrete data to continuous function, then the interpolated $g(x)$ is reduced by a constant value α and finally the approximated discontinuity value is calculated using the following equation

$$L(x) = g(x)/\alpha. \tag{14}$$

Where $\alpha = \sqrt{\sum g(x)^* \lambda}$. Here $g(x)$ is the linear interpolation of $g(x)$, λ is the x interval value. As a result, $L(x)$ is the approximated discontinuity value.

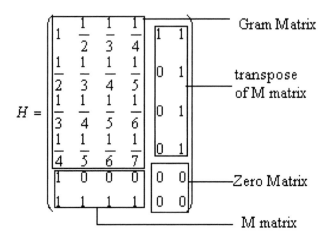

3.2   Threshold Calculation Algorithm

Most of the existing shot cut detection methods [1], [8] uses threshold parameter to distinguish shot boundaries and changes. The common challenge is the
selection of the threshold value for identifying the level of variation, which in
turn define a shot boundary. In order to avoid this problem, we have used an
algorithm proposed in [14] to compute threshold value (Th). The following steps
are carried out for calculating the threshold value.

Calculate the mean of the discontinuity values $\bar{x} = \frac{1}{N} \sum_{i=1}^{N} x_i$..

Find the deviation of x from the mean $d_x = (x_i - \bar{x})$.

Find the mean of i.e., $\bar{d}_x = \frac{1}{N} \sum_{i=1}^{N} d_{x_i}$.

Standard deviation of the deviation

$$\sigma_{d_x} = \left(\frac{\sum_{i=1}^{N}(d_{x_i} - \bar{d}_x)^2}{N} \right)^{1/2} \tag{15}$$

$$\text{Threshold} Th = \bar{x} + \sigma_{d_x}. \tag{16}$$

A cut is detected when the approximated value is higher than the Threshold Th.
The obtained result on comparing with the traditional cut detection methods
diminishes the rate of false hits occurred due to sensitivity of object motion and
the camera motion.

3.3   Proposed Algorithm

1. Extract features F for each frame from the existing methods discussed in section 2. Here, features are the dissimilarity value between the current frames
   i and next frame $i + 1$.
2. Apply least square polynomial approximation on the discontinuity values.
3. Calculate the threshold Th using the Eq. (16).
4. if approximated discontinuity value is greater than the threshold Th, the
   corresponding frame $i + 1$ is declared as cut frame.

4   Experimental Results

The proposed algorithm for detecting video hard cuts has been tested on various TRECVID video datasets. We have selected the video datasets which has more number of camera / object movements. The characteristics of the some of the TRECVID video datasets are listed in Table 1. The experimental results of the existing methods discussed in section 2 are compared with our proposed method. In addition comparisons are made with the cut detection using threshold T on the approximated discontinuity values.

Table 1. Description of the Video of the Test Sets

Video Sequence	Nimber of Frames	Duration(s)	Total number of Shot cuts
A	1380	60	8
B	1150	50	18
C	2200	88	36
D	1440	60	20
E	920	40	40
F	1150	46	32
G	1500	60	18
Total	9740	404	156

Table 2. Performance Results of Pixelwise Differences Method[3]

Video sequences	$T = \mu + k\sigma$			The Proposed Algorithm			Approximation and $T = \mu + k\sigma$		
	P	V	F1	P	V	F1	P	V	F1
A	0.33	1.0	0.50	0.67	1.0	0.80	0.67	1.0	0.80
B	1.0	0.67	0.80	0.89	0.89	0.89	1.0	0.44	0.61
C	0.86	0.67	0.75	0.87	0.78	0.82	1.0	0.67	0.80
D	0.33	0.40	0.36	0.43	0.60	0.50	0.57	0.80	0.67
E	1.0	0.58	0.73	1.0	0.58	0.73	1.0	0.58	0.73
F	0.85	0.87	0.86	0.91	1.0	0.96	0.88	1.0	0.94
G	1.0	1.0	1.0	1.0	1.0	1.0	1.0	1.0	1.0
AVERAGE			0.71			0.89			0.79

A correctly detected shot transition is called a hit, a not detected cut is a missed hit and a falsely detected shot transition is a false hit. For the evaluation of the proposed abrupt shot detection algorithm, the precision, recall and combined measures are calculated using the following equations.

$$\text{Precision}(P) = \frac{\text{No. of hits}}{\text{No. of hits + False hit}}. \tag{17}$$

$$\text{Recall}(V) = \frac{\text{No. of hits}}{\text{No. of hits + Missed hits}}. \tag{18}$$

Table 3. Performance Results of RBG Color Histogram Difference Method[2]

Video sequences	$T = \mu + k\sigma$			The Proposed Algorithm			Approximation and $T = \mu + k\sigma$		
	P	V	F1	P	V	F1	P	V	F1
A	1.0	0.50	0.67	1.0	0.50	0.67	1.0	0.50	0.67
B	1.0	0.67	0.80	1.0	0.89	0.94	1.0	0.67	0.80
C	1.0	0.44	0.61	1.0	0.89	0.94	1.0	0.44	0.61
D	1.0	0.60	0.75	0.75	0.60	0.67	1.0	0.60	0.75
E	1.0	0.67	0.80	1.0	0.67	0.80	1.0	0.67	0.80
F	1.0	0.87	0.94	1.0	0.97	0.98	1.0	0.94	0.97
G	1.0	1.0	1.0	1.0	1.0	1.0	1.0	1.0	1.0
AVERAGE			0.79			0.86			0.80

Table 4. Performance Results of Edge Change Ratio Method[6,7]

Video sequences	$T = \mu + k\sigma$			The Proposed Algorithm			Approximation and $T = \mu + k\sigma$		
	P	V	F1	P	V	F1	P	V	F1
A	0.50	0.50	0.50	1.0	1.0	1.0	1.0	1.0	1.0
B	1.0	0.33	0.50	1.0	0.33	0.50	1.0	0.33	0.50
C	1.0	0.33	0.50	1.0	0.55	0.71	1.0	0.33	0.50
D	1.0	0.40	0.57	1.0	0.40	0.57	1.0	0.40	0.57
E	0.86	0.50	0.62	1.0	0.50	0.67	0.83	0.42	0.56
F	0.85	0.87	0.86	0.91	1.0	0.96	0.88	1.0	0.94
G	1.0	1.0	1.0	1.0	1.0	1.0	1.0	1.0	1.0
AVERAGE			0.65			0.77			0.72

Table 5. Performance Results of HSV Histogram Differences Method[4]

Video sequences	$T = \mu + k\sigma$			The Proposed Algorithm			Approximation and $T = \mu + k\sigma$		
	P	V	F1	P	V	F1	P	V	F1
A	1.0	1.0	1.0	0.40	1.0	0.57	0.40	1.0	0.57
B	1.0	0.44	0.61	1.0	0.89	0.94	1.0	0.44	0.61
C	1.0	0.89	0.94	1.0	0.89	0.94	0.83	0.55	0.66
D	0.57	0.80	0.66	0.80	0.80	0.80	0.67	0.80	0.73
E	1.0	1.0	1.0	1.0	1.0	1.0	1.0	0.83	0.91
F	1.0	0.87	0.945	1.0	0.97	0.985	1.0	0.94	0.97
G	1.0	1.0	1.0	1.0	1.0	1.0	1.0	1.0	1.0
AVERAGE			0.87			0.89			0.78

Table 6. Performance Results of Statistical Method(likelihood ratio)[5]

Video sequences	$T = \mu + k\sigma$			The Proposed Algorithm			Approximation and $T = \mu + k\sigma$		
	P	V	F1	P	V	F1	P	V	F1
A	1.0	0.50	0.67	1.0	0.50	0.67	1.0	1.0	1.0
B	1.0	0.44	0.61	1.0	0.55	0.71	1.0	0.44	0.61
C	1.0	0.33	0.50	1.0	0.44	0.61	1.0	0.33	0.50
D	1.0	0.40	0.57	1.0	0.60	0.75	1.0	0.40	0.57
E	1.0	0.58	0.73	1.0	0.58	0.73	1.0	0.50	0.67
F	1.0	0.87	0.945	1.0	0.97	0.985	1.0	0.94	0.97
G	1.0	1.0	1.0	1.0	1.0	1.0	1.0	1.0	1.0
AVERAGE			0.72			0.78			0.76

Table 7. Performance Results of ExclusiveOR Method)[8]

Video sequences	$T = \mu + k\sigma$			The Proposed Algorithm			Approximation and $T = \mu + k\sigma$		
	P	V	F1	P	V	F1	P	V	F1
A	0.33	1.0	0.50	1.0	1.0	0.67	1.0	1.0	1.0
B	1.0	0.44	0.61	0.78	0.78	0.71	1.0	0.55	0.71
C	0.71	0.44	0.54	0.73	0.89	0.61	0.70	0.78	0.74
D	1.0	0.80	0.89	1.0	0.80	0.75	1.0	0.80	0.89
E	0.67	0.67	0.67	0.75	0.75	0.73	0.82	0.75	0.74
F	1.0	0.87	0.945	1.0	0.97	0.985	1.0	0.94	0.97
G	1.0	1.0	1.0	1.0	1.0	1.0	1.0	1.0	1.0
AVERAGE			0.73			0.88			0.86

Table 8. Comparative Results Using Average F1 Ratio of Various cut Detection Methods

Cut Detection Methods	$T = \mu + k\sigma$	The Proposed Algorithm	Approximation and $T = \mu + k\sigma$
Pixelwise	0.71	0.89	0.79
RGB Color Histogram	0.79	0.86	0.80
Edge Change Ratio	0.65	0.77	0.72
HSV Color Histogram	0.87	0.89	0.78
Statistical Method	0.72	0.78	0.76
Exclusive OR	0.73	0.88	0.86
AVERAGE	**0.74**	**0.84**	**0.78**

$$CombinedMeasure(F1) = \frac{2.P.V}{(V + P)}. \tag{19}$$

In Table [2-7], we provide the performance results of the different video cut detection methods using the threshold T, approximation and Th, approximation and T. For comparison purpose threshold T from Eq. 8 is used for other existing methods [2-8].

5   Conclusions

In this paper, we have proposed a new algorithm to improve the performance of the existing methods where initially features are extracted using the traditional shot detection methods. The extracted features are approximated using least square polynomial approximation method. Its main advantage is that it reduces sensitivity to camera and object motion where most of the cut detection methods are highly sensitive. The performance of various shot cut detection algorithms using different combinations are tested on a set of video sequences. For hard cuts, our method achieves average detection rates of 15% more than that of the existing methods. Thus, our future work will focus on improving this detection approach for the other shot transition types like dissolve, fade and special effects.

References

1. Boreczky, J.S., Rowe, L.A.: Comparison of Video Shot Boundary Detection Techniques, Storage and Retrieval for Still Image and Video Databases IV. In: Proceedings of the SPIE 2670, San Jose, CA, USA, pp. 170–179 (1996)
2. Lienhart, R.: Comparison of Automatic Shot Boundary Detection Algorithms. In: Image and Video Processing VII 1999, Proceedings of SPIE, vol. 3656, pp. 290–301 (1999)
3. Zhang, H.J., Kankanhalli, A., Smoliar, S.W., Tan, S.Y.: Automatic Partitioning of Full Motion Video. ACM Multimedia Systems 1(1), 10–28 (1993)
4. Zhang, W., Lin, J., Chen, X., Huang, Q., Liu, Y.: Video Shot Detection using Hidden Markov Models with Complementary Features. In: Proceedings of the First International Conference on Innovative Computing, Information and Control. IEEE Computer Society, Los Alamitos (2006)
5. Dugad, R., Ratakonda, K., Ahuja, N.: Robust Video Shot Change Detection. In: Proceedings of the IEEE workshop on Multimedia Signal Processing, Redondo Beach, CA, pp. 376–381 (1998)
6. Zabih, R., Miller, J., Mai, K.: A Feature Based Algorithm for Detecting and Classifying Scene Breaks. In: ACM Multimedia 1995, San Fransisco, CA, pp. 189–200 (1995)
7. Lienhart, R.: Reliable Transition Detection in Videos: A Survey and Practitioner's Guide. International Journal of Image and Graphics (IJIG) 1(3), 469–486 (2001)
8. Chantamunee, S., Gotoh, Y.: University of Shef eld at TRECVID 2007: Shot Boundary Detection and Rushes Summarisation (2007)
9. Kikukawa, T., Kawafuchi, S.: Development of an Automatic Summary Editing System for the Audio Visual Resources. Trans. Inst. Electron. Inform. Commun. Eng. J75-A(2), 204–212 (1992)
10. Otsuji, K., Tonomura, Y., Ohba, Y.: Video Browsing using Brightness Data. In: Proceedings SPIE/IS&T VCIP 1991, vol. 1606, pp. 980–989 (1991)
11. Canny, J.: A Computational Approach to Edge Detection. IEEE Transactions on Pattern Analysis and Machine Intelligence 8(6), 34–43 (1986)
12. Maheshkumar, H., Kolekar, S., Sengupta: Video Shot Boundary Detection: A Comparative Study of Three Popular Approaches. In: National Conference on Communication (NCC), IISc, Bangalore, India (2004)
13. Godfrey, M.D.: An Algorithm for Least squares Polynomial Approximations, (November 1970) amended (December 2009)
14. Lakshmi Priya, G.G., Domnic, S.: Video Cut Detection using Block based Histogram Differences in RGB Color Space. In: Proceedings of ICSIP, pp. 29–33 (2010)

Braille Character Recognition Using Generalized Feature Vector Approach

Bhattacharya J. and Majumder S.

Central Mechanical Engineering Research Institute, Durgapur, WestBengal, India
{bjhilik,sjm}@cmeri.res.in

Abstract. The paper uses a multi-parameter based feature detection algorithm which efficiently detects the embossed dots from a braille print.This is further utilized to make a vision based analysis of the achieved printing quality of the braille printer developed by Central Mechanical Engineering Research Institute (CMERI). A simple approach is also proposed for the recognition of the braille characters for converting them into normal text.The technique is further modified to apply it on character recognition from interpoint braille print.

Keywords: Braille Character Recognition, Color Matching, Feature Detection, Generalized Feature Vector.

1   Introduction

Braille system devised by Louis Braille in 1825, is commonly used by the visibly handicapped individuals to read and write. Braille represents normal text as a pattern consisting of raised dots arranged in cells. Each cell consisting of six dots in a 3 x 2 configuration represents an alphabet or number by protruding at one or more dot positions. There are three different grades of braille writing which are in use. Beginners use just 26 standard letters of english alphabet and punctuation. Books, signs in public places, menus, and most other Braille materials are written using contractions which are used for saving space. Personal letters, diaries, and notes are written as shorthand with entire words shortened to a few letters. Though the Roman alphabet (english braille) is accepted as the braille standard universally, different countries have adapted the coding system to suit their local languages also.

The Bharati Braille (the Braille scheme adopted by India and some South Asian countries) for instance uses phonetic equivalents from the english braille to represent hindi text. Development of multilingual braille code and braille printers have been an active area of research for a long period.Various braille printers have been developed through the generation using various technologies, some being improvement over their previous versions whereas some being totally novel[1–7]. Inspite of these advancements the number of Braille printing units in the country is a meagre figure owing to the fact that their purchasing costs inclusive of the import and courier charges, adds up to a huge sum. A cost effective indigenous

K.R. Venugopal and L.M. Patnaik (Eds.): ICIP 2011, CCIS 157, pp. 171–180, 2011.

Braille embossing unit is hence developed by CMERI to address this problem. Fig. 1 represents a braille printing using the braille printer developed by CMERI. A vision based approach where a multiparameter based feature detector is used to extract the braille dots from the digital braille print, is utilized to measure the dot spacings for examining the printing quality. This helps in providing the necessary feedback to the design team so that they can improve the printer prototypes accordingly. A simple but elegant approach to convert the braille code to running text is also proposed. The english text provided for printing and the reconverted english output can be compared to verify the accuracy of the braille coding system used during printing. Besides it can also be utilized in regenerating braille print from existing ones. This paper is organized in the following manner.

Section 1 discusses the basic background of the problem. Section 2 provides the analysis of the printing quality using a vision based approach whereas section 3 suggests a technique for braille character recognition. Section 4 further illustrates the modified algorithm for character recognition from interpoint braille print. Finally, discussion and conclusion is presented in section 5.

Fig. 1. A test print using the braille printer developed by CMERI

2   Vision Based Printing Analysis

A good quality print requires to have the same horizontal and vertical spacing between the dots of a cell and also in-between two cells. Inorder to calculate the inter-dot spacings the dots are required to be detected. This is further done using a digitized image of the print. It is obvious that detecting the dots from a similar colored background is an obscure task. A number of different techniques have been in use to obtaining a good quality digitized image of a braille print. Some of the previous research works done on braille character recognition reports the use of various image processing techniques like canny edge detection [8], image thresholding with beta distribution [9], template matching with cross correlation [10] for dot detection from the digital image.

The performance of these procedures depends on the digital image quality. It may give suitable results on a very high quality image but fail to give desired output for an ordinary scanned image like the one shown in Fig. 2 where a single parameter is not sufficient to detect the dots. Fig. 3 and 4 shows the result of applying edge detection and thresholding operations on Fig. 2 respectively. It is clearly visible that for both the procedures the dots are not clearly detected and needs further processing. For Fig. 3 the edges are detected as disjoint dots and requires grouping whereas other intensity based segmentation algorithms fail to give suitable results due to undistinguishable variations between the background and region of interests. This paper uses a feature detection algorithm called GFV (Generalized Feature Vector) which successfully detects the dots even for an ordinary scanned image as shown in Fig. 5. GFV can be defined as a multimodal

Fig. 2. Scanned image of a braille print using an ordinary scanner

Fig. 3. Application of canny edge detector for detecting dot boundaries from image shown in Fig. 2

Fig. 4. Application of multilevel thresholding for detecting dots from image shown in Fig. 2

Fig. 5. Application of GFV for detecting dot from image shown in Fig. 2

probability distribution in a multidimensional feature space which essentially encapsulates multiple features for consistent detection. The basic idea of GFV stems out from the fact that if detection relies on a single feature it may lead to multiple false alarms or wrong identification. This error can be greatly reduced to a large extent when a number of features are used instead of one, in an integrated framework. Though primarily applied to vision sensors GFV has the potential to include data obtained from other types of sensors. This approach is also found to be resilient to the extrinsic parametric variations with minimal false alarm. The algorithmic flow of the method is based on two steps [11]. In the first step a model is selected from the image and the parameters are calculated. In the second step the image is initially segmented with the color parameter and then remaining GFV parameters for each region is calculated. Different color matching techniques reported in literature basically uses histogram matching techniques. Color matching often suffers due to environmental variations. The same object looks different at two different lighting conditions. Even changing view positions at the same environmental conditions bring in changes in the appearance of the object. These problems are controlled to a great extent in the GFV algorithm by using a statistical gating for color matching. Instead of using the exact histogram of the model to match the color, matching is done over a scaled deviation of the dominant intensity range of the model as lighting variations mainly influence the recessive intensities. Each distinguishable region along with its multiple parameters is represented as a multivariate gaussian distribution.

The classification of an image frame into sample (i.e., region of interest) and non-sample (i.e., remaining regions of the image) is done using parameter estimation of the sample's multivariate gaussian distribution, which is grown iteratively over the subsequent image frames. The Maximum Likelihood Estimator (MLE) is chosen for parameter estimation as it is known to give an unbiased, minimum variance, consistent and convergent estimate for multivariate gaussian distributions, provided such an estimate can be determined for a particular sample. In principle GFV can include as many feature parameters as desired but for the present purpose only color and energy are considered. GFV reference model is created using the selected model shown in Fig. 6. The image is then segmented using the reference color parameter and energy for each segmented region is calculated. Regions which have a distance metrics less than the threshold value of 0.05 is extracted as dots as shown in Fig. 7. Once the dots are detected, the

Fig. 6. Braille print with a sample dot selected(shown using red rectangle) for calculating GFV parameter of model

Fig. 7. Detected dots using GFV method

next task lies in finding its spacing. The dots are represented using their centroid position which is based on the standard center of mass equation in discrete form. In order to find out the inter-dot spacing the dots are first marked in a sequential manner. This is done using the following steps:

(1) The dots are initially clustered using the k-means clustering algorithm where the number of clusters equals the number of lines. Fig. 8 shows the clusters.
(2) In each cluster the dots are again grouped into three according to their increasing x-distance. This is further depicted in Fig. 9.
(3) The dots are finally numbered using their y-distance. The final sequence is thus seen in Fig. 10. Once the numerical arrangement of the dots are complete they can be used to compute the spacings. It is evident from the Fig. 9 that the x-distance between dots of two groups j and $j + 1$ gives the inter-dot horizontal

spacing if j is odd and inter-cell horizontal spacing(i.e. inter-character spacing) if j is even. From Fig. 10 it is obvious that the y-distance between two dots k and $k+1$ for each group j gives the inter-dot vertical spacing.

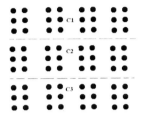

Fig. 8. Three clusters C1,C2 and C3 formed from k-means clustering

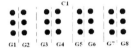

Fig. 9. Grouping of the dots in each cluster according to their x-distance

Fig. 10. Ordering of the dots in each group according to their y-distance

The results of dot spacing measurements computed using the above procedure for two prototypes are shown. It can be clearly visible from the results in Table 1 that the earlier model had some ambiguity. The prototype was thus modified according to the requirements. The horizontal and vertical spacings for three samples from the current printing unit are shown in Tables 2, 3 and 4. The pixel to metric scale conversion is done using the paper size and image dimension.

Table 1. Dot measurements of print from an earlier printer prototype

Horizontal spacing between characters	3.45	3.5	2.6	3.45	3.45	3.5	2.6	3.45
Horizontal spacing between dots	2.4	2.4	2.4	2.5	2.6	2.4	2.4	2.5
Vertical spacing between dots	2.14	2.21	2.14	2.28	2.14	2.14	2.28	2.21

Table 2. Horizontal spacing between two dots of a character

Sample1	2.4464	2.4464	2.4230	2.4230	2.4230	2.4464	2.4464	2.4464	2.4464	2.4464
Sample2	2.4230	2.4464	2.4464	2.4464	2.4464	2.4464	2.4464	2.4464	2.4230	2.4464
Sample3	2.4464	2.4464	2.4230	2.4464	2.4464	2.4464	2.4464	2.4464	2.4464	2.4464

Table 3. Vertical spacing between two dots of a character

Sample1	2.1427	2.1427	2.1341	2.1341	2.1341	2.1427	2.1427	2.1427	2.1427	2.1427
Sample2	2.1341	2.1427	2.1427	2.1427	2.1427	2.1427	2.1427	2.1427	2.1427	2.1427
Sample3	2.1427	2.1341	2.1427	2.1427	2.1427	2.1427	2.1427	2.1427	2.1427	2.1427

Table 4. Horizontal spacing between two characters

Sample1	3.5009	3.5009	3.5431	3.5009	3.5009
Sample2	3.5009	3.5009	3.5009	3.5009	3.5009
Sample3	3.5009	3.5009	3.5431	3.5009	3.5009

3   Vision Based Braille Character Recognition

The character recognition system consists of the following steps (i)Image acquisition,(ii)selection of sliding window dimension and interval, (iii) cell extraction with sliding window,(iv)dot detection of cell using GFV,(v)binary code generation,(vi)code lookup to reconstruct english text.

A sliding window as shown in Fig. 11 with a fixed interval is used to slide over the entire braille image to detect each cell. This operation does not give any anomaly as it is already verified that the inter-dot and inter-cell spacings are fixed.The dot positions for each cell is then detected using GFV as shown in Fig. 12 and 13. Each cell is divided into grids as shown in Fig. 14 and the

Fig. 11. Figure depicts a sliding window marked with the blue rectangle

Fig. 12. Dot position detected using GFV for each cell extracted using the sliding window

Fig. 13. Dot position detected using GFV for each cell extracted using the sliding window

corresponding code for the cell is generated according to the presence or absence of a dot centroid in each grid. The configuration followed is shown in Fig 15. English word reconstruction is then carried out from the generated binary code using a lookup table. Table 5 shows the generated code and corresponding english conversion for a sample(first line) from Fig. 1.

Table 5. Generated code and corresponding english conversion

010100	101110	100110	010100	100000	000000	010100	011100	000000		
I	N	D	I	A		I	S			
101010	101001	111010		100100	101010	101001	101110	011110	111010	101111
O	U	R		C	O	U	N	T	R	Y

Fig. 14. Figure shows griding of each cell

Fig. 15. Figure depicts the cell numbering order used for code generation

4   Braille Character Recognition for Interpoint Braille Print

Single sided braille writing generally consumes a lot of space hence interpoint printing is preferred to reduce the bulk of paper. However vision based character recognition now becomes an intricate task as both the front side and back side dots are visible in the digital image of the print. The dot detection algorithm thus detects both the dots as seen in Fig. 16 and Fig. 17. The algorithm described in

Fig. 16. An interpoint braille print

Fig. 17. Both front side and back side braille dots detected by GFV

the previous section is further modified to distinguish between the front side and back side dots and generate the binary code for the front page from the interpoint print. Similar to the previous case a fixed size sliding window is used to slide over the entire image and detect each cell as depicted in Fig. 18. As seen from the figure each window consists of both side dots. These dots are differentiated as front or back sided by a griding method further illustrated using Fig. 19. Each window shown using red colored rectangle is subdivided into 3 regions $R1,R2,R3$. The front side dots are numbered using 1-6 and back side dots are numbered using a-f. All the dots which lie in region $R1$ entirely (for example dot 3 in Fig. 19(i)) are accepted whereas dots which lie entirely in region $R3$(for example dot e in Fig. 19(i)) are rejected. Dots lying in both $R2$ and $R3$ are either front and back side merged dots (for example dot 6 and f in Fig. 19(i)) or front side dots(for example dot 6 in Fig. 19(ii)).For the former case the dot centroid is modified using the merged dot centroid and bottom extreme point of the dot. Again, dots lying in both $R1$ and $R2$ are either merged dots (for example dot 2 and b in Fig. 19(i)) or back side dots(for example dot b in Fig. 19(iii)). Here, for the former case the dot centroid is modified using the merged dot centroid and bottom extreme point of the dot whereas for the later case the dot is rejected. The GFV parameters for this case consists of size ratios along with color and energy in order to differentiate between a single dot and a merged dot. The algorithm is tested using some sample prints and some of the results

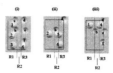

Fig. 18. Sliding window (shown using blue rectangle) to detect each cell

Fig. 19. Gridding of braille cells

are shown in Fig. 20.The binary code generation can then be done using the centroid of the accepted dots in each window in a similar manner as described for single sided print.

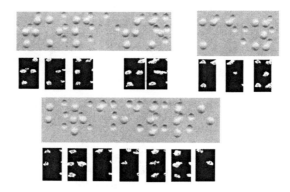

Fig. 20. The dots in each window is detected using GFV.The accepted dots are then marked with its centroid as shown using red colored circle.

5 Conclusions

The experimental results verify that the GFV approach efficiently detects the braille dots even from low quality digital braille image. The binary code generator for each Braille cell used for word reconstruction provides satisfactory result with a high accuracy and very low processing time. The modified algorithm for character recognition from interpoint braille print also works fine and successfully distinguishes between front side and back side dots. Work is in progress to generate the english text for both sides of the page simultaneously for interpoint braille print.

6   Appendix

(i)Color Parameter of Object of Interest

The object of interest (i.e., the model) is manually selected from image data $Img(m, n, c)$ using a selection window roi depicting the *region of interest*. The 3-dimensional data of the selected object $Img_{roi}(m, n, c)$ is represented using its probability density function $pdf(I, c)$. The *pdf* is calculated for all the three colors channels red, green and blue using the following equation.

$$pdf(I, c) = \frac{freq(I^c)}{\sum_{I=0}^{255} freq(I^c)}. \tag{1}$$

where $freq(I^c)$ represents the number of pixels of intensity I in the cth color channel. As the images used are 8-bit color images, I ranges from $0 - 255$ in each color channel. The *pdf* of each color channel is plotted and an intensity range $L^c : H^c$ is selected interactively to represent $Img_{roi}(m, n, c). L^c : H^c$ is selected such that $p(L : H, c) > \frac{1}{2} max(p(I, c))$. Color,being one of the GFV parameters of the model is represented using the mean and standard deviation of this intensity range. The mean $\mu_{L^c:H^c}^c$ and standard deviation $\sigma_{L^c:H^c}^c$ is calculated using standard formulas:

$$\mu_{L^c:H^c}^c = \frac{L^c + H^c}{2}. \tag{2}$$

$$\sigma_{L^c:H^c}^c = \sqrt{\sum_{I^c=L^c}^{H^c} (I^c - \mu_{Img_{roi}}^c)^2}. \tag{3}$$

Equation 2 can be used to calculate the mean of $L^c : H^c$ as the range is continuous.

(ii)Color Matching

The image intensities of the input image $Img(m, n, c)$ lying beyond the range specified by mean $\mu_{L^c:H^c}$,and scaled deviation $\delta\sigma_L^c : H^c$ of the reference model are marked as outliers O^c

$$O^c = |I - \mu_{L^c:H^c}| > \delta\sigma_L^c : H^c. \tag{4}$$

The regions representing the same color as the model can now be determined from Eq. 5

$$S(reg, c) = I - O^c. \tag{5}$$

(iii)Energy Calculation

The energy of an image is the measure of the number of intensity levels which its pixels have and can be statistically measured using Eq. 6.

$$energy = \sum_{I=0}^{255} pdf(I)^2. \tag{6}$$

Energy content of an image is inversely proportional to the number of intensity levels its pixels are distributed across. The equation shown above calculates the energy of a gray level image; for color images the red, green and blue color channels has to be considered separately. In the present work,instead of calculating the energy for the three color channels separately, an weighted average is used to represent the energy of the object $Img_{roi}(m, n, c)$

$$energy_{Img_{roi}(m,n,c)} = \sum_{c\epsilon\{red,green,blue\}} \alpha_c \sum_{I=0}^{255} pdf(I,c)^2. \tag{7}$$

where $\alpha_c = \frac{\mu_{Img_{roi}(m,n,c)}}{\sum_{c\epsilon\{red,green,blue\}} \mu_{Img_{roi}(m,n,c)}} . \mu_{Img_{roi}(m,n,c)}$ is the mean of the entire selected region and is given by $\sum_{I=0}^{255} I.pdf(I,c)$.

References

1. Lars-Eric, A.: Device for Printing Braille U. S Patent 4108066 (August 22, 1978)
2. Galarneau, R.: Printer Head for Braille Printer U.S Patent 4735516 (April 5, 1988)
3. Tsukuda, Y., Goto, I.: Braille Printer U.S Patent 5193921 (March 16, 1993)
4. Tsukuda, Y., Goto, I.: Braille Printer U.S Patent 5222819 (June 29, 1993)
5. Deng, J.-J., Sung, M.-H.: Apparatus for Inscribing Braille Characters on a Sheet of Paper U.S Patent 5803741 (September 8, 1998)
6. Ogawa, T., Tsukasa, T.: Braille Printing Apparatus U.S Patent 5876128 (March 2, 1999)
7. Emmert, J.R., Evans, C., Rencher, M.A., Keithley, D.G.: Laser Printer for Braille U.S Patent Appl. Publication 0055768 (March 16, 2006)
8. Al-Shamma, S.D., Fathi, S.: Arabic Braille Recognition and Transcription into Text and Voice. In: 5th Cairo International Biomedical Engineering Conference, Cairo, Egypt (2010)
9. Al-Salman, A.S., Al-Salman, A.S., El-Zaart, A., Al-Suhaibani, Y., Al-Hokail, K., Al-Qabbany, A.O.: An Efficient Braille Cells Recognition. IEEE, New York (2010)
10. Mennens, J., Tichenens, L.V., Francois, G., Engelen, J.J.: Optical Recognition of Braille Writing using standard Equipment. IEEE Transactions on Rehabilitation Engineering (1994)
11. Bhattacharya, J., Majumder, S.: The Generalized Feature Vector (GFV): A New Approach for Vision Based Navigation of Outdoor Mobile Robot, NAComm (2009)

Kernel Discriminative Embedding Technique with Entropy Component Analysis for Accurate Face Image Classification

Sharmila Kumari M.[1] and Shekar B.H.[2]

[1] Department of Computer Science & Engineering, P.A. College of Engineering,
Mangalore, Karnataka
[2] Department of Computer Science, Mangalore University, Mangalore, Karnataka
sharmilabp@gmail.com

Abstract. In this paper, we have reported a new face image classification algorithm based on Renyi entropy component analysis. In the proposed model, kernel discriminant analysis is integrated with entropy analysis to choose the best principal component vectors which are subsequently used for pattern projection to a lower dimensional space. Extensive experimentation on Yale and UMIST face database has been conducted to reveal the performance of the entropy based kernel discriminative embedding technique and comparative analysis is made with conventional kernel linear discriminant method to signify the importance of selection of principal component vectors based on entropy information rather based only on magnitude of eigenvalues.

Keywords: Biometrics, Entropy Component Analysis, Face Image Classification, Fisherface, Linear Discriminant Analysis.

1 Introduction

In the last two decades, we have witnessed the significant growth of research in the field of biometrics; in particular on face image classification because of its wide acceptability in several applications ranging from crime detection, identity authentication, access control, face based video indexing/retrieval to human computer interaction/ communication. Several models have been proposed for face image classification ranging from appearance based models to 3D techniques. Among the many techniques, appearance based models gain much popularity because of their robustness against noise, occlusion and simplicity in terms of feature representation. In these approaches, data transformation is a fundamental step and the goal is to obtain highly discriminative lower-dimensional data from high-dimensional data. Principal Component Analysis (PCA) and Linear Discriminate Analysis (LDA) are the widely used tools in face recognition domain that encodes high-dimensional face images as lower-dimensional eigenfaces [1] and fisherfaces [2] respectively. Although PCA ensures least reconstruction error, it may not be optimal from a discrimination stand point. Belhumeur et al., [3] have proposed the linear discriminative analysis technique (FLD) that

K.R. Venugopal and L.M. Patnaik (Eds.): ICIP 2011, CCIS 157, pp. 181–189, 2011.

extracts features which possess the best discrimination capability. The PCA based system is better for the databases of a smaller number of classes and the FLD is better for the databases of larger number of classes. Additionally, the effect of non-uniform illumination conditions on the face image classification performance is studied and the superiority of the FLD method over the PCA method has been shown in [4]. However, PCA/FLD are linear methods which ensures that the data transformed are uncorrelated and preserve maximally the second order statistics of the original data and hence is insensitive to the dependencies of multiple features in the patterns. To overcome this problem, kernel PCA [5],[6] kernel FLD [7] is proposed as a non linear extension that computes the principal components in a high-dimensional feature space.

More recently, in [8] it is observed that the kernel PCA /kernel FLD or any other PCA/FLD based models in general chose top eigenvalues and eigenvectors of the kernel matrix /co-variance matrix which does not reveal structure related to Renyi entropy of the input space data set. This issue motivated us to employ kernel entropy component analysis (kernel ECA) as an alternative to kernel LDA for efficient face representation and accurate classification. In kernel ECA, the data transformation from higher dimension to lower dimension is achieved by projecting onto the kernel FLD axes that contribute to the entropy estimate of the input space data set and these axes will, in general, not necessarily correspond to the top eigenvalues and eigenvectors of the kernel matrix. Based on these features, face representation and classification can then be performed using a simple nearest neighbor rule. Experimental results and comparisons with conventional kernel FLD show the effectiveness of the proposed method.

2   Kernel FLD: A Review

The kernel FLD is perhaps the best known data transformation method in a non-linear sense when class-wise information is available. Let $X = [x_1, x_2, \ldots, x_N]$, where $x_i \in R^d, i = 1, \ldots, N$ represent the set of N face images converted into a vector form of d dimension. It is further assumed that each image belongs to one of C classes. The basic idea of kernel FLD is to map the input data X into a feature space F *via* a nonlinear mapping Φ which is given by $\Phi : R^d \rightarrow F$ such that $x_t \rightarrow \Phi(x_t), t = 1, \ldots, N$ and then to perform an LDA in the feature space F instead of input space R^d. Let $\Phi = [\Phi(x_1), \Phi(x_2), \ldots \Phi(x_N)]$.

Let S_B and S_W be the between-class and within-class scatter matrices in the feature space F, respectively, expressed as follows:

$$S_B = \frac{1}{N} \sum_{i=1}^{C} C_i (\overline{\Phi}_i - \Phi_i)(\overline{\Phi}_i - \Phi_i)^T. \tag{1}$$

$$S_W = \frac{1}{N} \sum_{i=1}^{C} \sum_{j=1}^{C_i} (\Phi_{ij} - \overline{\Phi}_i)(\Phi_{ij} - \overline{\Phi}_i)^T. \tag{2}$$

where $\Phi_{ij} = \Phi(x_{ij})$, $\overline{\Phi}_i = (1/C_i) \sum_{j=1}^{C_i} \Phi(x_{ij})$ is the mean of the class C_i, $\overline{\Phi}_i = \frac{1}{N} \sum_{i=1}^{C} \sum_{j=1}^{C_i} \Phi(x_{ij})$ is the average of the ensemble, and X_i is the element number in x_i, which leads to $N = \sum_{i=1}^{C} \sum_{j=1}^{C_i} C_i$. LDA determines a set of optimal discriminant basis vectors, denoted by $\Psi_{k\,k=1}^{N}$, so that the ratio of the between class scatter matrix and within class scatter matrix is maximized [2]. Assuming $\Psi = [\Psi_1, \Psi_2, \ldots \Psi_N]$, the maximization can be achieved by solving the following eigen value problem:

$$\Psi = argmax \frac{|\Psi^T S_B \Psi|}{|\Psi^T S_W \Psi|}. \tag{3}$$

Subsequently, we project the vectors in R^d to a lower dimensional space spanned by the eigenvectors Ψ. Let x be a test sample whose projection is $\Phi(x)$ in R^d, then the projection of $\Phi(x)$ onto the eigenvectors Ψ is the non-linear Fisher's principal components corresponding to Φ:

$$\Psi.\Phi(x) = \sum_{i=1}^{q} \alpha_i(\Phi(x_i).\Phi(x)) = \sum_{i=1}^{q} \alpha_i k(x_i, x). \tag{4}$$

In other words, we can extract the first α non-linear principal components which are corresponding to the first q non-increasing eigenvalues using the kernel function.

In the case of kernel FLD, the top α eigenvectors associated with first q large eigenvalues are considered to transform high dimensional face image data into its lower dimensional data. Although kernel ECA is similar to kernel FLD in terms of obtaining the eigenvectors and eigenvalues, the procedure of feature extraction is based on the energy content of the eigenvectors and eigenvalues and the details are brought out in the following section.

3   Kernel Entropy Component Analysis for Face Feature Extraction

The Renyi quadratic entropy is given by

$$H(p) = -log \int p^2(x)dx. \tag{5}$$

where $p(x)$ is the probability density function generating the data set, or sample, $S = x_1, x_2, \ldots x_N$. Because of the monotonic nature of logarithmic function, one can consider the quantity:

$$V(p) = \int p^2(x)dx. \tag{6}$$

The estimation of $V(p)$ will be done using the Parzen window density estimator as suggested in [6] and is given below.

$$\widehat{p}(x) = \frac{1}{N} \sum_{x_t \in S} k_\sigma(x, x_t). \tag{7}$$

Here $k_\sigma(x, x_t)$ is the kernel centered at x_t and width governed by the parameter σ.

Hence,

$$\widehat{V}(p) = \frac{1}{N} \sum_{x_t \in S} \widehat{p}(x_t) = \frac{1}{N} \sum_{x_t \in S} \frac{1}{N} \sum_{x_t \in S} k_\sigma(x_t, x_{t'}) = \frac{1}{N^2} \mathbf{1}^T K \mathbf{1}. \tag{8}$$

Here, the element (t, t') of the $N \times N$ kernel matrix K is $k_\sigma(x_t, x_{t'})$ and $\mathbf{1}$ is an $(N \times 1)$ vector containing all ones.

Hence, the Renyi entropy estimator may be expressed in terms of the eigenvalues and eigenvectors of the kernel matrix, which may be decomposed as $K = EDE^T$ where D is the diagonal matrix containing the eigenvalues $\lambda_1, \lambda_2, \ldots, \lambda_N$ and E is a matrix with the corresponding eigenvectors $\alpha_1, \alpha_2, \ldots, \alpha_N$ as columns. Rewriting the above, we have:

$$\widehat{V}(p) = \frac{1}{N^2} \sum_{i=1}^{N} (\sqrt{\lambda_i} \alpha_i^T \mathbf{1})^2. \tag{9}$$

It shall be observed from the above expression that the certain eigenvalues and the corresponding eigenvectors will contribute more to the entropy estimate than others since the terms depend on different eigenvalues and eigenvectors. This is where one can notice the difference between kernel FLD and kernel ECA. That is Eq. (9) reveals that the Renyi entropy estimator is composed of projections onto all the kernel FLD axes, however, only a principal axis λ_i for which $\lambda_i \neq 0$ and $\alpha_i^T \neq 0$ contributes to the entropy estimate. Hence, kernel ECA is defined as an q-dimensional data transformation technique obtained by projecting Φ onto a subspace E_q spanned by those q kernel PCA axes contributing most to the Renyi entropy estimate of the data. Hence E_q is composed of subset of kernel FLD axes but not necessarily those corresponding to the top q eigenvalues. Hence in kernel ECA, for the purpose of principal component extraction, the projections of x are computed onto the eigenvectors in F which contributes more to Eq. (9).

4   Recognition

Let I be an image given for recognition. Let I^f be its projected image onto the q number of projection axes computed by $I^f = I.E$. Given two images, say i_1 and i_2 of any face(s), represented by feature matrices $Z_1 = [z_1^1, z_2^1, \ldots, z_q^1]$ and $Z_2 = [z_1^2, z_2^2, \ldots, z_q^2]$, the distance $d(Z_1, Z_2)$ is defined as

$$d(Z_1, Z_2) = \sum_{j=1}^{q} |z_j^1 - z_j^2|^2. \tag{10}$$

where $|a - b|_2$ denotes the Euclidean distance between the two vectors a and b. If the feature matrices of the training images are $F_1, F_2, \ldots, F_N$, and each image belongs to some face O_i, then for a given test image I, if $d(I^f, F_l) = min_j d(I^f, F_j)$ and $F_l \in O_i$, then the resulting decision is $I \in O_i$.

5   Experimental Results

This section presents the results of the experiments conducted to corroborate the success of the proposed model. We have conducted experimentation using two image databases. The Yale face database contains 165 images of 15 subjects that include variation in both facial expression and lighting. In Fig. 1, we have shown the closely cropped images which include internal facial structures. In addition, we have also chosen subset of UMIST face database consisting of 500 gray-scale images of 20 subjects, each covering a wide range of poses as well as race, gender and appearance. In Fig. 2, we have shown subset of one such subject of the UMIST database. All experiments are performed on a P-IV 2.99GHz Windows machine with 3GB of RAM.

Fig. 1. Subset of one subject of Yale face database

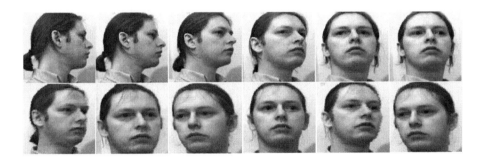

Fig. 2. Subset of one subject of UMIST face database

5.1   Experimental Setup -1

It is observed in [5] that the distribution of face patterns is highly non-convex and complex when the patterns are subjected to large variations in view points. Hence, in our first experimental set up, we have used subset of Yale face database to reveal the significance of ECA based kernel FLD over conventional kernel FLD [5] for face classification.

In order to visualize, we have used five randomly chosen subjects which contains 50 images. Kernel FLD and ECA based kernel FLD feature bases have been considered for projection of images. For each image, its projections in the first two most significant feature bases of each subspace are visualized in Figs. 3 and 4.

In Fig. 3, we have shown the projections on the first two most significant principal components extracted by kernel FLD and they provide a low-dimensional representation for the samples which can be used to capture the structure of the data. In Fig. 4 we have shown the projections on the first two most significant principal components extracted by ECA based kernel FLD which contribute more to the Renyi entropy (in this case, the 13th and 3rd principal component vectors) unlike kernel FLD where projection is by having the first and the second principal component vectors associated with first large and second large eigenvalues. In both the approaches, we have used the polynomial kernel as suggested in most of the works on face representation and classification.

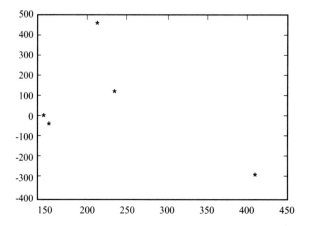

Fig. 3. Distribution of 9 samples of five subjects in kernel FLD based subspace

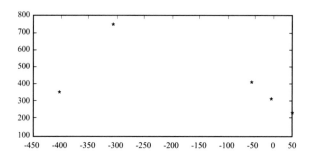

Fig. 4. Distribution of 9 samples of five subjects in ECA based kernel FLD subspace

It shall be observed from Figs. 3 and 4 that the cluster of face samples in ECA based kernel FLD is linearly separable and much better distinct from classification point of view when compared to kernel FLD. One can notice from Figs. 3 and 4 that the distance between cluster of face samples is quite high in the case of proposed model which gives clear idea that entropy component analysis is useful for the selection of principal component vectors.

5.2   Experimental Setup -2

In the second experimental set up, we have considered UMIST face database. Here we have taken alternate three samples per class for training (180) and the remaining samples for testing (320). In addition, we have also conducted experiments considering 140 faces as training faces choosing seven sample faces per class and the classification performance has been obtained considering the remaining faces as test faces (360). The classification performance of proposed model with varying dimension of feature vectors is given in Table 1. The classification performance obtained due to kernel FLD with similar experimental setup is given in Table 2 for UMIST database.

In the case of Yale face database, we have considered randomly chosen four samples per class for training (60) and the remaining samples for testing (105). Similarly, we have chosen three samples per class randomly for training (45) and the remaining samples for testing (120). The classification rate obtained due to the proposed model is reported in Table 3 and the classification results obtained due to kernel FLD with similar experimentation is given in Table 4.

It shall be observed from Tables 1, 2, 3 and 4 that the average classification rate of the proposed model is quite high when compared to kernel FLD

Table 1. Classification accuracy of the proposed model for UMIST face database

Polynomial kernel of degree	Classification accuracy for varying dimensions of feature vectors									
	Dimension of feature vector	3		5		7		9		11	
	No. of testing samples	320	360	320	360	320	360	320	360	320	360
2		88.13	80.83	93.13	91.67	95.00	94.17	95.94	96.11	97.50	95.83
3		89.38	86.94	94.06	93.46	94.69	94.44	97.19	95.28	96.56	96.67
4		85.31	78.33	91.25	85.83	93.75	93.33	94.06	94.72	95.94	94.72

Table 2. Classification accuracy of kernel FLD model for UMIST face database

Polynomial kernel of degree	Classification accuracy for varying dimensions of feature vectors									
	Dimension of feature vector	3		5		7		9		11	
	No. of testing samples	320	360	320	360	320	360	320	360	320	360
2		84.37	82.22	90.62	90.83	95.31	94.72	96.96	95.28	97.50	96.11
3		85.00	84.17	91.25	91.94	93.75	94.44	97.19	95.83	97.81	96.67
4		87.81	78.33	91.25	88.89	93.75	88.89	94.06	94.17	95.63	96.94

Table 3. Classification accuracy of proposed model model for YALE face database

Polynomial kernel of degree	Classification accuracy for varying dimensions of feature vectors									
	Dimension of feature vector	3		5		7		9		11
	No. of testing samples	105	120	105	120	105	120	105	120	105	120
2		75.15	81.21	81.21	93.33	86.06	98.79	87.88	99.39	90.90	99.39
3		63.33	75.76	80.00	83.64	85.45	93.34	87.88	98.78	89.09	99.39
4		73.33	75.16	82.21	87.88	81.81	96.97	86.67	92.73	89.09	98.78

Table 4. Classification accuracy of kernel FLD model for YALE face database

Polynomial kernel of degree	Classification accuracy for varying dimensions of feature vectors									
	Dimension of feature vector	3		5		7		9		11
	No. of testing samples	105	120	105	120	105	120	105	120	105	120
2		68.48	80.60	83.03	87.25	88.48	98.79	90.91	99.39	92.12	99.39
3		69.89	75.15	80.00	90.30	81.21	90.30	89.09	94.55	88.48	96.97
4		73.33	75.15	81.21	86.07	81.81	89.09	81.81	92.73	81.81	98.78

and hence choosing principal components based on Renyi entropy is more appropriate in face representation and classification problems.

6   Conclusions

A new face recognition algorithm based on Renyi entropy component analysis is proposed in this work. In the proposed model, FLD methodology is integrated with entropy analysis to choose the best principal component vectors which are subsequently used for pattern projection to a lower-dimensional space. Extensive experimentation on the standard face databases reveals that the entropy based principal component vectors selection is more appropriate rather than selecting principal component vectors based only on magnitude of eigenvalues.

Acknowledgements

The authors would like to thank the support provided by DST-RFBR, Govt. of India vide Ref. No. INT/RFBR/P-48 dated 19.06.2009.

References

1. Belhumeur, P.N., Hespanha, J.P., Kreigman, D.J.: Eigenfaces vs. Fisherfaces: Recognition using Class Specific Linear Projection. IEEE Transactions on Pattern Analysis and Machine Intelligence 19(7), 711–720 (1997)
2. Fisher, R.A.: The use of Multiple Measure in Taxonomic Problems. Annals of Eugenics 7, 179–188 (1936)
3. Jenssen, R.: Kernel Entropy Component Analysis. IEEE Transactions on Pattern Analysis and Machine Intelligence 32(5), 847–860 (2010)
4. Kim, K.I., Jung, K., Kim, H.J.: Face Recognition using Kernel Principal Component Analysis. IEEE Signal Processing Letters 9(2), 40–42 (2002)
5. Lu, J., Plataniotis, K.N., Venetsanopoulos, A.N.: Face Recognition using Kernel Direct Discriminant Analysis Algorithms. IEEE Transactions on Neural Networks 14(1), 117–126 (2003)
6. Parzen, E.: On the Estimation of a Probability Density Function and the Mode. The Annals of Math. Statistics 32, 1065–1076 (1962)
7. Schokopf, B., Mika, S., Burges, C.J.C., Knirsch, P., Muller, K.R., Ratsch, G., Mola, A.J.: Input Space Versus Feature Space in Kernel based Methods. IEEE Transactions on Neural Networks 10(5), 1299–1319 (1999)
8. Turk, M., Pentland, A.: Eigenfaces for Recognition. Journal of Cognitive Neuroscience 3(1), 71–86 (1991)

Convolutional Neural Network Based Segmentation

Leena Silvoster M. and Govindan V.K.

Department of Computer Science and Engineering
National Institute of Technology Calicut, Kerala, India
`leenasilvoster@gmail.com, vkg@nitc.ac.in`

Abstract. Machine learning system refers to the one which automatically accumulates knowledge about new environments based on experience to recognize complex patterns. This ability to learn from experience, analytical observation, and other means, results in a system that can improve its own speed and performance. In this work, Convolutional Neural Network is used for learning how to segment images. Convolutional Neural Networks (CNN) extract features directly from pixel images with minimal preprocessing. It can even able to recognize a pattern which has not been presented before, provided it resembles one of the training patterns. After learning (from ground-truth image), CNN automatically generate a good affinity graph from raw SEM images. This affinity graph can be then paired with any standard partitioning algorithm, such as N-cut, connected component to achieve improved segmentation. In this paper, we demonstrate the use of combined approach, where a Convolutional Neural Network and Connected Component algorithm(CC) are used to segment SEM images. F-score of this algorithm was found to be 78%.

Keywords: Convolutional Neural Network, Connected Components, SEM Image.

1 Introduction

The influence of imaging technologies on the study of biomedical and neuroscience lead a new research area. The present day automated imaging system is able to acquire and archive tons of image data. Scientists work on imaging not only need machines, but also must have an overlook of the properties of machines. Ideally, use a computer to analyze an image with little or no expertise.

Detection of neuronal tissues is one of the challenging problems of neuroscience. Scanning electron microscopy (SEM) delivers image stacks with a resolution adequate to identify the components in dense neuropil. They are difficult to distinguish from each other solely on the basis of local image statistics, especially when the signal-to-noise ratio of data is low. Recent developments in imaging technology have rendered possible automated acquisition of high quality volume electron microscopy data. However, purely manual or purely automated strategies to distinguish neural tissues are likely to fail.

K.R. Venugopal and L.M. Patnaik (Eds.): ICIP 2011, CCIS 157, pp. 190–197, 2011.
© Springer-Verlag Berlin Heidelberg 2011

Segmentation algorithm partitions the image into different sets of pixels which belong to distinct objects. A good segmentation algorithm will be able to answer the following:

1. Given two different segmentations of the same image, how can we differentiate the mismatches between them?
2. Given two different segmentations of two images, how can we minimize the disagreements with the ground truth?

In this paper, we present an innovative automated learning approach for the detection of the affinity graph using a Convolutional Neural Network (CNN) trained using ground truth generated by human experts. This learned CNN affinity graph can be combined with any partitioning algorithm which leads to an accurate segmentation result.

Convolutional Neural Network consists of a set of layers. Each layer contains one or more planes. Input of each unit in a plane is accepted from a small neighborhood in the planes of the previous layer. Shared weight concept is applicable to each plane. Multiple planes in each layer detect multiple features. After detecting the features, the image is passed to a subsampling layer which is used to perform a local averaging of the weights. Shared weights help to reduce the number of parameters of the network.

The first step in this approach of image segmentation is to generate an affinity graph. In the conventional approach, affinity functions used to design the edge weights depends on its local image features such as intensity, spatial derivatives, texture or colour. Machine learning architecture known as CNN is an important mile stone in learning affinity function. The CNN based approach trains the Convolutional Neural Network using the raw input image and the ground truth segmentation generated by human experts, and an affinity graph is obtained. This affinity graph can then be partitioned using any standard partition algorithm. It has been observed that supervised graph-methods outperform their unsupervised peers in various classification tasks. Supervised graphs are typically constructed by allowing two nodes to be adjacent only if they are of the same class. Learn a good affinity graph from raw EM images. The CN affinity graph can be then paired with any standard partitioning algorithm and improves segmentation. Performance of a graph based segmentation algorithm can be hampered by poor choices of affinity function.

The rest of this paper is organized as follows: Section 2 describes the related works in this area. Section 3 deals with the architecture of Convolutional Neural Network (CNN). Section 4 presents the algorithm. The performance metric and the results are presented in Section 5, and finally the paper is concluded in Section 6.

2   Related Work

The study of structure and connectivity of the nervous system is a challenging research area. Neurons are particularly challenging to segment, due to their highly branched, intertwined, and densely packed structure [1]. Axons are narrow as just as a few vowels. So only electron microscopy (EM) has sufficient resolution to reveal them [2]. Previous work of reconstruction of neurons ranges from manual tracing [2] to semi-automated interactive methods and fully automated methods. In semi-automated methods snakes or active deformable contours are used for the reconstruction [3]. In fully automated method, first detects the neuronal cell with multi-scale ridge detector. Short breaks in detected boundaries are then interpolated using anisotropic contour completion formulated in fuzzy-logic framework [4]. Active contours can provide smooth, accurate segmentations of cells. However, they are very sensitive to initialization. Almost all methods require an initialization and hence, these methods are impractical for segmenting cells. Some attempts had been done on fully automation which involves hand-designed architectures with some machine knowledge [5].

To eliminate the human interaction and parameter tuning, the CNN is introduced. Convolutional Neural Network consists of a set of layers. Each layer contains one or more planes. It can even able to recognize a pattern which has not presented before, provided it resembles one of the training patterns. Shared weights help to reduce the number of free parameters. CNN provides partial invariance to translation, rotation, scale and deformation. Three features of CNN are: local receptive fields, shared weights, and spatial sub-sampling.

Following are the applications of Convolutional Neural Network which inspired the present work. Steven Nowlan and Platt [6] have introduced Convolutional Neural Network to track hand in a sequence of video frames. This gesture recognition system is able to classify whether the hand is closed or open in 99.1% of the test frames. This system can detect a hand in 99.7% of the test frames. Garcia and Delakis [7] have successfully used Convolutional Neural Networks on face detection and reported a perfect recognition rate. The system can detect highly variable face patterns, even with rotated images [7]. Lawrence et al. [8], proposed CNN using 1D Haar wavelet at the first layer. The convolutional face features for MLP (multilayer perceptron) classifier is used to recognize face. In another work, the translation invariance feature of CNN was used by Waibel et al. [9] to recognize the dynamic structure of phonemes. LeCun et al. [10] showed that CNN outperforms all other techniques as it can recognize the variability in characters, and proposed a perfect hand written character recognizer based on CNN. Jain et al. [11] has successfully used CNN for Image restoration. Turanga et al. [1] used CNN to generate affinity graph suitable for segmentation.

3   Convolutional Neural Network

Convolutional Neural Network is defined as a directed graph. The nodes correspond to the image pixels. The edges correspond to filters. CNN is a multilayer perceptron (MLP) designed specifically to recognize two-dimensional shapes with a high degree of invariance to translation, scaling, skewing, and other forms of distortion. This is the advantage of Convolutional Neural Network over fully

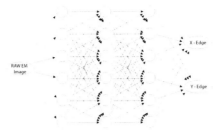

Fig. 1. Convolutional neural network

connected multilayer perceptron. The architecture is in Fig. 1. The use of weight sharing allows implementing the Convolutional Neural Network in parallel form. The reduction in the number of free parameters is achieved through the use of weight sharing. The capacity of the machine learning is thereby reduced, which in turn improves the machine's generalization ability. The adjustments to the free parameters of the network are made by using the stochastic mode of back propagation learning. Learning of CNN has two fold benefits. With the prior knowledge of the images, it is able to learn complex, high-dimensional, nonlinear mapping. Secondly, it's able to learn the syntactic weights and bias levels [12].

4   Algorithm

Initialization. The CNN contained 6 feature maps in each layer with sigmoid nonlinearities. All filters in the CNN were 5*5 in size. This led to an affinity classifier that uses a 17*17 raw image patch to classify an affinity edge. The weights are randomly selected from the elements of filters and biases from a normal distribution of standard deviation [1].

Online Stochastic Gradient Descent Learning Algorithm. Batch learning is inefficient since it is not practical to compute the gradient with respect to the entire training set for each update. Therefore, we used stochastic online learning for this problem. The back propagation algorithm for training the weights in a multi-layer net uses steepest descent minimization procedure and the sigmoid threshold function.

A Convolutional Neural Network is an alternating sequence of linear filtering and nonlinear transformation operations. The input is an EM image and output layers will contain two images, while intermediate layers (referred to as hidden layers) contain images called feature maps that are the internal computations of the algorithm. The CNN used corresponds to the directed graph, where the nodes represent images and the edges represent filters. By experimental work, it has been proved that three hidden layers are sufficient. Each hidden layer has six feature maps.

The input of the Convolutional Neural Network is the raw EM input image and the features of the image are automatically detected by the Convolutional Neural Network. CNN is learned using online stochastic gradient descent learning algorithm and it is adapted to new environments. The output of the Convolutional Neural Network gives two images. Using affinity function, the affinity graph is constructed from the edges.

Partitioning a Thresholded Affinity Graph by Connected Components. Connected components(CC) are an exceedingly simple method of graph partitioning. More sophisticated algorithms, such as spectral clustering or graph cuts, might be more robust to misclassifications of one or a few edges of the affinity graph. The advantage of this graph partitioning algorithm is its simplicity.

Our Approach. Combining the connected component algorithm with the affinity graph obtained from the Convolutional Neural Network yields a better result. From the output of CNN, our aim is to detect and localize boundaries of the image accurately.

Canny detector is insufficient to detect the boundary of the image when there is only a major change in average image brightness. In this approach, we are trying to learn real boundary of the image which is tightly peaked around the location of image boundaries marked by humans. Combine multiple cues of image to improve their detection and localization of boundaries. Thus, multiple detections in the vicinity of brightness edges produce smooth, spatially extended outputs.

5   Performance Evaluation and Results

Aim is to evaluate performance of the segmented image.
Precision is the fraction of the correct instances of the algorithm that believes to belong to the relevant subset. That is, proportion of predicted positives which are actual positive.

$$Precision = \frac{TP}{TP + FP} . \tag{1}$$

Recall is the fraction of the correct instances that actually belong to the relevant subset. That is, proportion of actual positives which are predicted positive.

$$Recall = \frac{TP}{TP + FN} . \tag{2}$$

F-score is the harmonic mean of the precision and the recall.

$$F - score = \frac{2 * precision * recall}{(precision + recall)} . \tag{3}$$

False positive rate is the proportion of absent events that yield positive test outcomes.

$$False\ positive\ rate = \frac{FP}{FP + TN} . \tag{4}$$

True positive rate measures the proportion of positives correctly classified.

$$True\ positive\ rate = \frac{TP}{TP + FN} . \tag{5}$$

Accuracy is defined as the ratio of the misclassified pixels to the total number of pixels.

$$Accuracy = \frac{TP + FN}{TP + FN + TN + FP} . \tag{6}$$

Where TP is the number of true positive predictions,
FP is the number of false positive predictions,
TN is the number of true negative predictions,
FN is the number of false negative predictions.

We demonstrate the training of Convolutional Neural Network to produce affinity graph from raw EM images. We are able to correctly predict the affinity graph when Connected Component algorithm is combined with the output of Convolutional Neural Network. Then, in the post processing step, contour of the image is detected and it is added to the image. F-score of this proposed work is obtained as 78%.

5.1   Data Set

We use the data set of the Drosophila first instar larva ventral nerve cord (VNC) with the serial section transmission electron microscopy. The microcube measures 2 x 2 x 1.5 microns approximately, with a resolution of 4 x 4 x 50 nm/pixel [13]. As a preprocessing step, the image distortion correction plugin for ImageJ [14] is used for correcting the distortion. *ImageJ* is a plugin of *TrakEM2* [14].

5.2   Results

The results are shown in Fig. 2, Fig. 3 and in the Table 1.

Table 1. Comparison of results

Method	Precision	Recall	F-score	FP	TP	Accuracy	Time
CC	0.05	0.11	.07	0.7	0.11	0.25	0.3
CC+CN	0.56	0.06	.10	0.07	0.06	0.37	0.3
Proposed combined work	0.64	1	0.78	0	1	0.64	0.3

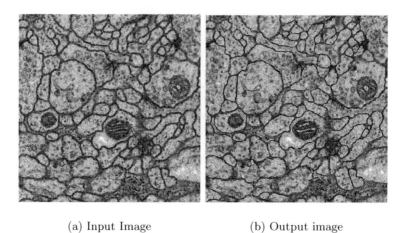

(a) Input Image   (b) Output image

Fig. 2. Results

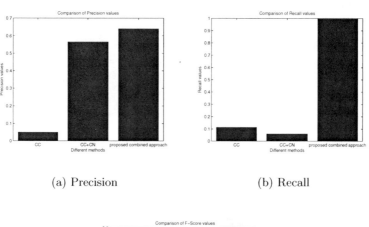

(a) Precision   (b) Recall

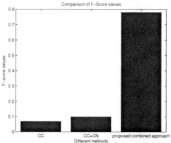

(c) F-score

Fig. 3. Various Plots

6   Conclusions

A combined Convolutional Neural Network and graph partition algorithm based segmentation approach is presented. The running time of finding the connected component is linear in the number of pixels. Therefore, this method is faster than many of the existing methods. The adjustable threshold parameter is independent of number of objects, so we need only the threshold value of the image. Thus, we conclude that this method is efficient as well as faster.

References

1. Turaga, S.C., Murray, J.F., Jain, V., Roth, F., Helmstaedter, M., Briggman, K., Denk, W., Seung, H.S.: Convolutional Networks can Learn to Generate Affinity Graphs for Image Segmentation. Neural Computation 22, 511–538 (2010)
2. Briggman, K.L., Denk, W.: Towards Neural Circuit Reconstruction with Volume Electron Microscopy Techniques. Current Opinion in Neurobiology 16, 562–570 (2006)
3. Carlbom, I., Terzopoulos, D., Harris, K.M.: Computer-Assisted Registration, Segmentation, and 3D Reconstruction from Images of Neuronal Tissue Sections. IEEE Transactions on Medical Imaging, 13, 351–362 (1994)
4. Mishchenko, Y.: Automation of 3D Reconstruction of Neural Tissue from Large Volume of Conventional Serial Section Transmission Electron Micrographs. Journal of Neuroscience Methods 176, 276–289 (2009)
5. Vasilevskiy, A., Siddiqi, K.: Flux Maximizing Geometric Flows. IEEE Transactions on Pattern Analysis and Machine Intelligence, 1565–1578 (2002)
6. Nowlan, S.J., Platt, J.C.: A Convolutional Neural Network Hand Tracker. Advances in Neural Information Processing Systems 7 (1995)
7. Garcia, C., Delakis, M.: Convolutional face finder. A Neural Architecture for Fast and Robust Face Detection. IEEE Transactions on Pattern Analysis and Machine Intelligence 26, 1408–1423 (2004)
8. Lawrence, S., Giles, C.L., Tsoi, A.C., Back, A.D.: Face Recognition: A Convolutional Neural-Network Approach. IEEE Transactions on Neural Networks 8, 98–113 (1997)
9. Waibel, A., Hanazawa, T., Hinton, G., Shikano, K., Lang, K.J.: Phoneme Recognition using Time-Delay Neural Networks. IEEE Transactions on Speech and Signal Processing 37, 328–339 (1989)
10. LeCun, Y., Bottou, L., Bengio, Y., Haffner, P.: Gradient-Based Learning Applied to Document Recognition. Proceedings of the IEEE 86, 2278–2324 (1998)
11. Jain, V., Murray, J.F., Roth, F., Turaga, S., Zhigulin, V., Briggman, K.L., Helmstaedter, M.N., Denk, W., Seung, H.S.: Supervised Learning of Image Restoration with Convolutional Networks. IEEE Press, Los Alamitos (2007)
12. Haykin, S.: Neural Networks and Learning Machines. Pearson Prentice Hall, USA (2008)
13. Cardona, A., Saalfeld, S., Preibisch, S., Schmid, B., Cheng, A., Pulokas, J., Tomancak, P., Hartenstein, V.: An Integrated Micro-and Macro-Architectural Analysis of the Drosophila Brain by Computer-Assisted Serial Section Electron Microscopy. PLoS Biol. 8: e1000502 (2010)
14. Cardona, A.: TrakEM2: An ImageJ-Based Program for Morphological Data Mining and 3D Modeling. In: Proc. ImageJ User and Developer Conference, vol. 4 (2006)

An Efficient Preprocessing Methodology for Discovering Patterns and Clustering of Web Users Using a Dynamic ART1 Neural Network

Ramya C.[1] and Kavitha G.[2]

[1] Department of Studies in Computer Science and Engineering,
U.B.D.T. College of Engineering, Davangere University, Davangere, India
[2] Lecturer, U.B.D.T.C.E, Davangere University, Davangere-04
cramyac@gmail.com

Abstract. In this paper, a complete preprocessing methodology for discovering patterns in web usage mining process to improve the quality of data by reducing the quantity of data has been proposed. A dynamic ART1 neural network clustering algorithm to group users according to their Web access patterns with its neat architecture is also proposed. Several experiments are conducted and the results show the proposed methodology reduces the size of Web log files down to 73-82% of the initial size and the proposed ART1 algorithm is dynamic and learns relatively stable quality clusters.

Keywords: Adaptive Resonance Theory (ART), ART1 Neural Network, Clustering, Preprocessing, Web Usage Mining.

1 Introduction

Web log data is usually diverse and voluminous. This data must be assembled into a consistent, integrated and comprehensive view, in order to be used for pattern discovery. Without properly cleaning, transforming and structuring the data prior to the analysis one cannot expect to find the meaningful patterns. Rushing to analyze usage data without a proper preprocessing method will lead to poor results or even to failure. So we go for preprocessing methodology [1]. The results show that the proposed methodology reduces the size of Web access log files down to 73-82% of the initial size and offers richer logs that are structured for further stages of Web Usage Mining (WUM).

We also present an ART1 based clustering algorithm to group users according to their Web access patterns. In our ART1 based clustering approach, each cluster of users is represented by a prototype vector that is a generalized representation of URLs frequently accessed by all the members of that cluster. One can control the degree of similarity between the members of each cluster by changing the value of the vigilance parameter. In our work, we analyze the clusters formed by using the ART1 technique by varying the vigilance parameter ρ between the values 0.3 and 0.5.

K.R. Venugopal and L.M. Patnaik (Eds.): ICIP 2011, CCIS 157, pp. 198–204, 2011.

2   Preprocessing Methodology

The main objectives of preprocessing are to reduce the quantity of data being analyzed while, at the same time, to enhance its quality [2]. Preprocessing comprises of the following steps Merging of Log files from Different Web Servers, Data cleaning, Identification of Users, Sessions, and Visits, Data formatting and Summarization as shown in Fig. 1.

2.1   Merging

At the beginning of the data preprocessing, the requests from all log files, put together into a joint log file with the Web server name to distinguish between requests made to different Web servers and taking into account the synchronization of Web server clocks, including time zone differences.

2.2   Data Cleaning

The second step of data preprocessing consists of removing useless requests from the log files. Since all the log entries are not valid, we need to eliminate the irrelevant entries. Usually, this process removes requests concerning non-analyzed resources such as images, multimedia files, and page style files.

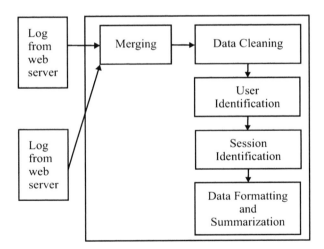

Fig. 1. Stages of Preprocessing

2.3   User Identification

In most cases, the log file provides only the computer address (name or IP) and the user agent (for the ECLF log files). For Web sites requiring user registration, the log file also contains the user login (as the third record in a log entry) that can be used for the user identification.

2.4   Session Identification

A user session is a directed list of page accesses performed by an individual user during a visit in a Web site A user may have a single (or multiple) session(s) during a period of time. The session identification problem is formulated as "Given the Web log file, capture the Web users navigation trends, typically expressed in the form of Web users sessions".

2.5   Data Formatting and Summarization

This is the last step of data preprocessing. Here, the structured file containing sessions and visits are transformed to a relational database model.

3   Clustering Methodology

A clustering algorithm takes as input a set of input vectors and gives as output a set of clusters thus mapping of each input vector to a cluster[3]. A novel based approach for dynamically grouping Web users based on their Web access patterns using ART1 NN clustering algorithm is presented in this paper. The proposed ART1 NN clustering methodology with a neat architecture is discussed.

3.1   The Clustering Model

The proposed clustering model involves two stages Feature Extraction stage and the Clustering Stage. First, the features from the preprocessed log data are extracted and a binary pattern vector P is generated. Then, ART1 NN clustering algorithm for creating the clusters in the form of prototype vectors is used. The feature extractor forms an input binary pattern vector P that is derived from the base vector D [5]. The procedure is given in Fig. 2. It generates the pattern vector which is the input vector for ART1 NN based clustering algorithm.

The architecture of ART1 NN based clustering is given in Fig. 3. Each input vector activates a winner node in the layer F2 that has highest value among the product of input vector and the bottom-up weight vector [6]. The F2 layer

```
Procedure Gen_Pattern()
Begin
      for each pattern vector P_H, where H = 1 to n
      for each element vector p_i in pattern vector P_H,
      i = 1 to m
      if URL_i requested by the host more twice then
            p_i = 1;
         else
            p_i = 0;
End
```

Fig. 2. Procedure for Generating Pattern Vector

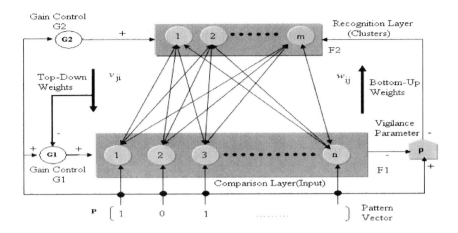

Fig. 3. Architecture of ART1 NN based Clustering

Table 1. Algorithm of ART1 NN Clustering

---

1. Initialize the vigilance parameter ρ, $0 \le \rho \le 1$, $w = 2/(1+n)$, $v = 1$ where w is $m \times n$ matrix (bottom-up weights and v is the $n \times m$ matrix (top-down weights), for n-tuple input vector and m clusters.

2. Binary unipolar input vector p is presented at input nodes. $p_i = \{0, 1\}$ for i=1,2,...,n

3. Computing matching scores $y_k^0 = \sum_{i=1}^n w_{ik} p_i$ for k=1,2,...,m. Select the best matching cluster j with $y_j^0 = Max(y_k^0)$ k=1,2,...,m.

4. Perform similarity test for the winning neuron $\dfrac{\sum_{i=1}^n v_{ij} p_i}{\|p\|_1} > \rho$, where ρ the vigilance parameter and the norm $\| p \|_1$ is the L_1 norm defined as,

$\| p \|_1 = \sum_{i=1}^n | p_i |$, if the test

is passed, the algorithm goes to step 5. If the test fails, then the algorithm goes to step 6, only if top layer has more than a single active node left otherwise, the algorithm goes to step 5.

5. Update the weight for index j passing the test (1). The updates are only for entries (i, j) where i=1,2,...m and computed as follows

$w_{ij}(t+1) = \dfrac{v_{ij}(t)p_i}{0.5 + \sum_{j=1}^n v_{ij}(t)p_i}$ and $v_{ij}(t+1) = p_i v_{ij}(t)$

This updates the weights of jth cluster (newly created or existing one). Algorithm returns to step 2.

6. The node j is deactivated by setting y_j to 0. Thus this node does not participate in the current cluster search. The algorithm goes back to step 3 and it will attempt to establish a new cluster different than j for the pattern under test.

---

then reads out the top-down expectation of the winning node to F1, where the expectation is normalized over the input pattern vector and compared with the vigilance parameter ρ. If the winner and input vector match within the tolerance allowed by the ρ, the ART1 algorithm sets the control gain G2 to 0 and updates the top-down weights corresponding to the winner. If a mismatch occurs, the gain controls G1 and G2 are set to 1 to disable the current node and process the input on another uncommitted node [7]. Once the network is stabilized, the top-down weights corresponding to each node in F2 layer represent the prototype vector for that node [8]. Summary of the steps involved in ART1 clustering algorithm is shown in Table 1.

4   Experimental Results

We have conducted several experiments on log files collected from NASA Web site during July 1995. Through these experiments, we show that our preprocessing methodology reduces significantly the size of the initial log files by eliminating unnecessary requests and increases their quality through better structuring. It

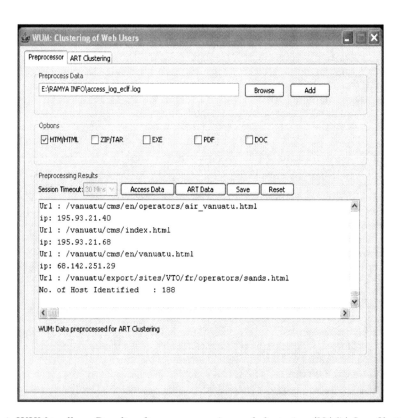

Fig. 4. WUM toolbox: Results after preprocessing and clustering (NASA Log file,1995)

Table 2. Results after Preprocessing

Website	Duration	Original Size	Size after Preprocessing	% Reduction in Size	No. of Sessions	No. of Users
NASA	$1\text{-}10^{th}$	75361 bytes	20362 bytes	72.98%	6821	5421
-	Aug 95	(7.6MB)	-	-	-	-
NASA	$20\text{-}24^{th}$	205532 bytes	57092 bytes	72.22%	16810	12525
-	July 95	(20.6MB)	-	-	-	-
Academic	$12\text{-}28^{th}$	28972 bytes	5043 bytes	82.5%	1645	936
Site	May 2001	(2.9MB)	-	-	-	-

is observed from the Table 2 that, the size of the log file is reduced to 73-82% of the initial size. The Fig. 4 shows the GUI of our toolbox with preprocessor tab and ART Clustering tab. The Preprocessor Tab allows the user to perform preprocessing operation. The ART Clustering tab allows the user to perform clustering operation. The pattern vector (corresponding to the preprocessed log file) and vigilance parameter values have to be specified as inputs. The prototype vectors of the clusters are displayed at the result panel. The results show that the proposed ART1 algorithm learns relatively stable quality clusters.

5   Conclusions

In this paper, we have presented an effective methodology for preprocessing required for WUM process. The experimental results illustrate the importance of the data preprocessing step and the effectiveness of our methodology. Next, we present ART1 clustering algorithm to group hosts according to their Web request patterns. The experimental results prove that the proposed ART1 algorithm learns relatively stable quality clusters.

References

1. Kosala, R.H., Blockeel: Web Mining Research: A Survey. Proceedings of Special Interest Group on Knowledge Discovery and Data Mining, SIGKDD 2(1), 1–15 (2000)
2. Kohavi, R., Parekh, R.: Ten Supplementary Analyses to Improve Ecommerce Web Sites. In: Proceedings of the Fifth WEBKDD Workshop (2003)
3. Cooley, R., Mobasher, B., Srivatsava, J.: Web Mining: Information and Pattern Discovery on the World Wide Web. In: ICTAI 1997 (1997)
4. Phoha, V.V., Iyengar, S.S., Kannan, R.: Faster Web Page Allocation with Neural Networks. IEEE Internet Computing 6(6), 18–26 (2002)
5. Garofalakis, M.N., Rastogi, R., Sheshadri, S., Shim, K.: Data Mining and the Web: Past, Present and Future. In: IWWIDM 1999 (1999)
6. Fu, Y., Sandhu, K., Shih, M.: Clustering of Web Users Based on Access Patterns. In: International Workshop on Web Usage Analysis and User Profiling (WEBKDD 1999), San Diego, CA (1999)

7. Zhang, T., Ramakrishnan, R., Livny, M., Birch: An Efficient Data Clustering Method for Very Large Databases. In: Proceedings of the ACM SIGMOD Conference on Management of Data, Montreal, Canada, pp. 103–114 (June 1996)
8. Cadez, I., Heckerman, D., Meek, C., Smyth, P., Whire, S.: Visualization of Navigation Patterns on a Website Using Model Based Clustering. Technical Report MSR-TR-00-18 (March 2002)
9. Paliouras, G., Papatheodorou, C., Karkaletsis, V., Spyropoulos, C.D.: Clustering the Users of Large Web Sites into Communities. In: ICML 2000, Stanford, California, pp. 719–726 (2000)
10. Xie, Y., Phoha, V.V.: Web User Clustering from Access Log Using Belief Function. In: KCAP 2001, British Columbia, Canada (October 2001)

Moving Object Segmentation Using Fuzzy C-Means Clustering Affine Parameters

Vivek Bhandari[1], Kapuriy B.R.[2], and Kuber M.M.[3]

[1] Department of Aerospace Engineering
[2] Department of Applied Mathematics
[3] Department of Computer Engineering
Defence Institute of Advanced Technology, Girinagar, Pune, India
v.bhandu@gmail.com

Abstract. Affine motion model is widely used in motion segmentation. This paper gives an approach for moving object segmentation by using Fuzzy C-Means clustering on Affine parameters. Here this algorithm has been simulated in Matlab. Fuzzy C-Means clustering has been applied on the affine parameters of the pixels. Affine parameters have been calculated from Optical Flow data. Here Lucas Kanade method has been used for Optical flow Velocity calculation. Comparison of proposed method with respect to K-Means clustering segmentation method has been presented. By proposed method reduction in segmentation computation time has been achieved to almost half of the time compared to K-Means clustering segmentation. Segmentation output of the proposed method on the test video *flower.yuv* has produced good results.

Keywords: Affine parameters, Fuzzy C-Means Clustering, K-Means Clustering, Lucas Kanade, Optical Flow.

1 Introduction

Moving object segmentation is carried out mainly by detecting the motion. This motion detection is mainly carried out either by Optical flow method or Block subtraction method between two frames. In this paper Lucas Kanade Optical Flow method has been used for motion detection. With the help of Optical Flow data Affine parameters have been computed. Similarly modelling can be done for projective and prospective parameters too. In this paper we have confined our domain to affine parameters. These affine parameters have been used by Fuzzy C-Means clustering for Moving Object Segmentation. Moving object segmentation has large area of application in the field varying from civil application to military application. It can be used for detecting certain task specific events.

2 Optical Flow

The most common method used for computing Optical flow are Lucas Kanade method and Horn and Schunck method [1], [2]. In our work we have used Lucas Kanade method for Optical flow computation. The expression for image velocity/ Optical flow is given by Eq. (1)

K.R. Venugopal and L.M. Patnaik (Eds.): ICIP 2011, CCIS 157, pp. 205–210, 2011.
© Springer-Verlag Berlin Heidelberg 2011

$$\vec{v} = [A^T W^2 A]^{-1} A^T W^2 \vec{b} . \tag{1}$$

where, $A = [\nabla I(x_1, y_1), ... \nabla I(x_N, y_N)]$ for neighbourhood N comprising $n \times n$ pixels
$W = diag[W(x_1, y_1), ... W(x_N, y_N))]$.
$\vec{b} = -(I_t(x_1, y_1), ... (x_N, y_N))$.

In order to compute optical flow, Intensity gradient with respect to x, y and t is computed. Neighbourhood window size is decided so as to calculate Optical Flow corresponding to any pixel. In the experiment two consecutive frames of test video have been taken as shown in Fig.(1) and the corresponding Optical flow computed using Lucas Kanade is plotted in Fig.(2). This optical flow data has been used in the later stage for segmentation purpose.

Fig. 1. LHS:Frame No.-200,   RHS:Frame No.-201

3   Motion Analysis

The most common type of transformations are Rigid, Affine, Projective, Prospective and Global polynomial transformation. Here in our study we have used affine transformation modelling [3], [4] of Optical flow velocity. Full velocity at each pixel location has been modelled for Affine Parameters. Affine transformation caters for shear, rotation, translation and scaling transformation. This affine transformation is composed of the cartesian operations of a scaling, a translation and a rotation.

$$\vec{p_2} = \vec{t} + sR \ \vec{p_1} . \tag{2}$$

where, $\vec{p_1}$ and $\vec{p_2}$ are the coordinate vectors of the two images; $\vec{t}$ is the translation vector; s is scale factor, and R is the rotation matrix.

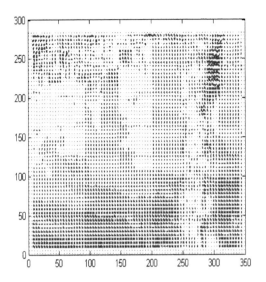

Fig. 2. Optical flow

Affine motion is defined by Eq. (3) and Eq. (4)

$$V_x(x,y) = a_{x0} + a_{xx}x + a_{xy}y. \tag{3}$$
$$V_y(x,y) = a_{y0} + a_{yx}x + a_{yy}y. \tag{4}$$

Affine parameters corresponding to i_{th} hypothesis of $\vec{V}_x$ are given in Eq. (5) and the Affine parameters of $\vec{V}_y$ are given in Eq. (6)

$$a^T_{x_i} = [\, a_{x\ 0_i},\ a_{x\ x_i},\ a_{x\ y_i}]. \tag{5}$$
$$a^T_{y_i} = [\, a_{y\ 0_i},\ a_{y\ x_i},\ a_{y\ y_i}]. \tag{6}$$
$$\phi^T = [1, x, y]. \tag{7}$$

The combination of Eq. (5) and Eq. (6) is given in Eq. (11) which forms the ith hypothesis vector in the six-Dimensional affine parameter space

$$a^T_i = [\, a_{x\ 0_i},\ a_{x\ x_i},\ a_{x\ y_i},\ a_{y\ 0_i},\ a_{y\ x_i},\ a_{y\ y_i}]. \tag{8}$$

Motion field as shown in Eq. (3) and Eq. (4) can be written as shown in Eq. (9) and Eq. (10)

$$V_x(x,y) = \phi^T\, a_{\ x_i}. \tag{9}$$
$$V_y(x,y) = \phi^T\, a_{\ y_i}. \tag{10}$$

Linear least square estimate of Affine parameters a_i for a given motion field is given by Eq. (11) for each region i

$$[\, a_{\ x_i},\ a_{\ y_i}] = [\sum_{p_i}\phi\phi^T]^{-1}\sum_{p_i}(\phi[\, V_x(x,y)\ V_y(x,y)]. \tag{11}$$

4   Proposed Work on Moving Object Segmentation

This paper presents a new approach for motion segmentation by applying Fuzzy C-Means clustering on Affine parameters for segmentation purpose. In paper [3] K-Means clustering method has been used for motion segmentation. In this paper we have recommended use of Fuzzy C-Means clustering on affine parameters for carrying out motion segmentation. There are different works using Fuzzy C-Means clustering exploiting different parameters for image segmentation. FCM iteratively moves the cluster centers to the optimised place within a dataset of Affine Parameters, by iteratively updating the cluster centers and the membership grades for each data point. The algorithm is an iterative optimization that minimizes the cost function/ objective function as defined in Eq. (12).

$$J_m = \sum_{i=1}^{N} \sum_{j=1}^{C} U_{ij}^m |X_i - C_j|^2. \tag{12}$$

where, m is any real number greater than 1, U_{ij} is the degree of membership of X_i in the cluster j, X_i is the six dimensional Affine Parameter of the i_{th} pixel, C_j is the six-dimension cluster center of the jth cluster. N is the total number of pixels which is to be partitioned in C clusters.

Membership functions and cluster centers are updated by the following.

$$U_{ij} = \frac{1}{\sum_{k=1}^{C} \frac{|X_i - C_j|}{|X_i - C_k|}^{\frac{2}{m-1}}}. \tag{13}$$

$$C_j = \frac{\sum_{i=1}^{N} U_{ij}{}^m \times X_i}{\sum_{i=1}^{N} U_{ij}}. \tag{14}$$

If $||U(k+1) - U(k)|| <$ threshold then stop; otherwise again find the membership function and cluster centers.

5   Results of Experiment

The simulation for both method i.e., the Fuzzy C-Means clustering method (proposed method)and the K-Means clustering method has been performed on the test video (flower.yuv)in Matlab. The test environment under which simulation was carried out is intel core 2 Duo, 2.26 G.Hz CPU with 32 bit Operating system. The picture size of the test video *flower. yuv* is 288 × 352 pixels. The moving object segmentation has been carried out by considering frame no. 200 and frame no. 201 of the test video *flower. yuv*. The results of segmentation by both methods are shown in Fig. 3, Fig. 4, and Fig. 5, where, LHS figures are segmented by Fuzzy C-Means clustering on Affine Parameters and the RHS figures are segmented by K-Means clustering on Affine Parameters. The comparison of both methods is shown in Table1.

Fig. 3. Segmentation using Fuzzy C-Means Clustering and K-Means Clustering (Flower bed Layer- LHS:FCM, RHS:K-Means)

Fig. 4. Segmentation using Fuzzy C-Means Clustering and K-Means Clustering (House Layer- LHS:FCM, RHS:K-Means)

Fig. 5. Segmentation using Fuzzy C-Means Clustering and K-Means Clustering (Tree Layer- LHS:Fuzzy C-Means, RHS:K-Means)

Table 1. Optical Flow and Segmentation Computation Time for Output Figures as shown in Fig. 3, Fig. 4, Fig. 5.

Segmentation Method	Optical Flow cal time(Sec)	Segmentation time(Sec)
K-Means Clustering	82.3103	331.8732
Fuzzy C-Means Clustering	82.3103	160.9266

6   Conclusions

The proposed Fuzzy C-Means algorithm for moving image segmentation is able to produce encouraging result with reduction in processing time as shown in Table 1. The segmented images can further be improved by applying pre-processing and post-processing on the subject video.

References

1. Barron, J.L., Fleet, D.J., Beauchemin, S.S.: Performance of Optical Flow Techniques. International Journal of Computer Vision, 43–77 (1994)
2. Barron, J.L., Thacker, N.A.: 2D and 3D Optical Flow, Imaging Science and Biomedical Engineering, University of Manchester (2005)
3. Wang, J.Y.A., Adelson, E.H.: Representing Moving Images with Layers. IEEE Trans. on Image Processing 3(5), 625–638 (1994)
4. orshukov, G.D., Bozdagi, G., Altunbasak, Y., Tekalp, A.M.: Motion Segmentation by Multistage Classication. IEEE Transactions on Image Processing 6(11), 1591–1594 (1997)

Age Estimation Using Gender Information

Lakshmiprabha N.S., Bhattacharya J., and Majumder S.

Surface Robotics Lab,
Central Mechanical Engineering Research Institute,
Durgapur - 713 209, West Bengal, India
{n_prabha_mech,bjhilik,sjm}@cmeri.res.in

Abstract. Estimating age from a facial image is a intriguing and exigent task. Aging changes both shape as well as texture and it is an irreversible, uncontrollable and personalized. The way of aging in male is different from female and hence the accuracy of age estimation process can be improved if it is preceded by gender classification. The work proposed in this paper takes care of this by using gender information for categorizing age range of the given face image. Appearance parameters (AAM), containing shape and texture variations is used for gender classification which is analyzed with two well known classifiers Neural Networks and Support Vector Machines (SVM). Gender classified appearance parameters are fed into male or female age estimator. Age estimation is then performed using Neural networks which classifies age range of the given face image. Experimental results on FG-NET age database demonstrate the effectiveness of the framework and validates that performance is better than existing approaches. The results also shows that appearance parameter from AAM increases the performance of the gender classification.

Keywords: Age Estimation, Active Appearance Model, Gender Classification, Neural Networks, Support Vector Machine.

1 Introduction

The human face conveys important information such as identity, expression, ethnicity, gender, age for example. Estimating age from a given face image has applications such as access control, surveillance, face recognition, age synthesis, electronic customer relationship management and thus has attracted many researchers attention. Face appearance of a person changes with the process of growing older. These changes increases the difficulty of computer based face recognition task. There are two stages of aging: (1) Early growth and development occurs from birth to adulthood where there are greater change in carniofacial growth (shape changes), (2) Adult aging from adult to old age is because of skin aging (texture changes). These changes in appearance vary from person to person and it is contributed by various factors like ancestry, health, lifestyle, race, gender, working environment, climate, decrease or increase in weight, smoking, drug use, diet, and emotional stress [1], [2].

K.R. Venugopal and L.M. Patnaik (Eds.): ICIP 2011, CCIS 157, pp. 211–216, 2011.
© Springer-Verlag Berlin Heidelberg 2011

Males and Females may also age differently as they have varying type of face aging pattern [1], [3]. This is due to the difference in makeup, hair style, accessories in female or mustache and beard in case of males. From the above facts it is assumed that the performance of the age estimator may be improved by using gender information. Thus, a new method where gender classification precedes age estimation is proposed. Gender recognition accuracy is affected significantly by aging variation [4]. This can be addressed by using appearance parameters from Active Appearances Model (AAM) [5] as input to the gender classifier.

The paper is organized in the following way, Section 2 details about the proposed method. Experimental results obtained using FG-NET database [6] is discussed in section 3.

2   Proposed Method

The proposed method consists of following steps: Face annotated images are read from the database followed by feature extraction using Active Appearance Model (AAM). AAM converts face images into appearance parameters, contains both shape and texture information. This is given as input for training the gender classifier. Depending upon the output from the gender classifier, the appearance parameters are fed into the corresponding age estimator. The block diagram of the proposed method is shown in Fig. 1(a). Gender classification is attempted with two classifiers: Neural network, Support vector machine. Age estimation is performed using Neural networks and the output is given in terms of age range.

2.1   Feature Extraction

Features from face images are extracted using Active Appearance Model (AAM) [5]. The training set consists of hand annotated face images from FG-NET database with sixty eight landmarks. Let $I = [I_1, I_2, \ldots, I_N]$ represents N training set images with landmark points as $x = [x_1, x_2, \ldots, x_N]$. Shape variations are obtained by aligning these landmark points and then Principal Components Analysis (PCA) is performed on those points. Any shape vector x in the training set can be represented as in Eq. 1.

$$x \approx \overline{x} + V_s b_s, b_s = V_s^T (x - \overline{x}). \tag{1}$$

where $\overline{x}$ is the mean shape, V_s contains the eigenvectors of largest eigenvalues (λ_s) and b_s represents weights or shape model parameters. By rewriting Eq. 1, it is possible to calculate shape model parameters corresponding to a given example. The shape can be changed by varying the elements of b_s using eigenvalues (λ_s). Given the mean face shape, the texture modeling is done by warping each training set images into the mean shape, to obtain a shape free patch. Let $g = [g_1, g_2, \ldots, g_N]$ be the shape free vectors of all the training set images. Similar to shape modeling, texture modeling is done by using PCA as in Eq. 2. where b_g is the weights or grey-level model parameter, V_g is the eigenvectors and $\overline{g}$ is

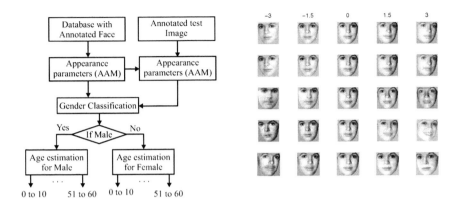

(a) Block diagram of the proposed method

(b) Effect of varying first five appearance parameters

Fig. 1. Proposed method and appearance parameters

the mean grey-level vector. Appearance model parameter can be obtained by combining shape model parameter and grey-level model parameter. Combined parameter vector is obtained by using Eq. 3. W_s is a diagonal matrix of weights for each shape parameter. PCA is applied on combined parameter vector and the appearance parameter controlling both shape and texture of the model is calculated.

$$b_g = V_g^T(g - \bar{g}). \tag{2}$$

$$b_{sg} = \begin{pmatrix} W_s b_s \\ b_g \end{pmatrix}. \tag{3}$$

$$b_{sg} = Qc. \tag{4}$$

where $Q = \begin{pmatrix} Q_s \\ Q_g \end{pmatrix}$ and c is the appearance parameter. By varying c, it is possible to achieve changes in both shape and texture. Fig. 1(b) shows the effect of varying first five appearance parameters by $\pm 3\sqrt{\lambda_{sg}}$, where λ_{sg} is the eigenvalues.

When an annotated test image (x_{test}) is given as input, it is converted into shape model parameter b_{stest} using Eq. 1 and multiplied with W_s. The test image is warped with the mean shape and converted into shape free patch. Using Eq. 2, grey-level model parameter b_{gtest} is calculated. Combining b_{stest} and b_{gtest} results in b_{sgtest} and the appearance parameter c_{test} is obtained using Eq. 4. c_{test} is used for classification purpose.

2.2 Gender Classification

The FG-NET [6] database consists of face images of people at different age. Gender recognition accuracy is affected significantly by age specially in case of young or senior faces [4]. This affects the performance of gender classifier as well as age estimation accuracy. To address this, Gender classification is performed on face appearance parameters from AAM and it is analyzed with two well known classifiers Neural Network [7] and Support Vector Machine [8], [9].

Gender Classification with Neural Network. In this paper, network consists of three layers and training is done using multilayer feedforward networks with gradient descent backpropagation algorithm. Number of input nodes is equal to the size of the feature vectors. Number of nodes in the hidden layer is experimental. 800 numbers of hidden nodes are used in this case. Number of output nodes is two. Tan-sigmoid is the transfer function used for both hidden as well as output layer. 1's and -1's are used as target values. This forms a vector called as target vector whose dimension is 2 x Y, where Y depends on the number of images in the training set. 6500 number of iteration is used for network training. 0.0001 is set as goal for the network to achieve.

The neural network is trained with the face appearance parameters (c) obtained from AAM. The face appearance parameter (c_{test}) of the test image is given as input to the network. The output from the network is checked for correctness.

Gender Classification with Support Vector Machine. A popular machine learning method Support Vector Machines (SVM) [8], [9] are devised to solve binary class pattern recognition task. The basic idea is to find a hyperplane which separates the d-dimensional data perfectly into its two classes. In many cases the data given for classification is not linearly separable. With the help of kernel, SVM represents the data into higher dimensional space where the data is easily separable.

Let N training data be $(c_1, y_1), (c_2, y_2), \ldots (c_N, y_N)$, c_i is the appearance parameters and y_i be the class label with 1 representing male and -1 representing female. The nonlinear decision surface is obtained as in Eq. 5. The SVM algorithm finds N_s support vectors s_i, coefficient weights α_i and constant b.

$$\sum_{i=1}^{N_s} \alpha_i y_i K(s_i, c) + b = 0 \tag{5}$$

$$f(c) = sign(\sum_{i=1}^{N_s} \alpha_i y_i K(s_i, c) + b) \tag{6}$$

where, $b = -\frac{1}{2}(w.c_r + w.c_s)$, c_r and c_s are support vectors satisfying $\alpha_r, \alpha_s > 0, y_r = 1, y_s = -1$. and $K(c_a, c_b) = \Phi(c_a).\Phi(c_b)$. A polynomial kernel with 2 is used as the tuning parameter. When an appearance parameters of the test image (c_{test}) is given as input, the sign of the Eq. 6 is checked for correctness.

2.3   Age Estimation

Age estimation is performed using neural networks. Gender classified face appearance parameters are given as input to the neural network and the output from the network is the age range. There are two separate age estimators, one for male and the other for female, which learns facial variation with respect to aging in male and female respectively.

The structure of the network is similar to the one explained in section 2.2. Number of input nodes is equal to size of the face appearance parameter. Number of output nodes is six (*i.e.*, $0 - 10, 11 - 20, \ldots, 51 - 60$) which indicates the age range. 1000 numbers of hidden neurons and 6500 number of iterations is used for age estimator. $1's$ and $0's$ are used as the target values, $1's$ in the position of the age range it represents and $0's$ everywhere else. The dimension of the target vectors is 6 x M (or 6 x F), where M (or F) represents number of male (or female) images. The performance of the proposed method is checked by providing appearance parameters (c_{test}) of the test image. The output is checked for correctness.

3   Experimental Results

The performance of the algorithm is tested using FG-NET database [6]. 321 images with age ranging from 5 - 69 are used in the dataset. The training set consists of 111 male and 107 female images. The test set consists of 50 male and 53 female images. The face images from the FG-NET database also have other variations such as pose, illumination, expression, self occlusion, shadow, out-of-focus etc. These variations affect the performance of the algorithm.

The recognition rate of gender classifier directly on face images using Neural network is 65.42 and using SVM is 64.679. Table 1 shows the results of gender classification performed on appearance parameters from AAM. This clearly shows that gender classification using appearance parameters increases the performance.

The proposed method is tested by providing annotated face image from both training and test set, followed by feature extraction and classification as shown in Fig. 1(a). Table 1 shows the results of gender classification, age estimation and gender classification followed by age estimation. Set A refers to gender classification using neural networks. Set B refers to gender classification using SVM. Age estimation is performed using neural networks for both cases.

The quality of images available in the FG-NET database is not that good and it affects the performance of the algorithm. Results clearly show that age estimation performed after gender classification increases the performance. The performance of the set A is higher than set B but training the neural network is

Table 1. Results of Gender classification followed by age estimation is compared with age estimation

Methods	Set A (%)	Set B (%)
Gender classification	92.523	87.850
Age estimation	72.274	72.274
Gender classification followed by age estimation	77.259	74.455

a time consuming step. Thus it is evident that incorporating gender information increases the performance of the age estimation process.

4   Conclusions and Future Work

It is easily observable from the results that the use of AAM steadily increases the performance of gender classification. Experimental results from FG-NET database show further that incorporating gender information for age estimation increases the age estimation performances. Work is in progress to modify the algorithm for age classification into more specific age ranges.

Acknowledgements

I would like to express my sincere gratitude to Mrs. S. Datta for the necessary support and assistance during various stages of work. I would also like to thank Prof. Gautam Biswas, Director of the Institute for his support and encouragement.

References

1. Fu, Y., Guo, G., Huang, T.S.: Age Synthesis and Estimation via Faces: A Survey. IEEE Transactions on Pattern Analysis And Machine Intelligence 32(11) (November 2010)
2. Patterson, E., Ricanek, K., Albert, M., Boone, E.C.: Automatic Representation of Adult Aging in Facial Images. In: Proc. 6th IASTED Int. Conf. on Visualization, Imaging, and Image Processing, pp. 171–176 (August 2006)
3. Guo, G., Fu, Y., Huang, T.S., Dyer, C.: Locally Adjusted Robust Regression for Human Age Estimation. In: Proc. IEEE Workshop Applications of Computer Vision (2008)
4. Guo, G., Dyer, C., Fu, Y., Huang, T.S.: Is Gender Recognition Affected by Age? In: IEEE Int. Workshop on Human Computer Interaction, (HCI 2009) (2009)
5. Cootes, T.F., Edwards, G.J., Taylor, C.J.: Active Appearance Models. In: Proc. European Conf. on Computer Vision, vol. 2, pp. 484–498. Springer, Heidelberg (1998)
6. The FG-NET Aging Database, http://www.fgnet.rsunit.com/.
7. Sun, Z., Yuan, X., Bebis, G., Louis, S.J.: Neural-Network-Based Gender Classification using Genetic Search for Eigen-Feature Selection. In: Proc. Int. Joint Conf. on Neural Networks, pp. 2433–2438 (2002)
8. Yang, M.H., Moghaddam, B.: Gender Classification with Support Vector Machines. In: Proc. of the Int. Conf. on Automatic Face and Gesture Recognition (FG) (2000)
9. Burges, C.J.: A Tutorial on Support Vector Machines for Pattern Recognition. Data Mining and Knowledge Discovery 2, 121–167 (1998)

Robustness of Serial and Parallel Biometric Fusion against Spoof Attacks

Zahid Akhtar[1] and Nasir Alfarid[2]

[1] Department of Electrical and Electronic Engineering, University of Cagliari (Italy)
[2] Cognizant Technology Solutions, Hyderabad (India)
z.momin@diee.unica.it

Abstract. In this paper, we empirically study the robustness of multimodal biometric systems against spoof attacks. A few recent studies have questioned, contrary to a common claim in the literature, that a multimodal biometric system in parallel fusion mode can be cracked even if a single biometric trait is spoofed. Robustness of multimodal biometric systems in serial fusion mode against spoof attacks has so far not been investigated. We compare the performance of the multimodal systems with each mode under different spoof attack scenarios. We empirically show that multimodal biometric systems in both fusion modes are not intrinsically robust against spoof attacks as believed so far. In particular, multimodal biometric systems in serial fusion mode can be even less robust than systems in parallel mode, when only the best individual matcher is spoofed. Nonetheless, systems in serial fusion mode can be more robust than systems in parallel mode, when all matchers are spoofed.

Keywords: Biometrics, Biometric Fusion, Multimodal Systems, Robustness Evaluation, Spoof Attacks.

1   Introduction

Biometrics is the automated method to recognize or to identify a person based on their physiological or behavioral traits such as face, fingerprint and so on. To deal with the security issues in the information age, individuals, governments and industries have greatly accepted and deployed biometrics as a legitimate technique. Each biometric trait is supposed to pose attributes like uniqueness, universality, acceptability and hard to forge [1]. Unfortunately, recent researches have shown that an impostor can steal, copy, capture and reproduce the biometric traits to attack the biometric systems [2,3,4]. This kind of attack, faking biometric trait input, to the system is known as *spoof attack*. Spoof attack is related to the sensor, and is also called as "direct attack".

Due to great acceptance and usage of biometric technologies based security systems, their issues about resilience and security against attacks are also raising. Several researchers are studying the vulnerabilities of biometric systems, the potential attack mechanisms with their counteractions. As pointed out in [5], a generic biometric system has eight vulnerable points that can be exploited by

K.R. Venugopal and L.M. Patnaik (Eds.): ICIP 2011, CCIS 157, pp. 217–225, 2011.
© Springer-Verlag Berlin Heidelberg 2011

an adversary to get unauthorized access to a system. Among the others, spoof attack is a growing concern. Spoof attack does not require developed technical skill and information about the system's internal operational mechanism, leading to increased number of potential attackers. For instance, 60% fake fingerprints reproduced using gum were accepted as legitimate user by the system in [2]. One possible counteraction suggested in literature is "liveness" detection (vitality testing) [4], but no method is fully matured yet.

Besides "liveness" detection, multimodal biometric systems have been proposed to enhance the recognition accuracy as well as security against attacks as compared to the unimodal (one single) biometric systems that made them up. Extensive empirical evidences have shown that they are effective to accuracy improvement. It is claimed that multimodal systems are more robust against spoof attacks, since evading several systems is more difficult than evading just one [6]. This claim implies that to evade a multimodal system it is necessary to evade *all* fused individual systems *simultaneously*. However, there is no experimental evidence to support this assumption, with the exception of [7], [8] where some evidences were provided that a multimodal biometric system in parallel fusion mode made up of a face and a fingerprint matcher can be cracked by spoofing only one of the matchers. Two possible fusion rules for parallel mode were proposed in [7] to improve robustness against spoofing attacks. Although the results were promising, the parameters on which such rules depend (the probability that each trait is subject to a spoofing attempt, and that the attempt succeeds) could be difficult to tune in practice, as pointed out in [7].

Multimodal biometric systems in serial fusion mode have advantages [9,10,11] such as : (a) the majority of the genuine users are accepted by using only one biometric trait (b) all available biometrics are required to unauthorized users, thus over coming the drawback of the systems in parallel fusion mode where all available biometrics are necessary to perform fusion, and the verification time depends on the slowest system. To the best of our knowledge, robustness of multimodal biometric systems in serial fusion mode against spoof attacks has so far not been investigated. Thus, it is of great interest to assess the performance and robustness of multimodal biometric systems against spoof attacks in serial fusion mode, as well.

In this work, we empirically investigate the possibility of evading a multimodal biometric systems in each fusion mode, by considering eight multimodal systems in serial mode and four systems with six score fusion rules in parallel mode. We specially analyze the behaviour of the systems made up of face and fingerprint matchers under spoofing scenarios when: (i) only the fingerprint trait has been spoofed; (ii) only face has been spoofed; (iii) both, fingerprint and face, have been spoofed. We compare the probability of an impostor being authenticated as genuine user under these scenarios in each fusion mode. Our results show that multimodal biometric systems in both fusion modes are not intrinsically robust against spoof attacks as believed so far. In particular, systems in serial fusion mode can be even less robust than systems in parallel mode, when only the best individual matcher is spoofed. However, systems in serial fusion mode can be more robust than systems in parallel mode, when all fused matchers are spoofed.

2   Multimodal Biometric Systems

The multimodal biometric systems considered in this paper are composed of a face and a fingerprint matchers and fusion is carried out at the matching score level. The performance of the system, at specified operating threshold value, is evaluated in terms of false acceptance rate (FAR): the percentage of accepted impostors, and false rejection rate (FRR): the percentage of rejected genuine users. Using the score distributions of impostors and genuine users ranging in [0,1] interval, the FAR and FRR are estimated, respectively, as follows:

$$FAR(s^*) = \int_{s^*}^{1} p(s|impostor)ds. \tag{1}$$

$$FRR(s^*) = \int_{0}^{s^*} p(s|genuine)ds. \tag{2}$$

2.1   Serial Fusion

We utilized the same two-stage serial fusion architecture presented in [10], as depicted in Fig. 1. The subject submits the first biometric to the system, which is processed and matched against the respective template. If the resulting score is greater than a predefined upper threshold (s_u^*), user is accepted as a genuine user. If the score is less than a predefined lower threshold (s_l^*), user is rejected as an impostor. If the score falls into the $(s_l^*, s_u^*]$ interval ("uncertainty region" - see Fig. 2), an additional biometric ("biometric 2") is required and the user is finally classified. This scheme can be extended to more than two biometrics as also pointed out in [10].

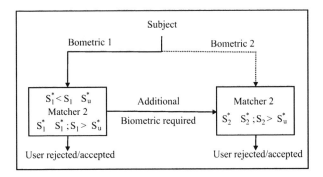

Fig. 1. The outline of multimodal biometric system in serial fusion mode

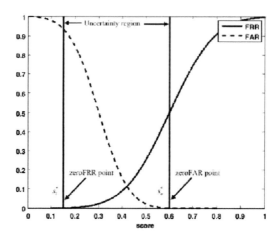

Fig. 2. FAR and FRR for each score value. The subject classification can be devoted to a secondary matcher in the uncertainty region.

2.2 Parallel Fusion

Fig. 3 depicts multimodal biometric system in parallel fusion mode with two matchers. The user has to submit the two biometrics simultaneously to the respective sensors, whose matching scores are combined through some score fusion rule. If the fused score (s) is equal or greater than a predefined threshold (s^*) then user is accepted as genuine user, otherwise classified as impostor.

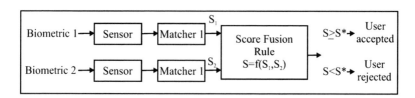

Fig. 3. The outline of multimodal biometric system in parallel fusion mode

2.3 Score Fusion Rules

We evaluated three fixed (sum, product and bayesian) and three trained (weighted sum, weighted product and exponential sum) score fusion rules. Let s_1, s_2 and s be the scores of face, fingerprint matchers and the fused score, respectively.

1. **Sum.** The sum rule is a direct summation of the matching scores produced by the matchers, and the fused score is computed as:

$$S = \sum_{i=1}^{2} s_i. \tag{3}$$

2. **Product.** The product rule is also applied directly to the matching scores produced by the matchers as:

$$S = \prod_{i=1}^{2} s_i.$$ (4)

3. **Bayesian.** The fused score by bayesian rule [12] is computed as follows:

$$s = \frac{\prod_{i=1}^{2} s_i}{\prod_{i=1}^{2} s_i + \prod_{i=1}^{2} (1 - s_i)}.$$ (5)

4. **Weighted Sum.** The weights for the weighted sum rule can be computed using linear discriminant analysis (LDA) [13]. The aim of using LDA based fusion rule is to obtain a fused score which provides minimum wthin-class and maximum between-class variations. The fused score are computed as:

$$s = \sum_{i=1}^{2} w_i s_i.$$ (6)

   where w_i is the weight of the matcher i.
5. **Exponential Sum.** The fused score of two matchers by using exponential sum is obtained as follows [14]:

$$S = \sum_{i=1}^{2} w_i exp(s_i).$$ (7)

   where w_i is the weight of biometric system i which was calculated by the same procedure discussed in weighted sum rule.
6. **Weighted Product.** The fused score of the set of two matchers using weighted product rule which is also know as logarithmic opinion pool, is computed as follows [14]:

$$S = \prod_{i=1}^{2} s_i^{w_i}.$$ (8)

The value of the weight $w_i \in [0,1]$ has been computed by maximizing the system performance on the chosen operational points, namely, by minimizing the FAR and FRR on the training data set. This rule accounts the varying discrimination ability and reliability of each matcher.

3   Experiments

3.1   Experimental Setup

We used benchmark NIST Biometric Score Set Release 1 (BSSR1) [15] data set. It contains similarity scores obtained from two different face matchers (denoted as C and G) and from one fingerprint matcher both using left and right index (denoted as RI and LI). We used set 2 and set 3 of the BSSR1 to create multimodal data sets of 3000 users, for each individual, one genuine score and 2999 impostor scores are available for each matcher and each modality. All the scores were normalized using the hyperbolic tangent method [6].

We simulated the spoof attacks at operation phase considering a worst case scenario, namely, we assume that impostors are able to exactly replicate the sample of the biometric traits of a genuine user. Therefore, to simulate a spoofed sample an impostor score was replaced with a randomly chosen genuine score. We point out that the same approach was used in [7]. Differently from [7], in this work we made no assumption about the probability of spoofing attacks and of their success. This is due to the fact that in practice it is quite difficult to quantify such probabilities, as pointed out also in [7].

Using the four sets of scores of the NIST BSSR1 data set, we fabricated four different multimodal systems in parallel fusion mode by pairing in all possible ways the face score set with the fingerprint score set. The resulting systems are therefore $FaceG - FingerprintLI$ (denoting the multimodal system made up by the face matcher G and the fingerprint matcher using the left index), $FaceG - FingerprintRI$, $FaceC - FingerprintLI$, and $FaceC - FingerprintRI$, which will be denoted for short with the corresponding symbols ($G-LI, G-RI, C-LI$ and $C-RI$). Eight multimodal systems in serial fusion mode were fabricated as follows, $G - LI$ (denoting the the face matcher G at the first stage and the fingerprint matcher using the left index at the second stage of the processing chain), $LI - G, G - RI, RI - G, C - LI, LI - C, C - RI$ and $RI - C$.

To provide high security the biometric systems operate at a low FAR operating point, we evaluated the robustness of the above multimodal systems at three different operating points: 0, 0.01% and 0.1% FAR, resulting the lowest threshold values that produce FAR on training data set equal to operating points, respectively. Accordingly, we set the lower threshold (s_l^*) in serial fusion mode to the zero FRR (see Fig. 2), which assures that genuine users are not rejected with 0% error probability (FRR=0%). All operating parameters were set on the original data sets (without spoof attacks).

3.2 Experimental Results

We report the results obtained on $G - RI, C - LI$ multimodal systems in parallel fusion mode in Tables 1 and 2 (top), respectively, using sum, weighted sum (with LDA) score fusion rules. The results obtained with product and bayesian rules were qualitatively very similar to sum rule while the results with exponential sum and weighted product rules were similar to weighted sum rule, hence are not reported. Results on $G - RI, RI - G$, and $C - LI, LI - C$ multimodal systems in serial fusion mode are reported in Tables 1 and 2 (bottom), respectively. For serial fusion mode, the results with "uncertainly region" (see Fig. 2) of interval $(s_l^*, 0.01]$ and $(s_l^*, 0.1]$, at second stage, were qualitatively similar to the result of the interval $(s_l^*, 0]$, hence we only report results of the internal $(s_l^*, 0]$.

Following observations can be made on Tables. 1 and 2.

Table 1. FAR (%) of the G-RI System in parallel fusion mode, with the Sum, Weighted Sum (top), and G-RI and RI-G Systems in serial fusion mode (bottom), when either the fingerprint, the face or both, the fingerprint and face are spoofed, at three operational points

| Operating | G-RI system in parallel fusion mode | | | | | |
| | Sum | | | W. Sum | | |
Point	Fing. Sp.	Face Sp.	Both Sp.	Fing. Sp.	Face Sp.	Both Sp.
0% FAR	67.25	0.00	77.03	68.10	0.00	70.16
0.01% FAR	82.56	0.48	89.90	83.03	0.02	84.87
0.1% FAR	86.47	3.27	93.06	88.00	0.16	88.96

| | G-RI system in serial fusion mode | | | RI-G system in serial fusion mode | | |
Operating Point	1st Stage Face Sp.	2nd Stage Fing. Sp.	Both Stages Both Sp.	1st Stage Fing. Sp.	2nd Stages Face Sp.	Both Stages Both Sp.
0% FAR	8.70	68.54	66.69	68.53	8.71	9.11
0.01% FAR	67.63	83.44	83.62	83.43	67.63	66.73
0.1% FAR	77.86	88.73	87.76	88.73	77.87	77.88

1. Our results on four multimodal systems in parallel and eight in serial fusion mode clearly show that spoofing only one biometric trait be sufficient to evade a multimodal system. For instance, from Table 1 it can be seen that even at 0.1% FAR operating point the FAR attained values up to 88.00% and 88.73% , in parallel and serial mode, respectively.

2. Spoofing only the best individual matcher (as the fingerprint one appears in both cases) creates serious security breaches. For example, in Table 1, when only the fingerprint is spoofed the FARs under attack, at 0.01% FAR operating point, are 82.56 % and 83.44%, in parallel (sum rule) and serial $(G-RI$ system) mode, respectively. Furthermore, serial mode turned out to be less resilient against best matcher spoofing as compare to parallel fusion mode.

3. In parallel fusion mode, we found that in training procedure much higher weight was always given to fingerprint matcher (the best individual one). The result was that, in trained rules, spoofing fingerprints lead to a increase in FAR even higher than in fixed rules. This means that, trained rules are less robust than fixed ones in best matcher spoofing scenario. However, trained rules are more resilient to spoof attacks than fixed rules, in the all matcher spoofing scenarios.

4. When all matcher are spoofed, systems in serial mode are more robust than in parallel fusion mode. Namely, in Table. 2 at 0.1% operating point, the FARs in serial $(C-LI)$ and parallel (weighted sum rule) fusion mode, when both face and fingerprint are spoofed, are 83.19% and 84.56%, respectively.

Table 2. FAR (%) of the $C - LI$ System in parallel fusion mode, with the Sum, Weighted Sum (top), and $C - LI$ and $LI - C$ Systems in serial fusion mode (bottom), when either the fingerprint, the face or both, the fingerprint and face are spoofed, at three operational points

Operating Point	C-LI system in parallel fusion mode					
	Sum			W. Sum		
	Fing. Sp.	Face Sp.	Both Sp.	Fing. Sp.	Face Sp.	Both Sp.
0% FAR	54.98	0.00	62.36	55.62	0.00	57.70
0.01% FAR	75.69	0.34	82.80	76.20	0.02	77.40
0.1% FAR	80.30	2.58	87.93	81.76	0.14	84.56

Operating Point	C-LI system in serial fusion mode			LI-C system in serial fusion mode		
	1st Stage	2nd Stage	Both Stages	1st Stage	2nd Stages	Both Stages
	Face Sp.	Fing. Sp.	Both Sp.	Fing. Sp.	Face Sp.	Both Sp.
0% FAR	46.42	56.53	56.15	56.53	46.47	45.90
0.01% FAR	75.46	76.50	76.42	76.50	75.48	76.12
0.1% FAR	82.00	82.54	83.19	82.53	82.01	83.38

5. In serial fusion mode, it is sufficient to keep the best matcher (fingerprint here) at the last stage in the processing chain [10], thus making system more robust against spoof attacks at first stage. Moreover, as the average verification time of parallel fusion is always equal to that of the slowest biometric, both in terms of cooperation required and matching time. Thus we argue that serial fusion mode with proper processing chain with "liveness" detection method is better choice to get the best trade-off between robustness and performance of the system.

4   Conclusions

Robustness of multimodal biometric systems against spoof attacks in serial fusion mode has been not investigated so far. In this paper, we empirical investigated and found that multimodal biometric systems, both in serial and parallel fusion mode, are not intrinsically robust against spoof attacks, as believed so far they can be evaded by spoofing *only one* biometric trait. In particular, systems in serial fusion mode can be even less robust than systems in parallel mode, when only the best individual matcher is spoofed.

In the future, we will further analyze the robustness of the systems by constructing proper large data set containing real spoof attacks, and also evaluate the robustness of the system in serial fusion mode with parallel fusion mode at it's last stage in the processing chain.

References

1. Jain, A.K., Ross, A., Prabhakar, S.: An Introduction to Biometric Recognition. IEEE Trans. on Circuits and Systems for Video Technology 14(1), 4–20 (2004)
2. Matsumoto, T., Matsumoto, H., Yamada, K., Hoshino, S.: Impact of Artificial Gummy Fingers on Fingerprint Systems. In: Proc. of SPIE. Optical Security and Counterfeit Deterrence Techniques IV, vol. 4677, pp. 275–289 (2002)
3. He, X., Lu, Y., Shi, P.: A Fake Iris Detection Method Based on FFT and Quality Assessment. In: Proc. Chinese Conf. on Pattern Recognition, pp. 316–319 (2008)
4. Kim, Y., Na, J., Yoon, S., Yi, J.: Masked Fake Face Detection using Radiance Measurements. J. Opt. Soc. Am. A, 26(4), 760–766 (2009)
5. Nalini, K.R., Jonathan, H.C., Ruud, M.B.: An analysis of Minutiae Matching Strength. In: Proc. of Third AVBPA, pp. 223–228 (2001)
6. Ross, A., Nandakumar, K., Jain, A.K.: Handbook of Multibiometrics. Springer, Heidelberg (2006)
7. Rodrigues, R.N., Ling, L.L., Govindaraju, V.: Robustness of Multimodal Biometric Methods against Spoof Attacks. J. Visual Languages and Computing 20(3), 169–179 (2009)
8. Rodrigues, R.N., Kamat, N., Govindaraju, V.: Evaluation of Biometric Spoofing in a Multimodal System. In: Proc. Fourth IEEE Int. Conf. Biometrics: Theory Applications and Systems, pp. 1–5 (2010)
9. Takabashi, K., Mimura, M., Isobe, Y., Seto, Y.: A Secure and User-Friendly Multimodal Biometric System. In: Proc. of SPIE on Biometric Technology for Human Identification, vol. 5404, pp. 12–19 (2004)
10. Marcialis, G.L., Roli, F., Didaci, L.: Personal Identity Verification by Serial Fusion of Fingerprint and Face Matchers. Pattern Recognition 42(11), 2807–2817 (2009)
11. Allano, L., Dorizzi, B., Garcia-Salicetti, S.: Tuning Cost and Performance in Multimodal Biometric Systems: A Novel and Consistent View of Fusion Strategies based on the Sequential Probability Ratio Test (SPRT). Pattern Recognition Letters 31(9), 884–890 (2010)
12. Suen, C.Y., Lam, L.: Multiple Classifier Combination Methodologies for Different Output Levels. In: Kittler, J., Roli, F. (eds.) MCS 2000. LNCS, vol. 1857, pp. 52–66. Springer, Heidelberg (2000)
13. Duda, R., Hart, P., Stork, D.: Pattern Classification. John Wiley Inc., Chichester (2001)
14. Kumar, A., Kanhangad, V., David, Z.: A New Framework for Adaptive Multimodal Biometrics Management. IEEE Trans. on Information Forensics and Security 5(1), 92–102 (2010)
15. NIST, http://www.itl.nist.gov/iad/894.03/biometricscores/index.html

Robust Two-Way Locking Protocol for Key Exchange

Shivaraj Shetty, Saumya Hegde, and Mohit P. Tahiliani

Department of Computer Science and Engineering
National Institute of Technology Karnataka, Surathkal, India
shettyshivaraj@gmail.com

Abstract. Sharing of symmetric key between the sender and receiver for encryption and decryption is considered to be one of the major issues in the communication networks. It is due to the fact that the strength of cryptosystem depends not only on the strength of the key, but also on the underlying key exchange protocol. In this paper, we propose a Robust Two-way Locking Protocol which overcomes the drawback of Diffie-Hellman key exchange protocol in terms of flexibility provided to the sender for selecting the desired key. Moreover we demonstrate the applicability of the proposed protocol in TCP handshake and compare it with Secure TCP which is based on Diffie-Hellman (DH) key exchange protocol. Based on the simulation results it is observed that Robust Two-way Locking (RoToLo) Protocol incurs negligible overhead in the network while providing greater flexibility of key selection to the sender as compared to Secure TCP.

Keywords: Diffie-Hellman, Flexibility, Key Exchange, Secure TCP.

1 Introduction

Widespread use of internet fostered by the advent of mobile computing devices has posed several challenging issues for securing data communication. Both Symmetric key cryptosystem and Asymmetric key cryptosystem are widely used by the applications of internet. However, Symmetric key cryptosystem is preferred for applications that are delay sensitive (*e.g.,*: telnet, web browsing *etc.,*) since Asymmetric cryptosystems are computation intensive.

The major concern while using Symmetric key cryptosystem is the *secure key exchange* between the communicating end hosts. Several key exchange algorithms have been proposed for the same, however, Diffie-Hellman (DH) algorithm and its variants remain the most popular and widely accepted ones. Though Diffie-Hellman algorithm and its variants [1], [2] have proved to be successful for several years, they provide limited flexibility to the end hosts in terms of key selection *i.e.,* the end hosts can select only the *key length* but not the *desired key* itself. Selecting only key length does not guarantee the desired strength of the key. Thus in this paper we propose a Robust Two-way Locking (RoToLo)

K.R. Venugopal and L.M. Patnaik (Eds.): ICIP 2011, CCIS 157, pp. 226–232, 2011.

Key Exchange Protocol that provides the flexibility of selecting the *desired key* to the end hosts.

There has been a lot of interest in enhancing the transport protocols such as Transmission Control Protocol (TCP) to provide security features for process to process communication [3], [4]. Since TCP is the most widely used transport protocol in internet for majority of the applications, it reduces the overhead of enhancing application protocols to provide security features. Thus, in this paper, we demonstrate the applicability of RoToLo Key Exchange protocol in TCP handshake procedure and compare it with Secure TCP[3] which is based on Diffie-Hellman key exchange protocol.

The remainder of the paper is organized as follows: Section 2 highlights the possible drawbacks of Diffie-Hellman key exchange protocol and the motivation for designing RoToLo key exchange protocol. The working of RoToLo key exchange protocol is described in Section 3. Section 4 explains the modifications required in TCP handshake procedure. Section 5 presents the simulation results and possible drawbacks of RoToLo key exchange protocol. Section 6 concludes the paper with future directions.

2   Motivation

Diffie-Hellman (DH) key exchange algorithm is the most widely accepted key exchange algorithm in many networking protocols including IP Security (IPsec), Secure Socket Layer (SSL) and Secure Shell (SSH). DH security depends on the difficulty in solving the Discrete Logarithm Problem (DLP) [5]. The basic working of Diffie-Hellman key exchange algorithm represented in Fig. 1.

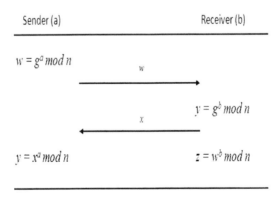

Fig. 1. Diffie-Hellman key sharing

Based on the algorithm it can be noted that in DH key exchange algorithm the strength of the shared key mainly depends on the combination of a and b.

Since a is selected and known only by sender and b is selected and known only by receiver, there is no control over the combination of a and b. Thus the major drawback of DH key exchange algorithm is that a poor combination of a and b may reduce the strength of the shared key significantly.

To overcome this drawback we propose RoToLo key exchange protocol which provides the flexibility of selecting the *desired key* to the sender. RoToLo protocol does not require key selection from the receiver. Instead it is designed to securely transfer the key selected by the sender to the receiver.

Since RoToLo protocol avoids selection of the key by the receiver (and hence a poor combination of a and b), it does not compromise with the strength of the shared key. The detailed description of RoToLo protocol is explained in the next section.

3   Robust Two-Way Locking Protocol

The proposed key exchange protocol is based on the two way locking mechanism. The name *Two way locking* stems from the fact that both sender and receiver lock (encrypt) and unlock (decrypt) the key to be shared. The proposed two way locking mechanism is *robust* since it does not compromise with the strength of the shared key. In this mechanism the sender has complete flexibility in selecting the desired key. However, unlike DH key exchange algorithm, RoToLo key exchange protocol requires three messages to be exchanged rather than two messages.

3.1   Algorithm

The proposed RoToLo key exchange algorithm is designed based on Discrete Logarithm Problem (DLP) using the concept of RSA. Sender generates its own $(e1, d1)$ pair while receiver generates its own $(e2, d2)$ pair. However, unlike RSA, in RoToLo algorithm, $\phi(n)$ is public and both pairs of e and d are private. Hence strength of RoToLo key exchange algorithm is same as that of Diffie-Hellman key exchange algorithm which is also based on DLP.

Following are some of the notations used in the proposed algorithm:

- n : large prime number
- $\phi(n) : n - 1$
- k: key to be shared, selected by sender
- $(e1, d1)$: key pair for sender; $gcd(e1, \phi(n)) = 1$ and $d1e1 \equiv 1 \, mod \, \phi(n)$
- $(e2, d2)$: key pair for receiver; $gcd(e2, \phi(n)) = 1$ and $d2e2 \equiv 1 \, mod \, \phi(n)$

The RoToLo algorithm is described as follows,

Step 1: Sender selects $e1$ and calculates the corresponding $d1$. It also selects k, the key to be shared and sends $w = k^{e1} mod \, n$ to the receiver.

Step 2: Receiver selects $e2$ and calculates the corresponding $d2$. It computes $x = w^{e2} mod\ n$ and sends it back to the sender.

Step 3: Sender computes $y = x^{d1} mod\ n$ and sends it to receiver.

Step 4: Receiver computes $w = y^{d1} mod\ n$, which is same as k to obtain the original key.

The above mentioned algorithm is represented in Fig. 2

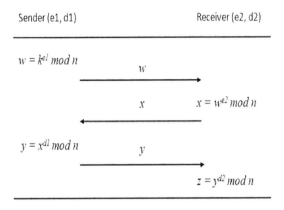

Fig. 2. RoToLo key exchange Protocol

4   Modification to TCP Handshake

The basic handshake procedure of TCP is modified so as to incorporate the proposed RoToLo key exchange protocol. The resulting TCP is named as Secure TCP with RoToLo protocol [STCP (RoToLo)] and has been implemented in Network Simulator-2 (NS-2) [6]. The modified TCP handshake procedure is explained below:

1. $w = k^{e1} mod\ n$ is sent from sender to receiver along with the SYN message.
2. $x = w^{e2} mod\ n$ is sent from receiver to sender along with the SYN+ACK message.
3. $y = x^{d1} mod\ n$ is sent from sender to receiver along with ACK message.

The handshake procedure of STCP(RoToLo) is as shown in Fig. 3. The key is inserted into the optional field of TCP header whose length is 40 bytes. The unused flag bits in TCP header are used for the negotiation between the sender and the receiver so as to use RoToLo key exchange protocol.

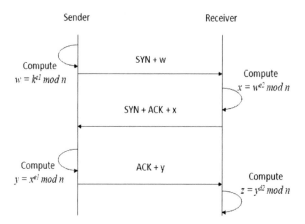

Fig. 3. STCP(RoToLo) handskahe procedure

5   Results and Analysis

In this section we compare the handshake delay of Secure TCP with STCP(DH) and STCP(RoToLo) with the handshake delay of basic TCP. Based on the results shown in Fig. 4 and Table 1 it is observed that the percentage increase in the handshake delay for STCP(DH) as compared to basic TCP is 0.37% and that of the proposed STCP(RoToLo) is 0.56%. Thus, an extra message in STCP(RoToLo) incurs negligible handshake delay while providing a greater flexibility to the user in terms of key selection.

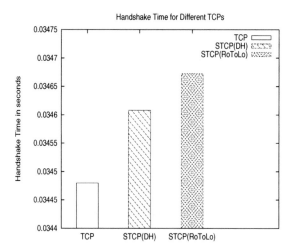

Fig. 4. Handshake time for different TCPs

Table 1. Handshake time for different TCPs

TCP	STCP(DH)	STCP(RoToLo)
0.03448s	0.034608s	0.034672s

Fig. 5 presents the handshake delay of basic TCP, STCP(DH) and STCP (RoToLo) by increasing the distance between the sender and the receiver. It can be observed that the handshake delay incurred by STCP(RoToLo) is almost similar to that of STCP(DH) though STCP(RoToLo) requires an extra message to be transmitted as compared to STCP(DH).

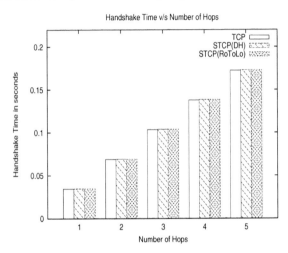

Fig. 5. Handshake time for different Hop count

6   Conclusions

In this paper we have proposed a Robust Two way Locking Protocol that provides greater flexibility to the sender in terms of key selection. Moreover we demonstrate the applicability of RoToLo key exchange protocol in TCP handshake procedure and show that the proposed algorithm incurs negligible overhead in the network. Also the unused flag bits in TCP header can be used for providing backward compatibility to Secure TCP and to change the key at a frequent interval of time for the connections that last for a long time. Although the proposed RoToLo protocol overcomes only one drawback of DH key exchange algorithm, it can be further extended to provide solutions for other drawbacks as well.

References

1. Jeong, I.R., Kwon, J.O., Lee, D.H.: Strong Diffie-Hellman-DSA Key Exchange. IEEE Communications Letters 11(5) (May 2007)
2. Prabir, B., Mourad, D., Hadi, O.: Improving the Diffie-Hellman Secure Key Exchange. In: Proceedings of the 2005 International Conference on Wireless Networks, Communications, and Mobile Computing, Wirelesscom (2005)

3. Toshiyuki, T., Suguru, Y.: Secure TCP-providing security functions in TCP layer. In: Proceedings INET 1995 (1995)
4. Swaminathan, P., Kumar, S.: On Implementing Security at the Transport Layer. In: COMSWARE (2008)
5. Nan, Li.: Research on Deffie-Hellman key Exchange Protocol. In: 2nd International Conference on Computer Engineering and Technology (ICCET) (2010)
6. Teerawat, I., Ekram, H.: Introduction to Network Simulator NS2., pp. 217–259. Springer Science, Heidelberg (2009)
7. Fang-Chun, K., Hannes, T., Fabian, M., Xiaoming, F.: Comparison Studies between Pre-Shared and Public Key Exchange Mechanisms for Transport Layer Security. In: 25th IEEE International Conference on Computer Communications. Proceedings, INFOCOM (2006)

Spam Control by Source Throttling Using Integer Factorization

Rochak Gupta, Vinay Kumar K., and Radhesh Mohandas

Department of Computer Science and Engineering
National Institute of Technology Karnataka, Surathkal, India
gupta.rochak@gmail.com

Abstract. Existing solutions for spam control that are limited to spam filtering at the receiver side underestimate the fact that the network bandwidth and processing time of the recipient email servers are wasted. To cut down these costs spam should be controlled before it reaches the receiving email server. In this paper, we propose a solution to control spam at the senders email server by throttling the client's CPU using integer factorization problem. Integer factorization is used to generate stamps as a proof of CPU cycles expended by the senders system for each email recipient. Cost of generating stamps is negligible when the client is sending emails to only a few recipients. However, as the number of recipients increases, the cost of generating stamps also increases which adversely affects the processing speed of the client. The server requires minimal processing time to verify stamps generated by the client.

Keywords: Integer Factorization, Source throttling, Spam, Spam control, Stamps.

1 Introduction

Techniques that control spam at the client side decrease only the costs associated with recipients. These techniques do not reduce the costs associated with network bandwidth to carry heavy load of spam and email servers to process spam emails.

Cost based spam control can be a solution to reduce the volume of spam by making the senders to pay for each email being sent. Nevertheless, forcing legitimate sender to pay money is not a good solution to achieve spam control. However, computational proof for spam fighting is an innovative solution that makes senders pay for sending email using computational effort rather than money [1], [2]. The idea is to make the sender pay some digital cost by performing a complex computation as evidence that email is worth receiving. This processing time is a minimal burden upon legitimate senders who send few emails every day. However, a spammer simply cannot afford to spend this additional time without slowing down spamming activity.

Our proposed solution is a cost based spam control. It controls spam at ingress point (sender email server) by throttling the client's CPU i.e., to make clients pay a stamp fee for each email recipient. The solution is based on integer factorization which is one of the most complex mathematical problems to solve.

K.R. Venugopal and L.M. Patnaik (Eds.): ICIP 2011, CCIS 157, pp. 233–239, 2011.

2   Related Work

The most common approaches are blacklist and whitelist. While whitelist is effective technique, it has several drawbacks. Any email sent by a stranger will be incorrectly classified as false positive (FP). The major flaw of blacklisting is that spammers tend to forge header information like sender information in spam emails and legitimate senders are also being added to blacklists.

Other spam filtering techniques are content based, phrase based and rule based. The problem with these techniques are that they need constant update and refinement because spammers use obfuscation techniques. Even some times constant updates do not work. One common obfuscation technique is using leet characters in content to disguise it from content based spam filters [3].

Researchers are working on spam filters to increase accuracy [4], [5]. Even though, the above mentioned approaches are good enough, they have two flaws. First, even if spam filters are fine tuned, they block or misclassified legitimate messages as spam (false positive) [6], [7]. The damage of a single false positive can be very serious [8]. Another problem is that they filter a message after it is delivered and stored in the receiver's email server. Cost of processing these emails at recipient email server and network bandwidth wastage are same.

3   Proposed Approach

The modified client server communication procedure with our proposed solution to achieve spam control is explained as follows:

1. At server, a list of prime numbers is generated and stored. Lists of composite numbers are generated by simply multiplying the prime numbers. e.g., $N= p * q$, where 'p' and 'q' are prime numbers and N is a composite number.
2. Sender composes an email and clicks on send. After the sender clicks on send, email client sends a 'helo' SMTP command and server replies with '250 ok'.
3. Client sends 'mail from' command and server replies with '250 ok' message.
4. For each recipient email id, client sends *rcpt to* command. Server maintains lists of composite numbers. For each session server selects one list and fetches a composite number from that list for each email recipient. Server injects the selected composite number with the reply message of *rcpt to*. Fig. 1 shows SMTP client server communication state diagram with our solution.
5. From each reply of *rcpt to* command, client extracts composite number injected by the email server. The client computes p and q using integer factorization algorithm given in section 5.1.
6. Client builds stamps using $<N, p, q>$ triplets. Following is format of stamps:

$$X\text{-}INTEGERFACT: p: q: N$$

   Client computes stamp for each recipient of the email, and appends the generated stamps with body of the email.
7. Client forwards the email to the sender's email server. The server extracts stamps appended with email body and verifies them. The server performs verification in two steps. In first step, the server checks whether $N = p * q$.

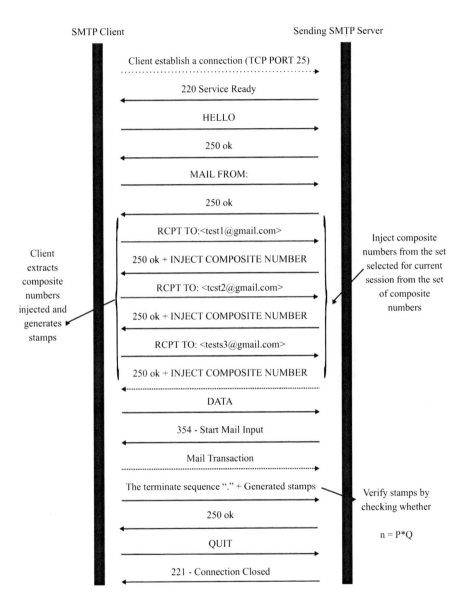

Fig. 1. SMTP Client Server Communication State Diagram with our Solution

In second step, the server stores all the composite numbers in the order they were sent and checks whether the received composite numbers are the same and in that order. The result of verification process is added as an extra header to the email, which indicates that email has passed integer factorization spam control.

4   Countermeasures against Attacks

We discuss various scenarios where a spammer tries to find the hole in proposed solution and the countermeasures that we have in place to defend such attacks.

Scenario 1: An attacker may calculate stamp once for one recipient and use the same stamp again for remaining email ids.

To counter this scenario, The server stores all the composite numbers in the order they were sent and while verifying checks whether the received composite numbers are the same and in that order.

Scenario 2: An attacker may guess the value of N by storing all possible combinations of <N, p, q> triplets.

For each session on the server side we select one list of composite numbers. When the server receives SMTP 'rcpt to' command, it chooses a composite number from selected list and appends this composite number with reply message of 'rcpt to' command. New list is selected periodically to avoid guesses. Table 1 gives details about possible composite numbers and memory requirement to store them. It is not possible for a client to store all possible combinations since it requires more than hundred million of TERA bytes memory.

Table 1. Memory required storing composite numbers

Length of Prime (Digit)	Possible n Digit Primes	Possible Composite Numbers C_2^n	Memory Required Storing Composite Numbers (TERA Byte)
7	586081	1717745176240	1.5
8	5096876	12989069931250	104
9	45086079	1016377237254081	8130
10	404204977	18446744073202533208	147573952

Scenario 3: The attacker may pre-compute all possible stamps and propagate stamps to other zombie machines.

As shown in Table 1, when we use primes of length 10 digits, nither it will be possible for attacker to store all possible numbers nor pre-compute the factors.

5   Implementation

We have implemented two modules for the Thunderbird email client and two modules for the Sendmail SMTP server. Using these modules we have modified existing client-server communication flow as mentioned in section 3. Details of these modules are discussed in the subsequent sections.

5.1 Algorithm Used for Integer Factorization

The proposed solution uses Fermats algorithm to perform the factorization task at client. This is one of the most famous factorization techniques.

5.2 Sendmail Module to Inject Composite Numbers

In order to inject composite numbers for an SMTP session, we have modified the Sendmail SMTP server. For each recipient, this module of SMTP server injects composite number into reply message of 'rcpt to' command.

5.3 Thunderbird Module to Extract Composite Numbers and to Calculate Stamps

Modified Thunderbird email client extracts composite numbers injected by the email server. This module uses algorithm given in section 5.1 for factorization. After factorization, this module generates stamp in format given in section 3.

5.4 Thunderbird Module to Append Stamps with Body Part

This module appends stamps with email body as evidence that the sender spent a certain amount of computational effort to send the email for each receiver.

5.5 Sendmail Module to Verify and to Add Extra Verification Message

Modified Sendmail server fetches stamps from email body and verifies them. Server performs verification in two steps as given in section 3. After verifying the stamps, this module adds extra header as mentioned in section 3.

6   Results

Proposed solution adds delay on the client side before the email is sent to the receiving email server. Delay depends on the number of email recipients. Fig. 2 shows Client Delay with Varying Number of Recipients. Our proposed solution depends on number of recipients but not on the mail body size. If we fix the number of recipients and vary the mail body size then we analyze that the delay on the client side remains same with or without proposed solution. Fig. 3 shows client delay with varying body size for 1 recipient. Client delay also depends on the length of composite numbers sent by the server. Fig. 4 shows the client delay with varying length of composite numbers for 20 recipients.

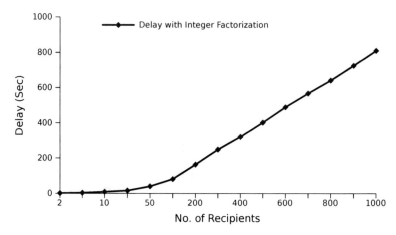

Fig. 2. Client Delay with Varying Number of Recipients

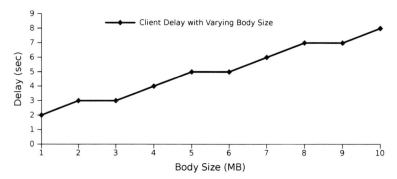

Fig. 3. Client delay with varying body size

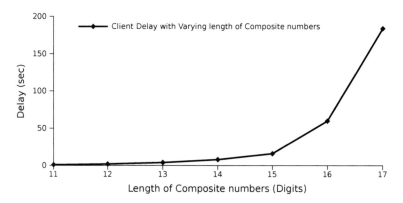

Fig. 4. Client delay with varying length of composite numbers

7   Conclusions

Proposed solution adds minor delay at the client of sending an email to each recipient. Delay is negligible when the client sends email to few recipients but reduces throughput of client by a huge factor if the client is sending an email to the large number of recipients. A spammer cannot afford to spend this additional time without slowing down spamming activity. Proposed solution adds a small overhead to the email server which is involved in the verification of stamps.

References

1. Zhong, Z., Huang, K., Li, K.: Throttling Outgoing SPAM for Webmail Services. In: Proceedings of the Second Conference on Email and Anti-Spam (June 2005)
2. Jagannath, S., Mohandas, R.: SPAM control using CPU Timestamps. In: Proceedings of the International Conference on Information Security and Artificial Intelligence (2010)
3. Hayes, B.: How many ways can you spell V1@gra? Scientific American 95(4), 298–302 (2007)
4. Yang, Y., Elfayoumy, S.: Anti-Spam Filtering Using Neural Networks and Baysian Classifiers. In: Proceedings of the 2007 IEEE International Symposium on Computational Intelligence in Robotics and Automation Jacksonville, FL, USA (June 2007)
5. Kanaris, I., Kanaris, K., Houvardas, I., Stamatatos, E.: Words vs. Character N-Grams For Anti-Spam Filtering. International Journal On Artificial Intelligence Tools, 1–20 (2006)
6. Delio, M.: Not All Asian E-Mail Is Spam. Wired News article (February 2002)
7. Williams, A.: Truth finally brought to light, Harvard acceptance letters discovered unkosher. Daily Princetonian (February 15 2002)
8. Jacob, P.: The Spam Problem: Moving Beyond RBLs,
   http://theory.whirlycott.com/~phil/antispam

Symmetric Encryption Using Sierpinski Fractal Geometry

Jhansi Rani P. and Durga Bhavani S.

Department of Computer and Information Sciences,
University of Hyderabad, Hyderabad, India
jhansirani.p@gmail.com

Abstract. Symmetric cryptography uses the same secret key for encryption and decryption. A desirable property of symmetric encryption is termed as avalanche effect by which two different keys produces different cipher text for the same message. Essential properties of fractals are sensitivity to initial conditions and self similarity, which makes two nearby keys to generate different cipher texts. Self similarity property of fractals can be exploited to produce avalanche effect. We propose a symmetric encryption algorithm which uses the fractal geometry of sierpinski triangle. We show that the keys that just differ by one bit generate different cipher texts. Cryptanalysis of the proposed algorithm shows that it is resistant to various attacks and stronger than existing encryption algorithms.

Keywords: Cipher Text, Cryptography, Fractals, Sierpinski Triangle, Symmetric Encryption.

1 Introduction

The cryptosystem in which the encryption key e is always equal to the decryption key is called a *symmetric* cryptosystem [1]. Symmetric encryption has five ingredients. *Plain text* is the original data or message which is given as input to the algorithm. *Encryption algorithm* performs various substitutions and transformations on the plain text. *Secret key* is given as input to the algorithm. The exact substitutions and transformations performed by the algorithm depend on the secret key. *Cipher text* is the scrambled message produced as output. It depends on the secret key and plain text. *Decryption algorithm* is the encryption algorithm run in reverse. It produces the plain text by taking cipher text and plain text.

Fractal is a geometric shape that is constituted of parts, each of which is at least approximately a reduced-size copy of the whole a property called self-similarity [2]. Fractals provide a potential avenue to look for secure encryptions [3]. The crucial property of sensitivity to initial conditions and self similarity prove to be very useful in this context [4]. An encryption algorithm is said to be sensitive, if two nearby keys generate different cipher texts. Hence sensitivity seems to be a required feature that satisfies the confidentiality requirement while constructing an encryption algorithm. An encryption algorithm proposed by [5]

K.R. Venugopal and L.M. Patnaik (Eds.): ICIP 2011, CCIS 157, pp. 240–245, 2011.

is vulnerable to all the four of cipher text only, known plain text, chosen plain text and chosen cipher text attacks. Several well-known encryption algorithms such as Blowfish, CAST, IDEA, RC5, Serpent, and Twofish too are not immune to attacks. We propose a novel algorithm that is resistant to all the four attacks.

Many symmetric encryption algorithms are proposed based on sensitivity of initial conditions using chaotic functions [5]. But very few are proposed using fractals [6,7,8] and fractal geometry [3]. We use fractal geometry to propose an encryption algorithm. The proposed encryption algorithm strengthens the basic idea given in [3] (unpublished).

2   Symmetric Encryption Using Sierpinski Triangle

Sierpinski triangle is a popular fractal which is generated by considering a triangle as an initiator and connecting the mid points of its three edges to form four small triangles. On iterating this process on the smaller triangles except the middle triangle, the mathematical limit set obtained is called a Sierpinski triangle [2]. For practical applications, we stop at certain n according to size of our requirement. The procedure followed for symmetric encryption is as follows: A Sierpinski triangle of required size is taken. The data that is present at the middle of a triangle is the secret key. The data which is surrounding the secret key is the plain text. The plain text and the key are placed in a chosen order such as middle, top, right and left. Based on the keys, the transformation of the plain text is carried out to obtain the encrypted text. Both the sender and receiver share the same key so this is symmetric encryption and is generally called as fractal symmetric encryption. First of all the inner triangles are filled with secret key, then the outer triangles are filled with plain text.

To elucidate the procedure in more detail, consider a sierpinski triangle which is having 81 sub triangles. The given plain text is divided into fixed size blocks of 80-bits each. Do 1-bit padding to the plain text. Secret key is of size 40-bits. Secret information shared by the sender and receiver is the secret key, order of storing the key and plain text further padding and masking operations are done if all bits in the triangle are 0's or 1's. Decryption procedure is exactly same as encryption done in reverse order.

The idea proposed by [3] (unpublished) consists of rotation operations which makes the algorithm prone to all the attacks. We strengthen the idea by mixing the bits using $\oplus$ and $\odot$ operations between the bits of plaintext and secret key respectively. Further left/right circular shift are applied which helps in randomising overall ciphertext in a significant way as seen in Step 6 of the algorithm.

2.1   Example

Plaintext : jhansirani
Plaintext in bits : 01101010011010000110000101101110011100110
110100101110010011000010110111001101001 1
Key : mango
Key in bits : 0110110101100001011011100110011101101111

Algorithm 1. Encryption Algorithm

1: Divide the plain text into fixed size blocks of 80-bits each.
2: Insert the secret key in the middle triangles in some order, say $MTRL$.
3: Insert the plain text around the middle triangle in some order, say TRL.
4: Recursively shift the sub-triangles of sierpinski triangle based on the middle bit. If the middle bit is 0, do right circular shift i.e, $T \leftarrow L$, $R \leftarrow T$ and $L \leftarrow R$. Otherwise do left circular shift i.e, $T \leftarrow R$, $R \leftarrow L$ and $L \leftarrow T$.
5: For each triangle do the following. If key $k = 0$ then $T = T \oplus K, L = L \oplus K, R = R \oplus K$. Otherwise $T = T \odot K, L = L \odot K, R = R \odot K$.
6: For each triangle do the following. If key $k = 0$, do left circular shift i.e, $T \leftarrow R$, $R \leftarrow L$ and $L \leftarrow T$. Otherwise do right circular shift i.e, $T \leftarrow L$, $R \leftarrow T$ and $L \leftarrow R$.

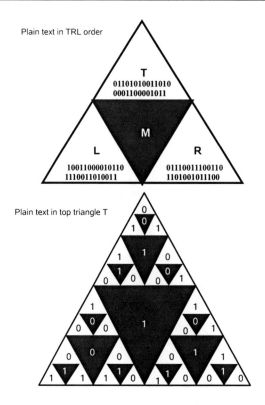

Fig. 1. Encryption Scheme

Figure 1 shows insertion of bits in $T\ R\ L$ order, and in the zoomed picture of the top triangle T, insertion the plaintext 01101010011010000110001011 along with the secret key is shown. Plain text is inserted in $T\ R\ L$ order recursively. Cipher text in bits : 11001101010100110011111000111101101111011 10111010000111111100010011001011110000100

3   Cryptanalysis

Cryptanalysis analyses the attacks that are possible based upon the characteristics of the design of the algorithm in order to deduce a specific plaintext or the secret key used.

3.1   Differential Cryptanalysis

Encryption algorithm is analysed by toggling one or two bits of secret key. Table 1 shows that the plaintexts that just differ by one or two bits generate different cipher texts. Bit difference of actual cipher text and cipher text obtained by toggling key is shown in the Table 1. For a sample we have done 10 experiments. Average bit difference is 38.2. The cipher texts obtained by changing secret key exhibit 49% of the bits different from the actual cipher text.

Table 1. Differential Cryptanalysis

Cipher text	Toggled bit position	No.of bits changed
110101011001110101000001001011111110111001 11111000011111100010101001000101011111110	1	39
110011010101001100111111000111110110111101 110111010000111111100010011001011111100010	2	39
110101011001110101000001011011111110111001 111111000011111011010101000111111111100100110	4	36
011011110001110101000001001011111110111001 11111000011111100010101001000101011111110	5	39
110101011101110010000001001011111110111001 11111000011111100010101001000101011111110	6	39
110101011001110101011000010011111110111001 11111000011111100010101001000101011111110	7	38
110101011001110101000001001111101100111001 11111000011111100010101001000101011111100	8	35
110101011001110101000001001011111110101011 10111000011111100010101001000101011111110	9	38
110101011001110101000001001011111110110011100 11111001110011110001010100100001010101011111	10	40
110101011001110101000001000011111110111001 11111000011110011111111100100010101111110	11	39

3.2   Ciphertext Only Attack

In this attack the cryptanalyst will know the encryption algorithm and the cipher text that has to be decoded. Suppose if the plaintext size is 9-bits, then the minimum number of bits in the secret key is 4-bits. So, the probability of finding the key is 1/16. Therefore the number of attempts that has to be made to find the key is 16. And if the plaintext size is of 27-bits, then the minimum number of bits in the secret key is 13-bits. So, the probability of finding the key is $1/2^{13}$. Extending the argument, if the plaintext size is 81-bits, then the minimum number of bits in the secret key is 40-bits. So, the probability of finding the key is $1/2^{40}$.

So in order to ensure security of the algorithm, we make an attack difficult we have considered the key size as 40-bits. In which case the number of alternative keys required is 2^{40}. Further we keep the order of storing the secret key in the subtriangles secret so that the number of alternative keys required rises to $24 * 2^{40}$.

3.3 Known Plaintext Attack

Here the attacker will have knowledge of the cipher text and one or more plaintext-ciphertext pairs and encryption algorithm.

Table 2, shows numbers of attempts required if the plain text size are 9, 27 and 81-bits respectively. They show that the plaintext that is known is more in size then the number of attempts will be less to find out the key.

Table 2. Known Plaintext Attack on a plaintext of different sizes

No of bits in the plain text	No of attempts required		
	9bits	27bits	81 bits
3	16	$2^5 * 256$	$24 * 2^{39}$
6	8	$2^5 * 128$	$24 * 2^{38}$
9	-	$2^5 * 64$	$24 * 2^{37}$

3.4 Chosen Plaintext/Ciphertext Attack

In the chosen plain text attack, the attacker selects the plaintext together with its ciphertext generated with the secret key. And in the chosen cipher text attack, the attacker selects the ciphertext together with its decrypted plaintext generated with the secret key. If we select a plaintext of size 9-bits we get different types of ciphertexts. We can see that for a plaintext/ cipher text of size 27-bits we get $24 * 2^9$ different types of cipher / plain texts and for a plain/ cipher text of size 81-bits we get $24 * 2^{27}$ different types of cipher / plain texts.

The proposed encryption algorithm is found to be secure against various attacks.

3.5 Comparison with DES

A desirable property of any encryption algorithm is that a small change in either plaintext or secret key should produce a significant change in the ciphertext which is called avalanche effect. We have taken plain texts of size 80-bits. Both the algorithms are run on ten plaintexts that differ by one bit. On average, the results show a difference of 34 bits in the case of DES and 38 bits for the proposed encryption algorithm. This shows that the proposed algorithm is on par with DES. Experiments have to be carried on large text messages in order to get a better idea of the strength of the algorithm.

4   Conclusions

There is immense literature that utilises chaotic functions in cryptography. To the best of authors knowledge there have not been much work on applying fractals to cryptography. In this paper a new symmetric encryption algorithm is developed that uses the strong recursive properties of sierpinski triangle and sierpinski carpet. Differential cryptanalysis is carried out to show that there is nearly 50% of diffusion with a single bit change in the plaintext. The algorithm is further analysed and shown to be resistant to all the four of cipher text only, known plain text, chosen plain text and chosen cipher text attacks. Evaluation has to be done using larger plain texts inorder to get a better estimate of the strength of the algorithm which forms part of ongoing work.

References

1. Buchmann, J.A.: Introduction to Cryptography, pp. 71–74. Springer, Heidelberg (2001)
2. Barnsley, M.F.: Fractals Everywhere. Academic Press, London (1986)
3. Peng, H., Guo, Q-p.: A Fractal Encryption Algorithm, Computer Processing and Distributing Laboratory, Wuhan University of Technology
4. Devaney, R.L.: Measure Topology and Fractal Geometry, pp. 65-75 (1990)
5. Kocarev, L.: Chaos-based Cryptography: A Brief Overview. IEEE Circuits and Systems Magazine 1(3), 6–21 (2001)
6. Kumar, S.: Public Key Cryptographic System using Mandelbrot Sets. In: IEEE Explore
7. Alia, M.A., Samsudin, A.B.: Generalized Scheme For Fractal Based Digital Signature (GFDS). IJCSNS International Journal of Computer Science and Network Security 7(7) (July 2007)
8. Rubesh Anand, P.M., Bajpai, G., Bhaskar, V.: Real-Time Symmetric Cryptography using Quaternion Julia Set. International Journal of Computer Science and Network Security 9(3), 20–26 (2009)

Recent Advances and Future Potential of Computer Aided Diagnosis of Liver Cancer on Computed Tomography Images

Megha P. Arakeri and Ram Mohana Reddy G.

Department of Information Technology
National Institute of Technology Karnataka, Surathkal, India
{meghalakshman,profgrmreddy}@gmail.com

Abstract. Liver cancer has been known as one of the deadliest diseases. It has become a major health issue in the world over the past 30 years and its occurrence has increased in the recent years. Early detection is necessary to diagnose and cure liver cancer. Advances in medical imaging and image processing techniques have greatly enhanced interpretation of medical images. Computer aided diagnosis (CAD) systems based on these techniques play a vital role in the early detection of liver cancer and hence reduce death rate. The concept of computer aided diagnosis is to provide a computer output as a second opinion in analysis of liver cancer. It assists radiologist's image interpretation by improving accuracy and consistency of radiological diagnosis and also by reducing image analysis time. The main objective of this paper is to provide an overview of recent advances in the development of CAD systems for analysis of liver cancer. Medical imaging system based on computer tomography will be focused as it is particularly suitable for detecting liver tumors. The paper begins with introduction to liver tumors and medical imaging techniques. Then the key CAD techniques developed recently for liver tumor detection, classification, case-based reasoning based on image retrieval and 3D reconstruction are presented. This article also explores the future key directions and highlights the research challenges that need to be addressed in the development of CAD system which can help the radiologist in improving the diagnostic accuracy.

Keywords: Computer Aided Diagnosis, Computed Tomography, Image Retrieval, Liver Cancer, Medical Imaging.

1 Introduction

For years, cancer has been one of the biggest threats to human life. It is expected to become the leading cause of death over the next few decades. Based on statistics from World Health Organization (WHO), deaths caused by cancer are projected to increase in the future, with an estimated 11 million people dying from cancer in the year 2030 [1]. Hence detection of this cancer in early stages becomes important to cure deadly disease. Currently, the only confirm diagnosis for the liver cancer is the needle biopsy which is an invasive technique and generally not recommended. Various imaging techniques like Computed Tomography (CT), Medical Resonance Imaging (MRI) and Ultra-Sonography (US) exist for acquiring the images of the liver [2]. Among all

K.R. Venugopal and L.M. Patnaik (Eds.): ICIP 2011, CCIS 157, pp. 246–251, 2011.
© Springer-Verlag Berlin Heidelberg 2011

these techniques CT has been identified as accurate noninvasive imaging modality in the diagnosis of liver cancer. The medical images interpreted by radiologists provide only about 75% of diagnostic accuracy. The advancements in image processing and artificial intelligence techniques have lead to the development of CAD system to ease image analysis task of radiologists. The components that can be made as part of CAD to provide complete assistance to the physician in diagnosis of liver cancer include segmentation, classification of tumor, image retrieval for case based reasoning and 3D reconstruction of tumor.

The aim of this paper is to provide an overview of recent advancements in the development of CAD systems for analysis of liver cancer and to present the major challenges in development of CAD.

This paper is organized as follows: Current techniques and related issues in different phases of CAD are discussed in section 2. Section 3 explores the various feature descriptors used in medical image retrieval systems. Finally, in section 4, the future research challenges are highlighted.

2   Computer Aided Diagnosis

A system for computer aided diagnosis of liver tumor on CT image is shown in Fig.1 . In the first step of CAD, suspicious regions of liver are detected. Next, the features such as texture, gray level intensity, shape and size of tumor are extracted which then assist the radiologist in classifying the suspicious liver region as benign or malign tissue.

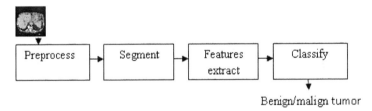

Fig. 1. Computer Aided Diagnosis System

2.1   Preprocessing

The noise can mask and blur important features in the image. Therefore, filtering techniques like median [3], wiener [4], and ICA [5] are proposed in the literature for noise elimination. However, the main problem of liver tumor detection from CT images is related to low contrast between tumor and liver intensities. Thus, contrast enhancement also should be done as part of CT image preprocessing through histogram processing as presented in [6].

2.2   Segmentation

The important task the radiologist face in medical image analysis is delineation of boundary of anatomical structures called segmentation. Kumar *et al.* [7] proposed a method that obtains a liver segmentation by using optimal gray level threshold within the mask area. The region growing is performed by extracting all pixels connected to the initial seed with intensity values within the threshold. Megha P A *et al.* [8] developed an algorithm to overcome the drawback of semi-automatic region growing by determining threshold and seed value automatically. The use of conventional watershed algorithm results in over segmentation. Jianhua Liu *et al.* [9] addresses the problem by combining watershed segmentation with region merging. H P Nagh *et al.* [10] demonstrated the use of *k*-means algorithm in clustering the medical images into several regions of interest.Mala *et al.* [11] extracts the liver tumor from liver region by applying fuzzy C-means clustering (FCM). Fuzzy membership function allows varying degree of membership and it require huge computational time. The deformable models or snake approach to image segmentation uses closed curves that deform under internal and external forces to delineate object boundaries. Rui Lu *et al.* [12] manually placed initial boundry outside the tumor region. Then the snake deforms to the tumor boundary with the minimization of energy function. The contour does not deform to the exact boundaries in the presence of blurred edges. Chetankumar *et al.* [13] formed initial contour of the snake using edge detection technique.

2.3 Feature Extraction

A reliable diagnosis of the cancer can be provided assisting the physician with computerized tissue classification. Yu-Len Huang *et al.* [14] extracted texture features on non enhanced liver CT image with 85% classification accuracy. Stavroula G *et al.* [15]improved the accuracy of the diagnosis of liver on CT images using three distinct feature sets extracted using first order statistics, spatial gray level dependence matrix and gray level difference method. The most robust features were derived from the original set using forward sequential search method. Tryphon Lambrou *et al.* [16] developed a CT liver image diagnostic system which extracts first and second order texture statistics from different scale wavelet transform coefficients and used leave-one-out method for feature selection. The feature set dimensionality can be reduced by popular methods like Principal Component Analysis (PCA) [17] and Independent Component Analysis [18].

2.4 Classification

The neural networks with their remarkable ability to derive meaning from complicated data can be used to extract patterns that are too complex to be noticed by humans. Megha P A *et al.* [19] used probabilistic neural network on CT abdominal images in conjuction with Co-occurrence texture features extracted from the segmented region and classified liver tissue as benign and malign with an accuracy of 94.6%. Chien Cheng Lee *et al.* [20] proposed classification of different types of liver tumor using support vector machine(SVM). Since SVM algorithm performs binary classification, it takes more time when many patterns have to be classified. The concept of neural network can be combined with fuzzy rules to provide fuzzy neural network [21].

3   Content Based Image Retrieval

Medical image retrieval is a very demanding application since it is expected to provide the physician a decision support for diagnosis by retrieving relevant cases. Most of the image retrieval methods used are text-based. This technique has its own disadvantages because the rich features present in an image cannot be described by keywords completely. The most effective method is content based image retrieval (CBIR) where images are retrieved based on visual similarity rather than keyword search [22].

Local features are more important than global features in medical image. Winnies Tsang *et al.* [23] used both local and global texture descriptors for tissue identification of CT abdominal images of liver and also experimented with several similarity measures. He achieved precision of 91.57% with combination of local features and Jeffery divergence similarity measure. Ajitha Gladis *et al.* [24] retrieves medical images based on image signature obtained by color histogram, texture and patterns of medical images by performing three level wavelet analyses with 97% retrieval accuracy. Pei-Cheng Cheng *et al.* [25] fills the gap between low level and high level semantics by considering the relevance feedback from the user and adjusting image weights. A comparative assessment of the performances of the medical CBIR systems is not possible as there is a lack of common database to evaluate different systems. The Image-CLEF med, is one of the few platforms to evaluate and compare different systems. The IRMA, the med-GIFT, and the VisMed projects are participants of Image-CLEF med [26]. Also,3D model of the tumor can be built for volume analysis [27].

4 Future Challeges

The future challenges in development of CAD system to assist the physician in making more accurate and reliable diagnostic decisions include:

(i) Development of fully automatic, accurate, robust and fast segmentation methods which can detect cancer in early stage. (ii) A reliable diagnosis with 100% classification should be achieved by feeding the more discriminative features of the tumor to the classifier and also by incorporating expert knowledge. (iii) There is a need to develop CBIR system which produces more meaningful results at faster retrieval rate (iv) 3D reconstruction methods that bring improvements in computation time and surface smoothness.

5 Conclusions

The use of quantitative image analysis tools, in conjunction with the experience of the physician, can improve diagnostic sensitivity and specificity and reduce interpretation time. This paper has provided extensive survey on CAD systems that have been proposed and developed in the recent years and also highlighted the future research challenges to develop more effective and efficient CAD systems that help in early diagnosis of liver cancer on computed tomography images.

References

1. World Health Organization Cancer FactSheets,
   http://www.who.int/mediacenter/factsheets/fs297/en/index.html
2. Bushberg, J.T., Anthony Seibert, J., Edmin, M., Leidholdt, J., John, M.: The Essential Physics of Medical Imaging, 2nd edn. Lippincott Williams and Williamsdition (2002)

3. Khryashchev, V.V., Priorov, A.L., Apalkov, I.V., Zvonarev, P.S.: Image Denoising using Adaptive Switching Median Filter. In: The Proceedings of IEEE International Conference on Image Processing, pp. 117–120 (2005)

4. Huang, X., Woolsey, G.A.: Image Denoising using Wiener Filtering and Wavelet Thresholding. In: The Proceedings of IEEE International Conference on Multimedia and Expo, pp. 1759–1762 (2000)

5. Jingtian, T., Xiaoli, Y., Meisen, P.: The Application of Independent Component Analysis in CT Image Denoising. In: The Proceedings of IEEE International Conference on Bioinformatics and Biomedical Engineering, pp. 1–4 (2009)

6. Ziaei., A., Yeganeh., H., Faez., K., Sargolzaei, S.: A Novel Approach for Contrast Enhancement in Biomedical Images Based on Histogram Equalization. In: The Proceedings of IEEE International Conference on BioMedical Engineering and Informatics, pp. 855–858 (2008)

7. Kumar, S.S., Moni, R.S., Rajeesh, J.: Automatic Segmentation of Liver and Tumor for CAD of Liver. Journal on Advances in Information Technology 2(1), 63–70 (2011)

8. Megha, P.A., Lakshmana, B.: Automatic Segmentation of Liver Tumor From Computed Tomography Images. In: The Proceedings of ACM International Conference and Workshop on Emerging Trends and Technology, pp. 234–238 (2010)

9. Liu, J., Wang, Z., Zhang, R.: Liver Cancer CT Image Segmentation Methods Based on Watershed Algorithm. In: The Proceedings of IEEE International Conference on Computational Intelligence and Software Engineering, vol. 1-4 (2009)

10. Nagh, H.P., Ong, S.H., Foong, K.W.C.: Medical Image Segmentation using k-means Clustering and Improved Watershed Algorithm. In: The Proceedings of IEEE Symposium on Image Analysis and Interpretation, pp. 61–65 (2006)

11. Mala, K.V., Sadasivam, Alagappan, S.: Neural Network based Texture Analysis of Liver Tumor from Computed Tomography Images. In: The Proceedings of World Academy of Science, Engineering and Technology, pp. 181–188 (2006)

12. Rui, L.U., Thng, C.H.: Tumor Volume Estimation by Semi-Automatic Segmentation Method. In: The Proceedings of IEEE International Conference on Engineering in Medicine and Biology, pp. 3296–3299 (2005)

13. Krishnamurthy, C., Jeffrey, J., Robert, J.: Snake-Based Liver Lesion Segmentation. In: The Proceedings of IEEE Symposium on Image Analysis and Interpretation, pp. 187–191 (2004)

14. Huang, Y., Chen, J.: Diagnosis of Hepatic Tumors with Texture Analysis in Non Enhanced Computed Tomography Images. Journal on Academic Radiology 13(6), 713–720 (2006)

15. Stavroula, G., Loannis, K.: Differential Diagnosis of CT Focal Liver Lesions using Texture Features, Feature Selection and Ensemble Driven Classifiers. Journal on Artificial Intelligence in Medicine 41(1), 25–37 (2007)

16. Lee, C.C., Sz, H.C., Tsai, H.M., Choo, P.: Discrimination of Liver Diseases from CT Images Based on Gabor Filters. In: The Proceedings of IEEE Symposium on Computer Based Medical Systems, pp. 203–206 (2006)

17. Poonguzhali, S., Deepalakshmi, B., Ravindran, G.: Optimal Feature Selection and Automatic Classification of Abnormal Masses in Ultrasound Liver Images. In: The Proceedings of IEEE International Conference on Signal Processing, Communications and Networking, pp. 503–506 (2007)

18. Prasad, M., Sowmya, A., Koch, I.: Efficient Feature Selection Based on Independent Component Analysis. In: The Proceedings of IEEE Conference on Intelligent Sensors, Sensor Networks and Information Processing, pp. 427–432 (2004)

19. Megha, P.A., Lakshmana, B.: Texture Based Characterization of Liver Tumor on Computed Tomography Images. In: The Proceedings of ACM International Conference and Workshop on Emerging Trends and Technology, pp. 123–127 (2011)

20. Lee, C.C., Sz, H.C.: Gabor Wavelets and SVM Classifier for Liver Diseases Classiflcation from CT Images. In: The Proceedings of IEEE International Conference on Systems, Man and Cybernetics, pp. 548–552 (2006)

21. Lin, C.T., Cheng, W.C., Liang, S.: An On-Line ICA-Mixture-Model-Based Self-Constructing Fuzzy Neaural Network. IEEE Transactions on Circuits and Systems 52(1), 207–221 (2005)

22. Muller, H., Michoux, N., Bandon, D., Antonie: A Review of Content-Based Image Retrieval Systems in Medical Applications-Clinical Benefits and Future Directions. Elsevier Journal on Medical Informatics 73, 1–23 (2004)

23. Tsang, W., Corboy, A.: Texture-based Image Retrieval for Computerized Tomography Databases. In: The Proceedings of IEEE Symposium on Computer-Based Medical systems, pp. 1–5 (2005)

24. Ajitha gladis, K.P., Ramar, K., Rajamony, J.: Content-Based Image Retrieval Using Templates of Medical Images. ICGST-GVIP Journal 10(4), 23–34 (2010)

25. Cheng, P.-C., Chien, B.-C., Ke, H.-R., Yang, W.-P.: A Two-Level Relevance Feedback Mechanism for Image Retrieval. Journal on Expert Systems with Applications 34(3), 2193–2200 (2008)

26. Mller, H., Deserno, T.M.: Content-Based Medical Image Retrieval. Springer, Heidelberg (2011)

27. Ai, H., Bo, S.: Automatic Segmentation and 3D Reconstruction of Human Liver Based on CT Image. In: The Proceedings of IEEE International Conference on Bioinformatics and Biomedical Engineering, pp. 1–4 (2010)

Computational Methods to Locate and Reconstruct Genes for Complexity Reduction in Comparative Genomics

Vidya A.[1], Usha D.[1], Rashma B.M.[1], Deepa Shenoy P.[1],
Raja K.B.[1], Venugopal K.R.[1], Iyengar S.S.[2], and Patnaik L.M.[3]

[1] Department of Computer Science and Engineering
University Visvesvaraya College of Engineering
Bangalore University, Bangalore, India
[2] Head of Wireless Sensor Networks and Robotics Research Laboratory
Department of Computer Science
Louisiana State University, Baton Rouge, USA
[3] Vice Chancellor, Defence Institute of Advanced Technology, Pune, India
vidyaananth16@gmail.com

Abstract. Discovering the functions of proteins in living organisms is an important tool for understanding cellular processes. The source data for such analysis are commonly the peptide sequences. Most common algorithms used to compare a pair of nucleotide sequence are Global alignment algorithm (Needleman-Wunch algorithm) or local alignment algorithm (Smith-Waterman algorithm). Analysis of these algorithms show that time complexity required to the above mentioned algorithms is $O(mn)$ and space complexity required is $O(mn)$, where m is size of one sequence and n is size of the other sequence. This is one of the major bottlenecks as most of the sequences are very large. The proposed Coding Region Sequence Analysis(CRSA) algorithm presents a method to reduce both time and space complexity by meaningfully reducing the size of sequences by removing not so significant *exons* using wavelet transforms. DSP techniques supply a strong basis for regions identification with three-base periodicity.

Keywords: BLAST, Coding Regions, HUMCS3, MGWT, Similarity Search.

1 Introduction

Bioinformatics has been gaining importance for their discoveries in the search for greater understanding of the organisms. With the completion of a host of genome sequencing projects, the amount of available genome data is increasing exponentially [1]. There is a greater need for development of novel methods and techniques of automatic sequencing of large volumes of DNA fragments, prediction of RNA secondary structure and construction of phylogenetic trees. A key

K.R. Venugopal and L.M. Patnaik (Eds.): ICIP 2011, CCIS 157, pp. 252–257, 2011.

step in this process is identification of all genes present in the DNA sequence. Gene Identification is to achieve the annotation in genomics and to look similar to those identified sequences[2], [3]. Different aspects of a sequence search includes search by content, search by signal (also referred as search by site), and search by similarity[4]. Computational methods are necessary to identify genes on the sequenced DNA and knowing the efficiency and reliability, the structure of genes and how they are expressed.

The task involved in the process of identification is the genomic signal processing where in the mapping of the chemical bases of DNA to a number set is achieved. A number of methods have been proposed for gene detection, based on distinctive features of protein-coding sequences. This effective DNA signal is analyzed by the Digital Signal Processing (DSP) concepts and techniques. A properly defined Fourier transform is a powerful predictor of both the existence and the reading frame of protein coding regions in DNA sequences [5].

DNA microarray technology is considered as one of the major step in genomic research due to its parallel processing feature[6]. Wavelet transforms are used to analyse DNA sequences is by taking advantage of multiscale approaches that consists of using small scales to analyze small protein coding regions, and using large scales for larger regions. Wavelet analysis is not suitable in this case since the frequency of the analyzing function varies with the scale parameter, while coding regions with Three Base-pair Periodicity (TBP) presents the same frequency content at different scales[7].

Motivation: Jesus *et* al., [7] presented Modified Gabor-Wavelet Transform (MGWT) for the identification of protein coding regions and it was tuned to analyze periodic signal components and presents the advantage of being independent of the window length. They compared the performance of the MGWT with other methods by using eukaryote data sets. The performance of MGWT is better when compared with all assessed model-independent methods in terms of identification accuracy. It is observed that combined approach of Basic Local Alignment Search Tool(BLAST) and MGWT can reduce time and space complexity by reducing the size of DNA sequence.

Contribution: CRSA algorithm proposed in this paper, reduces the time and space complexity of sequence alignemnt. The intermediate result of the algorithm is a number of homologous sequences. Time and space complexity is reduced by removing non-coding regions of both query and target sequences. The genes were reconstructed and sequence alignment is done for real time analysis.

Organization: The remainder of this paper is organized as follows: Section 2 presents the overview of Literature Survey. Section 3 describes the background. Section 4 describes the proposed method and implementation of reducing the time and space complexity of sequence similarity search. Section 5 presents the results and a comparative assessment of the proposed method with algorithms described in the literature. Concluding remarks are presented in section 6.

2   Related Work

Hwan and Choi [1] proposed the problems associated with gene identification and the prediction of gene structure in DNA sequences. A number of Predictive Methods have been developed to address these problems. Content-based methods rely on the overall, bulk properties of a sequence in making a determination [8]. Characteristics considered here include how often particular codons are used, the periodicity of repeats, and the compositional complexity of the sequence. Because different organisms use synonymous codons with different frequency, such clues can provide insight into determining regions that are more likely to be exons. Lopez-Villasenor et al., [9] proposed the studies consisting of statistical analysis that has the capacity to detect sequence periodicities in DNA.

Tiwari, et al., [5] investigated a Fourier technique based on a distinctive feature of protein-coding regions of DNA sequences, like the existence of short-range correlations in the nucleotide arrangement. The most promising of these is a $1/3$ periodicity, which is present in coding sequences. The presence of this periodicity can be seen most directly through the Fourier analysis. Authors focuses on the relative strength of this periodicity, which has been used later in order to form a simple technique to predict genes (with and without introns) in unknown genomic sequences of any organism.

Zhang et al., [6] presented an overview of applications of signal processing techniques for DNA detection, structure prediction, feature extraction and classification of differentially expressed genes.

3   Background

Identification of protein coding regions is an important topic in genomic sequence analysis. Model-Independent methods are not suitable due to their dependence on predefined window length required for a local analysis of a DNA region. Modified Gabor-wavelet Transform (MGWT) proposed by Jesus P et al., [7] for the identification of protein coding regions outperforms all assessed model-independent methods with respect to identification accuracy. This method avoids identification errors but also makes a tool available for detailed exploration of the nucleotide occurrence. A more precise identification of short coding regions is allowed in MGWT. The major problem in large scale data analysis is time and space complexity. With the application of the MGWT sequence length can by reduced by identification of protein coding regions and reconstruction of genes, which greatly enhances the reduction of time and space complexity in genomic data analysis.

4   The Proposed Method

4.1   Problem Statement

Given a raw DNA sequence, the objectives are:
(i) To find a homologous sequence of biological importance.

(ii) To identify a protein coding region.
(iii) To reduce time and space complexity of sequence alignment.

4.2   Algorithm

The raw DNA sequence identified cannot be directly subjected under BLAST. The FASTA format of the DNA sequence has to be fed to BLAST[10].The algorithm proposed Coding Region Sequence Analysis(CRSA) first analyses the sequences withot removing the coding regions. For the second time the algorithm analyses the sequences without non-coding regions.

Table 1. Algorithm: Coding Region Sequence Analysis(CRSA)

Step1: Obtain the FASTA format of the query sequence.
Step2: Find homologous gene for the same by blasting the query sequence.
Step3: Compare query sequence with homologous sequence using Needleman
         Wunch and Smith-Waterman algorithms using dynamic programming.
Step4: Record the result of comparison of two sequences.
Step5: Remove non-coding region by reconstructing Gene sequence
         using wavelet transform.
Step6: After removing non-coding regions from both query and target
         sequence, compare query and target sequences using
         Needleman Wunch and Smith-Waterman algorithms.
Step7: Record the result of comparison of two sequences
         after removing non-coding regions.

4.3   Implementation

We focused our study on the analysis of DNA sequences of Eukaryotics. Eukaryotics has been particularily considered for study in the context of coding region identification. For a detailed analysis, we used a sequence Human Chorionic Somatomammotropin hCS-3 gene(HUMCS3)[10]. HUMCS3 is a polypeptide placental hormone. Its function and structure is similar to that of human growth hormone. The target sequence for the further alignment function was identified. Comparison of query sequence with target sequence using Needleman Wunch and Smith-Waterman algorithms using dynamic programming was carried out[11].

   For the identification of coding regions on a given DNA sequence the following method is used [7]: (i) Numerically map the DNA sequence to four binary sequences. (ii) For each binary sequence apply the MGWT. (iii)Sequences spectra has to be projected onto the position axis and (iv) Thresholding the projection coefficients for location of the edges among coding regions. After removing non-coding regions from both query and target sequence, comparison of query and target sequences was done using Needleman Wunch and Smith-Waterman algorithms[10].

5   Results and Discussions

The FASTA format of the raw DNA sequence HUMCS3, has been subjected under BLAST[10] for the identification of the homologus sequence, which has resulted in a number of sequences. The homologous sequence obtained from BLAST is in good agreement with Homo sapiens placental lactogen hormone precursor (CSH1) gene, complete cds(HUMPLA). It modifies the metabolic state of the mother during pregnancy to supply the energy to the fetus. HUMPLA is considered as the target sequence with a 97% similarity against the query sequence. The two sequences have been aligned for similarity search[11]. The MGWT method extracts all *exons* and *introns*. The non-coding regions were removed using MGWT[7]. The protein coding regions of both query and target sequences are as shown in the Table 2.

The identity and similarity of query sequence and the target sequence was 90.6% before removal of the non-coding regions. The score of similarity search is found to be 13213.5. The Smith Waterman approach has minimum number of gaps when compared to Needleman Wunch approach. After removing the non-coding regions, the reconstructed genes are again aligned for similarity search[11]. The result obtained is depicted in Table 3.

The percentage of identity is found to be 90.0% in Needleman and Wunch algorithm, whereas it is 98.0% in Smith-Waterman approach. The percentage of similarity is 90.3% in Needleman and Wunch algorithm and it is found to be 98.0% in Smith-Waterman approach. The number of gaps were reduced to 3 in case of Smith waterman approach. The score after removing the non-coding regions is found to be 965. From the results obtained we observe that the similairty of the two sequences is almost equal in both the approaches. The time and space complexity of the sequence alignment is reduced in this approach.

Table 2. Protein Coding Region of HUMCS3 and HUMPLA

HUMCS3		HUMPLA	
Base Pair Count	No.of Base Pairs	Base Pair Count	No.of Base Pairs
1:1240-1261	22bp	1:1224-1273	50bp
2:1380-1582	203bp	2:1385-1595	211bp
3:1838-2029	192bp	3:1830-2019	190bp

Table 3. Results Obtained Before and After Removal of Non-Coding Regions

Factors	Before Removal		After Removal	
	HUMCS3	HUMPLA	HUMCS3	HUMPLA
	Needle	Water	Needle	Water
Length	2979	2754	217	200
Identity	2700/2979 (90.6%)	2700/2754 (98.0%)	196/217 (90.0%)	196/200 (98.0%)
Similarity	2700/2979 (90.6%)	2700/2754 (98.0%)	196/217 (90.3%)	196/200 (98.0%)
Gaps	251/2979 (8.4%)	26/2754 (0.9%)	20/217 (9.2%)	3/200 (1.5%)
Score	13213.5	3213.5	965.0	965.0

6   Conclusions

The role of signal processing in genomics is quite important. In the present work, a wavelet transformed method is adopted for finding coding regions in a query sequence (HUMCS3). Homologous sequence is found using BLAST. Homologous sequence HUMPLA is in good agreement with HUMCS3. A modified Gabor Wavelet Transform is adopted to remove the non-coding regions. The time and space complexity of sequence alignment is greatly reduced after removing non-coding regions.

References

1. Do, J.H., Choi, D.K.: Computational Approaches to Gene Prediction. The J. Microbiology 44(2), 137–144 (2006)
2. Zhang, M.Q.: Computational Prediction of Eukaryotic Protein Coding Genes. Nature Rev. Genetics 3(9), 698–709 (2002)
3. Dougherty, E.R., Shmulevich, I., Chen, J., Jane Wang, Z.: Genomic Signal Processing and Statistics, vol. 2. Hindawi Publishing Corp., (2005)
4. Blanco, E., Guigo, R.: Predictive Methods using DNA Sequences, Bioinformatics: A Practical Guide to the Analysis of Genes and Proteins, 3rd edn. John Wiley and Sons, Inc., Chichester (2004)
5. Tiwari, S., Ramachandran, S., Bhattacharya, A., Bhattacharya, S., Ramaswamy, R.: Prediction of Probable Genes by Fourier Analysis of Genomic Sequences. Bioinformatics 13(3), 263–270 (1997)
6. Zhang, X., Chen, F., Zhang, Y., Agner, S.C., Akay, M., Lu, Z., Waye, M. M. Y., Tsui, S. K.: Signal Processing Techniques in Genomic Engineering. In: IEEE, pp. 1822–1833 (2002)
7. Mena-Chalco, J.P., Carrer, H., Zena,Y., Cesar Jr., R.M.: Identification of Protein Coding Regions using the Modified Gabor-Wavelet Transform. IEEE/AMC Transactions on Computational Biology and Bioinformatics 5(2) (2008)
8. Baxevanis, A.D., Francis Ouellette, F.B.: Bioinformatics: A Practical Guide to the Analysis of Genes and Proteins, 2nd edn. A John Wiley and Sons, Inc., Chichester (2001)
9. Lopez-Villasenor, I., Jose, M.V., Sanchez, J.: Three-Base Periodicity Patterns and Self-Similarity in Whole Bacterial Chromosomes. Biochemical and Biophysical Research Comm. 325(2), 467–478 (2004)
10. National Center for Biotechnology Information, http://ncbi.nlm.nih.gov
11. http://www.ebi.ac.uk/Tools/Psa/

Identifying an Appropriate Requirements Prioritization Methodology Using Fuzzy Decision-Making

Gaur Vibha and Soni Anuja

Department of Computer Science, University of Delhi
{3.vibha,30.anuja}@gmail.com

Abstract. Requirements prioritization focuses primarily on determining right classification of requirements to meet stakeholders' apprehensions. But unless a rationally sound prioritization process is adopted, prioritizing requirements may become an arbitrary and unnecessary futile exercise. The key objective of the proposed work is to evaluate prioritization methods from literature and assist developer in identifying most suitable prioritization method. To comprehend the needs of stakeholders, this work captures the fuzzy requirements from stakeholders and employs Fuzzy Multi-Criteria Decision-Making approach to yield a rapid selection of an appropriate prioritization method. This will assist the developer to address stakeholders' expectations without squandering resources and hence in developing a system of high quality.

Keywords: Asymptotic Complexity, Attributes, Fuzzy Requirements, Requirements Prioritization, Stakeholders.

1 Introduction

Requirements prioritization is emerging as a critical and essential but challenging activity in software development. Requirements prioritization involves identifying most important requirements from the exhaustive list of requirements, both significant and trivial [1]. In case of a small project, industry may fine-tune with any of the informal technique for requirements prioritization. But for large projects, thousands of requirements with hundred of stakeholders may require a formal and well defined requirements prioritization method. This should address a number of issues *viz.*, size of the project, conflicts resolution, multiple perspectives and fuzzy concerns of stakeholders [1], [2], etc.. Various requirements prioritization techniques have been reported in literature [2-11]. Wieger' method takes account of various concerns of stakeholders with respect to cost, value, risk and penalty associated with requirements [2], [7]. Priority assessment method contemplates multiple perspectives of stakeholders and utilizes the concept of correlation to compute weighted priorities of requirements [4]. Analytical hierarchy Process is a Multi-Criteria Decision-Making technique with respect to a number of parameters that involves pair wise comparison of requirements

K.R. Venugopal and L.M. Patnaik (Eds.): ICIP 2011, CCIS 157, pp. 258–268, 2011.

[3], [11]. TOPSIS is also a Multi-Criteria Decision-Making method suitable for small sized projects where no hierarchical decisions are required [5]. Fuzzy AHP resolves the fuzziness associated with requirements by a single decision-maker [9], [10]. Requirements triage method expresses various concerns of stakeholders with respect to feature sets $viz.$, business goals, crosscutting etc..[8]. To resolve the feasibility problem and stakeholders' fuzzy concerns, an integrated approach for requirements prioritization was undertaken in our previous work with the objective of satisfying all stakeholders [6].

It is observed that none of the prioritization methods may be perfect to meet simultaneously all the requirements of an application. A most appropriate prioritization method for one application may not be a perfect fit for another application. A wrong selection of a requirements prioritization method may result in wastage of resources resulting in customers' dissatisfaction. This requires a methodology to identify a prioritization method that would address two aspects: (i) the assessment of attributes of an application and (ii) the characteristics exhibited by various prioritization methods. As these two aspects mentioned are often vague and ambiguous, therefore can be expressed in linguistic terms. This paper employs Fuzzy Decision Making in designing the proposed technique for identifying an appropriate requirements prioritization method that appears to be a logical choice.

The overall objective of this work is twofold: to evaluate various prioritization methods with respect to multiple attributes and to identify the prioritization method most suitable to an application. The rest of this paper is organized as follows. The section 2 gives overview of FMCDM. Section 3 evaluates these prioritization methods from literature against various characteristics and asymptotic complexity. Section 4 employs FMCDM to identify an appropriate prioritization method. Section 5 illustrates the proposed method with an experimental study and finally section 6 concludes the paper.

2   Fuzzy Multi-Criteria Decision-Making Method (FMCDM)

Multi-Criteria Decision-Making is an analytic method to necessitate the consideration of different courses of action under a number of criteria [12]. MCDM is assumed to yield the best choice out of relevant alternatives $X = (X_1, X_2 ..... X_n)$ with respect to a number of criteria $C = (C_1, C_2 ..... C_n)$. Various Multi Criteria Decision Making methods have been reported in literature $viz.$, AHP, Fuzzy AHP, TOPSIS etc.. Out of these TOPSIS is very simple and easy to implement. It is used when the user prefers a simple ranking approach [5], [13], [14].

As the appraisal of attributes required in an application and various characteristics of requirements prioritization methods are often subjective and require no hierarchical decision making, therefore this work employs TOPSIS method accompanied with few fuzzy operations to identify an appropriate prioritization method. According to this technique, the best alternative would be the one that is nearest to the positive ideal solution [5]. The positive ideal solution is a solution that maximizes the desired and minimizes undesired characteristics, whereas the negative ideal solution maximizes the undesired and minimizes the desired characteristics [5], [14]. The distance measure between two triangular fuzzy numbers in TOPSIS, employed in this work can be calculated using the vertex method (Chen, 2000) as follows [14]:

$$d(\widetilde{e}, \widetilde{f}) = \sqrt{1\backslash3[(e_1 - f_1)^2 + (e_2 - f_2)^2 + (e_3 - f_3)^2]}. \tag{1}$$

if $\widetilde{e}=(e_1,e_2,e_3)$ and $\widetilde{f}=(f_1,f_2,f_3)$ are two positive Triangular Fuzzy Numbers (TFNs) and p is a scalar value then, the various fuzzy operations on $\widetilde{e}$ and $\widetilde{f}$ employed in this work are given below [5], [14].

$$(\widetilde{e} + \widetilde{f}) = (e_1 + f_1, e_2 + f_2, e_3 + f_3). \tag{2}$$

$$(\widetilde{e} - \widetilde{f}) = (e_1 - f_1, e_2 - f_2, e_3 - f_3). \tag{3}$$

$$(\widetilde{e} * \widetilde{f}) = (e_1 f_1, e_2 f_2, e_3 f_3). \tag{4}$$

$$\widetilde{e}\backslash p = (e_1\backslash p, e_2\backslash p, e_3\backslash p). \tag{5}$$

The subsequent section evaluates above described requirements prioritization methods against a number of attributes identified.

3   Evaluating Requirements Prioritization Methods

The primary objective and challenge before any prioritization method is to ensure the delivery of most essential functionality on time while meeting high customer expectations and limited resources [11]. Presently a number of prioritization methods available in literature, may roughly be divided in two categories: methods based on Eq. 1 multiple criteria and Eq. 2 negotiation concept [7]. AHP, Fuzzy AHP, TOPSIS and Wieger's method belong to first category and priority assessment encompasses the negotiation approach to compute final priority of requirements. The integrated approach involves both as it satisfies all stakeholders with multiple criteria in the form of conflicting requirements. Requirements triage consists of various clusters *viz.*, feature sets, non functional requirements and business goals that may be treated as multiple criteria. The subsequent subsections evaluate various requirements prioritization methods against asymptotic complexity and multiple characteristics of an application *viz.*, size of the project, feasibility estimation, feature sets and conflicts resolution etc..

3.1   Complexity Analysis

This subsection analyses requirements prioritization methods *viz.*, AHP, wieger's method, Fuzzy AHP, priority assessment, requirements triage, integrated Approach and TOPSIS with respect to their asymptotic complexity. The upper bound of asymptotic complexity using big-Oh notation of all these prioritization methods was computed [15] as $O(n^2 \text{ x } m)$, $O(n)$, $O(n^2 \text{ x } m)$, $O(n^3/s^2)$, $O(n^3)$, $O(m^3 \text{ x } s)+ O(m \text{ x } n)$, $O(m \text{ x } m)$ respectively where number of conflicting requirements (m) is significantly lesser than number of candidate requirements (n) with number of stakeholders(s). It is clear from Fig. 1 that the wieger's and TOPSIS are the prioritisation methods with less complexity. If the least upper bound of asymptotic complexity $O(n)$ of weiger's method considered as an informal method is overlooked, then asymptotic complexity of TOPSIS is observed significantly less compared to other prioritization methods as shown in Fig. 1. But, TOPSIS is considered as a simple Multi-Criteria Decision-Making method suitable for small projects which does not deal with various stakeholders' concerns [5], therefore in spite of having slightly higher complexity in comparison to wieger's and TOPSIS methods and significantly lesser than remaining ones, an integrated approach appears to be one of the most suited methods in resolving stakeholders' individual and diverse concerns.

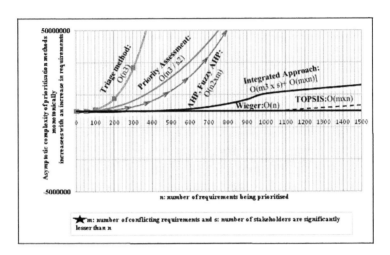

Fig. 1. Prioritization methods compared against complexity parameter

3.2   Comparative Analysis

Software requirements need to be prioritized when the elicitation process has produced sufficiently large number of requirements than can be implemented at once [1]. There exist a number of approaches for requirements prioritization. However, all are not suitable for every kind of application, therefore this subsection investigates various prioritization methods taken from literature [2-11] and illustrates their comparative analysis which would further assist developer in identifying most appropriate method for an application.

Ease of use: The requirements prioritization methods *viz.*, AHP, Fuzzy AHP, TOPSIS, priority assessment, requirements triage and integrated approach are easy to operate due to systematic and analytical guidelines. Wieger's method appears to be informal method due to lack of clarity for specifying the scales and missing structured directives [7].

Core concept: The requirements prioritization methods AHP and Fuzzy AHP work on the concept of pair wise comparison, TOPSIS employs distance measure, wieger's method utilizes value estimation and piority assessment involves multiple perspectives of stakeholders for obtaining prioritized list of requirements. Integrated approach incorporates agent cards, tasks and goals while triage method uses various clusters of feature sets etc..

Prioritization factors: In case of requirements prioritization methods AHP, Fuzzy AHP and TOPSIS, various prioritization factors may be specific to problem domain. Wieger's method addresses prioritization of requirements with respect to cost, value, risk and penalty parameters while priority assessment incorporates high level requirements *viz.* usability, security, reliability that further are mapped to low level requirements. Integrated approach incorporates various criteria formulated in the form of conflicting requirements *viz.* cost, schedule, risk etc., and triage method utilizes various clusters *viz.* feature sets, non functional requirements, business goals etc..

Automation: AHP and Fuzzy AHP both can be automated but requires a lot of efforts in pair wise comparison. wieger's method can partially be automated due to missing guidelines. TOPSIS, priority assessment, triage method and integrated approach can be automated to obtain a prioritized list of requirements.

Table 1. Comparative analysis of prioritization methods based on fuzzy characteristics

Prioritisation methods	Characteristics						
	A_1	A_2	A_3	A_4	A_5	A_6	A_7
	Project size	Feasibility estimation	Feature sets	Individual concerns	Conflicts resolution	Multiple perspectives	Fuzziness
AHP	*S*	*H*	*NGL*	*NGL*	*NGL*	*NG L*	*NGL*
Wieger's	*VS*	*L*	*NGL*	*NGL*	*L*	*NGL*	*NGL*
Fuzzy AHP	*S*	*H*	*NGL*	*NGL*	*NGL*	*NGL*	*VH*
Priority assessment	*H*	*M*	*M*	*NGL*	*L*	*VH*	*NGL*
Triage	*VH*	*H*	*VH*	*NGL*	*VL*	*VL*	*NGL*
Integrated	*H*	*VH*	*H*	*VH*	*VH*	*VL*	*VH*
TOPSIS	*S*	*L*	*NGL*	*NGL*	*NGL*	*NGL*	*VH*

A literature survey of prioritization methods [2-11] described above was carried out. As a result of comparative analysis, various characteristics of a software application *viz.* project size, feasibility estimation, feature sets, individual concerns, conflicts resolution, fuzziness and multiple perspectives were identified in consultation with fifteen software developers that may be considered for identifying the most suitable prioritization methodology and the results are reported in Table 1. These characteristics are explained in the following paragraph.

The project size may vary from small to very high determined by the nature of application. Feasibility estimation is an appraisal for implementing a requirement within assigned estimates. Feature set has emerged as one of the most important criteria utmost demanded in real time large applications [8]. Thousands of requirements in very large sized projects need to be clustered on feature sets such as business goals, functional requirements etc., Individual concerns are associated with resolving the personal concerns of stakeholders in decision-making. Fuzziness is concerned with capturing vagueness and uncertainty inherent in human thoughts. Conflicts resolution involves the concerns of multiple stakeholders over common issues and multiple perspectives involve various perceptions in elicitation of requirements. Since these attributes are often fuzzy and uncertain, therefore can be captured using linguistic terms *viz.* negligible (NGL), very less (VL), less (L) or small (S), moderate (M), high (H) and very high (VH) which further are mapped to triangular fuzzy numbers (TFNS) as shown in Fig. 3.

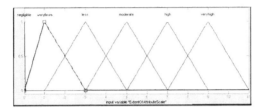

Fig. 2. Triangular fuzzy number scale for degree of attributes

Table 1 evidently illustrates that AHP is suitable for small sized projects with high level of feasibility estimation. Other parameters *viz.* feature sets, individual concerns and conflicts resolution etc., are missing in it. Triage method may deal with very large sized projects at their feature sets but lacks individual fuzzy concerns. Likewise feasibility estimation, individual concerns and conflict resolution are undertaken by an Integrated approach and multiple perspectives by priority Assessment. Out of all prescribed methods, only Fuzzy AHP, integrated approach and TOPSIS cope up with the fuzziness inherent in human thoughts. Because of distinguished features of these requirements prioritization methods, it is observed that one prioritization method is not always perfect to meet the demands of all software projects. Identification of an appropriate prioritization method always depends on the nature of the application, size of the project and many other characteristics prescribed above. Therefore there is a need for some systematic methodology that may facilitate to identify an appropriate requirements prioritization method. The subsequent section provides the guide lines to reach to the identification of an appropriate prioritization method.

4   Methodology for Identifying an Appropriate Requirements Prioritization Method

An effective prioritization method selection procedure for a specific software application is one of the most significant requirements for a software industry. The heavy cost incurred due to wrong selection of a prioritization method has forced the companies to be far more concerned regarding identification of a most suitable prioritization method [1]. The selection of an appropriate prioritization method (PM) from a given set of various prioritization methods is guided by comparing their profile with a required profile in terms of various attributes.

The proposed methodology based on the concept of fuzzy set theory is divided into two phases as illustrated in Fig. 3. In phase I, the stakeholders' concerns for an application are aggregated. In phase II, distance measure of all prioritization methods with respect to positive ideal and negative ideal solution is obtained to get their final ranking.

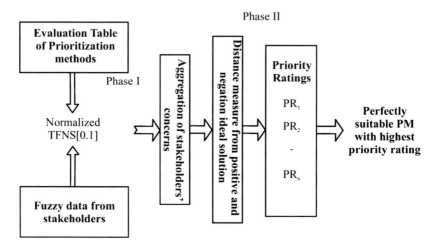

Fig. 3. FMCDM Framework for identifying most appropriate requirements prioritization method

A systematic representation of this methodology divided into Phase I and Phase II is given below.

Phase I:

1. Linguistic terms specifying the degree of attributes of various prioritisation methods specified in Table 1 are mapped to corresponding triangular fuzzy numbers using the scale exhibited in Fig. 2.
2. Solicit the weights of attributes $A_1, A_2, \ldots A_r$ from stakeholders as required in an application in linguistic terms as illustrated in Table 2, which further are mapped to corresponding triangular fuzzy numbers.
3. Normalize the fuzzy weights obtained in step1 and step 2, using the equation given below:

$$\widetilde{nw}_{Aij} = \left(\frac{a_{ij}}{\max a_{ij}}, \frac{b_{ij}}{\max b_{ij}}, \frac{c_{ij}}{\max c_{ij}} \right). \tag{6}$$

where r: number of attributes, p: number of prioritization methods and s: number of stakeholders with $1 \leq j \leq (p$ or $s)$ and $1 \leq i \leq r$. $\widetilde{nw}_{Aij} = (a_{ij}, b_{ij}, c_{ij})$ is the resulted normalized fuzzy weights of characteristics with $1 \leq j \leq p$ operated on evaluation Table 1 and with $1 \leq j \leq s$ operated on stakeholders apprehensions stored in Table 2.

4. Aggregate fuzzy weights of attributes [14] as $\widehat{ARF}_{WAi} = (w_{i1}, w_{i2}, w_{i3})$ with $i = 1,2,...,r$ obtained by s number of stakeholders with $1 \leq j \leq s$, where $w_{i1} = \min w_{ij}$, $w_{i2} = \frac{1}{s} * \sum w_{ij}$ and $w_{i3} = \max w_{ij}$
   The resultant weights thus obtained would incorporate the apprehensions of every stakeholder and thus satisfy all.

Phase II:
5. Construct weighted normalised fuzzy decision matrix over the normalised values of evaluation Table 3 using the equation given below [5], [14]:

$$\widehat{FDM}_{Aij} = [r_{ij}]_{rXp} = [\widetilde{nw}_{Aij} * \widehat{ARF}_{WAi}]_{rXp}. \tag{7}$$

6. Find out the fuzzy positive ideal solution denoted as PM^* and fuzzy negative ideal solution denoted as PM^- of various characteristics over prioritisation methods(PM) [5], [14] specified below:

$$PM^* = (r_1^*, r_2^*, r_3^* .... r_r^*). \tag{8}$$

$$PM^- = (r_1^-, r_2^-, r_3^- .... r_r^-). \tag{9}$$

   Where $r_j^* = \max r_{ij3}$ and $r_j^- = \min r_{ij1}$ with $i = 1,2.....r$ and $j = 1,2.....p$. The above formula facilitates to obtain PM^* and PM^- in the form of the largest and smallest possible values of TFNs termed as r_{ij} respectively over all prioritization methods.

7. Compute final Priority Rating (PR) of each PM with $j = 1,2..p$ with respect to all attributes using the equation given below [5], [14]:

$$PR_j = \frac{d_j^-}{d_j^* + d_j^-}. \tag{10}$$

Where d_j^* is the summation of the distance of attributes of PMs with respect to PM^* and d_j^- from PM^-. It can be observed that $d_j^* = \{0 \text{ if } PM_j = PM^*$, that causes PR_i as 1. Similarly $d_j^- = \{0 \text{ if } PM_j = PM^-$, that causes PR_i as 0. Hence highest Priority Rating (PR) will ensure the most suitability of PM for a given application.

5 Experimental Results

To illustrate the application of proposed method, a scenario was considered in a software industry to identify an appropriate requirement prioritization method out of multiple methods described in literature.

In this scenario, stakeholders were highly concerned for size of the project, frequently occurring feature sets, moderately concerned for feasibility estimation and little apprehensive for individual concerns, conflicts resolution and fuzziness. Various stakeholders involved in an application expressed their concerns for various attributes in linguistic terms as demonstrated in Table 2 which further after

Table 2. Stakeholders apprehensions in linguistic terms in an application

Stakeholders	Attributes						
	A_1	A_2	A_3	A_4	A_5	A_6	A_7
S_1	VH	M	VH	NGL	NGL	VL	NGL
S_2	VH	M	VH	VL	NGL	VL	NGL
S_3	VH	L	VH	NGL	VL	VL	NGL
S_4	VH	M	VH	NGL	NGL	VL	NGL

being mapped to TFNs were converted to normalized form using Eq. 6 and resulted in aggregate weight $\widetilde{ARF}_{WAi}$ as exhibited in Table 3. Table 1 elaborates the degree of various attributes in linguistic terms in requirements prioritization methods which are converted to normalized TFNs using Eq. 6 illustrated in Table 3.

Table 3. Normalised weights $\widetilde{nw}_{Aij}$ of characteristics of prioritisation methods

PM	Characteristics						
	A_1	A_2	A_3	A_4	A_5	A_6	A_7
PM_1	$(0.1, 0.3, 0.5)$	$(0.7, 0.8, 0.8)$	$(0, 0, 0)$	$(0, 0, 0)$	$(0, 0, 0)$	$(0, 0, 0)$	$(0, 0, 0)$
PM_2	$(0, 0.1, 0.3)$	$(0.1, 0.3, 0.5)$	$(0, 0, 0)$	$(0, 0, 0)$	$(0.1, 0.3, 0.5)$	$(0, 0, 0)$	$(0, 0, 0)$
PM_3	$(0.1, 0.3, 0.5)$	$(0.7, 0.8, 0.8)$	$(0, 0, 0)$	$(0, 0, 0)$	$(0, 0, 0)$	$(0, 0, 0)$	$(1, 1, 1)$
PM_4	$(0.7, 0.8, 0.8)$	$(0.4, 0.6, 0.6)$	$(0.4, 0.6, 0.6)$	$(0, 0, 0)$	$(0.1, 0.3, 0.5)$	$(1, 1, 1)$	$(0, 0, 0)$
PM_5	$(1, 1, 1)$	$(0.7, 0.8, 0.8)$	$(1, 1, 1)$	$(0, 0, 0)$	$(0, 0.1, 0.3)$	$(0, 0.1, 0.3)$	$(0, 0, 0)$
PM_6	$(0.7, 0.8, 0.8)$	$(1, 1, 1)$	$(0.7, 0.8, 0.8)$	$(1, 1, 1)$	$(1, 1, 1)$	$(0, 0.1, 0.3)$	$(1, 1, 1)$
PM_7	$(0.1, 0.3, 0.5)$	$(0.1, 0.3, 0.5)$	$(0, 0, 0)$	$(0, 0, 0)$	$(0, 0, 0)$	$(0, 0, 0)$	$(1, 1, 1)$
$\widetilde{ARF}_{WAi}$	$(1, 1, 1)$	$(0.1, 0.5, 0.6)$	$(1, 1, 1)$	$(0, 0, 0.3)$	$(0, 0, 0.3)$	$(0, 0.1, 0.3)$	$(0, 0, 0)$

The weighted normalized decision matrix obtained using Eq. 7 as exhibited in Table 4, illustrates that the aggregate weights of stakeholders $\widetilde{ARF}_{WAi}$ were used to balance out the effect of the attributes in various prioritization methods. Fuzzy positive ideal solution PM^* and fuzzy negative ideal solution PM^- were computed using Eq. 8 and Eq. 9.

PM^*=[(1,1,1), (0.6,0.6,0.6), (1,1,1), (0.3,0.3,0.3), (0.3,0.3,0.3), (0.3,0.3,0.3), (0,0,0), (0.3,0.3,0.3)]. and

PM^-=[(0,0,0), (0, 0, 0), (0,0,0), (0,0,0), (0,0,0), (0,0,0), (0,0,0), (0,0,0)].

Finally Eq. 10 was utilized to obtain final priority rating of aforesaid prioritization methods as illustrated in Table 5. Out of these values, triage with the highest priority rating PR equally 0.653 appears to be the most appropriate method for the application that would assist developer in efficiently prioritizing requirements.

Table 4. Weighted normalised fuzzy decision matrix i.e., $\widetilde{FDM}_{Aij} = [\widetilde{nw}_{Aij} * \widetilde{ARF}_{WAi}]$

PM	Characteristics						
	A_1	A_2	A_3	A_4	A_5	A_6	A_7
PM_1	$(0.1, 0.3, 0.5)$	$(0.1, 0.4, 0.5)$	$(0, 0, 0)$	$(0, 0, 0)$	$(0, 0, 0)$	$(0, 0, 0)$	$(0, 0, 0)$
PM_2	$(0, 0.1, 0.3)$	$(0, 0.2, 0.3)$	$(0, 0, 0)$	$(0, 0, 0)$	$(0, 0, 0.2)$	$(0, 0, 0)$	$(0, 0, 0)$
PM_3	$(0.1, 0.3, 0.5)$	$(0.1, 0.4, 0.5)$	$(0, 0, 0)$	$(0, 0, 0)$	$(0, 0, 0)$	$(0, 0, 0)$	$(0, 0, 0)$
PM_4	$(0.7, 0.8, 0.8)$	$(0, 0.3, 0.4)$	$(0.4, 0.6, 0.6)$	$(0, 0, 0)$	$(0, 0, 0.2)$	$(0, 0.1, 0.3)$	$(0, 0, 0)$
PM_5	$(1, 1, 1)$	$(0.1, 0.4, 0.5)$	$(1, 1, 1)$	$(0, 0, 0)$	$(0, 0, 0.1)$	$(0, 0, 0.1)$	$(0, 0, 0)$
PM_6	$(0.7, 0.8, 0.8)$	$(0.1, 0.5, 0.6)$	$(0.7, 0.8, 0.8)$	$(0, 0, 0.3)$	$(0, 0, 0.3)$	$(0, 0, 0.1)$	$(0, 0, 0)$
PM_7	$(0.1, 0.3, 0.5)$	$(0, 0.2, 0.3)$	$(0, 0, 0)$	$(0, 0, 0)$	$(0, 0, 0)$	$(0, 0, 0)$	$(0, 0, 0)$

Table 5. Computation of final priority rating

Prioritization methods	d_j^*	d_j^-	$PR_j^- = \frac{d_j^-}{d_j^* + d_j^-}$
$PM_1 : AHP$	2.78	0.715	0.205
$PM_2 : Wieger's$	3.028	0.505	0.143
$PM_3 : FuzzyAHP$	2.782	0.715	0.204
$PM_4 : Priority\ assessment$	1.711	1.89	0.525
$PM_5 : Triage$	1.320	2.488	0.653
$PM_6 : Integrated$	1.428	2.393	0.626
$PM_7 : TOPSIS$	2.917	0.549	0.158

6 Conclusions

A number of requirements prioritization methods have been in literature having their salient characteristics. However, all of them are not suitable for every type of application. Identifying right prioritization method involves considering the different attributes of an application at hand, and characteristics exhibited by various prioritization methods. As the appraisal of attributes required in an application and the characteristics depicted by these methods are often subjective, therefore can be articulated in linguistic terms. Therefore, the use of fuzzy set theory in designing the proposed technique for identifying an appropriate requirements prioritization method appeared to be rationally valid. Firstly, this paper characterizes various prioritization methods with respect to a number of aspects and eventually employs Fuzzy Multi-Criteria Decision-Making to synthesize a most suitable prioritization method for an application. This will assist developer to envisage these methods to address the needs of the stakeholders and provide him a sound underpinning in rapid selection of an appropriate prioritization method which consequently may eschew unnecessary overheads and enable him in developing system of high quality without depletion of resources.

References

1. Sarah, H.: Choosing the Right Prioritization Method. IEEE, Los Alamitos (2008) ISBN: 978-0-7695-3100-7
2. Wiegers, K.E.: Software Requirements, 2nd edn. Woodpecker publisher (2006) ISBN: 81-7853-071-6
3. Karlsson: Software Requirements Prioritizing, pp. 110–116. IEEE, Los Alamitos (1996) ISBN: 0-8186-7252-8
4. Kunia, N., Yuji, K.: Priority Assessment of Software Requirements from Multiple Perspective, vol. 1, pp. 410–415. IEEE, Los Alamitos (2004) ISBN: 0-7695-2209-2
5. Serkan, B.: Operating System Selection using Fuzzy AHP and TOPSIS Methods. Mathematical and Computational Applications 14(2), 119–130 (2009)
6. Vibha, G., Anuja, S.: An Integrated Approach to Prioritize Requirements using Fuzzy Decision Making, vol. 2(4) (August 2004) ISSN: 1793-8244
7. Laura, L.: Empirical Evaluation of Two Requirements Prioritization Methods in Product Development Projects, pp. 161–170. Springer, Heidelberg (2004)
8. Laurent, P.: Towards Automated Requirements Triage. In: Proc. IEEE, pp. 131–140 (2007) ISBN: 978-0-7695-2935-6
9. Yajun, Y.: Evaluation of English Textbook Using Fuzzy Analytic Hierarchy Process, pp. 30–33. IEEE, Los Alamitos (2008) ISBN: 978-0-7695-3563-0
10. Lin, Y.H.: Prioritization of Competitive Priority in Cleaner Production Implementation, pp. 104–108. IEEE, Los Alamitos (2007) ISBN: 978-1-4244-1529-8
11. Joachim, K.: An Evaluation of Methods for Prioritizing Software Requirements, vol. 39(14-15), pp. 939–947. Elsevier, Amsterdam (1998)
12. Klir, J.: Fuzzy Sets and Fuzzy Logic. PHI publications (1995) ISBN:81-203-1136-1
13. Yaodong, H.: Fuzzy Multi-Criteria Decision-Making TOPSIS for Distribution Center Location Selection (2009) ISBN: 978-0-7695-3610-1
14. Sreekumar: A fuzzy Multi-Criteria Decision-Making Approach for Supplier Selection in Supply Chain Management, vol. 3(4), pp. 168–177 (April 2009)
15. Cormen: Introduction to Algorithms, 2nd edn. PHI publications (2007)

Analyzing Design Patterns for Extensibility

Annappa B., Rabna Rajendran, Chandrasekaran K., and Shet K.C.

Department of Computer Science and Engineering,
National Institute of Technology Karnataka, Surathkal, India
annappa@ieee.org,rabna.rajendran@gmail.com

Abstract. A system is said to be extensible, if any changes can be made to any of the existing system functionalities and/or addition of new functionalities with minimum impact. To achieve extensibility, it has to be planned properly starting from the initial stage of the application development. Keeping in mind all the possible future changes to be made, the designer should select the proper design patterns and finish the design for the application. Once the application design is finished, it should be analyzed to make sure that the application is extensible.

Keywords: Design Analysis, Design Patterns, Extensible Application, Extensibility, Software Development.

1 Role of Design Patterns in Software Development

In software engineering, the functional and non functional requirements are taken into consideration during the design phase. During designing of the application, some unforeseen problems might arise. As the designer solves these problems, he might come across more problems. When the solutions for these problems are closely analyzed, lot of similarities can be found and these existing solutions can be adopted to satisfy new requirements with or without minor changes to the existing solutions. In such a situation, the designer can use a solution that is already proved to be a good solution, which can foresee the possible problems and take actions to avoid such a situation. That solution which is used again and again forms a particular pattern and the solution for these recurring problems are called as design pattern.

A design pattern can be described as a solution that is proved for a software design problem. It is an object model that serves as an abstraction of the implementation model and its source code. Patterns help designers in better communication using the known and understood terms in software engineering. Knowingly or unknowingly programmers are following some patterns while writing code for a similar problem. Patterns are reusable as it can be applied for similar problems whenever necessary and it can avoid most of the issues that can happen at the time of implementation [1].

A pattern is not a finished code which can be directly used in the implementation of similar problems, but it gives a hint to solve a problem effectively and thereby speedup the development process. A Pattern is not a method or a framework. In object oriented programming, they show the relations and interactions

K.R. Venugopal and L.M. Patnaik (Eds.): ICIP 2011, CCIS 157, pp. 269–278, 2011.

between the classes and their objects. Using patterns makes it easy for the architect or programmer to understand it later for extension or modification. All the existing patterns can be mainly grouped under 3 categories based on how they are used as: (i) Creational, (ii) Structural, (iii) Behavioral.

Creational patterns deals with mechanisms for instantiating objects. The structural patterns deal with the composition of objects and their organization to obtain new and varied functionality. Behavioral pattern explains the interaction between different objects. In this paper, more importance is given to patterns related to extensibility. There are mainly three patterns which come under extension patterns. They are decorator, visitor and iterator [2].

2   Software Extensibility

With the emerging technologies, requirements are also changing and increasing day-by-day. The innovations in the software field forces the language designers and tool builders to enrich their products to be compatible with these innovations. Making changes to an already deployed code might not be easy all the time. It may be easy for a small application to be recompiled and redeployed. But for large software with many users, recompilation and redeployment may take a reasonable time and results in wastage of resources. Modern software need to be expanded by other developers or users to fit in the customer requirements. Software teams do not want to touch the code base for each and every change because it is error prone.

It is at this situation that, the designers and developers start thinking about extensibility and extensible architectures or designs come to the help of software developers. The important feature of extensibility is to make any change in existing system functions with minimum impact. By extensions, it means either the addition of new functionality or modification of existing functionality. In Software Engineering context it appears as a set of techniques in Software Architecture and Software Design. In Programming Languages it appears as a set of mechanisms and concepts that make it easy to extend the software. When the software is extended there will be some added features along with the functionalities that were available previously.

Most of the time, extensibility is misunderstood for reusability. Code reusability is copy/paste of the code that already exists for a similar application and it is just modifying that code to add more features or to correct some problems in the existing version. So the resultant application will be a newer or more efficient version of the existing version. But in case of extensibility, it is not reuse of the available code. Extensible design supports the iterative development principles. It allows functionality to be implemented in small steps as required.

To achieve extensibility, it has to be planned properly starting from the initial stage of the application development. The designer should have an idea of possible future requirements and how the application will have to be modified in future. For example, if it is an application for a restaurant, provision should be there to add more variety items in the menu and calculate the bill according to the menu chosen by the customer or to accept the orders through internet or mobile or introduce different modes of payment etc., Many other changes can also happen as the time changes, say tax, rate of each item etc., So the designer should make sure that the application can accommodate all these changes without affecting the existing system.

3   Extensibility Versus Scalability

Scalability is often misunderstood with extensibility. Software is said to be scalable if it is able to handle the growing amount of work. In a web application, scalability is generally related to the increased number of users or visitors. As the quantity increases, if the design fails, then it does not scale. Most of the time, it happens because the software does not use the available resources efficiently.

Extensibility is a system design principle where the implementation takes into consideration the future growth [6-7]. Consider a banking application. A banking application will have different types of customers, accounts, loans and many related services. It is said to be extensible when it is possible to add more functions like new type of savings account or able to offer some new services like online banking, mobile banking, currency converter etc., without making much change in the existing system. The system should work the same even after the new features are added. As time passes, the number of customers increases. If the application is meant for a limited number of customers, then it is not fit for a banking purpose, because a bank grows with the increase in the number of people ready to do business with them. So the application should be able to handle as many numbers of customers as needed without any performance issue and there should not be any limit on that matter. That explains scalability.

Software can be efficient if it is both scalable and extensible. For making the system extensible it should be scalable. If it is not scalable, at the time of adding some more functionality, the requirements may be more and the system may not be capable of adjusting to the changes made. If a system is not efficient, then there is no point in extending it and trying to add more features to it. So it can be said that extensibility and scalability complements each other.

4   Designing an Application-A Case

An application is said to be extensible if any change can be made to the existing application without affecting the existing functionalities and how they are working [3]. Developing such an application starts with understanding what the application is for and what all changes have to be made in future and designing starts with breaking down the entire application into small modules to make it easy to design and selecting the proper design pattern for these small modules. Then design, analyze and implement these modules separately and finally join these modules together to complete the application.

This can be explained with an example. Consider the workflow of the application given in Fig. 1. The application is for a restaurant where different types of pizzas are being served and the bill is calculated according to the ingredients chosen by the customer. In the Fig. 1, it has only one module and it is for calculating the cost of the pizza. The design for this module is given in Fig. 2. It is designed using decorator pattern. After the designing and implementation of this module, it is analyzed for extensibility. Since it can accommodate changes without affecting the existing components, it is extensible.

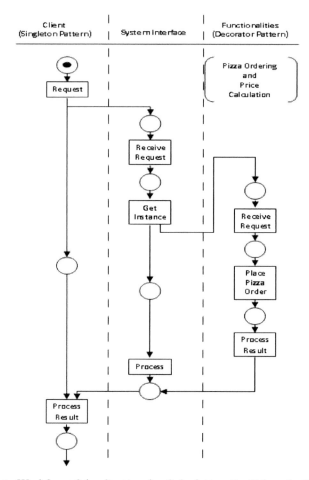

Fig. 1. Workflow of Application for Calculating the Price of a Pizza

Now consider the Fig. 3. This is an extension of the workflow given in Fig. 1. This extension has two modules (functionalities). One is for calculating the price and another one for the payment purpose. These modules are separated and implemented separately. The module for calculating the price remains the same where as one more module has been added to the existing version for the payment purposes. Each of these modules is made extensible using the proper design pattern. The design for payment module is given in Fig. 4. This module

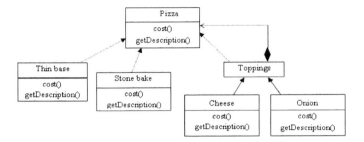

Fig. 2. Design of Module for Calculating the Price of a Pizza

is designed using strategy pattern. It can be seen from the design of this module that more methods can be added without affecting the existing methods. Similarly, if more functionality has to be added to this application, that can be added to it without affecting the working of the application. If the developer wants to modify or delete a module, it can also be performed without affecting the working of other modules.

5   Analysis

5.1   Design Patterns are Design Ideas

A Design pattern can be described as a solution that is proved for a software design problem. It is an object model that serves as an abstraction of the implementation model and its source code. Patterns help designers in better communication using the known and understood terms in software engineering. Each and every design pattern has a special purpose. Patterns are reusable as it can be applied for similar problems whenever necessary and it can avoid most of the issues that can happen at the time of implementation.

A design pattern is not a working code or a framework, but it is a method that gives the designer an idea on how the different modules in the design interact with each other. By using the design patterns, it can be made sure that there is no flaw in the design of application even before starting the coding for the application. Since design patterns clearly shows the interaction between the classes and its objects, it is easy for the designer to understand it easily. Also for making any changes later, if the complete design is available, it is easy to make the changes in the existing system and modify it according to the necessities.

5.2   Design Patterns and Extensibility

An application is said to be extensible, when it is possible to make any change in existing system functions with minimum impact. By extensions it means either the addition of new functionalities or modification of existing functionalities. When the software is extended, there will be some added features along with the functionalities that were available previously. To achieve extensibility, it

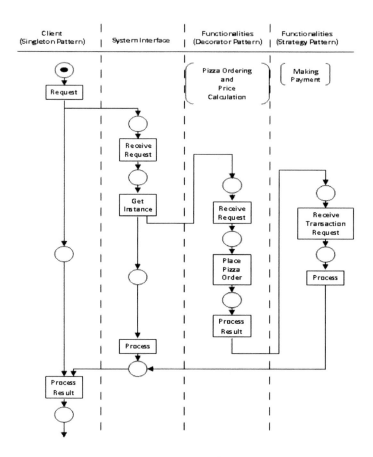

Fig. 3. Workflow of the Application for the Restaurant

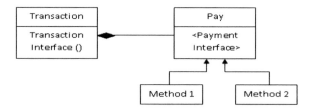

Fig. 4. Design of Module for Payment Purpose

has to be planned properly starting from the initial stage of the application development. Enough care should be taken at the time of design itself.

Design patterns make it easy for the designer to analyze the design of the application more efficiently before starting the implementation. For designing an application that is extensible, the designer should have an idea about the future needs and the changes that has to be made in the application to accommodate those changes. The designer has to choose patterns that allow changes in future without affecting the whole application. So the designer has to pay attention in choosing patterns for the design of application. There are certain things that he has to keep in mind. First is that, all the patterns are not extensible. And another fact is that, sometimes the design can be extensible but not scalable. Scalability and extensibility complements each other. So even if the application is extensible, there is no point in extending it if it cannot handle the increasing need for resources. So the designer has to make sure that the application is scalable as well as extensible.

Extensibility of the application depends much on the design pattern that is used in the design. So enough care should be taken to make sure that the suitable design pattern has been selected. Once the design has been analyzed for extensibility, implementation can be started [4].

5.3   Design Patterns Help to Evaluate Extensibility

Extensibility depends on how the different modules depend on each other, i.e., up to what extent they are coupled to each other. An extensible design should be loosely coupled which means low interdependency. As the coupling increases, the dependence between the modules also increases which means any change made to a module will result in changes in the other modules also. The main aim of extensibility is to minimize the impact once any change has been made to the existing system [2], [5].

Use of design patterns can help the designer to evaluate the design for extensibility even before starting the implementation. When some commonly used patterns such as factory pattern, strategy pattern, decorator pattern etc., are considered; by analyzing the structure itself the designer will get an idea whether any change can be made in the code without affecting the existing code. Consider the UML diagram of factory patten given in Fig. 5. In this pattern, Product is an interface and Concrete Product implements the Product. Factory is an abstract class and *ConcreteFactory* is the class which extends the factory class. Here there are mainly two concrete components. Each of these concrete components is tightly coupled to the other classes which show that adding a new class is not possible.

Now consider Strategy Pattern given in Fig. 6. This pattern is used when there are common situations when classes differ only in their behavior. From the UML structure, it can be seen that the *ConcreteStrategy* [8-9] is implementing the Strategy interface and it is not connected with any other class. More number of ConcreteStrategy can be added if needed. In the implementation, adding a class would not make any change in the existing features. Once a new class is

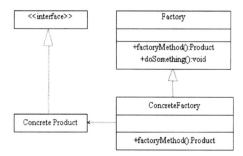

Fig. 5. Factory Pattern

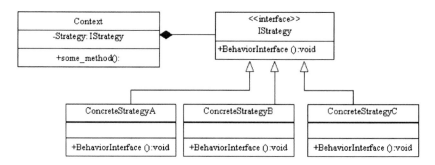

Fig. 6. Strategy Pattern

added, it can access other classes using its objects. Since adding a new class does not make any change to the existing functions, this pattern is suitable for adding some features in future.

The UML diagram of decorator pattern is given in Fig. 7. It is used when functionalities has to be added to an object dynamically at runtime. In this structure there are two concrete components which are loosely coupled, which makes it easy to add more classes or make any change in one of these classes without making any change to other classes. Concrete component and decorator implement the interface component while concrete decorator extends all the functionalities of the decorator. As many ConcreteDecorator components can be added, as needed without making any change to other classes.

Similarly each and every design pattern and check whether it allows changes without affecting the other parts of the application. It can be easily checked by how loosely or tightly the components are coupled. As the coupling increases, extensibility decreases. So the designer has to choose a design pattern for that particular purpose and which has the least coupling.

6   Analyzing an Application Design for Extensibility

Now, the extensibility for an application has to be analyzed. During the design phase, the application can be broken down into number of modules. Each module

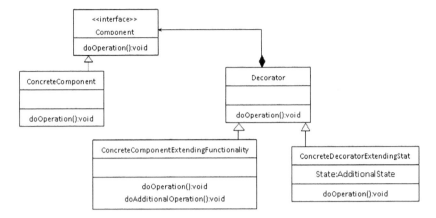

Fig. 7. Decorator Pattern

will perform a specific task. Designer can choose the proper design pattern for each and every module. If the chosen design patterns for each module are loosely coupled, mostly the entire application will also be extensible. But choosing an extensible pattern alone does not make the application extensible. So extensibility of an application depends on the extensibility of the design pattern as well as how much that particular pattern is suitable for the application.

Consider these designs given in Fig. 2 and Fig. 8. Both the designs are using decorator pattern. The first design is for calculating the bill for a pizza at a restaurant and the second design is for adding n numbers.

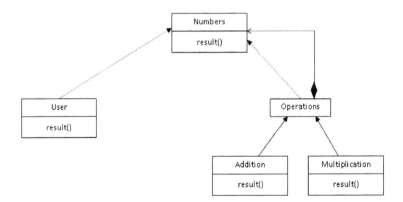

Fig. 8. Design of application for adding n numbers

In this design for calculating the price of pizza, as many number of toppings and bases can as needed, which makes it completely extensible. But in the second design, more number of operations such as subtraction, multiplication etc. can be added. But this will work only for a single user. If we want to make it work for multiple users, it is not possible.

From this, it can be understood that the design pattern to be chosen should be able to perform the functions that the application needs and it should be extensible. Considering about a large application which has many functionalities, the application will have different modules and each module will be using different patterns. If these modules are extensible separately, then the whole application will be extensible provided that these separated modules are joined together properly and that too in a loosely coupled fashion.

7 Conclusions

Nowadays extensibility is seen as a necessary aspect of software application requirement in the software engineering practices. In this paper, some design patterns are considered and analyzed these patterns for extensibility. The application will be extensible, if the design pattern chosen is suitable for the application and it allows the designer to make changes without affecting the existing code. Two small applications have been considered to understand this concept. So by choosing the appropriate design pattern for each module and finally connecting these modules in a loosely coupled fashion makes the application extensible.

References

1. Allan, K.: The Philosophy of Extensible Software (August 2002),
   http://accu.org/index.php/journals/391
2. Shriram, K., Matthias, F.: Toward a Formal Theory of Extensible Software. In: ACM SIGSOFT International Symposium on the Foundations of Software Engineering (1998)
3. Metsker, S.J., Wake, W.C.: Design Patterns in Java. Addison-Wesley Professional, Reading (2006)
4. Ellen, A., Aino, C.: How to Preserve the Benefits of Design Patterns. In: OOPSLA (1998)
5. Spiteri, Staines, A.: A Fundamental Modeling Concept Approach for Modeling UML Design Patterns. International Journal Of Computers 2(3) (2008)
6. Matthias, Z.: Evolving Software with Extensible Modules, vol. 17(5). ACM, New York (September 2005)
7. Raju, P., Browne, J.C.: Support for Extensibility and Reusability in a Concurrent Object Oriented Programming Language. In: IEEE-Proceedings of IPPS (1996)
8. Design Patterns, http://www.oodesign.com/
9. Design Patterns, http://www.dofactory.com/Patterns/Patterns.aspx

Quality Determinants in Offshored IS Projects: A Comparison between Projects Completed Within-Budget and Over-Budget

Sankaran K.[1], Nik Dalal[2], and Kannabiran G.[1]

[1] National Institute of Technology, Tiruchirappalli, India
{kb,msz0602}@nitt.edu
[2] William Spears School of Business, Oklahoma State University, Stillwater, USA
nik@okstate.edu

Abstract. Customers have shifted their focus to offshoring vendors ability to provide high quality software, in addition to the cost advantages. However, delivering projects within the budgets ensures profitability and growth of vendors. The present research highlights how meeting budget requirements is related to the impact of key determinants on software quality in offshore development projects executed by vendors. A survey of project managers engaged in off shoring at leading Indian software companies was carried out and the collected data were analysed using structural equations modelling techniques. Out of six determinants, in the case of projects completed within the budget, while process maturity is associated with functionality, reliability, usability and performance of the software and technical infrastructure is associated with reliability, maintainability, usability and performance in the case projects completed within the budget. However in the case of projects that exceeded the budget, it is found while requirements uncertainty is associated with maintainability, technical infrastructure is associated with maintainability and performance of the software.

Keywords: Budget, Determinants of quality, IS Offshoring, Software Process Maturity, Quality attributes.

1 Introduction

Offshore outsourcing has seen considerable growth during the past few years, especially due to easy access to skilled and qualified resources in developing countries like India. In recent times, managers of both outsourcing and vendor firms have realized that the focus to maintain quality is necessary in addition to cost savings from the outsourced development projects. Many researchers have observed that in view of the declining cost advantages, Indian offshore vendors need to change focus from cost to the quality related measures of the software services provided in [1], [2]. It is reported that there have been only few studies on factors that impact software quality; but quantitative survey-based research is lacking on the subject [3]. With this background, the objective of this paper is to empirically evaluate the key factors that determine the quality in offshore

K.R. Venugopal and L.M. Patnaik (Eds.): ICIP 2011, CCIS 157, pp. 279–286, 2011.

software development, through a survey of project managers of IT companies in India. The paper begins with a review of the relevant previous research, followed by research objectives and methodology. Subsequent sections cover the data analysis and interpretation, followed by the discussion on the relative importance of the determinants of software quality. The paper concludes with implications for practice and directions for future research.

2   Review of Previous Research

The importance of software quality (SQ) has been stressed by many researchers Luftman and Kempaiah [4], who all observed that SQ can determine the success in todays competitive market. Many researchers Gorla and Lin [3] observed that software quality as one of the critical issues of the decade but there is inadequacy of empirical studies investigating the management of quality of software development. Various approaches and frameworks, such as Total Quality Management (TQM), ISO, CMMI and Six Sigma have been proposed to improve software quality. The relevant previous research relating to software quality and its determinants are reviewed and presented in the following sections.

2.1   Software Quality Attributes

Of the Quality Models which have been developed in the past, the ones most widely known are Dromeys, McCalls and Boehms, and more recently, the ISO 9126. Behkamal et al., [5] customized the ISO 9126 model to desirable software quality attributes for web applications which are reliability, usability, security, availability, scalability, maintainability, and time to market. According to Andreou and Tziakouris [6], ISO 9126 model, having six major characteristics, namely, functionality, reliability, usability, efficiency, maintainability and portability, along with their associated sub-characteristics, can be suitably modified to a quality frame work for developing and evaluating original software components. Our current research study excluded portability and efficiency attributes as they deal with time behaviour and computing resources consumed [3]; hence, it has been modified by using more suitable term performance of the software to provide a comprehensive representation of the attribute in our chosen list of software quality attributes for the study. To sum up, therefore, we have finally considered five main attributes, viz., Functionality, Reliability, Maintainability, Usability and Performance as measures of Software Quality for our study.

2.2   Factors Impacting Software Quality

In the past, many researchers Dyba [7] and Pereira [8] et al., have identified the factors influencing the success of software projects. Further, software quality has been considered as a surrogate measure of the project success in [3]. Therefore, it is essential to study and analyse the factors which influence the software quality in the development projects. Key factors namely Requirements Uncertainty, Technical Infrastructure, Knowledge Transfer and Integration, Trained Personnel, Process Maturity, Communications and Control are identified from the previous research that impacts the software quality. Details on the previous research of the factors are given in the following sections.

Requirements uncertainty [RU] means that within a software system, requirements are not known until it is practically used. Previous studies Han and Huang [9] posit requirements uncertainty to be an important source of poor quality in software development. According to Pressman [10], as requirements keep changing in the project life cycle, subsequent changes in the design and rework can create disruptions in managing requirements and provide scope for defects. Gopal and Koka [11] observed while most studies have considered the effects of requirements uncertainty in in-house projects, its effects are magnified in the offshore domain due to barriers of geographical and organizational boundaries between the client and vendor. Li et al., [12] proposed Software Quality depends on availability Technical Infrastructure [TI], including good tools, material, methods and latest technological developments. Thus, TI capability has been recognized as one of the key dimensions of IT capability of the vendor in existing information systems research for promoting software quality in [13].

Knowledge Integration is defined as the process of absorbing knowledge from the external sources and blending it with the technical and business skills, know-how, and expertise that reside in the business and IS units of a firm by Tiwana et al., [14]. In the case of offshore projects, external integration would therefore measure the knowledge gained between the on shore and offshore unit as well as between the project teams, while internal integration would measure the knowledge gained within the teams [15]. Process maturity is defined as the indication of how close a developing process is being complete and capable of continuous improvement through quantitative measure and feedback by Jones [16]. Subramanian et al., [17] have endorsed the view that process improvements are vital for improving software quality.

Sahay et al., [18] have reported very significantly, the need of trained personnel and the effect of staff attrition in the offshore software development projects. It is shown that a large amount of software project failures are caused by personnel factors such as lack of proper training [9] and frequent shifting of personnel between projects [11]. Communication and control [CC] is viewed as more critical in executing offshore development projects, as the communication between on-site and offshore teams is to be really effective and well coordinated [19]. According to Gopal et al., [20], communication and control mechanisms in offshore development reduce project uncertainty and thereby improve quality of software developed. In light of the above findings reported by the previous research, it is argued that communication and control plays a key role in the in offshore development environment due to the challenges involved in achieving good between on-site and offshore teams.

2.3 Budget Requirements

One of the capabilities of a vendor is to ensure cost effective way to produce competitive products and services [21]. Globalization, outsourcing and open-source movements have intensified the competition in the software industry [22]. To succeed, software companies strive to get their jobs done faster for less money. Consequently, completing the project within budget has become the norm in todays software industry. Business users are charged same regardless of where the project is outsourced and that puts pressure on IT managers to persuade business users to allow their projects to be sent offshore. The difficulty rests in selecting service provider companies that are most likely to fit their financial budget and take their individual needs seriously. Therefore, meeting budget requirements is one the key objectives, in addition to meeting the quality requirements.

3 Research Objectives and Methodology

Based on a detailed review of the previous research on the factors impacting the Software Quality (SQ) attributes, within the context of offshore software development, the objectives of the research are to identify and evaluate the impact of the factors on the SQ attributes in the context of projects completed within budget and exceeded budget. The research covers the dependent variable, software quality and the independent variables, requirements uncertainty, process maturity, communication and control, knowledge transfer and integration, trained personnel and infrastructure facilities. The above stated research objectives along with the underlying conceptual research framework are translated into sets of hypotheses and presented below:

$H_{1.2B}$ and $H_{1.2B}$: Higher the requirements uncertainty lower will be the functionality of the software quality in the projects completed within the budget and exceeded the budget respectively. In the same way, $H_{1.2B}$, and $H_{1.2B}$, $H_{1.3B}$ and $H_{1.3B}$, $H_{1.4B}$ and $H_{1.4B}$ and $H_{1.5B}$ and $H_{1.5B}$ are related to requirements uncertainty with reliability, maintainability, usability and performance respectively. Likewise, the hypotheses are formulated to link other quality determinants with quality attributes.

A comprehensive research questionnaire was used to measure the constructs in the proposed research model. Items related to measure software quality attributes and the determinants were measured using a 5-point Likert Scale (*Strongly Disagree, Disagree, Neutral, Agree and Strongly Agree*). A pilot study was conducted involving senior managers, Project Managers and/or Leads from a midsize software firm to further refine the scales and develop a survey instrument. Based on inputs from the respondents of the pilot study, the modified final research questionnaire was designed. Sample size for the study was determined using the sample size determination for the fraction method and the organizations were chosen based on their size. HR-Head of ten leading software firms were contacted and 440 responses were considered for data analysis.

4   Data Analysis and Interpretation

Structural Equation Modelling (SEM) analysis was undertaken using statistical package. As a first step for theory testing, the validity of the instrument was tested using a two-stage factor analysis using first principal components analysis (PCA) and then SEM to test for convergent and discriminant validity. The reliability and validity tests are conducted for each construct. Cronbach's values all constructs are above 0.60 indicating that the scales have good reliability. Similarly, the Comparative Fit Index and Normed Fit Index above 0.90 indicates Unidimentionality and Convergent Validity respectively. After refining the scales, confirmatory factor analysis (CFA) on the new scales was performed using structural equation modelling to further test the discriminant validity. This was carried out using the software AMOS 16.0 and the measurement models for the same groups of variables. For discriminant validity, the square root of AVE should be greater than the correlations of the constructs. The average variance extracted was of 0.5 for all the constructs, which indicated discriminant validity.

The structural model tested for the SQ in projects completed within budget and exceeded budget was developed to test the hypotheses and those accepted are presented in Table 1. In the case of projects completed within the budget, the Goodness-of-fit index (GFI=0.865), Normed fit index (NFI=0.922), and the comparative fit index (CFI=0.926) are all above 0.90, suggesting a good fit between the structural model and the data. RMSEA =0.037 which is well below the suggested threshold value of 0.08. In the case of projects exceeded the budget, the Goodness-of-fit index (GFI=0.874), Normed fit index (NFI=0.912), and the comparative fit index (CFI=0.924) are all above 0.90, suggesting a good fit between the structural model and the data. RMSEA =0.046 which is well below the suggested threshold value of 0.08. All of these fit indices are acceptable, suggesting that the overall structural model provides a good fit with the data.

In the case of analysis relating to projects completed within the budget, it is found that process maturity is associated with functionality, reliability, usability and performance of the software. It is further found that it has strong association with functionality and usability, based on the values.

Technical Infrastructure is associated with reliability, maintainability, usability and performance of the software. As per the values, technical infrastructure has strong association with reliability, maintainability and performance. It is found that while requirements uncertainty is associated with maintainability, knowledge transfer and integration is associated with maintainability of the software, in the case projects completed within the budget. However, in the case of projects that exceeded the budget, it is found while requirements uncertainty is associated with maintainability and technical infrastructure is associated with maintainability and performance. As per the values, technical infrastructure has strong association with maintainability than performance of the software. It is also found that process maturity, trained personnel and knowledge transfer and integration have no association with any of the quality attributes.

It is found that TI is associated with reliability, maintainability, usability and performance of the software in the case of projects executed within the

Table 1. Summary of accepted hypothesis through structural model fit for projects completed within budget and exceeded budget (**p<0.01 (significant at 99% confidence level) ***p<0.001 (significant at 99.9% confidence level))

Structural Path	Hypo-thesis	Beta coefficient	t-value
Projects completed within Budget			
Requirements Uncertainty → Maintainability	$H_{1.3B}$	0.116	2.982***
Technical Infrastructure → Reliability	$H_{2.2B}$	0.299	4.942***
Technical Infrastructure → Maintainability	$H_{2.3B}$	0.375	4.600***
Technical Infrastructure → Usability	$H_{2.4B}$	0.161	3.038***
Technical Infrastructure → Performance	$H_{2.5B}$	0.212	3.016***
Knowledge transfer and integration → Maintainability	$H_{3.3B}$	0.143	2.231**
Process Maturity → Functionality	$H_{4.1B}$	0.225	4.309***
Process Maturity → Reliability	$H_{4.2B}$	0.131	2.086**
Process Maturity → Usability	$H_{4.4B}$	0.216	3.917***
Process Maturity → Performance	$H_{4.5B}$	0.167	2.247**
Projects completed with exceeded Budget			
Requirements Uncertainty → Maintainability	$H_{1.3EB}$	0.335	2.574***
Technical Infrastructure → Maintainability	$H_{2.3EB}$	0.380	2.716***
Technical Infrastructure → Performance	$H_{2.5EB}$	0.294	2.214***

budget. Further, technical infrastructure has strong association with reliability, maintainability and performance. The strong association is due to the fact that most of the Indian vendors have very strong TI, including tools for capturing requirements, analysis and code generation. However, in the case of projects that exceeded the budget, it is found technical infrastructure is associated only with maintainability and performance. Further, technical infrastructure has strong association with maintainability than performance of the software in this case. Practitioners may concentrate on improving TI so that in addition to maintainability and performance, it would help organizations to achieve reliability and usability while keeping the budgets within the limits. Our research shows that process maturity affects four out of five attributes of quality. Practitioners may take extra care to establish matured processes so that the four features may be achieved while the project will also get executed within budget. It is also found that requirements uncertainty is associated with maintainability attribute of the quality attribute in both cases of projects completed within budget and exceeded budget. This clearly indicates that requirements uncertainty is an important aspect to be managed for achieving maintainability. Our research shows that knowledge transfer and integration is associated with maintainability of the software, in the case projects completed within the budget. However, it is not associated with any quality attributes in the case of projects that exceeded the budget. Practitioners may focus on knowledge transfer and integration to complete the project within budget. Our research shows that trained personnel and communication and control have no significant association with any of the quality attributes in projects completed within budget as well as exceeded budgets.

Therefore, practitioners may focus more on these factors if they have to achieve specific schedule requirements.

5   Conclusions

The research study was conducted to evaluate and compare the impact of key determinants on the software quality in offshore development projects executed by Indian Vendors. The study is based on primary data collected from Project managers from ten software companies in India. The study has identified the key determinants which influence the specific attributes of the software quality by critically comparing the projects that are completed within budget and exceeded the budget. Out of six determinants, in the case of projects completed within the budget, while process maturity is associated with functionality, reliability, usability and performance of the software, technical infrastructure is associated with reliability, maintainability, usability and performance of the software. However in the case of projects that exceeded the budget, it is found while requirements uncertainty is associated with maintainability, technical Infrastructure is associated with maintainability and performance of the software. Future studies on software quality may explore the impact of the project size and type as variables affecting the quality of the project may be undertaken. Comparative study with respect to software projects relating to different industrial verticals like banking, healthcare, retail etc., may be useful to deploy appropriate quality management systems.

References

1. Davis, G.B., EinDor, P., King, W.R., Torkzadeh, R.: IT Off-Shoring: History, Prospects, Challenges. Journal of the AIS 7(11), 770–795 (2006)
2. Ethiraj, S.K., Kale, P., Krishnan, M.S., Singh, J.V.: Where Do Capabilities Come From and How Do They Matter? A Study in the Software Services Industry. Strategic Management Journal 26(1), 25–45 (2005)
3. Gorla, N., Lin, S.C.: Determinants of Software Quality: A Survey of Information Systems Project Managers. Information and Software Technology (2010)
4. Luftman, J., Kempaiah, R.: Key Issues for IT Executives 2007. MIS Quarterly Executive 7, 99–112 (2008)
5. Behkamal, B., Kahani, M., Akbari, M.K.: Customizing ISO 9126 Quality Model for Evaluation of B2B Applications. Information and Software Technology 51, 599–609 (2009)
6. Andreou, A.S., Tziakouris, M.: A Quality Framework for Developing and Evaluating Original Software Components. Information and Software Technology 49, 122–141 (2007)
7. Dyba, T.: An Empirical Investigation of the Key Factors for Success in Software Process Improvement. IEEE Transactions on Software Engineering 31(5), 410–424 (2005)
8. Pereira, J., Cerpa, N., Verner, J., Rivas, M., Procaccino, J.D.: What Do Software Practitioners Really Think about Project Success. The Journal of Systems and Software 81, 897–907 (2008)

9. Han, W.M., Huang, S.J.: An Empirical Analysis of Risk Components and Performance on Software Projects. The Journal of Systems and Software 80(1), 42–50 (2007)
10. Pressman, R.S.: Software Engineering: A Practitioners Approach. McGraw-Hill, NY (2005)
11. Gopal, A., Koka, B.: Determinants of Service Quality in Offshore Software Outsourcing. In: Information Systems Outsourcing Enduring Themes, New Perspectives and Global Challenges, 3rd edn. (2008)
12. Li, E.Y., Chen, H.G., Cheung, W.: Total Quality Management in Software Development Process. The Journal of Quality Assurance Institute 4, 5–41 (2000)
13. Santhanam, R., Hartono, E.: Issues in Linking Information Technology Capability to Firm Performance. MIS Quarterly 27(1), 125–153 (2003)
14. Tiwana, A., Bharadwaj, A., Sambamurthy, V.: The Antecedents Of Information Systems Development Capability In Firms: A Knowledge Integration perspective. In: Twenty-Fourth International Conference on Information Systems, pp. 246–258 (2003)
15. Prahalad, C., Krishnan, M.: The Dynamic Synchronization of Strategy and Information Technology. Sloan Management Review, 24–33 (Summer 2002)
16. Jones, S.: Toward an Acceptable Definition of Service. IEEE Software, 87–93 (May 2005)
17. Subramanian, G.H., James, J.J., Klein, G.: Software Quality and IS Project Performance Improvements from Software Development Process Maturity and IS implementation strategies. The Journal of Systems and Software 80, 616–627 (2007)
18. Sahay, S., Nicholson, B., Krishna, S.: Global IT Outsourcing-Software Development across Borders, 1st edn. Cambridge University Press, United Kingdom (2003)
19. Hong, H.-K., Kim, J.-S., Kim, T., Leem, B.-H.: The Effect of Knowledge on System Integration Project Performance. Industrial Management and Data Systems 108(3), 385–404 (2008)
20. Gopal, A., Mukhapadhyay, T., Krishnan, M.S.: Role of Software Processes and Communication in Offshore Software Development. Communications of the ACM 45(4), 193–200 (2002)
21. Gottschalk, P., Solli-Sther, H.: Critical Success Factors from IT Outsourcing Theories: An Empirical Study. Industrial Management and Data Systems 105(6), 685–702 (2005)
22. Nan, N., Harter, D.E.: Impact of Budget and Schedule Pressure on Software Development Cycle Time and Effort. IEEE Transactions on Software Engineering 35(5) (2009)

A Framework for Security Design Engineering Process

Kakali Chatterjee[1], Daya Gupta[1], and Asok De[2]

[1] Department of Computer Engineering, Delhi Technological University, India
[2] Ambedkar Institute of Technology, Delhi, India
kakali2008@gmail.com

Abstract. Adopting a security enhanced software development practices that includes secure development process will reduce the number of exploitable faults and weaknesses in the designed software. Current software development processes enforce security measures during design phase which may end up in specifying security related architecture constraints that are not really necessary. To eliminate this problem, we propose a Framework for Security Design Engineering Process that involves converting security requirements and threats into design decisions to mitigate the identified security threats. The identified design attributes are prioritized and a Security Design Template (SDT) is prepared to find out the specific cryptographic technique that would eventually help in the later stages of the design process by eliminating unnecessary design constraints in a particular scenario.

Keywords: Security Design Engineering, Security Design Template, Security Engineering Process, Security Requirement Engineering.

1 Introduction

Security Engineering is focused on implementing security in software or related systems. The security goals are traditionally classified into confidentiality, integrity and availability of information in an organisation [1]. A lot of work has been reported on discovering and eliciting of security requirements like abuse case [2], misuse case [3], common criteria [4], attack trees [5]. Secure tropos extension of tropos methodology [6] and intentional anti model extension of KAOS methodology with security requirement oriented construct [7] were discussed. The root cause of security requirements is the mitigation of different types of risk associated with the threats. To prioritize the elicited security requirements [8], one needs to measure underlying risks. There is Risk Management methods like EBIOS [9], OCTAVE [10], CRAMM [11] which enforce security levels based on risk measure. The well known process of Viewpoint Oriented Requirements Definition was explained in [12]. Eliciting security requirements using viewpoint oriented approach [13] and prioritizing this security requirement using techniques of CRAMM are discussed [14]. Once security requirement engineering is through, one needs to take proper design decision for security requirements analogues to

K.R. Venugopal and L.M. Patnaik (Eds.): ICIP 2011, CCIS 157, pp. 287–293, 2011.
© Springer-Verlag Berlin Heidelberg 2011

conventional design process for functional and nonfunctional requirements. If proper design decisions are not taken, then either it can lead to an underdeveloped system with unnecessary design constraints or makes the system vulnerable or unnecessary constraint overflowing the budget. These design decision for security requirement will require modeling of software environment from systems perspective. In this paper we propose a Framework for Security Design Engineering Process that involves converting security requirements and threats (which are identified during the security requirement elicitation stage) into design decisions to mitigate the identified security threats. The different types of security requirements are mapped to the different security services. The identified design attributes are prioritized and a Security Design Template (SDT) is prepared based upon the set of important security attributes that influences design choices at the various layers of security engineering process. Finally, we find out the specific cryptographic technique that would eventually help in the later stages of the design process by eliminating unnecessary design constraints in a particular scenario. The rest of the paper is organized as follows: In Section 2, Proposed Security Engineering Process is discussed; Section 3 provides Proposed Framework for Security Design Engineering; Section 4 provides Implementation Example; Finally we conclude the paper in Section 5.

2   Proposed Security Engineering Process

To design, build and deploy secure systems, we must integrate security into SDLC and adapt current software engineering practices and methodologies to include specific security-related activities. Security-related activities [15] include identifying security requirements, prioritizing and management of security requirements, security design, implementing security mechanisms, security testing. Our proposed framework for Security Engineering Process (SEP) is shown in Fig. 1. The concept of this framework for security engineering process is an attempt to propose a design framework taking the view of stakeholders as well as environmental constraints in the earlier software development phases.

3   Proposed Framework for Security Design Engineering

The proposed framework for Security Design Engineering Process is as shown in Fig. 2.

Step 1: Mapping of security requirements with security services. After the security requirements have been identified, we proceed to the design phase of the Security Engineering Process (SEP) i.e., prioritized security requirements are mapped with security services like Confidentiality, Integrity, Authentication and Non-repudiation services. This would eventually help in the later stages of the design process, by specifying which cryptographic techniques would be suitable in a particular scenario.

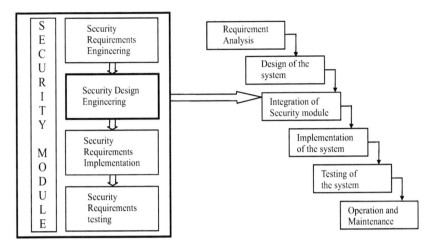

Fig. 1. Proposed Framework for Security Engineering Process integrated with SDLC

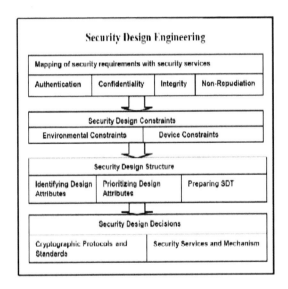

Fig. 2. Proposed Framework for Security Design Engineering Process

Step 2: Identifying Design Constraints. In this activity, different constraints are identified which affects the selection of cryptographic techniques. The Environmental Constraints of the target deployment system is considered here depending on whether the system would be implemented on a wired/wireless/embedded/Mobile environments or Desktop based systems. For instance, in a web based system, there are many communicational constraints (like channel capacity, bandwidth, power etc.,) and computational constraints (like memory, processing power, energy etc.,).

Step 3: Security Design Structuring. A good design demands a thorough understanding of the target platform, operating environment and performance and security requirements of the system. Table 1 lists important design attributes and their priorities for High-end and Low-end devices found in [16].

Table 1. List of design attributes and their priorities

High-end devices		Low-end devices	
High priority	**Low priority**	**High priority**	**Low priority**
Scalability	Cost	Security	Throughput
Security	Power consumption	Complexity	Flexibility
Throughput	Complexity	Power consumption	Algorithm agility
System architecture		Cost	Scalability
Target platform		System architecture	
Algorithm agility		Target platform	
Flexibility		HW/SW	
HW/SW			

Preparation of Security Design Template (SDT). Proposed Template contains the values of the design attributes. The values of the design attributes are classified into following categories as shown in Table 2.

Table 2. Proposed SDT containing the priorities of design attributes

Environment	Design Attribute	Priority			Cryptographic Technique
		High (Value 1.0)	**Medium (Value 0.5)**	**Low (Value 0.1)**	
Wired [ ]	Throughput	✓			Cryptographic Software [ ]
WLAN [✓]	Target platform	✓			File Encryption Tools [ ]
WPAN [ ]	Cost			✓	Disc Encryption Tools [ ]
WMAN [ ]	Power consumption			✓	Public key Encryption [✓]
Mobile [ ]	Storage	✓			Symmetric Encryption [ ]
Sensor [ ]	Scalability	✓			Block Ciphers [ ]
Embedded [ ]	Flexibility	✓			Stream Ciphers [ ]
	Algorithm agility		✓		Digital Signatures [ ]
	Complexity		✓		Biometric Authentication [ ]
	Bandwidth	✓			Hash Algorithms [ ]

Step-4: Security Design Decisions. We propose a template based decision approach to choose the best suitable cryptographic technique depending upon the design attributes supplied in the above Security Design Template. This has been done in the subsequent Section.

4   Implementation Example

In this section, we implement the security design engineering process in Web based Banking system. For a Web based Banking, the direct actors /stakeholders can be Customer, Bank Employee, Bank Database. We identify the banking services of each actor and their associated non-functional requirements applying Viewpoint Oriented Security Requirement Engineering Process (VOSREP) as below:

- From the viewpoints of Customer, the banking services are Balance inquiry, Transaction information, Fund transfer, Bill payment and non-functional requirements are Reliability, Performance, Supportability.
- From the viewpoints of Bank Employee, the banking services are Update Account, Transaction processing, User query process, Report generation, Maintenance and non-functional requirements are Correctness and Consistency of Information, Minimize response time in accessing account, Usability.
- From the viewpoints of Bank Database, the banking services are Maintaining reports of the database, Recovery system and non-functional requirements are Reliability, Integrity, Recovery, Performance.

Based on above analysis, Threats and associated Security Requirements have been identified as shown in Table 3. For prioritizing Security Requirements (SR), we have assumed certain values of Threat Rating (very low 0.10, low 0.33, medium 1.00, high 3.33, very high 10.00) and Vulnerability (low 0.1, medium 0.5, high 1.0) against each identified Threat and Asset Values (range 1 to 10) against each Asset affected which are project specific. The Risk is measured based on CRAMMs Risk Matrix [14] as Risk= value based on measure of (Threat, Vulnerability, Asset). Table 3 shows the SR'Prioritization in Web based Banking System. Table 4 below shows Decision Template containing the priorities of the design attributes in smart card environment. If we want to consider some public key algorithm in this environment, the design decision should depend upon which technique among various available techniques can be considered. The decision template provides necessary data of different public key algorithm which help us to choose a suitable cryptographic technique in a particular environment.

Table 3. SR Prioritization in Web based Banking System

Security Requirement	Threat	Threat Rating	Vulnerability	Assets affected	Asset Value	Risk	SR Prioritize
Authentication	1. T.PIN_Violated	3.33	0.1	User login info(1,2)	4	3,2	5
	2. T.Denial_of_service	0.10	0.5	Smart Card info(1,2,3)	9	6,5,5	16
	3. T.Impersonate	0.33	0.5	Account info(1,3)	6	4,4	8
Authorization	1. T.Change_Data	3.33	0.5	Certificate info(2)	7	5	5
	2. T.Certificate_steal	1.00	0.5	Account info(1,2)	6	5,4	9
Privacy	1. T.PIN_Violated	3.33	0.5	User login info(1,2)	4	4,2	6
	2. T.Unauthorize_access	0.10	0.5	Account info(1,2)	6	5,3	8
Integrity	1. T.Replace	1.00	0.1	Customers info(1,2)	5	3,3	6
	2. T.Data_Theft	1.00	0.1	Transaction info(1,2)	8	5,5	10
Non-Repudiation	1.T.Certificate_steal	3.33	0.5	Customers info(1)	5	4	4

Table 4. Decision Template for Web based Banking system

Public key Encryption Technique	Design Attribute	Priority			ECC operation on GF(p)		
		High (Value 1.0)	Medium (Value 0.5)	Low (Value 0.1)	Operation	Itera tions	Total Time (ms)
RSA	Throughput	✓			168 bit Encryption	269	42
ELGAMAL	Target platform	✓			168 bit Decryption	337	38
PohligHellman	Cost			✓	168 bit Signature	138	36
Rabin	Power consumption			✓	168 bit Verification	205	34
LUC	Storage	✓			155 bit Encryption	114	30
ECC ✓	Scalability	✓			155 bit Decryption	223	31
HECC	Flexibility	✓			155 bit Signature	336	30
	Algorithm agility		✓		155 bit Verification	281	38
	Complexity		✓				
	Bandwidth	✓					

We implemented some of the most common cryptographic algorithms using $Crypto++$ library. All were coded in C++ and ran on *Intel Core 2DUO* CPU T6400@2.00*GHz PC* with 4GB RAM and windows vista operating system. We used these data in the Decision Template.

5   Conclusion

We have developed a Framework for Security Design Engineering Process. The different types of security requirements are mapped to the different security services. The identified design attributes are prioritized and a security design template is prepared to find out the specific cryptographic technique that would eliminate unnecessary design constraints in a particular environment. This process is coherent with the conventional Software Engineering Process so that eliciting security requirements and security design become an integral part of system engineering and security engineering.

References

1. Fabian, B., Gurses, S., Heisel, M., Santen, T., Schmidt, H.: A Comparison of Security Requirement Engineering Methods. In: Requirements Engineering, vol. 15, pp. 7–40. Springer, Heidelberg (2010)
2. Dermott, J.M., Fox, C.: Using abuse Case Models for Security Requirements Analysis. Department of Computer Science, James Madison University (1999)
3. Sindre, G., Opdahl, A.L.: Eliciting Security Requirements with Misuse Cases. In: Requirements Engineering, vol. 10, pp. 34–44. Springer, Heidelberg (2005)
4. Ware, M., Bowles, J., Eastman, C.: Using the Common Criteria to Elicit Security Requirements with Use Cases. IEEE Computer Society, Los Alamitos (2006)

5. Robert, J., Ellison: Attack Trees. Software Engineering Institute, CMU (2005)
6. Giorgini, P., Manson, G., Mouratidis, H., Philip, I.: A Natural Extension of Tropos Methodology for Modelling Security. In: OOPSLA (2002)
7. Van Lamsweerde, A.: Elaborating Security Requirements by Construction of Intentional Anti-models. In: ICSE, pp. 148–157. IEEE Computer Society, Los Alamitos (2004)
8. Donald, G., Firesmith: Engineering Security Requirements. Journal of Object Technology 2(1), 53–68 (2003)
9. EBIOS: Expression of Need and Identification of Security Objectives. DCSSI, France (2004)
10. Christopher, A., Audrey, D.: OCTAVE Method Implementation Guide, vol. 2. Carnegie Mellon University, Pittsburgh, PA, SEI (2001)
11. The Logic behind CRAMMs Assessment of Measures of Risk and Determination of Appropriate Countermeasures, Siemens Enterprise (2005)
12. Kotonya, G., Sommerville, I.: Requirement Engineering with View Points (1995)
13. Gupta, D., Agarwal, A.: Security Requirement Elicitation using View Points for Online System. In: ICETET 2008, pp. 1238–1243. IEEE Computer Society, Los Alamitos (2008)
14. Gupta, D., Jaiswal, S.: Security Requirement Prioritization. Software Engineering Research and Practice, 673–679 (2009)
15. Sommerville, I.: Software Engineering. Pearson Education, London (2003) ISBN-8129708671
16. Hankerson, D., Menezes, A., Vanstone, S.: Guide to Elliptic Curve Cryptography. Springer publication, Heidelberg (2004) ISBN 0-387-95273-X

Software Piracy Prevention through SMS Gateway

Abhinav Kumar, Anant Kumar Rai, Ankur Kumar Shrivastava,
Dhirendra Yadav, Monark Bag, and Vrijendra Singh

Cyber Law and Information Security Division,
Indian Institute of Information Technology, Allahabad, India
{abhinavcool2,anantrai6feb}@gmail.com

Abstract. Software piracy is a main concerned for organization world-wide, not considering the numerous defence techniques in position and various others that have been anticipated to stop it, thus resulting in the loss of millions of revenue for such organization. This paper looks at the primary loop hole in the current scenario, follow-on from the static nature of defence and lack of ability to stop the duplication of digital data. A new method is presented here, that facilitates the dynamic nature of defence and thus making it harder to create a supplementary, similar functional copy.

Keywords: Anti-Piracy Method, Database Management System, Intellectual Property, SMS Gateway, Software Protection, Tailored Approach.

1 Introduction

Software Piracy is the process in which involves people creates unlawful copies of software that result in copyright violation of software.

The unlawful copying of software products was allowed before 1980, without facing any legal consequence. The U.S. Patent Office does not acknowledge copyright of software source code but still it's allowed copyright on software compiled version. In 1970, Bill Gates present evidences and formed a strong group which result in the formulation of regulation to safe the interest of software development organization.

According to the research work published reports so far suggested various protective measures to prevent software piracy although they addressed the problem associated with software piracy from legal, ethical technical means but still till date there is no effective measure to prevent software piracy.

Unlawful copying of copyrighted software becomes painless and free of cost by the development of file sharing program such as Bit Torrent and Napster. Add on to this the availability of high speed internet make any software just a click away from users.

According to seventh BSA global software piracy study, in global market the software piracy rate jumps from 2% to 43%. The major reason behind this drastic change is exponentially raising PC markets in emerging market likes Brazil, India

K.R. Venugopal and L.M. Patnaik (Eds.): ICIP 2011, CCIS 157, pp. 294–300, 2011.

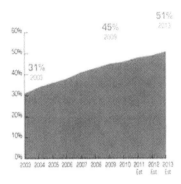

Fig. 1. Percentage of Worldwide Installed Base of PCs

and China. The PC market in these three nations registered an 86% growth in PC shipments [1]. Fig. 1 shows the percentage of worldwide installed PCS base except Australia, New Zeland, Japan, US, Canada and Western Europe, based on seventh annual BSA global software piracy study.

Source: Seventh Annual BSA Global Software Piracy Study, May 2010

2   Related Work

There are hundreds of copy protection techniques [2] and strategies that have been proposed in last two decade for software piracy prevention. Gopal and Sanders show that deterrent measures like legal punishment are more effective as compare to preventive measures like copy-protection techniques.

Yet various researches are going on in the field of preventive measures. In early 1980s software companies shared various protection techniques just to increase the number of users of their software, as the number of personal computer users was increasing exponentially [3]. More term which comes in our mind is Software diversity which was the most neglected aspect in academic environment until various organization face millions of dollars loss annually.

One can now feel an emergency in promoting awareness about it and promoting research to formulate ways to stop unlawful copying of software. If we are asked to segregate the entire software piracy prevention process on the bases of the approaches then three approaches can be derived.

The first approach can be considered as the basic way of software prevention and that is software piracy prevention through registration codes. Registration codes are unique string or combination of them required to be entered by the user while installing some software.

On the purchase of software these unique code is provided to the user, which they are required in order to install the software. It is almost next to impossible for user to generate these codes, making it an efficient way of preventing software piracy. Software companies can either produce a pre-generated catalogue of codes for clients to utilize, or produce a unique code based on the client's name or computers' signature. It is also possible to produce Registration codes from a computer signature. A computer signature is produced by collecting exclusive information of the computer and changing it into a code that can only be utilized by that particular machine. This prevent user from entering one code in more than one computer. Software pirates keep on finding ways to share pre-produced unique code over internet. Various software pirates groups are active and they reversed code generation mechanism to generate their own unique registration codes.

The second approach talks about online activation of software, thus adding an additional layer of protection in software suite. Online activation involves Software Company as clients are needed to contact them. The software company will allow activation of the software product only if it was not activate on other computer or if the client is lawful owner of the software. This prevent user from illegally installing software on more than one computer. Like the previous approach, this approach also have loop hole. Utilizing these drawbacks software pirate groups from time to time issue patches to bypass the online activation of softwares.

The last approach is of Media Protection. By media protection we mean safe guarding the physical media such as Floppy, CD and DVD Drives which can be very easily copied from one system to another without any point of concerned. Many clients try to install a software product on more than one computer from the same physical media or they pass the physical media to their friend to install the software products. In countries where software piracy rates are very high, software pirates create multiple copies of a single software product and sell them on the street for a modest price of $2.

Like the earlier two approaches media protection also not able to stop software pirates from duplicating downloaded version of software products. Tools like Daemon Tools and Alcohol 120% help software pirates to bypass the media protection media.

3   Effective Anti-piracy Methods

Effectively preventing software piracy requires multiple tactics. Software companies must ensure they protect their intellectual property, reduce consumer's desire to pirate their software, and implement software protection methods to stop those who wants to steal it.

3.1   Intellectual Protection

An essential part of employing anti-piracy methods is to ensure that intellectual property (IP) is properly protected. This requires effort from both the software companies and the national governments. First, the government must ensure that the required laws exist to protect company's intellectual property. Next, these laws must be enforced against infringers. Finally, the industry must educate and spread awareness among the public about the IP laws.

The first step in implementing proper IP protection lies on the active participation from the governments. The government must create the laws which will protect Intellectual Property against infringement. This includes software patents and copyrights. Software companies should know–what laws protect their IP in marketable countries, and lobby the governments if these laws are not adequate. Strong intellectual protection laws exist in most developed nations, and many other countries are developing these laws. The United States recently passed the Digital Millennium Copyright Act [4], which includes many provisions for protecting intellectual property.

World copyright protection laws include the World Trade Organization's Trade-Related Aspects of Intellectual Property [5] (TRIPS) and the World Intellectual Property Organization (WIPO) Copyright Treaty.

The next step in intellectual property protection is ensuring that there are measures in place to enforce the laws. Without the proper enforcement, the laws can do nothing. In the United States, both private companies (like Microsoft) and government agencies (like Department of Justice, FBI, police departments, postal service) can file criminal suites against alleged offenders [6].

The final step in implementing intellectual property laws is consumer education. Studies have shown that 54% of consumers are unaware any policies against redistribution of paid-for content exist [7]. Another study reveals that only 25% of college students take the position that piracy is wrong.

3.2   Reducing Consumers' Desire to Pirate the Software

A powerful and effective method to prevent software piracy is to make it less desirable to pirate at the very first place. Software companies can take several steps to do this, including making it easy to legally obtain the software, ensuring proper pricing, and changing social attitudes.

Making software easier to obtain legally is another way in reducing the piracy. The customers who find it difficult to obtain software legitimately will explore other means to acquire it. So, it's very important to offer the software though several venues. This may include offering downloadable versions in countries that do not offer the product in retail stores. If customer can find a product with an ease and legally then it's very likely he or she may acquire the software from a company. This approach may make the customer to explore the illegal means to get software.

Pricing is also plays an important role in piracy. If purchase price in obtaining software is more than the expectation then, the customer will definitely pirate it. Regional income considerations must be used when determining the price at which software will be sold. Piracy rates are often higher in developing countries, where consumers usually make considerably less income [8]. Consumers with less income will be more likely to pirate the software since they cannot afford the high price.

Finally, there are social considerations to take into account when selling software in different countries. An attitude on the morality of software piracy differs from region to region, due to cultural differences. In areas such as Hong Kong and China where piracy rates are high, social beliefs have long held that copying works of any kind is necessary and honorable, and a way to learn . A combined campaign of industry and government can help change these attitudes over time.

4 Tailored Approach

After reviewing the existing techniques for software piracy prevention we realize there is various flaws in them. With our tailored approach we tried to remove the flaws provide better security to software companies. We defined our approach in step wise as follows.

1. Purchase Software.
2. Each software product must have a serial number along with a hidden unique number.
3. Serial number matching is performed. MAC address and unique ID is fetch.
4. If the serial number does not match then an error message will be display and the installation process terminate.
5. An XOR function is perform on MAC address and current date is perform which will be display on screen.
6. User is required to SMS the display code to a mobile number along with the serial number of product on 67689.
7. Server will then store the serial number and MAC address (which the server will get by again performing XOR on the receiving code). The server will get unique ID from the database which will have unique ID associated with each serial number.
8. At server, a code will be generated by simply adding the unique number and current date.
9. This number will be forwarded to the user.
10. User will enter the code and then only can install the software. If the code differs then error message will be display.

With the help of Fig. 2 we try to explain our tailored approach through flow chart. It is the flowchart of complete process that is starting from the initial installation till the software installation complete.

– Unique Number is fetch internally during initial installation procedure.

Notes

1. 5th to 7th Step is part of the installation process and the installation will not be completed until you validate your software from the organization server.
2. At 8th step the organization server will generate a number (e.g., the combination of the unique number and Date of Installation), so as every time the user will get a different number and hence the chance of guessing is less.
3. On 9th step the server will send the number generated back to the user. We can design the installation process in such a way that it will also generate the same number (one which was generated by server) and when it verifies that the number is same then installation complete else it will display error message.

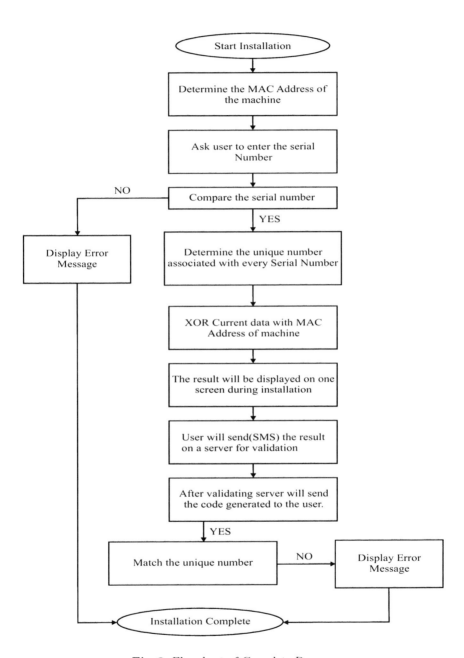

Fig. 2. Flowchart of Complete Process

4. At 10th step again a validation process will occur which will compare the code a user get from the server with the code generated on backside of installation process which will also the combination of date and unique id, which will be fetch through programming.

5 Conclusions

With the computer software becoming an indispensible among the various users like the home user or the medium or large enterprises, it is becoming more and more important to protect software companies' products against illegal activities. Software companies in today's market places should be aware of the methods that pirates use to steal software, and common tactics they can use to protect their intellectual property. Though piracy is not likely to stop completely with an immediate effect, but attacking the problem from different perspectives will result in increasing the sales and revenues of the organizations. The harder for a user to pirate a product is, the more likely that the product is purchased legally.

References

1. Seventh Annual BSA/IDC Global Software 09 Piracy Study (November 05, 2010)
2. Atallah, L., Jiangtao, L.: Enhanced Smart-card based License Management. In: Proc. of IEEE International Conference on E-Commerce, pp. 111–119 (June 2003)
3. Shy, O., Thisse, J.F.: A Strategic Approach to Software Protection. Journal of Economics Management Strategy 8(2), 163–190 (1999)
4. U.S. Copyright Office, The Digital Millennium Copyright Act of 1998. Washington, DC (October 28, 1998)
5. World Trade Organization. Agreement on Trade-Related Aspects of Intellectual Property Rights. Marrakesh, Morocco (April 15, 1994)
6. Software Information Industry Association, SIIA's Report on Global Software Piracy 2000. Washington, DC (2000)
7. Software Information Industry Association and KPMG LLP, Doesn't Everyone Do It? Internet Piracy Attitudes and Behaviors (Fall 2001)
8. Business Software Alliance, First Annual BSA and IDC Global Software Piracy Study. Washington, DC (July 07, 2004)

Estimating Strength of a DDoS Attack in Real Time Using ANN Based Scheme

P.K. Agrawal[1], B.B. Gupta[2,3], Satbir Jain[1], and M.K. Pattanshetti[2]

[1] Department of Computer Engineering, Netaji Subhas Institute of Technology,
Delhi University, New Delhi, India
[2] Department of Computer Engineering, Graphic Era University, Dehradun, India
[3] Department of Electronics and Computer Engineering,
Indian Institute of Technology, Roorkee, India
{pradeep.k.agrawal84,gupta.brij}@gmail.com

Abstract. At present, distributed denial of service attack (DDoS) is most common and harmful threat to Internet infrastructure. Many approaches are given in literature for handling these attacks; however there is no scheme that can completely prevent or detect these attacks. Estimating strength of a DDoS attack in real time is helpful to suppress the effect of a DDoS attack by filtering or rate limiting the most suspicious attack sources. In this paper, we present artificial neural network (ANN) based scheme to estimate strength of a DDoS attack. Datasets generated using NS-2 network simulator running on Linux platform are used for training and testing feed forward neural network. Feed forward neural network with different number of neurons are compared for their estimation performance using mean square error (MSE). Simulation results show proposed scheme can estimate strength of DDoS attack in real time efficiently.

Keywords: Artificial Neural Network, DDoS attack, Entropy, Intrusion detection, Mean Square Error.

1 Introduction

Today, World Wide Web (WWW) has become the mean for financial management, education, global information service center for news, advertisements, and for many other services. Distributed denial of service (DDoS) attack is most common and harmful threat to World Wide Web and Internet infrastructure. DDoS attacker mostly targets the network bandwidth or connectivity to prevent the legitimate use of service by producing an excessive surge of traffic toward a victim. Victim of DDoS attack can suffer damages like file corruption or system shutdown, *etc.*, [1]. The impact of DDoS attack can be minor inconvenience to user of a website or the financial losses for companies that run e-commerce website. An FBI affidavit [2] describes a DDoS attack on an e-commerce website using a 5,000 node zombies that caused a loss of several millions of dollars in revenue. System manager or researcher always tries to modify their approach

K.R. Venugopal and L.M. Patnaik (Eds.): ICIP 2011, CCIS 157, pp. 301–310, 2011.
© Springer-Verlag Berlin Heidelberg 2011

to handle new attacks and attackers also modify the attack tools to bypass the security system developed by researchers or system managers. These DDoS attacks and attack handling processes are running in a cycle. Unfortunately there is no scheme that can completely detect or prevent the DDoS attacks. Defending DDoS attacks on web server has become a very challenging problem. Real time estimation of strength of a DDoS attack is helpful to suppress the effect of DDoS Attack. In this paper, we proposed an ANN based scheme for estimating strength of a DDoS attack in real time. Real time estimation of strength of a DDoS attack can be utilized to suppress the effect of DDoS attack by filtering or rate limiting the most suspicious attack sources. Datasets generated using NS-2 network simulator running on Linux platform are used for training and testing feed forward neural network. Feed forward neural network with different number of neurons are compared for their estimation performance using mean square error (MSE). Results show proposed scheme can estimate strength of a DDoS attack in real time efficiently.

The remainder of this paper is organized as follows: Section 2 contains related work. Section 3 provides an overview of artificial neural networks (ANN). Section 4 describe the entropy based DDoS Detection. Section 5 contains experimental setup and performance analysis. Section 6 shows the results of ANN based scheme. Finally, Section 7 concludes the paper.

2   Related Work

In literature, there are many applications in which ANN based schemes are effectively used. In [3], Gupta et. al., have used ANN based scheme to predict number of zombies in a DDoS attack. In this ANN based scheme, feed forward neural network is used to predict number of zombies. In [4–6], ANN is trained using normal and attack traffic data and ANN is used to decide normal or presence of attack. In [5], feed forward neural network is used to detect different DDoS attacks. In [6], ANN is used to classify a network while under attack. This classification uses three layer feed forward neural network and it is trained to output 0 when there is no attack and output 1 when there is attack. In [3–10], various regression models, i.e., linear, polynomial, exponential, power and logarithmic, multiple are used to estimate strength of DDoS attack. In [11], backscatter analysis is used to estimate number of spoofed addresses involved in DDoS attack, but backscatter is an offline analysis. In this paper, we take a step further to concept of estimating strength of DDoS attack and we use ANN for estimating strength of DDoS attack in real time. We have calculated the mean square error (MSE) and test error in order to measure the performance of the proposed scheme. Results show proposed scheme can be used to estimate strength of DDoS attack efficiently.

3   Artificial Neural Networks

An Artificial Neural Network (ANN) is a mathematical or computational model that is inspired by the structure or functional aspects of biological nervous system

[7]. A neural network is a set of interconnected artificial neurons in which each connection has a weight associated with it. These associated weights are learned by iteratively processing a training dataset during the training phase. Neural networks are inherently parallel, used to speed up the computational process [8]. ANN based scheme particularly useful in applications where the complexity of the data or task makes impractical to humans or other computer techniques [7]. ANN can be applicable to broad categories like function approximation, classification including pattern or sequence recognition *etc.*

3.1 Multilayer Feed Forward Neural Network

Multilayer feed forward neural network is most popular network. It consists of an input layer, output layer and one or more hidden layer between input and output layer. A Multilayer feed forward network is shown in Fig. 1 [8]. Multilayer neural network shown in Fig. 1 is two layer neural network (input layer is not counted), a hidden layer with three neurons and output layer with two neurons. Each layer of feed forward network made up of neurons or units. Each neuron in a particular layer is connected with all neuron in the next layer except output layer. The network shown in Fig. 1 is known as feed forward because none of the weight cycles back to an input unit or output unit of a previous layer [8]. Multilayer feed forward neural network having enough number of neurons or layers and training sample can be used to approximate any function. The output O_j of unit j at hidden or output layer is computed as follows:

$$O_j = f(I_j) = 1/(1 + e^{-I_j}). \tag{1}$$

$$I_j = \sum W_{ij}O_i + \theta j. \tag{2}$$

where,
f is the activation function.
I_j is net input to jth unit.
W_{ij} is weight of connection between unit j and previous layer unit i.
O_i output of unit i from previous layer and θ_j is bias of the unit j.

3.2 Back Propagation Algorithm

Neural networks can be classified in many forms based on type of connection and algorithms used in learning process. Back propagation algorithm is most widely used to perform learning on a multilayer feed forward neural network. Multilayer feed forward network learn by repeatedly processing a training dataset. For each tuple in training dataset, weights are modified in order to minimize the mean square error (MSE) between the predicted values and actual target values. In back propagation algorithm the weights and biases are modified as follows:

$$W_{ij} = W_{ij} + \delta W_{ij}. \tag{3}$$

$$\theta j = \theta j + \delta\theta j. \tag{4}$$

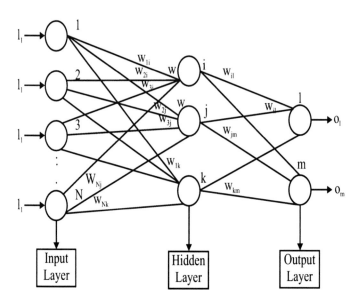

Fig. 1. Learning Process in Feed Forward Neural Network by Back Propagation Algorithm

where, $\delta\theta j$ is change in bias and δW_{ij} is change in weight. Changes in bias and weight is measured based on error of network prediction. Method of gradient descent is used to find a set of weights that fits the training data to minimize MSE.

4   Entropy Based DDoS Attack Detection

This section describes an entropy based DDoS detection scheme [9]. It can be implemented as a part of access router or implemented as separate unit that interact with access router to detect attack. Entropy based scheme is based on the assumption that the traffic normally seen in the network differs from traffic under attack. In order to detect attack, the value of entropy $H_c(X)$ (entropy at the time of detection) is calculated in continuous time interval δ; whenever there is deviation in entropy above the threshold value from $H_n(X)$ (normal entropy value) attack is detected. Sample entropy simply defined as a metric that capture the degree of dispersal or concentration of a distribution [4]. Sample entropy $H(X)$ is calculated as:

$$H(X) = -\sum p_i log_2(p_i)(5).$$ (5)

where, p_i is n_i /S. Here n_i is the total number of bytes arrival in a flow i in a continuous time interval δ and S is the total number of bytes arrival in N number of flows, represented as:

$$S = \sum_{i=1}^{N} n_i, i = 1, 2, 3...N.$$ (6)

5 Experimental Setup and Performance Analysis

In this section, we evaluate our proposed scheme using simulations. The simulations are carried out using NS2 network simulator. We show that false positives and false negatives triggered by our scheme are very less. This implies that profiles built are reasonably stable and are able to estimating strength of DDoS attack correctly [10].

5.1 Simulation Environment

Real-world Internet type topologies generated using Transit-Stub model of GT-ITM topology generator are used to test our proposed scheme, where transit domains are treated as different Internet Service Provider (ISP) networks i.e., Autonomous Systems (AS). For simulations, we use ISP level topology, which contains four transit domains with each domain containing twelve transit nodes i.e., transit routers. All the four transit domains have two peer links at transit nodes with adjacent transit domains. Remaining ten transit nodes are connected to ten stub domain, one stub domain per transit node. Stub domains are used to connect transit domains with customer domains, as each stub domain contains a customer domain with ten legitimate client machines. So total of four hundred legitimate client machines are used to generate background traffic. Total zombie machines range between 10 and 100 to generate attack traffic. Transit domain four contains the server machine to be attacked by zombie machines [10].

The legitimate clients are TCP agents that request files of size 1 Mbps with request inter-arrival times drawn from a Poisson distribution. The attackers are modeled by UDP agents. A UDP connection is used instead of a TCP one because in a practical attack flow, the attacker would normally never follow the basic rules of TCP, i.e., waiting for ACK packets before the next window of outstanding packets can be sent, etc. The attack traffic rate is fixed to 25 Mbps in total; therefore, mean attack rate per zombie is varied from 0.25Mbps to 2.5 Mbps. In our experiments, the monitoring time window was set to 200 ms. Total false positive alarms are minimum with high detection rate using this value of monitoring window. The simulations are repeated and different attack scenarios are compared by varying attack strength and at fixed total number of zombies.

6 Results and Discussions

6.1 Data Set Description

In our paper, in order to estimate strength of a DDoS attack, we utilize deviation in entropy. For validating our scheme, we have taken same dataset as used in [10]. Dataset samples contain the deviation in entropy and actual strength of DDoS attack. These dataset samples are generated using NS-2 network simulator on Linux platform. A transit stub model of GT-ITM topology generator is used to generate Internet type topology for simulation. In this experiment, total 100 zombies are used to generate attack traffic, attack traffic ranges from 10 Mbps to 100 Mbps.

Table 1. Training Data - Deviation in Entropy with Actual Strength of DDoS Attack

Actual strength of DDoS attack (Y)	Deviation in Entropy (X)
10M	0.149
15M	0.169
25M	0.192
30M	0.199
35M	0.197
40M	0.195
45M	0.195
55M	0.212
60M	0.233
65M	0.241
75M	0.253
80M	0.279
85M	0.280
90M	0.299
100M	0.319

Table 2. Testing Data: Deviation in Entropy with Actual Strength of DDoS Attack

Actual strength of DDoS attack (Y)	Deviation in Entropy (X)
20M	0.184
50M	0.208
70M	0.244
95M	0.296

In order to train and test the feed forward neural network, obtained datasets are divided into two parts. First part, training data, contains 78.95% of total data values for training the neural network. Training data values are shown in Table 1. Second part, testing data, contains randomly chosen data values from original dataset. Test data samples used for testing the feed forward neural network are shown in Table 2.

6.2   Network Training

In network training phase, a feed forward neural network has to be trained by providing deviation in entropy (x) as input and corresponding actual strength of DDoS attack (y) as target value. Generated output values by neural network are compared with actual target values to find the error in network prediction.

Back propagation learning algorithm iteratively calculate the change in weight and the bias based on the minimum error or other stopping criteria is meet and connections weight and bias are adjusted according to Fig. 2. There is no

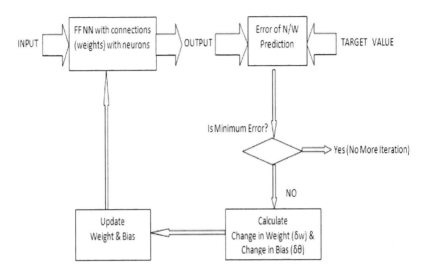

Fig. 2. Learning Process in Feed Forward Neural Network by Back Propagation Algorithm

direct method for deciding the size of network for a given problem. The size of network appropriate for a given problem basically decided based on experience or trial error method. Network size directly affect the training time as well as the implementation cost. As increase the network size, both the training time and implementation cost is also increases. In order to get good estimation results, two layers feed forward networks with 10, 15 and 20 neurons (units) are used. These networks are trained using Levenberg-Marquardt back propagation algorithm available in MATLABs neural network toolbox. Mean square error (MSE) is used to measure the performance of the training. MSE is the difference between the target value and the actual output value of neural network. In best situation the MSE is 0, Means network output is same as target value. Training results in Table 3 show that MSE in training decreases as the network size increases.

6.3   Network Testing

Once the training phase is completed, trained network is ready for testing. Using the testing data as given in Table 2, deviation in entropy (X) is fed as input to the trained network. MSE in testing for various two layers feed forward networks with 10, 15 and 20 neurons (units) is shown in Table 4.

Table 3. Training Results of Various Two Layer Feed Forward Networks

Network Used	Network Size	Number of Epochs	MSE in Testing
Two layer	10-1	100	1.57
feed forward	15-1	100	0.63
network	20-1	100	0.46

Table 4. Testing Results of Various Two Layer Feed Forward Networks

Network Used	Network Size	Number of Epochs	MSE in Testing
Two layer	10-1	100	4.9
feed forward	15-1	100	3.5
network	20-1	100	1.8

From the Table 4, we can see that MSE in testing decrease as the network size increases. Minimum the MSE means estimated values are closer to actual values. Fig. 3 shows the comparison between actual strength of DDoS attack and estimated strength of DDoS attack for various feed forward neural networks.

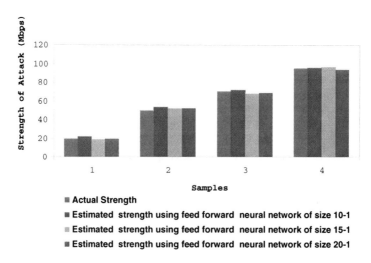

Fig. 3. Comparison between actual strength of DDoS attack and estimated strength of DDoS attack using various size feed forward neural networks

From Fig. 3 we can see the estimated strength of DDoS using two layers feed forward network with 20 neurons is much closer to the actual strength of DDoS attack as compared to the same network with 10 or 15 neurons. Test error for is calculated using the two layers forward neural network with 10, 15 and 20 neurons (units). Test error results are shown in Tables 5, 6 and 7.

Table 5. Summary of Test Error for Two Layer Feed Forward Neural Network of Size 10-1

Deviation in entropy (X)	Actual strength of DDoS attack(Y)	Test error
0.184	20	1.63
0.208	50	3.66
0.244	70	1.52
0.296	95	1.14

Table 6. Summary of Test Error for Two Layer Feed Forward Neural Network of Size 15-1

Deviation in entropy (X)	Actual strength of DDoS attack(Y)	Test error
0.184	20	-1.44
0.208	50	2.27
0.244	70	-1.82
0.296	95	1.92

Table 7. Summary of Test Error for Two Layer Feed Forward Neural Network of Size 20-1

Deviation in entropy (X)	Actual strength of DDoS attack(Y)	Test error
0.184	20	0.20
0.208	50	1.91
0.244	70	-1.01
0.296	95	-1.70

Results show that the estimating strength of a DDoS attack using ANN based scheme is very close to the actual strength of a DDoS attack. Hence ANN based scheme can be used for estimating the strength of DDoS attacks in real time.

7   Conclusions

In this paper, potential of Artificial Neural Network (ANN) for estimating strength of a DDoS attack has been investigated. The feed forward neural network with size of 10, 15 and 20 are used for estimating strength of DDoS Attack. The deviation in Entropy and strength of DDoS attack are used as an input and output to the two layer feed forward network, respectively. Results are very promising, as estimating strength of a DDoS attack using feed forward neural network is very close to actual strength of a DDoS attack.

References

1. Douligeris, C., Mitrokotsa, A.: DDoS Attacks and Defense Mechanisms: Classification and State of the Art. Elsevier Science Direct Computer Networks 44, 643–666 (2004)
2. CERT Incident note IN 2004-01 W32/Novarg. A Virus (2004)
3. Gupta, B.B., Joshi, R.C., Misra, M.: ANN Based Scheme to Predict Number of Zombies in DDoS Attack. International J. of Network Security 13(3), 216–225 (2011)
4. Gupta, B.B., Agrawal, P.K., Joshi, R.C., Misra, M.: Estimating Strength of a DDoS Attack Using Multiple Regression Analysis. In: Meghanathan, N., Kaushik, B.K., Nagamalai, D. (eds.) CCSIT 2011, Part III. CCIS, vol. 133, pp. 280–289. Springer, Heidelberg (2011)
5. Ahmad, I., Abdullah, A.B., Alghamdi, A.S.: Application of Artificial Neural Network in Detection of DoS Attacks. In: Proceedings of International Conference on Security of Information and Networks(SIN 2009), North Cyprus, Turkey, pp. 229–234 (2009)
6. Seufert, S., Brien, D.O.: Machine Learning for Automatic Defense Against Distributed Denial of Service Attacks. In: Proceedings of IEEE International Conference on Communications, ICC 2007, pp. 1217–1222 (June 2007)
7. Yegnanarayana, B.: Artificial Neural Networks. Prentice-Hall, New Delhi (1999)
8. Han, J., Kamber, M., Pei, J.: Data Mining Concepts and Techniques. Elsevier, Amsterdam (2006) ISBN: 978-1-55860-901-3
9. Shannon, C.E.: A Mathematical Theory of Communication. In: ACM SIGMOBILE Mobile Computing and Communication Review, vol. 5, pp. 3–55 (2001)
10. Gupta, B.B., Joshi, R.C., Misra, M.: Estimating Strength of DDoS Attack Using Various Regression Models. Int. J. Multimedia Intelligence and Security 1(4), 378–391 (2010)
11. Moore, D., Shannon, C., Brown, D.J., Voelker, G., Savage, S.: Inferring Internet Denial-of-Service Activity. ACM Transactions on Computer Systems 24(2), 115–139 (2006)

Performance Analysis of Multicarrier Code Division Multiple Access Transmission Techniques

Sarala B.[1] and Venkateshwarulu D.S.[2]

Department of ECE, MVSR Engineering College, Hyderabad, India
Department of ECE, Benaras Hindu University (BHU), Varanasi, India
b.sarala@rediffmail.com, dronamraju_sv@yahoo.com

Abstract. Recent advances in wireless communications have made use of Multicarrier Code Division Multiple Accesses (MC CDMA) technique to allow high data rate transmission for broadband communications. The Bit Error Rate (BER) and Signal to Noise Ratio (SNR) of MC CDMA considering three different spreading sequences in presence of Additive White Gaussian Noise (AWGN) and Rayleigh fading are studied and investigated. Bit Error Rate (BER) of MC CDMA transmission system depends strongly on Multiple Access Interference (MAI) due to cross correlation properties of applied spreading codes. The spreading codes for MC CDMA like Walsh codes, Gold codes, Maximal length Pseudo Noise (PN) codes are used in order to minimize the BER, and to reduce MAI.

Keywords: Additive White Gaussian Noise, Bit Error Rate, Multiple Access Interference, Multicarrier Code Divivsion Multiple Accesses.

1 Introduction

Multicarrier Code Division Multiple Access (MC CDMA) system is a dominant digital modulation technique for 4th generation (4G) wireless communication system. The conventional CDMA technique used in third generation system faces serious limitations by channel dispersion, causing Inter Symbol Interference (ISI), and it requires advanced signal processing algorithms to contain it [1]. The MC CDMA employing multiple stream of data channel can combat channel dispersion, hence ISI, thereby increasing system capability to accommodate a higher number of users and its data requirements. The pre-4G technology is example for 3rd generation partnership project (3 GPP) long terms Evolution (LTE) often branded 4G. The 4G provides a wide range of data rates up to $100mbps$ to 1 $Gbps$. The 4G is able to support interactive services like video conferencing, wireless internet etc., The bandwidth much wider (100 MHZ) and data transmitted with higher data rates [2]. The 4G broadband networks support IP telephony services, Ultra broadband internet access, gamming services and HDTV, streamed multimedia services.

MC CDMA is a multiple access scheme used in Orthogonal Frequency Division Multiplexing (OFDM) telecommunication systems, allowing the system

K.R. Venugopal and L.M. Patnaik (Eds.): ICIP 2011, CCIS 157, pp. 311–319, 2011.
© Springer-Verlag Berlin Heidelberg 2011

to support multiple users at the same time. The main idea of the OFDM is to split the data stream to be transmitted into N parallel streams of reduced data and to transmit each of them on a separate subcarrier made orthogonal by appropriately choosing the frequency spacing between them to obtain high spectral efficiency [3]. OFDM is an efficient modulation scheme for broadband wireless communications to obtain high data rates, accurate channel estimation is required. MC CDMA spreads each user in the frequency domain [4]. In 1993 a new multiple access schemes based on a combination of CDMA and multicarrier (OFDM) techniques are proposed, such as multicarrier-CDMA (MC-CDMA)[5]. MC CDMA technique transmitted a single data symbol at multiple narrowband subcarriers with each subcarrier encoded with a phase offset of 0 to π (180) based on a spreading code [6]. The set of frequency offsets form code to distinguish different users. Each bit is transmitted over N different subcarriers has its own phase offset determined by spreading code.

Frequency domain spreading schemes in which the chips of a spread data symbol are assigned across the subcarriers were also proposed independently by Yee etal (1993), Fazel and Papke (1993), and Chouly etal (1993).These schemes with frequency domain spreading have become simply as multicarrier CDMA [7]. An advantage of frequency domain spreading in comparison with time domain spreading is the inherent frequency diversity in frequency selective channel, which on other hand can also be disadvantages as the orthogonally between spreading codes deteriorates. MC CDMA has been usually considered to perform better than MC-DS-CDMA or single carrier Direct Sequence (DS_CDMA) CDMA in a synchronous downlink [8]. MC CDMA technique to deliver multirate services, variable bit rate transmission, multirate data streams in frequency selective channels [9].MC CDMA advantages are higher data rate application, simpler frequency domain equalization, better performance, higher spectral efficiency, minimize adjacent carrier spacing , to avoid Inter Symbol Interference (ISI), delay spread is minimum, alleviate multipath effects [10]. MC CDMA disadvantages are carrier offset between transmitter and receiver due to oscillator instability, Doppler Effect, incurs heavy loss in the performance of MC CDMA [9]. The high Peak to Average Power Ratio (PAPR) severely limits its application. Spreading codes play an important role in multiple access of MC CDMA system, M-sequences, Gold code sequences etc., has been traditionally used as spreading codes in MC CDMA. These sequences are generated by shift registers, which are periodic in nature. In order to spread the bandwidth of the transmitting signals, Pseudo Noise (PN) sequences have been extensively used in spread spectrum communication systems. The maximal length shift sequences, and Gold codes, Walsh codes are most popular spreading sequences in CDMA [11]. This paper is organized as follows. In section 1 introduced MC CDMA system model. In section 2 spreading sequences presented. Section 3 discusses the Rayleigh fading in presence of AWGN. Section 4 Performance Evaluation of MC CDMA System will be presented. Simulation and conclusion will be given on section 5 and 6.

2 MC CDMA System Model

A block diagram of simplified baseband model of MC CDMA transmitter is given in Fig. 1. The transmitter schematic of the MC CDMA system using frequency domain spreading which is based on Fig. 1 that the information bits to be transmitted from a particular user are firstly baseband modulated into BPSK modulation symbols and then they are spread by using a specific spreading sequence. In the case of MC CDMA, as the spreading codes Walsh codes, Gold codes, Orthogonal codes, maximal length PN codes, complementary Go lay codes are used mostly. The spread symbols are modulated by multicarrier modulation implemented by Inverse Fast Fourier Transformation operation(IFFT) [12]. The IFFT block outputs are fed to the guard insertion block and parallel to serial conversion represent the input of DAC. To overcome the effect of Inter Symbol Interference (ISI), baseband signal is cyclically extended to more than the channel delay spread to allow transmission of an interference free symbol. The transmitted signal is represented as

$$S_k(t) = \sum_{n=-\infty}^{\infty} \sum_{i=1}^{q} \sum_{j=1}^{N_c} \sqrt{\frac{2p}{N_c}} bk_i[n]c_k[j-1]PT_S(t-nT_s)cos(2\pi f_{ij}t+\theta_{ij}(k)). \quad (1)$$

$b_{ki}(n)$ represents the ith data stream of user k and $b_{ki}[n]$ is assumed to be random variable, assumes values of +1 or -1 with equal probability. $c_k(j)$ is the jth spreading code, $P_r(t)$ represents rectangular modulation, $\theta_{ij}(k)$ is the random phase introduced by the carrier modulation[13]. The basic structure of receiver sketched in Fig. 2. By using a guard interval, the receiver select the portion of the signal is free from ISI. This is processed by an FFT block to demodulate multiple carriers. When there are k active users, the received signal is represented by

$$r(t) = \sum_{k=0}^{K-1} \sum_{i=0}^{N-1} P_{n,i}C_k[i]\alpha_k(n)\left(cos2\pi f_c t + 2\pi i\frac{F}{t_b} + \theta_{k,i}\right) + n(t). \quad (2)$$

Where the effects of channel included in P_k, I and $_{k,I}$ and $n(t)$ is Additive White Gaussian Noise (AWGN) with a one sided power spectral density of N_0. MC CDMA can handle N simultaneous users with good BER, using standard receiver techniques.

Fig. 1. MC CDMA Transmitter Block Diagram

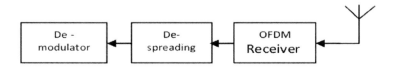

Fig. 2. MC CDMA Receiver block Diagram

3   Spreading Sequences

Consider MC CDMA system $a_k(n) \in \{+1, -1\}$ which denotes the nth information of the kth user, is multiplied by the chip of the users specific spreading sequence for example Walsh Hadamard code, $c_k[i](i = 0, --, N - 1)$. Walsh Hadamard orthogonal codes are used for spreading because of their good orthogonal cross-correlation property [14]. An m-sequence (PN code), can be generated by using a linear feedback shift register of length n that cycles through all possible $2^n - 1$ states. While the m-sequence have excellent autocorrelation properties, quasi-orthogonal and periodic. Gold sequences can be generated with a length of $2^n - 1$ is composed of a preferred pair of m-sequences, together with the element-wise multiplications of these two sequences in their different phases. The Gold sequences obtain low cross correlation property [15].

4   Channel Model

There are many models available in literature to characterize fading channel. Rayleigh fading channel model assumes a direct/dominant path and many reflected path [16], [17]. The probability density function of a Rayleigh fading channel is defined as follows.

$$f_p(p) = f_p(\sqrt{2}p)\frac{dp}{|dp|} = \frac{1}{\sigma 2} exp^{\left(\frac{-p}{\sigma 2}\right)}. \tag{3}$$

Where, p is instaneous power and is related to signal amplitude p as

$$p = 1/2 * p^2. \tag{4}$$

Noise Model. We consider an Additive White Gaussian Noise (AWGN) in presence of Rayleigh fading channel to simulate BER given by

$$\sigma^2 = w * N_0/N. \tag{5}$$

Where w is the total bandwidth, N_0 is the noise spectral density, N_c is total subcarriers. $BER Calculation$: The BER for ith subcarrier corresponding to BPSK is given by

$$BER_{BPSK\_AWGN} = \frac{1}{2} erfc(\sqrt{E_b}/N_0). \tag{6}$$

$$BER_{BPSK\_fading} = \frac{1}{2}erfc\left[1 - \frac{1}{\sqrt{1 + \frac{1}{E_b/N_0}}}\right]. \tag{7}$$

E_b/N_0 is the ratio between the energy per bit (E_b) and the noise power density N_0.

5   Performance Evaluation of MC CDMA System

Usually the spreading techniques are expected to be stronger against the ICI due to their wide bandwidth property produced in spreading the data symbols with the generated chip sequence. The spreading code provides the interference rejection capability. The use of Walsh Hadamard code with good autocorrelation properties can reduce the impact of interference. MC CDMA performance analysis based on different spreading sequences has been applied at AWGN channel and Rayleigh fading channel is studied and analyzed. Spreading sequences like Walsh codes, m-sequence PN codes, Gold codes have been chosen. Number of subcarriers Nc=8 and 16 are transmitted for the spread of BPSK modulation.

MC CDMA transmission system represented by BER versus E_b/N_0 (Signal to Noise Ratio) for different spreading sequences such as Walsh codes, m-sequence PN codes, and Gold codes are evaluated. This paper compares the performance of three types of spreading codes for MC CDMA. The result analysis is as shown in Figures numbered 3 to 14.The received symbol power is equal to the transmitted symbol power. Each user symbol is spread over 8 subcarriers and 16 subcarriers, 2 and 4 users with different spreading sequences with the guard interval. A guard interval of 20% of the MC CDMA symbol period employing BPSK is taken into consideration. The system is simulated in MATLAB.

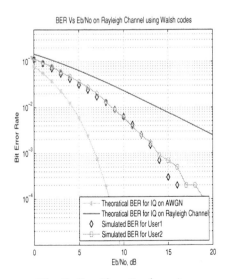

Fig. 3. For $N_c = 8$ subcarriers

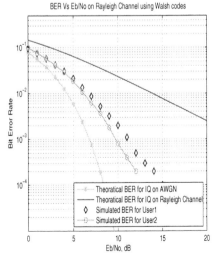

Fig. 4. For $N_c = 16$ subcarriers

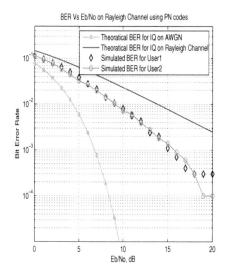

Fig. 5. For $N_c = 8$ subcarriers

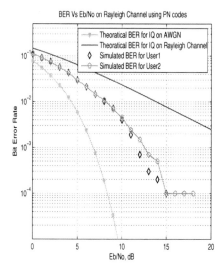

Fig. 6. For $N_c = 16$ subcarriers

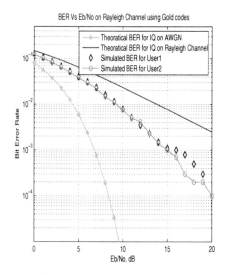

Fig. 7. For $N_c = 8$ subcarriers

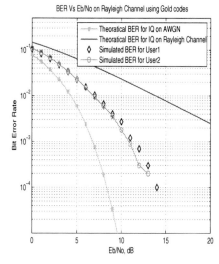

Fig. 8. For $N_c = 16$ subcarriers

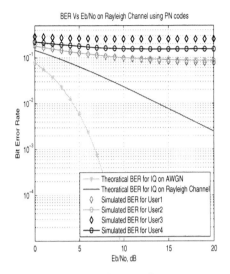

Fig. 9. For $N_c = 8$ subcarriers

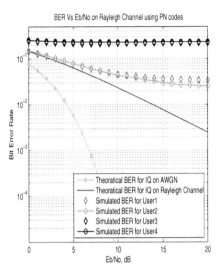

Fig. 10. For $N_c = 16$ subcarriers

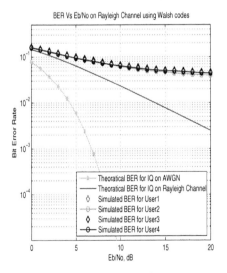

Fig. 11. For $N_c = 8$ subcarriers

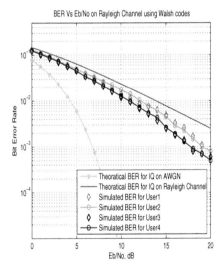

Fig. 12. For $N_c = 16$ subcarriers

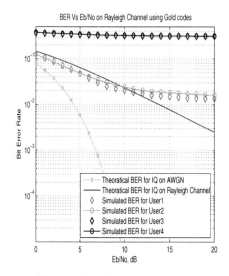

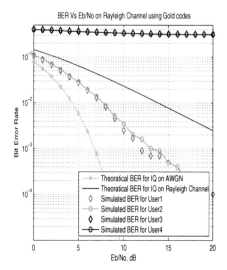

Fig. 13. For $N_c = 8$ subcarriers   **Fig. 14.** For $N_c = 16$ subcarriers

6   Results

The result analysis is as shown in Figures numbered 3 to 14 [18].

7   Conclusions

In this paper, we have studied and analyzed MC CDMA for different spreading sequences. Results are given for several variations of the available parameters of MC CDMA transmission systems for three spreading sequences of Walsh codes, PN codes, and Gold codes at AWGN and Rayleigh fading channel.

- The number of subcarriers increases to reduce BER and provides quality of service.
- As the number of users increases, BER increases, even though MC CDMA supports maximum number of users.
- Walsh codes provide better performance of MC CDMA.
- The Rayleigh fading channel is better for MC CDMA.

The performance of the both multi-user systems gauzed by the average BER and close analysis of the results concludes the following.

- Higher access capability obtained with MC CDMA.
- The results infer that larger code sequence length used in MC CDMA system leads to obtain a better performance but at the same time decreases the data rate of the system.

Therefore, there is also a trade-off between the number of multiplexed users and the desired system performance. Future work is focused on selecting the best subcarrier and transmitting the data through the subcarriers by adaptive modulation methods to achieve robust and spectrally efficient communication over the multipath fading channels.

References

1. Guenach, M., Steendam, H.: Performance Evaluation and Parameter Optimization of MC-CDMA. IEEE Transactions on Vehicular Technology 56(3) (May 2007)
2. OFDM and MC-CDMA-TELCOM, A Technologies Latest Telecom News GSM (March 18, 2011)
3. Multicarrier CDMA-Wikipedia
4. The Enhanced Performance of Combined Multi-Carrier and CDMA Technologies in Multi-path Fading Channels
5. Digital Implementation of ETSI OFDM Symbol Synchronization based on Sliding Correlation
6. Hara, S., Prasad, R.: Overview of Multi-Carrier CDMA. IEEE communications Magazine 35(12), 126–133 (1997)
7. Nobilet, S., Helard, J., Moltier, D.: Spreading Services in Up-link and Down-link MC-CDMA Systems. PAPR an MAI Minimization. European Transactions in Telecommunications (2002)
8. Claudio, S., Gianluca, G., Carlo, S.R.: Performance Evaluation of MC CDMA Techniques for Variable Bit-rate Transmission in Leo Satellite Networks
9. Drotar, P., Gazela, J., Galaija, P.: Effects of Spreading Sequences on the Performance of MC-CDMA System with Non-linear Models of HPA. Radio Engineering 18(1) (April 2009)
10. Taher, H.J., Salleh, M.F.M.: Multi-carrier Transmission for Wireless Communication Systems–A Survey. School of Electrical and Electronics Engineering, University Sains Malaysia, vol. 08(5) (May 2009) ISSN:1109-2742
11. Arsalan, T., Mccormick, A.C., Grant, P.M., Erdogan, A.T.: A Low Power MMSE Receiver for Multi-Carrier CDMA. In: ISCAS, (on Circuits and Systems) May 6-9, vol. 4, pp. 41–44 (2001)
12. Dinan, E.H., Jabbari: Spreading Codes for Direct Sequence CDMA and Wide-band CDMA Cellular Networks. IEEE communications 12 Magzine 36, 48–54 (1998)
13. Prasad, R., Hara, S.: Overview of Multi-Carrier CDMA. In: Proceeding of Fourth International Symposium in Spread Spectrum Techniques
14. Yang, Y., Lijong, S., Liu, J.c.: Performance Analysis of Carrier Frequency Offset on Up-link MC-CDMA System with Unbalanced EGC over Nakagami Fading Channels
15. Kunnari, E.: Multirate MC CDMA Performance Analysis in Stochastically Modeled Correlated Fading Channels with an Application to OFDM-UWB, pp. 56-58
16. Lee, W.C.Y.: Mobile Cellular Telecommunications, 2nd edn. McGrawHill, Newyork (1995)
17. Yee, N., paul, J., Linnartz: Multi-Carrier CDMA in an Indoor Wireless Radio Channel
18. John, G.P., Salehi, M., Bauch, G.: Contemporary Communication Systems using MATLAB and Simulink, 2nd edn. (1997)

Optical Chaos Synchronization and Spatio-temporal Digital Cryptography

Santo Banerjee[1] and Sumona Mukhopadhyay[2]

[1] Dipartimento di Matematica, Politecnico di Torino, Corso Duca degli Abruzzi 24,
10129 Torino, Italy
[2] Army Institute of Management, Judge's Court Road, Alipore, Kolkata, India
santo.banerjee@polito.it, sumona.mukhopadhyay@gmail.com

Abstract. The Optical chaotic systems, with infinite dimensionality, have gained a lot of attention for communication and cryptographic purposes. The semiconductor devices act as a cryptosystem with high bandwidth. We explore the synchronization phenomenon between two spatio-temporal chaotic semi conductor lasers with bi-directional coupling. The coupling facilitates two way simultaneous communication. The ease of modular implementation of optical feedback together with the randomness and ergodic properties of the infinite dimensional systems produces completely randomized chaotic time series. Such a system is an ideal candidate for cryptographic purposes of large streams of data such as a digital image. The system renders enough *confusion* and *diffusion* properties to the transmitted gray scaled image rendering the statistically disordered cipher image totally incoherent from the original message. Simulation result and statistical tests demonstrate the merit of the system in achieving robust and secure cryptography with deterministic chaos aiding in the correct recovery of the encoded image.

Keywords: Bi-directional Coupling, Image Cryptography, Semiconductor Laser, Spatio-Temporal Chaos Synchronization.

1 Introduction

The advancement in high speed telecommunication and the indispensable usage of internet capabilities has compelled to seek for efficient alternative techniques to securely communicate information.

The primary requirements for a secure cryptographic system are:

1. High dimensional system which remains chaotic in a continuous range of the parameter space[1].
2. The encryption methodology should incorporate properties like a huge key space [2], which should be very sensitive to any kind of perturbations and immune from statistical attacks.
3. Minimum transfer of system information.

An efficient and faster new breed of encryption technique operating in the physical layer of the transmission system is lately creating a lot of buzz. This is

K.R. Venugopal and L.M. Patnaik (Eds.): ICIP 2011, CCIS 157, pp. 320–328, 2011.
© Springer-Verlag Berlin Heidelberg 2011

achieved by using chaotic carriers obtained from semiconductor lasers to encode an information. Chaos Cryptography [3,4,5,6,7], an offshoot of traditional cryptography is realized with the synchronization of two coupled chaotic trajectories. The genesis of chaos based cryptography is attributed to the pioneering work of chaos synchronization by Pecora and Carroll [8]. Its principle of operation relies primarily on the fact that the chaotic nonlinear oscillator plays the role of a broadband signal generator and the chaotic waveform can mask the information.

Features of Chaotic Dynamics exploited in Chaos Based Cryptography are: ergodicity [9], sensitivity to initial condition, randomness, mixing, high dimensionality and complexity of the chaotic carrier. The high complexity of the chaotic carrier induced due to the high frequencies and the large number of degrees of freedom makes the recovery process difficult without an appropriate receiver. These higher dimensional nonlinear devices, due to the delay-induced dynamics [10], exhibit nonlinear dynamical behavior with fast irregular pulsations of the optical power, or wavelength hopping, with bandwidth ranging from a few gigahertz to tens of giga-hertz, large correlation dimension of chaotic carriers[11][12], preventing linear filtering and frequency-domain analysis. These key properties required for secure transmission makes chaos based cryptography an ideal choice. Chaos based cryptography renders the cipher deterministically disordered having a strong dependence on even minimal variations of initial conditions and parameter values, and makes them resistant to most of the attacks. In apropos to the above, the complexity and unpredictability of a yet another high dimensional chaotic system has been applied in this present work for symmetric mode cryptographic applications. Rest of the paper is organized as follows: Section 2 presents the system exhibiting spatio-temporal chaos followed by an investigation of the two way coupled synchronization phenomenon is demonstrated in section 3. Section 4 describes the implementation of the synchronized system in cryptographic application. In section 5, we perform a detailed statistical analysis of the encryption methodology followed by the conclusion in section 6.

2   The System and Spatio-temporal Chaos

A spatially extended system exhibiting extreme disordered phase in both space and time is labeled as a spatio-temporal chaotic system [13]. The disorder in space and time can be quantified by the rapid decay of spatial correlations and the positive Lyapunov exponents respectively. Excellent examples of this kind of system is a one dimensional coupled map lattices(CML) [14] and semiconductor laser system. Spatio-temporal chaotic systems overcome the problem of rapid degradation suffered by individual chaotic systems [15] and are found to exhibit sustained periodicity [16] with a performance edge [17]. This is also beneficial in communication [18]. Studies reveal that the short external cavities is responsible for producing multimodal dynamics [19] in the laser systems with delay induced optical feedback which results in increasing the dimensionality of the rate equations. Therefore, the system we consider takes the following form [20].

$$\pm \frac{\partial E_\pm}{\partial z} + \frac{\partial E_\pm}{\partial t} = i \left(\frac{D_p}{L_c} \right) \frac{\partial^2 E_\pm}{\partial z^2} - iWL_c E_\pm + \kappa \left[(N - 1) - i\alpha N \right] E_\pm,$$

$$\frac{\partial N}{\partial t} = \left(\frac{D_f T}{L_c^2} \right) \frac{\partial^2 N}{\partial z^2} + \frac{\Lambda T}{N_0} - \frac{T}{\tau} N_2 - aTE_0^2 (N - 1) \left(|E_+|^2 + |E_-|^2 \right). \quad (1)$$

$E_\pm$ are the forward (backward) electric fields normalized by the electric pump $E_0 \sim 10^{17} \text{v/m}$. N is the carrier density normalized by N_0. The space and the time variables are normalized respectively by $L_0 \sim 1\mu\text{m}$ and $T \sim 0.01$ ns. The system of Eq (1) describes the weakly nonlinear dynamics of slowly varying two counter propagating longitudinally high-frequency (hf) optical fields (traveling waves) interacting with low-frequency (lf) density perturbations associated with the electron-hole (total) charge carriers in the active semiconductor lasers. The amplitude of the optical wave envelope is modulated by the electrostatic small but finite amplitude electron-hole density fluctuations in which n_l represents the refractive index of the active layer. D_p stands for the diffraction which provides higher-order dispersion. The system exhibits spatio-temporal chaos as shown in Fig. 1. For rest of the parameters with their numerical values refer Table I in [13].

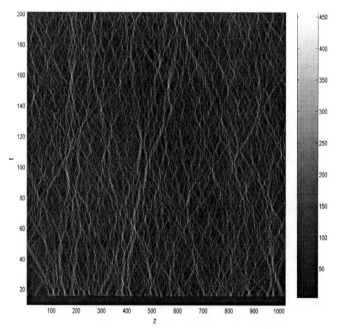

Fig. 1. Spatio-temporal contour plot corresponding to $|E_+|$=constant in Eq. 1 showing chaos

3   Synchronization of Spatio-temporal Semiconductor Lasers

The synchronized system exhibiting spatio-temporal chaos is formulated as below [13]

$$\pm \frac{\partial E_{\pm 1}}{\partial z} + \frac{\partial E_{\pm 1}}{\partial t} = i \left(\frac{D_p}{L_c} \right) \frac{\partial^2 E_{\pm 1}}{\partial z^2} - iWL_c E_{\pm 1} + \kappa \left[(N-1) - i\alpha N \right] E_{\pm 1}$$
$$+ \epsilon_1 \left(E_{\pm 2} - E_{\pm 1} \right),$$
$$\frac{\partial N_1}{\partial t} = \left(\frac{D_f T}{L_c^2} \right) \frac{\partial^2 N_1}{\partial z^2} + \frac{\Lambda T}{N_0} - \frac{T}{\tau} N_1 - aT E_0^2 \left(N_1 - 1 \right) \left(|E_{+1}|^2 + |E_{-1}|^2 \right). \quad (2)$$

and

$$\pm \frac{\partial E_{\pm 2}}{\partial z} + \frac{\partial E_{\pm 2}}{\partial t} = i \left(\frac{D_p}{L_c} \right) \frac{\partial^2 E_{\pm 2}}{\partial z^2} - iWL_c E_{\pm 2} + \kappa \left[(N-1) - i\alpha N \right] E_{\pm 2}$$
$$+ \epsilon_2 \left(E_{\pm 1} - E_{\pm 2} \right),$$
$$\frac{\partial N_2}{\partial t} = \left(\frac{D_f T}{L_c^2} \right) \frac{\partial^2 N_2}{\partial z^2} + \frac{\Lambda T}{N_0} - \frac{T}{\tau} N_2 - aT E_0^2 \left(N_2 - 1 \right) \left(|E_{+2}|^2 + |E_{-2}|^2 \right). \quad (3)$$

where the symbols $\kappa = \Gamma L_c N_0 a, \epsilon = \zeta L_c, L_c = Tc/n_l, \epsilon_1 = 1.5$ and $\epsilon_2 = 2.0$. By introducing the coupling term $\propto$ and ϵ, representing the non-radiative laser loss or gain by the driver or response field due to power reflectivity, the system described above is synchronized. Therefore, it is imperative to see whether synchronization of such high-dimensional chaotic systems is robust against noise and/or error signals for transmitted messages. The system is composed of three variables viz., the forward field E_{+1}, the backward field E_{-1} and the normalized carrier density function N. The wave number of modulation is represented k, β is a suitable constant taken as $1/500$ to make the perturbation small. $E_{\pm 0} = 2$ and $\tilde{E}_{\pm 1}, \tilde{N}$ are constants of the order of unity. $E_\pm$ are the forward (backward) electric fields normalized by the electric pump $E_0 \sim 10^{17}$v/m. N is the carrier density normalized by N_0. The space and the time variables are normalized respectively by $L_0 \sim 1\mu$m and $T \sim 0.01$ ns. The system of Eq. (2) and Eq.(3) represents the weakly non-linear dynamics of slowly varying two counter propagating longitudinally high-frequency (hf) optical fields. D_p stands for the diffraction which provides higher-order dispersion. The dynamical behaviors of the twin-strip lasers shows a transition from order to spatio-temporal chaos [20] by altering the inter-element distance of the coupled two strips of laser.

The system of equations describe the effect of local optical fields and the charged carriers along the longitudinal directions on the dynamics of the optical system. The simulation results after numerical integration with proper initial conditions are displayed in Fig. 2. which represents the synchronization error between the two lasers respectively .

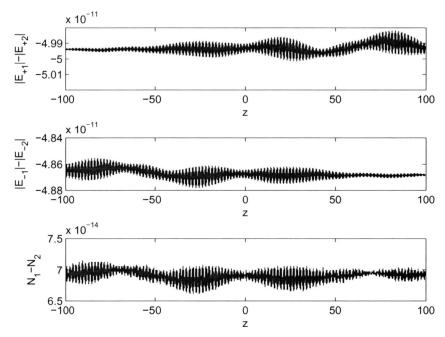

Fig. 2. Synchronization errors of coupled spatio-temporal semiconductor laser systems

It is interesting to note that due to bi-directional coupling the system represented through Eq. (2) and Eq.(3) can interchangeably play the role of transmitter and receiver. An interesting fact about the two-way coupled system is that the signals from the communicating parties contains information only pertaining to the electric field. This makes the scheme secure from the common "man-in-the-middle" attack. For efficient cryptography, the key space and the key length should be large in order to resist brute force attack. Moreover, for absolute secrecy the keys space should not be reused. The scheme adheres to Kirchoff's principle and the arrangement of the key set forms a Vignere cipher which is theoretically unbroken [7]. At synchronization, say at $t=t_{max}=20$ (dimensionless unit), the system will remain the same for any $t_i > t_{max}$ at which the error between $E_{\pm 1}$ and $E_{\pm 2}$ will approach zero. At this instant, infinitely many numbers are generated which are ergodic and randomized in nature. This is the state y_0 where both the sender and receiver can start collecting data used for cryptographic purpose from any time after t_{max}.

4   Application in Image Encryption

This section focusses on the application of the synchronized space time laser systems for digital cryptography of a monochrome image. Private/ secret key used by both the communicating parties are $\rightarrow N_1$, $\rightarrow N_2$. On the other hand, variables transmitted over the communication channel/ Public key are $\rightarrow E_{+1}, E_{-1}, E_{+2}, E_{-2}$.

4.1   Algorithm

A digital image $P(M, N)$ is basically composed of three sets of two-dimensional matrices containing integers in the range of $0 - 255$. Each matrix contains M number of rows and N number of columns.

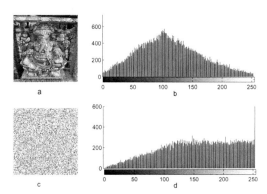

Fig. 3. The encryption process : (a) The original image (b)Histogram for the original image (c) The encrypted image (d) Histogram for the encrypted image.

Preprocessing Stage for both the communicating parties:-The system is subjected to a maximum number of iterations t_{max} after which an initial synchronized state y_0 is selected. The infinite number of chaotic sequences for the application are generated from variable N_1 at the transmitter end and N_2 at the receiver section as $Y = \{y_1, y_2, \ldots, y_\infty\}$. Then, each y_i is pre-processed as under $k_i \leftarrow integer(abs(10^3 \times |y_i|))Mod(M)$, The set $K = \{k_1, k_2, \ldots, k_\infty\}$ is used for cryptographic purpose.

Encryption

Encryption through Image Multiplication
Step 1:- Each of the pixels in a block of 8 bits of the image P is rotated through 5 bit positions by circular shift to produce the intermediate image A.

Encryption through Pixel Position Shuffling :- Diffusion phase
Step 2:- Permutation along the rows and columns - From the synchronized data set K, the pixel position of A is shuffled for each row r and column c through the following operation. $B_{rc} \leftarrow A_{kc}$, $B_{kc} \leftarrow A_{rk}$.

Encryption through Statistical Alternation :- Confusion phase
Step 3:- In this second phase, the key set K is used to change the pixel values of the image by additive operation expressed as under to obtain the cipher image CI. $CI_{rc} \leftarrow B_{rc} + k_i$.If $CI_{rc} > 256$ then $CI_{rc} \leftarrow CI_{rc} - 256$.

Decryption

The decryption steps are the reverse of the encryption process. The proposed method is simulated in Matlab 7.0 environment. The intensity plot in Fig. 3

shows that the cipher image is completely statistically disordered making it impossible to fathom any information about the original image.

5   Security Analysis

This section implements the algorithm for encrypting a 256×256 sized gray scale image and examines its efficiency. To ensure a large divergence of a chaotic trajectory from the initial condition, the number of iterations should be relatively large. The key space is generated after a considerable number of iterations using the variables of the system. The infinite dimensional system generates a huge key space which is large enough in order to withstand brute force attacks.

Fig. 4 (a),(b) shows that the incorrectly recovered image highly differs from the original due to a minor change in the key set obtained by changing the initial condition.This illustrates that the key sets are very sensitive to noise disturbances. Also from Fig. 4(c),(d) it can be observed that there is hardly any correlation between the adjacent pixels before and after cryptography among the randomly selected pixels placed adjacently along the horizontal direction.

Another quantifiable statistical measure of diffusion properties is the Unified Average Changing Intensity (UACI) which determines the average intensity of the differences between the pixel values of the original and encrypted image. Our scheme obtains a sufficiently high value of NPCR= 99.86 and UACI = 30.67. A higher value of NPCR is more desirable so as to prove that the system is resistant to differential attacks.

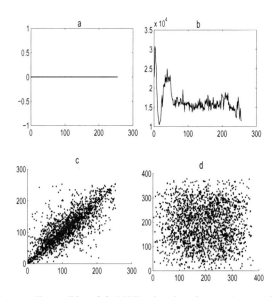

Fig. 4. Mean Square Error Plot (a) MSE plot for decryption with correct keys (b) MSE plot for decryption with incorrect keys; Scatter plot of correlation coefficients of adjacent pairs of pixels along the horizontal direction: (c) Correlation coefficient of the original image (d) Correlation coefficient of the cipher image

6   Conclusions

The paper investigates the synchronization phenomenon of a two way coupled laser systems exhibiting spatio-temporal chaos. We report the following results (a) For efficient cryptography, it is vital to choose a system which is robust and exhibits high dimensionality. (b) Cryptography with synchronized laser systems yields even better result without a need for several rounds of encryption, thus it is computationally inexpensive. (c)Bi-directional coupling facilitates a novel line of communication paradigm and our system being of infinite dimension renders additional security. Exhaustive statistical tests show that the proposed encryption scheme is tolerant to major brute force threats. These observations are vital from the perspective of real time communications and in high speed cryptography.

References

1. Banerjee, S., Yorke, J.A., Grebogi, C.: Robust Chaos. Physical Review Letters 80(14) (1998)
2. Schneier, B.: Applied Cryptography: Protocols, Algorithm, and Source Code in C. Wiley, New York (1996)
3. Alvarez, G., Monotoya, G., Pastor, F., Romera, M.: Chaotic Cryptosystems. In: Proc. IEEE Int. Carnahan Conf. Security Technology, pp. 332–338 (1999)
4. Banerjee, S., Ghosh, D., Ray, A., Chowdhury, A.R.: Europhysics Lett. 81, 20006 (2008)
5. Kocarev, L., Jakimoski, G., Stojanovski, T., Parlitz, I.: From Chaotic Maps to Encryption Schemes. In: Proc. IEEE Int. Symposium Circuits and Systems, vol. 4, pp. 514–517 (1998)
6. Kocarev, L.: Chaos-Based Cryptography:A brief overview. IEEE Circuits and Systems Magazine 1(3), 6–21 (2001)
7. Mukhopadhyay, S., Mitra, M., Banerjee, S.: Chaos Synchronization with Genetic Engineering Algorithm in Secure Communication. In: Banerjee, S. (ed.) Chaos Synchronization and Cryptography for Secure Communications: Applications for Encryption, pp. 476–509. IGI Global Publishers, U.S.A (2010)
8. Pecora, L.M., Carroll, T.L.: Phys. Rev. Lett. 64, 821 (1990)
9. Caponetto, R., Fortuna, L., Fazzino, S., Xibilia, M.G.: Chaotic Sequences to Improve the Performance of Evolutionary Algorithms. IEEE Transactions on Evolutionary Computation 7(3), 289–304 (2003)
10. Ikeda, K., Matsumoto, K.: High-Dimensional Chaotic Behavior in Systems with Time-Delayed Feedback. Physica D 29, 223–235 (1987)
11. Wang, A., Wang, Y., He, H.: Enhancing the Bandwidth of the Optical Chaotic Signal Generated by a Semiconductor Laser with Optical Feedback. IEEE Photonics Technol. Lett. 20(19), 1633–1635 (2008)
12. Kane, D.M., Toomey, J.P., Lee, M.W., Shore, K.A.: Correlation Dimension Signature of Wideband Chaos Synchronization of Semiconductor Lasers. Opt. Lett. 31(1), 20–22 (2006)
13. Banerjee, S., Rondoni, L., Mukhopadhyay, S., Misra, A.P.: Synchronization of Spatio-Temporal Semiconductor Lasers and It's Application in Color Image Encryption. Optics Communications 284(9), 2278–2291 (2011)

14. Li, P., Li, Z., Halang, W.A., Chen, G.: Chaos, Solitons Fractals 32, 1867 (2007)
15. Li, S., Chen, G., Mou, X.: Int. J. Bifurcation Chaos Appl. Sci. Eng. 15, 3119 (2005)
16. Wang, S., Liu, W., Lu, H., Kuang, J., Hu, G.: Int. J. Mod. Phys. B 18, 2617 (2004)
17. Wang, X., Zhan, M., Lai, C.H., Gang, H.: Chaos 14, 128 (2004)
18. Garca-Ojalvo, J., Roy, R.: Spatio-Temporal Communication with Synchronized Optical Chaos. Physical Review Letter 86(22), 5204 (2001)
19. Serrat, C., Prins, S., Vilaseca, R.: Dynamics and Coherence of a Multimode Semiconductor Laser with Optical Feedback in an Intermediate-Length External-Cavity regime. Physical Review A 68, 053804 (2003)
20. Hees, O., Scholl, E.: Physica D 70, 177 (1994)

Statistical Analysis of Network Traffic over LAN through IAMT

Shashank Srivastava, Abhinav Goyal, Rajeev Kumar, and Nandi G.C.

Indian Institute of Information Technology,
Allahabad, India
{Shashank12march,honeykool23,rajisstillhere,gcnandi}@gmail.com

Abstract. To overcome the problem of existing tools and mechanism, we developed a sophisticated and fast Internet Access Monitoring Tool (IAMT) which works as a handy tool for network administrators to monitor the users' activities on internet. Our main motive behind developing this tool comes from the need of a tool through which network administrator can analyze the users' net surfing habit, distribution/consumption of bandwidth and detection of suspicious activities from user's side. In our tool we analyzes both inbound and outbound traffic. This tool provides the feature of live packets analysis along with the functionality of storing the information in a database for future use. This tool can be very useful in organizations and institutions especially educational institutions where the number of peers is very high and their internet's consumption habits follow a certain pattern.

Keywords: Network Monitoring, Packet Analysis, Statistical Analysis, Traffic Monitoring.

1 Introduction

High demand of internet and IT applications have pressurized the organizations to monitor the network traffic to make their network infrastructure almost immune to various consequences of network overhead and failure. Heading with this problem, network traffic monitoring has become more crucial in current communication infrastructure. In general, to perform network monitoring, the network administrator sniffs the traffic flow with a program called sniffer which works in promiscuous mode [1] and examines captured traffic passing through selected network interface (NIC) [2]. Network monitoring describes the process that constantly monitors the activities performed on a network. It is an initial phase for network management. We developed a tool which provides following functionalities:

- Network Traffic Management
- Traffic Monitoring
- Network Management and optimization.

K.R. Venugopal and L.M. Patnaik (Eds.): ICIP 2011, CCIS 157, pp. 329–335, 2011.
© Springer-Verlag Berlin Heidelberg 2011

2   Proposed Algorithm for Capturing and Statistical Analysis of Traffic Pattern

The basic motivation behind to develop IAMT (Internet access and monitoring tool) tool was to analyze the behavior of internet traffic over LAN. Our tool provides the facilities of proper network monitoring to establish security and management of network resources to improve network efficiency. IAMT architecture is composed of three abstraction layer shown in Fig. 1.

1. Application Layer.
2. Kernel Layer.
3. Network Layer.

Network layer provides a set of network interface cards for capturing network traffic in promiscuous mode [1]. It provides captured traffic to kernel layer. Kernel layer acts as an interface between application layer and network layer. It stores captured traffic in memory buffer which can be read by user at application layer. Application layer analysis the data stored by the kernel layer from users' perspective.

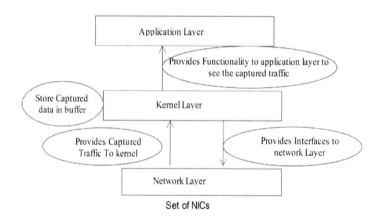

Fig. 1. Abstraction layers of architecture

2.1   Capturing and Statistical Analysis of Traffic Pattern

We devised an algorithm for internet traffic monitoring over LAN. Following steps are proposed to perform network analysis:

Step1: Details of all NICs (network interfaces cards). First lists out the NICs connected to the monitoring node (Monitor server). NULL or "any" is a type of device argument which is to be used for filtering the network traffic (captured packets) from all the network interface cards.
Class : GetDeviceName

Step2: Capture the packets through the selected network card interface or interfaces. Network administrator can select any interface for capturing network traffic. A queue is generated for buffering the captured packets and its size is specified according to bandwidth of concerning network. IAMT uses java library libpcap-0.9.8 [3] to capture the packets in promiscuous mode which pledges that the interface card transfers all the network traffic (passes through selected interface) towards monitor node or server.
Class : *OnlinePacketCapturing, QueuePacketClass*

Step3: Packets filtering phase. Since many types of packets travel across the network's interfaces,this tool applies filters which help in getting the only concerned packets to analyze. IAMT filters the packets by their IP Address, Mac address, protocol and port numbers contained in each individual packet [4].
Class : *SetFilter*

Step4: Analysis of captured (filtered) packets. IAMT uses jnetpcap-1.3.b0010-1.fc11.i386 java library [3] for capturing packets. A packet contains fixed size headers and data payload. Headers of a packet contain the information pertaining to its originator and destination. It also specifies the protocol details through which it travels across network. IAMT analyzes these captured packets by their sender and receivers address, protocols (used to transfers these) packets, port number etc.

Step 5: Analysis of Packet by tracking sequence number and acknowledgement. In this phase, IAMT takes out the details regarding IP Address, NIC Address[4], Latest Time of opened URL, and Upload/Download of each opened URL. Unlike other monitoring tools that have log manager, IAMT has capability to find bandwidth usage according to each and every URL opened. We devise an algorithm based upon Sequence and Acknowledge number of Packet. To find the details of uploading /downloading from different websites by a particular user, we devise a method which tracks the activities of users and their requests by analyzing the sequence and acknowledgment number hidden in packet header. Now using the concept of TCP handshaking [5] and TCP session maintenance we devise an approach which works in a following manner.

ProposedAlgorithm:

- Pick up a packet from the buffer.
- IAMT defines a data structure which maps Node's IP Address to a vector of current ACKs from all the active tcp session from that node. Each TCP sessions corresponds to the URL that has been accessed by that particular node.
- Extract sender and receiver IP addresses.One address will always be of the router or proxy server depending on which machine the IAMT is deployed.By using this information we can quickly find out for which node of the LAN this packet is meant to.

- Since ACK is nothing but the SEQ of next packet(belonging to same tcp session), hence with the help of IP address and SEQ of current packet we can easily find out the TCP session to which this current packet belongs. This is done by searching the ACK in the vector correspond to the IP Address of current vector.
- If SEQ of current packet matches to any ACK then we update the ACK saved in vector by the current ACK, else we add the current ACK in the vector marking the beginning of new TCP session.
- When ACK is updated or saved at that time IAMT also saves the relevant information like Packet size, URL information(only in SYN packets), port, Node's Address(to which this packet belongs).
  $Class : PacketDetailsExtract$

Step6: Create and update database with captured packet details. We used $MySql$ to create database. All the information extracted from $PacketDe-tailsExtract$ class is sent to Update Database class where information is saved in database.

Step7. Analysis of database. IAMT displays the data in ordered and categorized way. Whenever we want the data (information regarding network's traffic), first establish a connection with database and put the appropriate query to retrieve the relevant information regarding network's traffic.

3   Observation and Results

IAMT works in following phases.

Step1: Initial phase: In this phase, network administrator has to choose a network interface for capturing traffic from the set of available lists. User of the tool can select interface or a set of interfaces for capturing network or internet traffic.

Step2: Log Viewer: After capturing network traffic, the administrator analyzes the internet or network traffic through the log details. There are following options in front of administrator for log details like search with the help of IP, MAC and accessed site.

Step3: Analysis phase: Administrator analyzes the details of traffic current date and month wise and statistical analysis of users' behavior of accessing network, websites and network bandwidth usages in terms of various graphs shown in Figures 2, 3 and 4. (Fig. 2 presents the details regarding downloading /uploading data in terms of mega bytes by corresponding IP and MAC addresses) whereas (Fig. 3 shows the top ten bandwidth consuming websites) in which *symentic.liveupdate.com* consumes highest bandwidth among websites and (Fig. 4 shows top 7 users of network).

Current Month Analysis(MB)

Ip	Mac	Downl...	Upload	Downl...	Uploa...
172.16...	0:26:1...	3,338.78	255.87	14.11	16.86
172.16...	0:26:1...	2,615.74	55.74	11.06	3.67
172.16...	0:26:1...	2,177.91	45.33	9.21	2.99
172.16...	0:19:D...	1,813.84	88.14	7.67	5.81
172.16...	0:1E:E...	1,133.19	29.91	4.79	1.97
172.16...	0:1D:9...	1,106.09	29.72	4.67	1.96
172.16...	0:23:A...	1,090.64	46.85	4.61	3.09
172.16...	0:1D:B...	919.97	71.14	3.89	4.69
172.16...	0:25:B...	780.7	24.82	3.3	1.64
172.16...	0:19:D...	758.79	26.85	3.21	1.77
172.16...	0:26:1...	735.14	20.68	3.11	1.36
172.16...	0:19:D...	580.8	28.23	2.45	1.86
172.16...	0:1B:3...	479.71	20.27	2.03	1.34
172.16...	0:16:D...	422.82	15.97	1.79	1.05
172.16...	0:26:1...	362.89	14.44	1.53	0.95
172.16...	0:21:9...	361.16	9.33	1.53	0.61
172.16...	0:1D:6...	349.38	16.01	1.48	1.05
172.16...	0:1B:3...	345.98	10.97	1.46	0.72

Global Data(MB) Analysis (Excluding Current Month)

Ip	Mac	Downl...	Upload	Downl...	Uploa...
172.16...	0:26:1...	3967.0	1175.0	13.86	53.7
172.16...	0:1D:B...	2990.0	1.0	10.45	0.05
172.16...	0:21:9...	2625.0	68.0	9.17	3.11
172.16...	0:1D:9...	2064.0	1.0	7.21	0.05
172.16...	0:26:1...	1936.0	10.0	6.77	0.46
172.16...	0:23:A...	1646.0	15.0	5.75	0.69
172.16...	0:23:A...	1551.0	28.0	5.42	1.28
172.16...	0:21:9...	1516.0	56.0	5.3	2.56
172.16...	0:23:8...	1011.0	69.0	3.53	3.15
172.16...	0:26:1...	820.0	350.0	2.87	16.0
172.16...	0:23:8...	795.0	9.0	2.78	0.41
172.16...	0:25:B...	716.0	0.0	2.5	0.0
172.16...	0:26:1...	697.0	0.0	2.44	0.0
172.16...	0:1A:8...	633.0	13.0	2.21	0.59
172.16...	0:23:A...	495.0	0.0	1.73	0.0
172.16...	0:23:A...	491.0	25.0	1.72	1.14
172.16...	0:16:D...	475.0	1.0	1.66	0.05
172.16...	0:26:1...	394.0	0.0	1.38	0.0

Bar Graph

Pie Graph

Bar Graph

Pie Graph

Fig. 2. Current Month and Global Data Analysis

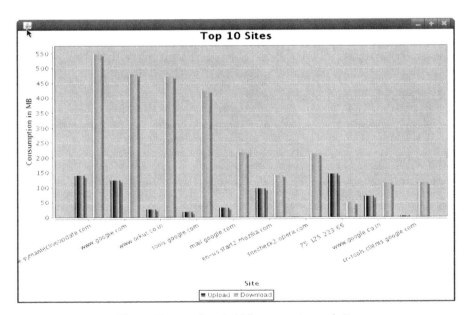

Fig. 3. Top ten bandwidth consuming websites

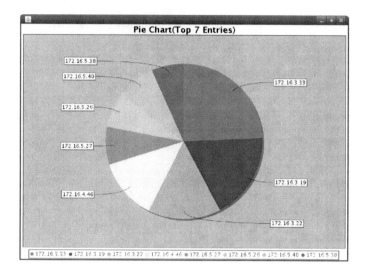

Fig. 4. Top seven bandwidth hosts in network

3.1 Advantages

- IAMT is a simple and sophisticated handy networking tool for network administrator.
- Since IAMT is using the layered approach, layer can be modified(keeping its interface same or compatible) according to the requirement without bothering about other layers.
- Effective analysis of bandwidth consumptions by websites which helps in banning those sites which are not required for curriculum purpose still users are using it.

4   Conclusions

In the competitive environment of developing software application for network administrator, we are up with the making of IAMT, a network statistical analyzer, which can be used for traffic monitoring by doing statistical analysis of the behavior of traffic flow and pattern. The various prospects which we have focused for network monitoring are Internet Traffic Management, Internet Traffic Monitoring, Network management and optimization with identifying network policy and security violations. The prominent area of network monitoring attracts the attention of various software organizations to help in building efficient and scalable network infrastructure to take the new challenges of network technologies.

References

1. Ansari, S., Rajeev, S.G., Chandrasekhar, H.S.: Packet Sniffing: A Brief Introduction. IEEE Potentials 21(5), 17–19 (2003)
2. Qadeer, M.A., Zahid, M.: Network Traffic Analysis and Intrusion Detection using Packet Sniffer. In: Second International Conference on Communication Software and Networks, pp. 313–317 (2010)
3. Libpcap: `http://www.tcpdump.org`
4. IP and Network addresses, `http://www.yale.edu/its/network/ip:andnic`.
5. Andrew, S.T.: Computer Networks, 4th edn. (2002)

PT: A Path Tracing and Filtering Mechanism to Defend against DDoS Attacks

Samant Saurabh, and Ashok Singh Sairam

Department of Computer Science, IIT Patna, Patliputra Colony, Patna
ssaurabh@iitp.ac.in

Abstract. Distributed Denial of Service Attack continues to plague the world. Defense against the DDoS attacks gets complicated due to IP spoofing. We propose a new packet marking technique PT (called Path Tracer) which imprints the fingerprint of the path taken by attack traffic in each packet, thereby enabling the victim to identify the attack traffic on per packet basis even in presence of IP Spoofing. Our Packet Marking Technique has many unique features. It helps the victim to proactively filter out the attack packets based on the unique path mark. A single packet contains information about complete attack path. The marking algorithm is very simple. Our approach does not create overhead in the packet and it does not require any extra storage. Analysis of our scheme proves the effectiveness of PT in filtering out DDoS traffic while allowing the legitimate traffic to be processed normally.

Keywords: DDoS, DoS Attacks, Deterministic Packet Marking, Internet Security, Hashing, and Path Identification.

1 Introduction

Distributed Denial of Service (DDoS) attacks [1], [2] continue to plague the Internet. In a typical DDoS attack, attackers compromise multiple machines and use them to send large numbers of packets to a single victim server to overwhelm its capacity. As an increasing number of businesses and services depend on the Internet, safeguarding them against attacks is a priority. DDoS attacks are among the hardest security problems to address as they are easy to implement, hard to prevent and difficult to trace.

1.1 IP Trace Back

A common solution for preventing DDoS attacks is IP traceback. Routers mark information on packets en-route to the victim, who can then use that information to reconstruct the path that the packets taken from the attacker through the Internet, despite IP address spoofing [3]. Most of the IP Traceback mechanism aims at finding the complete and exact path to the attacker. They also assume that the victim only initiates the traceback or passively receives traceback information.

K.R. Venugopal and L.M. Patnaik (Eds.): ICIP 2011, CCIS 157, pp. 336–341, 2011.
© Springer-Verlag Berlin Heidelberg 2011

1.2   Attack Path Fingerprint

We observe that reconstructing the exact path to the attacker is not necessary in defending against a DDoS attack. We only need to get an indication of the particular path that attack packets take [4], [5]. In addition, because our approach transmits path information in each packet, the victim can filter packets itself, based on its knowledge of the path information carried by a single prior attack packet. The victim need only classify a single packet as malicious to be able to filter out all subsequent packets with the same marking. What makes this possible is that our packet marking is deterministic; all packets traversing the same path carry the same marking.

1.3   Paper Organization

The remainder of the paper is organized as follows: In Section 2 we give the problem statement and evaluation metrics for solution. In Section 3 we provide design motivations in using particular marking scheme. In Section 4 we present the packet marking algorithm that we propose to deploy on Internet routers. In Section 5 we present packet filtering scheme for PT. In Section 6 we analyze the packet marking technique deployed in the routers and provide analytical results. Section 7 concludes the paper.

2   Problem Statement and Evaluation Metrics

Path Tracer and Filter is concerned with (a) Marking of Identification field of IP packets header with the fingerprint of the packets path and (b) Filtering of attack packet based on the marking. All routers in the path of the packet supply their fingerprint using the marking algorithm. As the path is assumed to be unique, so when IDS at the victim detects an attack, we can see the path mark of the attack packet and subsequently filter out the attack traffic based on the packet mark.

2.1   Evaluation Metrics

1. Marking process should be light weight in processing and memory.
2. Number of attack packets needed for filtering should be minimal.

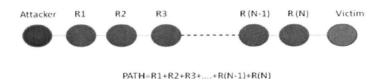

PATH=R1+R2+R3+....+R(N-1)+R(N)

Fig. 1. Aim of PTF is to mark a unique fingerprint for the given path FINGERPRINT(R1+R2+R3+...+R(N-1)+RN) in the ID field of the given packet header

3. Processing, bandwidth and memory requirements at the router and victim should be as low as possible.
4. Filtering of attack traffic should not block legitimate traffic directed towards the victim.Lemmas, Propositions, and Theorems.

3   Design Motivations

If all packets arriving at the victim have some distinctive marking, then the victim need only note the markings that correspond to attack packets and then drop all incoming packets matching those markings. We propose to construct a path identifier to be embedded by routers in the IP Identification field. The router marking in PT is deterministic such that every packet traversing a particular path is marked with the same path identifier, which is generated by each routers along the path from end-host to victim. One of notable feature of our scheme is that even though our marking space is limited, we can accommodate path length of any possible size. The marking for an entire path in PT is not guaranteed to be globally unique. However, we show that a globally unique identifier is not necessary in providing strong DDoS protection and that the benefits of having a single-packet, deterministic marking, allow the victim to develop rapidly responsive packet filters to protect itself during such attacks.

4   PT Marking Scheme

In this section, we present the PT packet marking scheme to be deployed on Internet routers. We assume, for the moment, that all routers in the Internet implement our scheme, however we can show by analysis and experimental results all routers need not take part in the marking, then also our scheme would give us quite satisfying results.

4.1   IP Address Hashing

We find that routers in a path of IP packets have very similar IP addresses which differ only in last few bits. This is problematic because it would make the PT markings for different paths less likely to be distinguishable from each other. Ideally, we would like to maximize the entropy of the bits that we mark with, to reduce the likelihood of marking collisions (where two different paths have the same PT marking). To solve this problem, we have routers mark packets using bits from the 16 bit hash of their IP addresses [6], rather than from their IP addresses alone.

4.2   Distinctive Marking Algorithm

Distinctive Marking Algorithm is described in Table 1. Algorithm Pt_Mark runs at each of the routers through which the packet traverses. Initially packetMark is set to be all zero. The intuition for using XOR operation is it can give us

Table 1. Algorithm: Distinctive Marking Algorithm

```
Input: Packet Mark, IP Address of Router
Output: Packet Mark
Following code is executed at each router in the IP packet path

Pt_Mark (IPAddress Router_IP, packetMark& pM) {
//16 bit hash of 32 bit IP address
HashMark hm = Hash(Router_IP);
for (int i=0; i¡=15; i++)
pM(i) = pM(i) XOR hm(i);
}
```

maximum uniqueness as opposed to AND and OR bitwise operations. Each router in the path xors its IP addresss hash with the already existing packet mark in the ID field. Finally when the packet arrives at the victim, the mark is the XOR summation of hash of IP address of each router in the path.

5   Filtering Scheme for PT

The most basic filter a victim can apply to packets with PT markings is to record the markings of identified attack packets and drop subsequent incoming packets matching any of those markings. We assume that we already have an Intrusion Detection Framework for detecting an attack packet. Although this filter provides little flexibility to the victim, it has a very fast attack reaction time, since all the victim has to do is classify a single packet as an attack packet before being able to filter out all subsequent packets sent by that attacker. The filter requires very little storage as one mark requires just 16 bits of memory. To store N attack signatures we just need 16*N bits of storage space(Table 2).

Table 2. Algorithm: Packet Filtering

```
Input: IP_Packet, attack Mark Vector
Output: Filter Result

FilterPackets(IP_Packet, attackMarkVector {
Mark m = IP_Packet.mark();
Iterator it = V.begin();
while (it.next() ) {
            if (it.mark() == m )
                        IP_Packet.discard();
                        break;
    }
}
```

6   Analysis of PT Marking Scheme

In PT, we identify the attack packets by just observing the mark on the packet. Our deterministic packet marking scheme marks the packets coming from the same path with a unique identifier or fingerprint. The performance of our algorithm depends upon the probability of collision of our path identifier with other paths identifier. It can easily be seen that probability of two different IP Packet paths having the same hash mark is $2\text{-}d$, where d is the number of bits used for marking. ID field is 16 bit, hence the probability of path identification mark of two path colliding is 2-16 which is very low.

6.1   Legacy Routers and Incremental Deployment

It is observed that our marking scheme will perform quite well even in case of incremental deployment. Even if some routers in the path dont take part in marking then also if we have sufficient routers deployed with our marking algorithm, then path identifier can be constructed successfully by the marking operation.

6.2   Analytical Results

1. **Number of Packets:** Our scheme is very fast. When Intrusion Detection System (IDS) detects attack, PT can filter out attack packet on per packet basis.It does not require to collect high number of packets.
2. **Amount of storage at victim:** We require 16 bits to store one packet mark corresponding to one attack signature. For N attacks we require N*16 bits.
3. **Marking complexity:** Our algorithm is very simple to implement at the routers. It requires very low processing overhead and no storage and bandwidth overhead.
4. **Filtering:** At victim side, it can filter out the attack traffic just by checking the packet mark in the ID field of the packet with the attack marks present in the victim table.
5. **Incremental Deployment:** Our scheme supports incremental deployment and does not require zero day complete installation.
6. **Independent of path length:** Our marking scheme is independent of path length and can imprint fingerprint of each router in the path.

Fig. 2. PT is able to construct path identifier even during incremental deployment as shown in the figure above. Legacy routers dont have PT deployed on them while PT compliant routers have PT deployed in them.

7 Conclusions

In this paper, we have presented PT, a novel approach to defend against DDoS attacks. Our proposal draws from elements of IP Traceback methods but is not concerned with reconstructing a path from a victim to an attacker, rather, it is concerned with marking paths with unique markings. This gives the victim of a DDoS attack the ability to filter, on a per-packet basis, any incoming packets that match known attacker marks. We believe that PT marking is the most general, flexible, and powerful of the packet marking schemes to date, and shows significant potential in reducing or eliminating the DDoS threat.

References

1. Savage, S., Wetherall, D., Karlin, A., Anderson, T.: Practical Network Support for IP Traceback. In: Proceedings of the 2000 ACM SIGCOMM Conference (August 2000)
2. Snoeren, A.C., Partridge, C., Sanchez, L.A., Jones, C.E., Tchakountio, F., Schwartz, B., Kent, S.T., Strayer, W.T.: Single-packet IP traceback. IEEE/ACM Transactions on Networking (ToN) 10(6) (December 2002)
3. Abraham, Y., Adrian, P., Dawn, S.: Pi: A Path Identification Mechanism to Defend Against DDoS Attacks. In: IEEE Symposium on Security and Privacy (May 2003)
4. Ansari, N., Belenky, A.: IP Traceback with Deterministic Packet Marking. IEEE Communication letters (April 2003)
5. Perrig, A., Yaar, A., Song, A.: StackPi: A New Defense Mechanism against IP Spoofing and DDoS Attacks, Technical Report, Carnegie Mellon University USA (2003)
6. Snoeren, A.C., Partridge, C.L., Sanchez, A., Jones, C.E., Tchakountio, F.S., Kent, T., Strayer, W.T.: Hash-based IP traceback. In: ACM SIGCOMM (August 2001)

Application of GA in Key Generation for Image Transposition Cipher Algorithm

Sandeep Bhowmik[1] and Sriyankar Acharyya[2]

[1] Department of Computer Science & Engineering, Hooghly Engineering & Technology College, West Bengal, India
to_sandeepb@yahoo.co.in
[2] Department of Computer Science & Engineering, West Bengal University of Technology, West Bengal,India
srikalpa8@yahoo.co.in

Abstract. With the increasing use of digital techniques for transmitting and storing images, the fundamental issue of protecting image data against unauthorized access, chaos-based encryption has enjoined a superb know-how to deal with the problem of fast and highly-secured image encryption. The effectiveness of the transposition cipher algorithm profusely depends on the trait of the *key*. If a *key* is badly designed or poorly selected, then the protection fails to provide proper security and improper access can be gained on the sensitive information. This work focuses on the application of a crucial Artificial Intelligence approach in block-based image transposition cipher generation. Here, Genetic Algorithm has been applied to search for effective keys to encrypt images through permutation of the pixel locations. This work also statistically analyses the effect of applying varied sizes of keys in block- based image transposition algorithm.

Keywords: Block Cipher, Correlation Coefficient, Genetic Algorithm, Image Cryptograph, Transposition Algorithm.

1 Introduction

The alluring progressions in digital image processing and network communications during the preceding decades have created immense demand for real-time secured image-transmission over the Internet and wireless networks. To meet this challenge, since early 1990s, many efforts have been initiated to explore specific solutions to image encryption [1] and they are categorized into two broad groups: substitution ciphers and transposition ciphers. Among them, chaos-based transposition algorithms have shown some exceptionally good properties in many concerned aspects regarding security and complexity. The idea of using chaos for data encryption is evidently not new and can be traced back to the classical Shannons paper [2], followed by several dissertations in this arena.

We know that *key* plays a vital role in any encryption method and often the security of a cipher depends on the quality of the *key*. This work focuses on a totally new development towards the *key*-generation algorithm for image

K.R. Venugopal and L.M. Patnaik (Eds.): ICIP 2011, CCIS 157, pp. 342–348, 2011.
© Springer-Verlag Berlin Heidelberg 2011

encryption. If we can design a *key* to be applied on an image that will largely decrease the correlation among the image elements, then obviously the generated cipher image will be further protected. In this work, we have tried to introduce a block-based transformation algorithm using chaos mapping, where the mapping is derived by applying one important Artificial Intelligence procedure, Genetic Algorithm and the transposition algorithm hides the original image through simple permutation of the pixel locations.

Genetic Algorithms originated from the studies of cellular automata, conducted by John Holland and his colleagues at the University of Michigan [3]. GA is a search technique used in computer science to find approximate solutions to combinatorial optimization problems, based on a particular class of evolutionary algorithms that use techniques inspired by evolutionary biology such as inheritance, mutation, natural selection, and crossover. Researchers have adopted GA as a solution to optimization in various fields in recent years. Its intrinsic parallelism allows the uses for potential processing. GA as a solution to optimization problem started gaining popularity at the end of the preceding century [4]. Problems which appear to be particularly appropriate for solution by GA include Scheduling [5] and State Assignment Problem [6]. It can be quite effective to combine GA with other optimization methods.

In this research we have tried to analyze an effective way for image encryption, by applying GA to generate keys. The rest of this paper is organized as follows: A brief discussion about the existing image transposition schemata is in Section 2. In Section 3, the proposed technique is described. Section 4 presents the experimental results and performance comparison and finally, Section 5 concludes the paper.

2   Transposition Ciphers for Image Encryption

Visual information and imagery play an important role in almost all areas of our lives. Cryptography is the knowledge of protecting the privacy of information during communication. A simple transposition or permutation cipher works by breaking a message into fixed size blocks, and then permuting the characters within each block according to a fixed permutation, say P. The *key* to the transposition cipher is simply the permutation P. So, the transposition cipher has the property that the encrypted message contains all the characters that were in the plaintext message. In other words, the unigram statistics for the message are unchanged by the encryption process. The size of the permutation is known as the period.

For the past years several chaotic image encryption algorithms have been proposed. The process of developing a chaos-based cipher can be summarized as follows. First, a chaotic map is generalized by introducing parameters into the map, and then that map is used to scatter the image pixels. The most obvious application is to use one, two or more dimensional maps to produce the cipher data. Several algorithms have been used to manipulate the pixels by using different maps, like Arnolds Cat Map, Tent Map, Baker map [7], other Chaotic Maps

[8], two dimensional chaotic maps [9] etc., Yen and Guo [10] proposed two chaotic image encryption algorithms where the images pixels are rearranged based on a random binary sequence generated by a chaotic system. Pixel shuffling expands diffusion property and dissipates correlation of two adjacent pixels.

3   The Proposed Technique

Image transposition cipher algorithm disturbs the arrangement of the pixels and quality of encryption depends on the rearrangement pattern. As this pattern is derived from a *key*, there is scope of improving the encryption quality by using proper *key*. Now if we want to rearrange a block of N-pixels we will have to use a *key* of length N. This *key* is actually an arrangement of N numbers among $N!$ possible patterns. To search for a good pattern, we have applied advance search technique GA, to get an optimum result, which can be applied as *key* to enhance the encryption quality.

In GA terminology, we are looking for the optimum chromosome of size N, where each element of the chromosome is indicating a new position of the image pixel within a block of size N. A trial solution is represented as a string of N integers lay between 1 and N. The $k - th$ integer from the left of the chromosome is the new position assigned to the pixel k. Pixels of the chromosome are considered as genes. The fitness function of the chromosomes is calculated on the basis of the sum of total variation of each gene from its initial position. The objective is to maximize the fitness value to minimize the pixel correlation. We have applied the chromosome first horizontally and then vertically on each block. As a simple pre-encryption technique which has been proved very effective for any image encryption algorithm [11], we scramble the image by breaking it into 16 equal size square blocks. Each block then has been rotated 90 degree counter clockwise as well as flipped upside down.

Performance has been analyses in terms of correlation coefficients among image pixels. We have tested the procedure for various sizes of keys, ranging from 8 bytes up to 64 bytes, by dividing the image with different block sizes of 8×8 pixels, 12×12 pixels, 16×16 pixels, 24×24 pixels, 32×32 pixels, 48×48 pixels, 64×64 pixels.

4   Experimental Analysis

To analyze the effect of the algorithm, it was applied on three different benchmark gray scale images *Cameraman*, *Lena* and *Peppers*. The images are bit mapped (bmp) images with size of 192×192 pixels. In order to evaluate the impact of the varying *key* size on the correlation value, seven different cases are tested. The keys were applied on square blocks, where block size is determined by the size of *key* being used. The sizes of keys generated using GA and their respective fitness values are shown in Table 1. It can be observed that the fitness of *key* increases significantly with *key* size.

The implementation of the work has been done on *Intel Pentium IV* platform, with *Microsoft Windows XP* as *OS*. The image processing tasks has

Table 1. Key Sizes used for different test cases and their corresponding Fitness values

Case No.	Key Size	Fitness Value
Case 1	8 bytes	31
Case 2	12 bytes	71
Case 3	16 bytes	127
Case 4	24 bytes	283
Case 5	32 bytes	635
Case 6	48 bytes	1139
Case 7	64 bytes	2035

   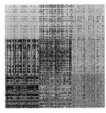

A　　　　　　A_{08}　　　　　　A_{24}　　　　　　A_{64}

Fig. 1. (A) Image *Cameraman*, (A_i) Encrypted image with key size of i-bytes(i=8,24,64)

  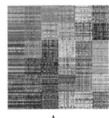 

A　　　　　　A_{12}　　　　　　A_{32}　　　　　　A_{64}

Fig. 2. (A) Image *Lena*, (A_i) Encrypted image with key size of i-bytes(i=12,32,64)

been done using *Matlab* 7.5 and keys have been generated through GA using *TurboC* + + compiler.

Statistical test includes the comparative performance analysis on the basis of correlation coefficient. We have tested the correlation between horizontally and vertically adjacent pixels of the ciphered images according to the Eq. 1.

$$r = (n \sum (xy) - \sum x \sum y)/\sqrt{([n \sum (x^2) - (\sum x)^2] \times [n \sum (y^2) - (\sum y)^2])}. \quad (1)$$

where n is the number of total pairs of data and x, y are values of two adjacent pixels.

We analyze the described chaotic algorithm on images *Cameraman*, *Lena* and *Peppers*. Fig. 1, Fig. 2 & Fig. 3 show few sample encrypted images on applying the block-based transposition algorithm with different size of keys.

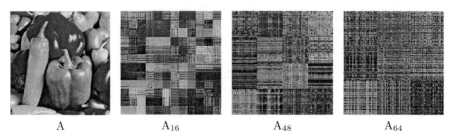

A   A$_{16}$ A$_{48}$ A$_{64}$

Fig. 3. (A) Image *Peppers*, (A$_i$) Encrypted image with key size of i-bytes(i=16,48,64)

Table 2. Correlation Coefficient results of image *Cameraman*, *Lena* and *Peppers*

Processed Image	Correlation Coefficient								
	Image *Cameraman*			Image *Lena*			Image *Peppers*		
	Hor	Ver	Avg	Hor	Ver	Avg	Hor	Ver	Avg
Original	0.9235	0.9361	0.9298	0.9327	0.9446	0.93865	0.9483	0.9446	0.94645
Case 1	0.6945	0.6849	0.6897	0.7431	0.5208	0.63195	0.6952	0.5208	0.608
Case 2	0.6255	0.6439	0.6347	0.6718	0.4895	0.58065	0.6041	0.4895	0.5468
Case 3	0.5880	0.5892	0.5886	0.6101	0.3040	0.45705	0.5015	0.304	0.40275
Case 4	0.5600	0.5477	0.55385	0.5293	0.2194	0.37435	0.3835	0.2194	0.30145
Case 5	0.3277	0.3058	0.31675	0.3270	0.1276	0.2273	0.207	0.1276	0.1673
Case 6	0.3629	0.2450	0.30395	0.2889	0.0634	0.17615	0.2661	0.0634	0.16475
Case 7	0.0969	0.2714	0.18415	0.0629	0.0729	0.0679	0.1072	0.0729	0.09005

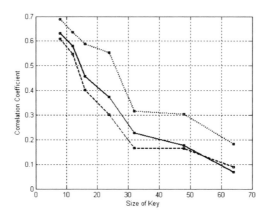

Fig. 4. Relationship between Correlation Coefficient and Size of Keys. The dotted-line is for *Cameraman* image, the solid-line is for image *Lena* and the dashed-line is for image *Peppers*.

Table 2 summarizes the Correlation Coefficient results of the different cases applied for the three images *Cameraman*, *Lena* and *Peppers*. In the table Hor, Ver, Avg meaning Horizontal, Vertical and Average Correlation Coefficient respectively.

Fig. 4 summarizes the effect on the correlation coefficient values of the three images for applying different sizes of keys in the encryption process. The figure shows that Correlation Coefficient values among image pixels decrease as the *key* size increases. But it is also clear that for individual images the decrease rate is not same as the *key* size increases. Table 1 state all the *key* size used and their corresponding Fitness values. From Table 1 it can be observed that the increment rate of the fitness value is not linear. The rate of increment in fitness varies as the *key* size changes. So it is evident that the Correlation Coefficient of image pixels in Fig. 4 do not only decrease depending on the size of the *key*, but the decrease also depends on the fitness value of the *key* being applied. Correlation among image pixels decreases as the Fitness of *key* increases.

5 Conclusions

In this paper a simple and effective encryption method has been analyzed and examined for image data security process using a block-based transformation cipher technique. The *key* that is being applied for the encryption purpose has been generated using Genetic Algorithm, an important method of Artificial Intelligence. Here we have examined different cases on three different benchmark images. Size of the block depends on the *key* size in the process of transformation. The purpose is to generate keys with maximum fitness values, so that it can disturb the arrangement of pixels significantly, and enhance the encryption quality. Experimental observations show, though the correlation coefficient value is inversely proportional to the *key* size, the rate of decrease in correlation value is not linear. Further study can be made to investigate how the *key* size and *key* fitness value together contributes to the change in correlation among image pixels.

References

1. Bourbakis, N., Alexopoulos, C.: Picture Data Encryption using Scan Patterns. Pattern Recognition 25(6), 567–581 (1992)
2. Shannon, C.E.: Communication Theory of Secrecy System. Bell System Technical Journal 28, 656–715 (1949)
3. Holland, J.H.: Adaptation in Natural and Artificial Systems, 2nd edn. MIT Press, Cambridge (1992)
4. Al-Tabtabai, H., Alex, P.: Using Genetic Algorithms to solve Optimization Problems in Construction. Engineering, Construction and Architectural Management 6(2), 121–132 (1999)
5. Man, Z., Wei, T., Xiang, L., Lishan, K.: Research on Multi-Project Scheduling Problem Based on Hybrid Genetic Algorithm. In: International Conference on Computer Science and Software Engineering, vol. 1, pp. 390–394 (2008)
6. Kumar, A.: A Novel Genetic Algorithm Approach to Solve Map Colour Problem. In: Emerging Trends in Engineering and Technology, ICETET, pp. 288–291 (2008)
7. Pichler, F., Scharinger, J.: Efficient Image Encryption based on Chaotic Maps. In: Workshop of the AAPR, Pattern Recognition, pp. 159–170. Oldenbourg, Munchen (1996)

8. Fridrich, J.: Image Encryption based on Chaotic Maps. In: IEEE Conf. on Systems, Man, and Cybernetics, Orlando, Florida, pp. 1105–1110 (1997)
9. Fridrich, J.: Symmetric Ciphers based on Two-Dimensional Chaotic Maps. International Journal of Bifurcation and Chaos 8(6), 1259–1284 (1998)
10. Yen, J.C., Guo, J.I.: A New Chaotic Mirror-Like Image Encryption Algorithm and its VLSI Architecture. Pattern Recognition and Image Analysis 10(2), 236–247 (2000)
11. Younes, M.A.B., Jantan, A.: Image Encryption using Block-Based Transformation Algorithm. IAENG International Journal of Computer Science 35(1) (2008)

A Novel Reversible Data Embedding Method for Source Authentication and Tamper Detection of H.264/AVC Video

Sutanu Maiti and Mahendra Pratap Singh

Department of Computer Science and Engineering
National Institute of Technology Karnataka, Surathkal, India
maiti.sutanu.cs09@gmail.com, mps_82@aol.in

Abstract. Authentication of multimedia content is required to proof the data integrity and establish the identity of the content creator. In this paper, we propose a source authentication and tamper detection scheme under the framework of H.264/AVC. To overcome the burden of sending authentication information separately, a novel reversible data embedding method is proposed. In this scheme, content based digital signature is generated and embedded in each frame of the video. Since human eyes are more sensitive to luminance than chrominance components of an image, only luminance components are used in this scheme to produce the digital signature. Proposed scheme is a hard authentication method, which is robust to luminance components of the video sequence.

Keywords: H.264/AVC, Integer Transformation, Reversible Data Embedding, Tamper Detection, Video Authentication.

1   Introduction

Multimedia applications use H.264/AVC (MPEG-4 Part-10) [1-3] video coding standard to transmit high definition videos with low bit-rate. As large number of users rely on the multimedia applications, the security of such systems has become a great challenge. Recent advances in high speed processors and distributed systems allow attackers to alter and forge transmitted video contents without leaving any trace. To protect sensitive videos from such attacks, content authentication is a widely used technique. Authentication is required for integrity and verifying the senders [4]. In this paper, a hard authentication scheme using Reversible Data Embedding method is proposed for H.264/AVC video.

Reversible or lossless data embedding [5-6] method embeds invisible data (also called as payload) into a digital image in reversible fashion. In this method the image before embedding payload and image after extracting payload does not differ even in a single bit and so the payload. In this proposed scheme, the encoder embeds the encrypted hash digest of each frame of the video sequence into the corresponding frame. At the decoder, after extracting the payload, hash digest is calculated and compared with the embedded one. As the embedding

K.R. Venugopal and L.M. Patnaik (Eds.): ICIP 2011, CCIS 157, pp. 349–355, 2011.
© Springer-Verlag Berlin Heidelberg 2011

process is reversible both the digests must match. At encoder, hash digest is encrypted using RSA algorithm whose decryption key is made public. Decoder decrypts the payload using the public key and gets the hash digest. Then it compares this hash digest with its calculated hash digest. To embed and extract the payload, a new transformation method is proposed.

2   The Proposed Authentication Scheme

The proposed method is an extension of the authentication scheme based on reversible data embedding used for digital images [5]. For a video sequence the proposed reversible data embedding method is applied for each frame. Deblocking filter is used to reconstruct the frame from quantized residues of predicted macroblock. As soon as deblocking filter finishes its work, luma blocks are collected and used as feature data from each macroblock of frames. After collecting the entire feature data, hash digest and using that hash digest digital signature is calculated. After completion of encoding of frame, signature is embedded within the frame using proposed reversible data embedding method. The entire process can be divided into two parts, signature generation and signature verification.

2.1   Signature Generation

Feature data cannot be taken before quantization process since it is not reversible. In this scheme, feature data are collected from output image of the deblocking filter that is applied after quantization process. Deblocking filter reconstructs the image from encoded macroblocks. Because of this reconstruction process, edges of macroblocks will also change. Due to the above mentioned change, the hash value calculated before deblocking filter will differ from the hash value calculated after applying deblocking filter.

Basic coding structure for H.264/AVC for a macroblock is given by G. J. Sullivan and T. Wiegand [2]. Fig. 1 denotes the modified structure of the encoding process of H.264/AVC for a macroblock. In this modified encoder, calculated digital signature is embedded within the frame using proposed reversible data embedding method.

2.2   Signature Verification

After decoding each frame, the payload extraction method is called, which gives embedded signature and original frame. From all the macroblocks of the frame, feature data is collected and from that data, signature is calculated again. If calculated signature is same to the extracted signature, then the frame is authentic otherwise tampered. In Fig. 2, the signature verification process is described in a flow chart.

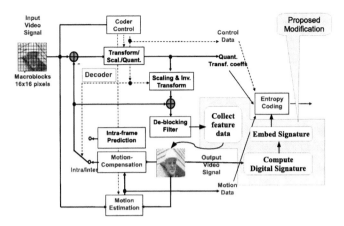

Fig. 1. Modified Coding Structure of H.264/AVC for a macroblock

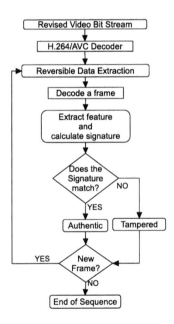

Fig. 2. Signature Verification Process

3   Reversible Data Embedding

Reversible data embedding or lossless watermarking is the process of extracting the embedded information from the watermarked image and allows exact recovery of the original image. It is mainly used for content authentication of digital images or videos. In this process, secret information is embedded into the image and any attempt to change the watermarked image fails the authentication.

4   The Proposed Method

One way to embed a bit in a pair (or a group) of pixels is to arrange that pair (or the group) in such a way that the orientation itself will denote whether the embedded bit is 0 or 1. The orientation used here is as follows, for a pair of integers, the left integer will always be greater than the right integer. To embed a 0 bit, keep the pair intact and to embed a 1, swap the pair. At the decoder, if a pair is swapped, then read 1 otherwise 0. In this paper, an integer transformation[7] is proposed to make the required orientation. The transformation method takes a pair of integers (A, B) and outputs (X, Y) with the required orientation. The algorithm is given below.

Forward Transformation:

$X = 2 * A;$
$Y = 2 * B;$
If $X \leq Y$ Then
      $X = 2 * Y - X + 1;$
$Y = Y/2;$
$X = X - Y;$

The Inverse Transformation method performs the reverse operation. It takes (X, Y) and outputs (A, B). The algorithm is given below.

Inverse Transformation:

$X = X + Y;$
$Y = 2 * Y;$
If X is odd Then
      $X = 2 * Y - X + 1;$
$A = X/2;$
$B = Y/2;$

4.1   Embedding Algorithm

Table 1 describes the algorithm that embeds the payload in a digital image.

Table 1. Embedding Algorithm

Step 1: Read the next pair of integers.
Step 2: Apply Forward Transformation method on the pair.
Step 3: Read the bit to be embedded.
Step 4: If the bit read in step 3 is 0, goto step 6.
Step 5: Swap the pair.
Step 6: If there are remaining bits in payload, goto step 1.

4.2   Extraction Algorithm

Table 2 describes the algorithm that extracts the payload from the watermarked image and reconstructs the watermarked image to the original image.

Table 2. Extraction Algorithm

Step 1: Read the next pair of integers.
Step 2: For the pair (a, b) if $a < b$, goto step 3.
Otherwise goto step 5.
Step 3: Write a 0 bit as payload.
Step 4: goto step 7.
Step 5: Write a 1 bit as payload.
Step 6: Swap the pair.
Step 7: Apply Inverse Transformation on the pair.
Step 8: If there are more pairs to read, goto step 1.

5   Results

The latest H.264/AVC reference software (JM 17.2) is used to implement our proposed scheme. To calculate hash digest SHA-1 and RSA based digital signature is used for the following results.

Table 3 shows the result of lena image after applying the proposed Reversible Data Embedding method with maximum payload size.

Table 3. Sample output of the proposed Reversible Data Embedding Method

Original Image   Watermarked Image   Decoded Image

The transformation method changes pixel value of first pixel of each pairs. So, the watermarked image looks distorted. Distortion of the image is directly proportional to the size of the payload. Fig. 3 displays the payload vs. PSNR graph of the watermarked image. For a multimedia application, encoder is called only once while the decoder is called each time the video has to be displayed. So, the delay produced by the decoder is an important issue. Fig. 4 displays the difference of execution time of modified decoder and original decoder applied on the different video sequences.

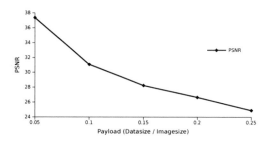

Fig. 3. Payload vs. PSNR graph of the watermarked image

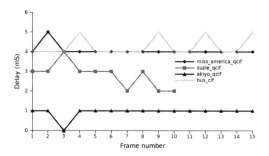

Fig. 4. Delay of the decoder on different videos

6   Conclusions

In this paper, a reversible data embedding technique based on the concept of pixel orientation is proposed whichdoes not use location map.Since embedding and extraction algorithms are linear in time, and compression of location map is also not required for this scheme, it executes faster than existing methods. The proposed transformation method enlarges first value of each pair. As the luma values do not differ much with their neighbors for a natural image, enlargement of pixel value does not exceed the upper limit (i.e., 255).

References

1. Sullivan, G.J., Topiwala, P., Luthara, A.: The H.264/AVC Video Coding Standard: Overview and Introduction to the Fidelity Range Extentions. In: SPIE Conferences on Applications of Digital Image Processing XXVII (August 2004)
2. Sullivan, G.J., Wiegand, T.: Video Compression From Concepts to the H.264/AVC Standard. Proceedings of the IEEE 93(1) (January 2005)
3. Wiegand, T., Sullivan, G.J., Bjontegaard, G., Luthara, A.: Overview of the H.264/AVC Video Coding Standard. IEEE Transactions on Circuits and Systems for Video Technology (July 2003)
4. Ramaswamy, N., Rao, K.R.: Video Authentication for H.264/AVC using Digital Signature and Secure Hash Algorithm. In: NOSSDAV 2006, Rhode Island, USA, May 22-23 (2006)

5. Awrangjeb, M.: An Overview of Reversible Data Hiding. In: ICCIT 2003, Jahangir-nagar University, Bangladesh, December 19-21, pp. 75–79 (2003)
6. Shi, Y.Q.: Reversible data hiding. In: Cox, I., Kalker, T., Lee, H.-K. (eds.) IWDW 2004. LNCS, vol. 3304, pp. 1–12. Springer, Heidelberg (2005)
7. Tian, J.: Reversible Data Embedding Using a Difference Expansion. IEEE Transaction on Circuits ans Systems for Video Technology 13(8) (August 2003)

Ant-CAMP: Ant Based Congestion Adaptive Multi-Path Routing Protocol for Wireless Networks

Chirag Raval, Saumya Hegde, and Mohit P Tahiliani

Department of Computer Science and Engineering
National Institute of Technology, Surathkal, Karnataka, India
chiragraval1109@gmail.com

Abstract. The advent of mobile computing devices and wide deployment of wireless networks have led to an exponential increase in the internet traffic. Long congestion epochs and frequent link failures in wireless network lead to more number of packets being dropped and incur high end-to-end delay, thereby degrading the overall performance of the network. Congestion control, though mainly incorporated at the transport layer, if coupled with the routing protocols, can significantly improve overall performance of the network. In this paper we propose Ant based Congestion Adaptive Multipath (Ant-CAMP) routing protocol that aims to avoid congestion by proactively sending *congestion notification* to the sender. The proposed Ant-CAMP routing protocol is implemented in Network Simulator-2 (NS-2) and its performance is compared with Ad-hoc On Demand Multi-Path Distance Vector (AOMDV) in terms of Packet Drops due to Congestion, Packet Delivery Fraction and Average End-to-End Delay.

Keywords: Ant Colony Optimization, Congestion Control, End-to-End Delay, Multi-Path Routing Protocols, Packet Delivery Fraction.

1 Introduction

Wide deployment of wireless networks and a high demand for continuous network connectivity has led to an exponential increase in the internet traffic. Efficiently allocating resources in wireless networks is a challenging task since the characteristics of the wireless medium vary continuously due to the interference effects.

Packet drops in wireless networks are frequent events caused by congestion, link failures, channel errors, hand-offs etc., Congestion control is mainly coupled with transport protocols such as Transmission Control Protocol (TCP), Datagram Congestion Control Protocol (DCCP) etc., However it has been shown that TCP as well as DCCP cannot differentiate congestion packet losses and non-congestion packet losses. Thus a lot of research has focused on designing congestion aware/adaptive routing protocols in wireless networks [1].

Frequent link failures lead to considerable amount of packets to be dropped and incur high end to end delay in the network. Several multipath routing protocols have been proposed to reduce the overall end to end delay caused by

K.R. Venugopal and L.M. Patnaik (Eds.): ICIP 2011, CCIS 157, pp. 356–366, 2011.

link failures [2]. Moreover, multipath routing protocols also enhance the overall performance of the network by providing fault tolerance and load balancing features [3].

In this paper, we propose a Ant Colony Optimization (ACO) [4] based congestion adaptive multipath routing protocol called Ant based Congestion Adaptive Multipath (Ant-CAMP) routing protocol that aims not only to reduce the packet drops caused by congestion but also to reduce the overall end to end delay by exploiting the advantages of multipath routing protocol.

ACO is a widely accepted branch of swarm intelligence based on which several routing protocols (including multipath routing protocols) for wireless networks have been designed [5]. ACO is based on foraging principle of ants that walk randomly in search of food. On the way to destination (food source), they lay a chemical substance called *pheromone* to mark the path followed by them. When any ant finds the food source, it returns on the same path laying *pheromone* with high intensity which in turn increases the overall intensity of *pheromone* on that path. Other ants moving randomly detect and start following this path which has high probability to reach the destination. While returning back from destination, they too lay their *pheromone* on the same path which further increase the intensity of the path and attract more ants to follow this path.

The proposed Ant-CAMP routing protocol is implemented in NS-2 and its performance is compared with AOMDV [6] routing protocol. The performance comparison is based on Packet drops due to Congestion, Packet Delivery Fraction and Average End-to-End Delay.

The remainder of the paper is organized as follows. Section 2 gives a detailed description of Ant-CAMP routing protocol. Section 3 and 4 presents the simulation environment and results respectively. Section 5 concludes the paper with future directions.

2   Ant Based Congestion Adaptive Multipath Routing Protocol (Ant-CAMP)

2.1   Overview

Ant-CAMP is a hybrid node disjoint multipath routing protocol which includes reactive route discovery, proactive route maintenance and aims to avoid congestion by proactively sending *congestion notifications* to the sender. Shortest path from sender to receiver is discovered considering "average queue length" as a routing metric. Since Ant-CAMP is a multipath routing protocol it finds multiple paths from source to destination in a single route discovery. Once the route is discovered it is proactively probed by the route maintenance phase of Ant-CAMP to update the routing table. Moreover, every node in the network calculates its average queue size and when it exceeds a predetermined *threshold*, it sends a *congestion notification* to the sender. On receiving *congestion notification* from the intermediate nodes, the sender switches to next optimal path available in the routing table. If there exists no path, route discovery phase is re-initiated.

2.2 Route Discovery

Route discovery phase of Ant-CAMP is initiated only when source wants to send data to the destination. In single route discovery multiple node disjoint paths from source to destination are discovered and stored in a routing table. Only if all these paths fail, route discovery phase is re-initiated.

Route discovery phase of Ant-CAMP uses two control packets called *reactive_forward_ant* (RF-Ant) and *reactive_backward_ant* (RB-Ant). Source initiates the route discovery phase by broadcasting RF-Ant to all its neighbours. All intermediate nodes, on receiving RF-Ant, check whether they are the destination of the RF-Ant packet. If they are the destination, they reply back to the source by converting RF-Ant to RB-Ant which propagates in the reverse path. If they are not the destination, they re-broadcast the RF-Ant. RF-Ant contains following information:

(source_address, destination_address, generation_number, average_queue_size, hop_count, first_hop)

Every node maintains *(source_address, generation_number)* pair to identify duplicate RF-Ant. Each time a sender initiates new route discovery phase, *generation_number* is increased by one. The *average_queue_size* in RF-Ant contains the maximum average queue size on the path. *hop_count* field represents the total number of hops between source and destination.

When a node receives RF-Ant, it checks whether it is a duplicate RF-Ant or not by comparing the *generation_number* and *source_address* with information stored in its routing table. When an intermediate node detects duplicate RF-Ant it drops the RF-Ant reducing its further propagation. Before re-broadcasting RF-Ant, every intermediate node stores following information in its routing table.

(source_address, destination_address, generation_number, expiration of reverse path)

This information is useful in forwarding RB-Ant from destination to the source. Thus, the reverse path (from destination to source) is set up while propagating RF-Ant towards destination.

A duplicate RF-Ant received at the destination denotes that it may have traversed disjoint paths. To ensure whether RF-Ant has traversed node disjoint path or not, destination node stores the *first_hop* information. If *first_hop* of RF-Ant is different from the one which is stored, the destination node generates the RB-Ant. Fig. 1. shows the route discovery from source (S) to destination (D). Source broadcasts RF-Ant to its neighbour nodes 1, 2 and 3. These nodes check whether the received RF-Ant is duplicate or not. If the received RF-Ant is not duplicate and they are not the destination, then they re-broadcast the RF-Ant. Otherwise if the RF-Ant is duplicate then it is dropped. Assume that node-4 receives first copy of RF-Ant from node-2. It establishes the reverse path and forwards the RF-Ant. Later when node-4 receives duplicate copy of RF-Ant from node-3 it simply discards the duplicate RF-Ant rather than re-broadcasting it. When destination (D) receives the RF-Ant from node-1 it stores the *first_hop* field of RF-Ant (in our example node-1) in its routing table, converts RF-Ant into RB-Ant and sends it on the reverse path which was previously set up during

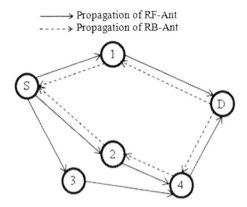

Fig. 1. Path formation from Source (S) to Destination (D)

propagation of RF-Ant. Later when destination (D) receives duplicate RF-Ant from node-4, it checks the *first_hop* of RF-Ant with the one which is stored in its routing table. If the *first_hop* of the received RF-Ant is different, D generates RB-Ant and sends it back to the source otherwise simply discards the received RF-Ant. Thus, Ant-CAMP forms the node disjoint multiple paths between source and destination.

2.3   Calculating Average Queue Size

The routing metric used by Ant-CAMP to find shortest path between source and destination is average queue size. Every node in the network calculates its average queue size based on Exponential Weighted Moving Average (EWMA) as shown in Eq. 1

$$avg = ((1 - q\_w) \times avg') + (q\_w \times cur\_que). \qquad (1)$$

Variables:
avg: new average queue size in packets
avg': old average queue size in packets
q_w: queue weight (0 < q_w ≤ 1)
cur_que: current occupied queue size in packets
The value of q_w can be set statically or dynamically. However, Ant-CAMP routing protocol dynamically sets the value of q_w based on Eq. 2 as shown below.

$$q\_w = \frac{current\_queue}{total\_queue}. \qquad (2)$$

From Eq. 2, it can be observed that the value of q_w mainly depends on the value of current_queue. If the queue is almost full (congestion building up), q_w value will be higher and hence more weightage will be given to *cur_que* in Eq. 1. Similarly if queue is almost empty, q_w value will be low and hence more weightage will be given to *avg'* in Eq. 1). Thus the avg value directly reflects the

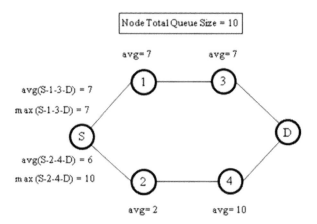

Fig. 2. Difference between aggregate and maximum queue size of the path

amount of congestion at the node. Ant-CAMP relies on the maximum average queue size *(avg)* of the path rather than the aggregate queue size of the entire path. The motivation for the same is explained below.

Consider the scenario shown in Fig. 2. Suppose each node has total queue size of 10 packets. There are two paths from source (S) to the destination (D). If RB-Ant carries aggregate of average queue size of all nodes on the path, then route table of S consists of avg (S-1-3-D) set to 7 packets and avg(S-2-4-D) set to 6 packets. Source selects the path $S-2-4-D$ since it has less overall queue size. But the queue of node-4 is full and hence congestion occurs resulting in packet drops. Thus the aggregate queue size does not provide accurate information about the amount of congestion on the path.

Instead if RB-Ant carries maximum average queue size of the path, then information stored in source's routing table is: $max(S-1-3-D)$ set to 7 packets and $max(S-2-4-D)$ set to 10 packets. In this case, $S-1-3-D$ path is selected since the probability of congestion occurrence on this path is less compared to other path. Thus the maximum queue size provides accurate information about the congestion on the path.

2.4   Route Maintenance

Route maintenance phase of Ant-CAMP uses two control packets called *monitor_forward_ant* (MF-Ant) and *monitor_backward_ant* (MB-Ant). These control packets ensure path availability and path optimality in terms of average queue size. Since the average queue size at all intermediate nodes keeps varying, frequently updating the routing table is very crucial. To update the routing table source generates MF-Ant which travels the path established during the route discovery phase. On receiving MF-Ant, the destination converts MF-Ant to MB-Ant and sends it back to the source which contains maximum average queue size information for that path. Thus MF-Ant ensures the path optimality by traversing all the paths periodically.

Table 1. Algorithm for Generating Congestion Notification

On arrival of each packet
Calculate average queue size (avg)
if avg > threshold
    Generate CN-Ant to source
endif
if source receives CN-Ant
    Mark the route as congested route
endif
if source is sending data
    Select alternate path from route table
endif

The source expects one MB-Ant for each MF-Ant. If a MB-Ant is not received by source within certain period of time, it assumes that the path is not available and hence updates its routing table.

2.5   Congestion Notification

Ant-CAMP uses a special control packet called *congestion_notification_ant* (CN-Ant) to notify the sources about congestion on the path. The CN-Ants are sent by the intermediate node based on the following algorithm:

As shown in algorithm, for arrival of each data packet, the node calculates average queue size and compares it with predetermined threshold *"threshold"*. If the average is more than the *threshold*, the intermediate node sends CN-Ant to the source to notify about the congestion. If the average is less than the *threshold*, the incoming packet is en-queued and CN-Ant is not generated.

On receiving CN-Ant from intermediate nodes, the source marks that path as *congested path* and switches to next optimal path in the routing table. If alternate paths do not exist, source reinitiates route discovery phase and the entire mechanism of Ant-CAMP is repeated. The propagation of CN-Ant is explained below.

Consider the example shown in Fig. 3. Source (S) is transmitting data to the destination (D) via path $S - 2 - 4 - D$. When data packet arrives at node-4, it calculates its average queue size and compares it with the *threshold*. Assume the *threshold* is set to 8 packets. Thus when node-4 encounters that its average queue size (9 packets) is more than the *threshold* (8 packets), it notifies the source about congestion by sending CN-Ant. On receiving CN-Ant, source marks $S - 2 - 4 - D$ path as congested and switches to an alternative path i.e., $S - 1 - 3 - D$. Thus by proactively sending *congestion notification* to the source, Ant-CAMP routing protocol avoids congestion and hence reduces the number of dropped packets.

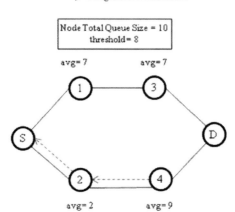

Fig. 3. Congestion Notification

3   Simulation Environment

The simulation is carried out on two different topologies. One topology consists of 16 nodes placed in 4x4 grid while other topology consists of 25 nodes placed in 5x5 grid in network. The number of connections is varied across 5, 10, 15. Table 1 lists the details about the simulation environment [7], [8].

Table 2. Simulation Environment

Parameter	Setup
Simulator	Network Simulator 2
Total Nodes	16, 25
Simulation Time	200 seconds
Simulation Area	1000m x 1000m
Data Packet Size	512 bytes
Traffic Model	FTP
Number of Connections	5,10,15

4   Results and Analysis

In this section, we compare the performance of Ant-CAMP routing protocol with AOMDV in terms of Packet Drops due to Congestion, Packet Delivery Fraction and Average End to End Delay.

4.1   Packet Drops Due to Congestion

From Fig. 4.a it is observed that Ant-CAMP significantly reduces the number of packet drops due to congestion as compared to AOMDV for 16 nodes with

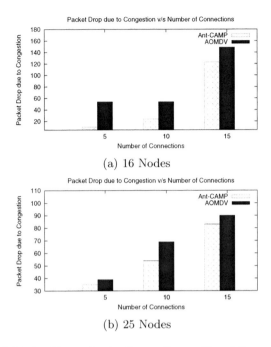

Fig. 4. Packet Drops due to Congestion vs No. of Connections

varying number of connections (5, 10, 15). Since AOMDV is not congestion-adaptive, it continuously sends data on the path even if congestion occurs and hence results in more number of packets being dropped.

Fig. 4.b shows Packet Drops due to Congestion in case of AOMDV and Ant-CAMP for 25 nodes with varying number of connections (5, 10, 15). Table. 3 shows the percentage decrease in Packet Drops due to Congestion with Ant-CAMP as compared to AOMDV for 16-nodes and 25-nodes with varying number of connections (5, 10, 15).

4.2   Packet Delivery Fraction

Fig. 5.a and 5.b demonstrate the effectiveness of Ant-CAMP in terms of Packet Delivery Fraction for 16 nodes and 25 nodes with varying number of connections

Table 3. Decrease in Packet Drop due to Congestion

No. of Connections	Improvement of Packet Drops due to Congestion (%)	
	16 Nodes	25 Nodes
5	81.48	10.25
10	55.55	21.74
15	17.45	7.77

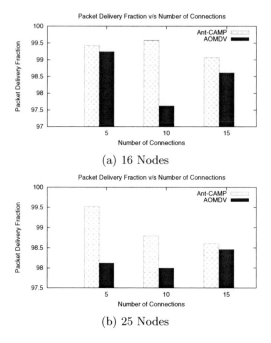

(a) 16 Nodes

(b) 25 Nodes

Fig. 5. Packet Delivery Fraction vs No. of Connections

(5, 10, 15). As the number of connection increases in network, the network becomes congested. As a result, PDF of AOMDV reduces because of its congestion-un-adaptive nature.

Table. 4 shows the percentage increase in terms of PDF with Ant-CAMP as compared to AOMDV for 16-nodes and 25-nodes with varying number of connections (5, 10, 15).

Table 4. Increase in Packet Delivery Fraction

No. of Connections	Improvement of Packet Delivery Fraction (%)	
	16 Nodes	25 Nodes
5	0.19	1.43
10	2.00	0.82
15	0.46	0.15

4.3   Average End to End Delay

Fig. 6.a shows average End to End Delay of AOMDV and Ant-CAMP for 16 nodes with varying number of connections (5, 10, 15). The Ant-CAMP monitors the path in terms of average queue size by periodically sending *monitor ants*.

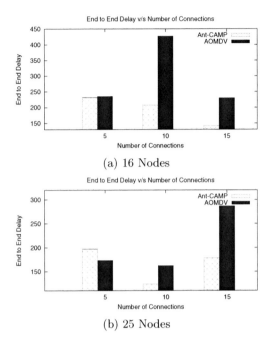

(a) 16 Nodes

(b) 25 Nodes

Fig. 6. Average End to End Delay vs No. of Connections

Table 5. Decrease in Average End to End Delay

No. of Connections	Improvement of Average End to End Delay (%)	
	16 Nodes	25 Nodes
5	1.63	-13.60
10	51.46	23.86
15	38.33	37.82

Source sends data on the path with minimal average queue size which in turn results in reducing end to end delay [7], [8].

Fig. 6.b shows Average End to End Delay of AOMDV and Ant-CAMP for 25 nodes with varying number of connections across (5, 10, 15). Table. 5 shows the percentage decrease in terms of PDF of Ant-CAMP compared to AOMDV for 16-nodes and 25-nodes topology.

5   Conclusions and Future Work

In this paper, we have proposed a bio inspired congestion adaptive multipath routing protocol called Ant-CAMP that not only aims to avoid network congestion by proactively sending *congestion notifications* but also aims to reduce the overall average end to end delay of the network by expoiting the benefits of multipath routing protocols. The proposed Ant-CAMP routing protocol is implemented in NS-2 and its performance is evaluated based on the comparative study between Ant-CAMP and AOMDV in terms of Packet Drops due to Congestion, Packet Delivery Fraction and Average End to End Delay. Based on simulation results it is observed that Ant-CAMP routing protocol reduces the number of packet drops due to congestion and improves the overall packet delivery ratio while minimizing the average end to end delay of the network. However, Ant-CAMP can be further optimized by dynamically varying the predetermined threshold and accurately selecting queue weight for average queue size calculation.

References

1. Tran, D.A., Harish, R.: Congestion Adaptive Routing in Mobile Ad Hoc Network. IEEE Transactions on Parallel and Distributed Systems 17(11) (November 2006)
2. Mohammed, T., Kemal, E.T., Sasan, A., Shervin, E.: Survey of Multipath Routing Protocols for Mobile Ad Hoc networks. Journal of Network and Computer Applications 32, 1125–1143 (2009)
3. Jack, T., Tim, M.: A Review of Multipath Routing Protocols: From Wireless Ad Hoc to Mesh Network. In: Proc. ACoRN Early Career Researcher Workshop on Wireless Multihop Networking, pp. 17–18 (July 2006)
4. Marco, D., Vittorio, M., Alberto, C.: Ant System: Optimization by a Colony of Co-operating agents. IEEE Transactions on Systems, Man, and Cybernetics-Part B 26(1), 1–13 (1996)
5. Falko, D., Ozgur, B.A.: A Survey on Bio-inspired Networking. Computer Networks 54(6), 881–900 (2010)
6. Marina, M.K., Das, S.R.: Ad Hoc On-demand Multipath Distance Vector Routing. Computer Science Department, Stony Brook University (2003)
7. NS, The Network Simulator, http://www.isi.edu/nsnam/ns/
8. http://mohittahiliani.blogspot.com/2009/12/awk-script-for-ns2.html

Man-in-the-Middle Attack
and Its Countermeasure in
Bluetooth Secure Simple Pairing

Thrinatha R. Mutchukota, Saroj Kumar Panigrahy, and Sanjay Kumar Jena

Department of Computer Science and Engineering
National Institute of Technology Rourkela, Rourkela-769 008, Odisha, India
{thrinathr,skp.nitrkl}gmail.com,skjena@nitrkl.ac.in

Abstract. This paper describes the countermeasure of man-in-the-middle attack in Bluetooth secure simple pairing. The attack is based on sending random signals to jam the physical layer of legitimate user and then by falsification of information sent during the input/output capabilities exchange; also the fact that the security of the protocol is likely to be limited by the capabilities of the least powerful or the least secure device type. In addition, a new countermeasure is devised that render the attack impractical, as well as it is an improvement to the existing Bluetooth secure simple pairing in order to make it more secure.

Keywords: Attack, Bluetooth, MITM, NINO, Security.

1 Introduction

Bluetooth is a technology for short range wireless data and real time two-way audio/video transfer providing data rates up to 24 Mbps. It operates at 2.4 GHz frequency in the free Industrial, Scientific, and Medical (ISM) band. Bluetooth devices that communicate with each other form a piconet. The device that initiates a connection is the piconet master and all other devices within that piconet are slaves. The radio frequency (RF) waves can penetrate obstacles, because of this reason the use of wireless communication systems have grown rapidly in recent years. The wireless devices can communicate with no direct line-of-sight between them. This makes RF communication easier to use than wired or infrared communication, but it also makes eavesdropping easier. Moreover, it is easier to disrupt and jam wireless RF communication than wired communication. Because wireless RF communication can suffer from these threats, additional countermeasures are needed to protect against them.

The basic Bluetooth security configuration is done by the user who decides how a Bluetooth device will implement its connectability and discoverability options. The different combinations of connectability and discoverability capabilities can be divided into three categories, or security levels: Silent, Private and Public [1]. In Bluetooth versions up to 2.0+EDR, pairing is based exclusively on the fact that both devices share the same Personal Identification Number (PIN)

K.R. Venugopal and L.M. Patnaik (Eds.): ICIP 2011, CCIS 157, pp. 367–376, 2011.
© Springer-Verlag Berlin Heidelberg 2011

or passkey. As the PINs often contain only four decimal digits, the strength of the resulting keys is not enough for protection against passive eavesdropping on communication. It has been shown that MITM attacks on Bluetooth communications (versions up to 2.0+EDR) can be performed [1,2,3,4,5]. Bluetooth versions 2.1+EDR (Enhanced Data Rate) and 3.0+HS (High Speed) add a new specification for the pairing procedure, namely Secure Simple Pairing (SSP) [1]. Its main goal is to improve the security of pairing by providing protection against passive eavesdropping and Man-in-the-Middle attack (MITM) attacks. Instead of using (often short) passkeys as the only source of entropy for building the link keys, SSP employs Elliptic Curve Diffie-Hellman public-key cryptography. To construct the link key, devices use public-private key pairs, a number of nonces, and Bluetooth addresses of the devices. Passive eavesdropping is effectively thwarted by SSP, as running an exhaustive search on a private key with approximately 95 bits of entropy is currently considered to be infeasible in short time. In order to provide protection against MITM attacks, SSP either asks for user's help or uses an Out-Of-Band (OOB) channel. The SSP uses four association models named OOB, Numerical Comparision (NC), Passkey Entry (PE) and Just Works (JW). Fig. 1 shows the Bluetooth SSP with NC method. The six phases of SSP are explained below:

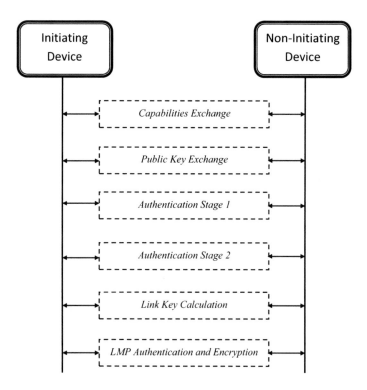

Fig. 1. Bluetooth Secure Simple Pairing with Numerical Comparision

- Capabilities Exchange: The devices that have never met before or want to perform re-pairing for some reason, first exchange their Input/Output (IO) capabilities to determine the proper association model to be used.
- Public Key Exchange: The devices generate their public private key pairs and send the public keys to each other. They also compute the Diffie-Hellman key.
- Authentication Stage-1: The protocol that is run at this stage depends on the association model. One of the goals of this stage is to ensure that there is no MITM in the communication between the devices. This is achieved by using a series of nonces, commitments to the nonces, and a final check of integrity checksums performed either through the OOB channel or with the help of user.
- Authentication Stage-2: The devices complete the exchange of values (public keys and nonces) and verify the integrity of them.
- Link Key Calculation: The parties compute the link key using their Bluetooth addresses, the previously exchanged values and the Diffie-Hellman key constructed in public key exchange phase.
- Link Management Protocol Authentication and Encryption: Encryption keys are generated in this phase, which is the same as the final steps of pairing in Bluetooth versions up to 2.0+EDR.

The rest of the paper is organized as follows. The reported literature on various MITM attacks on Bluetooth are summarized in Section 2. Existing countermeasures and proposed countermeasure against MITM attacks are discussed in Section 3 and 4 respectively. Section 5 provides the concluding remarks.

2   MITM Attacks on Bluetooth

The First MITM attack on Bluetooth assumes that the link key used by two victim devices is known to the attacker was devised by Jakobsson and Wetzel [2]. This attack will work for the version 1.0B and as well as all versions upto 2.0+EDR, because of no security improvements were implemented in those specifications. The authors also showed how to obtain the link key using offline PIN crunching, by passive eavesdropping on the initialization key establishment protocol.

By manipulating with the clock settings, the attacker forces both victim devices to use the same channel hopping sequence but different clocks. This is an improvement of the attack of [2] by Kugler [3]. In addition, Kugler shows how a MITM attack can be performed during the paging procedure. The attacker responds to the page request of the master victim faster than the slave victim, and restarts the paging procedure with the slave using a different clock.

Reflection (relay) attacks aim at impersonating the victim devices [4]. The attacker does not need to know any secret information, because she only relays (reflects) the received information from one victim device to another during the authentication.

The versions 2.1+EDR and 3.0+HS of Bluetooth provide protection against the MITM attacks described above, by the means of SSP. However, it has been shown that MITM attacks against Bluetooth 2.1+EDR and 3.0+HS devices are also possible [5,6,7,8,9]. Because SSP supports several association models, selection of which depends on the capabilities of the target devices, the attacker can force the devices into the use of a less secure mode by changing the capabilities information.

Haataja and Toivanen proposed two new MITM attacks on Bluetooth SSP [1]. The first attack is based on the falsification of information sent during the IO capabilities exchange. The second attack requires some kind of visual contact to the victim devices in order to mislead the user to select a less secure option instead of using a more secure OOB channel. Now the situation has changed— Bluetooth devices with an adjustable Bluetooth device addresses are readily available and techniques for finding hidden (non-discoverable) Bluetooth devices have been invented. Therefore, the danger of MITM attacks has recently increased.

MITM attacks can be possible on these Bluetooth connection methods— (i) SSP with just works, (ii) if one of the devices does not have IO devices or the MITM impersonates as legitimate user and tells "no-input and no-output" as its capabilities to connect and (iii) by creating Jam in physical layer (PHY) when legitimate users know each other. Table 1 shows the bluetooth connection methods and the possibility of the MITM attacks on those methods. Possible solutions to the above attacks are presented in Table 2.

The various jammers used for jamming the PHY layer of Bluetooth devices are— constant jammer, deceptive jammer, random jammer, reactive jammer [10,11]. The jamming activities of various jammers are given in Table 3. There exist different intrusion detection schemes (IDS) are: Signal Strength Measurements, Carrier Sensing Time, Measuring the PDR and Consistency Checks [10,11,12]. Discoverability of different types of jammers using different intrusion detection schemes (IDS) are shown in Table 4. With these IDS, one can be able to

Table 1. The Bluetooth connection methods and possibility of the MITM attacks

Sl. No.	Bluetooth Connection Methods	Possibility of MITM Attacks
1	SSP with Just Works	YES
2	SSP-OOB as mandatory	NO
3	SSP- Numeric comparison with both devices have IO capabilities	NO
4	One of the devices does not have IO devices or the MITM impersonates as legitimate user and tells "no-input and no-output" as its capabilities to connect.	YES
5	By creating Jam in PHY when legitimate users know each other	YES
6	By using RF fingerprints as Keys	NO
7	By Adding an additional window at the user interface level	NO

detect all types of jammers and overcome the problem of distinguishing between network dynamics and jamming attacks. However, there are still open issues. For example, the frequency of the location advertisements can significantly affect the performance of the location consistency check system. In addition, wireless propagation effects (e.g., Fading) should be taken into consideration for accurately computing the false alarm rate of the IDS.

There exist also various intrusion prevention schemes— simple PHY layer techniques [10], directional antennas [13], spread spectrum [14], cyber mines and FEC (Forward Error Correction) [15], [16], and use of covert channels in the presence of a jammer [17], [18]. Table 5 shows the prevention schemes for the jamming attacks.

Table 2. The possible solutions to the attacks which are presented in Table 1

Sl. No.	Problems	Solutions
1	SSP with Just Works	By not allowing the devices for the JW option association model (the users should have key sharing) OR by allowing the devices by adding an additional window at the user interface level.
2	One of the devices don't have IO devices OR The MITM impersonates as legitimate user and tells "no-input and no-output" as its capabilities to connect.	OOB as a mandatory association model (i.e., the communication will be very secure by using near field communication like infrared).
3	By creating Jam in PHY layer when legitimate users know each other	By using one of Anti-Jamming techniques like frequency hopping, direct sequence spread spectrum and uncoordinated spread spectrum.

Table 3. The types of jammers and their activities

Sl. No	Type of Jammers	Activity
1	Constant Jammer	A jammer continually emits radio signals on the wireless medium. The signals can consist of a completely random sequence of bits.
2	Deceptive Jammer	Similar to the constant jammer. Their similarity is due to the fact that both constantly transmit bits. The main difference is that with the deceptive jammer, the transmitted bits are not random. The deceptive jammer continually injects regular packets on the channel without any gaps between the transmissions.
3	Random Jammer	An attacker employing random jamming, jams for t_j seconds and then sleeps for t_s seconds. During the jamming intervals, the jammer can follow any of the approaches.
4	Reactive Jammer	This jammer is constantly sensing the channel and upon sensing a packet transmission immediately transmits a radio signal in order to cause a collision at the receiver.

Table 4. Discoverability of various jammers using different intrusion detection schemes

Sl. No.	Intrusion Detection Schemes [10,11,12]	Constant Jammer	Deceptive Jammer	Random Jammer	Reactive Jammer
1	Signal Strength Measurements	Yes	Yes	No	No
2	Carrier Sensing Time	Yes	Yes	No	No
3	Measuring the PDR*	Yes	Yes	Yes	Yes
4	Consistency Checks**	Yes	Yes	Yes	Yes

* PDR measurements can not always distinguish between jamming and network failures and/or poor link conditions.
** Consistency Checks introduce two detection techniques:
(a) Signal Strength Consistency Check
(b) Location Consistency Check

Table 5. Intrusion prevention schemes

Sl. No.	Intrusion Prevention Schemes	Activities [10,15,16]
1	Simple PHY Layer Techniques	By reducing the distance between legitimate transceiver pair or by increasing the transmission power, we can reduce the jamming-to-signal ratio and make the link more robust to jamming attacks.
2	Directional Antennas [13]	Jamming interference coming from directions other than the direction of transmission does not stimulate transmission deferrals due to carrier sensing.
3	Spread Spectrum [14]	The most well known techniques are based on the use of Spread Spectrum communications. Here signal processing techniques used as jamming countermeasures.
4	Cyber Mines and FEC (Forward Error Correction) [15,16]	Low energy long-lived jamming units are called cyber-mines. For handing these there are some methods like Low Density Parity Codes (LDPC) and Turbo-Codes etc.
5	Use of covert channels in the presence of a jammer [17,18]	When the reception of a packet is affected by jammer, the receiver can identify the reception of a (corrupted) packet. By encoding data based on the inter-arrival times between received corrupted packets, a low rate channel under jamming can be established.

Schemes 1 and 2 do not perform any processing of the transmitted signal while, Schemes 3-5 perform processing of transmitted signal.

2.1   MITM Attack in Bluetooth SSP

The MITM first disrupts (jams) the PHY by hopping along with the victim devices and sending random data in every time slot. In this way, the MITM shuts down all piconets within the range of susceptibility and there is no need to use a Bluetooth chipset to generate hopping patterns. Finally, a frustrated user thinks that something is wrong with his/her Bluetooth devices and deletes previously

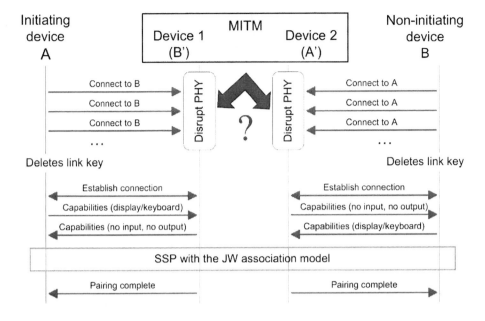

Fig. 2. MITM Attack on Bluetooth SSP

stored link keys. After that the user initiates a new pairing process by using SSP, and the MITM can forge messages exchanged during the I/O capabilities exchange phase by pretending as legitimate user, because the legitimate user's information is deleted. While using the SSP, also the MITM attacks are going to be possible by using the PHY layer jamming and falsification of information. Fig. 2 shows the problem of MITM attacks on physical layer of bluetooth devices.

3   Existing Countermeasures

3.1   By Adding an Additional Window at the User Interface Level

It is recommend that an additional window, "The second device has no display and keyboard! Is this true?", should be displayed at the user interface level of SSP when the JW association model is to be used. The user is asked to choose either "Proceed" or "Stop". The advantage of this approach is that the JW association model can still be a part of the future Bluetooth SSP specifications without any changes [1].

3.2   SSP-OOB as Mandatory

Future Bluetooth specifications should make OOB a mandatory association model in order to radically improve the security and usability of SSP. Therefore, future Bluetooth specifications should at least strongly recommend the use of an OOB channel (e.g., NFC) to all Bluetooth device manufacturers [1].

4   Proposed Countermeasure

The proposed approach is as follows. While one of the initiating or non-initiating devices is trying to connect with each other, the attacker will send wrong signals which leads to the corruption of the original signal. So, the legitimate users thinks that, there may be some sort of genuine jam in the network and gets frustrated, and deletes all the information about the other devices. We have to stop these jamming attacks which are attacking PHY layer. By considering the prevention schemes of jamming attack explained in Table 5, we can avoid the MITM attack. After that, the process of SSP will be followed for the secure communication. The prevention schemes of PHY layer are also called anti-jamming techniques. Fig. 3 shows the solution for the countermeasure against MITM attack.

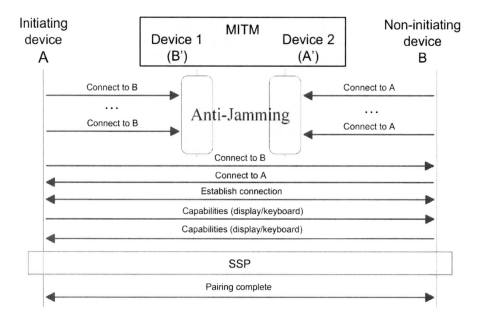

Fig. 3. Countermeasure to MITM Attack

5   Conclusions

It is shown that the MITM attack on PHY layer can be avoided by applying the anti-jamming techniques on SSP model. That will give MITM-attack-free method for secure communication. Still the problem area is open for more research on how to make Bluetooth connections more secure.

Acknowledgment

The authors are indebted to Information Security Education and Awareness (ISEA) Project, Department of Information Technology, Ministry of Communication and Information Technology, Government of India, for sponsoring this research and development activity.

References

1. Haataja, K., Toivanen, P.: Two Practical Man-in-the-Middle Attacks on Bluetooth Secure Simple Pairing and Countermeasures. IEEE Transactions on Wireless Communications 9(1), 384–392 (2010),
   http://dx.doi.org/10.1109/TWC.2010.01.090935
2. Jakobsson, M., Wetzel, S.: Security Weaknesses in Bluetooth. In: Naccache, D. (ed.) CT-RSA 2001. LNCS, vol. 2020, pp. 176–191. Springer, Heidelberg (2001),
   http://dx.doi.org/10.1007/3-540-45353-9_14
3. Kugler, D.: Man in the middle attacks on bluetooth. In: Wright, R.N. (ed.) FC 2003. LNCS, vol. 2742, pp. 149–161. Springer, Heidelberg (2003),
   http://dx.doi.org/10.1007/978-3-540-45126-6_11
4. Levi, A., Çetintaş, E., Aydos, M., Koç, c.K., Çağlayan, M.U.: Relay Attacks on Bluetooth Authentication and Solutions. In: Aykanat, C., Dayar, T., Körpeoğlu, İ. (eds.) ISCIS 2004. LNCS, vol. 3280, pp. 278–288. Springer, Heidelberg (2004),
   http://dx.doi.org/10.1007/978-3-540-30182-0_29
5. Haataja, K.: Security Threats and Countermeasures in Bluetooth-Enabled Systems. Ph.D. thesis, University of Kuopio, Department of Computer Science (February 2009)
6. Suomalainen, J., Valkonen, J., Asokan, N.: Security associations in personal networks: A comparative analysis. In: Stajano, F., Meadows, C., Capkun, S., Moore, T. (eds.) ESAS 2007. LNCS, vol. 4572, pp. 43–57. Springer, Heidelberg (2007),
   http://dx.doi.org/10.1007/978-3-540-73275-4_4
7. Hypponen, K., Haataja, K.: Nino: Man-in-the-Middle Attack on Bluetooth Secure Simple Pairing. In: 3rd IEEE/IFIP International Conference in Central Asia on Internet, ICI 2007, pp. 1–5 (September 2007),
   http://dx.doi.org/10.1109/CANET.2007.4401672
8. Haataja, K., Hypponen, K.: Man-in-the-Middle Attacks on Bluetooth: A Comparative Analysis, A Novel Attack, and Countermeasures. In: Proc. IEEE Third International Symposium on Communications, Control and Signal Processing (ISCCSP 2008), St. Julians, Malta (March 2008)
9. Haataja, K., Toivanen, P.: Practical Man-in-the-Middle Attacks Against Bluetooth Secure Simple Pairing. In: 4th International Conference on Wireless Communications, Networking and Mobile Computing, WiCOM 2008, pp. 1–5 (October 2008),
   http://dx.doi.org/10.1109/WiCom.2008.1153
10. Pelechrinis, K., Iliofotou, M., Krishnamurthy, V.: Denial of Service Attacks in Wireless Networks: The case of Jammers. IEEE Communications Surveys Tutorials 99, 1–13 (2010), http://dx.doi.org/10.1109/SURV.2011.041110.00022
11. Xu, W., Trappe, W., Zhang, Y., Wood, T.: The Feasibility of Launching and Detecting Jamming Attacks in Wireless Networks. In: Proceedings of the 6th ACM international symposium on Mobile Ad Hoc Networking and Computing MobiHoc 2005, pp. 46–57. ACM, New York (2005),
    http://doi.acm.org/10.1145/1062689.1062697

12. Xu, W., Ma, K., Trappe, W., Zhang, Y.: Jamming Sensor Networks: Attack and Defense Strategies. IEEE Network 20(3), 41–47 (2006),
    http://dx.doi.org/10.1109/MNET.2006.1637931
13. Noubir, G.: On connectivity in ad hoc networks under jamming using directional antennas and mobility. In: Langendoerfer, P., Liu, M., Matta, I., Tsaoussidis, V. (eds.) WWIC 2004. LNCS, vol. 2957, pp. 186–200. Springer, Heidelberg (2004),
    http://dx.doi.org/10.1007/978-3-540-24643-5_17
14. Viterbi, A.J.: Principles of Spread Spectrum Communication. Addison-Wesley Wireless Communications Series. Addison-Wesley, Reading (1995)
15. Noubir, G., Lin, G.: Low-Power Dos Attacks in Data Wireless Lans and Counter-measures. SIGMOBILE Mob. Comput. Commun. Rev. 7, 29–30 (2003),
    http://doi.acm.org/10.1145/961268.961277
16. Lin, G., Noubir, G.: On Link Layer Denial of Service in Data Wireless Lans: Research Articles. Wirel. Commun. Mob. Comput. 5, 273–284 (2005),
    http://portal.acm.org/citation.cfm?id=1072503.1072505
17. Xu, W., Trappe, W., Zhang, Y.: Anti-Jamming Timing Channels for Wireless Networks. In: Proceedings of the first ACM conference on Wireless network security, WiSec 2008, pp. 203–213. ACM, New York (2008),
    http://doi.acm.org/10.1145/1352533.1352567
18. Chung, F., Salehi, J., Wei, V.: Optical Orthogonal Codes: Design, Analysis and Applications. IEEE Transactions on Information Theory 35(3), 595–604 (1989),
    http://dx.doi.org/10.1109/18.30982

On Downlink Inter Cell Interference Modeling in Cellular OFDMA Networks

Ranjan Bala Jain

Department of Electrical Engineering, IIT Bombay, India
ranjanbala@gmail.com

Abstract. The most important issue in Orthogonal Frequency Division Multiple Access (OFDMA) cellular network is inter-cell interference (ICI) due to universal frequency reuse. In this work, we derive the analytical expression for interference on a particular user in a reference cell from all interfering cells irrespective of the position of user. We consider the effect of path loss, shadowing and fading on interference from three tiers of cells. Then we calculate ICI for two hop relay network. OFDMA downlink involves the sum of correlated random variables. Therefore a general expression is derived to solve the problems of correlated random variables irrespective of the system. The analytical and simulation results show the correctness of derivation.

Keywords: Correlated Random Variables, ICI, OFDMA, SIR, SINR.

1 Introduction

Wireless communication systems experience physical characteristics such as time varying multipath and shadowing due to obstructions in the propagation path. Also the performance of wireless cellular network is limited by interference from other users, and for this reason, it is important to have accurate techniques for modeling interference.

OFDMA is a promising multiple access technique for next generation mobile networks. The technology for OFDMA based system is OFDM. With OFDM, available spectrum is split in to a number of parallel orthogonal narrowband subcarriers to combat multipath. These subcarriers are allocated to different users in a cell independently. In order to utilize the spectrum efficiently, frequency reuse of one is considered in OFDMA based network which introduces more severe Inter Cell Interference (ICI) among users using the same subcarriers. ICI is considered as one of the major factors which affects the performance in terms of outage probability, blocking probability and hence the capacity of OFDMA cellular system. Therefore it is necessary to understand the effects of ICI on the performance and capacity of the network when deploying or when system is analyzed and designed to mitigate the undesired effects of ICI. This is also dependent on channel characteristic such as path loss and shadow fading and these effects also vary with the location of users. Typically, a user is said to be in

K.R. Venugopal and L.M. Patnaik (Eds.): ICIP 2011, CCIS 157, pp. 377–388, 2011.

outage when the required SINR is not achieved. In order to compute the outage probability of a user, it is essential to know the distribution of the SINR.

The modeling of ICI for cellular OFDMA has been recently considered in the literature. Traditionally time consuming simulations are used to find the Signal to Interference Ratio (SIR) statistics. In some work either the large path loss [1] or multipath propagation [2] is taken which are incomplete for the study of real wireless environment. The authors in [2] calculate the capacity of Nakagami multipath fading channels assuming that the SNR is gamma distributed. In this the effect of shadowing and path loss is neglected. In [3], ICI resulting from multiple cells has been approximated by Gaussian and Binomial distribution. The results have been verified by simulations. The distribution of ICI for various positions of the user has been calculated in [4]. In this semi-analytical approach, impact of power allocation on downlink intercell interference has been presented.

More recently, in [5], a model is presented for outage probability computation in a packet switched cellular mobile radio network. In this work, outage probability is defined with respect to the threshold data rate or equivalently bandwidth demand for a single cell and multiple cells. In [6], an iterative method is presented to calculate the distribution of ICI for a universal frequency reuse cellular OFDMA system with voice over IP traffic. In [7], it is shown that for random subcarrier allocation, the overall interference on all subcarriers will be the geometric mean of the interferences on individual subcarriers. We follow this approach to calculate the overall interference distribution on a subchannel.

In [8], the performance of OFDMA system is investigated in terms of outage probability and system throughput under different frequency reuse by considering average SINR. Here the effect of fading is not considered. In [9], the performance of multicell OFDMA is presented to calculate the Erlang capacity by considering independent interferences. Also number of users is known. However it is necessary to consider the randomness of users and interferences from various cells are not independent but they are correlated. In [10], the Tele-traffic performance of OFDM-TDMA system in terms of time congestion, Traffic congestion and call congestion is analyzed using Adaptive Modulation and Coding(AMC) and state dependent blocking for various traffic streams. Here, it is assumed that each subcarrier is affected by Rayleigh fading only. The analytic expression for SINR cumulative distribution function in multicellular system is derived with full transmit diversity using Alamouti scheme in [11]. In [12], an analytic model is proposed to calculate the uplink Erlang capacity of multi-class multi-hop relay networks with AMC scheme for flat Rayleigh fading channels.

The effect of ICI is estimated by the SIR of the communication link. It is defined as the ratio of the power of the desired signal S to the power of the total interference signal, I. Since both power levels S and I are random variables due to RF propagation effects (path loss, shadowing and fading), user mobility and traffic variation, the SIR is also a random variable. In modeling of interference, it is difficult to find the distribution of the sum of several signal powers (not necessarily independent or identical distributed) received from various interferes. The OFDMA downlink involves the sum of correlated random variables (power received from various interferes), to the best of our knowledge, there has not been any work done to derive the CDF of SIR in downlink of OFDMA network using correlated as well as mutually independent effects multipath fading, shadowing and path loss together. The rest of the paper is organized as follows. In section 2, the system model and problem description is presented and sections 2.1, 2.2 and 2.3 present the ICI modeling without power control, with power control and subcarrier activity factor. Section 3 discusses the architecture and ICI modeling for two hop cellular OFDMA relay network. Section 4 provides the numerical and simulation results. Section 5 presents the conclusion of the work.

2   System Model and Problem Description

In interference limited environment, the quality of received signal at the receiver is typically measured by means of achieved SIR, which is the ratio of power of desired signal to the total power of the interference signals.

We consider the downlink of a cellular OFDMA system with hexagonally shaped cells of the radius R as shown in Fig. 1. The BSs are marked with a small circle and some user positions are marked by crosses. The BSs are located at the centre of the cells and are equipped with Omni-directional antennas. For simplicity in calculation we approximate the hexagonal cell by a circular cell and without loss of generality, we assume the radius of the cell to be unity. We consider interference from the first three tiers surrounding the reference cell. The reference cell and the six neighboring cells in first, second and third tier are numbered as 0 and 1,...,6, 7,...,18 and 19,...,36 respectively.

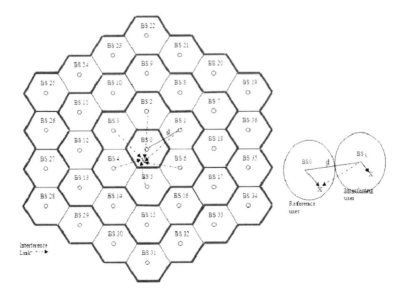

Fig. 1. Architecture of Conventional Cellular OFDMA System

A network with universal frequency reuse is considered, i.e., all the cells use the same spectrum. This relaxes the advanced frequency planning otherwise necessary among different cells. However, universal frequency reuse introduces more severe ICI. A simple path loss based channel model is assumed in this work. If the power transmitted by the BS is P, then a user at a distance d receives power $Pd^{-\beta}$ where β is path loss exponent. The signal coming from BSs experiences Rayleigh fading and long term shadowing (which follows a lognormal law with σ (dB) $= 6$ to 12 dB spread). All paths are assumed to be independently faded and shadowed. We use the natural base for lognormal Random Variables.

In a cellular OFDMA system, available spectrum is divided into orthogonal subcarriers. Every user is allocated a set of subcarriers commonly known as subchannel. The assignment of subcarriers to sub-channel is random and differs independently from cell to cell. We assume that the users are uniformly distributed over the cell. When a user enters into the system, it has some QOS requirement (Bit Error Rate, data rate or Signal to Interference Noise Ratio). Depending on these user is allocated a set of subcarriers to satisfy QOS, commonly called a sub-channel. On a particular subcarrier, the user receives interference from the users in the neighboring cells, who are allocated the same subcarrier. The interference power depends on the distance between neighboring BS and user. The position of user is a random variable and hence the interference on a subcarrier. We derive the Cumulative Distributive Function (CDF) of this interference on a subcarrier analytically. Then we use the fact that for random subcarriers allocation, the overall interference on all subcarriers in a sub-channel is the geometric mean of the interference on individual sub-carriers [7].

2.1 Inter-cell Interference Modeling without Power Control

This section derives the CDF of interference on a subcarrier from all the cells in first three tiers. Consider a user in the reference cell at a distance r from the BS and at an angle θ from the axis as shown in Fig. 1. Depending upon QOS requirement, a set of orthogonal subcarriers is assigned to the user. Let us analyze the interference received by it on one of the subcarriers. The SIR for desired user u, at a distance r on a subcarrier m in a reference cell is expressed as,

$$\gamma_{u,r,m} = \frac{Pr^{-\beta}\xi\alpha^2}{\sum_{i=1}^{N} Pd_i^{-\beta}\xi_i\alpha_i^2} = \frac{1}{\sum_{i=1}^{N}\left(\frac{d_i}{r}\right)^{-\beta}\frac{\xi_i}{\xi}\left(\frac{\alpha_i}{\alpha}\right)^2} .$$

Where, d_i is the distance between i^{th} interfering BS and reference user. β is the path loss exponent and N is the number of interferers from neighboring cells. Where, $d_i = \sqrt{(x - x_i)^2 + (y - y_i)^2}$, (x, y) and (x_i, y_i) are the coordinates of the user in reference cell and the ith interfering BS respectively. Since the position of user in reference cell (x, y) is random variable therefore d_is have different distribution and is not independent. ξ_i and $\alpha_i{}^2$ represent shadowing and fading between i^{th} interfering BS and reference user. ξ and α represents the shadowing and fading between reference BS and reference user. N is the number of interferers in the number of tiers considered. In general, the number of interferers in n tiers is given by $6n$.

We assume that all BSs transmit at the same power P. Thus $\gamma_{u,r,m}$ can be represented as reciprocal of interference as follows:

$$\gamma_{u,r,m} = \frac{1}{I}.$$

And the problem is now to calculate the distribution function of the total interference I. We solve it by the method of moments in two steps.

Since d_is are not independent therefore, first, we group the interference into two components B_is, which are having different distributions and C_is, which are *iid* random variables.

$$I = \sum_{i=1}^{N} B_i C_i.$$

$B_i = \left(\frac{d_i}{r}\right)^{-\beta} = \left[\frac{(x-x_i)^2+(y-y_i)^2}{x^2+y^2}\right]^{\frac{-\beta}{2}}$ and $C_i = \frac{\xi_i}{\xi}\left(\frac{\alpha_i}{\alpha}\right)^2$ and we find the exact moments of the interference power. Second, we match the obtained moments to lognormal distribution, as it is often used to model the total interference in cellular systems. The first and second order moments of total interference I are calculated as, $E[I] = E[C_i]E[\sum_{i=1}^{N} B_i]$., since C_is are *iids* and

$$E[I^2] = E\left[\sum_{i=1}^{N} B_i^2\right]E[C_i^2] + (E[C_i])^2\left[E\left(\sum_{i=1}^{N} B_i\right)^2 - E\left(\sum_{i=1}^{N} B_i^2\right)\right].$$

Let $M_n = E[\sum_{i=1}^{N} B_i^n] = \frac{2}{3\sqrt{3}} \int \int_{x,y\in H_0} \left(\sqrt{\frac{(x-x_i)^2+(y-y_i)^2}{x^2+y^2}}\right)^{-n\beta} dxdy$ where, expectation is taken over the position of mobiles being uniformly distributed over their respective sub-cells. And, H_0 is a hexagon of unit side, (Its area is $3\sqrt{3}/2$) centered at *(0, 0)* and i^{th} interfering BS is located at (x_i, y_i). These integrals are evaluated separately for each interfering BS and then summed for all integrals to get M_n. Since the distance between a reference user and the interfering fixed BSs are not independent, therefore can not be separated into a sum of terms, therefore it is integrated for the entire geometry as follows:

$$A_s = E\left(\sum_{i=1}^{N} B_i\right)^2 = \frac{2}{3\sqrt{3}} \int \int_{x,y\in H_0} \left(\sum_{i=1}^{N}\left(\sqrt{\frac{(x-x_i)^2+(y-y_i)^2}{x^2+y^2}}\right)^{\frac{-B}{2}}\right)^2 dxdy.$$

Where (x_i, y_i) and H_0 are the same as defined previously. Since C_i has four random variable components, shadowing and fading from the interfering BS to the reference user and from reference BS to user. To find the exact moments of C_i, the moment of individual components, their ratios and products are to be determined. Since the ratio of the two independent lognormal random variables is itself a lognormal distributed RV with statistics are defined by $(0,\sigma^2)$. Since the components of C_is are independent and all C_i are *iid*, the P - coefficients can be expressed as:

$$P_n = E[C_i^n] = E\left[\left(\frac{\xi_i}{\xi}\right)^n\right]E\left[\left(\frac{\alpha_i}{\alpha}\right)^n\right] = \bar{\xi}\bar{\alpha}.$$

2.2   Inter-cell Interference Modeling with Power Control

With power control, the power transmitted will be proportional to the path loss between the mobile and its BS. That is the power transmitted by the BS is Pd^β, then a user at a distance d receives power P. where β is path loss exponent. The signal coming from BSs experiences Rayleigh fading and long term shadowing (which follows a lognormal law with $\sigma(dB) = 6$ to 12 dB spread), the power control mechanism will compensate this. All paths are assumed to be independently faded and shadowed. We model this by a lognormal random variable with statistics $(0,\ \sigma^2 + \sigma_e^2)$. We use the natural base for lognormal Random Variables. The SIR for desired user u, at a distance r on a subcarrier m in a reference cell is expressed as

$$\gamma_{u,r,m} = \frac{P\xi\alpha^2}{\sum_{i=1}^{N} Pr_i^\beta d_i^{-\beta}\xi_i\alpha_i^2} = \frac{1}{\sum_{i=1}^{N}\left(\frac{d_i}{r_i}\right)^{-\beta}\frac{\xi_i}{\xi}\left(\frac{\alpha_i}{\alpha}\right)^2}.$$

Where r_i is the distance of user in i^{th} cell from BS i, who is using the same subcarrier as allocated in reference cell. The procedure to calculate the exact moments of I is same as done in without power control. Here one more term in denominator is introduced. Thus interference is divided into two groups as follows,

$$B_i = (d_i)^{-\beta} = [(x - x_i)^2 + (y - y_i)^2]^{\frac{-\beta}{2}}.$$

$$C_i = \frac{\xi_i}{\xi}\left(\frac{\alpha_i}{\alpha}\right)^2 r_i^\beta.$$

The other parameters are already evaluated, only the Expected value of r_i^β is to be determined. Since the position of mobile users has uniform distribution over its cell i.

$$f(r_i) = \frac{2r_i}{R^2}, \qquad 0 < r_i \le R.$$

Then $E[r_i^{n\beta}] = \frac{2R^{n\beta}}{\beta+2}$ and $E[(\frac{\xi_i}{\xi})^n] = exp[\frac{n\sigma\ ln\ 10}{10}]^2$. In Table 1, all M and P coefficients are calculated for various β and n for both power and without power control. Since the components of C_is are independent and all C_is are *iids*, the $P-$ coefficients can be expressed as,

$$P_n = E[C_i^n] = E\left[\left(\frac{\xi_i}{\xi}\right)^n\right]E\left[\left(\frac{\alpha_i}{\alpha}\right)^n\right]E[r_i^{n\beta}].$$

Now the obtained moments are matched by approximating I by a lognormal random variable of parameters $(\mu_I,\ \sigma_I^2)$.

$$E[I^n] = e^{n\mu_I + \frac{n^2}{2}\sigma_I^2}.$$

On inverting we obtain, $\mu_I = 2\ ln\ E[I] - \frac{1}{2}\ ln\ E[I^2]$ and $\sigma_I^2 = -2lnE[I] + lnE[I^2]$. Using μ_I and σ_I^2, we find the distribution as,

$$F_I(x) = N\left[\frac{ln\ x - \mu_I}{\sigma_I}\right], \qquad x > 0.$$

Here $N(x)$ is the standard normal cumulative distribution function. We have thus determined the distribution of interference on a subcarrier for the reference user present in the reference cell.

2.3 Inter-cell Interference Modeling with Subcarrier Activity Factor

In the last sections, we considered that all subcarriers which are allocated to the reference users are being used in the neighboring cells. However it is not true, this subcarrier activity is considered by a Bernoulli R.V. Let λ_i is the Bernoulli distributed R.V. and it is unity when a subcarrier is being used in the neighboring cells. Thus the SIR can be written as follows.

$$\gamma_{u,r,m} = \frac{P\xi\alpha^2}{\sum_{i=1}^{N} P\lambda_i r_i^\beta d_i^{-\beta} \xi_i \alpha_i^2} = \frac{1}{\sum_{i=1}^{N} \left(\frac{d_i}{r_i}\right)^{-\beta} \frac{\xi_i}{\xi} \lambda_i \left(\frac{\alpha_i}{\alpha}\right)^2} .$$

Notations are same as used previously, only subcarrier activity factor is included as given by, $B_i = (d_i)^{-\beta}$ and $C_i = \frac{\xi_i}{\xi}\left(\frac{\alpha_i}{\alpha}\right)^2 \lambda_i r_i^\beta$.

$$P_n = E[C_i^n] = E\left[\left(\frac{\xi_i}{\xi}\right)^n\right] E\left[\left(\frac{\alpha_i}{\alpha}\right)^n\right] E\left[r_i^{n\beta}\right] E(\lambda_i^n) \text{ where, } E(\lambda_i^n) = n!p \text{ and}$$

p is the probability that a subcarrier is in use in the neighboring cells.

3   OFDMA Multi-Hop Cellular Model

In this section, we present the architecture of multi-hop cellular OFDMA network. We consider the downlink of the network, six fixed relay stations (FRS) are added in the conventional single hop cellular network. We define the reference cell as the combination of central sub-cell and containing a BS and its surrounding six sub-cells containing relay stations. The RS are deployed in the network such that there is a good channel condition between BS and FRS as Line of Sight (LOS) environment. And the BS-MS link and FRS-MS link are in non line of sight environment. All FRS are regenerative repeaters so they decode the data from BS and then forward to the target MS. Two hop relay system is the most efficient multi-hop system in terms of system capacity. Hence we assume that if MS are located in central sub-cell, (Inner region) they will be served by BS and transmit in single hop only. And if MSs are located in surrounding sub-cells (relay region), they will be served by corresponding relays and transmit in two hops only.

We assume that BS is having N, number of subcarriers and each RS and BS is allocated N_{RS} and N_{BS} such that $N = N_{BS} + 6\,N_{RS}$. Since in the reference cells all users have allocated subcarriers so no inter sub-cell interference will occur. We also assume that FRS transmit and receive data at different frequency band. However the frequency reuse of one is used, so the users will experience interference from RS and BS of out of reference cell. We analyze this interference on FRS-MS. Let user(MS) is present in one of the relay region, the SIR between reference BS and FRS link (γ_{BS-FRS}) is given by

$$\gamma_{BS-FRS} = \frac{P_{BS}(d_{BS-FRS})^{-\beta}10^{\frac{\xi}{10}}\alpha^2}{\sum_{i=1}^{N} P_{BS}(d_{i\ BS-FRS})^{-\beta}10^{\frac{\xi_i}{10}}\alpha_i^2}$$

$$= \frac{1}{\sum_{i=1}^{N}\left(\frac{d_{BS-FRS}}{d_{i\ BS-FRS}}\right)^{-\beta}10^{\frac{\xi_i-\xi}{10}}\left(\frac{\alpha_i}{\alpha}\right)^2}$$

Now the SIR on the FRS and MS link (γ_{FRS-MS})is given by

$$\gamma_{FRS-MS} = \frac{P_{FRS}(d_{FRS-MS})^{-\beta}10^{\frac{\xi}{10}}}{\sum_{i=1}^{N} P_{FRS}(d_{i\ FRS-MS})^{-\beta}10^{\frac{\xi_i}{10}}}$$

$$= \frac{1}{\sum_{i=1}^{N}\left(\frac{d_{FRS-MS}}{d_{i\ FRS-MS}}\right)^{-\beta}10^{\frac{\xi_i-\xi}{10}}\left(\frac{\alpha_i}{\alpha}\right)^2}$$

Where, P_{BS} is the power transmitted by BS to the FRS and P_{FRS} is the power transmitted by FRS to the MS. d_{BS-FRS} is the distance between the BS and FRS in which user is present. $d_{i\ BS-FRS}$ is the distance between i^{th} BS and FRS serving the user. d_{FRS-MS} is the distance between serving FRS and MS and $d_{i\ FRS-MS}$ is the distance between FRS of ith cell who is using the same subcarrier as used by FRS of reference cell and β is path loss exponent. The complete architecture of relay system is shown in Fig. 2.

The calculation of interferences are same as done in single hop cellular OFDMA networks, because the geometry for relay network is modified version of conventional cellular network. Here we consider 3 tiers of interfering cells. As in the cells of first tier fixed relay stations are kept and interferences are obtained from some cells of second, third and fourth tiers where FRS are kept (See Fig. 2.). However it can also be seen that the multi-hop relay network is scaled version of unit radius Hexagonal cell surrounded by six interfering cells. The distance between centre cell and interfering cell is given by $d_{new} = \sqrt{d^2 + H^2 - 2dH cos(15°)}$ and $H = dcos30°/cos75°$ Where, d is the distance between reference cell and interfering cells in conventional cellular OFDMA network, $d = \sqrt{3}R$, R is radius of cell.

4 Numerical and Simulation Results

We validate our analytical results by Monte-Carlo simulations. We calculate the M and P parameters in Table 1. We observe the downlink interference for a reference user from three tiers of the cells. We plot the normalized interference CDF in log-log scale for both conventional and multi hop relay network. We consider the cases, $\beta = 2$, 3 and 4 and vary the shadowing parameter over the range of 6-12 dB (σ =1.382 to 2.763) with and without power control and various subcarrier activity factor as shown in Fig. 3, 4, 5 and 6. We take power control error at 1 dB ($\sigma_e = 0.2303$).

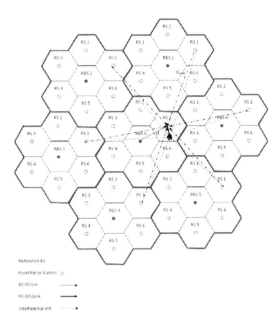

Fig. 2. Architecture of Multi Hop Relay Cellular OFDMA System

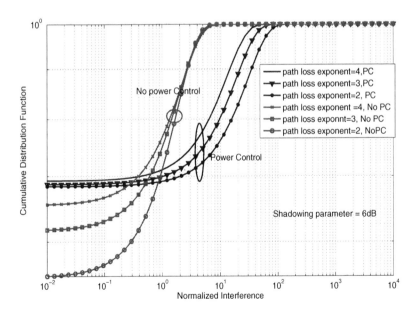

Fig. 3. CDF of normalized interference for various path loss exponents and shadowing parameter = 6 dB with power control (power control error = 1 dB) and without power control

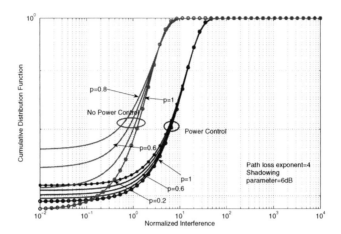

Fig. 4. CDF of normalized interference for path loss exponents = 4 and shadowing parameter= 6 dB with power control (power control error = 1 dB) and without power control in for various subcarrier activity factor p = (0.2, 0.4, 0.6, 0.8 and 1)

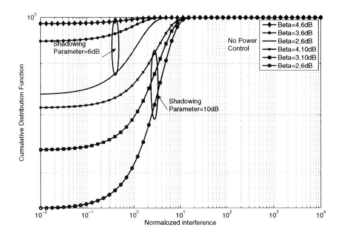

Fig. 5. CDF of normalized interference for various path loss exponents (2, 3 and 4) and shadowing parameters (6 and 10 dB) without power control in two hop relay network

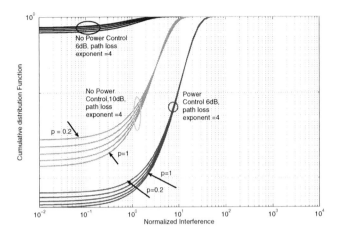

Fig. 6. CDF of normalized interference for path loss exponents = 4 and shadowing parameter = 6 and 10 dB with power control (power control error = 1 dB) and without power control in two hop relay network for various subcarrier activity factor $p = (0.2, 0.4, 0.6, 0.8, 1)$

Table 1. M parameter for various lay-out and path loss

Layout	Conventional Cellular Network			Two Hop Relay Network		
β	2	3	4	2	3	4
M_1	0.9184	0.6663	0.5281	0.1381	0.0345	0.0007
M_2	0.5281	0.4107	0.3876	0.0087	0.0006	0.0004
A_s	2.215	1.215	0.8341	0.0495	0.0031	1.98×10^{-4}

5   Conclusions

We derived a general expression for CDF of interference in single hop and two hop relay cellular OFDMA network analytically and determined it for three tiers of cells including Log normal shadowing and Rayleigh fading. The Rayleigh fading model can be replaced by any other fading model. The computation is very simple as it involves only numerical integrations which depend upon the position of the reference users and path loss exponent β. They are calculated once and used to calculate exact moments. This method of analysis is a tool in systematic planning and design, to solve the problem of correlated random variables, to understand interference in a real wireless scenario, to find better interference mitigation techniques and to compute outage and blocking probability accurately and hence capacity.

Acknowledgement. The author would like to thank Prof. Abhay Karandikar, IIT Bombay for his invaluable support, guidance and discussions.

References

1. Rappaport, T.S.: Wireless Communications: Principles and Practice, 2nd edn. Prentice-Hall PTR, Englewood Cliffs (2001)
2. Alouni, M.S., Goldsmith, A.: Capacity of Nakagami Multipath Fading Channels. In: Proceedings of the IEEE Vehicular Technology Conference, vol. 1(12), pp. 133–147 (2000)
3. Plass, X.D.S., Legouable, R.: Investigations on Link-Level Inter-cell Interference in OFDMA systems. In: Symposium on Communication and Vehicular Technology, pp. 49–52 (November 2006)
4. Castaneda, J.N.I.V.M., Ivrlac, M., Klein, A.: On Downlink Inter-cell Interference in a Cellular System. In: PIMRC 2007, pp. 5720–5725 (2007)
5. Hasselbach, P., Klein, A.: An Analytic Model for Outage Probability and Bandwidth Demand of the Downlink in Packet Switched Cellular Mobile Radio Networks. In: ICC 2008, pp. 252–256 (2008)
6. Bi, Q., Vitebsky, S., Yang, Y., Yuan, Y., Zhang, Q.: Performance and Capacity of Cellular OFDMA Systems with Voice-Over-IP Traffic. IEEE Transactions on Vehicular Technology 57, 3641–3652 (2008)
7. Cioffi, J.: A Multicarrier Primer. Amati Communications Corporation and Stanford University, Tech. Report, T1E1, 4/91-157 (1991)
8. Jia, H., Zhang, Z., Yu, G., Cheng, P., Li, S.: On the Performance of IEEE 802.16 OFDMA System under Different Frequency Reuse and Subcarrier Patterns. In: ICC 2007, pp. 5720–5725 (2007)
9. Elayoubi, S.E., Fourestie, B.: Performance Evaluation of Admission Control and Adaptive Modulation in OFDMA Wimax Systems. IEEE/ACM Transactions on Networking 16(5), 1200–1211 (2008)
10. Wang, H., Iverson, V.B.: Erlang Capacity of Multiclass TDMA Systems with Adaptive Modulation and Coding. In: ICC 2008, vol. 4, pp. 115–119. IEEE, Los Alamitos (2008)
11. Cheikh, D.B., Kelif, J.-M., Coupechoux, M., Godlewski, P.: Outage Probability in a Multi-Cellular Network Using Alamouti Scheme. In: Proceedings of the 33rd IEEE conference on Sarnoff, pp. 26–30 (2010)
12. Wang, H., Xiong, C., Iverson, V.B.: Uplink Capacity of Multiclass IEEE 802.16j Relay Networks with Adaptive Modulation and Coding. In: ICC 2009, pp. 1–6 (2009)

AMul: Adaptive Multicast Routing Protocol for Multi-hop Wireless Networks

Vaidehi Panwala, Saumya Hegde, and Mohit P Tahiliani

Department of Computer Science and Engineering
National Institute of Technology Karnataka, Surathkal
India
vaidehi.p99@gmail.com

Abstract. Wireless Networks have evolved as promising technology for numerous applications to provide Internet access to fixed and mobile wireless devices. Multicasting plays a crucial role in many applications of Wireless Networks. Several routing protocols have been proposed for multicast communication in mobile wireless networks. In this paper we propose a reactive and receiver initiated multicast routing protocol called Adaptive Multicast (AMul) to provide better Quality of Service (QoS) in Wireless Networks. Using simulations, we compare AMul with Protocol for Unified Multicasting through Announcements (PUMA) which is also a reactive and receiver initiated multicast routing protocol for Multi-Hop Wireless Networks. Based on the simulation results, we observe that AMul reduces the overall end to end delay while inducing negligible control overhead in the network.

Keywords: Control Overhead, End to End delay, Multicast Routing Protocols, Multi-hop Wireless Networks, QoS, Total Overhead.

1 Introduction

Tremendous growth in the number of mobile computing devices has lead to the widespread deployment of wireless networks. With the advances in recent technologies and an increasingly sophisticated mobile work force worldwide, content and service providers are interested in supporting group communications over wireless networks.

Data transmission modes are mainly categorized into unicast, multicast and broadcast. Majority of the applications use unicast transmission mode for data transfer. However if real-time multimedia applications such as live video streaming are shared among multiple clients using unicast communications, it could result in network resources starvation. Multicasting is an efficient method of supporting group communication as compared to unicasting or broadcasting since it allows transmission of packets to multiple destinations using fewer network resources [1], [2]. Moreover multicast communications over wireless networks have gained a lot of attention recently and have posed several important and challenging issues.

K.R. Venugopal and L.M. Patnaik (Eds.): ICIP 2011, CCIS 157, pp. 389–395, 2011.
© Springer-Verlag Berlin Heidelberg 2011

Multimedia applications demand high Quality of Service (QoS) as compared to other applications such as file transfer and email, where per packet delay and control overhead have minimal impact. Thus to enhance the QoS for multimedia applications, multicast routing protocols must be tailored towards minimal packet delay and control overhead in the network.

In this paper we propose a reactive and receiver initiated multicast routing protocol named Adaptive Multicast (AMul) Routing Protocol which aims to provide better QoS in multi-hop wireless networks by minimizing per packet delay and control overhead. The proposed AMul routing protocol is implemented in Network Simulator-2 (NS-2) and the results are compared with Protocol for Unified Multicasting through Announcements (PUMA) in terms of average end to end delay, control overhead and total overhead.

The remainder of the paper is organized as follows. In Section 2 we discuss the basic guidelines of AMul protocol. Section 3 presents the Simulation Environment and Section 4 discusses the Results and Analysis. Section 5 concludes the paper with future directions.

2 Adaptive Multicast (AMul) Routing Protocol

2.1 Overview

AMul routing protocol is a mesh based, reactive, receiver initiated multicast routing protocol in which receivers join a multicast group using the address of a Core. AMul routing protocol aims to reduce the overall end to end delay of the network by minimizing per packet queuing delay.

AMul is a modification of PUMA[3-6] and thus eliminates the need for a unicast routing protocol and the pre-assignment of cores to multicast groups. The major difference between AMul and PUMA is that AMul uses average remaining queue as a routing metric while PUMA uses distance to core as a routing metric. The rest of the working of AMul is exactly similar to that of PUMA.

In AMul, every node of the network is expected to calculate its average remaining queue and send this information to other nodes by using Multicast Announcement Packet (MAP). MAP of AMul contains an extra field called average remaining queue as compared to multicast announcement of PUMA. Multicast announcement packets are used by nodes to notify other nodes about joining or leaving a group, maintain the group, elect core nodes and to establish routes for sources outside the multicast group.

The MAP formats of PUMA and AMul are shown in Fig. 1 and Fig. 2 below:

Core ID	Group ID	Seq. Num.	Dist. to Core	Parent	Mesh Member Flag

Fig. 1. PUMAs Multicast Announcement Packet Format

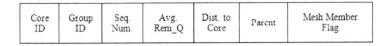

Core ID	Group ID	Seq. Num.	Avg. Rem_Q	Dist. to Core	Parent	Mesh Member Flag

Fig. 2. AMuls Multicast Announcement Packet Format

The fields contained in AMuls MAP are:

- *Core ID*: The Core ID is the address of the special node i.e. the core of a multicast group.
- *Group ID*: Group ID specifies the address of the multicast group
- *Sequence Number*: Sequence numbers are used so that only fresher multicast announcements are considered by the nodes.
- *Average Remaining Queue*: Average remaining queue is used as a routing metric. For the same core ID and sequence number, multicast announcements with higher average remaining queue are considered better.
- *Distance to Core*: Distance to the core specifies the distance of a node to the core node in terms of number of hops.
- *Parent*: It states the preferred neighbor to reach the core.
- *Mesh Member Flag*: It is set when the sending node belongs to the mesh.

2.2   Propagation of MAPs and Formation of Routing Table

MAPs are initiated by the core node of a particular group and traverse the entire network. Every node in a network forms a routing table (by using MAPs) which is required to establish a mesh and route the packets from senders to receivers. Once the routing table is formed, every node generates its MAP based on the best entry in its routing table and sends it to its neighboring nodes.

Fig.3(a) illustrates the propagation of MAPs and building of routing table. Solid arrows indicate the neighbor from which a node receives its best MAP. An example routing table of node 8 is shown in Fig.3(b). Routing table of node 8 has three entries for its neighbors 6, 9 and 5. The entries in the routing table are arranged based on the descending order of average remaining queue size.

Routing table at any node is updated only if the sequence number of MAP is higher than the sequence number stored in the routing table i.e., the MAP is a fresh MAP and not a duplicate MAP. The entries in a routing table are sorted based on the maximum average remaining queue. If average remaining queue is same, then the entries are sorted based on the minimum distance to core.

2.3   Calculating Remaining Queue Size

Every node in the network calculates its average remaining queue size. It is calculated based on Exponential Weighted Moving Average (EWMA) as shown in Eq. (1)

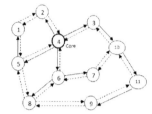

Neighbour	Remaining Queue Size	Distance to Core	Parent
6	38	1	4
9	27	4	11
5	12	1	4

(a)   Propagation   of   (b) Routing Table of Node 8
MAPs

Fig. 3. Propagation of MAPs and Example Routing Table

$$new\_avg = ((1 - \alpha) \times old\_avg) + (\alpha \times rem\_q\_size). \tag{1}$$

where,

$$rem\_q\_size = max\_q\_size - cur\_q\_size.$$

Here *new_avg* represents average remaining queue size and is calculated on arrival of each packet at the node. *old_avg* represents average remaining queue size of previous iteration.

The value of α ($0 < \alpha \leq 1$) can be either static or dynamic. However we recommend α to be dynamic so as to be adaptive to the current traffic load.

α varies dynamically as shown below

$$\alpha = \frac{rem\_q\_size}{max\_q\_size}. \tag{2}$$

where *rem_q_size* is the remaining queue size and *max_q_size* is the maximum queue size.

Based on Eq. (2), when *rem_q_size* is less (i.e., queue is almost full), *new_avg* is the reflection of *old_avg* whereas when *rem_q_size* is more (i.e., queue is almost empty) *new_avg* is the reflection of *curr_rem_q_size* where *curr_rem_q_size* is the current remaining queue size .

3   Simulation Environment

A single multicast group with 5 senders in a multi-hop wireless network is simulated using NS-2. Every sender generates a traffic load of 10 packets/sec. Total number of multicast receivers are varied from 5, 10, 15 to 20. All nodes are configured to move with a uniform speed of 1 m/s.

The details of simulation environment are listed in Table 1.

Table 1. Simulation Environment

Simulator	Network Simulator 2
Total Nodes	20
Simulation Time	700 seconds
Simulation Area	1500m x 300m
Node Placement	Random
Pause Time	0
Mobility Model	Random Waypoint
Radio Range	250m
Data Packet Size	512 bytes

4   Results and Analysis

In this section we compare the performance of AMul and PUMA based on average end to end delay, control overhead and total overhead. First we compare the performance of AMul and PUMA by assigning a static value for α ($\alpha = 0.002$) in Eq. (1). Later we demonstrate the performance improvement by selecting dynamic value (based on Eq. (2)) for α in Eq. (1).

4.1   For $\alpha = 0.002$

As shown in Fig. 4(a), AMul reduces the overall end to end delay in the network as compared to PUMA.

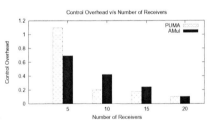

(a) Average End to End Delay v/s Number of Receivers

(b) Control Overhead v/s Number of Receivers

Fig. 4. $\alpha = 0.002$

Moreover, as shown in Fig. 4(b) and Fig. 5, control overhead and total overhead incurred by AMul is negligibly higher than that of PUMA for some scenarios. This is because of the extra field included in MAP of AMul.

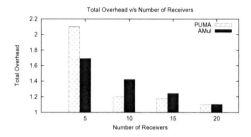

Fig. 5. Total Overhead v/s Number of Receivers for $\alpha = 0.002$

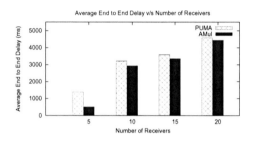

(a) Dynamic α

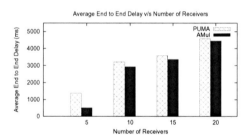

(b) Static α v/s Dynamic α

Fig. 6. Average End to End Delay v/s Number of Receivers

4.2 $\alpha = \text{rem\_q\_size} / \text{max\_queue\_size}$

In this section we compare the performance of AMul with static value of α and AMul with dynamic value of α . As shown in Fig. 6(b), better performance is obtained when α is selected dynamically.

Dynamic selection of α enables AMul to react to abrupt changes in the traffic load and hence improves the overall performance of AMul.

5   Conclusions

In this paper we have proposed a reactive, receiver initiated and mesh based multicast routing protocol called Adaptive Multicast (AMul) to provide better Quality of Service (QoS) in Wireless Networks. AMul uses average remaining queue as a routing metric to efficiently route the multicast packets. Based on the comparative study between AMul and Protocol for Unified Multicasting through Announcements (PUMA) which is also a reactive, receiver initiated and mesh based multicast routing protocol we observe that AMul reduces the overall end to end delay while inducing negligible control overhead in the network. However the value of α can be optimized further to improve the overall performance of the network.

References

1. Varshney, U.: Multicast Over Wireless Networks. Communications of the ACM 45(12) (2002)
2. Badarneh, O.S., Kadoch, M.: Multicast Routing Protocols in Mobile Ad Hoc Networks. A Comparative Survey and Taxonom, EURASIP Journal on Wireless Communications and Networking (2009)
3. Vaishampayan, R., Garcia-Luna-Aceves, J.J.: Efficient and Robust Multicast Routing in Mobile Ad Hoc Networks. In: IEEE International Conference on Mobile Adhoc and Sensor Systems (2004)
4. Royer, E.M., Perkins, C.E.: Multicast Operation of the Ad-hoc On-Demand Distance Vector Routing Protocol. In: Mobicom 1999, Seattle, Washington, USA. ACM, New York (1999)
5. Fall, K., Vardhan, K.: The ns Manual, The VINT Project (2010)
6. Tahiliani, M.P.: Network Simulator 2 Blog, http://mohittahiliani.blogspot.com/2009/12/awk-script-for-ns2.html

Performance Evaluation of Multipath Source Routing Protocols in MANET

Jayalakshmi V.[1], Ramesh Kumar R.[2], and Geetha S.[3]

[1] Dravidian University, Kuppam,Andhra Pradesh
[2] As Salam College of Engineering, Aaduthurai, Tamil Nadu
[3] Anna University of Engineering and Technology, Thiruchirapalli
jayasekar1996@yahoo.co.in

Abstract. Multipath routing in mobile ad-hoc networks allows the establishment of multiple paths for routing between a source-destination pair. A common characteristic of all popular multi-path routing algorithms in Mobile Ad-hoc networks is to find Route Discovery procedure and is carried out only when there is a packet to be transferred and there exists no valid path. There are numerous Multi-path on-demand routing algorithm exists to discover several paths instead of one, once the routing is performed. In this paper various multipath protocols like SMR, ZD-MDSR, DSR, SMS, are compared. The efficiency of these protocols has been evaluated on different scenarios using performance metrics such as packet delivery ratio, routing load and end-to-end delay. The analyses of the routing performance are tested and the results are compared and represented graphically.

Keywords: DSR, Mobile Ad-hoc Networks, Multihop Wireless, SMR, SMS, ZD-MDSR.

1 Introduction

MANET is the network completely self-organizing and self-configuring, requiring no existing network infrastructure or administration. Some routing policies [1], [2] and [3] have been proposed in order to establish and maintain the routes in MANET, and DSR is a generally utilized one. There are many common routing algorithms used in Adhoc networks but AODV [4], [5] and DSR [6], which both are on-demand algorithms. In some multi-path algorithms once different paths are discovered, they are all stored but only one of them is used for transferring the data. The other stored paths will become useful once the current one is broken. There are also other multi-path algorithms that transfer data over all discovered paths concurrently which reduces end to end delay and increases end to end bandwidth. Some key challenges Associated with an ad-hoc environment, and some specific characteristics are *Dynamic topology, Multi-hop, Bandwidth-constrained, variable capacity links*, etc.. The typical problems encountered in designing single path protocols for a mobile wireless environment also arise in designing multipath protocols. Mobility makes it difficult or impossible to maintain a global view of the network. Mobility also has implications in terms of

K.R. Venugopal and L.M. Patnaik (Eds.): ICIP 2011, CCIS 157, pp. 396–402, 2011.

caching policies. If cached information at intermediate nodes is frequently out of date, caching can degrade routing performance because detecting inaccurate routing, information is not instantaneous. In addition to the dynamic topology, unreliable and range limited wireless transmission makes resiliency a requirement rather than an enhancement in a routing solution. Since mobile transmitters are likely to be battery powered, routing protocols need to minimize the communication for coordinating network nodes. At the protocol level, The design of multipath routing needs to consider failure models, Characteristics of redundant routes, Coordinating nodes to construct routes, Mechanisms for locating mobile destination and intermediate forwarding nodes and failure recovery.

The paper is organized in 4 sections. Section 2 gives the review of Multipath Routing Protocols Section 3 illustrates the simulation results of the comparison of the protocols. We conclude the paper in Section 4.

2   Review of Routing Protocols

2.1   Dynamic Source Routing (DSR)

Dynamic Source Routing (DSR) [6] is a routing protocol for wireless mesh networks and is based on a method known as *source routing*. It is designed specially for use in multihop ad-hoc networks of mobile nodes. It allows the network to be completely selforganizing and self-configuring and does not need any existing network infrastructure or administration. DSR uses no periodic routing messages which reduces network bandwidth overhead, conserves battery power and avoids large routing updates. It needs support from the MAC layer to identify link failure. DSR is composed of the two mechanisms of Route Discovery and Route Maintenance, which work together to allow nodes to discover and maintain source routes to arbitrary destinations in the network. DSR enables multiple routes to be learnt for a particular destination. DSR does not require any periodic update messages, thus avoiding wastage of bandwidth.

2.2   Split Multi Path Routing(SMR)

SMR [7] protocol provides a way of determining maximally disjoints paths. Paths are maximally disjoint when they are node disjoint, but when there are no node-disjoint paths available, the protocol minimizes the number of common nodes. Multiple routes are discovered on demand, one of which is the path with the shortest delay. The routes established by the protocol are not necessarily equal in length. When a source needs a route to a destination but no information is available, it floods a RREQ message on the entire network. Because of this flooding, several duplicates that traversed through the network over different routes reach the destination. The destination then selects multiple disjoint paths, and sends RREP packets back via the chosen routes. Since the destination needs to select disjoint paths, source routing is used. The complete route information is in the RREQ packets. Furthermore, intermediate nodes are not allowed to send RREPs, even when they have route information to the destination The

SMR algorithm is optimized when the destination selects the two routes that are maximally. One of the two routes is the route with the shortest delay; the path taken by the first RREQ the destination receives. This path is used to minimize route acquisition latency required by on-demand protocols. The destination knows route information from all possible routes and it can determine the maximally disjoint route to the already replied route.

2.3   Shortest Multipath Source (SMS)

SMS routing protocol is proposed based on DSR. It builds multiple partial-disjoint paths from source S to destination D in order to avoid the overhead of additional route discoveries and to quick recovery in case of route breaks. Improved performance in terms of Fraction of packets delivered, end-to-end delay and routing overheads is obtained. SMS earns multiple partial-disjoint paths that will bypass at least one intermediate node on the primary path that is shown in Fig. 1.a.Consider the case of traffic flowing between nodes S and D using link A-B as a segment of the path. In case of a link failure between A and B, the source node will search for an alternate route that does not contain node B that is shown in Fig. 1.b. An alternative route between source S and destination D is (S, A, F, C, D).

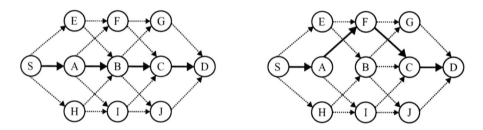

Fig. 1. (a) Partial Disjoint Multiple Paths (b) Select the alternate path

2.4   Zone Disjoint Multi-Path Dynamic Source Routing (ZD-MPDSR)

A Multi-Path Routing Algorithm by the name of ZD-MPDSR has been offered in [8]. ZD-MPDSR discovers Zone-Disjoint paths between source and destination nodes, and source node uses these paths for simultaneous sending of data to destination. In [9], [10] multi-path routing with directional antenna is proposed. In this protocol directional antenna is used for finding Zone-Disjoint paths between a source and destination.Due to low transmission zone of directional antenna, it is easier to get two physically close paths that may not interfere with each other during communication. Destination in both ZD-MPDSR [9] and ZDAOMDV [11] tries to choose the Zone-Disjoint paths from received RREQs and send the RREPs to the source for these RREQs. In ZD-MPDSR, for recognizing zone-disjoint paths between source and destination, a new field is established in RREQ packet, which is called ActiveNeighborCount and it is initiated by zero. As a matter of fact this field shows the number of active neighbors for nodes on a path. In order to set the ZD-MPDSR up, the entire nodes should keep a table which is called RREQ-Seen and this table records the characteristics of received RREQs by every node. In ZD-MPDSR intermediate node shouldnt send RREP to any source and in fact should let the destination receive all RREQs and choose the best paths and send RREPs to the source.

3   Performance Evaluation Results

3.1   Simulation Environment

The simulation environment is NS2 [12] and it consists of N mobile nodes in a rectangular region of size 1000 meters by 1000 meters. Each node has a radio propagation range of 250 m and channel capacity was 2Mbps. The IEEE 802.11 Distribution Coordination Function (DCF) is used as Medium Access Control (MAC). The random waypoint model was adopted as the mobility model. In the random waypoint model, a node randomly selects a destination from the physical terrain. It moves in the direction of the destination in a speed uniformly chosen between a minimum and maximum speed specified. After it reaches its destination, the node stays there for a time period specified as the pause time. In our simulation, minimum speed was set constant to zero. The simulated traffic is Constant Bit Rate (CBR) and all data packets are 512 Bytes. Each simulation is run for 300 seconds.Three important metrics evaluated are *throughput,end-to-end delay* and *routing loads.*

3.2   Simulation Scenarios

We ran experiments with two different base settings. In the first setting, 100 nodes are randomly placed inside an area of 1000 x 1000 m². For the second setting, then number of nodes and the size of the simulation area are varied, while keeping the average node density constant.

3.3   Simulation Results

In the first scenario, to evaluate capability of the protocols for different node mobility, we change node mobility by varying the maximum speed. The number of nodes and pause time was fixed at 100 nodes and 1 second, respectively. Fig. 2.a. and Fig. 2.b. shows the evolution of the delivery ratio and average delay for increasing node speed (from 10 to 50 m/s) in a random waypoint model.

In Fig. 2.a. from the results SMR outperform DSR especially when the mobility increases. In DSR only one route is used for each session and when that route is invalidated the source uses the cached route that is learned from overhearing packets and the cached routes may be stale. SMS outperforms DSR, SMR due to lower overheads in the route discovery process since the destination node sends multiple RREP while DSR sends only one RREP. But in ZD-MPDSR zone disjoint paths are used for sending data , it has greater packet delivery ratio than the all the other three routing protocols.

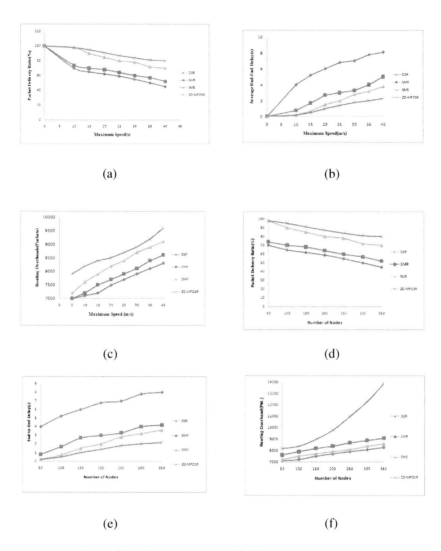

Fig. 2. (a)-(c)Varying speed, (d)-(f)Varying Network size

Since in ZD-MPDSR, zone disjoint paths are used for sending data the end-to-end delay is less than all the other protocols (Fig. 2.b.). DSR has the longest delay in mobile scenarios because it delivers data packets on routes longer than those of SMR. In addition, DSR yields longer delays in reconstructing routes and the period of time the data packets are buffered at the source node during route recovery results in larger end-to-end delays. SMR uses the remaining valid route when one of the multiple routes is disconnected, and hence no route acquisition latency is required. The availability of shorter alternate routing paths in the former eliminates route discovery latency that contributes to the delay when an active route fails. When a congestion state occurs in a path, the source node can re-distrbiute incoming data packets to alternative routing paths, thereby reducing the queue waiting time of data packets.

Fig. 2.c. shows the overhead in the considered test scenarios with variable speed for Random way point mobility model. Overhead is expressed as the number of control packets forwarded. Since the ZD-MPDSR uses the RREQ-Query and RREQ-Query-Reply in route discovery, its overhead is more than DSR and SMR.

In the Second set of experiments, of which the results are visualized in figures 2.d, 2.e, 2.f. In this scenario, the number of nodes and the size of the simulation area are varied, while keeping the average node density constant. In this case, ZD-MPDSR has lower end-to-end delay than SMS, DSR and SMR (Fig. 2.d.), and also exhibits greater packet delivery ratio than SMS, DSR and SMR (Fig. 2.e). The experimental results represent that if the size of network increase, the amount of receiving data packets by destination nodes will be decreased. In this scenario, the DSR has greater control overhead than the all the other protocols (Fig. 2.f.).

4   Conclusion

Any form of multipath technique always performs substantially better than single path routing. Providing multiple paths is useful in Adhoc networks because when one of the routes is disconnected, the source can simply use other available routes without performing the route recovery process. The simulation study demonstrates that there is a subtle tradeoffs between delay and routing load. Some of the multi-path routing algorithms in MANET in order to decline the end-to-end delay divide the data in the source and send different sections to the destination by several routes simultaneously. In ZD-MPDSR zone disjoint paths are used for sending data, it gives the higher packet delivery ratio and the lower end-to-end delay than the other protocols. Simulation results indicate that ZD-MPDSR outperforms DSR, SMR, SMS in terms of packet delivery ratio and end-to-delay and DSR outperforms all the other three protocols when routing overhead is considered. SMS gives good packet delivery ratio, end-to end delay and also lower routing head which makes it suitable for protocol suitable for real-time data and multimedia services.

References

1. Johnson, D., Maltz, D.: Dynamic Source Routing in Ad-hoc Wireless Wetworks. In: Imielinski, T., Korth, H. (eds.) Mobile Computing. Kluwer Academic, Hingham
2. Park, V.D., Corson, M.S.: A Highly Adaptive Distributed Routing Algorithm for Mobile Wireless Networks. In: Proceedings of IEEE Infocom (1997)

3. Perkins, C.E., Bhagwat, P.: Highly Dynamic Destination-Sequenced Distance-Vector Routing (DSDV) for Mobile Computers. In: Proceedings of ACM Sigcomm (1994)
4. Perkins, C.E., Royer, E.M.: Ad-hoc On-demand Distance Vector Routing. In: Proceedings of IEEE Workshop on Mobile Computing Systems and Applications, WM-CSA (1999)
5. Perkins, C.E., Belding-Royer, E., Das, S.R.: Ad-hoc On-demand Distance Vector (AODV) Routing RFC 3561 (July 2003), http://www.ietf.org/rfc/rfc3561.txt
6. Johnson, D.B., Maltz, D.A., Hu, Y.: The Dynamic Source Routing Protocol for Mobile Ad-hoc Networks
7. Lee, S.j., Gerla, M.: Split Multipath Routing with Maximally Disjoint Paths in Ad-hoc Networks. In: Proceedings of IEEE International Conference on Communication (ICC), Helsinki, Finland, pp. 3201–3205 (2001)
8. Taheri, N., Javan, D.: Reducing End-to-End Delay in Multipath Routing Algorithms for Mobile Ad-Hoc Networks. In: Zhang, H., Olariu, S., Cao, J., Johnson, D.B. (eds.) MSN 2007. LNCS, vol. 4864, pp. 715–724. Springer, Heidelberg (2007)
9. Roy, S., Saha, D., Bandyopadhyay, S., Ueda, T., Tanaka, S.: Improving End-to-End Delay through Load Balancing with Multipath Routing in Ad-hoc Wireless Networks using Directional Antenna. In: Das, S.R., Das, S.K. (eds.) IWDC 2003. LNCS, vol. 2918, pp. 225–234. Springer, Heidelberg (2003)
10. Bandyopadhyay, S., Roy, S., Ueda, T., Hasuike, K.: Multipath Routing in Ad-hoc Wireless Networks with Directional Antenna. Personal Wireless Communication 234, 45–52 (2002)
11. Taheri Javan, N., Kiaeifar, R., Hakhamaneshi, B., Dehghan, M.: ZDAOMDV: A New Routing Algorithm for Mobile Ad-Hoc Networks. In: Proceedings of 8th IEEE ICIS (International Conference on Computer and Information Science), Shanghai, China, pp. 852–857 (2009)
12. Network Simulator-2, http://www.isi.edu/nsnam/ns

Steiner Tree-Based Decentralization Mechanism (STDM) for Privacy Protection in Wireless Sensor Networks

Jayashree N. and Sathish Babu B.

Department of Computer Science and Engineering
Siddaganga Institute of Technology, Tumkur-572 103, Karnataka, India
darecse@gmail.com,bsb@sit.ac.in

Abstract. Privacy and Security of the data are the major concern in Wireless Sensor Networks (WSN). Many applications which are based on WSN require data exchanges with data privacy intact of the sensed data. Using minimum tree structure can significantly reduce the number of nodes in data transmission. In this paper, we propose a privacy mechanism, STDM, for WSN based on Steiner tree and decentralization mechanism in order to provide privacy of the data with minimum number of hops to the sink. Simulation results show that STDM performs efficiently compared to some of the existing approaches. It gives high path diversity which guarantees the increase in data privacy.

Keywords: Data Privacy, Decentralization, Security, Steiner Tree, WSN.

1   Introduction

A data privacy is to share the data only with the trusted users. The common attacks against sensor privacy are [1]: Monitor and Eavesdropping; Traffic Analysis; and Camouflages Adversaries. Some of the mechanisms which are available to address privacy risks in WSN are given in [2,3,4]. They are: Anonymity Mechanisms: Depersonalizing the data before the data is released. The techniques under this mechanism are: data decentralization, change data traffic and node mobility; Policy-based Approaches: Based on the specifications of the privacy policies, the access control decisions and authentication are made [5,6,7]; and Information Flooding: It includes the anti-traffic analysis mechanisms to prevent an outside attacker tracking the location of a data source as the location of sensed objects can be revealed [8].

A Steiner tree is a minimum weight tree connecting a designated set of vertices, in an undirected, weighted graph [9] which results in minimum cost tree. It is optimal in terms of bandwidth utilization [10]. In this paper, a secure multicast scheme incarporating the Steiner tree and the data decentralization mechanisms to obtain an efficient data transmission against privacy attacks in WSN is proposed.

K.R. Venugopal and L.M. Patnaik (Eds.): ICIP 2011, CCIS 157, pp. 403–409, 2011.
© Springer-Verlag Berlin Heidelberg 2011

Rest of the paper is organised as follows: section 2 for related works on decentralization mechanism and Steiner tree; section 3 for the proposed scheme and mechanisms used in it; section 4 for simulation with results, and finally, section 5 draws conclusions.

2   Related Work

In [11], a secure routing multicast using Steiner tree approach is proposed where an adversary cannot access data without a key. In [12], a decentralized intrusion detection based on the inference of the network behavior obtained from the analysis of events detected by a node is proposed with minimum resource utilization. In [13], a decentralized data transmission mechanism optimizing the energy efficiency in WSN and reducing latency is presented. In [14], an approach of a secured decentralized data transfer against node capture attacks for WSN using secret sharing scheme is proposed.

3   Proposed Scheme

In this approach WSN has Steiner tree structure over which data decentralization mechanism is applied.

3.1   Network Model

Consider a WSN, $V = (G, E)$, where G is a set of nodes and $E \subseteq V^2$ is the set of communication links (Fig. 1). There exists a pair $(a, b) \in E$ i.e., a is able to communicate with b. The neighborhood set of a is given by

$$N(a) = b \neq a \wedge (a, b) \in E \quad . \tag{1}$$

The Node-state Information Table (NIT) of a node to store location information is given in Table 1, where, PID- global ID; DID- location information or Dynamic ID; Cluster Head Flag (CHF)- 0 or 1; Height Value- length of the path to the source node; Membership Flag (MF)- 0 or 1; and Father Node-local routing information.

3.2   Steiner Tree Construction

In this approach, the WSN is converted to a Steiner Tree structure.There are five phases in construction of a Steiner tree [11]: Node information gathering phase; Steiner tree construction phase; Steiner sub-tree distribution phase; Data delivery phase; and Steiner tree maintains phase.

Table 1. Node-state Information Table

PID	DID	Cluster Head Flag	Height Value value	Membership Flag	Father Node
Node23	(23,49)	1	2	1	(13,33)

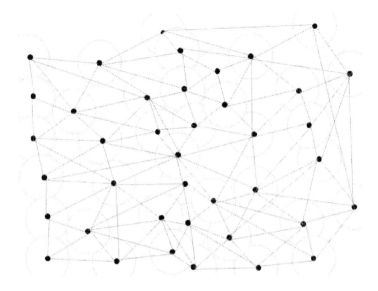

Fig. 1. Network Model

3.3   Sensed Data Decentralization Mechanism

The data is distributed along different paths from source S to the sink T and are distinguished with an identifier. S sets a threshold number k where $n \geq k$ [14].

The two phases in this mechanism are: (a) Encryption phase: The divisions of the data are encrypted using $f(x)$ and transmitted with redundancy check code C(D).

$$f(x) = D + a_1 x + a_2 x^2 + \dots + a_{k-1} x^{k-1} mod \quad q \quad . \tag{2}$$

where $q \geq max(n, D)$ and $a_i (i = 1, 2, 3, \dots n)$ are random images and q is a large prime number. (b) Decryption phase: When k divisions are collected, the original data D can be decrypted using the Lagrange's interpolation method shown in equations (2) and (3) and decrypted data D' is compared with decrypted C(D) for obtaining accuracy.

$$D = \lambda_1 v_1 + \lambda_2 v_2 + \dots + \lambda_k v_k \quad . \tag{3}$$

where, $\lambda_j = \prod_{i \neq j}^{i=1} \frac{u_i}{u_i - u_j} mod \quad q$. Three cases are assumed for the data decentralization in WSN: without any attacks; with one or more privacy attacks; and without any attacks but re-routing because of mismatch between data sent and received.

An algorithm depicting STDM combining the Steiner tree and data decentralization mechanisms is given in Table 2. In STDM, since incomplete data and communication pattern are obtained at any node, an adversary cannot trace back to the source node with incomplete information; High path diversities are obtained; An adversary cannot compromise a node without a key.

Table 2. Algorithm for Steiner tree-based decentralization mechanism

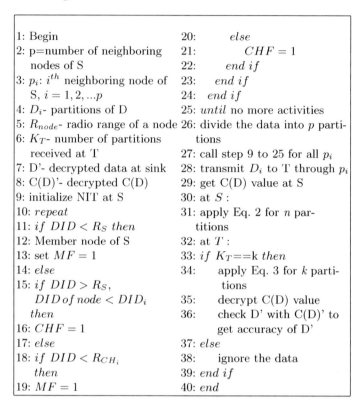

1: Begin	20: *else*
2: p=number of neighboring	21: $CHF = 1$
nodes of S	22: *end if*
3: p_i: i^{th} neighboring node of	23: *end if*
S, $i = 1, 2, ...p$	24: *end if*
4: D_i- partitions of D	25: *until* no more activities
5: R_{node}- radio range of a node	26: divide the data into p partitions
6: K_T- number of partitions	
received at T	27: call step 9 to 25 for all p_i
7: D'- decrypted data at sink	28: transmit D_i to T through p_i
8: C(D)'- decrypted C(D)	29: get C(D) value at S
9: initialize NIT at S	30: at S :
10: *repeat*	31: apply Eq. 2 for n partitions
11: *if* $DID < R_S$ *then*	
12: Member node of S	32: at T :
13: set $MF = 1$	33: *if* K_T==k *then*
14: *else*	34: apply Eq. 3 for k partitions
15: *if* $DID > R_S$,	
$DID\,of\,node < DID_i$	35: decrypt C(D) value
then	36: check D' with C(D)' to
16: $CHF = 1$	get accuracy of D'
17: *else*	37: *else*
18: *if* $DID < R_{CH_i}$	38: ignore the data
then	39: *end if*
19: $MF = 1$	40: *end*

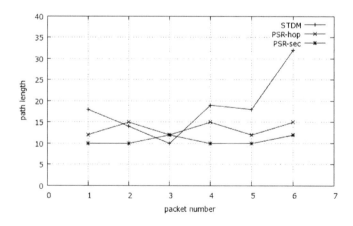

Fig. 2. Path diversity in privacy schemes

4   Simulation and Results

For simulation purpose we assume the communication range of each node as 50m, the area of simulation of 500*500m, the density as 10 nodes per communication range, and a total of 300 nodes to be deployed. Higher the path diversity, better the privacy provided in WSN. The path diversity of STDM is compared with the existing approaches PSR-hop (Phantom Single-path Routing with hop-based approach) and PSR-sec (sector-based approach) for 6 nodes [15] as shown in Fig. 2, where STDM gives higher path diversities. The energy consumption for the decentralization of data over Steiner tree can be analysed as follows: Most of the data partitions may use the same nodes for transmission which slightly increases the energy consumed over those nodes; The cluster head node in Steiner tree of one neighboring node may be a member node in that of other neighboring node which makes the energy consumption being shared by different nodes at each path; and the energy consumption increases with the number of destinations and their locations. This analysis for STDM is compared with one of the existing approaches of Steiner tree as shown in Fig. 3a.

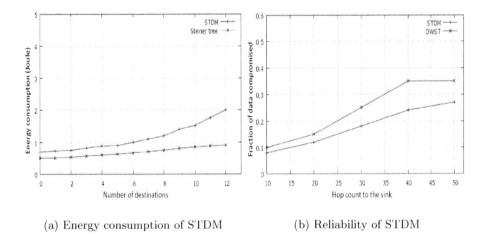

(a) Energy consumption of STDM   (b) Reliability of STDM

Fig. 3. Results

The probability of the data compromised, P, is obtained by the ratio of number of nodes that collect all shares of each node to the sink node, N_p, to the number of combinations of nodes compromised, N_c. It is given by

$$P = \frac{N_p}{N_c} \quad .$$

(4)

The number of combinations of nodes,where, N is the number of sensor nodes and *l* is the number of nodes compromised. *P* gives the reliability of STDM. The node compromise in STDM is compared with the decentralization mechanism without Steiner tree (DWST). The node compromising decreases in STDM as shown in Fig. 3b.

5   Conclusions

This paper presents a Steiner Tree-based Decentralization Mechanism for Privacy in WSN (STDM), which mainly aims at the privacy of sensed data and data transmission along shortest path. STDM achieves a better performance in protecting privacy of the sensed data, when compared to other existing approaches, along with the lower costs for transmission. The decentralization mechanism over Steiner tree results in high path diversities and hence, reduces the possibilities of occurrence and success of the privacy attacks.

References

1. Padmavathi, G., Shanmugapriya, D.: A Survey of Attacks, Security Mechanisms and Challenges in Wireless Sensor Networks. International Journal of Computer Science and Information Security (2009)
2. Sharma, S.: Energy-efficient Secure Routing in Wireless Sensor Networks (2009)
3. Gruteser, M., Schelle, G., Jain, A., Han, R., Grunwald, D.: Privacy-Aware Location Sensor Networks. In: 9th USENIX Workshop on Hot Topics in Operating Systems (HotOS IX) (2003)
4. Gruteser, M., Grunwald, D.: A Methodological Assessment of Location Privacy Risks in Wireless Hotspot Networks. In: Hutter, D., Müller, G., Stephan, W., Ullmann, M. (eds.) Security in Pervasive Computing. LNCS, vol. 2802, pp. 10–24. Springer, Heidelberg (2004)
5. Molnar, D., Wagner, D.: Privacy and Security in Library RFID: Issues, Practices, and Architectures. In: ACMCCS (2004)
6. Duri, S., Gruteser, M., Liu, X., Moskowitz, P., Perez, R., Singh, R., Tang, J.: Framework for Security and Privacy in Automotive Telematics. In: 2nd ACM International Workshop on Mobile Commerce (2000)
7. Snekkenes, E.: Concepts for Personal Location Privacy Policies. In: Proceedings of the 3rd ACM Conference on Electronic Commerce, pp. 48–57 (2001)
8. Ozturk, C., Zhang, Y., Trappe, W.: Source-Location Privacy in Energy-Constrained Sensor Network Routing. In: Proceedings of the 2nd ACM Workshop on Security of Adhoc and Sensor Networks (2004)
9. Steiner Tree, http://xw2k.nist.gov/dads/html/steinertree.html/
10. Tehranipoor, M.: Steiner Tree Problem (September 2008)
11. Fan, R., Chen, J., Fu, J.-Q., Ping, L.-D.: A Steiner-Based Secure Multicast Routing Protocol for WSN. In: 2nd International Conference on Future Networks (2010)
12. da Silva, A.P.R., Martins, M.H.T., Rocha, B.P.S.: Decentralized Intrusion Detection in Wireless Sensor Networks. In: ACM 1-59593-241-0/05/0010, Q2S Winet (2005)

13. Mihaylov, M., Tuyls, K., Now, A., Tuyls, T.: Decentralized Learning in Wireless Sensor Networks. In: Taylor, M.E., Tuyls, K. (eds.) ALA 2009. LNCS, vol. 5924, pp. 60–73. Springer, Heidelberg (2010)
14. Kohno, E., Ohta, T., Kajuda, Y.: Secure Decentralized Data Transfer Against Node Capture Attacks for Wireless Sensor Networks. In: International Symposium on Autonomous Decentralized Systems, ISADS (2009)
15. Kamat, P., Zhang, Y., Trappe, W., Ozturk, C.: Enhancing Source-Location Privacy in Sensor Network Routing. In: Proceedings of 25th IEEE International Conference on Distributed Computing Systems, Columbus, OH, USA, pp. 599–608 (2005)

MFTR: Multipath Fault Tolerant Routing in Wireless Sensor Networks

Indrajit Banerjee[1], Prasenjit Chanak[2], and Hafizur Rahaman

[1] Department of Information Technology
[2] Purabi Das School of Information Technology,
Bengal Engineering and Science University, Shibpur, Howrah, India
{ibanerjee,rahaman_h}@it.becs.ac.in, prasenjit.chanak@gmail.com

Abstract. In the modern age huge amount of wireless sensor networks is used for security surveillance and environments monitoring. The main challenge is to improve fault tolerance percentage of wireless sensor networks and also provide an energy efficient fast data routing service. In wireless sensor networks energy conservation is most significant because every sensor node has a constant power supply. In this paper we propose an energy efficient multipath fault tolerant routing protocol in wireless sensor networks referred as MFTR. The MFTR use multiple data routing path for fault tolerance and traffic control. One shortest path is use for main data routing in MFTR technique and other two backup paths are used as alternative path for faulty network and to handle the overloaded traffic on main channel. The performances analysis of MFTR depicts better result compare to other popular fault tolerant techniques in wireless sensor networks.

Keywords: Base Station(BS), Fault Tolerant(FT), Routing, Wireless Sensor Network(WSN).

1   Introduction

Wireless sensor network is a collection of hundreds and thousands of low cost, low power smart sensing devices. In WSN fault occurrences probability is very high compare to traditional networking [1]. These features motivate researchers to make automatic fault management techniques in wireless sensor networks. As a result now a day's different types fault detection and fault tolerance technique have been proposed [2], [3]. The wireless sensor networks occurrences of fault largely classify in two groups; one transmission fault another is node fault. The node fault [4], [5], and [6] is further classified into five groups. These are power fault, sensor circuit fault, microcontroller fault, transmitter circuit fault and receive circuit fault [7].

   In this paper, we propose a fault tolerant routing which involves fault recovery process with fault detection scheme, referred as multipath fault tolerance routing in wireless sensor networks (MFTR). In MFTR technique every sensor nodes transmit their data to base station through shortest path. If data and nodes fault

K.R. Venugopal and L.M. Patnaik (Eds.): ICIP 2011, CCIS 157, pp. 410–415, 2011.

occur in the network, these are recovered very fast and data are transmitted to base station with minimum time and energy loss. The MFTR also control the data traffic when data are transmitted to cluster head or base station.

The rest of this paper is organized as follows. Section 2 describe mathematical model. In Section 3, we propose MFTR fault tolerance scheme. Performances and comparison result are showed in Section 4. Finally, the paper is concluded in Section 5.

2   Mathematical Model

In MFTR technique we are used standard data communication model as we have used in [8]. In MFTR technique clusters size are calculated with the help of Theorem 1 and Theorem 2. Theorem 1 establish a relation between number of message passing through a node and nodes energy. The Theorem 2 establish a relation between numbers of nodes connection of a particular node with number of message passing in a particular time. The load of a node is directly affected by the number of node connected to a particular node. If number of node connection is increased then load on that particular node is increased, if number of connection is decreased then load of the particular node is decreased. On the other hand if load of sensor nodes is increase then energy loss of the sensor node is increased, if load of the sensor node is decreased then sensor node energy loss is decreased.

Definition 1: The load P_j of a node is depending on number of data packet receives and transmits by a particular node. The data load on a particular node is depends on number of sensor nodes connected with it and amount of data sensed by this particular node. The S_p denoted a single connection data packet receive and transmit data packet S_d for single connection. $P_j = \sum_{i=0}^{n} S_p + S_d$

Theorem 1: If initial energy of a sensor node is U, then partial derivative of the total energy of a sensor node expressed in terms of number of message passing Δ_j at node j is equal to the load P_j at sensor node j. This theorem expressed symbolically as $\frac{\partial U}{\partial \Delta_j} = P_j$

Proof: Consider a series of loads $P_1, P_2, P_3, ..., P_j, ...P_n$ are acting on node $1, 2, ..., j, ..., n$ who are producing number of message $\Delta_1, \Delta_2...\Delta_j, ...\Delta_n$.

Now impose a small increment $\partial \Delta_j$ to the message passing at the node j keeping all other load unchanged. As a consequence, the increments in the loads are $\delta P_1, \delta P_2, ...\delta P_j, ...\delta P_n$. The increment in the number of message at node j and consequent increments in loads at all the neighbor nodes. Therefore, $P_j \, \delta \Delta_j = \Delta_1 \delta P_1 + \Delta_2 \delta P_2 + ... + \Delta_j \, \delta P_j + ... + \Delta_n \delta P_n$, $\frac{\delta U}{\delta \Delta_j} = P_j$. In the limit $\delta \Delta_j \to 0$, the above equation becomes $\frac{\partial U}{\partial \Delta_j} = P_j$

Theorem 2: Partial derivative of the energy loss in sensor nodes expressed in terms of load with respect to any load P_j at any sensor nodes j is equal to the number of message passing Δ_j through the jth node. This theorem may be expressed symbolically as $\frac{\partial U}{\partial P_j} = \Delta_j$

Proof: Consider a series of loads $P_1, P_2, P_3, ..., P_j, ..., P_n$ acting on a node j and for this section the message passed are $\Delta_1, \Delta_2, ...\Delta_j, ...\Delta_n$. Now impose a small increment δP_j to the load at the node j keeping all other factors unchanged. As a consequence, the message passing increases by $\delta\Delta_1, \delta\Delta_2...., \delta\Delta_j, ..., \delta\Delta_n$. However, due to increments in the load at node j, there is a consequent increment in message passing in all the neighboring nodes. Therefore, $P_1\delta_1 + P_2\delta_2 + ... + P_j\delta_j + ... + P_n\delta_n = \Delta_j\delta P_j$, $\frac{\delta U}{\delta P_j} = \Delta_j$ In the limit $\delta P_j \rightarrow 0$, the above equation becomes $\frac{\partial U}{\partial P_j} = \Delta_j$

3   MFTR: Multipath Fault Tolerant Routing

In MFTR technique cluster size are calculated base on the cluster head load using Theorem 1 and Theorem 2. The clusters head load depends on number of message received in cluster head and number of data transmitted from cluster head.

In MFTR technique sensor nodes are arranged into small clusters. Cluster member nodes are capable to send data over multiples paths. Cluster member nodes sent their data in a shortest path to CH; other paths are used for duplicated data transmission. Within a cluster a cluster member nodes send their data to other cluster member nodes through three alternative paths. One of them is shortest which is responsible for fast data transmission to cluster head(Fig. 1).

In MFTR technique when a data is received by the destination node, they compare the received data with own sensed data. If the comparison result is less than threshold value then sensor circuit of the node is good. If sensor node receive data from neighbor nodes then sensor node receiver circuit is good. If a

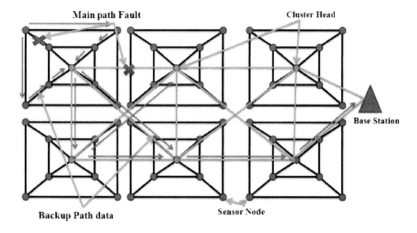

Fig. 1. Alternative path data routing in MFRT

Table 1. Fault Detection Algorithm

```
while network is alive do
    for each node do
        if node receive data from neighbour then
            Receiving data transmitted to shortest path
        else
            Send health message all neighbour nodes
            if receive replay all neighbour nodes then
                Transmission fault occurs in previous transmission
            else if not receives replay from communication node
                then
                Communication node is dead
                Inform to all neighbour node
            else if not receives replay from all neighbour then
                nodes receiver circuit fault
            end if
        end if
        if Neighbor node data >= threshold value then
            Sensor circuit node is good
        else
            Sensor circuit of comparision nodes is faulty
            Inform to cluster head
        end if
    end for
end while
```

sensor node is not received any data from its neighbor nodes for a long period of time then they send a message to neighbor nodes to check the health of the neighbors. If all neighbor nodes reply then the sending node consider there is some transmission fault occurs between communicating neighbors. However, if any neighbor node do not respond then sensor confirm it receiver circuit is faulty. On the other hand if communication node is not replay then sensor nodes decide a communication node is dead and inform to all neighbor nodes. The fault detection algorithm is discussed next.

4   Performance of MFTR

In order to evaluate the performance of MFTR four traditional metrics of WSN have been considered. Global Energy of Network: this is the sum of residual energy of each node in the network. Average delay: average latency from the moment of data transmitted from source node to base station. Average packet delivery ratio: number of packet transmitted to source node and number of packet receive at destination node. Average dissipated Energy: total energy loss of the network to total number of sensor nodes ratio. The simulation parameters we have taken same as our previous work [8].

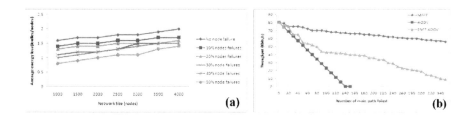

Fig. 2. (a)Average delay in different percentage of nodes failures.(b) Average packet delivery in different percentage of nodes failures

Fig. 2.a. shows the average packet transmission delay from sensor nodes to base station in different networks size. In MFTR technique data delivery time increase very slowly when nodes faults occurs.

The Fig. 2.b. shows the average packet delivery ratio from sender to base station. In the MFTR technique number of packet receives percentage in base station with respect to source node data transmission is very high. If any packet loss by nodes fault and path fault then backup path transmit duplicate data to cluster head as well as base station.

In MFTR technique energy loss rate of each node in different network size with different percentage of node failures. When node fault percentage is low then energy loss of the network is high because maximum data is delivered to base station.

The through put of the sensor nodes with respect to main routing path failures. In MFRT technique through put of sensor nodes is 49% batter comparison to the fault-tolerant routing protocol for high failure rate wireless sensor networks (ENFT- AODV) [9] technique and 70% batter comparison to ad-hoc on-demand distance vector (AODV) [10] techniques.

5   Conclusions

In this paper, we present MFTR as a multipath fault tolerant control routing technique. The MFTR technique recovers node fault and transmission fault in energy efficient manner. In MFTR technique fault tolerant percentage is very high compare to other fault tolerant techniques. Data routing time in MFTR is very fast in high percentage of nodes fault. The MFTR sensor nodes perform multi-hop packet routing in WSN. The simulation results establish that the proposed routing give better monitoring of the nodes that effectively leads to an energy efficient maximally fault tolerant in sensor network.

References

1. Akyildiz, I.F., Su, W., Sankarasubramaniam, Y., Cayirci, E.: A Survey on Sensor Networks. IEEE Communications Magazine 40(8), 102–114 (2002)
2. Paradis, L., Han, Q.: A Survey of Fault Management in Wireless Sensor Networks. Journal of Network and System Management 15(2), 170–190 (2007)

3. Yu, M., Mokhar, H., Merabti, M.: A Survey on Fault Management in Wireless Sensor Networks. In: Proceedings of Annual Post-Graduate Symposium on the Convergence of Telecommunications, Networking and Broadcasting, (PGNet) (2007)
4. Lee, W.L., Cardell Oliver, R.: WinMS: Wireless Sensor Network-Management System. An Adaptive Policy-Based Management for Wireless Sensor Networks (2006)
5. Chessa, S., Santi, P.: Crash Fault Identification in Wireless Sensor Networks. Computational Communications 14, 1273–1282 (2002)
6. Gupta, G., Younis, M.: Fault Tolerant Clustering of Wireless Sensor Networks. In: WCNC, pp. 1579-1584 (2003)
7. Banerjee, I., Chanak, P., Sikdar, B.K., Rahaman, H.: DFDNM: Distributed Fault Detection and Node Management Scheme in Wireless Sensor Network. In: Springer Link International Conference on Advances in Computing and Communications, pp. 22–23 (2011)
8. Banerjee, I., Chanak, P., Sikdar, B.K., Rahaman, H.: EERIH: Energy Efficient Routing via Information Highway in Sensor Network. In: IEEE International Conference on Emerging Trends in Electrical and Computer Technology (2011)
9. Che-Aron, Z., Al-Khateeb, W.F.M., Anwar, F.: ENFAT-AODV: The Fault-Tolerant Routing Protocol for High Failure Rate Wireless Sensor Networks. In: IEEE (2010)
10. Wheeler, A.: Commercial Application of Wireless Sensor Networks using ZigBee. IEEE Communications Magazine (2007)

Authentication in Wireless Sensor Networks Using Zero Knowledge Protocol

Muneera Hashim, Santhosh Kumar G., and Sreekumar A.

Department of Computer Science,
Cochin University of Science and Technology, Cochin
muneeraycet@gmail.com

Abstract. Effective functioning of Wireless Sensor Networks requires the nodes to be able to identify malicious nodes from genuine ones. Hence these networks have always been in quest for efficient and inexpensive authentication mechanisms. As cryptographic schemes tend to exhaust sensor network resources, this paper investigates the use of zero knowledge protocol for the authentication of sensor nodes. The proposed scheme was evaluated based on the simulation results. A comparative analysis with a similar approach was done and the proposed scheme was seen to be nine orders of magnitude faster.

Keywords: Authentication, Malicious Node, Security, Wireless Sensor Network, Zero Knowledge Protocol.

1 Introduction

Wireless Sensor Networks (WSN) are deployed in applications where they cooperate to accomplish certain tasks. Effective authentication mechanisms are vital for their successful operation, designing of which is extremely challenging due their resource constrained and physically insecure nature.

Majority of the existing works proposed for the security of sensor networks are based on cryptographic solutions. SPINS [1] includes SNEP and μTESLA. SNEP requires each communicating pair to share a secret masker key from which the remaining set of keys are derived whereas μTESLA needs the base station and the nodes to be loosely time synchronized. LEAP [2] involves derivation and maintenance of a set of keys by each node and works fine if attacks do not occur until the neighbor discovery phase is over. TinySec [3] provides authentication using MAC computed with shared secret keys. Above approaches rely on symmetric encryption, secure establishment of whose keys is yet another serious issue. At the same time, attempts for enabling the use of public key encryption [5] for authentication in Sensor Networks are progressing at a fast pace; at least for the secure establishment of symmetric keys [11].

Zero knowledge proof method [6], its implementation in identification schemes [7], and its variants [8-10] have been suggested for authentication purposes in various domains. Their use in WSN was proposed by [4], an Identification scheme for Base Nodes (IBN) where a group of sensor nodes cooperatively authenticates

K.R. Venugopal and L.M. Patnaik (Eds.): ICIP 2011, CCIS 157, pp. 416–421, 2011.
© Springer-Verlag Berlin Heidelberg 2011

the base station periodically. This paper verifies the applicability of Zero knowledge protocol for the Authentication of Sensor nodes (ZAS) using the FFS [7]
scheme and prove its efficiency as compared with IBN through simulation and
analysis.

Rest of the paper is organized as follows: Section 2 describes the system assumptions; Section 3 presents the proposed scheme and section 4 analyses the
resources overhead. Section 5 evaluates the simulation results and the paper
concludes with section 6.

2 System Model

A layered architecture is assumed in which the static sensor nodes communicate
with each other as well as with the base station to carry out the assigned job.
The average neighborhood size is not allowed to exceed a design parameter 'p'
as each node needs to store its neighbor's verification keys. Nodes as well as the
base station obtain data from each other only after successful authentication.

The trust assumptions are:

- The authority responsible for generating and distributing the secret keys
  among the nodes is trustworthy and cannot be compromised.
- A node that is legitimate performs no malicious activity unless it is compromised.

Power model for the Mica2:

As the radio withdraws 21.5 mA for transmitting and 7 mA for receiving and
the CPU uses 8 mA in the active state [12], the amount of energy spent for
transmission and reception is:

- Energy Tx $= (8 + 21.5) * 10^{-3}A * 3V * 416 * 10^{-6}sec/8bits = 4.602 \ \mu J$ /bit
- Energy Rx $= (8 + 7) * 10^{-3}A * 3V * 416 * 10^{-6}sec/8bits = 2.34 \ \mu J$ /bit

3 Proposed Scheme (ZAS)

At the network deployment phase, a trusted authority carries out the initial
settings:

- Chooses two primes p and q to yield the modulus $n = pq$, of infeasible
  factorization.
- Provides k unique secret keys $s_1, .., s_k$ at each node such that $gcd(s_i, n) = 1$,
  where k is the multiplicity of challenge (moc).
- Computes the verification keys v_i of each node, $v_i = s_i^2 \pmod n$.
- Provides each node with the modulus and the verification keys of its
  neighbors.

The authority is shut down soon after the deployment phase, as it has no further role in the network. Nodes execute the Authentication Protocol:

- Node i, the prover picks a random integer r, and sends $x = r^2 \pmod{n}$.
- Verifier challenges back the prover with a random binary set b of order k.
- Prover responses with $y = r \prod_{b_j=1} s_{ij} \pmod{n}$
- Verifier checks for $y^2 == x \prod_{b_j=1} v_{ij}$

The authentication procedure is repeated for 't' rounds with different 'r' values until the Verifier is convinced that the Prover does indeed possess the secret and is the node which it claims to be.

4   Overhead Analysis

4.1   Memory Consumption

As each node is to keep the verification keys of its single hop neighbors, and the key size being 512 bits, the estimated storage overhead incurred by ZAS is given by p x k x 512 bits per node; where 'p' is the number of neighbors and 'k', the multiplicity of challenge. Though IBN need not have to store more than one verification key for each of its neighbors, it involves extra storage overhead if the random values, to be used for successive authentication periods, are required to be stored at the nodes.

4.2   Communication Overhead

As the communication subsystem dominates the energy cost in Wireless Sensor Networks, a 6 and 1 for k and t respectively is suggested to obtain a security of 2^{-6}. In a single authentication, communication overhead is then 1024 bits. The energy required for transmitting a bit being 4.602 J, total communication energy spent for an authentication using ZAS would be 4.7 mJ. IBN due to its larger challenge value and the need to broadcast the random number of each authentication period would require 2048 bits of communication, equivalent to 9.4 mJ of energy.

4.3   Computational Complexity

Modular exponentiation is the most expensive of the operations involved in the schemes. Average number of modular operations per authentication required for ZAS is only $t (k+2)/2 = 4$ whereas IBN needs at an average $(3v - 1)/2 \approx 1.5v$ modular operations. As $3 \leq v \leq$ euler's totient of N, v would be huge. As exponentiation by repeated squaring involves $log_2 N$ operations, and Karastuba multiplication has a complexity of $O(N^{1.585})$, ZAS has a total time complexity of $O(N^{1.585})$; whereas IBN has $O(N^{1.585} log_2 N)$, where 'N' is the size of the modulus. Hence, for an optimum key size of 512 bits ZAS is seen to be nine orders of magnitude faster than IBN. Table 1 summarizes the resources overhead analysis.

Table 1. Resources comparison between ZAS and IBN; p, being the number of neighbors r, size of the random number set and N, size of the modulus

	ZAS	IBN
Memory Requirement (byte)	$64.p.k$	$64.p+64.r$
Communication Overhead (bit)	$1024.t$	2048
Computational Complexity	$O(N^{1.585})$	$O(N^{1.585}.log_2 N)$

4.4   Security Resilience Analysis

Security of the scheme rests on the difficulty of extracting square roots modulo an unknown factorization and the zero knowledge property of the protocol. The only cheating possibility for a malicious prover is to guess the challenge and prepare the witness accordingly. A malicious verifier could learn anything regarding the secret of the prover only if he attains both the responses for the same random number. Hence the implementation is to make sure that a proving pair never uses the same random number. Security is also related to the key size. Increasing the key size can offer better security but demands more memory. Fig. 1 shows the amount of memory used for various key and neighborhood sizes. A key size of 512 bits would be sufficient for sensor networks.

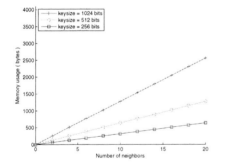
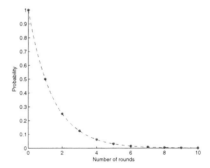

Fig. 1. Amount of memory used for various key and neighborhood sizes

Fig. 2. Success probability of malicious authentication

Impersonation is the root cause of the majority of sensor network attacks, prevention of which is vital for the existence and the very purpose of the system. In the proposed scheme any external malicious node can successfully impersonate with a probability of 2^{-kt} where $'k'$ is the multiplicity of challenge and $'t'$ the number of protocol rounds. The probability of success of an impersonation decreases exponentially with the number of rounds as in Fig. 2, which shows that a security of 2^{-10} is more than enough to deter cheaters in sensor network applications. The scheme also enjoys the property that, compromise of a single node does not affect the security of the remaining nodes. The interactive nature of the protocol prevents relay attacks as well.

5   Simulation Results

Simulation was performed on a customized WSN simulator build using Matlab. The simulation environment was setup for the sensor node platform MICA2 MPR 400CB. Simulation parameters are presented in the Table 2. Nodes were randomly distributed with a uniform density and assuring full connectivity.

Table 2. Simulation Parameters

Simulation Area	500 x 500 m
Number of nodes	100
Number of base stations	1
Transmission range	100 m
Initial energy	200 J
Average neighborhood size	7

Pairs of neighboring nodes were randomly selected for communication which exchanged data only if the authentication was successful. Authentication was simulated using ZAS with a moc value set as 6 and number of rounds, 1. Authentication was also simulated using IBN for the purpose of comparison. Computational times for successive authentications were compared as in Fig. 3 and IBN was found to spend more time for computation. The average computational energy consumed per authentication is 7.4 μJ for IBN and 4.8 μJ for ZAS. The total energy spent by a node for an authentication is hence calculated as 4.717 mJ for ZAS and 9.434 mJ for IBN. Total energy of the network depletes as authentication process progresses among the nodes, as depicted in Fig. 4.

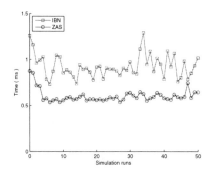 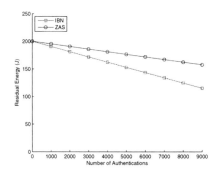

Fig. 3. Simulated computational time   **Fig. 4.** Residual energy in the network

6   Conclusions

As cryptographic security solutions are too complex for the sensor networks, the use of zero knowledge protocol for the authentication of sensor nodes is proposed. The scheme was evaluated to be computationally simpler, secure and power efficient based on the simulation results. A comparative analysis was made with a similar approach and the proposed scheme was seen to be nine orders of magnitude faster. The scheme also offers greater flexibility as the design parameters can be chosen based on the security requirement of the application.

References

1. Perrig, A., Szewczyk, R., Tygar, D., Wen, V., Culler, D.: Spins: Security Protocols for Sensor Networks. J. Wireless Networks 8, 521–534 (2002)
2. Zhu, S., Setia, S., Jajodia, S.: Leap: Efficient Security Mechanism for Large-Scale Distributed Sensor Networks. In: 10th ACM Conference on Computer and Communications Security, pp. 62–72. ACM Press, New York (2003)
3. Karlof, C., Sastry, N., Wagner, D.: TinySec: a Link Layer Security Architecture for Wireless Sensor Networks. In: 2nd International ACM Conference on Embedded Networked Sensor Systems, pp. 162–175. ACM Press, New York (2004)
4. Anshul, D., Roy, S.S.: A ZKP-based Identification for Base Nodes in Wireless Sensor Networks. In: 2005 ACM Symposium on Applied Computing, pp. 319–323. ACM Press, New York (2005)
5. Blab, E.O., Zitterbart, M.: Towards Acceptable Public Key Cryptography in Sensor Networks. In: 2nd ACM International Workshop on Ubiquitous Computing, pp. 88–93. ACM Press, New York (2005)
6. Goldwasser, S., Micali, S., Rackoff, C.: The Knowledge Complexity of Interactive Proof Systems. SIAM J. Computing 18, 186–208 (1989)
7. Feige, U., Fiat, A., Shamir, A.: Zero Knowledge Proofs of Identity. J. Cryptology 1, 77–94 (1988)
8. Schnorr, C.: Efficient Signature Generation by Smart Cards. J. Cryptology 4, 161–174 (1991)
9. Brickell, E., McCurley, K.S.: An Interactive Identification Scheme based on Discrete Logarithms and Factoring. J. Cryptology 5, 29–39 (1992)
10. Guillou, L.C., Quisquater, J.J.: A Practical Zero-Knowledge Protocol Fitted to Security Microprocessor Minimizing both Transmission and Memory. In: Günther, C.G. (ed.) EUROCRYPT 1988. LNCS, vol. 330, pp. 123–128. Springer, Heidelberg (1988)
11. Malan, D.J., Wells, M., Smith, M.D.: A Public Key Infrastructure for Key Distribution in TinyOS based Elliptic Curve Cryptography. In: 1st IEEE International Conference on Sensor and Adhoc Communications and Networks, pp. 71–80. IEEE Press, New York (2004)
12. Shnayder, V., Hempstead, M., Chen, B., Allen, G.W., Welsh, M.: Simulating the Power Consumption of Large Scale Sensor Network Applications. J. ACM transactions on sensor networks 7, 188–200 (2010)

Energy Efficient Load Sharing Mechanism for Multipath Routing Protocol in Wireless Sensor Networks

Kulkarni Prasanna, Saumya Hegde, and Shiva Murthy G.

Deparatment of Computer Science and Engineering, National Institute of Technology Karnataka, Surathkal, India
{kulkarni.prasanna87,kgshivam}@gmail.com

Abstract. Many existing energy efficient routing protocols in wireless sensor networks attempt to reduce the energy usage in data routing from source to sink node. Energy efficient routing in wireless sensor network is a paramount requirement to prolong the lifetime of the network. To increase the network lifetime, effective distribution of the traffic from the source node is very much necessary. We would like to propose a novel energy efficient load sharing mechanism in multipath routing for wireless sensor networks. The load sharing mechanism improves the wireless sensor network effectively.

Keywords: Load Sharing, Multipath Routing, Wireless Sensor Networks.

1   Introduction

A wireless sensor network consists of light-weight, low power, small size sensor nodes. The areas of applications of sensor networks vary from military, civil, healthcare, and environmental to commercial. Examples of application include forest fire detection, inventory control, energy management, surveillance and reconnaissance, and so on [1-4]. The sensor nodes perform desired measurements, process the measured data and transmit it to a base station, commonly referred to as the sink node, over a wireless channel. Recent past researchers proposed a single path routing protocol to transmit data. The optimal path is selected based on the metrics, such as the gradient of information, the distance to the destination, or the node residual energy level.

Some other routing protocols that use multiple paths choose the network reliability as their design priority [5]. Multipath routing protocols enhances the network lifetime effectively compared to single optimal path routing by distributing the traffic among multiple paths. To increase the network lifetime, uniform expenditure of network resources such as energy, bandwidth is much necessary. This work proposes an effective load sharing mechanism for multipath routing protocols. The load sharing mechanism distributes the traffic from the source node to its multiple paths to sink node based its available residual energy.

K.R. Venugopal and L.M. Patnaik (Eds.): ICIP 2011, CCIS 157, pp. 422–427, 2011.

The rest of this paper is organized as follows. In Section 2, it discusses the related work. The multipath routing scheme in Section 3. In Section 4 the load balanced algorithm for multipath routing. In Section 5 results and discussions are provided and conclusions are drawn in Section 6.

2   Related Works

Ad-hoc On-demand Multipath Distance Vector Routing (AOMDV) is an extension of AODV. AOMDV is a multi-path routing protocol [6]. In the route discovery mechanism every RREP is being considered by the source node and thus multiple paths can be discovered in one route discovery. When the source node wants to send the traffic to the destination node, route discovery is initiated by locally flooding the route request packets (RREQ) targeting the destination and waiting for the route reply packet. A reverse path to the source is found by the intermediate nodes using previous hop of the RREQ as the next hop on the reverse path. Intermediate node generates route reply only when valid route to the destination is available, else the RREQ is rebroadcast. Duplicate copies of the RREQ packet received at any node are discarded. When the destination receives a RREQ, it also generates a Route Reply (RREP). When a link failure is detected, a Route Error (RERR) is sent back via separately maintained predecessor links to all sources using that failed link. When the source receives the RERR, it initiates a new route discovery if the route is still needed. AOMDV selects the paths to route the in random. There is no fixed mechanism to share the load among the multiple paths.

3   Multipath Routing Scheme

The sensor nodes are distributed randomly in the sensing field. A network composed of a sink node and many wireless sensor nodes in an interesting area is considered. Assume that all nodes in the network are assigned with a unique ID and all nodes are participating in the network and forward the given data. The sensor nodes are assumed to be fixed for their lifetimes, and the identifier of sensor nodes is determined a priori. Additionally, these sensor nodes have limited processing power, storage and energy, while the sink nodes have powerful resources to perform any tasks or communicate with the sensor nodes. Once the nodes are deployed, they remain at their locations for sensing tasks. The sensor nodes can receive messages from other nodes. The Energy Efficient Load Balanced Multipath Routing Protocol (EELBMRP) assumes the network into number of stages based on the number of hops between source and destination as assumed in [7]. The sink is stage 0 node. Every node that can communicate with sink node is in stage 1. We assume that stage N node can communicate with nodes on the same stage and next stage $i.e.$, $n + 1$ stage but cannot with the $n - 1$ stage nodes. This back communication prevents the formation of loop paths.

3.1   Multipath Construction

The sink node starts the multipath path construction phase to create a set of neighbors that is the address of all nodes that are able to transmit data from the source. During this process route request messages are exchanged between the nodes. Each sensor node broadcast the route request packet once and maintains its own routing table. As it is a proactive routing protocol where it is necessary to store the routing information, the format of the route construction packet is as shown in the Fig. 1. The sink node initiates the route construction by flooding the route construction packet to its neighboring nodes. After the HopCount field is incremented it is compared with the nodes hop value. If there is no route to sink via that node or if HopCount field is smaller than node's hop value, route request message is processed otherwise drops the message. The total size of the route construction packet is 13 bytes. The packet type, *Beacon_Hop_count*, *Beacon_Src*, *Node_Energylevel*, *Seq_Num* and *Path* has one byte, two bytes, two bytes, four bytes, two bytes and two bytes respectively.

Packet_Type	Beacon_Hopcount	Beacon_Src	Node_Energylevel
		Seq_Num	Path

Fig. 1. The format of the Beacon packet

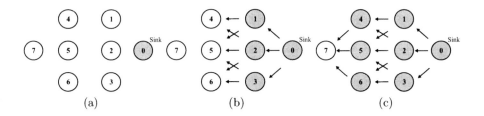

Fig. 2. (a), (b) and (c) shows route construction phase

The multipath construction phase is illustrated with an example given in Fig. 2. The Fig. 2(a) indicate the broadcasting of route construction packet to its neighboring nodes i.e., node 1, node 2 and node 3. The Fig. 2(b) indicates the generation of routing table in node 1, node 2 and node 3. These nodes update the route construction packet with the updated hop count and rebroadcast the route construction packet to its neighboring nodes. The Fig. 2(c) represents, when all the neighboring nodes have generated the routing table, the node received the route construction packet stops rebroadcasting the route construction packet.

4   Load Balanced Algorithm

This section discusses the proposing load sharing algorithm for the multipath routing protocol. The Load sharing algorithm increases the wireless sensor network life by distributing the traffic among the multiple paths based on its available residual energy level.

4.1   Algorithm

Load Sharing Algorithm
i) When a particular node wants to send data to sink it   should get $R.E's$ of all nodes which are participating   in its multiple paths.
ii) $RE_1, RE_2....RE_m$ are the minimum residual energies of the k multiple paths respectively.
iii) $\overline{X} = \sum_{i=1}^{M} RE_i/K$
iv) $X = \sum_{i=1}^{M} RE_i^2/K$
v) $Std.Dev = \sqrt{X - \overline{X}}$
vi) While (Std.Dev! $= 0$)
$\quad\quad$ $for\ i = 1$ to k
$\quad\quad\quad$ $if((RE_i - \overline{X}) > 0)$
$\quad\quad\quad\quad$ $diff\_energy = RE_i - \overline{X}$
$\quad\quad\quad\quad$ $no\_pkts\_to\_send = (diff\_energy/(E_{tx} + E_{rx}))$
$\quad\quad\quad\quad$ send no_pkts_to_send packets through multiple path 'i'
$\quad\quad\quad\quad$ $RE_i = RE_i - diff\_energy$
$\quad\quad\quad$ end if
$\quad\quad$ end for
$\quad\quad$ $\overline{X} = \sum_{i=1}^{M} RE_i/K$
$\quad\quad$ $X = \sum_{i=1}^{M} RE_i^2/K$
$\quad\quad$ $Std.Dev = \sqrt{X - \overline{X}}$
$\quad$ end While

5   Results and Discussions

The simulations are conducted using NS 2.34 simulator. The simulation parameters are 200 x 200 sq mm area, 10 to 100 numbers of nodes with grid topology, 802.15.4 mac layer and two ray ground radio propagation models. The energy model set to following values: *rxpower* is 0.02W, *txpower* is 0.035, *idlepower* 0.02 and sleep power is 0.001. The initial energy in sensor nodes is 5 Joules. The Fig. 3 and Fig. 4 show that, the residual energy levels before and after the data transmission, when the number of nodes is set to 100 both in AOMDV and EELBMRP respectively. The average number of nodes in multipath between the source and destination is 8 both in EELBMRP and AOMDV. After

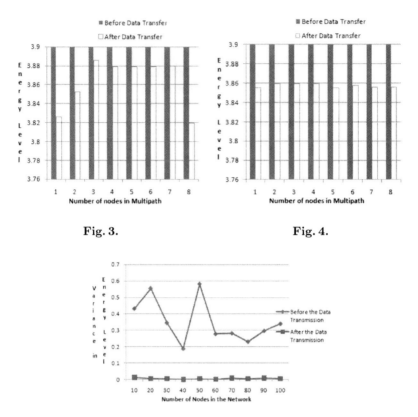

Fig. 3.   **Fig. 4.**

Fig. 5. Variance in the residual energy level of the nodes

the data transmission the residual energy level of the nodes in the multipath between the source and destination in AOMDV is not in equal levels i.e., from 3.820 to 3.883 Joules as shown in the Fig. 3. In case of EELBMRP the residual energy levels in the nodes on the multipath between the source and destination is almost equal to 3.848 Joules. There is an improvement of 93.3% of variance among the residual energy level of the nodes in EELBMRP compared to AOMDV.

The Fig. 5 shows the variance in the residual energy level in the nodes on multipath between the source node to sink node before the data transfer and after the data transfer in EELBMRP multiple paths. The number of nodes considered for the simulation is 10 to 100 nodes. The variance in the residual energy level before the simulation is 0.392 Joules and after the data transfer is 0.0008 Joules. This because of the load sharing algorithm which sends the data traffic through the paths based on its deviation in energy level from the residual energy level to the mean residual energy level. The standard deviation is calculated among the residual energy levels of the multiple paths. The data traffic is sent to spend only the defined amount of energy in that path.

6   Conclusions

To increase the network operational lifetime is a critical research issue in Wireless Sensor Networks. Many multipath routing protocols for Wireless Sensor Networks proposed the effective mechanism to increase the network lifetime by selecting the optimum route selection criteria. The work proposes EELBMRP to increase the network operational lifetime by distributing the data traffic among the multiple paths effectively. The load sharing algorithm in EELBMRP reduces the variance among the residual energy level in the nodes on multipath by 93.3%. The energy level after the data transfer lies around 3.848 Joules. The effective results can be seen by setting the varied initial energy levels for the nodes in the wireless sensor network.

References

1. Mainwaring, A., Culler, D., Polastre, J., Szewczyk, R., Anderson, J.: Wireless sensor networks for habitat monitoring. In: First ACM International Workshop on Wireless Sensor Networks and Applications WSNA (2002)
2. Gsottberger, Y., Shi, X., Stromberg, G., Sturm, T.F., Weber, W.: Embedding Low-Cost Wireless Sensors into Universal Plug and Play Environments. In: Karl, H., Wolisz, A., Willig, A. (eds.) EWSN 2004. LNCS, vol. 2920, pp. 291–306. Springer, Heidelberg (2004)
3. Delin, K.A.: Sensor web in Antarctica.: Developing and Intelligent, Autonomous Platform for Locating Biological Flourishes in Cryogenic Environments. In: 34th Lunar and Planetary Science Conference (2003)
4. Lewis, F.L.: Wireless Sensor Networks. In: Cook, D.J., Das, S.K. (eds.) Smart Environments: Technologies, Protocols, and Applications. John Wiley, New York (2004)
5. Intanagonwiwat, C., Govindan, R., Estrin, D.: Directed Diffusion: A Scalable and Robust Communication Paradigm for Sensor Networks. In: Proc. of ACM MobiCom 2000, Boston, MA, USA, pp. 56–67 (2000)
6. Maria, M., Das, S.: On-Demand Multipath Distance Vector Routing in Ad-hoc Networks. In: Proc. of Ninth International Conference for Network Protocols, pp. 14–23 (2001)

Global Distributed Indexing for In-Network Storage in Sensor Networks

Samant Saurabh[1], Shashi Shekhar Singh[2], and Ashok Singh Sairam[1]

[1] Department of Computer Science, IIT Patna, Patilputra Colony, Patna
[2] Department of Computer Science, University of Massachusetts, Amherst, USA
{ssaurabh,ashok}@iitp.ac.in, shashi.singh@gmail.com

Abstract. The Introduction of energy-efficient flash memory has greatly facilitated archival storage of sensor data that is necessary for applications that query, mine, and analyze such data for interesting features and trends. This trend has necessitated the need for a global distributed index for in-network storage in power constrained sensor networks. We propose and evaluate the architecture for such networks and a distributed indexing for the architecture that allows distributed queries to proceed in a fault-tolerant and energy efficient manner with low latency. We discuss the rationale behind the choice of our indexing scheme and evaluate some of the characteristics of the scheme.

Keywords: Bloom Filtering, Flash Based Storage, Global Distributed Indexing, Network Querying, Sensor Networks.

1 Introduction

A typical sensor application needs access to both present and past sensor data. Access to past data is necessary for applications such as mining of sensor logs to detect unusual pattern, analysis of historical trends, and post-mortem analysis of particular events. In the earlier approaches, when the storage costs at the sensor nodes were comparable to communication costs, sensors streamed data or events to a server for long-term archival storage [1], where the server often indexes the data to permit efficient access at a later time. Capacities of flash memories continue to rise as per Moores Law, while their costs continue to plummet. The energy cost of flash storage can be as much as two orders of magnitude lower than that for communication. These trends, together with the energy constrained nature of un-tethered sensors, indicate that local storage offers a viable, energy-efficient alternative to communication in sensor networks. This paper attempts to address the problem of distributed indexing in such sensor networks. We assume that the data sensed at the sensors are integral values e.g., pressure, humidity, wind direction, light intensity etc. The data is immutable and is sensed periodically. The distributed index should support retrospective queries. An example query could be: Find all nodes which recorded value v in the last seven days. Rest of the paper is organized as follows: Section 2 discusses the system architecture. Section 3 discusses the detailed design of

K.R. Venugopal and L.M. Patnaik (Eds.): ICIP 2011, CCIS 157, pp. 428–437, 2011.
© Springer-Verlag Berlin Heidelberg 2011

the distributed index. Section 4 discusses *bloom filters* being used as signature. Section 5 presents the results of our evaluation. Finally, section 6 concludes the paper and discusses future work.

2   System Architecture

We assume a homogeneous sensor network, where all the nodes are resource constrained. A canonical sensor node is equipped with low-power sensors, a microcontroller, and a radio as well as a significant amount of flash memory. The common constraint is energy, and the need for a long lifetime in spite of a finite energy constraint. The use of radio, processor, RAM, and the flash memory all consume energy, which needs to be limited. In general, radio communication is substantially more expensive than accesses to flash memory. A uniform distributed in-network storage treats all nodes equally. This makes it harder to design an energy efficient distributed index. Taking a leaf from TSAR design, we try to come up with a hierarchy, wherein the upper-layer nodes maintain a distributed index, and the lower-layer nodes actually sense raw data and send periodical summary of the data to the upper-layer nodes. Unlike TSAR [2], our upper-layer nodes are also resource constrained. The nodes are first clustered based on communication latencies. The geographically closer nodes are clustered into a single cluster. A *leader* is selected in each cluster. The nodes in a cluster send periodically to the leader of the cluster, a summary of the sensed data.

To reduce the burden on the resource constrained leaders, they are used only for maintaining a distributed index among themselves; they do not actually sense any data, unlike the local nodes. A query may arrive at any leader node. A leader maintains two kinds of data: (1) *Summary* data of all nodes within its cluster, and (2) a concise summary of the data stored at all other leaders. The leaders share among themselves a summary of data stored at them. So, this essentially is the summary of summaries sent by the local nodes.

3   Distributed Indexing and Design Consideration

In this section, we first enumerate the questions that we attempt to answer in this paper. Answers to these questions are then considered one by one.

3.1   Questions to Answer

1. What is the *summary* being sent to the leader node?
2. How is the summary stored in flash memory at the leader? What is the index for this summary data?
3. What summary do the leaders share among themselves to support distributed queries?

Summary Being Sent to the Leader. Suppose a cluster has n nodes. One of these nodes will be the leader, and the rest n-1 will be local nodes. All the local nodes periodically sense data (say every minute), and store it locally in their flash memories. A summary of this data is to be sent to the leader periodically (say every 30 minutes). Let this period be T. A simple summary for integral values may just be the *min-max* range of the sensed data in each interval of T time units. The leader receives every T time units, the *min-max* summary from each of the n-1 nodes within its cluster. Each summary sent by a node i is a 3-tuple $<i$, *min, max*$>$. The size of this summary is 3*sizeof(int) = 12 Bytes. We note that, since the time period T is fixed, sending timestamp values will be redundant. To save upon power, we would want to minimize summary size. Leader can just maintain a sequence number per node. Successive sequence numbers would indicate successive time periods. To support retrospective queries, the leader needs to archive all past summaries from all local nodes. History will be limited by the size of flash memory at the leader. The data arrival rate at the leader is given by the expression below. $R = \frac{(3*4)*(n-1)}{T}$ *bytes per second.*

Storage of Summary Data at Leader. The leader maintains n-1 in-memory current-values of a series of n-1 sequence numbers. Val_i ($1 \leq i \leq n$-1) denotes the next assignable sequence number for the summary arriving from node i. When a summary $<i$, *min, max*$>$ arrives, the leader assigns sequence number Val_i to it, and then increments Val_i. To store the summaries of n-1 local nodes, two design choices are given in [3]: (1) store the summaries of all streams (arriving from n-1 nodes) in an interleaved fashion on flash; (2) have the flash partitioned into n-1 partitions, where partition i stores the summaries of ith node contiguously in order of increasing sequence numbers. Log structured file system perfectly accommodates the peculiarities of a flash storage. Each partition is treated as a circular log file. Clearly option two is a cleaner way: it segregates the summaries from different nodes into different partitions, and also assigns storage space equally among the nodes.

Indexing of Summary Data Stored at Leader. Tuples $<min, max, seq\_no>$ are written sequentially in the ith partition for the summaries of the ith node. We note that the temporal summaries are *immutable*. Maintaining an explicit exact index like a B-Tree would be overkill. Moreover, the indexing would require implementing inserts most efficiently in an online fashion. There are no updates, and deletions occur only when a partition gets full. To accommodate for flash peculiarities, we would want a simple indexing scheme that could be computed online, as the summaries arrive. We take the idea from the Hyperion paper [2]. A summary stream from a node is partitioned into blocks and one of more signatures is computed for each block. We will generate a two-level signature-index over the summary data stored in a partition: the more accurate and numerous 1st level signatures will be stored on flash itself (in special index-blocks), while the coarser and relatively compact 2nd level signatures will be stored in RAM.

Indexing of Summary Data Stored at Leader: Level 1 Signature. To match flash properties, we choose the size of a block equal to a page/block size in flash. The data in our case is range data (*min-max* summaries). A suitable signature for such data is the aggregate functions MIN and MAX. MIN is the minimum of all *min* values of the ranges stored in the block. Similarly MAX is the maximum of all *max* values. The tuple <*MIN,MAX*> constitutes the signature for a block. Size of this level-1 signature = 2*sizeof(int)=8 bytes. These 8 bytes level-1 signatures are stored on flash in special blocks called index blocks. In [3], the signature of a block was stored within the block itself. This solved the problem of removing records from the index as they age out. When an aged-out block is deleted, the signature associated with that data block is also deleted. But we adopted index blocks for the following reason: On disks, the head can move to the portion of the block containing the signature and retrieve it exclusively. But a read operation on flash is block based, and hence reading each signature will incur cost of reading a full block. It may appear that the choice of index blocks for flash may complicate the process of deleting signatures associated with deleted blocks. But this task is facilitated by the fixed sizes of the summary data and the signatures. Suppose an index block can contain m level-1 signatures (corresponding to m data blocks). Then the signature of ith data block is stored in the $\lfloor \frac{m}{i} \rfloor^{th}$ index block at offset $(m\%i)$. So, if the ith data block is deleted, we retrieve this particular index block and mark the entry at the particular offset within this block as invalid. When the free space available for index blocks falls below a threshold, flash-specific storage reclamation policies may be applied over the erase units containing the index blocks. We note that we have a level-1 signature per block. Hence it may not be feasible to store the level-1 signatures in RAM. This necessitates that they be stored on flash.

Indexing of Summary Data Stored at Leader: Level 2 Signature. This is computed over k contiguous data blocks. For matching physical properties of flash, we choose k to be equal to the number of blocks within an erase unit. Thus, we have an 8 byte <*MIN,MAX*> signature over a whole erase unit. This signature will be coarser than the per block signature. And this 2nd level of signature will fit into RAM for faster access.

Characteristics of Signature (Aggregate Function). It is easy to observe that there will be false positives but no false negatives. False positives arise when the signatures show a match when there is none. This will be corrected when the actual data records are scanned. We want to minimize the probability of false positives. Fig. 1 shows an example showing the probability of false positives. Suppose a signature is generated for five range data (denoted by green intervals in the Fig. 1). The signature generated is <*MIN,MAX*>. The ranges denoted by red intervals indicate intervals not covered by any of the range data. For simplicity, we assume that all red and green intervals are equal in size. Probability of false positives =(Sum of lengths of all red intervals)/*(MAX-MIN)*.

We can expand the signature to include more than one disjoint intervals: <(MIN_1,MAX_1),(MIN_2,MAX_2),..., (MIN_r,MAX_r)>. There is a tradeoff between size of signature and accuracy of signature. We want to minimize size and

Fig. 1. An example showing probability of false positive

maximize accuracy; but higher the accuracy, higher the size. In the example given in the Fig. 2. Pr(False Positives) $= 4/9$. If the signature expanded to $<(MIN_1,MAX_1),(MIN_2,MAX_2),...,(MIN_r,MAX_r)>$: Pr(False Positives for 1st interval $(MIN_1,MAX_1) = $ p $= {}^1/_4$. Pr(False Positives for 2nd interval (MIN_2,MAX_2) $= $ q $= 0/2 = 0$.Pr(False Positives for expanded signature) $= p + q - pq = {}^1/_4$.

Intuition of Choosing Appropriate Signature Size

1. If the probability of false positives is less than an acceptable threshold, do not expand the signature.
2. If not, look for long stretches of red intervals. It is reasonable to exclude such long stretches from the signature by splitting the interval in the signature covering this stretch into two subintervals that exclude the stretch. If such long stretches of red intervals are not present, the betterment in probability of false positives may not be worth the extra storage used by the expanded signature. It is reasonable to fix a threshold on the length of the stretch. Anything above this threshold would be worth considering.

Progress of Search for a Query. A search scans the level-2 signatures (stored in RAM), and when a match is found, the corresponding k level-1 signatures are retrieved (from the index blocks on flash) and tested; data blocks are retrieved and scanned only when a match is found in a level-1 signature.

Note1: We are only interested in knowing if the relevant node i contains any data relevant to the query. So, as soon as we find an exact match with any summary data (stored on the actual data blocks), we cease further enquiry and forward the query to node i.

Note2: Since level-1 signatures are computed only when a data block gets full, we always test the last non-full data block for matches. For similar reason, the last non-full index block is also always tested (because level-2 signatures for it might not be computed).

Distributed Indexing among the Leaders. A query may be fired at any leader. We want to handle such queries without resorting to query flooding. The in-memory level-2 signatures stored at a leader provides a summary of the data stored at the leader.

Possible design choices

1. Use the idea employed within a cluster: choose a super-leader whom all leaders send the summaries. All queries first arrive at the super-leader which then forwards it to the leaders showing a match. However, we do not use this approach because of the following disadvantages: super-leader is the single point of failure. This defeats our fundamental target of being able to support distributed queries in a fault tolerant manner.

2. Use sparse skip interval graph (as suggested in [2]): This data structure is particularly useful against other distributed data structures (like distributed B-trees) for the following two reasons: (i) load balancing and fault tolerant: the query may arrive at any of the nodes, and not necessarily at the node where the root of the data structure is hosted; (ii) rebalancing is not required: a probabilistic balancing method is used, which trades off a small amount of overhead in the expected case in return for simple update and deletion (which does not require rebalancing). Using this approach, the probability of the structure being significantly out of balance is extremely small. In spite of these advantages, we do not use this for the following reasons: For a distributed data of size n, though the index has a desirable search cost $O(log\ n)$, it also incurs an exchange of $O(log\ n)$ messages among the nodes. Insertions also necessitate exchange of $O(log\ n)$ messages. For power constrained leader nodes, we are not ready to incur these communication costs. We note that [2] did not have this bottleneck because the data structure was distributed among the resource rich proxy nodes.

Our Design Choice. What we want is a combination of two things: support for distributed queries in a fault tolerant manner and no message exchange overhead for search operations. We employ a simple scheme which achieves these two objectives at the cost of increased message overhead for inserts. Each leader broadcasts its level-2 in-memory signature index to all other leaders. Whenever a new signature is added at level-2 (that happens only when a whole erase unit has been written), it is broadcast to all other leaders. Also, when an old signature is invalidated, the change is broadcast. Each leader stores its own level-2 signature in RAM, and those of the other leaders are stored on flash. When a query arrives at a leader, the following actions are taken: (i) if the query was forwarded by another leader, then just scan own signatures; (ii) if the query arrived directly from an application, apart from scanning own signatures, all scan other leader's level-2 signatures (from flash) one by one, and forward the query to leaders showing a match. Upon finding that a leader is not reachable, the application can forward the query to any other reachable leader (fault tolerance).

4   Bloom Filters as Signature

With aggregate functions being used as signatures, the results found were just about OK (see evaluation in section 5). We would want the false positives to be much lower. Moreover, it was found that the *min-max* summary of the sensor data was also very coarse. We then used bloom filters [3], which proved to be a much more accurate signature. A bloom filter creates a compact signature for one or more records, which may be tested to determine whether a particular key is present in the associated records. We used a set of k hash functions which together hashed each key into an m-bit word, of which k bits are set to 1. To check for the presence of a particular key, the hash for that key h_0 is calculated and compared with the signature for the record h_s; if any bit is set in h_0 but not set in h_s, then the value cannot be present in the corresponding data record. To calculate the false positive probability, we note that if the fraction of 1 bits in the signature for a set of records is r and the number of 1 bits in any individual hash is k, then the chance that a match could occur by chance is *1-(1-r)^k*; e.g., if the fraction of 1 bits is 1/2, then the probability is 2-k. A limitation with using bloom signatures is that the summary data present at the leaders should be scalar and not ranges. This renders *min-max* summary inapplicable. So, a sensor node sends a bloom signature of the raw data that it sensed in a time interval. A leader can then construct level-1 and level-2 bloom signatures over these scalar summaries. We found much better results with these bloom signatures.

5   Evaluation and Results

We simulated in Java. We had two clusters with 4 nodes each. Each cluster had a leader and 3 local sensor nodes. Each leader maintains 3 partitions on flash for its 3 local nodes. We used weather data from [4], [5]. In particular, we chose wind direction, which ranges from 1 to 360 degrees. We had 6 level-2 signatures and 51 level-1 signatures. Table 1 shows the results when aggregate functions are used as signatures. The number of false positives (both at level-1 and level-2) has been tabulated for 100 consecutive queries. The results have been averaged over the two clusters and over the 3 partitions within each cluster. For 100 queries 6*100=600 level-2 signatures and 51*100=5100 level-1 signatures may need to be matched. Though the number of false positives at level-1 is larger than that at level-2, percentage wise level-1 has much less false positives. Query values indicate the actual values v being queried.

These results are not very encouraging. We would want the false positives to be lesser. In most of the cases it turned out that *min = max*. Hence the summaries were very coarse, with long stretches of red intervals, and very short

Table 1. False Positives for aggregate function signature

#Queries	#False positives at level 1	#False positives at level 2	Number of real hits at leader	Query values	#Matches at other leader
100	80	110	76	1-100	0
100	100	148	128	101-200	1
100	76	90	110	201-300	1
100	74	92	68	301-400	0

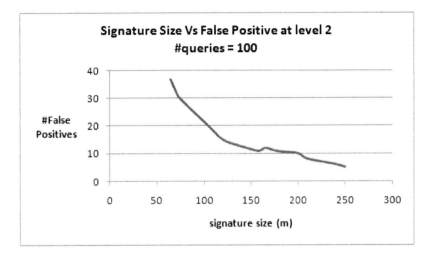

Fig. 2. Signature Vs False Positive at Level 2

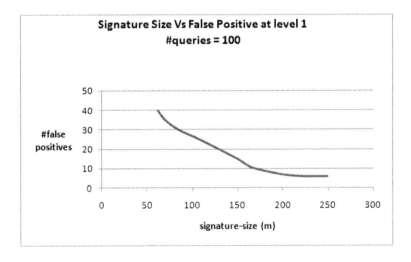

Fig. 3. Signature Vs False Positive at Level 1

sized (sometimes zero) green intervals. Moreover, we did not implement the expanding of signature to increase the accuracy (as explained in section 3.5). This is because the ideas proposed are still vague in terms of threshold for suitable lengths of red intervals. So, one of the limitations with aggregate functions is that it is not easily tunable to trade signature size with accuracy. *Min-max* summaries are also very susceptible to errors.

Next we show results for the same set of data when bloom filters are used by local nodes for summarizing and when the leaders computed two levels of bloom signatures with these summaries. We find much better results. The number of false

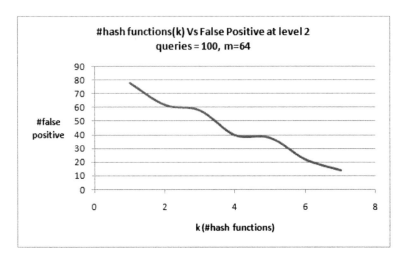

Fig. 4. Number of hash functions Vs False Positive at level 2

positives has substantially decreased. Moreover, bloom filters are easily tunable to trade signature size against accuracy. As we increased the signature size, the number of false positives decreased substantially. These results encourage the use of bloom filters for both summarizing local nodes data as well as for creating the index at the leaders. Fig. 2. shows the plot of signature-size versus false-positives at level-2. We observe almost an exponential drop in the number of false-positives as the signature size increases from 64 to 128 bits. Fig. 3. shows a similar trend for the false positives at level-1. Fig. 4. shows the plot of k (number of hash functions used) against false positives at level-2. We observe that the number of false-positives decreases substantially as k increases. This is because when k is small, there is a higher probability that though a key is not a member of the set, its k positions are set to 1 by other keys present in the set.

6   Conclusions

We designed the architecture for distributed indexing in an energy constrained uniform sensor network, where recent advances in flash memories have significantly reduced the local storage cost as compared to the communication cost. We evaluated two schemes: one in which nodes send *min-max* summaries and the leader computes signatures using aggregate functions over these range summaries; and in the other scheme, the nodes send bloom filters as the summary and the leader computes a two-level bloom signature index over these scalar summaries. We found that the latter scheme gave much better results. Moreover, it was easily tunable to trade signature size against accuracy (i.e., minimizing false positives) for the latter scheme.

References

1. Bonnet, P., Gehrke, J.E., Seshadri, P.: Towards Sensor Database Systems. In: Proceedings of the Second International Conference on Mobile Data Management (January 2001)
2. Desnoyers, P., Ganesan, D., Shenoy, P.: TSAR: A Two Tier Sensor Storage Architecture Using Interval Skip Graphs. In: Proceedings of the Third International Conference on Embedded Networked Sensor Systems (SenSys 2005), pp. 39–50 (2005)
3. Desnoyers, P., Shenoy, P.: Hyperion: High Volume Stream Archival for Retrospective Querying. In: Proceedings of the 2007 USENIX Annual Technical Conference, Santa Clara CA, pp. 17–22 (June 2007)
4. http://www.weather.cs.umass.edu
5. http://traces.cs.umass.edu/index.php/Sensors/Sensors

An Efficient Approach for Storage Migration of Virtual Machines Using Bitmap

Suresh Chandra Moharana and Madhu Kumar S.D.

Department of Computer Science and Engineering,
National Institute of Technology Calicut,
Kerala, India
{suresh_mcs09,madhu}@nitc.ac.in

Abstract. Cloud computing is an emerging technique to provide computing environment and services on-demand over web. Virtualization is the key technology used by cloud computing to employ virtual machines to satisfy the user demands for computing resources dynamically. The migration of the virtual machines in between physical hosts is necessary for balancing the load and minimizing the service disruption during system maintenance. The virtual machines with local storage have advantages of higher availability, improved performance and higher security over the virtual machines sharing centralized storage. So, the virtual machines need to have local storage and hence the storage need to be migrated along with virtual machine migration across physical hosts. The existing approaches of storage migration suffers from increased total migration time and reduced service performance. In this paper, we propose a five phase storage migration approach that will migrate virtual machines with storage across physical hosts. Our objective is to improve the service performance and reduce the total migration time during the storage migration of virtual machines. We have used the block bitmap to synchronize the virtual machine storage during migration. The synchronization time during the memory transfer is absent in our approach unlike previous approaches.

Keywords: Cloud Computing, Service Performance, Storage, Virtual Machine, Virtualization.

1 Introduction

Cloud computing is an emerging technological advancement in the computing domain allowing users to obtain hardware, software and applications as services on-demand over Internet. The ability to pay for use of computing resources on short-term basis as needed makes cloud computing more popular [1]. The computing resources need to scale-up and scale-down as per the user demand. Virtualization is the key technology that enables scalability in cloud. Virtualization is the process of running multiple guest operating system known as virtual machines (VMs) on top of hardware by sharing the underlying resources [2].

K.R. Venugopal and L.M. Patnaik (Eds.): ICIP 2011, CCIS 157, pp. 438–447, 2011.
© Springer-Verlag Berlin Heidelberg 2011

The virtual machines will be initiated or suspended as per the load conditions to satisfy the user requirements.

The virtual machine migration takes a running virtual machine and moves it from one physical host to another host [3]. The virtual machines need to be migrated for balancing the load and minimizing the service disruption during system maintenance [4]. The current approach of virtual machine migration only migrates the runtime memory image of the virtual machines. There is no need of transferring the virtual machine storage as the virtual machines share a centralized storage known as network attached storage [4]. The virtual machines with local storage have advantages of higher availability, improved performance and higher security [5]. Hence, the virtual machines should have independent storage and the virtual machine storage need to be migrated along with virtual machine migration.

The storage migration of virtual machines raises some serious challenges. The size of virtual machine storage is huge, so the entire storage transfer increases the total migration time significantly. The consumption of resources during the storage migration degrades the services provided by the migrated virtual machine. The storage need to be synchronized between the physical hosts involved in migration which may lead to redundant storage transfer.

In this paper, we propose a five phase virtual machine storage migration approach that reduces the total migration time and improves the service performance. Our approach is a modification to the approach provided by Bradford *et al.* [5] and it uses few techniques of virtual machine migration proposed by Luo *et al.* [6]. We have used the block bitmap to synchronize the storage of the migrated virtual machine. Our approach eliminates the synchronization time during memory transfer unlike previous approaches.

The paper is organized as follows. Related work is provided in Section 2. Section 3 provides the system design of storage migration. In Section 4 the conclusion and the future work are discussed.

2   Related Work

The virtualization tools such as Xen [2-10] and KVM [8] facilitates live virtual machine migration. The virtual machine migration approach transfers the memory pages iteratively to the destination host and the updated memory pages are identified during each iteration. The modified pages are transferred in subsequent iterations. Then, the virtual machine is stopped at the source host and the memory pages updated in the last iteration is transferred to the destination host and the virtual machine is restarted at the destination host.

There is another method known as freeze-and-copy [9] to transfer local storage of the virtual machine. In this method the virtual machine is suspended first and the whole virtual machine storage is copied to the destination host Then the virtual machine resumes its execution at the destination host. Kozuch *et al.* [9] proposed a virtual machine migration approach that uses the freeze-and-copy approach. A single copy of virtual machine is transferred to the destination without any redundancy.

Bradford *et al.* [1] proposed a pre-copy approach for storage migration of the virtual machines. The virtual machine storage is transferred to the destination in the bulk transfer phase. During the bulk transfer the consumption of resources degrades the services provided by the migrated virtual machine. The communication units known as *delta* is used to maintain synchronization between the source and the destination host. These *deltas* are transferred at regular intervals to the destination host. The virtual machine memory image is transferred iteratively to the destination after the bulk transfer phase and it has an impact on total migration time. It has the same downtime as in the shared storage migration but the total migration time is huge.

Luo *et al.* [5] proposed an approach for whole system migration of virtual machines. In this approach the storage and memory of the virtual machine is transferred iteratively to the destination host in the pre-move phase. The iterative transfer of virtual machine storage and memory reduces the service performance and increases the total migration time. Then, the virtual machine is suspended and the runtime memory image of the virtual machine is synchronized. The memory synchronization time has a direct effect on the total migration time. The block bitmap is used to maintain synchronization between the source and the destination host.

3   System Design

The system has to migrate the local storage of a virtual machine from the source to the destination machine. The following section describes the metrics for performance measurement of the proposed storage migration approach.

3.1   Performance Metrics

Downtime. It is the time interval during which services are not provided by the virtual machines [4]. It is the time during which the virtual machine halts at the source and restarts at the destination host. Synchronization is performed usually at downtime.

$$Downtime = M_t + S_t \qquad (1)$$

where M_t : Memory transfer time
S_t : Synchronization time

Service Degradation Time. The time interval during which the services provided by the virtual machine observes degradation. This can happen when virtual machine with huge storage is migrated from the source to the destination machine. Transfer rate has a direct impact on degradation time.

$$Service\ degradation\ time = D_{total}/D_{rate} \qquad (2)$$

where D_{total}: Total data transferred
D_{rate}: Data transfer rate

Total Migration Time. It is the duration of complete transfer of virtual machine from source to the destination host [4]. The amount of data to be transferred affects the total migration time. So we have to reduce the amount of data to be transferred.

$$Total\ migration\ time = D_t + M_t + S_t \tag{3}$$

where D_t: Disk transfer time

3.2   Block Bitmap

We have used the block bitmap in the proposed approach for storage migration of virtual machines. A block bitmap [6] consist of set of bits where each bit represents a disk block. The bitmap is used to record the location of dirty disk blocks during migration. The bit is set to 1 if the disk block is dirty otherwise bit is set to 0 as shown in Fig. 1. Bit granularity means the size of a storage unit described by a bit [6]. The size of bitmap directly depends upon bit granularity.

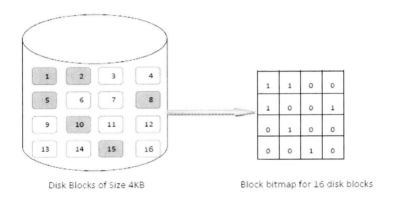

Disk Blocks of Size 4KB   Block bitmap for 16 disk blocks

Fig. 1. Block bitmap for disk blocks

3.3   Proposed System Architecture

The virtual machine migration without shared memory is not a new concept. Many researchers have suggested different mechanisms for storage migration. Bradford *et al.* [5] suggested a mechanism for storage migration of virtual machines. The modified disk blocks are maintained in communication unit known as *delta* [5] and they are transferred at regular intervals to synchronize the virtual machine storage. Then, the memory is transferred without suspending the services provided by the virtual machine. We have identified the problems associated with this approach. Those are the whole disk transfer in the bulk transfer phase takes large time increasing the total migration time. During the storage transfer the consumption of virtual machine resources degrades the services provided by the virtual machine increasing the service degradation time. *Deltas* used for synchronization which will cause some redundancy. After the bulk transfer phase, the memory migration incurs some time for synchronization increasing the total migration time.

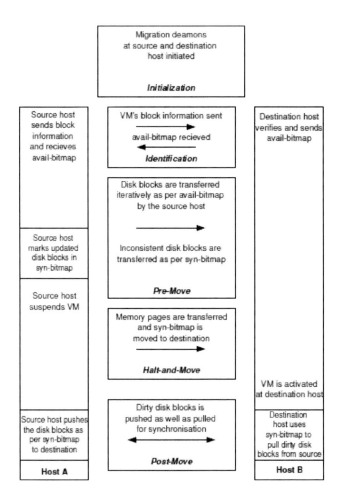

Fig. 2. Disk migration system architecture

Our approach is a modification to the approach provided by Bradford *et al.* [5] and it uses few techniques of virtual machine migration proposed by Luo *et al.* [6]. We aim at minimizing the total migration time and the service degradation time incurred during the storage migration of virtual machines. The synchronization time for the memory migration is absent in our approach.

The suggested approach consists of five phases to transfer the whole disk from the source to the destination host. Fig. 2 describes the system architecture for storage migration of virtual machines. The functionalities of each of those phases are described below.

Initialization. The migration daemons at the source and at the destination host are initiated. The migration daemons establishes a connection between the hosts involved in migration to begin virtual machine migration.

Identification. The identification phase is responsible for identifying the disk blocks of the virtual machines running at the destination host similar to the disk blocks of the migrated virtual machine. There can be similar disk blocks at both the ends due to similarity in operating system or applications. We have used algorithm given in Table 1 for this purpose.

Table 1. Algorithm: Identification Phase

1. Map the disk blocks of the migrated virtual machine to its digest using SHA-1
2. Transfer block digests to the destination host
3. Match the digest with the digest of the virtual machines running at the destination host
4. Mark the matched disk blocks in the avail-bitmap
5. Send the avail-bitmap back to the source host

We have extended the memory page identification approach proposed by Riteau *et al.* [10] for identifying the similar disk blocks. The approach followed in the algorithm is to calculate the digest of disk blocks of the migrated virtual machine using SHA-1 [11] and send it to the destination. Then, the destination host matches these digests with the block digests of the running virtual machines. The unavailable disk blocks are marked in the *avail-bitmap*. The *avail-bitmap* is sent back to the source host to begin the storage migration.

Pre-Move. The *pre-move* phase is responsible for transferring the unavailable disk blocks as per the *avail-bitmap* from the source to the destination host. The algorithm given in Table 2 describes the *pre-move* phase of storage migration. The virtual machine storage is transferred iteratively to maintain synchronization. The first iteration transfers the disk blocks marked in the *avail-bitmap*. The *syn-bitmap* is introduced to mark the modified disk blocks during each iteration and these updated blocks are transferred in subsequent iterations. The number of iterations of the storage transfer is determined by the dynamic rate limiting algorithm [4].

Step 2 to 7 in the *pre-move* phase algorithm transfers the unmarked disk blocks to the destination host as per the *avail-bitmap* and marks the disk blocks in the *syn-bitmap* modified during the transfer. Step 8 to 12 describes the dynamic rate limiting algorithm [4] to determine the number of iterations of disk transfer. The *dirtying rate* is a major factor in determining the number of iterations. The *dirtying rate* can be calculated dividing the number of dirty pages in a iteration by the time taken to complete that iteration [4]. Step 13 to 18 transfers the disk blocks in each iteration and marks the updated disk blocks in *syn-bitmap* during each round of the storage transfer.

Table 2. Algorithm: Pre-Move Phase

1. Receive avail-bitmap from the destination host
2. **for** each block N
3.   **if** avail-bitmap[N] == 0 then
4.   transfer block N to the destination host
5.   avail-bitmap[N] = 1
6.   **for** each modified block N
7.   syn-bitmap[N] = 1
8. Set minimum and maximum data transfer rate
9. Initialize data transfer rate with minimum data transfer rate
10. **if** transfer rate > maximum data transfer rate
11.   suspend the virtual machine
12.   goto step-21
13. **for** each block N
14. **if** syn-bitmap[N] == 1 then
15.   transfer block N to the destination host
16.   syn-bitmap[N] = 0
17.   **for** each modified block N
18.   syn-bitmap[N] = 1
19. transfer rate = transfer rate + dirtying rate
20. goto step-10
21. End of pre-move phase

Halt-and-Move. This phase is responsible for transferring the *syn-bitmap* and virtual machine memory image to the destination host. The *syn-bitmap* having the inconsistent disk block information is transferred to the destination host. Then, the consistent memory image of the migrated virtual machine is moved to the destination and the virtual machine is restarted at the destination host.

Post-Move. The inconsistent virtual machine disk blocks in the last iteration of the *pre-move* phase is synchronized in this phase after resuming the virtual machine at the destination host. The source host pushes the inconsistent disk blocks as per *syn-bitmap* to the destination host. The virtual machine running at the destination, if require any inconsistent disk block as per the *syn-bitmap* is pulled from the source host. The block request present in the pull list are pushed on priority to the destination host. The part of synchronization handled by the source host in the *post-move* phase is defined in the algorithm given in Table 3.

We have used the synchronization mechanism proposed by Luo *et al.* [6] to achieve synchronization at the destination host. The destination host provides disk blocks as per I/O request. The I/O request is a three tuple such as virtual machine id (VM_{id}), block number (N), operation (O).

Table 3. Algorithm: Synchronization at Source Host

```
1. Queue block M in the pull list L_p,
2. for each block N
3.     if syn-bitmap[N] == 1 then
4.         if L_p is not empty then
5.             for each M in L_p,
6.                 push block M to the destination host
7.                 syn-bitmap[M] = 0
8.         else
9.             push block N to the destination host
10.            syn-bitmap[N] = 0
```

When write operation is requested the corresponding disk blocks are provided from the destination host. The inconsistent disk blocks are pulled from the source host whenever read operation is requested. The algorithm used for synchronizing the destination host is given in Table 4.

Table 4. Algorithm: Synchronization at Destination Host

```
1. Receive an I/O request R(VM_id, N, O)
2. Insert R into the request list L_r
3. if R.VM_id != migrated VM_id then
4.     goto step-11
5. if syn-bitmap[N] == 0 then
6.     goto step-11
7. if R.O == Write then
8.     syn-bitmap[N] = 0
9.     goto step-11
10. Send pull request to the source host for block N
11. Remove R from L_r
```

3.4   Performance Analysis

We have simulated the proposed storage migration approach in CloudSim [12] toolkit. The machine we have used for simulation have *Intel Core 2 Duo* 2.10 *GHz* processor and 3 *GB* of RAM. We have used *Ubuntu* 9.10 operating system and *Java* 1.6 for running the simulation code.

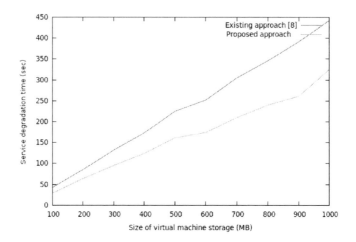

Fig. 3. Comparing Service Degradation Time

We have computed the service degradation time and the total migration time in our approach and in the existing approach [5] by varying the size of virtual machine storage in the range of 100 to 1000 MB. We have plotted the graphs for sevice degradation time and total migration time as shown in Fig. 3 and Fig. 4. We have observed that the proposed approach improves the service performance and decreases the total migration time for different sizes of virtual machine storage.

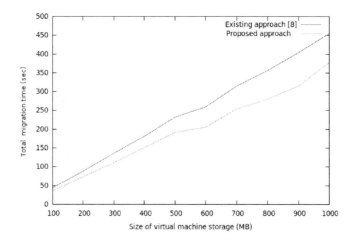

Fig. 4. Comparing Total Migration Time

4   Conclusions

The objective of the proposed approach for storage migration of virtual machines is to reduce the total migration time and to improve the service performance. The reduction in size of data transferred in the *pre-move* phase improves the service performance and decreases the total migration time. The storage migration approach avoids the memory synchronization time in the *halt-and-move* phase and as a result the total migration time reduces significantly.

In future, we plan to implement the proposed prototype for storage migration of virtual machines in Xen framework. We also plan to extend our algorithm to include data compression techniques in the *pre-move* phase to improve the total migration time.

References

1. Armbrust, M., Fox, A., Griffith, R., Joseph, A., Katz, R., Konwinski, A., Lee, G., Patterson, D., Rabkin, A., Stoica, I., Zaharia, M.: Above the Clouds: A Berkeley View of Cloud Computing. University of California at Berkeley Technical Report No. UCB/EECS-209-28, USA (February 2009)
2. Barham, P., Dragovic, B., Fraser, K., Hand, S., Harris, T., Ho, A., Neugebauer, R., Pratt, I., Warfield, A.: Xen and the Art of Virtualization. In: SOSP (2003)
3. Nelson, M., Lim, B., Hutchins, G.: Fast Transparent Migration for Virtual Machines. In: USENIX Annual Technical Conference, California, USA (April 2005)
4. Clark, C., Fraser, K., Hand, S., Hansen, J., Jul, E., Limpach, C., Pratt, I., Warfield, A.: Live Migration of Virtual Machines. In: Proceedings of the 2nd Conference on Symposium on Networked Systems Design and Implementation, CA, USA (May 2005)
5. Bradford, R., Kotsovinos, E., Feldmann, A., Schioberg, H.: Live Wide-Area Migration of Virtual Machines with Local Persistent State. In: Proceedings of the 3rd International Conference on Virtual Execution Environments, NY, USA (June 2007)
6. Luo, Y., Zhang, B., Wang, X., Wang, Z., Sun, Y.: Live and Incremental Whole-System Migration of Virtual Machines Using Block-Bitmap. In: 2008 IEEE International Conference on Cluster Computing, Tsukuba, Japan (September 2008)
7. XEN, http://www.cl.cam.ac.uk/research/srg/netos/xen
8. Kivity, A., Kamay, Y., Laor, D., Lublin, U., Liguori, A.: kvm: The Linux Virtual Machine Monitor. In: Proceedings of the Linux Symposium, Ottawa, Canada (June 2007)
9. Kozuch, M., Satyanarayanan, M.: Internet Suspend/Resume. In: Fourth IEEE Workshop on Mobile Computing Systems and Applications, Callicoon, NY (June 2002)
10. Riteau, P., Morin, C., Priol, T.: Shrinker: Efficient Wide Area Live Virtual Machine Migration Using Distributed Content-based Addressing. INIRIA-00454727, Version 1 (February 2010)
11. SHA-1, http://www.itl.nist.gov/fipspubs/fip180-1.htm
12. Buyya, R., Ranjan, R., Calheiros, R.N.: Modeling and Simulation of Scalable Cloud Computing Environments and the CloudSim Toolkit: Challenges and Opportunities. In: Proceedings of the 7th High Performance Computing and Simulation Conference. IEEE Computer Society, Los Alamitos (June 2009)

Cloud Computing Privacy Issues and User-Centric Solution

Lijo V.P. and Saidalavi Kalady

Department of Computer Science and Engineering,
National Institute of Technology, Calicut, India
lijovpaul@yahoo.co.in

Abstract. Recently, the most announced word in the world of computation is 'Cloud Computing'. In cloud computing, the services are provided by some vendors and the customers are unaware about the storage and maintenance of their data. So, logically speaking, the client has no control over the cloud. When the service providers process the data being provided by the customers, issues like privacy loss and data leakage may arise. This is an important barrier for the adoption of cloud services. A user-centric approach is essential to overcome this barrier. In this paper we present a solution which provides the control, over the data being submitted in the cloud, to the user.

Keywords: Cloud Computing, Cloud Security, Data Security, Privacy, Software as Service.

1 Introduction

Cloud computing offers a future in which we completely depends on some remote centralized facilities which have computing and storage utilities, instead of local computers. In this cloud computing environment the users can utilize the services such as the computing and storage provided by some service providers. The users are unaware about where the computing element resides and how the stored data is being used. Since the users have no control over it, maintaining the levels of protection of sensitive data is a new challenge. This challenge become very significant when the cloud computing involves a cross-border data transfers.

Cloud computing become very popular now a days, majority of the IT companies pursuing in to the cloud. Even though cloud provides cost effective service to customers, the hackers feel it as a honey pot. While sharing same platform there are chances of data leakage and privacy loss. To advance the cloud computing, we should take proactive measures to ensure security [1].

In cloud computing environment the services are carried out by the software on behalf of users. The users send their data, which may have sensitive information that helps to identify the user, to the cloud service and this data is processed by the application provided by the service provider, and the result is given back to the user. The cloud computing environment is suitable for business, as they can use hardware and software from cloud to meet their computing requirements, at

K.R. Venugopal and L.M. Patnaik (Eds.): ICIP 2011, CCIS 157, pp. 448–456, 2011.

a low cost. In Software as a Service (SaaS), data is processed in decrypted form and the result may be stored in the machine as plain text. So, this scenario may lead to leakage of sensitive data from the cloud [2].

In SaaS, the user submit their data to the cloud machine for processing, and the user has no control over the submitted data. So the user has no knowledge about where their data resides, how it is stored(as plain text or cipher text), and how the submitted data is used. The service provider may use the data against the wishes of the user. Service provider can share the sensitive information with others without the permission of the user. This may lead to privacy loss and data leakage. As Dan Lin's opinion [3], users fear of confidential data leakage and privacy loss becomes an important barrier to the wide adoption of cloud computing. So, to overcome this barrier a user-centric solution has to be developed, which provides the control, over the submitted data in cloud, to the users. Privacy is a major issue when designing a cloud service. As privacy is a fundamental human right, there should be proper measures for protecting sensitive data. There are different forms of privacy, including 'the right to be isolated from others' and 'the right to keep and control information about ourself'. Current legislation place many restrictions on processing of personal and sensitive data/ information by third parties. These restrictions limits the use of cloud computing service as currently designed [2].

In this paper, we present a user-centric solution to avoid fear of data leakage and privacy loss. This solution incorporate a client-agent module at service side, so service providers cooperation is needed. We present a user-centric trust model that helps the user to control their data and assumes the service provider cooperate with this client-agent.

In section 2, we present our solution and detailed description about its components. In section 3, we give a brief idea about other approaches and related works and in section 4, gives conclusion and future work.

2   Our Solution

In this section we present the overall architecture of our solution, provide more detail about the functionality provided by a central component of this solution, and then consider how this solution may address certain issues raised in the previous section.

2.1   Overall Architecture

The overall architecture of our solution is shown in Fig. 1. A user-centric approach for preventing privacy loss and data leakage is modelled. The central component of this approach is the client-agent. The client-agent resides at service provider to provide the knowledge about the submitted user data-how the data is actually used, stored and the actual location of the data. This approach assumes that user have service provider's consent to incorporate the client-agent module in the cloud application.

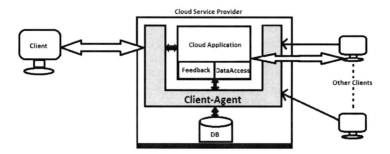

Fig. 1. A User-Centric Approach: Overall Architecture

2.2   Client-Agent

In this section we discuss features of the client-agent in more detail.

The client-agent has many features as shown in Fig. 2. for protecting the data in cloud. The client-agent mainly has three features: Encryption/Decryption, Key management and Filtering

Encryption/Decryption: This feature helps the client to transfer his data to and from the provider securely and ensure that the data stored in cloud database is encrypted. Symmetric key encryption algorithms like AES or DES can be used. The choice of selection of the algorithm is left to the user. User can select the algorithm, depending on his application's security preferences. The client can generate the symmetric key and encrypt the data. This encrypted data is send to the cloud along with the key. The symmetric key is encrypted using public key of client-agent. Public key encryptions such as RSA can be used for secure transferring of the symmetric key. At service provider, the client-agent decrypt the data by using symmetric key which is decrypted using client agent's private key. The cloud application can process the decrypted data and submit the result to the client-agent. The agent encrypts the result and sends it to the client. This feature gives control to the client over the data being submitted to the cloud.

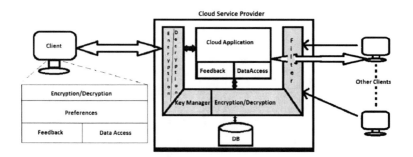

Fig. 2. Features of Client-Agent

This feature ensure that the data from the application to the database is encrypted and data from database to the application is decrypted. This feature improves the data security in cloud.

Key Management: The key manager generates the public and private key for RSA and keeps the private key securely. The symmetric key from client is also protected from other clients and even from the cloud application. The keys are embedded in a software and retrieving key by unauthorised person is tedious. For better protection, the key manager can generate RSA's public and private keys within a fixed intervals as regular fashion. So new keys replace old keys and encrypt the symmetric key with this new public key. Even though unauthorised person got private key, that key will not useful after a little time span. Because of this active refreshment of the keys, data in the cloud are secure.

Filtering: This will monitor other clients request to the database and report the client, if any attempt at unauthorized access to the data is made. This feature helps to preserve privacy in cloud. In current situation, the cloud user runs his application in an isolated virtual machine which is provided by the cloud service provider. As virtual machines are isolated from other virtual machines, unauthorised people may not have access on data in others virtual machines. And the feature Encryption/Decryption described above keeps the data as encrypted. So data are secured in cloud application, even this filtering is not active. But we place this feature to make sure that privacy preserved even if the virtualization security violated.

Preferences: This feature helps the user to set his security preferences. As per users security preference the key length and encryption algorithms can be decided. The user can set his security preferences as low, medium or high, depends on which data he transfer to cloud and whether it contains sensitive information or not.

This feature offers a choice for the user to get involved in maintaining security in cloud.

Other Features:

a. Data Access This feature allows users to access personal information in the cloud, in order to see what is being held about them, and to check its accuracy. Legislative authorities also suggested to add this feature in cloud applications to access the user's data, which are kept in the cloud, for checking whether the service provider follows privacy rules.

b. Feedback The Feedback feature manages and displays feedback to the user regarding usage of his personal information, including notification of data usage in the cloud. This feedback is provided by the cloud application periodically, by default, the cloud user can trigger the cloud application to get feedback about their data usage, location.

To incorporate these two features in cloud needs more modification in cloud application, so these should be included during development of the cloud application. These features are very same as features named Feedback and Data Access in Client-Based Privacy Manger by Mowbray [4].

2.3   Assumptions

Service Provider Cooperation: The service providers consent is needed to incorporate the client agent into the cloud application. The service provider should trust the user as he insert the client-agent in cloud application.

Proper Interface Provided: Client-Agent will be added as a plugin, so proper application interface should be provided by the service provider. Proper communication system is needed to get correct and valid information about the interface which is provided by the service provider. This would help the user to design and develop the client-agent properly, and incorporate this module in cloud application.

Semi-trusted Provider: The provider respect the security preferences of the client and adhere to the privacy policies. The sensitive data is not intentionally shared with other clients without permission. Malicious clients may access data without the permission of the provider.

Data: The data may contain sensitive information, such as sales data, healthcare information. So disclosure of this information may lead to privacy loss.

2.4   When this Proposed Solution is Not Suitable?

In the cloud applications which are not providing proper interface for client-agents, cannot implement this solution. Proper cooperation of service provider is needed for this solution. Some cloud may use other clouds to fulfil client's needs. In this case other cloud applications also has to provide the consent and support to incorporate agents in their applications. This may create some barriers for achieving scalability and virtualization.

As we know the cloud computing offers a future in which we compute on third parties centralized machines which have computing and storage facilities. In this case, the user needed only a web browser to use cloud applications, so user's machine need only minimum computing power. But for our solution the client needed some computational power to do encryption and decryption. It should have storage capacity to keep the counter parts of features of the client-agent. So our solution is not suit in the case of very thin client.

3   Other Approaches and Related Works

Many cloud applications allow the customers to install firewalls to prevent unauthorized access to the data. But this is not a final solution to prevent data leakage. In Amazon's Simple Storage Service (*S3*), while the data at rest is not encrypted by default, users can encrypt their data before it is uploaded to Amazon *S3*, so that it is not accessed or tampered with by any unauthorized party [5].

It is very important that the stored data in the cloud should be in encrypted form, to ensure data security. Many encryption schemes are available now. Cong

Wang [6], presented many aspects of storage security and suggested a distributed scheme to ensure integrity of user's data in cloud. To ensure privacy in cloud proper security of storage is essential. Even though the data storage is secure, there are lots of chances of attacks during mining data. Similarity checking is needed to mine exact data, this was done on plain text. So this will reveals the secrecy of the data. But recently Meena Dilip Singh [7], propose a cryptography based privacy preserving solution to mine cloud data. This gives a method to Mine cloud data in encrypted form itself, but it is not a generalized solution. Security in crypto-system mainly depends on the key. So key management is a significant task in security system. Weichao Wang [8], is presented a secure key management system and he suggested a fine grained encryption, which is more effective in cloud environment. Even though this proposed solution is capable to provide more security for the stored data, it has less control, over the data that is being processed in SaaS, by the data owner. Anonymization is one of the methods to preserve privacy. Querying heterogeneous databases using distributed anonymization is good idea to preserve privacy. But client has no control over his data that is submitted to the cloud.

The importance of privacy in cloud computing and many privacy issues related to the cloud computing are mentioned by Siani Pearson. He presented privacy as an important issue for cloud computing, both in terms of legal compliance and user trust. In the view of these issues privacy definitions are provided as "the right to be left alone" and "control of information about ourself" [2]. As the cloud computing is in a booming stage, many security issues are in concern. How the data is transferred and stored securely in a cloud are challenging concerns. Service Level Agreement(SLA) has an important role in security [9]. He suggested that SLA has to discuss about security policies, methods and their implementations.

In cloud environment many clients share same platform to store and process their data. Even though virtual machine isolation is protect their data from being shareable, it is essential introspection monitoring which is capable to monitor the guest OS to list black and white kernel functions [10]. They invoke cloud vendors to monitor guest OS functions to prevent Malware, instead of relaying virtualization security. Considering security and privacy in each stage of the development cycle is one of the best practices in the design of cloud [11]. Information and data security requirements in different modes of cloud computing (SaaS, PaaS, IaaS) are considered separately, is one of the best practice [12].

Wenjuan Li [13], introduced a frame work which consists of a trust module to ensure security in cloud environemnt. But this model do nothing for preserving privacy in SaaS. Hiroyuki Sato [14], proposed another trust model of security in terms of social security. These security problems are solved by hierarchical trust model. But Sato did not address privacy in SaaS.

Juan et al., [15], introduced a secure data flow processing system which is capable of preventing various attacks on data flow. But this system does not take care of the data leakage and privacy in SaaS.

Table 1. Comparison Between Our Solution and CBPM

Characteristics	Our Solution	CBPM
Privacy preserving	Yes	Yes
Need of service provider's cooperation	Yes	Yes
User's control over the data in the cloud	Yes	No
Need of Obfuscation of original data	No	Yes
Applicable on all type of data	Yes	No

Lombardi [16], presented a Transparent Cloud Protection System (TCPS) for increased security of cloud resources. Even though the TCPS provides protection from various attacks, it does not give an effective mechanism for detecting a larger possible number of threats.

Xu.J [17], proposed the security problem of sensitive data in management-type SaaS and used the encryption and signature to keep data security. Both the service provider and tenants are involved in the security establishment.

The Feedback and Data Access features described in section 2 build upon similar approaches used in Client-Based Privacy Manager (CBPM) [7]. Mowbrays suggestion is a client-based solution, which make sure users involvement for achieving privacy. In his proposed solution for privacy preservation, he uses a technique known as obfuscation which aims at reducing the amount of sensitive information available in the data being passed to the cloud. But in this proposal too, there is no control over the data that is being submitted to the applications in the cloud. And also, obfuscation is not a generalized solution.

Comparison between the related work client-based privacy manager [4] and our solution shown in Table 1. Both the solutions preserve the privacy with the cooperation of the providers. Service providers consent is needed to incorporate the privacy manager's features in the cloud application. The privacy manger has no control over the data being submitted in the cloud. But our client-agent has control over the data in the cloud. The user can take decision to hide the data from the cloud application even after left the data from the client. client-agent can take decision whether the data keep in encrypted form itself or data decrypt to present in the cloud application. Data is safe until the client-agent present it as a plain-text. In Privacy manager, obfuscate the data before sending the data as cipher text. But this is not needed in our solution. Arithmetic operations over the obfuscated data may create some problems such as overflow. So obfuscation limit the applicability of all types of data, so privacy manager as well. But in our solution, obfuscation is not using over original data. So our application is applicable on all types of data in which encryption and decryption are supported.

4   Conclusions and Future Work

In this paper, we present a user-centric solution which provides the user control over the data being submitted in the cloud. Our user-centric approach present a solution which incorporate a client-agent in cloud application which controls and manages data in the cloud. The client-agent makes sure that the data stored in the cloud is in encrypted form and the to and fro data flow is under control of the client-agent. This ensures data security and may motivate the users to adopt the cloud application without fear of data leakage and privacy loss.

As part of future work, we would like to investigate a solution for protecting data in the cloud without any cooperation of the cloud application and to derive better key management method at cloud application for fine grained encryption to gain better security.

References

1. Kaufman, L.: Data Security in the World of Cloud Computing. IEEE Security and Privacy 7(4), 61–64 (2009)
2. Pearson, S.: Taking Account of Privacy when Designing Cloud Computing services. In: ICSE Workshop on Software Engineering Challenges of Cloud Computing, CLOUD 2009, pp. 44–52. IEEE, Los Alamitos (2009)
3. Lin, D., Squicciarini, A.: Data Protection Models for Service Provisioning in the Cloud. In: Proceedings of the 15th ACM Symposium on Access Control Models and Technologies, pp. 183–192. ACM, New York (2010)
4. Mowbray, M., Pearson, S.: A Client-Based Privacy Manager for Cloud Computing. In: Proceedings of the Fourth International ICST Conference on Communication System Software and Middleware, pp. 1–8. ACM, New York (2009)
5. Subashini, S., Kavitha, V.: A Survey on Security Issues in Service Delivery Models of Cloud Computing. Journal of Network and Computer Applications (2010)
6. Wang, C., Wang, Q., Ren, K., Lou, W.: Ensuring Data Storage Security in Cloud Computing. In: 17th International Workshop on Quality of Service, pp. 1–9. IEEE, Los Alamitos (2009)
7. Singh, M., Krishna, P., Saxena, A.: A Cryptography Based Privacy Preserving Solution to Mine Cloud Data. In: Proceedings of the Third Annual ACM Bangalore Conference, pp. 1–4. ACM, New York (2010)
8. Wang, W., Li, Z., Owens, R., Bhargava, B.: Secure and Efficient Access to Outsourced Data. In: Proceedings of the 2009 ACM Workshop on Cloud Computing Security, pp. 55–66. ACM, New York (2009)
9. Kandukuri, B., Paturi, V., Rakshit, A.: Cloud Security Issues. In: IEEE International Conference on Services Computing, SCC 2009, pp. 517–520. IEEE, Los Alamitos (2009)
10. Christodorescu, M., Sailer, R., Schales, D., Sgandurra, D., Zamboni, D.: Cloud Security is not (just) Virtualization Security. In: Cloud Computing Security Workshop, Chicago, IL, (November 2009)
11. Lennon, R., Skår, L., Udnæs, M., Berre, A., Zeid, A., Roman, D., Landre, E., Van Den Heuvel, W.: Best Practices in Cloud Computing: Designing for the Cloud. In: Proceedings of the 24th ACM SIGPLAN Conference Companion on Object Oriented Programming Systems Languages and Applications, pp. 775–776. ACM, New York (2009)
12. Ramgovind, S., Eloff, M., Smith, E.: The Management of Security in Cloud Computing. In: Information Security for South Africa (ISSA), pp. 1-7 (2010)
13. Li, W., Ping, L., Pan, X.: Use Trust Management Module to Achieve Effective Security Mechanisms in Cloud Environment. In: 2010 International Conference On Electronics and Information Engineering (ICEIE), vol. 1. IEEE, Los Alamitos (2010)

14. Sato, H., Kanai, A., Tanimoto, S.: A Cloud Trust Model in a Security Aware Cloud
15. Du, J., Wei, W., Gu, X., Yu, T.: Towards Secure Dataflow Processing in Open Distributed Systems. In: Proceedings of the 2009 ACM Workshop on Scalable Trusted Computing, pp. 67–72. ACM, New York (2009)
16. Lombardi, F., Di Pietro, R.: Transparent Security for Cloud. In: Proceedings of the 2010 ACM Symposium on Applied Computing, pp. 414–415. ACM, New York (2010)
17. Xu, J., Jinglei, T.D.H.Y.Z.: Security Scheme for Sensitive Data in Management-Type SaaS. In: Procedings of the 2009 International Conference on Information Management, Innovation Management and Industrial Engineering, pp. 83–92. IEEE, Los Alamitos (2009)

Kerberos Style Authentication and Authorization through CTES Model for Distributed Systems

Aruna Kumari[1] and Dharmender Singh Kushwaha[2]

[1] Department of Computer Science and Engineering
Bharati Vidhyapeeth College of Engineering, Delhi, India
aruna.5183@gmail.com
[2] Department of Computer Science and Engineering
MNNIT, Allahabad, U.P., India
dsk@mnnit.ac.in

Abstract. With the rapid increase in the use of distributed systems, the user authentication and authorization and the protection of resources are the major concerns that need consideration. Various solutions are available for this in terms of approaches, models and protocols but each of these has some flaws. In this paper, we have made an attempt to address the associated concerns through an authentication and authorization model for distributed systems. The paper also describes an improvement over Kerberos protocol to authenticate the users and to access the services and resources that offsets certain limitations of Kerberos.

Keywords: Authentication, Authorization, Distributed Systems, Kerberos.

1 Introduction

In many organizations, most of the work considerably depends upon effective use of computational resources of geographically distributed systems and the level of their protection. Distributed system works here as a collection of computers linked via some network. Many problems, such as data storage, data transfer, automation of information processing, and complex problems solving are entrusted on the protection mechanisms deployed in the distributed systems. Several security policies are used to govern these components. These are also used to authenticate and authorize the users and to protect the resources and services of the system. Another issue is about the basis for authentication and access control? It can be the user identity, the network address the user operates from or the distributed service the user is invoking, i.e., the access operation. In this paper, we focus on Kerberos-style authentication and authorization with some additional functionality using CTES model [1-2]. We compare the proposed approach with the overhead concerned with various messages used in this model for the above said functions.

K.R. Venugopal and L.M. Patnaik (Eds.): ICIP 2011, CCIS 157, pp. 457–462, 2011.
© Springer-Verlag Berlin Heidelberg 2011

2   Previous Works on Kerberos

A lot of research work has been performed on Kerberos by several researchers because Kerberos is a time-tested and widely used lightweight protocol based on inexpensive symmetric key cryptography [1-9]. It allows a user to be authenticated once and later connect to application servers within the Kerberos realm without authenticating again for a period of time. The predominance of Kerberos involves independent development platform, high-speed communication of authentication, mutual authentication between entities and transferable relationship of trust, and a relatively strong compatibility with heterogeneous domains, which may adopt various trust policies [3], [8]. Chuang [10] gives a definition to the trusted intermediaries as the systems that authenticate clients and servers such as the Certificate Authorities in public key based systems and KDC (Key Distribution Center) in Kerberos Phillip [7] includes a pre-authentication approach as a Kerberos extension. The authors in [10] have used Kerberos for distributed authentication using public key cryptography.

2.1   Kerberos Protocol

Kerberos is a network authentication protocol and consists of Authentication Server (AS), Ticket-Granting-Server (TGS) as the part of Key Distribution Center (KDC) and Kerberos Authentication Database. The complete Kerberos authentication protocol also covers the client and server. Kerberos authenticates the client identity for which multiple messages are exchanged between different entities of the system. Client makes a request for TGT to AS with its own ID, ID of TGT and a timestamp, and authenticates its identity with AS. As a result, client gets the encrypted TGT and then requests the TGS for getting a SGT before accessing service.

2.2   Overview to CTES Model

The CTES model represents a collaborative trust approach where all the users are trustworthy and work under the mutual authentication and authorization to users with their dynamic nature of joining and leaving the distributed systems. The model is based on hybrid approach that consists of four components -Coordinators (Superhost and Agent), KDC Key Distribution Center (AS- Authentication Server and TGS- Ticket-Granting Server), Server and Client. The coordinators and KDC are the reliable controller systems around which all the activities are scattered. There is a mutual communication between the controller systems. Superhost maintains records of the clients and the servers of the distributed system, monitors the life time of the clients and servers and also controls the other controller systems. Agent manages the registry of service provided by servers, monitors clients behaviour, handles client requests for services and balances the load of servers.

The KDC is responsible for authenticating and authorizing the client when it requires a service. Client is a registered node of the distributed system that

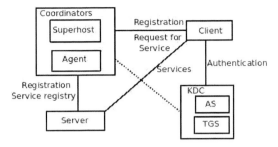

Fig. 1. Components of Proposed Model

can access the services and resources. The server creates a service and publishes its interface and access information to the service registry maintained by Agent. The major functions of the various components of the CTES model Fig. 1 are enumerated into the following classification:

1. Registration of users with Superhost,
2. Obtaining TGT from AS,
3. Obtaining SGT from TGS,
4. Obtaining servers reference from Agent,
5. Registration of services with Agent and
6. Accessing service from Server

2.3   Messages Used in the CTES Model

In our model, the messages involved for authentication and authorization are developed using the similar functionality as of Kerberos. As described in Fig. 2 the complete client authentication process involves 4 messages ($m1$, $m2$, $m3$ and $m4$). In its first message, client requests AS for authentication where AS using m2 contacts Superhost to verify the client and to obtain password, IP address and trust level of client using $m3$ and the result of this process is TGT assigned by AS to client by $m4$. We are using 2 messages ($m5$ and $m6$) to obtain SGT and to authorize the client. Here, client makes a new request to TGS with TGT

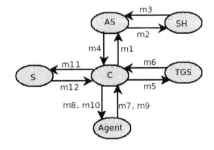

Fig. 2. Messages used in proposed model

(obtained in message m4) and an additional message, known as m_4) and an additional message, known as authenticator. In our architecture, after obtaining SGT (using message $m6$), client requests agent instead of Server to get the list of services for which client is authorized, and the list of servers for a service, using messages $m7, m8, m9$ and $m10$. The client uses messages $m11$ and $m12$ to access the service from server.

3   Results

3.1   CTES Model is Effective Than Kerberos

Kerberos requires 6 messages whereas the proposed system works on 12 messages but provides new dimension of services. Although, Kerberos uses 2 messages each for authenticating the identity of client and obtaining TGT; for obtaining SGT; and for accessing service whereas our architecture uses 4 messages for authenticating the identity of client and obtaining TGT, 2 messages for obtaining SGT, 4 for obtaining reference of server from agent and 2 for accessing service from server.

By using four additional messages for accessing service, we focus on the availability of services and servers of the distributed system that is not touched by any of the message of Kerberos. Here, agent is involved for providing the reference of server to the client on the basis of the requested service. Before transferring message m8 to client, agent analyzes the behaviour of client in the system along with sending intimation to Superhost to update the trust level of client. These additional features help in making our architecture efficient than Kerberos even when the number of messages increases. A relative discussion about the said issue proves that the proposed approach is efficient than Kerberos.

1. In the proposed system, initially the ID of TGS (in message $m1$) and ID of Server (in message $m5$) are not available with the client and it has been assumed that client (especially new client) is unknown to the system.
2. In the proposed system, Kerberos authentication database at KDC is not required to maintain the user ID and password of all the users of the distributed system. Superhost accomplishes this task. Superhost maintains the record of all clients who may access services and thus required to authenticate. Instead of a big database for Kerberos authentication, a file is used to keep the secret keys for trusted intermediaries. It is easy to secure and makes the proposed system efficient.
3. In the proposed system, instead of providing the ID and IP address of Server system to access a particular service, TGS provides the reference of Agent system to client, as in message $m6$. Here, Servers are transparent to TGS. Agent works as another trusted intermediary that registers the services of servers. Client has to contact Agent before making any request to Server.
4. We are considering dual encryption at client and server side to maintain data confidentiality. A malicious user may alter the network address of a system to redirect the messages but due to both ID and IP address, messages cannot be decrypted.

3.2   Offsetting Kerberos Limitations

1. *Password Guessing Attack*: Kerberos has limitation of password guessing attack. Since no authentication is required to request a ticket in Kerberos and unencrypted password is send to Authentication Server, the attacker can guess password and request many tickets. In CTES model this problem is resolved with the help of Superhost. Here, client does not transfer his/her password and its location to Authentication Server. AS takes this information from Superhost that verifies the client in the distributed network. Along with this, AS compares the extracted client IP address and the IP address stored at Superhost to authenticate the client. Hence, CTES model works against password guessing attack.

2. *Service Registries*: Service registries are the unique identifiers for services running on servers. In Kerberos authentication, every service must have a service registry so that clients can identify the service on the network. If a service registry is not set for a service, it is difficult to locate that service. Kerberos authentication is not possible if these service registries are not managed properly. In our collaborative approach, agent has given the responsibility to manage and control these service registries keeping the knowledge of active and underloaded servers of the distributed network.

3. *Platform dependence*: Kerberos authentication relies on client functionality that is built in to the Windows Server 2003 Operating System, the Microsoft Windows XP Operating System and the Windows 2000 Operating System. It makes the use of Kerberos rigid. Our CTES model is implemented in JAVA RMI and Java has feature of platform independency.

4. *Access Authorization*: Kerberos gives the benefits only in terms of authentication rather than access authorization. This additional feature is handled in proposed CTES model using different controller entities. Kerberos (version 4 and version 5) and CTES model are briefly enumerated in Table 1.

Table 1. Kerberos version and CTES model

Particulars	Kerberos V4	Kerberos V5	CTES Model
Single Sign on	Yes	Yes	Yes
Password guessing	Yes	Yes	No
Requierment of database for storing key	Yes	Yes	No
Adequate service registry maintenance	No	No	Yes
Use of symmetric key	Yes	Yes	Yes
Opreating system dependency	Yes	Yes	No
Mutual authentication between entities	No	Yes	Yes
ne Access authorization	No	No	Yes

4   Conclusions

The CTES model is briefly explained in this paper along with the messages involved in the process of user authentication and authorization. A Kerberos-style authentication and authorization has been proposed through a collaborative approach. We have been able to show that the CTES model is more efficient than Kerberos despite of increase number of messages. We establish 3-level trust hierarchy for securing services and reduced the Kerberos authentication database that stores the details of all the users of distributed systems and their respective secret keys with comparable message exchange. Apart from this, we have also reduced the overhead of Kerberos in keeping track of active users of the network. For all this, coordinator systems are introduced in CTES model to make the approach effective than Kerberos. It has also been ascertained that the various messages and the functionality used in CTES model overcomes the drawbacks of Kerberos like password guessing attack, platform dependency, etc.. Kerberos (version 4 and version 5) and CTES model are briefly enumerated in Table 1.

References

1. Kumari, A., Mishra, S., Kushwaha, D.S. : A New Collaborative Trust Enhanced Security Model for Distributed Systems. International Journal of Computer Applications., (International Conference on Futuristic Computer Applications - ACM) Published by Foundation of Computer Science, vol. 1, no. 26, pp. 127-134 (Febraury 2010)
2. Kumari, A., Mishra, S., Kushwaha, D.S.: A Collaborative Trust Enhanced Security Model for Distributed Systems Services. In: International Conference on Advances in Communication, Network and Computing- CNC 2010, pp. 260–264. IEEE Computer Society, Los Alamitos (2010)
3. Schneider, F.B., Bellovin, S.M., Inouye, A.S.: Building Trustworthy Systems: Lessons from the PTN and Internet. IEEE Internet Computing (November-December 1999)
4. Tei-hua, W., Shi-wem, G.: An Improved method of Enhancing Kerberos Protocol Security. Journal of China Institute of Communications 25(6), 76–79 (2004)
5. Neuman, B.C., Yu, T., Hartman, S., Raeburn, K.: RFC 4120: The Kerberos Network Authentication Service (V5) (July 2005)
6. Lin, C., Varadharajan, V.: Trust Based Risk Management for Distributed System Security- A New Approach. In: Proceedings of the IEEE First International Conference on Availability, Reliability and Security (2006)
7. Hellewell, P.L., Horst, T.W., Seamons, K.E.: Extensible Preauthentication in Kerberos. In: 23rd Annual Computer Security Applications Conference, pp. 201–210 (2007)
8. Liu, P., Zong, R., Liu, S.: A New Model for Authentication and Authorization across Heterogeneous Trust-Domain. In: International Conference on Computer Science and Software Engineering, vol. 03, pp. 789–792. IEEE Computer Society, Los Alamitos (2008)
9. Neuman, B.C., Tso, T.: Kerberos: An Authentication Service for Computer Networks. IEEE Communications Magazine 32(9), 33–38 (1994)
10. Sirbu, M.A., Chuang, J.C.: Distributed Authentication in Kerberos using Public Key Cryptography. In: Symposium on Network and Distributed System Security, SNDSS, p. 134 (1997)

Self Monitoring Analysis and Reporting Technology (SMART) Copyback

Rajashekarappa[1] and Sunjiv Soyjaudah K.M.[2]

[1] Department of Computer Science and Engineering,
JSS Academy of Technical Education,
Bonne Terre, Vacoas, Mauritius
rajashekarmb@gmail.com
[2] Department of Electrical and Electronic Engineering,
University of Mauritius, Reduit, Mauritius

Abstract. Users have variety of requirements of data storage that can be addressed using Self Monitoring Analysis and Reporting Technology (SMART) Copyback. It is estimated that over 94% of all new information produced in the world is being stored on magnetic media, most of it on Physical Disks (PD). Moreover, larger population studies rarely have the infrastructure in place to collect health signals from components in operation, which is critical information for detailed failure analysis. It presents the data collected from detailed observations of a large disk drive population in production Internet services deployment. Analysis identifies several parameters from the Physical Disks (PD), self monitoring facility (SMART) that correlate highly with failures. Despite this high correlation conclude that models based on SMART parameters alone are unlikely to be useful for predicting individual drive failures. Surprisingly, it found that temperature and activity levels were much less correlated with Physical Disk (PD) failures.

Keywords: Firmware, Physical Disk, RAID, Rebuild, Self Monitoring Analysis and Reporting Technology.

1 Introduction

The purpose of this paper is to explain the SMART (Self Monitoring Analysis and Reporting Technology) Copyback feature being introduced into MegaRAID (Redundant Array of Inexpensive Disk) SAS (Serial Attached SCSI) products and provide the detailed design[1]. The drive vendors builds a logic in to the drives to make drives smart so that the user gets warning signal as a predictive failure whenever the drive is about to go bad for some reason. The drives built with this kind of logic are called SMART drives which is an acronym for Self-Monitoring Analysis and Reporting Technology. Example: The drive monitors the number of ECC (Error Checking and Correction) errors and based on the analysis data it can give predictive failure if the ECC error threshold exceeds internal to the drive.

K.R. Venugopal and L.M. Patnaik (Eds.): ICIP 2011, CCIS 157, pp. 463–469, 2011.

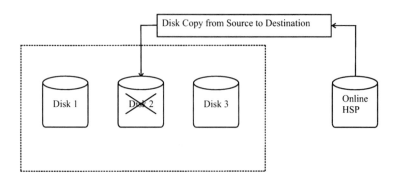

Fig. 1. Copyback data from a HSP drive to replaced failed drive

Copyback is a feature wherein a data from an ONLINE PD is copied to a destination Hotspare(HSP) or Unconfigured-Good PD. After successful completion, the destination Physical Disk(PD) becomes ONLINE (part of the array) while the source PD becomes Hotspare(HSP) or Unconfigured. Copyback can be initiated in any of the following ways:

– *Automatically by FW (Firmware) for revertible Hotspare(HSP)*: Copyback is automatically initiated on replacement of the failed PD whose arm position has now been taken by a Hotspare(HSP). The source of copyback would be the now ONLINE HSP drive and the destination, the newly replaced disk. After copyback completes, the ONLINE HSP is reverted back to HSP and the replaced drive becomes ONLINE [2].
– *Automatically by FW for SMART errors*: If a configured PD has SMART errors and there exists a HSP that can replace this drive, then copyback is started from the SMART error PD to the HSP. After copyback the source PD is marked Unconfigured Bad.
– *Manually by Applications*: The applications need to send a direct command with the source and destination PDs.

1.1   Terminologies

a) *Self-Monitoring Analysis and Reporting Technology (SMART)*: The drive vendors builds a logic in to the drives to make drives smart so that the user gets warning signal as a predictive failure whenever the drive is about to go bad for some reason. The drives built with this kind of logic are called SMART drives which is an acronym for Self-Monitoring Analysis and Reporting Technology. Example: The drive monitors the number of ECC (Error Checking and Correction) errors and based on the analysis data it can give predictive failure if the ECC error threshold exceeds internal to the drive.

b) *Hotspare*: Hotspare is a drive that is not part of any array, but can be commissioned to replace any failed disk of redundant array. The hotspare becomes part of the array once the rebuild is completed on it.

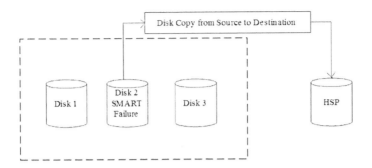

Fig. 2. Copyback data from SMART failure drive to HSP(hotspare)

c) *Rebuild*: Rebuild is process of reconstructing data on either a failed disk or a newly inserted disk or a hotspare in a RAID subsystem. The method to reconstruct depends on the RAID level. There are RAID Levels 1, 2, 3, 4, 5, 6, 10 etc., according to their requirements. In case of RAID1 the mirror copy is read from the other drive, for RAID5/RAID6, the peer drives are read and XORed to reconstruct the data on the rebuilding drive.

d) *Copy Back*: Copyback is a process for copying data from a given source disk to the destination disk. This operation is much faster than rebuild since it is a direct disk-to-disk copy unlike the rebuild where the data is read from peer drives and reconstructed.

e) *Firmware(FW)*: Firmware (FW) is a computer program that is embedded in Controller that operates the controller.

f) *Physical Disk(PD)*: A physical disk state is a property indicating the status of the disk. The physical drive states are: *Online* : Online A physical disk that can be accessed by the RAID controller and is part of the virtual disk.

Offline : A physical disk is offline when it is part of a virtual disk but its data is not accessible to the virtual disk. *U*nconfigured Good : A physical drive that is functioning normally but is not configured as a part of a Virtual Disk (VD) or as a hot spare. *HotSpare(HSP)*: A physical drive that is powered up and ready for use as a spare in case an online drive fails.

g) *Redundant Array of Independent Disks (RAID)*: is a technology that employs the simultaneous use of two or more hard disk drives to achieve greater levels of performance, reliability, and/or larger data volume sizes. When several physical disks are set up to use RAID technology, they are said to be in a RAID array [3]. The RAID controller supports RAID levels 0, 1, 5, 6, 10, 50, and 60.

RAID0: (striped disks) distributes data across several disks in a way that gives improved speed and full capacity, but all data on all disks will be lost if any one disk fails.

*RAID*1: (mirrored disks) could be described as a backup solution, using two (possibly more) disks that each store the same data so that data is not lost as long as one disk survives. Total capacity of the array is just the capacity of a single disk [4]. The failure of one drive, in the event of a hardware or software malfunction, does not increase the chance of a failure nor decrease the reliability of the remaining drives (second, third, etc.,).

*RAID*5: (striped disks with parity) combines three or more disks in a way that protects data against loss of any one disk; the storage capacity of the array is reduced by one disk.

The rest of the paper is organized as follows: Section 2 gives idea of design goal. Section 3 explains the implementation. Experimental observation and results are discussed in Section 4 and 5. Conclusion is made in Section 6.

2   Design

Copyback will use the rebuild rate which can be configured by the user to control host IO verses the rebuild/copyback operation. User can enable or disable copyback in the controller properties. There will be no MFC settings for copyback. SMARTer copyback can also be controlled via controller properties apart from revertible/DCMD copyback.

PD Allowed operations (startCopyback/stopCopyback) will have bits set by the firmware for the applications to expose copyback operations in the GUI. The firmware supports revertible hotspares at a controller level meaning if Ctrl-Prop.copybackDisabled is FALSE, then all HSPs are assumed revertible [5]. There is no control on a per HSP PD basis. Upon successful completion (automatic/manual) of copyback from the source ONLINE drive(previously HSP) to another drive(destination), the ONLINE hotspare will be reverted back to HSP.

Drives experiencing SMART errors will be a candidate for copyback source to an available best fit hot spare, if controller property SMARTerEnabled is TRUE. During SMARTer copyback, if any array becomes non-optimal(partially degraded/degraded) and there are no other HSPs other than copyback destination, copyback will be aborted and HSP commissioned for the array. No other background operations except rebuild are allowed on an array when copy back is active to avoid thrashing. However for rebuild on the same array, copyback will be aborted. Automatic copyback(revertible or SMARTer) will be restarted after rebuild is completed on the array. Log events to indicate copyback start, abort, progress and successful completion. Recovery of data for the destination drive due to errors on reads for the source drive will be handled similar to the host read commands. If the logical drive becomes non-optimal (partially degraded or degraded) due to source copyback drive failure, copyback will be aborted and rebuild will start on the destination copyback drive from PD. Copyback takes a higher priority over restoreHotspareOnInsertion(if both are enabled).

As of now We can not Enable SMART CopyBack without enable CopyBack function. So we were working on in implementing a independent switch to enable only SMART CopyBack. Without depending on the Normal Copyback functionality. The setting could be

CopyBack : Disabled

SMART CopyBack : Enabled.

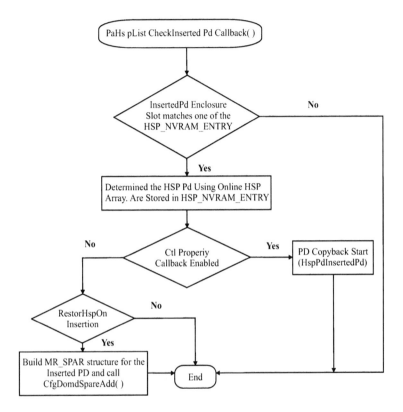

Fig. 3. Restore Hotspare on Insertion and Copyback Initiation for Revertible Hotspares

3   Implementation

Implementation of any software is always preceded by important decisions regarding selection of the platform, the language used, etc., These decisions are often influenced by several factors such as the real environment in which the system works the speed that is required, the security concerns, the memory requirements and other implementation specific details etc., Fig. 3 illustrate that Whenever a disk is inserted in failed HSP_NVRAM_ENTRY encl or slot, FW finds the disk whose previous state was hot spare using *onlineHspAr*, Once it finds the hot spare the copy back primitive is called with sourcePD set to hot spare drive and destination PD set to the inserted disk [6]. The flowchart in Fig. 3 describes the implementation.

4   Results and Discussion

Here we have taken snapshot as reference for the results. Fig. 4 shows that the drive vendors builds a logic in to the drives to make drives smart so that the user gets warning signal as a predictive failure whenever the drive is about to go bad for some reason. The drives built with this kind of logic are called SMART drives.

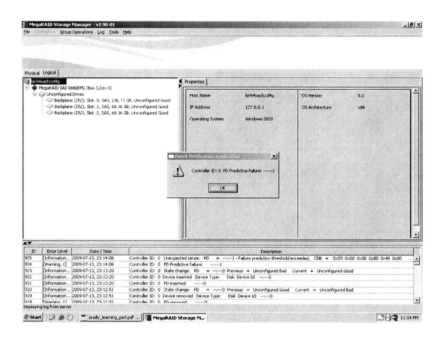

Fig. 4. SMART Drives showing Predictive Failure Message

5   Conclusions

In this study we report on the failure characteristics of consumer-grade Physical Disks(PD). The drive vendors builds a logic in to the drives to make drives smart so that the user gets warning signal as a predictive failure whenever the drive is about to go bad for some reason. The drives built with this kind of logic are called SMART drives which is an acronym for Self-Monitoring Analysis and Reporting Technology. Analysis is made possible by a new highly parallel health data collection and analysis infrastructure, and by the sheer size of our computing deployment.

Our results confirm the findings of some of the SMART Copyback parameters are well-correlated with higher failure probabilities. First errors in reallocation, offline reallocation, and probational counts are also strongly correlated to higher failure probabilities. Despite those strong correlations, we find that failure prediction models based on SMART Copyback parameters alone are a likely to be severely limited in their prediction accuracy, given that a large fraction of our failed Physical Disks have shown no SMART error signals whatsoever. This results suggests that SMART Copyback models are more useful in predicting trends for large aggregate populations than for individual components. It also suggests that powerful predictive models need to make use of signals beyond those provided by SMART Copyback.

References

1. Rob, P., Sean, D., Robert, G., Sean, Q.: Interpreting the data: Parallel Analysis with Sawzall. J. Scientific Programming, Special Issue on Grids and Worldwide Computing Programming Models and Infrastructure 13(4), 227–298 (2010)
2. Elerath, J.G., Shah, S.: Server Class Disk Drives: How Reliable are they? In: Proceedings of the Annual Symposium on Reliability and Maintainability, pp. 151–156 (January 2004)
3. Navathe, E.: Fundamentals of Database Systems, 3rd edn. Pearson Education, London (2003)
4. Sudarshan, S.K.: Database System Concepts, 3rd edn. McGraw-Hill, New York (2003)
5. Sommerville, L.: Software Engineering, 6th edn. Pearson Education Asia, London (2006)
6. Jalote, P.: An Integrated Approach to Software Engineering, 3rd edn. Springer publishers, Heidelberg (2005)

Hierarchical DHT to Efficiently Load Balancing in Dynamic Peer-to-Peer Environment

Kakulte Bhushan Santosh and Santhi Thilagam P.

Department of Computer Engineering, NITK Surathkal, Karnataka, India
b_kakulte@yahoo.com, santhisocrates@gmail.com

Abstract. There has been tremendous interest in emerging Peer-to-Peer (P2P) network overlays because they provide a good substrate for creating large-scale data sharing, content distribution and application-level multicast applications. P2P networks offer an efficient routing architecture that is massively scalable, self-organizing, and robust. It also provides fault tolerance. Structured peer-to-peer (P2P) such as Chord organizes peers into a flat overlay network and offer distributed hash table (DHT) functionality. Basically in this system, data is associated with keys and each peer is responsible for a subset of the keys. In Hierarchical DHTs peers are arranged into groups, and each group has its autonomous intra-group overlay network and lookup service. Compare to flat DHT systems, hierarchical systems can efficiently distribute the load among different peers. It is also observed that peers join and leave the P2P network frequently, which affect the structured network. In this paper, we are proposing the architecture which can efficiently balance the load among peers, also it can handle the frequent joining and leaving of peers in P2P system.

Keywords: Chord, Hierarchical DHT, Load Balancing, P2P System, Superpeer.

1 Introduction

Peer-to-Peer (P2P) applications are gaining increased popularity and deployment for their conspicuous advantages. As P2P network do not rely on dedicated servers, it is free from single point of failure and bandwidth bottleneck. P2P network has advantages of scalability, reliability, self-organizing and resistance to attack like DOS to some extent. P2P networks can be categorized as structured and unstructured overlays based on topology. In un-structured P2P network the overlay topology is completely unrelated to the placement of content while in structured networks the overlay topology is tightly controlled and files are placed at precisely specified locations based on the key generated by hash. In unstructured P2P overlays, such as Gnutella, Kazza, peers use flooding or random walks to resolve queries. These routing techniques can be used for complex searches since they are not limited to indexed data in the network. The main problem of these systems is that search cost does not scale well, as it grows linearly with the

K.R. Venugopal and L.M. Patnaik (Eds.): ICIP 2011, CCIS 157, pp. 470–475, 2011.

size of the network. In structured P2P system, node is responsible for a certain set of items and the system has an appropriate protocol for efficient routing of queries for items. The design objective of these overlays is to have every node store pointers to certain other nodes in the system such that a query for an item reaches the destination node in as few hops as possible.

Hierarchical P2P systems, offer a range of benefits in comparison with their flat structured system. They fit better the underlying physical network and are more appropriate for heterogeneous environments. The hierarchical distributed hash table (DHT) systems are generally organised into two layers, a superlayer built by superpeers and a leaf-peer layer built by rest of peers. The superlayer is implemented using a DHT algorithm such as chord. Each superpeer responsible for managing a group of leaf peers. Superpeer also responsible for delivering queries on behalf of the leaf peers in its group.

Chord is structured DHT protocol that organizes peers into a flat overlay network and offers DHT functionality. In the chord protocol each peer has to maintain finger table (routing information) to efficiently route the query, also it has to maintain successor info for repairing chord ring. As a node joins or leaves the system, the finger table must be created on this node; the affected finger table entry on several other nodes must be modified accordingly. To make the system work properly, each node periodically send message to its neighbours to check their availability.

In large system this communication overhead can be very high. In the environment where node joins and leaves very frequently, system generates considerable routing information traffic. Besides this, in conventional chord protocol it is assumed that all the nodes (peers) have equal capability, but in real scenario thats not the case. In reality each node has different bandwidth, CPU power, storage capacity, uptime in P2P overlay and so on.

In this paper we attempt to present an improved chord algorithm using hierarchical architecture. Propose architecture can efficiently balance load among different peers. It also considers the frequent joining and leaving of the node, so that there will be minimum affect on existing routing information which in terns reduces the network traffic.

The rest of this paper is structured as follows. Section 2 describes related work in hierarchical architecture. Section 3 discusses the proposed architecture. Section 4 shows the simulation and evaluation results of proposed architecture. In section 5 conclusion is presented.

2   Related Work

There is the growing interest in hierarchical DHTs. Although many hierarchical DHTs have been proposed in the literature, most of the works addressing the problem of building and configuring hierarchical P2P networks deal with un-structured networks and generally it do not consider frequent joining and leaving of nodes in network. In our work, we basically concentrate on the load balancing and peers behaviour of frequent joining and leaving the P2P network.

Recent Hierarchical DHT to efficiently Load Balancing 3 work has extensively examined hierarchical architectures. They are described below.

[1,2,3,4] focus on reducing the network traffic. It is influenced by Kazza which is un-structured P2P system. It considers three state of node in system such as super node, ordinary node and index node. It assumes that superpeers are stable and static.

[5] is two-tier chord system. It maintains the chord ring at the top tier. Top tier has the responsibility of handling request from tier-2. In this algorithm author did not consider frequent joining and leaving of peers. [6] solve multi attribute query and range using hierarchical architecture. It uses clustering phe- nomenon.

Based on responsibility assign to node, [7] consider three states of nodes such as temp, stable and fully stable. In this architecture, temporary node can leave anytime, they have minimum responsibility. Problem with this architecture is that it does not consider load balancing, also it assume stable and static super- peer. [8] provides inter-operation between different domain required to provide global multimedia service. It considers key structure such as prefix domain iden- tity and suffix represent node identity in domain.

3   Proposed Architecture

In this paper, we designed novel algorithm for chord overlay protocol that can perform efficiently even if in dynamic environment. In this architecture, we will consider 3-tier hierarchy see Fig. 1. Tier-3 represents new peers which send request to join. Tier-2 represents leaf peers which has less capability. Tier-1 represents the superpeers which maintain chord ring. Each tier has different responsibility. All the peers will start from tier-3 where node tries to connect with overlay (chord ring). When bootstrap node receive join request it will transfer that request to responsible node (superpeer) in tier-1. After receiving the request superpeer wait for some time which is stabilization time for node and then promote that node to tier-2 (leaf nodes).

When query arrives at tier-2 nodes then query then query will be transfer to its superpeer to take care of that query. Result of that query will be send back to original node where query had generated.

The basic idea behind our load balancing algorithm is that each superpeer has the responsibility to maintain routing information (finger table entries) for tier-1, tier-2 (leaf peers) interval and tier-2 information in terms of leaf peers which are directly connected to this superpeer.

When superpeer say S1 receive the request, it checks whether requested key is within its range of tier-2 interval. If yes, then it route's the query to exact peer in tier-2, otherwise S1 pass that request to the superpeer S2 by looking into its finger table entry.

3.1   Load Balancing

When superpeer S1 reached its maximum capacity either because of joining request or because more and more routing request, it initiates election algorithm

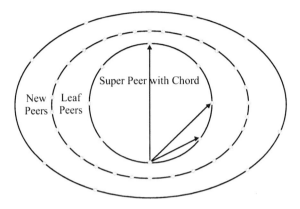

Fig. 1. An example showing probability of false positive

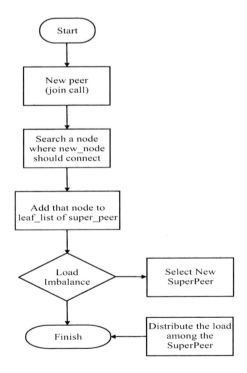

Fig. 2. An example showing probability of false positive

among the leaf peers in tier-2 which are connected to superpeer S1. For election of new superpeer we will find the mid of the interval say *(a, b)* for which S1 is responsible. In the second step, we will choose the peer from interval *(mid, b)* with maximum capacity in terms of bandwidth and processing power. Let new superpeer be S2 then we assign leaf in the interval *(mid, b)* to this new superpeer. Also we will update interval of S1 to *(a, mid)*. As new node is added to tier-1 which is chord ring it will repair it by stabilize call. In this way we can achieve the load balancing among the peers as well as it will generate minimum ring maintenance traffic. (Fig. 2.)

4   Simulation and Result

To check the performance of improved architecture, we did simulation. For this purpose we used oversim simulator. Oversim is an open source overlay network simulation framework over Omnet++, which contain several models for structured (e.g., chord, pastry) and un-structured P2P protocol. We compare the result of proposed architecture with existing chord. Fig. 3. shows one of the graphs.

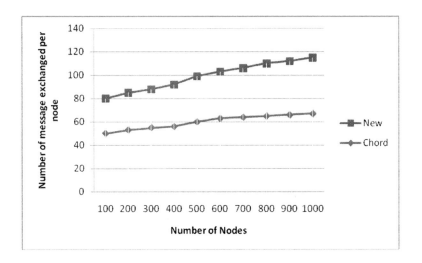

Fig. 3. An example showing probability of false positive

As we mentioned, when node joins the system, the corresponding routing information must be created. Also when node leaves system or fail, the affected routing information must change. When this happen very frequently, cost of maintenance (message need to communicate) will be very high. In our evaluation we compare this crucial parameter as in Fig. 3. From graph we can easily identify that improved architecture considerably reduce cost of maintaining overlay.

5 Conclusions

The traditional chord protocol has drawback in terms of ring maintenance traffic and load balancing. In our work, we analyze this problem and proposed improved algorithm using hierarchical structure. We discuss how this algorithm handles the load balancing and how node maintains the routing information at different node. To evaluate the performance of our improved algorithm we give a performance comparison with the standard chord protocol from the aspect of routing state maintenance overhead. From result we can see the improved algorithm perform better especially in maintaining routing state information. Propose architecture also do efficient load balancing among different peers.

References

1. Lupu, M., Ooi, B.C., Tay, Y.C.: Paths to Stardom: Calibrating the Potential of a Peer-Based Data Management System. In: Proceedings of the 2008 ACM SIGMOD International Conference on Management of Data, SIGMOD 2008, pp. 265–278 (2008)
2. Zoels, S., Despotovic, Z., Kellerer, W.: On Hierarchical DHT Systems: An Analytical Approach for Optimal Designs. Journal Computer Communications 31(3) (February 2008)
3. Artigas, M.S., Lpez, P.G., Ahull, J.P., Skarmeta, A.F.: Cyclone: A Novel Design Schema for Hierarchical DHTS. In: Proceedings of the Fifth IEEE International Conference on Peer-To-Peer Computing (P2P 2005), Konstanz, Germany (September 2005)
4. Zhang, Y.X., Luo, H.B., Zhang, H.K.: Load Balancing for Two-Tier Chord System. IEEE Electronics Letters 46(10), 685–686 (2010) ISSN: 0013-5194
5. Tian, Z., Wen, X., Sun, Y.: Improved Bamboo Algorithm Based on Hierarchical Network Model. In: ISECS International Colloquium Computing, Communication, Control, and Management, CCCM 2009 (2009)
6. Zhang, H., Ma, H.: An Efficient Hierarchical DHT-Based Complex Query for Multimedia Information. In: 2007 IEEE International Conference Multimedia and Expo (July 2007)
7. Shrivastava, B.K., Khataniar, G., Goswami, D.: Perfor- mance Enhancement in Hierarchical Peer-To-Peer Systems. In: Second International Conference on Communication Systems Software and Middleware, COMSWARE (January 2007)
8. Martinez-Yelmo, I., Bikfalvi, A., Guerrero, C.: Enabling Global Multi- Media Distributed Services Based on Hierarchical DHT Overlay Networks. In: The Second International Conference on Next Generation Mobile Applications, Services and Technologies, NGMAST 2008 (September 2008)

Remote Scan Using Secure Automated Client Server Model

Venkateshwarlu Gogikaru and Mahendra Pratap Singh

Department of Computer Science and Engineering
National Institute of Technology Karnataka, Surathkal, India
{gvenkateshwarlu7,mahoo15}@gmail.com

Abstract. In recent years, attackers gain entry into computer systems frequently with the help of Rootkit's. Detection of these Rootkits is not a simple task in early days. To detect Rootkits we need to run many scanning tools manually. This is not feasible many times and it is time consuming process for each client. We propose a secure automated client/server model to scan remote clients present in local area network. This model allows us to run the scanning tools automatically and periodically, to know the Rootkits present in the client system. For our experiment purpose we automated *RootkitRevealer* tool.

Keywords: Client Server Model, Rootkits, Remote Scan.

1 Introduction

Attackers wish to attack the systems with the help of malwares like viruses, Trojans horses, spywares, rootkits and etc.. Among these rootkit is the one sophisticated method of attack. Important feature of the rootkit is hiding their presence in a system. This makes detection of these malware much difficult. Recently, a number of attacks have surfaced all related to the rootkits with more sophisticated technology. One among them is Stuxnet [1], which targeted on industrial systems.

The term rootkit has been around for more than 15 years. Rootkit is a program that provides the means to create an undetectable presence on a computer [2]. Rootkits are not inherently "bad," and they are not always used by the "bad guys." It is important to understand that a rootkit is just a technology. But now a day's many bad guys using this technology to gain access into computer systems in an organization to access the important information.

Most of the attackers wish to gain entry into computer systems frequently by injecting illicit functionality to maintain control, gather information, or neutralize the defenses of the target system, among other objectives. While past attacks often focused on modifications to userlevel libraries or system binaries, the operating system kernel is an increasingly popular target from many days. Attackers typically modify the kernel using these rootkits either to implement their illicit functionality directly or indirectly.

K.R. Venugopal and L.M. Patnaik (Eds.): ICIP 2011, CCIS 157, pp. 476–481, 2011.

To detect these rootkits many companies developed different rootkit detection tools (RDTs) [3]. But we have to run all these tools manually. When there is large number of systems in an Organization, this is not possible many times. To achieve this we need an automated scanning mechanism.

To achieve this we proposed and implemented secure automated client server model with the help of RootKitRevealer (RKR) tool. RKR is one of the very first advanced rootkit detection tool. RKR successfully detects many persistent rootkits including AFX, Vanquish and HackerDefender [4]. This tool is very pretty simple to use, no installation required, so we use this tool in our experiment. In this experiment secure communication is maintained with the help of SSL in client server communication.

The rest of the paper is structured as follows. In section 2, tells the motivation of work, In Section 3, we give overview of SSL/TLS between client and server. In Section 4, we present the proposed model. In Section 4, the detailed implementation issues are discussed, and Section 5 concludes.

2   Motivation

Now days many company people developing different products and tools to detect the malwares. But these tools are not supporting the needs of an organization. For a person (say administrator) to detect malwares in an organization which consists of many systems is not a simple task. To do so, administrator has to install different tools in every system manually and scan them which is not feasible many times. This motivated us to make an automated model, to perform scan, updating the software and other things, in all the systems present in an Organization from a single system.

3   Overview of SSL/TLS

This section describes the SSL/TLS handshake protocol [5],[6]. In the remainder of the paper, the term "SSL" is used to refer to both SSL and TLS standards. SSL is the most widely used protocol to ensure secure communication in a network. It is typically employed by web servers to protect electronic transactions. SSL uses the RSA cryptosystem during an initial client/server handshake to establish a shared symmetric key for use during an SSL session

3.1   SSL Handshake Protocol Description

The simplest version of the SSL handshake (key-establishment) protocol [5],[6] consists of two communication rounds that contain the following messages and computations:

1. Client sends a "client hello" message to server. This indicates that client wants to initialize a SSL/TLS session and the message includes the cipher suites client supports and a random nonce r_c.

2. Server responds with a "server hello" message that includes server's public-key certificate and random nonce r_s. It also specifies server's choice of cipher suite from among client's candidates.
3. Client chooses a secret random 48-byte pre-master secret x and computes the shared master secret k by inputting values x, r_c, r_s into hash function f. It then encrypts x with the server's RSA public key and attaches the cipher text to a "client key exchange" message that is sent to server.
4. Server decrypts the pre-master secret using its private RSA key, and uses it to compute the shared master secret as f(x, r_c, r_s). To conclude the handshake, server sends a "server finished" message that includes a keyed hash of all handshake messages.

According to SSL specifications Diffie-Hellman also supported [5], like RSA. RSA is typically employed by web servers to protect electronic transactions. Based on the application specific method has to follow.

4   Proposed Automated Client-Server Model

The automated (Proposed) system is based on the TCP/IP based Client-Server Model. As shown in the Fig. 1 one of the system works as the server and remaining all other systems work as the clients. Whenever client is up, SSL handshake done with the server and secure connection establishes between them. Our model includes 3 phases: (1) Grouping phase, (2) Working phase, (3) Regrouping phase.

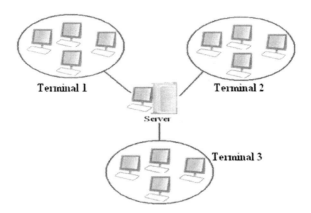

Fig. 1. Proposed Client-Server Model

4.1   Grouping Phase

This phase is meant for dividing the total number of clients in to the groups so that administrator can work easily on them [7]. As shown in Fig. 1, each group consists of approximately equal number of clients. In this server follows a strategy, in which it uses a threshold value $'x'$. Where $'x'$ represents maximum number of clients a group can accommodate. If the number of clients is less than or equal to the threshold value, it treats the total number of clients into a group. If the number of clients is greater than threshold value it divides the clients into groups. The value of 'x' depends up on the number of clients which connects to the server at a time, which is set by the administrator.

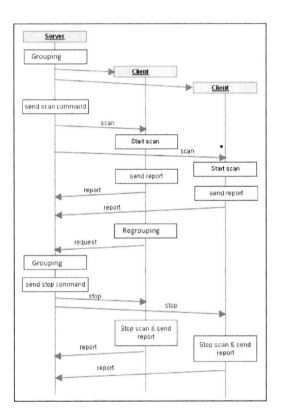

Fig. 2. Process of Automated Client-Server Model

4.2   Working Phase

Fig. 2 shows the working phase of the automated client-server model. In this phase administrator from server system sends scan, stop or update command to the selected or all the clients in a group. When client receives any of this command, sends acknowledgement back to the server. After receiving the scan command starts the scanning of computer with the help of tool, after finishing the scan it sends output file to the server. If administrator wants to stop the scanning, sends stop command to that particular client, whenever client receives stop command it stops the scanning and sends the output file back to the server. When it receives update command it checks for any updates of the tool, if updates are there it updates the tool. At server side administrator has to check the output files to find the malware presence.

4.3   Regrouping Phase

Whenever number of clients in a particular group becomes less than $x/2$, server combines all the clients and adjusts the $'x'$ value and divides it into number of groups.

5   Implementation and Working

Proposed model has been implemented with the help of RKR tool. Presently, this tool has to run manually in each system. Proposed model automate this tool in all the systems (clients) present in an organization from the server machine. As per our proposed model, we developed TCP/IP based server and client programs in java. Secure communication between client and server is maintained with the help of SSL.

At first client program has to be installed on all the computers manually. Whenever client is up it will connect to the server. Whenever client connects with the server, it receives the client information like; IP address, host name, user name, and MAC address, and display this information on graphical user interface (GUI) as shown in the Fig. 3. All clients divide into Groups as stated in the model.

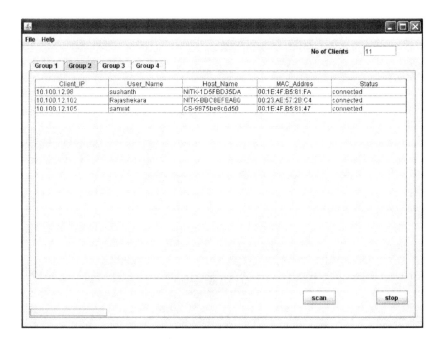

Fig. 3. Server side GUI

Administrator with the help of GUI selects the clients and sends the scan/stop command. When client receives any command it sends acknowledgement back to the server. Whenever a client receives the scan command, RKR tool starts the scanning of the system and sends output file back the server when it finish the scan. When a client receives the stop command, RKR tool ends the process and sends output file back to the server. Administrator has to analyze this output files to find the rootkit's presence in the particular system and has to take proper action.

6 Conclusions

Rootkit is the technique whereby malware, including viruses, spyware, and trojans, attempt to hide their presence from spyware blockers, antivirus, and system management utilities. To detect these rootkits many tools are available, but we need to run these tools manually. For administrator, it is not possible to safeguard all the systems which are present in an organization, with the help of these tools. In this paper we proposed a secure automated client server model to automate this type of tools. We applied our proposed model on RootkitRevealer tool.

References

1. Stuxnet, http://en.wikipedia.org/wiki/Stuxnet
2. Greg, H., Jamie, B.: Rootkits: Subverting the Windows Kernel. Addison-Wesley Professional, Reading (2005)
3. Todd, A., Benson, J., Peterson, G., Franz, T., Stevens, M., Raines, R.: In: Craiger, P., Shenoi, S. (eds.) IFIP International Federation for Information Processing. Advances in Digital Forensics III, vol. 242, pp. 89–105. Springer, Boston (2007)
4. Cogswell, B., Russinovich, M.: RootkitRevealer v1.71, http://technet.microsoft.com/en-us/sysinternals/bb897445.aspx
5. Network Working Group, RFC 2246 - The TLS Protocol Version 1.0 Internet RFC/STD/FYI/BCP Archives (1999), http://www.faqs.org/rfcs/rfc2246.html
6. Claude, C., Einar, M., Gene, T.: Improving Secure Server Performance by Rebalancing SSL/TLS Handshakes. In: ASIACCS 2006, pp. 26–34 (2006)
7. Kojima, K., Kawamata, W., Matsuo, H., Ishigame, M.: Network based Parallel Genetic Algorithm using Client-Server Model. In: Proceedings of the 2000 Congress Evolutionary Computation, vol. 1, pp. 244–250 (2000)

A Joint DWT-DCT Based Robust Digital Watermarking Algorithm for Ownership Verification of Digital Images

R.H. Laskar, Madhuchanda Choudhury, Krishna Chakraborty, and Shoubhik Chakraborty

Department of Electronics and Communication Engineering
National Institute of Technology Silchar, Silchar-788010, Assam, India
rabul18@yahoo.com

Abstract. In this paper, a robust digital image watermarking algorithm based on joint Discrete Wavelet Transform and Discrete Cosine Transform (DWT-DCT) is proposed. The proposed system provides imperceptibility and higher robustness against common signal processing attacks. A binary watermarked image is embedded in certain subbands of a 3-level DWT transformed coefficients of a host image. Then, DCT coefficients of each selected DWT subband is computed. A randomly generated two-dimensional key is used to encrypt the watermark. This 2D key provides security to the image and ownership copyrights. The PN-sequences of the encrypted watermark bits are embedded in the coefficients of the corresponding DCT middle frequencies providing higher security. In extraction stage, the same approach as that of the embedding process is used to extract the DCT middle frequencies of each subband. Finally, correlation between mid-band coefficients and PN-sequences is calculated to determine watermark bit which is again post-processed by the two-dimensional key generated to derive the actual watermark. Experimental results show that the proposed method based on joint procedure of DWT-DCT may be used for watermarking the digital images.

Keywords: Discrete Cosine Transform, Encryption, Kernel, PN-Sequences, Watermarking, Wavelet.

1 Introduction

In recent years, access to multimedia data has become much easier due to the rapid growth of the Internet. While this is usually considered an improvement of everyday life, it also makes unauthorized copying and distribution of multimedia data much easier, therefore presenting a challenge in the field of copyright protection. Digital watermarking, which is inserting copyright information into the data, has been proposed to solve the problem. During recent years, digital watermarking has drawn a lot of attention as a solution of this problem [1,2,3,4,5,6]. In general, a digital watermarking algorithm tries to adhere some copyright information to the original data. Although watermarks can be visible, invisible

K.R. Venugopal and L.M. Patnaik (Eds.): ICIP 2011, CCIS 157, pp. 482–491, 2011.
© Springer-Verlag Berlin Heidelberg 2011

watermarks are usually preferred. Hence, this paper, like many others, will focus on invisible watermarking schemes. Another requirement for digital watermarking algorithms is robustness. In other words, the watermark should survive the common signal processing operations and counterfeit attempts. A few digital image watermarking schemes have been proposed in the 1990s [1,2,3,4,5,6]

The early algorithms usually require the subtraction of the original image from the test image to detect the watermark [1,2,3,4]. Recent work showed that for ownership verification, the above subtraction would create severe problems [5]. Basically, an "original" image can either be the original image or obtained by subtracting the counterfeiter's watermark from the original image, and there is no way to distinguish one from the other. Therefore, a watermarking algorithm for ownership verification should avoid performing such subtraction in the detection process. Most of the papers in the literature on digital watermarking are proposing new algorithms. Some of these algorithms, although very clever, cannot be used in a practical system. Therefore, before proposing our algorithm, we want to discuss the requirements of a practical image watermarking system for ownership verification of digital images.

The rest of this paper is organized as follows: Section 2 discusses the necessary features that a real world digital watermarking system should posses for ownership verification. Section 3 discusses the proposed watermarking algorithm. Section 4 presents the simulated results and performance evaluation of the proposed system. The conclusions are given in section 5.

2   Requirements of Practical Watermarking Systems

In a practical digital image watermarking system for ownership verification, there should be at least two parties: the owner of the images and a legal authority. The responsibilities for maintaining security of the digital images is divided between these two parties. The first question is what each of the two parties should store. We begin with the storage requirement for the legal authority. The need to register the watermark is obvious. Otherwise, if one can claim anything to be his watermark, he can claim the ownership of any image. However, we do not think that it is practical to require the registration of each image. A system only makes sense when it serves a fairly large number of owners. Each of these owners possesses many images and keeps producing new images every day. So, the total number of images will be huge, and the storage of all the images is too expensive. Besides the storage problem, when a new image comes in, the authority also needs to check all the registered images to make sure that it has not been registered. This is expensive as well. Therefore, even if the registration of each image is possible, it will increase the cost of the registration. Some of the owners may give up the registration process and few others may register some of their images because of the expenses involved. In general, a copyright protection system works better when everybody complies because there is less ambiguity. On the other hand, if only the watermark requires registration, an owner can register one or several watermarks at the beginning and only pay a very small annual fee. The burden on the authority also decreases. The storage requirement is much lower, and the authority only needs to make sure the watermark of a new user does not coincide with the old ones. Then, what should the owner store? It seems that the owner only needs to store the images. However, we do not think that it is so simple. We model the watermarking insertion procedure by, $X' = X + W$, where X' is the watermarked image, X is the original image, and W is the added watermark. The owner will have private keys. Basically, even the authority itself cannot remove the watermarks without the private keys. The second question is who should perform the watermark detection procedure. There is no doubt that the authority should perform the detection procedure and provide testimony when a copyright dispute is taken to the court. However, it is not realistic to ask the authority to detect all the copyright violations in the first place, because it would require that the legal authority process all images and try to detect the watermarks of all owners in an image. This is very resource consuming and will increase the operation cost dramatically.

Particularly, if the system provides owners private control of the watermark, this may become impossible. A more realistic way is that the owner should first try to find any counterfeiters of his images. Because the owner is more familiar with his images, it is usually easy for him to recognize the images even if they have been manipulated. In addition, the number of images and the number of watermarks of one owner are much smaller than those of all owners. When the owner is suspicious of an image, he/she may perform the watermark detection procedure on that image. If he/she detects his/her watermark in the image, he/she will take the matter to the court of law. The court may ask the authority to verify the owner's claim, and the owner will provide the private key for the particular image to enable the authority to perform the detection procedure. The cost of such verification can be easily added to the punishment of the counterfeiter if the court decides that the copyright violation has really been taken place. Therefore, the operating cost of the system will stay low.

Now, we discuss what kind of algorithm the system should use. It is apparent that the algorithm(s) used by the system should be standardized. Most of the algorithms proposed in the literature use some sort of pattern recognition algorithm in the detection procedure. For any algorithm, there will be a probability of false alarm. In other words, given an arbitrary un-watermarked image, there is a chance that the detection procedure will claim that there is a watermark in it. To make a watermarking algorithm work, such false alarm probability should be very small. If the owner uses any algorithm and when a case is taken to the court of law, a lot of resources will be spent to verify if the false alarm probability of the owner's algorithm is small enough. To avoid doing this on a case by case basis, the algorithm(s) should be standardized. The probability of false alarm is known and consented to by all parties. Then question arises, what should a standardized algorithm satisfy? Besides the common requirements of invisible watermarks and robustness, it has already been mentioned that the algorithm should not depend on the subtraction of the original image in the detection procedure. The algorithm should have the ability to create a private key for each image and insert the watermark according to the key. However, this also adds another requirement for the algorithm. Given an arbitrary un-watermarked image, the owner must not be able to create a key so that he can detect his watermark in the image. In other words, there should not exist a reverse engineering algorithm to create the key based on the image.

The distribution of responsibilities shared by both the parties are summarized as follows:

The legal authority:
1. Stores the watermarks.
2. Does not store all the images.
3. Performs the final watermark detection.
4. Does not search for copyright violations in the first place.
5. Cannot remove the watermark from the Image.

The owner:
1. Stores images and private keys.
2. Searches for counterfeiters of his images.

The algorithm:
1. Should be standardized.
2. Achieves watermark invisibility.
3. Achieves robustness.
4. Does not require subtraction of the original image in watermark detection.
5. Gives owner private control of the watermark.
6. Prevents reverse engineering of the private keys.

3   Proposed Watermarking Algorithm

The proposed watermarking algorithm based on joint DWT-DCT based approach is discussed in this section. The algorithm consists of two procedures: watermark embedding and watermark extraction. The watermark embedding procedure starts with the generation of a random matrix. The random matrix equal to the size of the watermark (i.e., nxn, say), is generated. The original watermark is now XORed with this randomly generated matrix and a new encrypted version of the watermark is generated. The randomly generated matrix act as a key for the owner. For the sake of convenience, the encrypted watermark is mentioned as watermark in the rest of the paper. The watermarking is implemented by altering the wavelet coefficients of middle frequency subbands of a 3-level decomposed host image, followed by the application of the DCT on the selected subbands.

3.1   Watermark Embedding

The watermarking process is implemented by applying DWT to the host image, and then performing the DCT to the selected DWT subbands. The technique adopted by different DWT-based watermarking methods, is to embed the water-mark in the middle frequency subbands HL_{x3} and LH_{x3} (where, x may be 1 or 2). This is because, the modification of mid-frequency subbands is better in the perspective of imperceptibility and robustness. Consequently, HL_{x3} and LH_{x3} subbands in level three are chosen for performing DCT on them. If X denotes a vector of mid-band coefficients of the DCT transformed block and X' denotes a vector of the modified DCT coefficients of the same block after embedding, then the embedded sequence X' is given by Eq. 1.

$$X' = \begin{cases} \alpha * PN0 & \text{watermak bit } \bar{0}; \\ \alpha * PN1, & \text{watermak bit } \bar{1}. \end{cases} \tag{1}$$

The steps involved in the process of embedding the watermark in a host image is summarized in Table 1.

3.2 Watermark Extraction

The flowchart for watermark extraction is shown in Fig. 4, and the algorithm is described in details in Table 2. It is to be noted that the joint DWT-DCT algorithm is a blind watermarking algorithm, and thus the original host image is not required to extract the watermark.

Fig. 1. Four DWT subbands of the original image in level 2, to apply DWT to another level (shown in gray)

Fig. 2. Four selected multi-resolution DWT coefficient sets of the host image in level 3 (shown in gray)

4 Results and Discussion

The test images used for this study are Lena, Airplane, Baboon, Owl and Peppers. All the gray scale images are of size 512x512. The performance are judged in terms of visual observation and peak signal to noise ratio (PSNR) for both the watermarked image and the extracted watermark. The PSNR value for the gray images is given by:

$$PSNR = 10 \log_{10} \left(\frac{I_{MAX}^2}{MSE} \right). \tag{2}$$

Table 1. Steps for embedding the watermark

1. Perform DWT on the host image to decompose it into four non-overlapping multi-resolution coefficient sets: LL_1, HL_1, LH_1 and HH_1.
2. Perform DWT again on two HL_1 and LH_1 subbands to get eight smaller subbands and choose four coefficient sets: HL_{12}, LH_{12}, HL_{22} and LH_{22} as shown in Fig. 1.
3. Perform DWT again on four subbands: HL_{12}, LH_{12}, HL_{22} and LH_{22} to get sixteen smaller subbands and choose four coefficient sets: HL_{13}, LH_{13}, HL_{23} and LH_{23} as shown in Fig. 2.
4. Divide four coefficient sets: HL_{13}, LH_{13}, HL_{23} and LH_{23} into 4x4 blocks.
5. Perform DCT to each block in the chosen coefficient sets (HL_{13}, LH_{13}, HL_{23} and LH_{23}).
6. Re-formulate the grey-scale watermark image of size nxn into a vector of zeros and ones.
7. Generate two pseudo random sequences. One sequence is used to embed the watermark bit 0 (PN_0) and the other sequence is used to embed the watermark bit 1 (PN_1). Number of elements in each of the two pseudo-random sequences must be equal to the number of mid-band elements of the DCT-transformed, DWT coefficient sets. These two pseudo-random sequences (PN_0) and (PN_1) are passed to the receiver side.
   The mid-band is chosen and replaced because of the following two reasons:
   (i)It provides additional resistance to lossy compression techniques.
   (ii)Avoid significant modification of the cover image.
8. Embed the two pseudo random sequences, PN_0 and PN_1, with a gain factor α in the DCT transformed 4x4 blocks of the selected DWT coefficient sets of the host image. Instead of embedding in all coefficients of the DCT block, it applied only to the mid-band DCT coefficients. If we denote X as a vector of the mid-band coefficients of the DCT transformed block, then embedding is done as Equation 1.
9. Perform inverse DCT (IDCT) on each block after its mid-band coefficients have been modified to embed the watermark bits as described in the previous step.
10. Perform the inverse DWT (IDWT) on the DWT transformed image, including the modified coefficient sets, to produce the watermarked host image. The whole procedure is elucidated in Fig. 3.

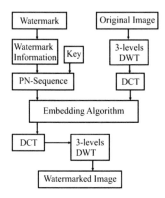

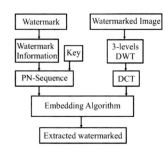

Fig. 3. Joint DWT-DCT water-mark embedding procedure

Fig. 4. Joint DWT-DCT water-mark extraction procedure

Table 2. Steps for extraction of the watermark

1. Perform DWT on the watermarked image to decompose it into four non-overlapping multi-resolution coefficient sets: LL_1, HL_1, LH_1 and HH_1.
2. Perform DWT again on two subbands HL_1 and LH_1 to get eight smaller subbands and choose four coefficient sets: HL_{12}, LH_{12}, HL_{22} and LH_{22} as shown in Fig. 2 and decompose each of the subbands to obtain the subbands HL_{13}, LH_{13}, HL_{23} and LH_{23}.
3. Divide four coefficient sets: HL_{13}, LH_{13}, HL_{23} and LH_{23} into 4x4 blocks.
4. Perform DCT on each block in the chosen coefficient sets: HL_{13}, LH_{13}, HL_{23} and LH_{23}.
5. The two pseudo-random sequences used to embed the watermark bit 0, (PN_0) and the watermark bit 1, (PN_1) are reused again.
6. For each block in the coefficient sets: $HL_{13}, LH_{13}, HL_{23}$ and LH_{23}, calculate the correlation between the mid-band coefficients and the two generated pseudo random sequences PN_0 and PN_1. If the correlation with the PN_0 was higher than the correlation with PN_1,then the extracted bit is considered 0, otherwise the extracted bit is considered 1.
7. The 2-dimensional nxn matrix is reconstructed using the extracted bits. This is the encrypted watermark.
8. The two dimensional key retained by the owner is XORed with the encrypted watermark to obtain the actual extracted watermark.
9. The similarity between the original and extracted watermark is calculated.

where I_{MAX} is the maximum pixel value of the component of the vector pixel of the original image. MSE represents the mean square error between the original image and the filtered image, which is given by:

$$MSE = \frac{1}{MNS} \left[\sum_{p=1}^{M} \sum_{q=1}^{N} \sum_{t=1}^{S} (Y_{p,q,t} - Y'_{p,q,t})^2 \right]. \tag{3}$$

Performances are compared for both the watermarked images and the watermark extracted images for different values of α. The α is the gain factor in the DCT transformed 4x4 blocks of the selected DWT coefficient sets of the host image and is chosen as one of the parameter for performance comparison. From the experimental results (shown in Table 3 and Table 4) and visual observation (as shown in Fig. 5 and Fig. 6), it has been observed that the performance of the proposed algorithm for watermarking is satisfactory. Moreover, by choosing a suitable value of α, it has been observed that the algorithm work for different variety of gray scale images. However, a trade-off has to be made between the quality of the watermarked image and the extracted watermark while choosing the value of α. Higher value of α degrades the quality of the watermarked image but gives a better extracted watermark image and vice versa. A value of 10 can be selected for α for acceptable quality of the images. Abbreviations used in Table 3 and Table 4, are as follows:

IMG: IMAGE; BAB: BABOON; PEP: PEPPERS; AIR: AIRPLANE.

Table 3. Performance comparison of the watermarked image for different values of α applied to five different test images

IMG	$\alpha = 5$ MSE	$\alpha = 5$ PSNR	$\alpha = 8$ MSE	$\alpha = 8$ PSNR	$\alpha = 10$ MSE	$\alpha = 10$ PSNR
LENA	1.1747	47.432	1.4644	46.474	1.7294	45.75
OWL	0.5316	50.875	0.8742	48.715	1.0534	47.905
BAB	2.4503	44.239	2.7664	43.712	3.0633	43.269
PEP	0.6882	49.754	1.0448	49.940	1.2911	47.021
AIR	1.1322	47.591	1.4445	46.534	1.7180	45.781

Table 4. Performance comparison of the extracted watermarked image for different values of α applied to five different test images

IMG	$\alpha = 5$ MSE	$\alpha = 5$ PSNR	$\alpha = 8$ MSE	$\alpha = 8$ PSNR	$\alpha = 10$ MSE	$\alpha = 10$ PSNR
LENA	0.0322	14.92	0.000976	30.10	0	HIGH
OWL	0.0029	25.376	0.0029	25.376	0	HIGH
BAB	0.0029	25.376	0.0039	24.089	0	HIGH
PEP	0.0635	11.972	0.000976	30.10	0	HIGH
AIR	0.0557	12.541	0.0039	24.089	0	HIGH

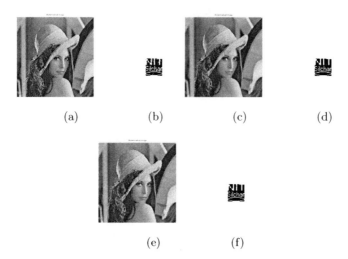

Fig. 5. Comparison of the result of proposed watermaking algorithm for different values of α (a) Watermarked LENA image for $\alpha=5$, (b) Extracted watermark for $\alpha=5$, (c) Watermarked LENA image $\alpha=8$, (d) Extracted watermark for $\alpha=8$, (e) Watermarked LENA image for $\alpha=10$, (f) Extracted watermark for $\alpha=10$.

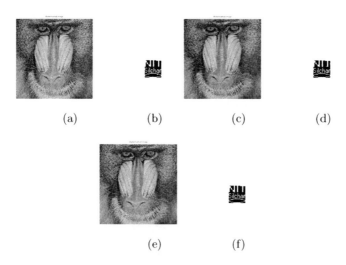

Fig. 6. Comparison of the result of proposed watermaking algorithm for different values of α (a) Watermarked BABOON image for $\alpha=5$, (b) Extracted watermark for $\alpha=5$, (c) Watermarked BABOON image $\alpha=8$, (d) Extracted watermark for $\alpha=8$, (e) Watermarked BABOON image for $\alpha=10$, (f) Extracted watermark for $\alpha=10$.

5   Conclusions

This work presents an algorithm for watermarking the digital images. It uses a joint DWT-DCT based approach. The DCT coefficients of the mid-frequency bands of 3-level DWT decomposed host image is embedded with the final watermark generated from the original watermark and the key. The extraction algorithm uses the key to recover the mid-frequency subbands. Both the subjective and objective evaluation results show that the performance of the proposed watermarking algorithm is satisfactory. It has been observed that by suitably selecting the value of α, a trade-off may be made between the quality of the watermarked image and the extracted watermarked image. The α also provides robustness to the algorithm. The observations are made for gray scale images. However, this algorithm may be extended for watermarking the color images.

References

1. Kim, Y., Kwon, O., Park, R.: Wavelet Based Watermarking Method for Digital Images Using the Human Visual System. In: IEEE International Symposium on Circuits and Systems, vol. 4, pp. 80–83 (July 1999)
2. Lin, S., Chin, C.: A Robust DCT-based Watermarking for Copyright Protection. IEEE Transactions on Consumer Electronics 46(3), 415–421 (2000)
3. Wang, Y., Doherty, J.F., Dyck, R.E.V.: A Wavelet-Based Watermarking Algorithm for Ownership Verification of Digital Images. IEEE Transactions on Image Processing 11(2), 77–88 (2002)
4. Nikolaidis, A., Pitas, I.: Asymptotically Optimal Detection for Additive Watermarking in the DCT and DWT Domains. IEEE Transactions on Image Processing 2(10), 563–571 (2003)
5. Chu, W.: DCT-Based Image Watermarking Using Sub sampling. IEEE Transactions on Multimedia 5(1), 34–38 (2003)
6. Deng, W., Wang, B.: A Novel Technique For Robust Image Watermarking in the DCT Domain. In: Proceedings of IEEE International Conference on Neural Networks and Signal Processing, vol. 2, pp. 1525–1528 (2003)
7. Gonzalez, R.C., Woods, R.E.: Digital Image Processing, 2nd edn. Prentice Hall Inc., Englewood Cliffs (2003)

New Curvelet Features for Image Indexing and Retrieval

Lakshmi A. and Subrata Rakshit

Center for Artificial Intelligence and Robotics, Bangalore, India
lachuv@yahoo.co.in

Abstract. In image retrieval, Curvelet global features have been used so
far. They have shown promising results in characterizing texture because
of its inherent ability to capture edge information more accurately than
Wavelet and Gabor. Global feature fails to characterize the local features
of the images. So, we have proposed a technique to combine the global
texture (Curvelet) and color features with local features derived from
Salient regions. We present a Salient region detector (based on Curvelet)
that extracts the regions where variations occur. We show that using the
global distribution of local features in addition to global features provides
better retrieval performance than those features which represents the
global nature of the image alone.

Keywords: Curvelet, Feature Extraction, Gabor, Image Indexing.

1   Introduction

With the rapid proliferation of large storage spaces, huge number of images have
been produced and stored. With this huge image database, there is a growing
need for efficient image retrieval systems. Image retrieval systems are broadly
classified as text based and content based. In text based retrieval system, human
supplied text is used as basis for searching, using text search algorithms. This
approach has many disadvantages. For example, annotation depends highly on
the user's perspective and it is excessively time consuming. To overcome the
drawbacks of text based retrieval system, content based image retrieval (*CBIR*)
system came into existence. It follows two step approach, indexing and searching. During indexing phase, a feature vector closely representing the image is
computed for each image in the database and stored in the feature base. In
searching phase, feature vector is computed for given query image and images
similar to the query image are returned to the user. CBIR uses low level features
such as color, texture, shape. A variety of techniques have been proposed to extract texture features. Texture feature extraction algorithms can be grouped as
statistical, geometrical, model-based and signal processing. Some of the statistical features [1-4] used are Sobel feature, co-occurrence matrix and run-length
matrix. Statistic techniques are sensitive to noise. In geometric methods, images
are converted into binary images of n grey levels and statistical features of connected areas are computed. In model-based approaches [5-8] Gaussian Markov

K.R. Venugopal and L.M. Patnaik (Eds.): ICIP 2011, CCIS 157, pp. 492–501, 2011.

random fields or Gibbs random fields were used to model textures. Some of the signal processing methods [9-14] employed linear transformations, Gabor filters and Wavelet filters.

One dimensional wavelets [15] are localized in time and frequency in one dimension. It can be extended to two dimension by applying it along x and y directions individually. The directional selectivity of multi dimensional wavelet obtained in this fashion is very poor. To resolve this issue, complex wavelet transforms are introduced. The support of theses wavelets are square, which is referred as isotropic scaling. This isotropic scaling implies that these wavelets become point like in the limit of infinite frequency. Thus they are good at approximating point singularities alone, where as images are characterized mainly by 2D singularities (lines and curves). Curvelets [16-18] are anisotropic extensions to wavelets. In contrast to fixed number of directions in complex wavelets, curvelets have more number of directions as the scale increases, thus providing better directional selectivity. In frequency domain, the length and width of curvelets follow parabolic scaling. Curvelets provide sparse representation along 2D singularities. Local slopes of the images are built into curvelet representation.

Gabor is oval in nature, where as curvelets are linear along edge direction. The oval shapes of the Gabor filters don't allow it to completely cover the frequency spectrum, whereas curvelets cover the entire frequency spectrum.

Curvelets have been used for character recognition [19], [20]. Ni and Leng [21] tried to use Curvelet feature for color image retrieval, but they have not used any benchmark database and not reported retrieval accuracy. These problems were recovered in [22] First and second order moments of Curvelet transform at various scales and orientations were used as features. Sumana et. al., showed that these Curvelet features outperforms Gabor features. Other works [23], [24] on Curvelet based texture retrieval parameterizes the distribution of Curvelet transform using higher order moments and these parameters are used as features for texture retrieval. These Curvelet texture features are made rotation invariant in [24]. In [25], an edge map is constructed from Curvelet Transform coefficients and used Hu invariants of each scale as feature vector for CBIR application. All the above mentioned methods describe the global texture feature in an image. In most of the cases, global features are very sensitive to occlusion and clutter. Thus, they will give rise to false matches in addition to the correct ones. To overcome the disadvantages of global features, image retrieval using local features were proposed. Local features are those that are extracted from a subset of image regions (called salient regions) where the image information content is supposedly important. Retrieval techniques that are solely based on local features are likely to be sensitive to large appearance changes. In order to counteract the disadvantages of global and local features, we have proposed a CBIR system which is based on the combination of global features and global distribution of local features. Texture features (using Curvelet) are used in conjunction with color feature to achieve better retrieval results. In this paper, texture features are used in conjunction with color feature to achieve better retrieval results.

The proposed Curvelet feature vector is comprised of four different set of features, i) global texture feature, ii) global color feature, global distribution of iii) local texture feature and iv) local color feature. In this paper, Curvelet coefficients are used to detect salient regions in a given image. Local features are computed on those detected salient regions.

Section 1 gives an overview of Curvelet transform. Section 2 and 3 explains the steps involved in feature extraction and feature matching respectively. Sections 4 furnishes the results of the experiments conducted to validate the performance superiority of the proposed method over some state of the art methods.

2   Curvelet Transform

In this section, we give an overview of the multi resolution Curvelet transform, its digital version and its spectral properties. Candes and Donoho [15] introduced multi-resolution transform named as Curvelet transform to represent 2 dimensional singularities in images better than other traditional transforms. The digital Curvelet coefficient of an image $f(N \times N$ pixels) at pixel $k = [k_1, k_2] k_1 \in [0, N-1], k_2 \in [0, N-1]$ can be calculated as

$$C(j, l, k) = \sum_{m_1=0}^{M_1} \sum_{m_2=0}^{M_2} \phi_{j,l,k_1,k_2}(m_1, m_2) f(m_1, m_2). \tag{1}$$

$j (\succ 0)$ is the scale. l is the orientation parameter. $l \in [0, \theta_a \times 2^{\frac{j}{2}}]$. θ_a is the angular spacing of coarser scale. ϕ_{j,l,k_1,k_2} is the curvelet waveform of span M_1, M_2 (Eq. 2).

$$C(j, l, k) = \psi_{j,k} \circledast \delta_{l,k}. \tag{2}$$

where $\psi_{j,k}$ is the wavelet waveform at scale j and translation k, $\delta_{\theta,k}$ is the line along direction θ and translation k

3   Feature Extraction

The details of the steps involved in the extraction of the proposed feature is given in this section. The proposed feature consists of four subsets of features, namely i) global texture feature, ii) global color feature, global distribution of iii) local texture feature and iv) local color feature. Each image in the database is converted to $YCbCr$. Features are calculated on Y, Cb and Cr individually. In the forthcoming sections, feature extraction is explained with Y component alone.

3.1   Global Features

This section describes the generation of global texture and color features. Five level (L) Curvelet transform is applied to Y ($N \times N$ pixels) componenet of the image. This decomposes Y into different scales and angles. The number of orientations from coarser to finer scale are $1, 8, 16, 16, 32$ (anisotropic scaling of Curvelet). The row and col size of the Curvelet coefficient image $s_x(j,l), s_y(j,l)$ respectively at a given scale $j \in [0, L-1]$ and orientation l are

$$s_x(j,l) = \frac{N}{2^j}. \tag{3}$$

$$s_y(j,l) = \frac{\frac{N}{2^j}}{\frac{\theta_j}{2}}. \tag{4}$$

where θ_j is the total number of orientations in scale j. Texture features are calculated as energy $\mathbb{E}_{j,l}$ of Curvelet coefficient at each scale and angle(Eq. 5). Color features are computed as energy $\mathbb{E}_Y$ of pixel values of Y (Eq. 6).

$$E_{j,l} = \sum_{k_1=0}^{s_x(j,l)} \sum_{k_2=0}^{s_y(j,l)} |C(j,l,k_1,k_2)|^2. \tag{5}$$

$$E(Y) = \sum_{m=0}^{N} \sum_{n=0}^{N} f(m,n)^2. \tag{6}$$

3.2   Global Distribution of Local Features

This section gives the details involved in the generation of feature vector elements based on the global distribution of local features. The steps involved in computing this feature are i) Detecting salient regions, ii) Assigning a descriptor for each salient region, iii) Computing the global distribution of the individual elements of this local descriptor. These three steps need to be done for Y, Cb and Cr components to generate the feature vector. In the forthcoming paragraphs, we have explained the feature generation of Y component alone.

The first and second step involves Curvelet transform. Curvelet transform is a multi resolution directional representation that expresses image variation at different scales and orientations.

Salient Region Detection: This section explains the extraction process of salient regions. Local features are of interest as they lead to image retrieval based on local properties of the image. In our CBIR system, we try to extract salient regions from the image, where information content is high at any resolution and orientation. Besides saving time, extracting features in salinet regions alone lead to more discriminant indexing. To detect salient regions, we decompose the image into different angles and scales as given in the previous section. The Y component of the image is considered to be composed of M^2 regions of size $n \times n (n \ll N)$ pixels, where

$$M = \frac{N}{n}. \tag{7}$$

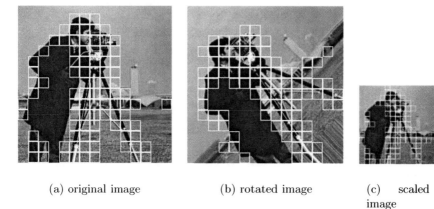

(a) original image   (b) rotated image   (c)   scaled
                                                        image

Fig. 1. Salient regions marked as box

We know the Curvelet coefficients that have been generated from each region at each scale and orientation. The tracked Curvelet coefficient vector $\mathbf{T}_{a,b}$ (Eq. 8) and saliency value $SV_{a,b}$ (Eq. 12) are computed for each region $a \in [0, M-1], b \in [0, M-1]$. The tracked coefficient vector for a particular region is a vector of curvelet coefficients generated by that region at various scales and orientations. Saliency value of a particular region is the l_1 norm of the corresponding tracked coefficient vector.

$$T_{a,b} = C(j, l, k_1, k_2). \tag{8}$$

$$j \in [0, L-1], l \in [0, \theta j]. \tag{9}$$

$$k_1 \in [a \times s_x(j,l), (a+1) \times s_x(j,l)]. \tag{10}$$

$$k_2 \in [b \times s_x(j,l), (b+1) \times s_x(j,l)]. \tag{11}$$

$$SV_{a,b} = |T_{a,b}|_1. \tag{12}$$

The region related to global variation (along all scales and orientations) will result in a higher saliency value. The regions with higher saliency value are termed as salient regions. We have restricted the number of salient regions to 100. The salient regions detected are scale and rotation invariant. It can be seen in Fig. 3.2 that most of the salient regions detected remain the same irrespective of the scale and orientation of the cameraman image. Fig. 1(b) and Fig. 1(c) are 45 degree rotated and scaled versions of cameraman image respectively.

Salient Region Descriptor: Once the salient regions have been detected, the next step is to assign a descriptor to each region. In this paper, each region was described with a feature vector of dimension 10 (9 local texture features and 1 local color feature). To extract texture feature, each salient region of Y component is decomposed individually to coarser and finer scale (with 8 different orientation in finer scale) using Curvelet transform. The energy of the Curvelet coefficients in coarser scale (a_1) and all eight angles of finer scale $(a_2, a_3, a_4, a_5, a_6, a_7, a_8, a_9)$ are taken as texture feature of that particular region. Energy of the individual salient region of $Y(a_{10})$ is computed as local color features.

Global Distribution: The third and final step is to compute the global distribution of the local features of the detected salient regions. Feature extraction based on global distribution aids in ignoring the geometry and allows for translation of objects.

Gaussian radial basis function is constructed for each individual element of the local feature descriptor, considering all the salient regions in the given image. The parameters mean and variance that characterize the individual radial basis function are computed as local feature vector (detailed explanation follows).

Let $a_{1i}, a_{2i} \ldots, a_{10i}$ be the 10 feature elements of the salient regions, with $i \in [0, 99]$ representing the region number. We model 10 different Gaussian radial basis function based on $a_{1i}, a_{2i} \ldots a_{10i}$ individually. Each basis function gives us indication of the distribution of local structures across the image. The parameters mean μ and variance σ^2 (Eq. 15) that characterize these basis function are computed as feature vector.

$$\mu_k = \frac{1}{100} \sum_{i=0}^{100} a_{ki}. \tag{13}$$

$$\sigma_k^2 = \frac{1}{100^2} \sum_{i=0}^{100} (a_{ki} - \mu_k)^2. \tag{14}$$

$$\text{where}, k \in [1, 10]. \tag{15}$$

3.3   Feature Matching

The feature extraction method mentioned above is applied to each and every image in the database. Each image is represented and indexed using the extracted feature vector $x_j, j \in [1, P]$, where P is the number of images in the database. When user submits a query, the same feature extraction process is carried out to extract query feature vector q. Similarity function $S(q, x_j)$ is computed for each and every image in the database as

$$S(q, x_j) = (q - x_j)^t (q - x_j). \tag{16}$$

The search ends in an ordered list of images according to their distance to the submitted query image. Top few images $p \ll P$ are returned to the user as relevant images.

3.4   Experimental Results

The indexing and query mechanism proposed in this paper have been implemented using **C** language. Digital curvelet transform is implemented using wrapping based fast discrete curvelet transform [16]. To assess the performance of the proposed CBIR, several experiments were conducted using the standard database coral. We have presented the results of two sets of experiments.

(a)

(b)

Fig. 2. Retrieval Results of Bus and Natural Scenery

Experiment 1: This is conducted to prove the retrieval efficacy of the proposed feature vector based CBIR. Fig. 2(a) and Fig. 2(b) shows few retrieval results for the given query images (top row, left image). In all these situations, proposed Curvelet features give good results

Experiment 2: This experiment shows the superiority of the proposed feature over other Curvelet features. In order to evaluate the proposed CBIR system, we have used the common performance metrics, Retrieval Accuracy (RA) (Eq. 17) and Precision-Recall pair (Eq. 18 and Eq. 19). RA is the average percentage of relevant retrieved images among the top 20 retrieved images. Precision P is the ratio between the number of relevant retrieved images and total number of retrieved images, where as recall is the ratio between the number of relevant retrieved images to the total number of relevant images in the database.

$$RA(\%) = \frac{\text{relevant images}}{20} \times 100. \tag{17}$$

$$Recall = \frac{\text{Relevant retrieved images}}{\text{Total relevant images in database}}. \tag{18}$$

$$Precision = \frac{\text{Relevant retrieved images}}{\text{Total retrieved images}}. \tag{19}$$

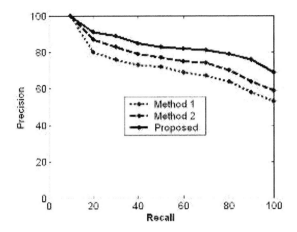

Fig. 3. Recall-Precision Graph

The images in the coral database can be divided into 10 different classes. As test case, we chose 50 images, 10 images from 5 different classes such as food, bus, tribals, dinosaurs, flowers. We computed the retrieval accuracy (for these 50 images) of our method and the method [22] which uses only global features. When the salient region features were included for CBIR as proposed, it was able to capture the foreground object details even if there is any clutter in background or change in the position of the object or background. Due to the above mentioned fact, the proposed method results in higher retrieval accuracy, especially for classes food, bus and tribals (Table 1).

Table 1. Comparison of Retrieval acuuracy

Class	Proposed	Global
Food	80	66
Bus	95	82
Tribals	90	79
Dinosaurs	96	94
Flowers	96	92

We have given the recall-precision graph in Fig. 3, computed with different numbers of return images. For this purpose, we have used a different test set from coral database. The test set has 50 images, 10 from 5 different classes. The classes are buildings, horses, elephants, seashore, mountains. Fig. 3 gives a comparison of the recall-precision curves of the proposed method, global Curvelet features method [22] and Wavelet features [26]. Note the huge fall in the precision of global Curvelet features and Wavelet features with increase in the recall, where as the proposed feature is able to maintain good precision even for higher levels of recall.

4 Conclusions

A novel feature extraction scheme is introduced for image retrieval. In this feature extraction method, we combined the global features with local features as an alternative to global features alone. Local features are texture and color feature extracted in the salient regions. Salient regions are detected (based on curvelet transform) as those regions where information is high in all scales and orientation. Curvelet based salient regions are located in visual focus points and they are scale and rotation invariant. The proposed method was compared with wavelet feature and global curvelet feature. The superiority of the proposed method was established using coral dataset in terms of retrieval accuracy and recall-precision graph.

References

1. Vickers, A.L., Modestino, J.W.: A Maximum Likelyhood Approach to Texture Classification. IEEE Trans. Pattern Anal. Machine Intell. PAMI 4(1), 61–68 (1982)
2. Haralick, R.M.: Statastical and Structural Approach to Texture. In: Proceedings of the IEEE Trans. vol. 67, pp. 786–804 (1979)
3. Lakshmi, A., Rakshit, S.: New Wavelet Features for Image Indexing and Retrival. In: IEEE Second International Advance Computing Conference, pp. 66–71 (2010)
4. Islam, M.M., Zang, D., Lu, G.: Rotation Invariant Curvelet Features for Texture Image Retrieval. In: Proc. of IEEE International Conference on Multimedia and Expo, pp. 562–565 (2009)
5. Cohen, P., Ledinh, C.T., Lacasse, V.: Classification of Natural Textures by Means of Two-dimensional Orthogonal Masks. IEEE Trans. Acoust, Speech, and Signal Proc. 37, 125–128 (1989)
6. Dum, D., Higgins, W.E., Wakeley, J.: Texture Segmentation using 2-D Gabor Elementary Functions. IEEE Trans. Pattem Anal. Machine Intell. 16, 130–149 (1994)
7. Bovik, A., Clark, M., Geisler, W.S.: Multichannel Texture Analysis using Localized Spatial Filters. IEEE Trans. Pattern Anal. Machine Intell. 12, 55–73 (1990)
8. Chellappa, R., Chatterjee, S.: Classification of Textures using Gaussian Markov Random fields. IEEE Trans. Acoust. Speech, Signal Processing ASSP-33(4), 959–963 (1986)
9. Conners, R.W., Harlow, C.A.: A Theoretical Comparison of Texture Algorithms. IEEE Trans. Pattern Anal. Machine Intell. PAMI-2, 204–222 (1980)
10. Haralick, R.M., Shanmugam, K., Dinstein, I.: Textural Features for Image Classification. IEEE Trans. Syst. Man, Cybern. SMC-3(6), 610–621 (1973)
11. Cands, E.J., Demanet, L.: The Curvelet Representation of Wave Propagators is Optimally Sparse. Communications on Pure and Applied Mathematics 58(11), 1472–1528 (2005)
12. Arivazhaga, S., Kumar, T.G.S., Ganesan, L.: Texture Classification Using Curvelet Transform. International Journal of Wavelets, Multiresolution and Info. Processing 513, 451–464 (2003)
13. Chang, T., Jay Kuo, C.C.: Texture Analysis and Classification with Tree-structured Wavelet Transform. IEEE Trans. Image Processing PAMI-2(10), 429–441 (1993)
14. Unser, M., Eden, M.: Multiresolution Feature Extraction and Selection for Texture Segmentation. IEEE Trans. Pattern Anal. Machine Intell. 2, 717–728 (1989)

15. Cands, E.J., Demanet, L., Donoho, D.L., Ying, L.: Fast Discrete Curvelet Trans-forms. SIAM Multiscale Modeling and Simulation 3(1), 861–899 (2006)
16. Joutel, G., Eglin, V., Bres, S., Emptoz, H.: Curvelet Based Feature Extraction of Handwritten Shapes for Ancient Manuscripts Classification. In: Proc. of SPIE-IS and T Electronic Imaging. SPIE, vol. 6500 (2007)
17. Murtagh, F., Starck, J.L.: Wavelet and Curvelet Moments for Image Classification, Application to Aggregate Mixture Grading. Pattern Recognition Letters 10(15), 1557–1564 (2008)
18. Weszka, J.S., Dyer, C.R., Rosenfeld, A.: A Comparative Study of Texture Measures for Terrain Classification. IEEE Trans. Syst. Man, Cybem. SMC-6(4), 269–285 (1976)
19. Majumdar, A.: Bangla Basic Character Recognition Using Digital Curvelet Trans-form. Journal of Pattern Recognition Research 1, 17–26 (2007)
20. Unser, M.: Local Linear Transforms for Texture Measurements. Signal Process-ing 11(1), 61–79 (1986)
21. Ni, L., Leng, H.C.: Curvelet Transform and its Application in Image Retrieval. In: 3rd International Symposium on Multispectral Image Processing and Pattern Recognition. Proceedings of SPIE, vol. 5286 (2003)
22. Sumana, I.J., Islam, M.M., Zhang, D., Lu, G.: Content Based Image Retrieval using Curvelet Transform. In: The Proc. of Int. Workshop on MMSP, pp. 11–16 (2008)
23. Derin, H., Elliott, H.: Modeling and Segmentation of Noisy and Textured Images using Gibbs Random Fields. IEEE Trans. Pattem Anal. Machine Intell. PAMI-9, 39–55 (1987)
24. Mallat, S.G.: A Wavelet Tour of Signal Processing. Academic Press, Inc., California (1998)
25. Cross, G.R., Jain, A.K.: Markov Random Field Texture Models. IEEE Trans. Pat-tern Anal. Machine Intell. PAMI-5(1), 25–39 (1983)
26. Cands, E.J., Donoho, D.L.: Curvelets A Surprisingly Effective Nonadaptive Rep-resentation for Objects with Edges. In: Rabut, C., Cohen, A., Schumacher, L.L. (eds.), pp. 105–120. Vanderbilt University Press, Nashville (2000)

Expert System Design Based on Wavelet Transform and Linear Feature Selection

Pritish Ranjan Pal, Gitartha Goswami, and Niladri Prasad Mohanty

Department of Biomedical Engineering, National Institute of Technology,
Raipur, Chhattisgarh, India
gitartha.nitrr@gmail.com

Abstract. Electromyography (EMG) signal is electrical manifestation of neuromuscular activation due to which physiological processes are accessible which cause the muscle to generate force and produce movement and help us to interact with the world. EMGs have large variation and nonstationary properties. There are two issues in the classification of EMG signals. One is the feature selection, and the other is classifier design. In EMGs diseases recognition, the first and the most important step is feature extraction. In this paper, we have selected Symlet of order five mother wavelet for EMG signal analysis and later we have selected eight features to classify EMG signals of isometric contraction for two different abnormalities namely ALS (Amyotrophic Lateral Sclerosis) which is coming under Neuropathy and Myopathy and the classification approach is termed as Muscular Atrophy Diagnostic Approach (MADA) by authors. From the experimental results, waveform length is the best feature comparing with the other features. Root mean square, spectrogram, kurtosis, entropy and power are other useful augmenting features.

Keywords: ALS, Isometric Contraction, Kurtosis, MADA, Myopathy.

1 Introduction

Human muscle consists of large number of fibers functionally arranged into individual motor unit which are all activated by nerve impulse from the nervous system which propagate through the length of the nerve fiber [1],[2]. Electrodes placed at the region of these muscles pick up different voltages in different region of these impulses. A plot of these voltages is called as Electromyogram (EMG). These signals have the properties of nonstationary, nonlinear, complexity, and large variation [1]. EMG can be recorded by two types of electrodes which are an invasive electrode called as wire or needle electrodes and a noninvasive electrode called as surface electrode [3]. Use of lotions and creams on skins for 24 hour is avoided prior to EMG recording. EMG is a main nerve diagnostic tool used in Electro diagnostics medicine and in clinical neurophysiology. EMG test collect information about injured nerves, damaged nerves and muscle disorders leading to symptoms like numbness stinging, burning pain and weakness. EMG test is a valuable diagnostics tool which provides a real map for physicians which will

K.R. Venugopal and L.M. Patnaik (Eds.): ICIP 2011, CCIS 157, pp. 502–510, 2011.

help to evaluate locate and treat neuromuscular disorders [4]. Muscle diseases are mainly categorized by their clinical appearance. At the beginning of 1990s long lasting classifications of disease were based on the genetic abnormalities muscle and further it is also classified on the basis molecular abnormalities.

Myopathy and Amyotrophic lateral sclerosis (ALS) are the two main muscular disorders and 20,000 Americans have ALS, and an estimated 5,000 people in the United States are diagnosed with the disease each year. Myopathy is diseases of skeletal muscle which are not the cause of nervous disorder [5],[6]. These diseases cause the skeletal or voluntary muscle to become weak or weakest.

Myopathy is usually degenerative, but they are sometime caused by drug side effects, chemical poisonings, or a chronic disorder of the immune system. Amyotrophic lateral sclerosis (ALS), sometimes called Lou Gehrig's disease, is a rapidly progressive, invariably fatal neurological disease that attacks the nerve cells(neurons)responsible for controlling voluntary muscles characterized by the gradual degeneration and death of motor neurons [7].About 5 to 10 percent of all ALS cases are inherited. Electromyogram is an important test for the detection of Myopathy and ALS.

In this paper, we propose a new technique, Muscular Atrophy Diagnostic Approach (MADA) which is based on feature extraction from acquired EMG for muscular diseases classification. EMG classification is one of the most difficult pattern recognition problems because there usually exists small but numerous variations in EMG features, which leads to difficulty in analyzing EMG signals. In muscles diseases recognition, there are two main points, namely feature selection and classifier design. We analyze EMG data by using Symlet wavelet order five before extracting the feature. In general, the methods of feature selection can be divided into two types: the measure of classification accuracy and the valuation using statistical criterion. After that the selection of the best features based on the proposed statistical criterion method is investigated.

For this purpose, we evaluate different kinds of features that have been widely used in EMG diseases recognition. The results of this evaluation and the proposed statistic method can be widely used in EMG applications such as control of EMG robots and prostheses or the EMG diagnosis of nerve and muscle diseases.

Various features were found in the literatures [8]. For example, features based on time domain are Mean Absolute Value, Modified Mean Absolute Value, Root Mean Square, Integrated of EMG, Simple Square integral, Variance, and Waveform Length. The brachial biceps muscles where used in this study because they were the most frequently investigated in the two abnormal patients.

The section 2 explains the data selection. In section 3 we discuss about the wavelet analysis for EMG signal and the features extracted (standard deviation, variance, root mean square, logarithmic root mean square, power, entropy, kurtosis, spectrogram). Section 4 explains the use of Support Vector Machine as a classifier. The section 5 gives the results and discussion about the result which leads to classification of signal. The section 6 gives the conclusion of the context.

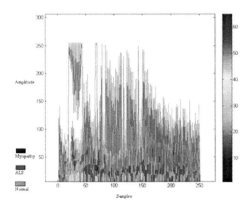

Fig. 1. *EMG* Signal of Normal, *ALS*, Myopathy patient from Biceps Brachii region

2   Data Selection

2.1   Subjects

For our study, we have chosen 3 groups. First group consisted of 10 normal subjects aged 21-35 years, 4 females and 6 males. All of the 10 subjects are in very good physical condition except one. None in this group had signs or history of neuromuscular disorders. The group with myopathy consisted of 7 patients; 2 females and 5 males aged 19-63 years. The *ALS* group consisted of 8 subjects; 4 females and 4 males aged 35-67 years. Besides clinical and electrophysiological signs compatible with *ALS*, 5 of them died within a few years after onset of the disorder, supporting the diagnosis of *ALS*.

3   Proposed Method

3.1   Expermental Protocol

The *EMG* signals were recorded under usual conditions for MUAP analysis. The recordings were made at low (just above threshold) voluntary and constant level of contraction.A standard concentric needle electrode was used. The *EMG* signals were recorded from bicep brachii of bicep. The high and low pass filters of the *EMG* amplifier were set at 2 Hz and 10 kHz for 11msec [9].

3.2   Proposed Method

In this paper, we describe each of the following steps involved for the classification of the acquired *EMG* signal. These steps are: (A) Base line shift for accurate estimation of parameters. (B) Wavelet analysis for *EMG* signal (C) Various parameters/features calculation (D) Classifier design.

A. Base Line Shifting: Generally human being produces static current which will interfere while recording EMG signal. Due to this problem EMG signal shifts upper side from the base line. This defect occurs due to the muscle tension, body movement or some environmental noise. For removing this problem, base line of EMG is shifted to zero line. This will optimize the result.

B. Wavelet analysis for EMG signal: Wavelet analysis was performed for short time period and the size of window is can be varied by using the real time frequency analysis. So the result at low and high frequency will gives us the same result. Here we have used the Symlet mother wavelet of order five for EMG signal analysis. The level of decomposition is three. Each wavelet is based on function called mother wavelet and subset are operated with scaling (a) and translation (b) is represented by equation

$$\phi(t) = \frac{1}{\sqrt{a}}\phi(\frac{t-b}{a}) = \phi(scale, position, t). \tag{1}$$

To extract the required EMG band, wavelet decomposition [4], [10], [11] is done which has certain advantages over other analysis like time-frequency localization, multi rate filtering and scale-space analysis. Variable window size is taken to compress and stretches the wave with decomposition is done up to third level to get the required bands by means of multi resolution analysis using complementary low and high pass filter. The original signal is decomposed and two sequences will be found out with high and low resolution frequency. Then the lower frequency component is decomposed to get the second level of component of higher and lower frequency and the same process will carry on up to fourth level to get the required frequency levels. After the step the statistical parameters will be calculated for the bands as described below. The required band for our analysis after reconstruction is $S = Ca_3 + Cd_1 + Cd_2 + Cd_3$,

where Ca is the approximated value and Cd are the detail values. It is represented in Fig. 2, Fig. 3 and Fig. 4.

C. Feature Extraction and Calculation: In present study, feature extraction of EMG was carried on S signal which is the reconstructed signal. Usually features stated below are used for detecting isometric contraction of biceps brachii muscles. These features are described below:

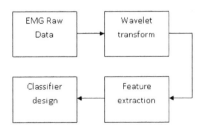

Fig. 2. Block diagram describing the process

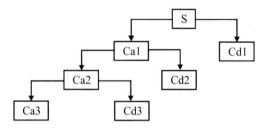

Fig. 3. Wavelet decomposition upto level three

Standard Deviation (SD). It is a parameter which gives us the deviation from the mean value around the origin axis for the segment of the given signal. It can be calculated as:

$$SD = \sqrt{E[(n - M)]^2} \ . \tag{2}$$

Variance (VAR). It gives power of the selected segment of the signal. Generally, variance is average of the square of the standard deviation (SD) for the selected segment of the signal. It can be defined as:

$$VAR = \frac{1}{N - 1} \sum_{n=1}^{N} x_n^{\ 2} \ . \tag{3}$$

Root Mean Square (RMS) and Logarithmic Root Mean Square. RMS is used to calculate constant force and non-fatiguing contraction. It can be defined as:

$$RMS = \sqrt{\frac{1}{N} \sum_{n=1}^{N} x_n^{\ 2}} \ . \tag{4}$$

The logarithmic transform of the above feature (RMS) that is Log RMS gives uniform scattering of points in selected segment of EMG which is better than RMSs scattering information. It can be explained as below:

$$Log \ RMS = \log(RMS) \ . \tag{5}$$

Power (P). The Fast Fourier transform (FFT) is determined with Hann Window for calculating Power Spectral Density P(f) for the chosen segment of EMG signal. This feature can be used for characterizing signals of different diseases. The PSD is determined by multiplying the Fourier transform of the filtered signal with the conjugate of that filtered EMG signal and is given by:

$$FFT[r_{(xx)}(1)] = \frac{1}{N}\{F[x_N(1)^* x_N^*(-1)]\} \ . \tag{6}$$

$$I_N(\omega) = \frac{1}{N}|X_N(e_{jw})^2| \ .$$

$$(7)$$

where Eq. 7 is known as Periodogram. $x_N(n)$ is a finite length N defined as:

$$x_N(n) = \begin{cases} x(n) & ;0 \leq n \leq N-1 \\ 0 & ;otherwise \end{cases} \ .$$

$$(8)$$

$r_{xx}(1)$ is the biased autocorrelation estimate.

Entropy (EN). One of the important features is entropy which is first introduced by Shannon. It is used for measuring order of the signal or randomness of the signal. In this paper, we are calculating Shannon Entropy which is calculated by using PDF (Probability Distribution Function) and can be calculated as below:

$$SHEN = \sum_i p_i(\log(p_i)) \ .$$

$$(9)$$

where
i = Total number of amplitudes over the segment (window) of the signal,
p_i = Probability of finding amplitudes over the segment (window) of the signal.

Kurtosis (KUR). It is a method to determine whether data sets are at peak or flat with respect to normal distribution. Data sets having high kurtosis have a distinct peak near the mean but afterwards that will decline rapidly and vice versa for low kurtosis data sets.

$$KUR = \frac{\sum_{n=1}^{N}(x_n - M)^4}{(N-1)SD^4} \ .$$

$$(10)$$

Spectrogram (SPEC). It is a plot between frequency content of signal and time progression of signal. From Fig. 7, Fig. 8, and Fig. 9, it is clear that all three groups have (ALS, Myopathy, and Normal) different spectrograms.

4   Support Vector Machine as a Classifier

After feature extraction, feature matrix is normalized in order to have features in a same range. Simply, SVM classifier was trained by the train-train data and then used for classifying the train-test data. SVM creates a separating hyper plane between two clusters of data, thus classifying data falling into two different classes. In non-linear classification, same operation was performed by non-linear kernel function, in our case, Gaussian-RBF kernel, given by

$$K(x_i, x_j) = \exp(-||x_i - x_j||^2/2\sigma^2) \ .$$

$$(11)$$

In this work we take two different group i.e. normal and abnormal (Myopathy and Neuropathy) signal for the classification purpose .We take 70% of signal to train the expert model using SVMStruct a structure with the Kernel Function

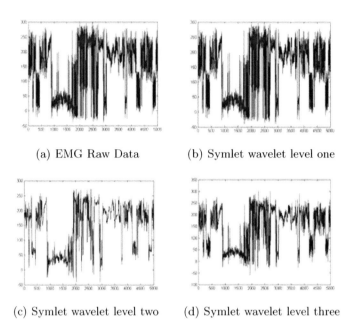

(a) EMG Raw Data   (b) Symlet wavelet level one

(c) Symlet wavelet level two   (d) Symlet wavelet level three

Fig. 4. Various levels of wavelet analysis

fields [4],[6]. Kernel function Value is Gaussian Radial Basis Function kernel (RBF) function handle with a scaling factor, sigma which is varying from 0 values to 10 and takes those which give maximum accuracy. After classifying using the SVM classifier, we conclude that the parameters like rms, kurtosis and entropy are the best features for distinction purpose. By taking the combination of features rms and entropy gives us the best result. Overall the classification accuracy comes around 93.36%. 5 Result and Discussion For classifying the EMG signals of different classes we calculated the parameters of the reconstructed signal S. During experiment we have taken 450 samples of 25 subjects which consist of normal and abnormal patients. Our classification uses features which has described above. So we are spotting some of the features which produce demarcation between different subjects.

(i) Kurtosis can be used to classify three different groups. The Kurtosis varies in following order which is visible in graph. $MYO > NOR > ALS$.

(ii) Next Entropy of the signal can be successfully used to measure the order of signal or randomness of signal. The entropy contents vary in following order which is visible in the following graph. $MYO > ALS > NOR$.

(iii) Constant force and non-fatiguing contraction indicated by RMS can be used as classifying feature as shown in the graph below. The RMS varies in following order which is visible in graph. $MYO > NOR > ALS$.

(iv) Spectrogram is a feature which can be used for demarcation between different diseases. Fig. 8 gives large demarcation by which diseases are clearly distinct.

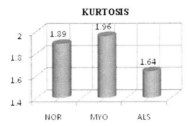

Fig. 5. Kurtosis representation of different groups of EMG Signal

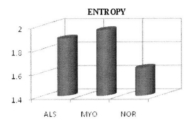

Fig. 6. Entropy representation of different groups of EMG Signal

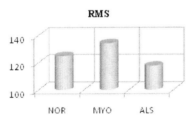

Fig. 7. RMS representation of different groups of EMG Signal

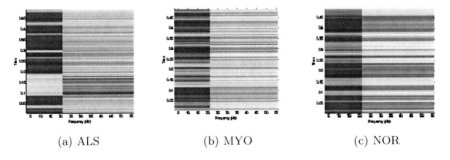

(a) ALS   (b) MYO   (c) NOR

Fig. 8. Spectrogram of ALS, Myopathy and Normal signals

5   Conclusions

In this present study we address the problem taking the statistical properties after wavelet reconstruction. The parameters like entropy, RMS, kurtosis and spectrogram will gives us a clear distinction for classifying and detecting the abnormality in EMG signals. The technique described is a cost effective as well as time effective approach to design an automated classifier for MADA. The future work lies with the classifier i.e., we will take different classifier and compare the results with each other.

References

1. Boisset, S., Goubel, F.: Integrated Electromygraphy Activity and Muscle Work. J Applied Physiol 35, 695–702 (1972)
2. Plonsey, V.: The Active Fiber in a Volume Conductor. IEEE Transactions on Biomedical Engineering 21, 371–381 (1974)
3. De Luca, C.: Electromyography. In: Webster, J.G. (ed.) Encyclopedia of Medical Devices and Instrumentation. John Wiley Publisher, Chichester (2006)
4. De Luca, C.J.: Use of the Surface EMG Signal for Performance Evaluation of Back Muscle. Muscle and Nerve 16, 210–216 (1993)
5. Jones, R.S., et al.: Online Analysis of Neuro-Muscular Function. IEEE Proceedings of Engineering in Medical Biology 10, 1607 (1988)
6. McGill, K., et al.: Automatic Decomposition of the Clinical Electromyogram. IEEE Transactions on Biomedical Engineering 32(7), 470–477 (1985)
7. Japan Amyotrophic Lateral Sclerosis Association, http://www.alsjapan.org/
8. Phinyomark, A., Hirunviriya, S., Limsakul, C., Phukpattaranont, P.: Evaluation of EMG Feature Extraction for Hand Movement Recognition Based on Euclidean Distance and Standard Deviation
9. Englehart, K., Hudgins, B., Parker, P.A.: A Wavelet-Based Continuous Classification Scheme for Multi-Function Myoelectric Control. IEEE Transactions on Biomedical Engineering 48(3), 302–311 (2001)
10. Aldroubi, A., Unser, M.: Wavelets in Medicine and Biology. CRC Press, Boca Raton (1996)
11. Rioul, O., Vetterli, M.: Wavelets and Signal Processing. IEEE Signal Processing Magazine (1991)

Binarization of the Noisy Document Images: A New Approach

Samir Malakar[1], Dheeraj Mohanta[2], Ram Sarkar[3], Nibaran Das[3],
Mita Nasipuri[3], and Basu D.K.[4]

[1] Dept. of Master of Computer Application, M.C.K.V. Institute of Engineering,
Howrah, India
[2] Dept. of Information Technology, Jadavpur University, Kolkata, India
[3] Dept. of Computer Science and Engineering, Jadavpur University, Kolkata, India
[4] A.I.C.T.E. Emeritus Fellow, Dept. of Computer Science and Engineering,
Jadavpur University, Kolkata, India
malakarsamir@gmail.com

Abstract. The work reported here, proposes a new methodology for
determination of the threshold value to binarize noisy/noise free digitized document images. First, Middle of Modal Class (MMC) filtering [1]
technique, one of our earlier works, is applied on the digitized document
images for smoothing the noisy pixels. Then, from that information, we
have identified two sets of gray-level values, one obviously representing
objects and another obviously representing background. Rest of the gray-
level values has been left for calculation of the threshold value. Then, we
have determined the mean gray-level value of the all these pixels with
gray-levels of the third set which will finally be used as threshold for
binarization. A comparison of our results with iterative thresholding [2]
and Otsus thresholding [2], [3] is done, and it is evident from the output
images that present methodology provides a satisfactory result.

Keywords: Binarization Technique, Global Thresholding, Handwritten
Document Image, MMC Filtering, Noise/Noise Free Document Image.

1 Introduction

Research interest in the field of image processing, has been growing fast during
the past few decades due to its application in various fields like satellite image
processing, medical imaging, security related applications(face, fingerprint, iris
etc.,), archiving of old document or manuscript images, etc., The key modules of
image processing system are image acquisition, enhancement, segmentation and
analysis. Out of these, image enhancement techniques, which include removal
of noise, stretching of contrast or binarization, are essential for preprocessing of
acquired images for almost every application domain.

Optical Character Recognition (OCR), a sub field of image processing and
pattern recognition, is a challenge to the researchers from long time before [4].
There are several issues in developing an OCR system. One such issue is related

K.R. Venugopal and L.M. Patnaik (Eds.): ICIP 2011, CCIS 157, pp. 511–520, 2011.
© Springer-Verlag Berlin Heidelberg 2011

to the enhancement of acquired document images which may be of poor quality due to low quality original document (e.g., old blue-prints, etc.,), quantization errors in digitization process, non-optimal light and contrast settings during copying/scanning process, transmission errors, paper defects and/or dirty optics, etc.. To overcome these problems, a proper image binarization algorithm is needed to produce a high contrast document image. The problem of binarization can be defined as separating the objects from the background in a gray level image $I(x, y)$, where objects appear darker (or lighter) than the background. A lot of techniques have already been proposed to solve this problem. The fastest way of solving this problem, among all available techniques, can be done by constructing a threshold surface $T(x, y)$, and then forming the binarized image $B(x, y)$ by comparing the value of the image $I(x, y)$ with $T(x, y)$ at every pixel position (x, y), via

$$B(x,y) = \begin{cases} 1 & I(x,y) > T(x,y) \\ 0 & I(x,y) \end{cases} \qquad (1)$$

It is clear that a fixed value of the threshold surface $T(x, y) =$ constant, cant yield satisfactory binarization results for images obtained under non-uniform illumination and/or with a non-uniform background. Mainly, $T(x, y)$ is calculated using any one of the global, local and adaptive thresholding technique approaches. The choice of $T(x, y)$ optimally is a real challenge for the researchers. To choose $T(x, y)$ optimally mainly iterative, recursive multi- spectral, hierarchical, histogram equalization, edge image, edge relaxation thresholding etc., are used. Here, we have developed a new global thresholding technique to find an optimal threshold $T(x, y)$, which can finally be used for binarization of digitized document images.

2   Previous Work

Lot of works has been done so far on image binarization techniques, which are applicable for digitized text pages, photographs, video signals, medical images etc.. One of the older methods of image binarization is Otsus [2],[3], which uses variance of pixel intensity calculates a global threshold. This technique applies clustering analysis of the gray scale data of input image and models clustering of two Gaussian distributions of gray-level values of pixels in the image. The threshold minimizes the class variance of the two classes of pixels. Kavallieratou [5] used histogram equalization technique to find global threshold. In this work it was considered that percentage of foreground pixel with respect to total image pixels is nearly 10%. Bresnan [6] calculated threshold using neighbors pixels intensity inside a window. The work determined the average of maximum and minimum intensity of pixels inside a window to achieve local threshold of the window.

Niblack [7] used local mean and standard deviation to calculate the local thresholds. Souvola et al., [8] presented an adaptive thresholding method specialized on document images that applies two algorithms in order to calculate local threshold for each pixel. Yanowitz et al., [9] motivated by the approach of Chow et al., [10], proposed a method which constructed a threshold surface by interpolating the image gray levels at the points where the image gradient is high. Indeed, high image gradients indicate probable object edges, where the image gray levels are between the object and the background level. The threshold surface was required to interpolate the image gray levels at all the support points and to satisfy the Laplace equation at non-edge pixels. Such a surface was determined by a Successive Over-Relaxation method (SOR)[9], [11].

Performance evaluation of several binarization methods by Trier et al.,[12]has shown that the technique developed in [9] was one of the best binarization methods. However, the computational complexity of successive over relaxation method is expensive: O (N3) for an N X N image and the resulting binarization process is slow, especially for large images. Furthermore, the threshold surface tends to have sharp extrema at the support points, and this could degrade binarization performance. However, the work proposed in [13] followed the approach of work in [9] i.e., adaptive thresholding method and used image values at support points with high gradients to construct a threshold surface. They defined a threshold surface via a method inspired by multi resolution representations, like Laplacian Pyramids [14] or wavelets [15]. The threshold surface was constructed as a sum of functions, formed by scaling and shifting of a predetermined function. The complexity of this technique is O(Nlog(N)) of image size N X N.

3   Motivation

All the works discussed above are no doubt good techniques, but none of them are applicable for all kind of digital images. Work proposed in [3], [5] used global threshold technique. The technique is not very much applicable if the image contains a very low variance among object and background pixels. Even ratio of background, foreground and noisy pixels plays a great deal towards the success. In the works [6], [8]local thresholding technique has been discussed. Again in the works[6,7,8] adaptive thresholding technique has been depicted. They are effective but little bit time consuming. Again, now a day it is considered that iterative thresholding technique [2] and Otsus thresholding technique [2],[3]is more effective for determining global threshold and subsequent binarization. But here also the choice of initial threshold is a real challenge. Even none of them considered how their technique will work on any noise free document images. In the light of the above facts, we have developed a new global threshold finding technique to find an optimal threshold, which can finally be used for binarization of digitized noisy document images as well as digitized noise free document images.

4   Present Work

In the present work, we have introduced a new methodology to determine a global threshold value to binarize noisy/noise free digitized document images.

First, MMC filtering [1] technique is applied on original digitized document images for removal of noisy pixels. From that information we have identified a set of gray-level values representing obvious objects and another set of gray-level values representing the background. Rest of the gray-level values has been left for calculation of the threshold value. Then, we have determined the mean gray-level value of the all these pixels with gray-levels of the third set which will finally be used as threshold for binarization. We have also compared our results for binarization with iterative thresholding [2] and Otsus thresholding [2], [3] techniques. For implementing iterative thresholding [2] technique initial threshold has been taken as the mean of 4 corner pixels and for Otsus thresholding [2], [3] technique it is 0 (zero). The Basic flow diagram of the present work is depicted in Fig. 1.

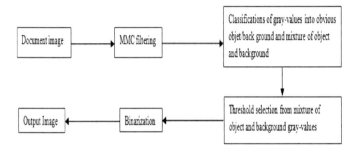

Fig. 1. Block diagram of present work

4.1   Window Selection

For MMC filtering [1] techniques, we have considered a window of size MxM pixels, where M is an odd positive integer number. Each square of the window are assigned with equal weight. We have applied MMC filtering technique [1] on each window and we have slid the window over the document image from left to right and from top to bottom and for each window position we have applied the MMC filtering techniques in order to achieve enhanced document image.

4.2   MMC Filtering

In MMC filtering technique [1], we have observed maximum occurrence of gray level values i.e., modal gray level value in a selected window. Now at the time of selecting the modal gray value for filtering it may so happen that all the pixels in the window may contain different gray level values as there are 256 different gray values. So to overcome this problem first we have searched the maximum (say, b) and minimum (say, a) gray level values in a document image and have partitioned the interval $[a, b]$ equally, subject to the window size. Then we have applied pigeonhole principle [16]. In this principle it is stated that if m pigeons fly into n pigeonholes ($m>n$), then at least one pigeonhole will contain two or more pigeons. Since we have selected window size as M x M pixels, therefore we have partitioned the interval into $(M*M)$-1 equal partitions keeping pigeonhole principle in mind, each of length $(b\text{-}a)/M*M$-1. We have called each partition as modal class and length of partition as range of the class. After that, we have put all the gray level values of the selected window into the proper class using the range information of the classes. Then we have searched for the class with maximum occurrence of gray level values i.e., the class with highest frequency and called it as modal class (MC). Next we have calculated the middle value *(Midval)* of the range of modal class i.e., if the range of MC is $[m, n]$ then $Midval = |m + n|/2$. Finally, we have modified the central gray level value of the selected window with this *Midval*. In our earlier work [1], we have shown that MMC filtering works better for window size of 3X3 pixels. Each cell of square window was assigned with equal weight i.e., 1. In our present work also we have applied same rule for the window selection and middle of modal class selection.

4.3   Threshold Computation

Applying our MMC filtering technique [1], we are left with only 8 distinct gray level values. Then, we have divided these 8 distinct gray level values into three categories namely; Obvious Object (OO), Obvious Background (OB) and Mixture of Object and Background (MOB).

Let,

$$OO : MOB : OB = M : N : P. \qquad (2)$$

Where M, N, P are natural numbers and

$$M + N + P = 8. \qquad (3)$$

Finally, we have calculated the mean of these N gray level values representing the category MOB. This mean value is considered as the final threshold value for binarization of MOBs. The original gray level image is finally binarized using this threshold value.

5   Experimental Result and Discussion

We have collected 50 text document images for our experimental procedure. Some of the sample images are collected from DIBCO (Document Image Binarization Contest) 2009 [17] and rest are prepared in the CMATER laboratory, Dept. of CSE, Jadavpur University. For experimentation, we have classified the document images, by visual inspection, into 2 categories, such as noise free document images and noisy document images. We have chosen the size of the window as 3x3 pixels for MMC filter as it was provided the best result of filtering in our earlier work [1].

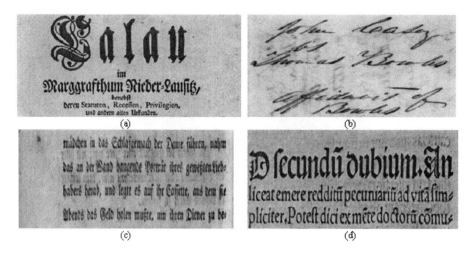

Fig. 2. [a-d] Four sample gray level document images

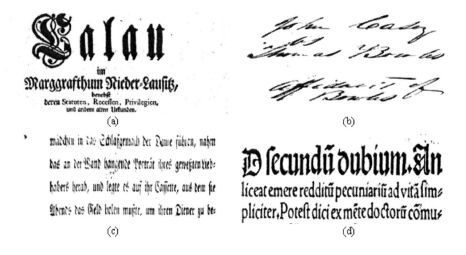

Fig. 3. [a-d] Corresponding binarized document pages of Fig. 2 [a-d] obtained by present technique considering as OO: MOB: OB= 2:2:4

From Eq. (2) and Eq (3), its clear that M: N: P contains all total 45 combinations. Among these 45 cases results for three suitable combinations are depicted in Fig. 3-5 (a-d). From these above said figures its obvious that combination 2: 3: 3 gives the best result. As we have compared our technique with iterative and Otsus method for selection of threshold and consequent binarization, the output are shown in Fig. 6-7(a-d). From the figures in Fig. 5-7(a-d) it is said that we have achieved satisfactory result with the application of present technique over iterative [2] and [3] and Otsus [2], [3] threshold selection technique.

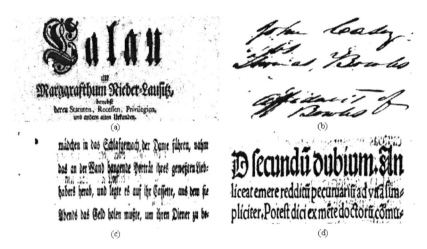

Fig. 4. [a-d] Corresponding binarized document pages of Fig. 2 (a-d) obtained by present technique considering as OO: MOB: OB= 3:2:3

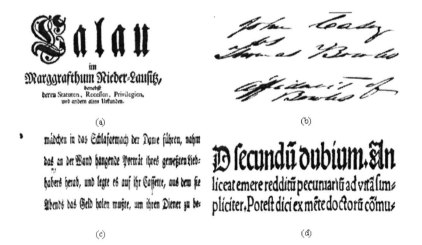

Fig. 5. [a-d] Corresponding binarized document pages of Fig. 2 (a-d) obtained by present technique considering as OO: MOB: OB= 2:3:3

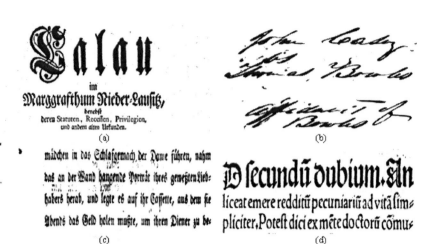

Fig. 6. [a-d] Corresponding binarized document pages of Fig. 2 (a-d) by Otsus thresholding technique

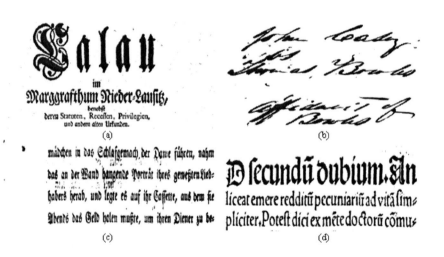

Fig. 7. [a-d] Corresponding binarized document pages of Fig. 2 (a-d) by Otsus thresholding technique

We have compared our technique by visual inspection. We cant provide Mean Square Error (MSE) result as the original noise-free text document images are not available.

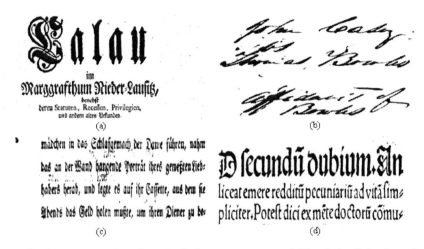

Fig. 8. [a-d] Corresponding binarized document pages of Fig. 2 (a-d) by Iterative thresholding technique

6   Conclusions

Image enhancement technique, which includes filtering, binarization etc., are essential for preprocessing of acquired images for almost every application in image processing domain. In the work reported here, a new global thresholding technique for binarization the input images is developed. The binarization technique is applicable for both the noisy and noise free text document images. A comparison of our results with iterative [2] and Otsus [2], [3] thresholding is done, and it is evident from the output images that the developed methodology provides better result. In the future development of the work, inclusion of more number and varieties of document pages, window size optimization for MMC filtering [1] and improved binarization techniques will be attempted.

Acknowledgments. Authors are thankful to the Center for Microprocessor Applications for Training Education and Research (CMATER), Project on Storage Retrieval and Understanding of Video for Multimedia (SRUVM) of Computer Science & Engineering Department, Jadavpur University, India, for providing infrastructure facilities during progress of the work. The work reported here, has been partially funded by DST, Govt. of India, PURSE (Promotion of University Research and Scientific Excellence) Programme.

References

1. Malakar, S., Mohanta, D., Sarkar, R., Nasipuri, M.: A Novel Noise-Removal Technique for Document Images. IJCCT 2(Special Issue 2-4), 120–124 (2010)
2. Gonzalez, R.C., Woods, R.E.: Digital Image Processing, vol. 1. Prentice-Hall, India (1992)

3. Otsu, N.: A Threshold Selection Method from Gray-Level Histogram. J. IEEE TSMC 9(1), 62–66 (1979)
4. Casey, R.G., Lecolinet, E.: A Survey of Method and Strategies in Character System. J. IEEE TPAMI 18(7), 690–706 (1996)
5. Kavallieratou, E.: A Binarization Algorithm Specialized on Document Images and Photos. In: 8th International Conference on Document Analysis and Recognition (ICDAR 2005). Proc. ICDAR, Seoul, Korea, August 29-September 1, pp. 463–467 (2005)
6. Bernsen, J.: Dynamic Thresholding of Gray-Level Images. In: International Conference Pattern Recognision (ICPR). Proc. ICPR, Paris, France, pp. 1251–1255 (1986)
7. Niblack, W.: An Introduction to Digital Image Processing. Prentice-Hall, Denmark (1986)
8. Sauvola, J., Pietikainen, M.: Adaptive Document Image Binarization. J. PR. 33(2), 225–236 (2000)
9. Yanowitz, S.D., Bruckstein, A.M.: A New Method for Image Segmentation. J. CVGIP 46(1), 82–95 (1989)
10. Chow, C.K., Kaneko, T.: Automatic Boundary Detection of the Left-Ventricle from Cineangiograms. J. Com. Biomed. 5(4), 388–410 (1972)
11. Southwell, V.R.: Relaxation Methods in Theoretical Physics. Oxford University Press, Oxford (1946)
12. Trier, D., Taxt, T.: Evaluation of Binarizaiton Methods for Document Images. J. IEEE TPAMI. 17(3), 312–315 (1995)
13. Blayvas, I., Bruckstein, A., Kimmel, R.: Efficient Computation of Adaptive Threshold Surfaces for Image Binarization. J. PR. 39(1), 89–101 (2006)
14. Burt, P.J., Adelson, E.H.: The Laplacian Pyramid as a Compact Image Crode. J. IEEE TCOM. 31(4), 532–540 (1983)
15. Mallat, S.: A Wavelet Tour of Signal Processing, vol. 3. Academic Press, London (1999)
16. Pigeonhole Principle, http://en.wikipedia.org/wiki/Pigeonhole_principle
17. Document Image Binarization Contest (DIBCO) (2009), http://users.iit.demokritos.gr/bgat/DIBCO2009/

Laser Communication Using High Speed Digital Design

Walasang S.S. and Kale S.N.

Defence Institute of Advanced Technology, Girinagar, Pune, India
sswalasang@yahoo.com

Abstract. The laser communication provides very high bandwidth enabling real time transmission of data, voice and video through free space. We have designed a laser transmitter which can switch at 155 Mbps [E3,T3,FE,ATM, OC-3/STM-1] with average power of 10-30mw across all frequency range upto 155Mbps, further the circuit incorporates safety of ESD(electro static discharge), slow start, over current protection and temp control. The receiver has been tested independently and in an integrated setup (with transmitter) starting from APD, comparator and pulse shaping circuit by stimulated input. The power budget is calculated for the link taking into account fade margin(Tx power, Rx aperture, Rx sensitivity, atmospheric losses due to absorption, scattering, scintillation etc).The optical lenses will be utilized to make the beam divergent limited and for focusing the light onto the receiver active area.

Keywords: High Speed Digital Logic, Laser Communication, Optical Communication, Optical Wireless.

1   Introduction

Communications using light is not a new science. Back in 1880, Alexander Graham Bell experimented with his photo phone that used sunlight reflected off a vibrating mirror and a selenium photo cell to send telephone like signals over a range of 600 feet. Laser communication or optical Wireless, refers to the transmission of modulated visible or IR beams through the atmosphere to achieve optical communications. Like traditional fiber optic communications, Laser communication uses lasers to transmit data, but instead of enclosing the data stream in a glass fiber, it is transmitted through the air. Currently RF is used as a technology[1] for communication for mobile elements. The disadvantage with RF is, the bit rates achieved are low unsecure and lower bandwidth will not be able to transmit real time information hence Laser communication which is highly secure and offers high bandwidth capability for real time communication needs would meet the requirement of mobile elements in real time decision making process[2]. The specification aimed to achieve for the laser communication are

(a) Window of operation : 1550nm
(b) Data Rate : 155Mbps

K.R. Venugopal and L.M. Patnaik (Eds.): ICIP 2011, CCIS 157, pp. 521–526, 2011.

(c) Laser power :≅30mw
(d) Bit Error Rate : 10^{-12}
(e) Divergence : 3mrad
(f) Optical Source : Semiconductor Laser Diode
(g) Receiver : InGaAs PIN /APD
(h) Receiver sensitivity :≺-30dBm
(i) Modulation : OOK(On -Off keying)

The basic block diagram of Laser communication is shown in Fig. 1.

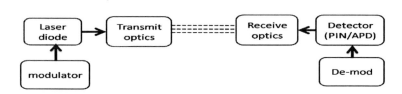

Fig. 1. Laser Communication block diagram

The key aspect of the design was the choice of modulation and the choice of laser source. The data rate being low in the 100's of MHz, we have chosen OOK(on off keying) and the Wavelength as 1550nm which is eye safe and do not penetrate the ocular media of the eye. The choice of 155Mbps [E3, T3, FE, ATM, OC-3/STM-1] is sufficient to demonstrate the transmission of data, voice and video through free space[3]. The laser diode is semiconductor laser source. Dual pole laser driver is chosen so that through one pole it is biased just at threshold and through second pole is used to drive the laser diode current based on the information arrival rate thus reducing the delay in switching time. The stability of the laser diode (wavelength shift)[4] with temperature variation is maintained by the use of the thermoelectric cooler. The output light is elliptical pattern and is made circular by the use of cylindrical lens. The receiver circuitry consists of collecting optics which is designed to collect the optical light and reject all wavelengths other than the wavelength of interest. The choice of the detector in the optical receiver is APD owing to its high sensitivity, which is essential as the propagation of the wave through free space leads to the degradation of the signal due to rain, fog, turbulence, scintillation etc., [5], [6], [7]. Post reception of optical signal by APD[8] the current equivalent to the light incident is passed through trans-impedance amplifier(owing to advantage of low thermal noise and high bandwidth), threshold comparator and decision making circuit for extracting the information from the received signal. The bias of the APD is varied based on the temp of the device so as to have a common gain or multiplication factor. The Transmitter waveforms[9] for various modulation frequency from few Hz to 150 MHz are as depicted in Fig. 2 and The receiver waveforms[10] for different threshold value are shown in Fig. 3.

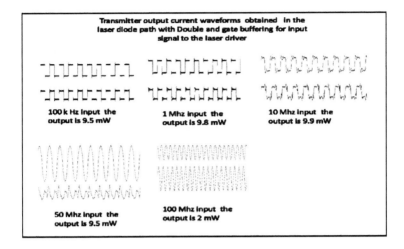

Fig. 2. Transmitter output waveform recorded at laser diode of two layer PCB

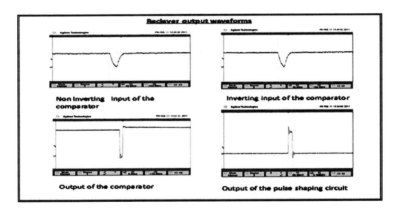

Fig. 3. Receiver output waveform at different stages

2   Performance Issues

Issues that have been considered in the design for optimal performance are :

(a) *Direct sunlight:* This may cause break of communication and thus affect the link availability. The solution is to establish the link in the North South direction or else use filter to suppress all wavelengths other than the wave length of interest penetrating the system if it is required to be located in the East-West direction.

(b) *Prevention of receiver saturation:* This can be prevented by the use of automatic power adjustment based on the link distance.

(c) *Temperature control:* The variation in temperature leads to wavelength shift and this is taken care by having thermoelectric cooler that either in creases/decreases the temperature based on the input from the temperature sensor (thermistor) using the peltier effect.

(d) *Transmitter Power:* To increase the transmission power use multiple transmitter.

(e) The optimal distance to be maintained in case of multiple transmitter is obtained from the following relation.

$$D = \sqrt{\lambda * R} \tag{1}$$

where $'D'$ is the separation between transmitter, λ is wavelength and R is the range

(f) *Electro Static Discharge:* The Laser sources and detectors are prone to damage due to static charges Electro Static Discharge protection needs to be used both positive and negative ESD protection.

(g) *Collecting Optics:* The light at the detector needs to be focused onto the receiver active area, the most suitable for focusing would be cassegrain device(telescope front end).

3   High Speed Design Issues for Operating at More Than 100 MHZ

Noise due to cross talk, mutual inductance, mutual capacitance, connectors, line terminations, characteristic impedance will introduce Noise at high frequency especially reflections from the load, ringing and ground bounce leading to abnormal functioning. To address these issues the PCB design should incorporate measures to avoid these effects. It is difficult to eliminate them but it can be minimized by addressing the high speed design issues in the PCB. We have designed circuit using multilayer PCB for addressing the issues involving high frequency f.

(a) Avoid loops as these will lead to the magnetic lines of force inducing voltage in the adjacent circuit

(b) The lines of the path from the driver to the laser diode needs to be short, else will introduce series inductance.

(c) The size of *via* needs to carefully chosen to avoid excessive mutual capacitance effect.

(d) Avoid parallel line as this will introduce cross talk at high frequency. If parallel paths used, incorporate minimum of 2 mm separation.

(e) The thickness and width of the electric path on the circuit is chosen based on the characteristic impedance desired.

$$R = \frac{0.65 * 10^{-6}}{WT} \tag{2}$$

Where R is characteristic impedance, W is the width of the path and T is the thickness.

(f) If the power distribution network is far then use decoupling capacitor at high and low frequency for storage of power and making the power available as and when required by the sink.

(g) To avoid problem of ringing and reflection use resistive termination.

(h) Ground bounce: The use of capacitive load will lead to shift in internal ground reference due to change in current through the ground pin. This can be solved by having lower supply voltage.

4   Multilayer PCB

The multilayer PCB has been designed incorporating the high speed design issues and the output recorded at all the frequency range along with the output power levels. There was tremendous improvement in the waveform and there was consistent in the output power in all the frequency range. The waveforms of the same are shown in Fig. 4

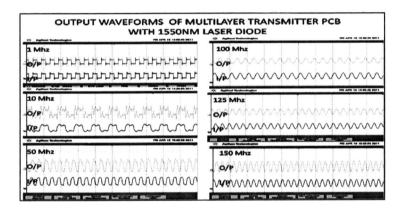

Fig. 4. Multi layer PCB output waveform recorded in the laser diode path

5   Applications

(a) Last-mile telecommunications link
(b) LAN link between buildings
(c) Intrusion detection
(d) Point to Point connectivity between two mobile towers
(e) Weather monitors
(f) Traffic counting and monitoring
(g) Optical bypass(in case of optical cable break)

6   Conclusions

The communication system designed meets the transmission requirement of 155Mhz for voice, data and video, catering to basic protocols of OC-3/STM-1 and for a distance upto 1km for 10-30mw laser output. To enhance the system for OC-48/STM-16 the circuit needs to be design utilizing the components with rise/fall time in pico-second with the choice of high power laser diode or multiple transmitter for higher distance. The laser communication requirement helps to tap the unutilized electromagnetic spectrum band without the issue of licensing added with no EMI, Immune to jamming and free from digging(As light guided through free space) and bandwidth offered is unmatched with any of the wireless communication technologies available in the market(2G, 3G, RF, Wi-Fi, Wi-Max etc) making it an ideal choice for rapid deployment in unfavorable terrain and for meeting the last mile connectivity of the defence real time applications. The system being designed is for static links if the platform of one link is mobile then you need to consider acquisition, tracking and pointing issues, which is presently not addressed.

Acknowledgments. Special thanks to Mr Rajender Singh and Mr Srikanth for their support in evaluation of this work.

References

1. Stotts, L., Stadler, B., Graves, B., Young, D., Kolodzy, P., Alan Pike, H., Lee, G.: Optical RF Communications Adjunct (ORCA). In: SPIE, vol. 7091 (2008)
2. Bloom, S.: The Physics of Free-Space Optics (2002)
3. Al-Akkoumi, M.K., Harris, A., Huck, R.C., Sluss Jr., J.J., Giuma, T.A.: Performance of a Wavelength-Diversified FSO Tracking Algorithm for Real-Time Battled Communicatios. In: SPIE, vol. 6877 (2008)
4. Achour, M.: Stimulating Atmospheric Free-Space Optical Propogation. PART-II: Haze, Fog and Low Clouds Attenuations. In: SPIE, vol. 4873 (2002)
5. Achour, M.: Stimulating Atmospheric Free-Space Optical Propogation. PART-I: Rainfall Attenuation. In: SPIE, vol. 4635 (2002)
6. Johnson, H.: High Speed Digital Design. Pearson Education, London (2009)
7. Gangl, M.E., Fisher, D.S., Zimmermann, J., Durham, L.M.: Default Airborne Laser Communication Terminal for Intelligence, Surveillance and Reconnaissance. In: SPIE, vol. 5550 (2004)
8. Al-Akdoumi, M.K., Huck, R.C., Sluss Jr., J.J.: High-speed Communications Enabling Real-time Video for Battlefield Commanders Using Tracked FSO. In: SPIE, vol. 6551 (2007)
9. Bloom, S.: The Physics of Free-Space Optics (2001)
10. Achour, M.: Stimulating Atmospheric Free-Space Optical Propogation, PART-II: Haze. In: SPIE, vol. 4873 (2002)

Stability of Electromagnetic Waves in Solid Chiral Materials

Shivamurthy K.P.[1], Rudraiah N.[2], and Satyanaga Kumar V.[3]

[1] Department of Electrical and Electronics Engineering,
Siddaganga Institute of Technology, Tumkur, Karnataka, India
[2] UGC-CAS in Fluid Mechanics, Department of Mathematics,
Bangalore University, Bangalore, India
[3] Department of Electrical Engineering, UVCE, Bangalore, India
kpsmurthy1@gmail.com

Abstract. In this paper, the linear stability of Electromagnetic Waves (EMWs) in a source free, homogeneous, isotropic, Solid Chiral Material (SCM) is studied. The linear stability of EMWs is investigated using normal mode technique. The dispersion relation for frequency, of EMWs with horizontal basic electric field a function of y only is obtained. From this dispersion relation, the nature of stability (i.e., stable, unstable and neutrally stable) of EMWs are obtained for the cases namely or where the wave number is in the horizontal x-direction.

Keywords: Electro Magnetic Waves, Isotropic, Linear Stability, Normal Mode Solutions, Solid Chiral Material (SCM).

1 Introduction

In this paper we develop a systematic analysis of the stability of electromagnetic waves in SCM considering source free, homogeneous, isotropic material. The results obtained have many applications in optics, remote sensing in the design of an effective antenna as well as artificial organs in biomedical engineering, joints, endothelium in coronary arteries and in other wave propagation problems. By definition [1], a chiral material is a three dimensional body consisting of molecules that cannot be brought into congruence with its mirror image by any amount of translation and rotation. Therefore, an object of chiral material has the property of handedness and hence must be either left-handed or right-handed. Some chiral materials occur naturally and related to each other as chiral material and its mirror image. Such materials are called enantiomorphism of each other.

Electromagnetic wave propagation, as handedness, is a wave polarization and described in terms of Helicity. Polarization of electromagnetic wave is the property that describes the time varying, direction and amplitude of electric field vector. It is important to note that when a polarized wave fall on the slab of chiral medium the waves are generated namely left circularly polarized wave and the other is right circularly polarized wave of different phase velocity. It is known that behind the slab the two waves combined to yield a linearly polarized wave whose plane of polarization is rotated with respect to the plane of polarization of the incident wave. The amount of rotation depends on the distance traveled in the medium which implies that optical activity occurs

K.R. Venugopal and L.M. Patnaik (Eds.): ICIP 2011, CCIS 157, pp. 527–532, 2011.

throughout the slab. The experiment and theoretical optical activities were well established by the end of nineteenth century and many theoretical physicists and applied
mathematicians have developed a theory to explain the interaction between electromagnetic waves with chiral material. In this paper, we explain the interaction between solid
chiral materials with Maxwells equations using suitable constitutive equations for chiral
media. For proper functioning of practical devices like antennas, machineries involving
chiral material and so on require the condition under which these devices are stable.
The study of it using normal mode technique is the objective of this paper.

To achieve this objective, the required basic equations are developed in section 2.
In section 3, we study the stability of EMWs in the x direction, considering the basic
applied electric field in the y direction which is purely a function of y. In section 4, we
study the stability of the basic state by superimposing infinitesimal symmetrical disturbances on the basic state. From this we obtain the required stability equation using
the linearization process. From this equation we obtain the dispersion equation from
which we discuss the nature of stability (i.e., stable, unstable, neutrally stable) for the
two cases, namely $l^2 > \lambda^2$ and $l^2 < \lambda^2$ and $\gamma^2 > \varepsilon(l^2 - \lambda^2)$ where l is the wave number
in the x-direction and λ is the growth rate of basic applied electric field E_b.

2   Mathematical Formulation

We consider a physical configuration as shown in Fig. 1. It consists of rectangular channel with Cartesian coordinates (x, y, z) as shown in Fig. 1.

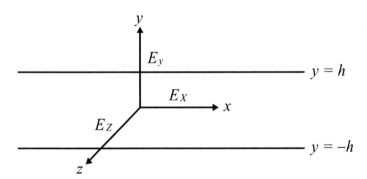

Fig. 1. Physical Configuration

It extending to infinity in the x and z directions and SCM is bounded between $y = \pm h$ in y-direction.

The Maxwell equations for this configuration assuming the physical quantities execute harmonic oscillations of the form $e^{-i\omega t}$ are:

Faraday's Law :

$$\nabla \times E = -\frac{\partial B}{\partial t}. \tag{1}$$

Ampere's Law in the presence of displacement current, $\frac{\partial D}{\partial t}$, is

$$\nabla \times H = \frac{\partial D}{\partial t}. \tag{2}$$

Gauss's law due to source free is

$$\nabla \cdot D = 0. \tag{3}$$

Assuming the physical quantities execute harmonic oscillation of the form $e^{-i\omega t}$, where ω, the frequency of oscillation is a complex quantity of the form

$$\omega = \omega_r + i\omega_i. \tag{4}$$

The Eq. 1 and Eq. 2 using this harmonic oscillation take the form

$$\nabla \times E = i\omega B. \tag{5}$$

$$\nabla \times H = -i\omega D. \tag{6}$$

The solenoidal property of B is

$$\nabla \cdot B = 0. \tag{7}$$

These have to be supplemented with the constitutive Eq. 2 and Eq. 3 for a chiral material are:

$$D = \varepsilon E + i\gamma B. \tag{8}$$

$$H = i\gamma E + \frac{1}{\mu}B. \tag{9}$$

where D is dielectric field, E is the electric field, B is the magnetic induction, μ is the magnetic permeability, ε the dielectric constant and γ is the chirality parameter. Eq. 6, using Eq. 8 and Eq. 9, takes the form

$$\nabla \times \left(i\gamma E + \frac{1}{\mu}B\right) = -i\omega(\varepsilon E + i\gamma B).$$

That is

$$i\gamma \nabla \times E + \frac{1}{\mu}\nabla \times B = -i\varepsilon\omega E. \tag{10}$$

Operating curl on Eq. 5, we get

$$\nabla \times \nabla \times E = i\omega \nabla \times B.$$

Substituting this $\nabla \times B$ in Eq. 10, we get

$$i\gamma \nabla \times E + \frac{1}{i\mu\omega}\nabla \times \nabla \times E = -i\varepsilon\omega E + \gamma\omega B.$$

Multiplying this equation by $i\mu\omega$, we get

$$\nabla \times \nabla \times E - k^2 E - \mu\gamma\omega\nabla \times E + i\mu\gamma\omega^2 B = 0.$$

Rearranging this, using Eq. 5 for $i\omega B$, we get

$$\nabla \times \nabla \times E - k^2 E - 2\mu\gamma\omega\nabla \times E = 0. \tag{11}$$

where

$$k^2 = \mu\varepsilon\omega^2. \tag{12}$$

Using the Vector Identity,

$$\nabla \times \nabla \times E = \nabla(\nabla \cdot E) - \nabla^2 E = -\nabla^2 E (\because \nabla \cdot E = 0).$$

Eq. 11, takes the form

$$\nabla^2 E + k^2 E + 2\mu\gamma\omega\nabla \times E = 0. \tag{13}$$

Since the SCM is assumed to be isotropic, means there is no preferred direction of propagation; and hence, without loss of generality, we assume that a plane wave is propagating along the positive x-axis.

3   Basic State

To study the stability of the wave in the x-direction, we consider the basic applied electric field, E_b in the y-direction, which is a function of y only. Then from Eq. 7, we have:

$$\frac{d^2 E_b}{d y^2} + k^2 E_b = 0. \tag{14}$$

Its solution, satisfying the boundary conditions,

$$E_b = \frac{v - v_0}{h} \quad at \quad y = h \quad and \quad E_b = \frac{v}{h} \quad at \quad y = -h. \tag{15}$$

where v and v_0 are the applied voltages due to embedded electrodes of different potentials at the boundaries, is

$$E_b = \frac{(2v - v_0)\cos ky}{2h\cos kh} - \frac{v_0 \sin ky}{2h\sin kh}. \tag{16}$$

4   Perturbed State

To study the stability of the basic state we superimpose a symmetric disturbance on the basic state of the form

$$E_x = E'_x, \quad E_y = E'_x + E_b, \quad E_z = E_0. \tag{17}$$

where E_0 is an applied electric field in the y-direction and primes($'$) denote the perturbed quantities. Eq. 13 for two dimensional scalar form,

$$\frac{\partial^2 E'_x}{\partial x^2} + \frac{\partial^2 E'_x}{\partial y^2} + k^2 E'_x + 2\mu\gamma\omega\frac{\partial E_0}{\partial y} = 0. \tag{18}$$

$$\frac{\partial^2 E_y'}{\partial x^2} + \frac{\partial^2 E_y'}{\partial y^2} + k^2 E_b + k^2 E_y' - 2\mu\gamma\omega\frac{\partial E_0}{\partial x} = 0. \tag{19}$$

$$\frac{\partial E_y'}{\partial x} - \frac{\partial E_x'}{\partial y} = 0. \tag{20}$$

Substituting Eq. 17 into Eq. 18 and Eq. 19, using Eq. 14 and linearizing them by neglecting the terms containing the product and higher order of prime quantities and assuming $E_o = a_0 x + a_1 y$, we get

$$\frac{\partial^2 E_x'}{\partial x^2} + \frac{\partial^2 E_x'}{\partial y^2} + k^2 E_x' + 2\mu\gamma\omega a_1 = 0. \tag{21}$$

$$\frac{\partial^2 E_y'}{\partial x^2} + \frac{\partial^2 E_y'}{\partial y^2} + k^2 E_x' - 2\mu\gamma\omega a_0 = 0. \tag{22}$$

We use the normal mode solution of the form

$$\left(E_x', E_y'\right) = \left[E_x(y), E_y(y)\right] e^{-ilx}. \tag{23}$$

Eq. 13 and Eq. 14 and the Gauss law for source free $\frac{\partial E_x'}{\partial x} + \frac{\partial E_y'}{\partial y} = 0$, using Eq. 23 and after some simplification, we get

$$\frac{d^2 E_x}{dy^2} + \alpha_1^2 E_x = -2\mu\gamma\omega a_1 e^{-ilx}. \tag{24}$$

where $\alpha_1^2 = \mu\varepsilon\omega^2 - l^2$. Let $a_1 = e^{\lambda y + ilx}$ and $E_x = e^{\lambda y}$ then Eq. 24 gives the dispersion relation

$$\omega^2 + \frac{2\gamma}{\varepsilon}\omega + \frac{\lambda^2 - l^2}{\mu\varepsilon} = 0. \tag{25}$$

whose roots are

$$\omega = -\frac{\gamma}{\varepsilon} \pm \sqrt{\frac{\gamma^2}{\varepsilon^2} + \frac{l^2 - \lambda^2}{\mu\varepsilon}}. \tag{26}$$

Let

$$\omega_1 = -\frac{\gamma}{\varepsilon} + \sqrt{\frac{\gamma^2}{\varepsilon^2} + \frac{l^2 - \lambda^2}{\mu\varepsilon}}. \tag{27}$$

$$\omega_2 = -\frac{\gamma}{\varepsilon} - \sqrt{\frac{\gamma^2}{\varepsilon^2} + \frac{l^2 - \lambda^2}{\mu\varepsilon}}. \tag{28}$$

5   Results and Discussions

From Eq. (26) we consider the following two cases:

Case 1: If $l^2 - \lambda^2 > 0$ and $\gamma^2 > \varepsilon(l^2 - \mu^2)$ then ω is positive and real. In harmonic case we have $e^{-i\omega t}$, $-i\omega = -i(\omega_r + i\omega_i) = -i\omega_r + \omega_i$.ω real means $\omega_i = 0$. Then the EMW is neutrally stable.

Case 2: If $l^2 < \lambda^2$, then Eq. 26 becomes $\omega = -\left(\frac{\gamma}{\varepsilon}\right) \pm \sqrt{\frac{\gamma^2}{\varepsilon^2} - \frac{\lambda^2 - l^2}{\mu\varepsilon}}$. Further if $\frac{\gamma^2}{\varepsilon^2} < \frac{\lambda^2 - l^2}{\mu\varepsilon}$. then we have,

$$\omega = \omega_r + i\omega_i = -\frac{\gamma}{\varepsilon} \pm i\sqrt{\frac{\lambda^2 - l^2}{\mu\varepsilon} - \frac{\gamma^2}{\varepsilon^2}}. \tag{29}$$

This means $\omega_r = -\frac{\gamma}{\varepsilon}$ and $\omega_i = \pm\sqrt{\frac{\lambda^2 - l^2}{\mu\varepsilon} - \frac{\gamma^2}{\varepsilon^2}}$.

For positive sign, $\omega_i > 0$ implying the amplitude increases with an increase in time t, then the system is unstable. For negative sign in Eq. 29 $\omega_i < 0$ and as time t increases the amplitude decreases and hence the system is stable.

Finally we conclude that the suitable values of l, λ and γ control the nature of the stability of EMWs.

Acknowledgement. The authors are grateful to the Director Dr. Chanbassappa M N, Prof. Basvarajaiah Dean, planning and development and the Principal Dr. Shivakumara-iah for their encouragement. This work is supported by UGC-CAS in Fluid Mechanics and also by ISRO Respond Project.

References

1. Rudraiah, N., Sudheer, M.L., Suresh, G.K.: Effect of External Constraints of Magnetic Field and Velocity Shear on the Propagation of Internal Waves in a Chiral Fluid (2011)
2. Lakhtakia, A., Varadan, V., Varadan, V.K.: Field Equations, Huygens's Principal, Integral Equations and Theorem for Radiation and Scattering of Electromagnetic Waves in Isotropic Chiral Media. J. Opt. Soc. Am. 5, 175–184 (1998)
3. Sivakumara, I.S., Venkatachalappa, M.V.: Advances in Fluid Mechanics. Tata McGraw Hill, India (2004)

Fusion of Cryptographic Watermarking Medical Image System with Reversible Property

Viswanathan P. and Venkata Krishna P.

School of Information Technology and Computer Science Engineering, VIT
University, Vellore 632014
pviswanathan@vit.ac.in

Abstract. In todays world large amount of medical information of patients are uploaded through internet, which needs more amount of time
and the information may be easily pirated and grabbed by the hackers.
One of the solutions to solve this problem is using watermarking and
cryptography in a single system, which is proposed in this article. In this
technique, first, the document of the patient is encrypted and then the
cipher is embedded in the medical image using bit wise operation for authentication. Due to embedding, some of the details of the medical image
may be corrupted, which can be recovered by using reversible property.
The proposed algorithm provides high payload capacity, less computational complexity, security, validation, reversible quality and privacy of
the patient.

Keywords: Cryptography, Embedding, Fusion, Reversible Property,
Watermarking.

1 Introduction

The watermarking [1] is done in two domain namely spatial domain and frequency domain [2]. The spatial domain is based on methods [3] like Etrellis
method and Basic message coding [4] in which the detector correlates the received image against each of the eight reference patterns. The Spread spectrum
[5] watermarking method is based on frequency domain such as discrete fourier
transform and discrete cosine transform based watermarking [6] embed the watermark in low frequency, high frequency or middle frequency components.

The differential expansion embedding algorithm with reversible property is
closely related to our proposed work, but the major drawbacks in this technique
is that the quality of the image will be radically corrupted due to under stream,
over stream and round up error problem and also have less hiding capacity [7].
The robustness depends on the dimension of bit plane. In order to secure the
data, some work has been done using cryptographic system based on symmetric
key system and asymmetric key system such as data encryption system, advance
encryption system, RC2 and RC4 etc., [8].

K.R. Venugopal and L.M. Patnaik (Eds.): ICIP 2011, CCIS 157, pp. 533–540, 2011.
© Springer-Verlag Berlin Heidelberg 2011

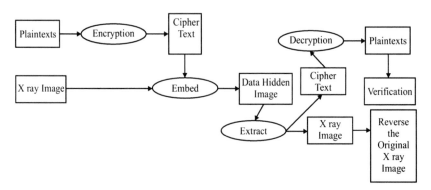

Fig. 1. Result of reference image

2   Cryptographic and Watermarking Fusion System

The medical image verification is the crucial course of action where the information of the patient must be maintained securely and certified without any distortion online. For this we developed an encrypted data embedding process known as fusion of cryptographic watermarking system shown in Fig. 1. This system provides high secure, high payload capacity and confidentiality to the patient data. Once authenticated the original image is retained by this model. The drawbacks of the system are, it only supports the image of range 0 to 255 and if additive or removal of information in the medical image, affects the watermarking.

In this paper, the fusion of cryptographic and watermarking medical image system with reversible property consist of six modules 1. Encryption, 2. Hiding, 3. Extracting, 4. Decryption, 5. Reversible, and 6. Verification. At last the mathematical evaluation and performance evaluation of the proposed work is statistically evaluated.

2.1   Encryption

In this module, we introduce an encryption algorithm based on the private symmetric key cryptographic system, which is used to encrypt the patient information. The encryption algorithm converts the information into ASCII value and then it is converted to Binary data of 8 digit using Eq. 1, Eq. 2 and Eq. 3.

$$bin_m sg(k + j) = bitand(z, 128).$$ (1)

$$z = bitshift(z, 1).$$ (2)

$$bin_m sg(k + j) = bin_m sg(j + k)/128.$$ (3)

By using the key of four bit binary data the information will be changed into cipher using (4), (5) and (6).

$$Qbin() = Rev(bin)/key.$$ (4)

$$Rbin() = Rev(bin)\%key. \tag{5}$$

$$Cbin_msg(i) = Qbin() + Rbin(). \tag{6}$$

where, $Qbin()$ is the Quotient of binary digits and $Rbin()$ is the Remainder of binary digits, $+$ is concatenation, key was 4 binary digit , $Rev()$ is reverse the binary digits and $Cbin()$ is the ciphered binary digits of the text.

2.2 Embedding Process

The transformed binary data called cipher has been taken as watermarking data which has to be hidden in the medical image. In this, the source image has 8bit per pixel, the grey level intensity range from 0 to 255. The course of action of this process is changing a particular bit of the medical image by the corresponding bit. The cipher binary data is embedded in the image with reversible property using Eq. 7, Eq. 8 and Eq. 9.

$$Image(m,k) = Oimage(m,k)\&\&, 254. \tag{7}$$

$$If Oimage(m,k)! = Image(m,k)i = m, j = k. \tag{8}$$

$$Hd_img(m,k) = Image(m,k)||Cbin_msg(i). \tag{9}$$

Where $OImage()$ is the source image and $Hd_img()$ represent the watermarked image. Thus the cipher binary data will be hidden in the medical image until the count moves to an end, where the number of characters will be considered as count.

2.3 Extraction Process

This process mainly focussed on certification and validation using watermarked image through embedding process. Here, we consider the source as the water-marked image and count as key for extracting the cipher text using Eq. 10.

$$Cbin_msg(i) = Hd_img \&\& 1. \tag{10}$$

2.4 Decryption

The medical image of a particular patient will be guaranteed at this stage by converting the cipher data to plain data using Eq. 11 and Eq. 12.

$$Q1bin() = Qbin()Xkey. \tag{11}$$

$$Pbin() = Rev(Q1bin + Rbin). \tag{12}$$

Where $Pbin()$ is the binary data of the plain text. The obtained data will be further converted into ASCII value and then to character. The resultant data will be used for authentication and verification of the patient.

2.5   Reversible Operation

The reversible operation is used to remove the watermarking and get back the original medical image. Initially the embedded region of watermarked image will be converted to an intermediate image which will be processed using Eq. 13. The resultant image and the extracted key, which contains the $(i,j)th$ position of the image where changes occur due to Eq. 11, will be processed further by Eq. 14 for reconstruction.

$$Image(m,k) = Hd_img(m,k)Cbin_msg(). \qquad (13)$$

$$OImage(m,k) = Image(i,j)||1. \qquad (14)$$

2.6   Authentication

In order to validate the ownership of the patient, multiple validations will be carried out. First, we check the count of characters and spaces in the notepad key by comparing the decrypted data with the data which is present before extraction process. Next we check the deciphered data using the private key of 4 digit binary number. Finally, we compare the decrypted text with the patient information. If the text matches with the patient information then the medical image will be certified or else the image will be disqualified. Once validated, Eq. 13 and Eq. 14 will be used for reconstruction. Due to multiple validations the patient information will be maintained secure and private. If any one of the input is wrong then the entire system will fail.

3   Case Study

We have taken the sample of image data as $105, 205, 100, 125, 224, 221, 123, 112$ and the text data as a. Initially the text data a having the ASCII value of 97 is encrypted to the ASCII value of 179 by using the Eq. 1, Eq. 2 and Eq. 3 shown in Table 2. The conversion of all ASCII value to binary format is done by bitwise operation using Eq. 4, Eq. 5 and Eq. 6 shown in Table 1.

Table 1. Binary conversion

Bitand(179,128)=128	Bitshift(179,1)=358	128/128=1
Bitand(358,128)=0	Bitshift(358,1)=716	0/128=0
Bitand(716,128)=128	Bitshift(716,1)=1432	128/128=1
Bitand(1432,128)=128	Bitshift(1432,1)=2864	128/128=1
Bitand(2864,128)=0	Bitshift(2864,1)=5728	0/128=0
Bitand(5728,128)=0	Bitland(5728,1)=11456	0/128=0
Bitand(11456,128)=0		

Table 2. Encryption

'a'=01100001	key='1001'
Reverse=10110000	Qbin=10110000/1001=10011
Rbin=10110000%1001=101	Encryped data=10110011=179

The sample cipher data 179 of the text data in binary format is embedded in the image using the Eq. 7, Eq. 8 and Eq. 9. The mathematical computation performed between the image and cipher data is shown in the Table 3. Due to embedding the original sample data is changed into $105, 205, 101, 125, 224, 221, 123, 113$ which is called watermarked data.

Table 3. Embedding

$Original image$	$Bitland(image, 254)$	179	$BitXOR(image, bin)$
105 01101001	104 01101000	1	105 01101001
205 11001101	204 11001100	0	204 11001100
100 01100100	100 01100100	1	101 01100101
125 01111101	124 01111100	1	125 01111101
224 11100000	224 11100000	0	224 11100000
221 011011101	220 01101110	0	220 11011100
123 01111011	122 01111010	1	123 01111011
112 01110000	112 01110000	1	113 01110001

The watermarked image data $105, 205, 101, 125, 224, 221, 123, 113$ is taken as input for extraction and for reconstruction of image. The sample watermarked data is processed by the Eq. 10 such that embedded data will be comes out from the image which is used for authentication shown in Table 4. For reconstruction this extracted data is processed with the watermarked image using Eq. 11 and by using the index table and the Eq. 12 the image is reconstructed is shown in Table 4.

Table 4. Extraction and Reconstruction

Original Image	Embedded	Extraction BitAND(Image,1)	Reconstruction BitXOR(Img,R)	BitOR(Img,1)
105 01101001	105 01101001	1	104	105
205 11001101	204 11001100	0	204	205
100 01100100	101 01100101	1	100	100
125 01111101	125 01111101	0	124	125
224 11100000	224 11100000	0	224	224
221 011011101	220 11011100	0	220	221
123 01111011	123 01111011	1	122	123
112 01110000	113 01110001	1	112	112

Fig. 2. Input Tested Images

Fig. 3. Watermarked Images

Fig. 4. Plain and Decrypted Test

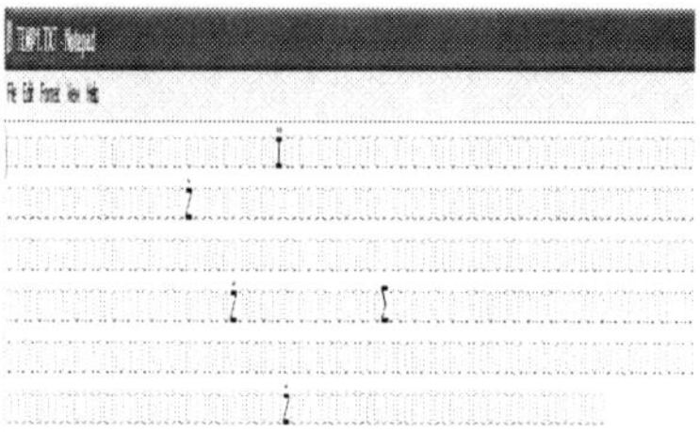

Fig. 5. Encrypt and Embedded Test

The extracted binary data 10100011 is decrypted by using Eq. 13, Eq. 14 converted ASCII value of 179 to 97 represent the character 'a' as shown in Table 5.

Table 5. Decryption

Encrypted data :179'= 10110011	key=1001
Qbin=10011*1001	Added 101=101=10110000
Right Shift= 01100001	Plain text='a'

4   Performance Evaluation

We used the medical image of a patient of $0 - 255$ grey level image shown in Fig. 2 and the details of the patient like, personal and diagnosed details in a text file shown in Fig. 4. The effectiveness of the fusion of cryptographic watermarking system is demonstrated as follows. Initially, the text in the source record encrypted into cipher binary data shown in Fig. 5 seems that difficult to read the data. It is hidden in the medical image in the source record shown in Fig. 3 have less distortion. The image is authenticated by the extracted cipher data from the watermarked image and decrypted as shown in Fig. 4. Further, the obtained cipher data and watermarked data with the extracted key were processed to recover the original medical image shown in Fig. 6 seems that there is no distortion in the medical image.

The record is validated with the information of the patient and decrypted information. Further the image contrast is improved by the frequency domain

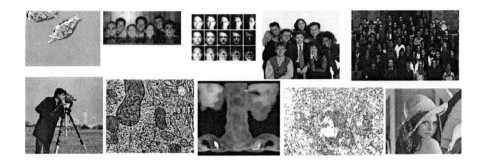

Fig. 6. Result of segmentation on reference image

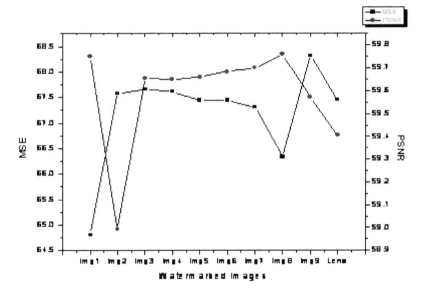

Fig. 7. Result of segmentation on reference image

technique called discrete wavelet transform. The image quality analysis is done by Peak signal Noise ratio using Eq. 15 and mean square error using Eq. 16 shown in Fig. 7 provides highest PSNR and for the reconstructed image Peak signal noise ratio is infinity and Mean square error is zero. Hence the original Image is recovered without any distortion.

$$PSNR = 20Xlog_{10}(\frac{255}{\sqrt{(MSE)}}). \tag{15}$$

$$MSE = \frac{1}{MN} \sum_{x=1}^{M} \sum_{y=1}^{N} [I(x,y) - I'(x,y)]^2. \tag{16}$$

5   Conclusions

The fusion of cryptographic watermarking system ensures security to the patient information in keeping the information confidentially by encrypting and hiding the data within the medical image. This system reduces the need of multiple documents less storage compatibility. The cost is minimal, since all the operations are performed using bitwise operations and the reversible operation recovered the medical images from distortion due to data hiding.

References

1. Hsu, C.-T., Wu, J.-L.: Hidden Digital Watermarks in Images. IEEE Trans. on Image Processing 8(1) (January 1999)
2. Cox, I., Bloom, J., Miller, M.: Digital, Watermarking, Principles and practice. Morgan Kauffman Publishers, San Francisco (2001)
3. Viswanathan, P.: Text Fusion Watermarking in Medical Image with Semi-reversible for Secure Transfer and Authentication. AIEEE Advance Recent Technology in Communication System. IEEE Explore (2009)
4. Fridrich, J., Goljan, M., Du, R.: Lossless Data Embedding new Paradigm in Digital Watermarking. EURASIP Journal on Applied Signal Processing Special Issue on Emerging Applications of Multimedia Data Hiding (2002)
5. Improved Spread Spectrum: A New Modulation Technique for Robust Watermarking. IEEE Trans. On Signal Processing (April 2003)
6. Rajendra Acharya, U., Niranjan, U.C., Iyengar, S.S., Kannathal, N., Min, L.C.: Simultaneous Storage of Patient Information with Medical Images in the Frequency Domain. Computer Methods and Programs in Biomedicine 76, 13–19 (2009)
7. Tian, J.: Reversible Watermarking by Difference Expansion. In: Proceedings of Workshop on Multimedia and Security: Authentication, Secrecy, and Steganalysis, pp. 19–22 (December 2002)
8. Jablon, D.: Strong Password Only Authenticated KeyExchange. Computer Communication Review, ACM SIGCOMM 26(5), 5–26 (1997)

A Comparative Analysis of Multilevel Daubechie Wavelet Based Image Fusion

Jharna Majumdar, Chetan K.T., and Sai Shankar Nag

Department of Computer Science and Engineering, NMIT,
Bangalore, Karnataka, India
jharna.majumdar@gmail.com

Abstract. Daubechie wavelet based image fusion scheme for various images at different levels applying several fusion rules is presented. The image fusion using Daubechie coefficients includes three steps: First, decomposition of source images by Discrete Wavelet Transform (DWT), then selecting fusion rules and fusing coefficients in DWT domain. Finally composing fused image by IDWT (Inverse DWT). For assessing the quality of image fusion, we have performed subjective measurements and objective measurements include reference as well as non-reference based schemes.

Keywords: Daubechie Wavelet, Discrete Wavelet Transform (DWT), Gemma Piella QM, Image Fusion, Multi-Resolution.

1 Introduction

Combining multiple input images of the same scene into a single fused image which preserves full content information, retaining the features from each of original images forms image fusion. Various fusion rules have been proposed which mainly include pixel based and region based and their performance varies for different variety of images. Image processing techniques with a multi-resolution analysis have been proved better than a normal analysis. Multi-resolution analysis included the pyramidal representation, wavelet transformations.

The Fast Fourier Transform (FFT) and the discrete wavelet transform (DWT) are both linear operations that generate a data structure that contains $log_2 n$ segments of various lengths, usually filling and transforming it into a different data vector of length 2^n [1].

A wavelet is defined by a name and the number of levels of decomposition. Image fusion in this paper includes the decomposition of images by DWT, applying fusion rules and finally performing IDWT. The fused image should contain more useful information compared to the input images and in order to assess the fused image a reference based and non-reference based algorithms have been developed which shows how a fused image retains information from the input images. These are called fusion parameters [2], [3] and each parameter varies due to different fusion rule.

K.R. Venugopal and L.M. Patnaik (Eds.): ICIP 2011, CCIS 157, pp. 541–547, 2011.
© Springer-Verlag Berlin Heidelberg 2011

2   Wavelet Based Image Fusion

2.1   The Daubechie Wavelet

Stephane G Mallats algorithm [4] provides us the multi-resolution image analysis technique, which is based on the Quadrature Mirror Filter (QMF) implementation of the discrete wavelet transform. Conceptually, the scaling and wavelet functions are two variable functions, denoted $\Phi(x, y)$ and $\Psi(x, y)$. There are three different wavelet functions, $\Psi^H(x, y)$, $\Psi^V(x, y)$ and $\Psi^D(x, y)$. The scaling function is the low frequency component and wavelet function is the high frequency component. However the wavelet function is related to the order to apply the filters. If the wavelet function is separable, i.e., $f(x, y) = f_1(x)f_2(y)$. These functions can be easily rewritten as follows.

$$\Phi(x, y) = \Phi(x)\Phi(y), \quad \Psi^H(x, y) = \Psi(x)\Phi(y)$$
$$\Psi^V(x, y) = \Phi(x)\Psi(y), \quad \Psi^D(x, y) = \Psi(x)\Psi(y)$$

Ingrid Daubechies found a systematical method to construct the compact support orthogonal wavelet [5]. For the Daubechies wavelet transforms, the scaling signals and wavelets have slightly longer supports, i.e., they produce averages and differences using just a few more values from the signal. This slight change, however, provides a tremendous improvement in the capabilities of these new transforms. They provide us with a set of powerful tools for performing basic signal processing tasks. These tasks include compression and noise removal for audio signals and for images, and include image enhancement and signal recognition. In this section we shall concentrate on the simplest one, the Daub4 wavelet transform. The Daub4 wavelet transform is defined in essentially the same way as the Haar wavelet transform. [6] the *Daub4 wavelet transform*, like the Haar transform, can be extended to multiple levels as many times as the signal length can be divided by 2. Let the scaling coefficients α_1, α_2, α_3, α_4 be defined by

$$\alpha_1 = \frac{1+\sqrt{3}}{4\sqrt{2}}, \alpha_2 = \frac{3+\sqrt{3}}{4\sqrt{2}}, \alpha_3 = \frac{3-\sqrt{3}}{4\sqrt{2}}, \alpha_4 = \frac{1-\sqrt{3}}{4\sqrt{2}}.$$

The wavelet coefficients are defined by

$$\beta_1 = \alpha_4, \ \beta_2 = -\alpha_3, \ \beta_1 = \alpha_2, \ \beta_2 = -\alpha_1.$$

2.2   Image Fusion Flow Diagram

The fusion frame work using Daubechies transform is shown in the Fig. 1. The Daubechies wavelet based fusion approach is given as follows:

1. The two images taking part in the fusion are geometrically registered to each other.
2. The wavelet coefficients are extracted from input images A and B by applying Discrete Wavelet Transform (DWT) with the same decomposition scale.
3. Making use of pyramid structure different fusion rules in different frequency domains are applied to get the fused image.
4. The last output image is generated by applying Inverse Wavelet Transform with reconstructed wavelet coefficients.

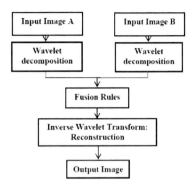

Fig. 1. Wavelet based image fusion flow diagram

3   Fusion Rules

In our paper we have used four different fusion rules which are basically pixel based fusion algorithms namely,

1. **Simple Average:** In this method of fusion the average of the intensity level of pixels of the input images are considered. The formula is given by:

$$C_{i,j} = I1_{i,j} + I2_{i,j}/2.0.$$

2. **Weighted Average:** When weights are given to the input images the probability of getting the fused images with a higher quality will be more [3]. The fusion functions as follows:

$$C_{i,j} = (0.54 * I1_{i,j} + 0.46 * I2_{i,j}).$$

3. **Cross Band:** In this method of fusion, the fused image is obtained as the higher value calculated as the sum of the absolute values of the three detailed coefficients, *i.e.*, HL, LH, HH.

4. **Intensity Band:** In the pixel-based selection, the absolute values of the two coefficients of the two input images are compared and the maximum value is taken for the fused image.

4   Evaluation Criteria for Fused Images

Image fusion results can be evaluated by visually called subjective measures or objectively by image-quality measures. Reference based measures included MAE, MSE, PSNR, RMSE, SNR, SSIM, MI *etc.*. In [3], Gemma Piella and Heijmans employed a universal image quality index to construct a new fusion quality metric without requiring a reference image. They improved UQI and added a saliency factor for each pair of corresponding blocks (a block from each input image) being examined against the corresponding block in the fused image. In this paper subjective analysis, reference and non-reference based quality metrics have been employed.

4.1   Reference Based

1. **Mean Average Error (MAE):** The large value of Mean Average Error (MAE) means that image is poor quality. MAE is defined as follows:

$$MAE = \frac{1}{M*N} \Sigma_{i=1}^{M} \Sigma_{j=1}^{N} \mid X_{ij} - Y_{ij} \mid.$$

2. **Mean Square Error (MSE):** The simplest of image quality measurement is Mean Square Error (MSE). The large value of MSE means that image is poor quality. MSE is defined as follows:

$$MSE = \frac{1}{M*N} \Sigma_{i=1}^{M} \Sigma_{j=1}^{N} \mid X_{ij} - Y_{ij} \mid^2.$$

3. **Peak Signal to Noise Ratio (PSNR):** The small value of Peak Signal to Noise Ratio (PSNR) means that image is poor quality. PSNR for an 8-bit image is defined as follows:

$$PSNR = 10log_{10}\left[\frac{255*255}{MSE}\right].$$

4.2   Non-reference Based

For the non-reference based quality metrics we have considered gemma-piella QM [5], where the saliencies considered are entropy, spatial frequency, cross entropy, variance and visibility.

The quality measures of image fusion as proposed by Gemma Piella are as follows.

$$Q(a, b, f) = (1/\mid W \mid)\Sigma_{w \in W}(\lambda_a(w)Q_0(a, f\backslash w) + \lambda_b(w)Q_0(b, f\backslash w))$$
$$\lambda_a(w) = s_a(w)/(s_a(w) + s_b(w)), \quad \lambda_b(w) = s_b(w)/(s_a(w) + s_b(w))$$

Where $s_a(w)$ represents some saliency of image as within the window w.

5   Simulation Results and Assessments

For the reference based assessment image considered here is the fused image by intensity-band rule with Haar wavelet at level 3 for all types of images except for the multi-spectral images where image considered here is the fused image by simple average rule with Haar wavelet at level 3. The results at Table 1 infer that intensity band performs better for all set of images except for the multi-spectral images where simple average outperforms. The implementation of fusion algorithms and the quality metrices has been done in Visual C++ 6.0 SDI GUI application.

For multi-sensor images, a set of 2 multi-sensor images, CT-MR are taken in the study, the subjective measures indicate the cross-band rule out-performs than other rules and is in difference with an average of 11.33% against intensity-band. For fusion of multi-spectral images, the subjective measures indicate the intensity-band rule out-performs than other rules and is in difference with an

Table 1. Reference based analysis of images

Images	Fusion Rule	MAE	MSE	PSNR
Multi-sensor	Cross-band	3.5481	126.7911	27.0999
images, CT and	Intensity-band	**3.4715**	**118.7314**	**27.3551**
MR (252x246)	Simple Avg	5.4151	186.1377	25.4325
	Weighted Avg	5.6043	196.2953	25.2017
Multi-spectral	Cross-band	12.9065	310.0444	23.2166
images (265x230)	Intensity-band	12.9760	310.5002	23.2102
	Simple Avg	**4.9275**	**55.1464**	**30.7156**
	Weighted Avg	5.2170	60.4586	30.3162
Multi-focal	Cross-band	**3.1115**	**35.3198**	**32.6506**
images,clock	Intensity-band	3.1225	35.6463	32.6107
(512x512)	Simple Avg	3.5830	43.5377	31.7422
	Weighted Avg	3.5756	42.7365	31.8228

Table 2. Multi-sensor Images, CT and MR(252x246)

↓Quality Metrics Fusion Rule→	Cross Band	Intensity Band	Simple Average	Weighted Average
Entropy	4.2764	**4.2874**	4.3339	4.3035
Spatial Frequency	19.242	**19.4638**	11.3044	11.2364
Cross Entropy	1.2431	**1.2329**	1.3733	1.4328
GP (Entropy)	0.7176	**0.7236**	0.5549	0.5114
GP (S-F)	0.7336	**0.7395**	0.5567	0.5175
GP (Contrast)	0.7323	**0.7383**	0.5549	0.5161
GP (Variance)	0.7442	**0.7504**	0.5618	0.5231
GP (Visibility)	0.6882	**0.6942**	0.5323	0.4910

Table 3. Multi-spectral Images(265x230)

↓Quality Metrics Fusion Rule→	Cross Band	Intensity Band	Simple Average	Weighted Average
Entropy	7.3991	**7.4451**	7.2331	7.2437
Spatial Frequency	42.453	**44.3339**	26.0471	26.1867
Cross Entropy	**2.4005**	2.5247	2.5625	2.6093
GP (Entropy)	0.6495	0.6677	**0.6930**	0.6882
GP (S-F)	0.6640	0.6672	**0.6822**	0.6791
GP (Contrast)	0.6755	0.6766	**0.6878**	0.6844
GP (Variance)	**0.7111**	0.7071	0.7040	0.7000
GP (Visibility)	0.6684	0.6690	**0.6783**	0.6773

Table 4. Multi-focal Images, Clock(512x512)

↓Quality Metrics Fusion Rule→	Cross Band	Intensity Band	Simple Average	Weighted Average
Entropy	**7.4074**	7.3907	7.3468	7.3547
Spatial Frequency	10.3805	**10.449**	6.3850	6.4994
Cross Entropy	0.0576	0.0607	**0.0365**	0.0395
GP (Entropy)	0.6816	0.6862	**0.7296**	0.7292
GP (S-F)	0.7346	0.7383	0.7551	**0.7563**
GP (Contrast)	0.7295	0.7336	0.7564	**0.7572**
GP (Variance)	0.7618	0.7654	0.7726	**0.7747**
GP (Visibility)	0.7332	0.7373	0.7584	**0.7587**

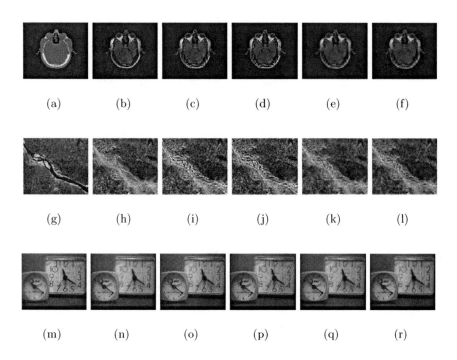

Fig. 2. (a)CT image, (b)MR image (c)cross band, (d)intensity band, (e)simple average, (f)weighted average, (g), (h)multi-spectral source images (i)cross band, (j)intensity band, (k)simple average, (l)weighted average,(m)right focus source image, (n)left focus source image (o)cross band, (p)intensity band, (q)simple average, (r)weighted average

average of 3.38% against cross-band. For multi-focal images, the subjective measures indicate the intensity-band rule out-performs than other rules and is in difference with an average of 5.81% against cross-band. The objective measures indicate that intensity band at lower levels out-performs for multi-sensor and multi-spectral, but simple average for multi-focal images.

6   Conclusions

The Daubechie wavelet based image fusion with different fusion rules has been implemented as the results have been analyzed. Selection of the decomposition levels and fusion rules depend on the type of images, multi-temporal and multi-sensor images perform well in intensity-band at lower levels whereas multi-spectral and multi-focal images perform better in simple average at higher levels of decomposition. The selection of the performance measures also plays a vital role in the assessment of fused image.

Acknowledgement

The authors express their sincere gratitude to the Director Dr. N.R. Shetty, and Principal Dr. H.C. Nagraj, Nitte Meenakshi Institute of Technology for their constant support in completing this research work. The authors are also thankful to Visveswaraya Technical University, Belgaum for their financial support for the completion of this research.

References

1. Graps, A.: An Introduction to Wavelets. IEEE Computational Science and Engineering 2(2) (Summer 1995)
2. Ghrare, S.E., Ali, M.A.M., Jumari, K., Ismail, M.: The Effect of Image Data Compression on the Clinical Information Quality of Compressed Computed Tomography Images for Tele-Radiology Applications. European Journal of Scientific Research 23(1), 6–12 (2008)
3. Gemma, P., Heijmans, H.: A New Quality Metric for Image Fusion (2006)
4. Mallat, S.G.: A Theory for Multi-Resolution Signal Decomposition, the Wavelet Representation. IEEE Trans. on Pattern Analysis Machine Intelligence 11, 674–693 (1989)
5. Nason, R.G.: Wavelet Methods in Statics, p. 55 (2008)
6. Walker, J.S.: Premier on Wavelets and their Scientific Applications (2006)

Automatic Detection of Texture Defects Using Texture-Periodicity and Gabor Wavelets

Asha V.[1], Bhajantri N.U.[2], and Nagabhushan P.[3]

[1] New Horizon College of Engineering, Bangalore, Karnataka, India
asha.gurudath@yahoo.com
[2] Govt. College of Engineering, Chamarajanagar, Mysore District, Karnataka, India
bhajan3nu@yahoo.com
[3] University of Mysore, Mysore, Karnataka, India
pnagabushan@hotmail.com

Abstract. In this paper, we propose a machine vision algorithm for automatically detecting defects in textures belonging to 16 out of 17 wallpaper groups using texture-periodicity and a family of Gabor wavelets. Input defective images are subjected to Gabor wavelet transformation in multi-scales and multi-orientations and a resultant image is obtained in $L2$ norm. The resultant image is split into several periodic blocks and energy of each block is used as a feature space to automatically identify defective and defect-free blocks using Ward's hierarchical clustering. Experiments on defective fabric images of three major wallpaper groups, namely, pmm, $p2$ and $p4m$, show that the proposed method is robust in finding fabric defects without human intervention and can be used for automatic defect detection in fabric industries.

Keywords: Cluster, Gabor wavelet, Periodicity, Texture Defects.

1 Introduction

Product inspection is a major concern in quality control of various industrial products. Textile industry is one of the biggest traditional industries where automated inspection system will help in reduced inspection time and increased production rate. Though patterned fabric designs being produced by modern textile industries are plenty, all patterned fabrics can be classified into only 17 wallpaper groups (denoted as $p1$, $p2$, $p3$, $p3m1$, $p31m$, $p4$, $p4m$, $p4g$, pm,pg, pmg, pgg, $p6$, $p6m$, cm, cmm and pmm) that are composed of lattices of parallelogram, rectangular, rhombic, square or hexagonal shape [1]. Strictly speaking, $p1$ defines a texture with just one lattice repeating itself over the complete image such as plain and twill fabrics. Among the other 16 wallpaper groups, pmm, $p2$ and $p4m$ are called major wallpaper groups as other groups can be transformed into these 3 major groups through geometric transformation [2]. Inspection on patterned textures belonging to wallpaper groups other than $p1$ group is more complicated than that in textures belonging to $p1$ group due to complexity in the design, existence of numerous categories of patterns, and similarity between the

K.R. Venugopal and L.M. Patnaik (Eds.): ICIP 2011, CCIS 157, pp. 548–553, 2011.
© Springer-Verlag Berlin Heidelberg 2011

defect and background [3]. So, most of the methods in literature rely on train-ing stage with numerous defect-free samples for obtaining decision-boundaries or thresholds [3-7]. Moreover, conventional human vision based inspection has the following shortfalls:

- Lack of reproducibility of inspection results due to fatigue and subjective nature of human inspections
- Prolonged inspection time
- Lack of perfect defect detection due to complicated design in fabric patterns manufactured by modern textile industries

Motivated by the fact that the response of the Gabor wavelets is similar to human visual system [8], we make use of Gabor-space of the defective image to discriminate between defect-free and defective zones and propose a method of defect detection on patterned textures belonging to 16 out of 17 wallpaper groups without any training stage. The main contributions of this research are summarized as follows:

- The proposed method is more generic as it can be applied to periodic images belonging to 16 out of 17 wallpaper groups (other than $p1$ group).
- The proposed method does not need any training stage with defect-free sam-ples for decision boundaries or thresholds unlike other methods.
- Detection of defective periodic blocks is automatically carried out based on cluster analysis without human intervention.

The organization of this paper is as follows: Section 2 gives a brief review on Gabor wavelets, proposed algorithm for defect detection and experiments on various real fabric images with defects. Section 3 has the conclusions.

2 Proposed Model for Defect Detection

2.1 Gabor Wavelets

In visual perception of real-world, Gabor wavelets capture the properties of spa-tial localization, orientation selectivity, spatial frequency selectivity, and quadra-ture phase relationship and are good approximation to the filter response profiles

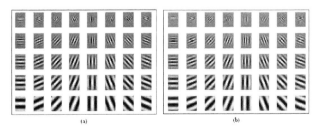

Fig. 1. (a) Real Gabor wavelets; (b) Imaginary Gabor wavelets. From left to right, the orientations are 0, $\pi/8$, $\pi/4$, $3\pi/8$, $\pi/2$, $5\pi/8$, $3\pi/4$, and $7\pi/8$ radians and from top to bottom, the scales are 0, 1, 2, 3, and 4 for both real and imaginary wavelets.

encountered experimentally in cortical neurons [8]. Gabor wavelets are widely used for image analysis because of their biological relevance and computational properties and are defined as follows [9]:

$$\psi_{\theta,\nu}(z) = \frac{k_{\theta,\nu}^2}{\sigma^2} \exp(-\frac{k_{\theta,\nu}^2 z^2}{2\sigma^2})[\exp(ik_{\theta,\nu}) - \exp(-\frac{\sigma^2}{2})]. \tag{1}$$

where θ and ν represent the orientation and the scale of the Gabor wavelet respectively in the spatial domain $z = (x,\ y)$ and the wave vector $k_{\theta,\nu}$ is given by

$$k_{\theta,\nu} = k_\nu \exp(i\theta). \tag{2}$$

where $k_\nu = k_{max}/f_\nu, k_{max} = \pi/2, f = \sqrt{2}$. The Gabor wavelets are self-similar as these can be generated from one wavelet through scaling and rotation via the wave vector. Each Gabor wavelet is a product of a Gaussian envelope and a complex wave with real and imaginary parts. Fig. 1 shows typical Gabor wavelets (real and imaginary parts) of size 36×26 generated using 5 scales $\nu \in \{0, 1, 2, 3, 4\}$ and 8 orientations $\theta \in \{0, \pi/8, \pi/4, 3\pi/8, \pi/2, 5\pi/8, 3\pi/4, 7\pi/8\}$.

2.2   Description of the Algorithm

There are three main assumptions in the proposed algorithm as follows:

- The image under inspection has at least two periodic units in horizontal direction and two in vertical direction of known dimensions.
- Number of defective periodic units is always less than the number of defect-free periodic units.
- Images under inspection are from imaging system oriented perpendicular to the surface of the product such as textile fabric.

As far as images of $p1$ wallpaper group (such as plain and twill fabrics) are concerned, there is a flexibility in selecting the size of the Gabor kernels [10]. However, in general, more reliable measurement of texture features calls for larger window sizes, whereas, extracting finer details calls for smaller windows [11]. For a periodic patterned texture, size of the filter can be chosen to be same as the size of the periodic unit. For images belonging to wallpaper groups other than $p1$, there are sub-patterns within a periodic pattern. Hence, for all the test images, size of the kernel is selected to be half the size of the periodic unit and each input defective image is subjected to Gabor wavelet transformation using Gabor kernels in 5 scales $\nu \in \{0, 1, 2, 3, 4\}$ and 8 orientations $\theta \in \{0, \pi/8, \pi/4, 3\pi/8, \pi/2, 5\pi/8, 3\pi/4, 7\pi/8\}$ to get a resultant image in $L2$ norm [12]. Since the proposed method is periodicity-based, from the the resultant Gabor filtered image of size $M \times N$, four cropped images of size $M_{crop} \times N_{crop}$ are obtained by cropping the resultant image from all 4 corners (top-left, bottom-left, top-right and bottom-right). Size of each cropped image ($M_{crop} \times N_{crop}$) is calculated using the following equations:

$$M_{crop} = floor(M/P_c) \times P_c. \tag{3}$$

$$N_{crop} = floor(N/P_r) \times P_r. \tag{4}$$

where P_r is the row periodicity (i.e., number of columns in a periodic unit) and P_c is the column periodicity (i.e., number of rows in a periodic unit). Each cropped image is split into several periodic blocks and energy of each block in $L1$ norm [12] is used as a feature space for Ward's hierarchical clustering [13] to get defective and defect-free clusters.

2.3 Illustration of the Algorithm, Experiments and Results

In order to illustrate the proposed method of defect detection, let us consider a defective image ($p4m$ image with *thick bar* defect) as shown in Fig. 2(a). The resultant image after Gabor wavelet transformation using Gabor kernels (in 5 scales and 8 different orientations) is shown in Fig. 2 (b). Defective and defect-free blocks are automatically identified from all cropped images obtained from the Gabor filtered image using Ward's clustering with energy of periodic blocks as feature space as shown in Fig. 2(c)-(f). In order to get the overview of the total defects in the input image, we use *fusion* of defects. The boundaries of the defective periodic blocks identified from each cropped image when superimposed on the Gabor-space of the original image (as shown in Fig. 3 (a)) can give an overview of the total defects. However, in order to extract the edges of the total defects, boundaries of the defective periodic blocks are taken on a plain

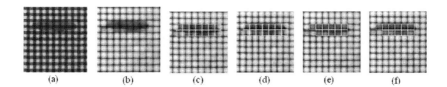

Fig. 2. (a) $p4m$ test image with *thick bar* defect; (b) Gabor-space of the image; (c), (d), (e) and (f) highlight the boundaries of the defective periodic blocks (in white pixels) identified from the cropped images.

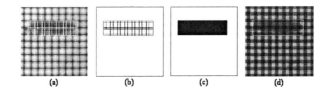

Fig. 3. Illustration of defect fusion: (a) Boundaries extracted from all cropped images shown superimposed on the Gabor-space of the original defective image; (b) Boundaries extracted from all cropped images shown separately on a plain background; (c) Result of morphological filling; (d) Edges of the fused defective blocks identified using Canny edge operator and shown superimposed on the original defective image.

background as shown in Fig. 3(b) and are morphologically filled [14] to get fused defective zones as shown in Fig. 3(c). Edges of these fused defecs are extracted using Canny edge operator [14] and are superimposed on the original defective image to get the overview of the total defects in the input image as shown in Fig. 3(d). Real fabric images of 3 major wallpaper groups (*pmm*, *p2* and *p4m*) with defects such as *broken end*, *hole*, *thin bar* and *thick bar* are also tested using the proposed method. Fig. 4 shows the final test results from experiments on these defective fabric images.

In order to access the performance of the proposed method, performance parameters [15], namely, precision, recall and accuracy are all calculated in terms of true positive (TP), true negative (TN), false positive (FP), and false negative (FN), where true positive is the number of defective periodic blocks identified as defective, true negative is the number of defect-free periodic blocks identified as defect-free, false positive is the number of defect-free periodic blocks identified as defective and false negative is the number of defective periodic blocks identified as defect-free. Precision is calculated as TP/(TP+FP). Recall is calculated as TP/(TP+FN). Accuracy is calculated as (TP+TN)/(TP+TN+FP+FN). The average metrics (precision, recall and accuracy), calculated for *pmm*, *p2* and *p4m* groups, are (100%, 68.6% and 93.9%), (100%, 90.2% and 99.6%), and (100%, 78.9% and 99.0%) respectively (based on total number of samples - 864, 2640 and 1440 for *pmm*, *p2* and *p4m* groups). Relatively less recall rates indicate that there are few false negatives identified by the proposed method. However, since the proposed method yields high precision and accuracy, the proposed method can contribute to automatic defect detection in fabric industries.

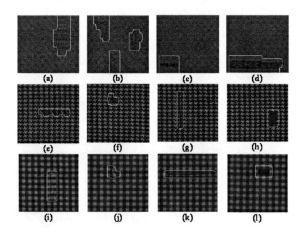

Fig. 4. Result of the proposed method of defect detection on real fabric images. First, second and third rows show *pmm*, *p2* and *p4* images respectivelty. Defects in first, second, third and fourth columns are *broken end*, *hole*, *thin bar* and *thick bar* respectivelty.

3 Conclusions

In the proposed method of defect detection, texture-periodicity has been effectively utilized for determining the size of the Gabor kernels for each test image and for analyzing the defective blocks in Gabor-space using hierarchical clustering. Fusion of defects identified from four cropped images generated from the input image helps in getting an overview of the total defects. Experiments on defective fabric images that belong to three major wallpaper groups ($pmm, p2$ and $p4m$) illustrate that the proposed method can contribute to the development of computerized defect detection in fabric industries.

Acknowledgments. The authors would like to thank Dr. Henry Y. T. Ngan, Research Associate of Industrial Automation Research Laboratory, Department of Electrical and Electronic Engineering, The University of Hong Kong, for providing the database of patterned fabrics.

References

1. Wikipedia, `http://en.wikipedia.org/wiki/Wallpaper_group`
2. Ngan, H.Y.T., Pang, G.H.K., Yung, N.H.C.: Performance Evaluation for Motif-Based Patterned Texture Defect Detection. IEEE Trans. on Autom. Sci. and Eng. 7(1), 58–72 (2010)
3. Ngan, H.Y.T., Pang, G.H.K.: Regularity Analysis for Patterned Texture Inspection. IEEE Trans. on Autom. Sci. and Eng. 6(1), 131–144 (2009)
4. Ngan, H.Y.T., Pang, G.H.K.: Novel Method for Patterned Fabric Inspection Using Bollinger Bands. Opt. Eng. 45(8), 087202, 1–15 (2006)
5. Tajeripour, F., Kabir, E., Sheikhi, A.: Fabric Defect Detection Using Modified Local Binary Patterns. In: Proc. of the Int. Conf. on Comput. Intel. and Multimed. Appl., pp. 261–267 (2007)
6. Ngan, H.Y.T., Pang, G.H.K., Yung, N.H.C.: Motif-based Defect Detection for Patterned Fabric. Pattern Recognition 41, 1878–1894 (2008)
7. Ngan, H.Y.T., Pang, G.H.K., Yung, N.H.C.: Ellipsoidal Decision Regions for Motif-Based Patterned Fabric Defect Detection. Pattern Recognition 43, 2132–2144 (2010)
8. Wikipedia, `http://en.wikipedia.org/wiki/Gaborfilter`
9. Lee, T.S.: Image Representation Using 2D Gabor Wavelets. IEEE Trans. Pattern Anal. Machine Intell. 18, 959–971 (1996)
10. Kumar, A.: Automated Defect Detection in Textured Materials. Ph.D Thesis. The University of Hong Kong (2001)
11. Jain, A.K., Farrokhnia, F.: Unsupervised Texture Segmentation Using Gabor Filters. In: Proc. of the IEEE Conf. on Syst. Man and Cybern., pp. 14–19 (1990)
12. Wikipedia, `http://en.wikipedia.org/wiki/Lp_space`
13. Wikipedia, `http://en.wikipedia.org/wiki/Cluster_analysis`
14. Gonzalez, R.C., Woods, R.E.: Digital Image Processing. Pearson Prentice Hall, New Delhi (2008)
15. Wikipedia, `http://en.wikipedia.org/wiki/Precision_and_recall`

Facial Emotion Recognition in Curvelet Domain

Gyanendra K. Verma and Bhupesh Kumar Singh

Indian Institute of Information Technology,
Allahabad, India
gyanendra@iiita.ac.in, rs65@iiita.ac.in

Abstract. The work being presented here describes a novel approach for human emotion recognition based on curvelet transform. Our approach of the emotion recognition is motivated by the fact that emotions expressed more obviously by the facial curves, hence the technique proficient in capturing the edge singularity as well as the curve singularities i.e., curvelets shall yield the better results. Curvelet coefficients were obtained by applying discrete curvelet transform on the facial expression image set JAFFE. The features were calculated by applying common statistics and classification was performed using support vector machine (SVM). The results obtained are promising, leading towards the inference that proposed method is more effective for the emotion recognition problem than the other comparable methods. Our approach was also applied on another In-House dataset and performance over the same is also included in the result.

Keywords: Curvelet Transform (CT), Emotion Recognition, Support Vector Machine, Jaffe.

1 Introduction

Facial expressions play a significant role in our social and emotional lives [1]. Todays researches are more focus on how to improve better human computer interaction. Recognizing facial expression and emotion by computer is an interesting and challenging problem. Emotion recognition is one of the prime applications of Human-computer Interaction. Computational scientists suggested three ways of emotion detection (i) emotion form facial expression (ii) emotion detection from speech and (iii) multimodal emotion detection i.e., combining facial and speech emotion. Physiological signals represent the most promising and objective manner for detecting emotions in computer science [2]. Major application areas of facial emotion recognition are security, behavioral science, medicine, communication, and education.

The emotional expression by a human face is an integrated visual impact of the various image subcomponents of the facial image mosaic like eyes, mouth, nose, eye brows etc. Hence in order to extract and follow the variation in the facial features, we have to take into account these characteristic points, and model facial gestures using anatomic information about the face as well [3]. It involves several preprocessing steps to track these facial regions. Once face image

K.R. Venugopal and L.M. Patnaik (Eds.): ICIP 2011, CCIS 157, pp. 554–559, 2011.

is registered it is subjected to curvelet transform yielding the curvelet coefficient. The features are extracted from the curvelet coefficient for their discriminating and auto association capability. The optimal set of the feature is being extracted using Support Vector Machine (SVM) classifier. In the present work has been executed for evaluation on two different data sets- JAFFE and our In-House dataset of facial emotion.

A lot of research work already done in the area of facial emotion recognition. Gabor filter have been used to recognize emotion from still images are reported in [4]. Curvelet Transform is relatively new approach used in multi-scale image analysis. Recently Curvelet based work is proposed by [5] for facial emotion recognition. Wavelet Transform based Emotion recognition system is presented in [6]. The rest of the paper is organized as follows: In Section 2, review of curvelet transform is being discussed. Proposed approach is presented in Section 3. Experiment results are discussed in Section 5. Concluding remarks and future work are outlined in Section 6.

2   The Curvelet Transform

The Curvelet transform is extension of the wavelet concept [7]. Wavelet transform often fails to represent the objects containing line singularities, resulting in the poor performance on the objects containing randomly oriented edges and curves. The higher dimensional generalization of the wavelet, the curvelet is designed to represent images at varying scales and angles. The key benefit of applying curvelet transform is that curved singularities can be approximated in non adoptive manner [8], that too with very few coefficients. The curvelet transform is able to catch the edge singularities in images.The DCT can be applied using two algorithms:

1. Unequispaced FFT transform and
2. Wrapping transform

3   Proposed Approach

The central problem of classification is developing a decision function partitioning the measurement space in regions, containing the samples of the corresponding class. The performances of the classifiers are improved by maximizing the interest distance and minimizing the intraset distances in the measured space. Hence performance of the face recognition system too depends upon the features extracted from images. The features should have high interclass similarity and low interclass similarity. In the present work the discrete curvelet transform (4th and 6th level) are being utilized for extracting features from the images. Features so extracted provide multi scale representation. Hence we have used the basic framework of Curvelab-2.1.2 [8] apply fast discrete curvelet transform with some our additional modification to extract the curvelet coefficient from 4th and 6th level decomposition.

Table 1. The Algorithm (USFFTs)

Algorithm for finding the curvelet coefficients:

1. First apply 2D FFT on an object f and obtain Fourier samples
$$f[n_1, n_2] - \tfrac{n}{2} \leq n_1, n_2 < \tfrac{n}{2} .$$

2. Then for each pair of scale/angle (j, l) resample the $f[n_1, n_2]$ to obtain sampled values of form for
$$f[n_1, n_2 - n_1 \tan \theta_l] \; for \; (n_1, n_2) \epsilon \; P_j .$$

3. After that the interpolated object or the sheared object f is multiplied with the parabolic window f_j called Cartesian window, effectively localizing near the parallelogram with the orientation θ_l, and obtains
$$f[n_1, n_2 - n_1 \tan \theta_l] U_j[n_1, n_2] .$$

4. The last step is, take the inverse 2D FFT of each $f_{j,l}$ hence collecting the discrete coefficients $C^D(j, k, l)$

Discrete curvelet coefficient can be given by the following equation.

$$C^D(j, l, k_1, k_2) = \sum_{\substack{0 \leq m < M \\ 0 \leq n < N}} f[m, n] \; \varphi^D_{j,l,k_1,k_2}[m, n] .$$

Here $\varphi^D_{j,l,k_1,k_2}[m, n]$ is digital curvelet transform. j is scale, l is orientation and $(k1, k2)$ are location parameters.

Digital curvelet transform here implemented by fast discrete curvelet transform. Its computation in spectral domain yields the advantage of FFT. For any given image, when image and the corresponding curvelet transformed into Fourier domain, there product is equivalent to convolution of the curvelet and image in spatial domain. Finally the curvelet coefficients are obtainable by applying inverse Fourier transform on the spectral product. Since the frequency response of a curvelet is a non-rectangular wedge; the wedge needs to be wrapped into a rectangle to perform the inverse Fourier transform. The wrapping is done by periodic tiling of the spectrum using the wedge, and then collecting the rectangular coefficient area in the center. Through this periodic tiling, the rectangular region collects the wedges corresponding portions from the surrounding periodic wedges.

After obtaining the curvelet coefficients, the mean and standard deviation are computed as the texture features for the curvelet. Hence, for every curvelet, two texture features were obtained. Let n curvelets be used for the transform, we get $2n$ texture features. Hence we need to use $2n$ dimension texture feature vector representing an image from the database. The features are extracted from very image of the database. Now onwards every image in the database is represented and indexed by the corresponding curvelet feature vector. The complete system model is illustrated in Fig. 1.

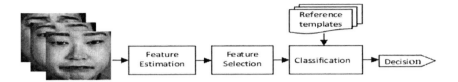

Fig. 1. System model for emotion detection

3.1 Feature Matching

The SVM classifier has been rated as the most effective classifier. SVM classification procedure is situated on VC dimension theory. The central objective of SVM is to track down hyper planes $(H1, H2)$ with largest obtainable margin M that separates the data points $x = <x1, x2, x3, ..., xi> \epsilon R^{th}$ two classes $y_i \epsilon \{1, -1\}$ by finding a weight vector $w \epsilon R^d$ and offset b. The hyper planes $(H1, H2)$ are forced to move apart until they meet similar class of data points which are named support vectors [9].

$$M = \frac{2}{||w||} .$$ (1)

$$((x, w) + b) \leq -1 \; for \; y_i = -1 .$$ (2)

Maximization of margin M beseeches minimization of $||W||$. So,

$$min_{w \epsilon R^d} (w, w) .$$ (3)

subject to:

$$y_i(<x, w> +b) - 1 => \geq 0 .$$ (4)

One of the variant of the very algorithm is soft margin SVM. It tolerates minimum effect of misclassification and/or error for dataset, not linearly divisible by hyper planes and brings the following optimization problem.

$$min_{w \epsilon R^d} (w, w) + c^{\sum_{i=1}^{n} \xi_i^2} .$$ (5)

subject to:

$$y_i(<x, w> +b) \geq 1 - \xi_i \; and \; \xi_i \geq 0; \; \forall i .$$ (6)

where specifications ξ_i is the slack variables that embody total training error. The trade-off intervening training error and maximal margin M is restrained by the governing parameter C.

4 Experiment and Results

The experiments were performed on JAFFE [10] and our In-House database. The JAFFE database contains 213 images of 7 facial expressions (6 basic facial

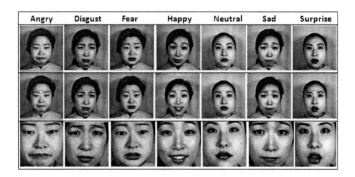

Fig. 2. Face detection of different emotion states

Table 2. Classification results(%)

	Anger	Surprise	Disgust	Fear	Happy	Neutral	Sad
Anger	90.0	9.0	5.2	8.0	6.2	9.0	9.5
Surprise		64.0	6.2	5.7	87.5	5.0	8.2
Disgust			50.4	4.7	4.5	7.0	8.7
Fear				80.0	6.7	5.7	7.2
Happy					95.8	8.7	9.7
Neutral						95.2	8.2
Sad							57.5

expressions and one neutral) posed by 10 Japanese female models. Each image has been rated on 6 emotion adjectives by 60 Japanese subjects. The images are acquired against a homogeneous background having the farthest expression variation. The images are of size 256×256.

The experiments comprise two steps: training and testing. Curvelet Transform decomposes each image into various levels. The 4th and 6th level decompositions are used to extract the curvelet coefficients as described in Section 3. We have applied some face detection algorithm to detect face from facial expression image as shown in Fig. 2. Then Discrete Curvelet Transform (DCT) has applied on cropped facial part in order to extract curvelet coefficients. Some statistical methods applied on curvelet coefficients at each subband level to get features. The subbands at 4th level decomposition are {1x1 cell} {1x16 cell} {1x32 cell} {1x1 cell} and 6th level decomposition {1x1 cell} {1x16 cell} {1x32 cell} {1x32 cell} {1x64 cell} {1x1 cell}.

For classification purpose image of same emotion state is assigned one class i.e., thirty images of angry emotion assigned the class 1 and similarly other emotion states assigned class. The whole database is grouped in seven emotion class for different emotional states. SVM classifier is used for classification purpose. The performance result of curvelet coefficients is shown in Table 1 for JAFFE database. All the experiments are performed on *Matlab* 7.0

5   Conclusions and Future Work

A Curvelet transform based facial emotion recognition approach has been proposed in this paper. The discrete curvelet transform is used to extract the curvelet coefficients for feature extraction and SVM classifier for pattern matching. The experimental results are promising and good in this category of systems: see [5]. As a comparison, we have also evaluated our system with In-House database. Clearly, the curvelet based approach achieved the highest recognition rate in this study.

References

1. Pantic, M., Rothkrantz, L.J.M.: Facial Action Recognition for Facial Expression Analysis From Static Face Images. IEEE Transactions on Systems, Man and Cybernetics 34(3) (2004)
2. Cheng, B., Liu, G.: Emotion Recognition from Surface EMG Signal Using Wavelet Transform and Neural Network. In: The 2nd International Conference on Bioinformatics and Biomedical Engineering, ICBBE 2008, pp. 1363–1366 (2008)
3. Cowie, R., et al.: Emotion Recognition in Human-computer Interaction. IEEE Signal Processing Magazine (2001)
4. Bartlett, M.S., Littlewort, G., Frank, M., Lainscsek, C., Fasel, I., Movellan, J.: Recognizing Facial Expression: Machine Learning and Application to Spontaneous Behavior. In: IEEE Computer Society Conference on Computer Vision and Pattern Recognition, vol. 2, pp. 568–573 (2005)
5. Saha, A., Jonathan Wu, Q.M.: Facial Expression Recognition using Curvelet Based Local Binary Patterns. In: IEEE International Conference on Acoustics Speech and Signal Processing, pp. 2470–2473 (2010)
6. Long, Z., Liu, G., Dai, X.: Extracting Emotional Features from ECG by Using Wavelet Transform. In: International Conference on Biomedical Engineering and Computer Science, pp. 1–4 (2010)
7. http://en.wikipedia.org/wiki/Curvelet
8. Curvelet Tutorial and Software, http://www.curvelet.org
9. Prasad, S., Kudiri, K.M.: Relative Sub-Image Based Features for Leaf Recognition using Support Vector Machine. In: International Conference on Communication, Computing and Security. ACM, New York (2011)
10. Lyons, M.J., Akamatsu, S., Kamachi, M., Goba, J.: Coding Facial Expressions with Gabor Wavelets. In: IEEE International Conference on Automatic Face and Gesture Recognition, pp. 200–205 (1998)

Automatic Identification of Instrument Type in Music Signal Using Wavelet and MFCC

Arijit Ghosal[1], Rudrasis Chakraborty[2], Bibhas Chandra Dhara[3],
and Sanjoy Kumar Saha[4]

[1] CSE Dept., Institute of Technology and Marine Engg.
24 Parganas (South), West Bengal, India
ghosal.arijit@yahoo.com
[2] Indian Statistical Institute, Kolkata, India
rudrasischa@gmail.com
[3] IT Dept., Jadavpur University, Kolkata, India
bcdhara@gmail.com
[4] CSE Dept., Jadavpur University, Kolkata, India

Abstract. In this work, we have presented a simple but novel scheme for Automatic Identification of Instrument Type present in the Music Signal. A hierarchical approach has been devised by observing the characteristics of different types of instruments. Accordingly, suitable features are deployed at different stages. In the first stage, wavelet based features are used to subdivide the instruments into two groups which are then classified using MFCC based features at second stage. RANSAC has been used to classify the data. Thus, a system has been proposed which unlike the previous system relies on very low dimensional feature.

Keywords: Audio Classification, Instrument Identification, MFCC, Music Retrieval, RANSAC, Wavelet Feature.

1 Introduction

An efficient audio classification system can serve as the foundation for various applications like audio indexing, content based audio retrieval, music genre classification. In the context of a music retrieval system, at first level it is necessary to classify them as music without voice *i.e.,* instrumental and music with voice *i.e.,* song. A few works [1], [2] have been reported in this direction. At subsequent stages further sub-classification can be carried out. Automatic recognition of instrument or its type like string, woodwind, keyboard is an important issue in dealing with instrument signals. In several works like [3], isolated musical notes have been considered as input to the system. But, in the signal arising out of a performance, the notes are not separated [4]. On the other hand recognition of musical instruments in a polyphonic, multi-instrumental music is a difficult challenge and a successful recognition system for a single instrument music may help in addressing the case [4].

A comprehensive study made by Deng [5] indicates that a wide variety of features and classification schemes have been reported by the researchers. Mel

K.R. Venugopal and L.M. Patnaik (Eds.): ICIP 2011, CCIS 157, pp. 560–565, 2011.
© Springer-Verlag Berlin Heidelberg 2011

Frequency Cepstral Coefficient(MFCC) have been used in different manner in number of systems. Brown et al. [6] have relied on MFCC, spectral centroid, auto correlation coefficients and adopted Bayes decision rules for classification. Agostini et al. [7] have dealt with timbre classification based on spectral features. A set of 62-dimensional temporal, spectral, harmonic and perceptual features is used by Livshin et al. [4] and k-NN classification is tried for recognition. Kaminskyj et al. [8] have initially considered 710 features including MFCC, rms, spectral centroid, amplitude envelope and dimensionality is reduced by performing PCA. Finally, k-NN classifier is used. The branch and bound search technique and non negative matrix factorization have been tried by Benetos et al. [9] respectively for feature selection and classification.

Past study reveals that different schemes have tried with various combination of the features with high dimensionality and classification techniques. Still the task of instrument recognition system, even for single instrument signal, is an open issue. In this work, we have classified instrumental signal based on the instrument type. The paper is organized as follows. The brief introduction is followed by the description of proposed methodology in section 2. Experimental result and concluding remarks are put in sections 3 and 4 respectively.

2   Proposed Methodology

The proposed scheme deals with recorded signals of single instrument. A hierarchical framework is presented to classify the signal according to the type of instrument used in generating the music. Instruments are commonly categorized as *String (Violin, Guitar etc.,), Woodwind (Flute, Saxophone etc.,), Percussion (Drum, Tabla etc.,)* and *Keyboard (Piano, Organ etc.,)*. Sound produced by different instruments bear different acoustics. Sound envelopes produced by a note may reflect signature of the instrument. Shape of the envelope is determined by the variation in sound level of the note and represents the timbral characteristics. The envelope includes attack *i.e.,* time from silence to peak, sustain *i.e.,* time length for which the amplitude level is maintained and decay *i.e.,* time the sound fades to silence. As in a continuous signal, it is difficult to isolate a note, a higher level features are designed that can exploit the underlying characteristics.

In our effort, we try to deal with small number of features and rely on the basic perception of the sound generated by the instruments. As we perceive, sound generated by a string or percussion instrument persists longer till it gradually fades away completely and it is not so for a conventional keyboard or woodwind type instrument. This observation has motivated us to classify the signals into two groups at first stage. The first group consists of keyboard and woodwind whereas the second group consists of string and percussion. At subsequent level, we take up the task of classifying the individual groups. In the following subsections we discuss about the features and classification technique that we have used.

2.1   Extraction of Features

At the first level of classification we have opted for features that can reflect the difference in the sound envelope of the two groups of instruments as discussed earlier. Basically, the envelope is formed by the variation in amplitude. It has motivated us to look for wavelet based feature. Audio signal is decomposed following Haar Wavelet transform [10]. As it has been shown in Fig. 1, a signal is first decomposed in low (L_1) and High (H_1) bands. Low band is successively decomposed giving rise to L_2 and H_2 and so on. In general, high band contains the variation details at each level. Wavelet decomposed signals (after 3rd level of decomposition) for different types of instruments have been shown in Fig. 2. Sustain phase of audio envelope is mostly reflected in low band. On the other hand, amplitude variation during attack and decay have substantial impact on the high bands. A fast attack or decay will give rise to sharp change in amplitude in the high band and a steady rise or fall is reflected by uniform amplitude in high bands. As it appears in Fig. 2, the high bands show discriminating characteristics for the two group of instruments. There is a uniform variation of amplitudes for the first group of instruments. On the other hand, for the second group a noticeable phase of uniform amplitude without much variation is reflected.

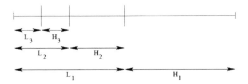

Fig. 1. Schematic Diagram for Wavelet Decomposition

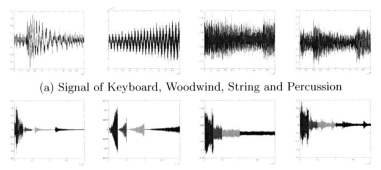

(a) Signal of Keyboard, Woodwind, String and Percussion

(b) Signal after wavelet decomposition of corresponding signal shown in (a)

Fig. 2. Signal of different instruments and corresponding signal after wavelet decomposition

Features are computed based on short time energy (STE) for the decomposed signals in H_1, H_2, H_3 and L_3 bands. For each band, signal is first divided into frames consisting of 400 samples. For each frame, short time energy (STE) is computed. Finally, the average and standard deviation of STE of all frames in the band are taken to form 8-dimensional feature.

(a)   (b)   (c)   (d)

Fig. 3. MFCC plots for different instrument signal shown in Fig. 2: (a) Keyboard, (b) Woodwind, (c) String and (d) Percussion

For the second stage, in order to discriminate the instrument types within the groups, we have considered Mel Frequency Cepstral Co-efficients (MFCC) as the features. As the instruments within each group differs in terms of distribution of spectral power, we have considered 13-dimensional MFCC features. The steps for computing the features are same as elaborated in [11]. Features are obtained by taking the average of first 13 co-efficients obtained for each frame. The plot of MFCC co-efficients for different signals have been shown in Fig. 3. It clearly shows that the plots for a keyboard and woodwind are quite distinctive and same is also observed for a string and percussion instrument.

2.2   Classification

The variety in the audio database under consideration makes the task of classification critical. The variation even within a class poses problem for NN based classification. For SVM, the tuning of parameters for optimal performance is very critical. It has motivated us to look for a robust estimator capable of handling the diversity of data and can model the data satisfactorily. RANdom Sample And Consensus (RANSAC) appears as a suitable alternative to fulfill the requirement.

RANSAC [12] is an iterative method to estimate the parameters of a certain model from a set of data contaminated by large number of outliers. The major strength of RANSAC over other estimators lies in the fact that the estimation is made based on inliers *i.e.* whose distribution can be explained by a set of model parameters. It can produce reasonably good model provided a data set contains a sizable amount of inliers. It may be noted that RANSAC can work satisfactorily even with outliers amounting to 50% of entire data set [13]. Classically, RANSAC is an estimator for the parameters of a model from a given data set. In this work, the evolved model has been used for classification.

3   Experimental Result

In order to carry out the experiment, we have prepared a database consisting of 334 instrumental files. 86 files corresponds to different keyboard instruments like piano, organ. 82 files corresponds to woodwind instrument like flute, saxophone. String instrument like guitar, violin, sitar contribute 84 files and remaining 82 files represent percussion instruments like drum, tabla. The database thus reflects appreciable variety in each class of instrument. Each file has the audio of around 40-45 seconds duration. Sampling frequency for the data is 22050 Hz. Samples are of 16-bits and of type mono.

Table 1. Classification Accuracy (in %) at First Stage

Classific. Scheme	Keyboard and Woodwind	String and Percussion
MLP	81.95	85.94
SVM	88.40	85.54
RANSAC	91.50	92.67

Table 2. Classification Accuracy (in %) at Second Stage

Classific. Scheme	Keyboard	Woodwind	String	Percussion
MLP	81.40	76.74	71.43	75.61
SVM	82.55	79.26	73.80	90.69
RANSAC	87.21	85.37	84.52	89.02

Tables 1 and 2 show the performance of the proposed scheme at two stages. We have used 50% data of each class as training set and remaining data for testing. Experiment is once again repeated by reversing the training and test set. Average accuracy has been shown in the tables. For MLP, there are 8 and 13 nodes in the input layers at first and second stage respectively. Number of output nodes is 2. we have considered single hidden layer with 6 and 8 internal nodes at first and second stage respectively. For SVM we have considered RBF kernel. Tables clearly show that performance of RANSAC based classification (with default parameter setting) is better.

4   Conclusions

We have presented a hierarchical scheme for automatic identification of instrument type in a music signal. Unlike other systems, proposed system works with features which are simple and of very low dimension. Wavelet based features categorizes the instruments in two groups and finally, MFCC based features classify the individual instrument classes in each group. RANSAC has been utilized as a classification tool which is quite robust in handling the variety of data. Experimental result also indicates the effectiveness of this simple but novel scheme.

Acknowledgment

The work is partially supported by the facilities created under DST-PURSE program in Computer Science and Engineering Department of Jadavpur University.

References

1. Zhang, T., Kuo, C.C.J.: Content-based Audio Classification and Retrieval for Audiovisual Data Parsing. Kluwer Academic, Dordrecht (2001)
2. Ghosal, A., Chakraborty, R., Dhara, B.C., Saha, S.K.: Instrumental/song Classification of Music Signal using RANSAC. In: 3rd International Conference on Electronic Computer Technology, India. IEEE CS Press, Los Alamitos (2011)
3. Herrera, P., Peeters, G., Dubnov, S.: Automatic Classification of Musical Instrument Sounds. New Music Research (2000)
4. Livshin, A.A., Rodet, X.: Musical Instrument Identification in Continuous Recordings. In: International Conference Digital Audio Effects, pp. 222–226 (2004)
5. Deng, J.D., Simmermacher, C., Cranefield, S.: A study on Feature Analysis for Musical Instrument Classification. IEEE Trans. on System, Man and Cybernatics – Part B 38, 429–438 (2008)
6. Brown, J.C., Houix, O., McAdams, S.: Feature Dependence in the Automatic Identification of Musical Woodwind Instruments. Journal of Acoustic Soc. America 109, 1064–1072 (2001)
7. Agostini, G., Longari, M., Poolastri, E.: Musical Instrument Timbres Classification with Spectral Features. EURASIP Journal Appl. Signal Process., 5–14 (2003)
8. Kaminskyj, L., Czaszejko, T.: Automatic Recognition of Isolated Monophonic Musical Instrument using KNNC. J. Intell. Inf. Syst. 24, 199–221 (2005)
9. Kotti, E.B.M., Kotropoulos, C.: Musical Instrument Classification using Nonnegative Matrix Factorization Algorithms and Subset Feature Selection. In: ICASSP (2006)
10. Gonzalez, C.R., Woods, E.R.: Digital Image Processing, 3rd edn. Prentice-Hall Inc., NJ (2006)
11. Rabiner, L.R., Juang, B.H.: Fundamentals of Speech Recoognition. Prentice-Hall, Englewood Cliffs (1993)
12. Fischler, M.A., Bolles, R.C.: Random Sample Consensus: A Paradigm for Model Fitting with Applications to Image Analysis and Automated Cartography. ACM Communications 24, 381–395 (1981)
13. Zuliani, M., Kenney, C.S., Manjunath, B.S.: The Multiransac Algorithm and its Application to Detect Planar Homographies. In: IEEE Conference on Image Processing (2005)

Design of Fuzzy Logic Based PID Controller for an Unstable System

Mahima Rastogi[1], Ashish Arora[1], and Yogesh V. Hote[2]

[1] Department of Instrumentation and Control Engineering,
Netaji Subhas Institute of Technology, Dwarka Sector-3, New Delhi, India
[2] Department of Electrical Engineering, Indian Institute of Technology,
IIT- Roorkee, Uttarakhand -247667, India
mahima.rastogi4@gmail.com

Abstract. This paper lay emphasis on the design of Fuzzy logic controller for an unstable electronic circuit. The results of Fuzzy Logic controller are compared with the results of Classical PID Controller that is being tuned by Zeigler-Nichols (Z-N) and Genetic Algorithm (GA) techniques using MATLAB / SIMULINK environment. The result reflects that the system can be more stable with the Fuzzy-logic based controller compared to the Genetic Algorithm based controller.

Keywords: Fuzzy Logic Controller, Fuzzy Sets, Linguistic Variables, PID Controller.

1 Introduction

The Fuzzy logic was initiated in 1965 by Lotfi A.Zadeh [1]. Fuzzy control system is a system based on fuzzy logic-a mathematical system that analyses analog input variables in terms of logical variables and takes on continuous values between 0 and 1, in contrast to classical or digital logic which operates on either 0 or 1 [2]. Fuzzy logic is widely used in machine control. Although genetic algorithm can perform just as well as fuzzy logic in many cases, fuzzy logic has an additional advantage that solution to the problem can be cast in those terms that human operator can understand, so that their experience can be used in the design of the controller. This makes it easier to mechanize tasks that are already successfully performed by humans.

In this paper, our main focus is to design a fuzzy logic controller for an unstable system and compare its result with classical PID Controller that is being tuned by Genetic Algorithm (GA), and Zeigler-Nichols (Z-N) [1-9]. Finally, based on the results of fuzzy logic controller and PID Controller, various parameters such as overshoot, rise time, settling time, and steady state error are calculated and compared.

2 Classical and Fuzzy PID Controller

As PID is regarded as standard control structure of the classical control theory, and fuzzy controllers have positioned themselves as a counterpart of classical

K.R. Venugopal and L.M. Patnaik (Eds.): ICIP 2011, CCIS 157, pp. 566–571, 2011.

PID controllers. PID Controllers are designed only for linear systems and they provide a preferable cost/benefit ratio [5]. However, the presence of non-linear effects limits their performance. Fuzzy controllers are successfully applied to non-linear structural characteristics. PID control law states that the output of the controller is combination of the proportional action, integral action, and the derivative action and is given by Eq. 1.

$$u(t) = K_p \left[e(t) + \frac{1}{T_i} \int_0^t e(u)du + T_d \frac{d}{dt} e(t) \right].$$ (1)

But in discrete domain output can be expressed as :

$$u(k) = K \left[e(k) + \frac{1}{T_i} (e(k) + e(k-1) + ...) \Delta t + T_d \left(\frac{e(k) - e(k-1)}{\Delta t} \right) \right].$$ (2)

$$u(k-1) = K \left[e(k-1) + \frac{1}{T_i} (e(k-1) + e(k-2) + ...) \Delta t + T_d \left(\frac{e(k-1) - e(k-2)}{\Delta t} \right) \right].$$ (3)

from Eq. (2) and Eq. (3), it can be shown that

$$u(k) = u(k-1) + \Delta u(k).$$ (4)

where $\Delta u(k)$ is incremental control action, and can be defined as, $\Delta u(k) = f(e(k), \Delta e(k), ...)$. Hence from above Eq. (4) we can say that, similar to classical PID Controller can have the following structure.

$$u(k) = u(k-1) + \Delta u(k).$$

However, $\Delta u(k)$ is obtained using fuzzy rule base that provides incremental control action, which is a function of e and Δe.

3   Design Consideration

In this paper, to show the comparison of Fuzzy Controller and Classical PID Controller we have considered an unstable system [3], having transfer function given by Eq. (5) and is shown below in Fig. 1. The step response of the unstable system is shown in Fig. 2.

$$G(s) = \frac{P(s)}{1 - P(s)H(s)} = \frac{1}{0.001s^3 + 0.04s^2 + 0.6s - 3}.$$ (5)

Further we have designed Fuzzy Logic based PID Controller and Genetic Algorithm (GA), Z-N tuned PID Controller for the above mentioned unstable system.

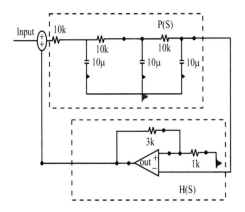

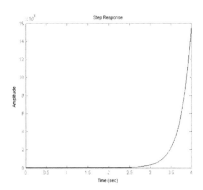

Fig. 1. Proposed Plant

Fig. 2. Step Response of unstable system

4   Design of PID Controller

Simulink model of the PID Controller for the above mentioned unstable system is shown below in Fig. 3.

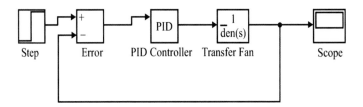

Fig. 3. PID Controller

By considering the values of the tuning parameters for both Zeigler-Nichols (Z-N) and Genetic Algorithm (GA) [3]. The step response of the plant with Controller is shown below in Fig. 4 and Fig. 5.

5   Design of Fuzzy Logic Controller

Simulink model of the fuzzy controller and plant with unity feedback is shown in Fig. 6.

In this paper we have used three membership functions for error input and three for the rate of change of error (errordot) input and are shown below in Fig. 7 and Fig. 8, here n means Negative, z means Zero and p means Positive.

According to the input membership functions the fuzzy rule matrix is obtained and shown below in Table 1. The response of the Fuzzy Controlled process is

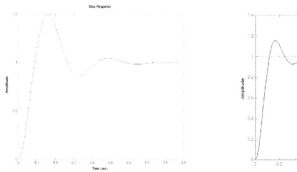

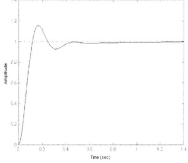

Fig. 4. Zeigler Nichols(Z-N)   **Fig. 5.** Genentic Algorithm

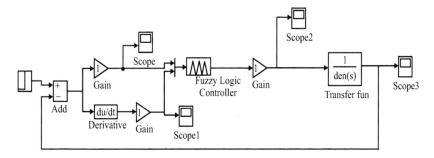

Fig. 6. Fuzzy Logic Controller

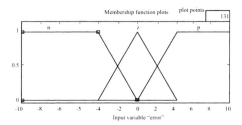

Fig. 7. Membership functions for error input

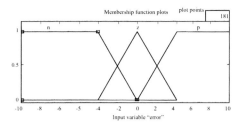

Fig. 8. Membership function for errordot input

Table 1. Rule Matrix

errordot → error ↓	n	z	p
n	Pb	p	z
z	P	Z	n
P	Z	n	nb

Table 2. Comparision of performance parameter

Types of Controller	M_p	T_s	T_r	e_{ss}
Z-N	0.5	2	0.17	0
GA	0.17	1.5	0.17	0
FLC	0	1.2	1	0

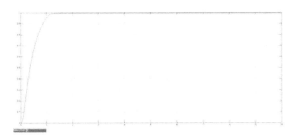

Fig. 9. Step Response with FLC

presented in Fig. 9. There is no Overshoot; settling time is 1.2sec and no steady state error.

The response parameters Overshoot(M_p), settling time(T_s), rise time(T_r), and steady state error(e_{ss}) for Zeigler-Nichols($Z - N$) tuned PID Controller, Genetic Algorithm tuned, and Fuzzy Logic Controller(FLC) are given below in Table 2.

6   Conclusions

The comparison of fuzzy logic based PID Controller with Classical PID Controller is presented in this paper. The classical PID Controller has been tuned through Zeigler-Nichols and Genetic Algorithm techniques. Fuzzy logic control process has been proved superior than the other two techniques. Zeigler-Nichols technique gives high overshoot, high settling time with zero steady state error. Genetic algorithm technique gives zero steady state error and smaller overshoot as compared to Z-N. Fuzzy logic controller shows no overshoot, zero steady state error and smaller settling time than that obtained from Zeigler Nichols tuned PID controller and Genetic Algorithm tuned PID controller. The results confirm that Fuzzy logic controller is simple in design and is prone to fewer errors. Further, we are working on neural network technology for the tuning a controller which gives better results in terms of settling time, rise time and steady state error than the fuzzy logic technique.

References

1. Zadeh, L.A.: Fuzzy Sets. Information and Control 8, 338–353 (1965)
2. http://www.wikipedia.org
3. Arora, A., Hote, Y.V., Rastogi, M.: Design of PID controller for unstable system. In: Balasubramaniam, P. (ed.) ICLICC 2011. CCIS, vol. 140, pp. 19–26. Springer, Heidelberg (2011)
4. Vaishnav, S.R., Khan, Z.J.: Design and Performance of PID and Fuzzy Logic Controller with Smaller Rule Set for Higher Order System. In: WCECS 2007, San Francisco, USA (2007)
5. Ying, H.: Fuzzy Control and Modeling: Analytical Foundations and Applications. IEEE Press, New York (2000)
6. Chopra, S., Mitra, R., Kumar, V.: Fuzzy Controller: Choosing an Appropriate and Smallest Rule Set. International Journal of Computational Cognition 3(4), 73–78 (2005)
7. Jain, A., Dutt, A., Saraiya, A., Pandey, P.: Genetic Algorithm based Tuning of PID Controller for Unstable system. B.E., Project, University of Delhi (2006)
8. Mittal, R., Gupta, S., Pokhriyal, S., Bhardwaj, V.: Design of PID Controller for Unstable System using Internal Model Control Technique. B.E., Project, University of Delhi (2006)
9. Biswas, A., Majumder, D., Sahu, S.: Assessing Morningness of a Group of People by using Fuzzy Expert System and Adaptive Neuro Fuzzy Inference Model. In: Balasubramaniam, P. (ed.) ICLICC 2011. CCIS, vol. 140, pp. 47–56. Springer, Heidelberg (2011)

Analysis of Spatio-temporal Relationship of Multiple Energy Spectra of EEG Data for Emotion Recognition

Theus H. Aspiras and Vijayan K. Asari

Department of Electrical and Computer Engineering, University of Dayton
Dayton, OH 45469, USA
aspirast1@notes.udayton.edu, vijayan.asari@notes.udayton.edu

Abstract. Evaluation of several feature metrics derived from decomposed wavelet coefficients of electroencephalographic data for emotion recognition is presented in this paper. Five different emotions (joy, sadness, disgust, fear, and neutral) are elicited by providing stimulus patterns and EEG data is recorded for each participant. The collected dataset is preprocessed through a band-pass filter, a notch filter, and a Laplacian Montage for noise and artifact removal. Discrete Wavelet Transform based spectral decomposition is employed to separate each of the 256-channel data into 5 specific frequency bands (Delta, Theta, Alpha, Beta, and Gamma bands), and several feature metrics are calculated to represent different emotions. A multi-layer perceptron neural network is used to classify the feature data into different emotions. Experimental evaluations performed on EEG data captured by a 256 channel EGI data acquisition system shows promising results with an average emotion recognition rate of 91.73% for 5 subjects.

Keywords: Discrete Wavelet Transform, Electroencephalography, Emotion Recognition, Multi-layer Perceptron Network, Spectral Analysis.

1 Introduction

Emotions influence our daily lives constantly, affecting our cognitive processes and communication with the world. Several studies have been conducted on the interaction between cognition and emotion and how it affects decision making. Naqvi et al., [1] discussed the somatic-maker hypothesis, which theorizes that decisions made for uncertain outcomes are influenced by emotions through bodily states. Another theory suggests that the variety of emotions that we experience is a result of this interaction between cognition and emotion [2]. Emotions can also occur simultaneously with physiological changes, according to James-Lange theory [3]. For example, shivering may occur while being in fear or sweating when nervous, but due to the theory from Lazarus [4], these reactions only occur after a cognitive assessment of the situation. Several efforts have been taken to understand emotion from a computer's perspective using different methods.

K.R. Venugopal and L.M. Patnaik (Eds.): ICIP 2011, CCIS 157, pp. 572–581, 2011.

Essa and Pentland [5] used a facial action coding system, but used a computer vision system to develop better representations of emotions in the system. Other researchers tried to find emotion through the sound waves produced from speech [6], [7]. To utilize all these sources, some have experimented with hybrid systems to provide a multi-modal emotion recognition system [8,9,10]. Using electroencephalographic recordings (EEGs) as a way to detect states of mind has been a growing area of research. Tran and Asari [11] used Independent Component Analysis of EEG data to detect 4 mental tasks (rest, imagined movement, visual spelling, and solving math problem). One of the biggest focuses in using EEGs for emotion recognition and several other applications are using frequency spectra as a means for feature extraction. Kostyunina and Kulikov [12] found that emotions have some distinct frequency characteristics, which can be found in the Alpha frequency band ($8Hz$ to $13Hz$). Others found that the Alpha band is for attention while the Beta frequency band ($13Hz$ to $30Hz$) is for emotion and cognition [13]. Ko et al. [14] had almost 70% recognition rate for some emotions and 10% for others using relative power values with different frequency bands. Murugappan et al. [15] used relative wavelet energy called Recoursing Energy Efficiency (REE) and Absolute Logarithm REE (ALREE) [16] for representing emotions. We propose a different strategy for energy representation of various spectral bands for more effective feature classification of emotional states.

2   Data Acquistion

To capture the EEG data for usage in our system, we use the Geodesic EEG System from EGI, Inc. containing a 256-channel high density sensor network and several algorithms to process the data. The system has a stimuli presentation software called E-Prime from Psychology Software Tools to present stimuli to our subjects. For each data capture session, we gave each participating subject an Institutional Review Board (IRB) approved consent form to sign for analysis of their EEG data. We used a total of 25 images, 5 images for each of the 5 distinct emotions (joy, sadness, disgust, fear, and neutral), to display as stimuli for each subject. All of the images were taken from the International Affective Picture System (IAPS), which provides a range of emotional stimuli. During the study, each participant would view each image for 30 seconds at random and be given a 10 second rest period in between each image. To provide enough spectral data for frequency analysis, the sampling rate used was $250Hz$.

3   Data Preprocessing

To prepare the EEG data for the feature extraction algorithms, the EEG data goes through three different preprocessing steps to remove unwanted noise and artifacts. The first preprocessing step is the band-pass filter. It is used to remove biases and to provide a frequency spectrum of interest. We used a second-order Butterworth band-pass filter to get a frequency range of $0.1Hz$ to $100Hz$. The second preprocessing step is the notch filter. This is used to remove line noises from electrical equipment that may be corrupting the signal. We applied a $60Hz$ Notch filter to remove these noises. The third preprocessing step is the Laplacian Montage. Montages are used in EEGs to allow different representations of the channels in the EEG. Several of these montages offer normalization methods to mitigate some of the noise that may be present. A popular EEG montage is the Average Reference montage which takes the mean of all the channels in the EEG and shows it as a separate channel. The Laplacian Montage is similar to the Average Reference in which a mean is taken from all channels, but it takes a weighted mean from surrounding electrodes and subtracts it from each channel. Eq. 1 shows each channel being subtracted by the weighted mean.

$$x_m = x_m - \frac{1}{N} \sum_{n=1}^{N} w_{mn} x_n. \tag{1}$$

where x_m is the channel of interest, x_n is the surround channels, w_{mn} is the weight matrix for each channel corresponding to every other channel, and N is the number of channels.

4   Feature Extraction

4.1   Discrete Wavelet Transform

The Discrete Wavelet Transform is a tool used to decompose the data into separate wavelets. These wavelets contain specific frequency bands for joint time-frequency analysis of the signals. To obtain these wavelets, the mother wavelet is processed into sets of coefficients. These coefficients can be further processed into other sets of coefficients. Repeating this process will yield a series of wavelets containing coefficients from different frequency bands. To calculate the DWT of a signal, we will pass the signal through a set of filters. A low-pass filter is applied with impulse response $g[n]$ which is modeled from half of the Nyquist frequency of the signal.

$$y[n] = x[n] * g[n] = \sum_{k=-\infty}^{\infty} x[k]g[n - k]. \tag{2}$$

where $x[n]$ is the original signal, $y[n]$ is resulting channel, and $*$ is the convolution operator. We then applied a high-pass filter with impulse response $h[n]$. This results in two signals containing half of the frequency band of the original signal. According to the Nyquist theorem, the maximum frequency that can be detected is half of the sampling frequency. Since both signals now have half of the frequencies, we can discard half of the frequencies, resulting in sub-sampled signals containing approximation coefficients (Eq. 3, lower frequencies) and detail coefficients (Eq.4, higher frequencies).

$$y_{low}[n] = \sum_{k=-\infty}^{\infty} x[k]g[2n - k]. \tag{3}$$

$$y_{high}[n] = \sum_{k=-\infty}^{\infty} x[k]h[2n + 1 - k]. \tag{4}$$

By continuously decomposing the approximation coefficients using several filters into sets of coefficients, we can obtain a set of sub-sampled wavelets. For our feature extraction, we used Daubechies wavelet of order 2 for fast computation of coefficients. Since we can decide how many levels to decompose the signal into, we decomposed the signal into five frequency bands shown in Table 1.

Table 1. The decomposed signals (Delta, Theta, Alpha, Beta, and Gamma bands) and the actual and standard ranges for each frequency band

Decomposed Signal	Frequency Bands(Hz)	Std. Frequency Bands (Hz)
Gamma (D2)	31.25 - 62.5	30.0 - 100.0
Beta (D3)	15.625 - 31.25	13.0 - 30.0
Alpha (D4)	7.8125 - 15.625	8.0 - 13.0
Theta (D5)	3.90625 - 7.8125	4.0 - 8.0
Delta (A5)	0 - 3.90625	0 - 4.0

4.2   Spectral Descriptors

To characterize the features from the Discrete Wavelet Transform, we can calculate several different metrics for recognition. Among the classical metrics for signals are minimum, maximum, mean, standard deviation, energy, power, and RMS. We can use these metrics as features for processing in the classifier.

4.3   Descriptor Normalization

Applying normalization to the classical metrics may give higher recognition rates. Murugappan et al., [15] uses Recousing Energy Efficiency (REE) which is a normalization of the wavelet energy in each respective frequency band. This technique is the same as Relative Wavelet Energy used by Salwani and Jasmy [16]. We first compute the energy in each frequency, as shown in Eq. 5.

$$E_f = \sum_{n=1}^{N} (x_{n_f})^2. \tag{5}$$

where x_{n_f} is each sample in the signal, N is the number of samples, and E_f is the energy in the given frequency band. Once we have the energy calculations, we find the total wavelet energy by the sum of the energy of all frequency bands, shown in Eq. 6.

$$E_{total} = \sum E_f. \tag{6}$$

where E_{total} is the total wavelet energy of the signal. We then divide the energy of the frequency bands by the total energy, shown in Eq. 7, resulting in a percentage calculation of energy.

$$REE_f = \frac{E_f}{E_{total}}. \tag{7}$$

where REE_f is the Recoursing Energy Efficiency for each frequency band. Murugappan et al., [17] also proposed the Absolute Logarithm Recoursing Energy Efficiency (ALREE) which is shown in Eq. 8.

$$ALREE_f = \left| \log \left(\frac{E_f}{E_{total}} \right) \right|. \tag{8}$$

We propose using the root mean square value (RMS) of the wavelet coefficients rather than the energy values for usage in the normalization. Due to the sub-sampling of the DWT algorithm in each frequency band, the energy calculation would be skewed, so normalization of this energy is needed to improve recognition. The RMS value offers this normalization and can be used in the same algorithms. Eq. 9 shows the calculation for the RMS value of each frequency band, Eq. 10 shows total frequency RMS, Eq. 11 shows the normalized root mean squared value (NRMS), and Eq. 12 shows the absolute logarithm normalized root mean squared value (ALRMS).

$$RMS_f = \sqrt{\frac{\sum_{n=1}^{N}(x_{n_f})^2}{N}}. \tag{9}$$

$$RMS_{total} = \sum RMS_f. \tag{10}$$

$$NMRS_f = \frac{RMS_f}{RMS_{total}}. \tag{11}$$

$$ALRMS_f = \left| \log \left(\frac{RMS_f}{RMS_{total}} \right) \right|. \tag{12}$$

where x_{n_f} is each sample in the signal, N is the number of samples, RMS_f is the root mean square value in the given frequency band, RMS_{total} is the total RMS value of the signal, $NRMS_f$ is the normalized RMS value of each frequency band, and $ALRMS_f$ is the absolute logarithm normalized RMS value of each frequency band.

5   Classification

The classifier used for our experiments was the Multi-layer Perceptron Network (MLP) which is a powerful classification tool which can be trained to learn non-linear manifolds and has the ability to generalize data well. The two-layer MLP network contains N inputs, L hidden nodes, M outputs, and is connected by two sets of weights. To update the weights, we must derive weights by minimizing the mean-squared error equation given by Eq. 13.

$$E = \frac{1}{M} \sum_{j=1}^{M} (d_j - y_j)^2. \tag{13}$$

where d_j are the target outputs, y_j are the actual outputs, M is the number of outputs, and E is the error of the network. When the chain rule is applied several times to the derivative of the error with respect to the weights, we can derive weight updates for output layer and the hidden layer, as shown in Eq. 14 and Eq. 15, respectively.

$$\Delta w_{jk}(t) = \eta \cdot (d_j - y_j) \cdot f'(Net_j) \cdot u_k. \tag{14}$$

$$\Delta v_{ki}(t) = \eta \cdot \sum_{j=1}^{M} (d_j - y_j) \cdot f'(Net_j) \cdot w_{jk} \cdot f'(Net_k) \cdot x_i. \tag{15}$$

where $\Delta w_{jk}(t)$ is the output layer weight update, η is the learning rate parameter such that $0 < \eta < 1$, $f'(Net_k)$ is the derivative of the transfer function of the hidden layer, u_k is the input to output layer, $\Delta v_{ki}(t)$ is the hidden layer weight update, w_{jk} are the weights of the output layer, $f'(Net_j)$ is the derivative of the transfer function of the output layer, and x_i are the inputs to the hidden layer.

6   Results

The collected dataset contains 5 instances of 5 elicited emotions for each of the 5 subjects. Each instance is preprocessed and the Discrete Wavelet Transform is applied. Each instance is then divided into one-second intervals and feature metrics are calculated, resulting in 1280 features for a 256-channel EEG recording using 5 frequency bands and 750 epochs of features for each subject. The MLP network was trained using 1280 inputs, 20 hidden nodes, 5 output nodes, and a dataset separated into a training set (40%), a validation set (20%), and a testing set (40%) to provide cross-validation of data and to generalize the dataset.

6.1   Experiment 1

For our first experiment, we will train the MLP network for each of the feature types for 10000 iterations using the gradient descent method. Table 2 shows the classification rates for all of the feature types. The normalized feature types provided the best overall recognition rates across all emotions. The ALREE had the highest total recognition of 90.00% followed by the ALRMS, the normalized RMS (NRMS), and the REE features with 89.40%, 86.67%, and 83.47% total recognition respectively. We can see that minimum and maximum metrics provided the highest classification for the classical features, 72.04% and 75.51% respectively, while power and energy gave the lowest percentage.

Table 2. Recognition rates for all feature types. The normalized features types are shown to have the highest recognition rates across all emotions. The ALREE and the ALRMS features gave the highest total recognition, reaching 90.00% and 89.40% recognition respectively.

Feature Type	Joy	Disgust	Sadness	Fear	Neutral	Total
Minimum	81.02	74.94	68.40	69.57	83.26	75.51
Maximum	82.27	65.86	72.05	61.39	77.61	72.04
Mean	55.61	50.11	71.40	60.18	54.87	58.27
Std. Deviation	74.94	50.34	42.24	61.90	83.84	62.98
RMS	78.68	58.72	52.76	50.82	74.54	62.76
Power	41.52	50.96	40.55	49.46	52.50	47.07
Energy	63.09	51.28	52.55	54.55	68.34	57.87
REE	84.99	91.56	70.80	86.73	83.30	83.47
NRMS	86.71	89.12	82.68	84.03	91.43	86.67
ALREE	89.72	90.40	88.67	90.46	90.72	90.00
ALRMS	90.00	93.93	87.82	85.25	90.44	89.40

6.2 Experiment 2

We can see that in experiment 1, using the RMS value instead of the energy of the signal boosted the recognition up to 3-4% in both normalized and non-normalized situations, but for the absolute logarithm case, ALREE provided better recognition over ALRMS. To verify this result, we trained the MLP network to minimize the mean-squared error to 0.01 for each case. Results for the normalized feature types are shown in Table 3.

Table 3. Recognition rates for the normalized feature types. The ALRMS feature extraction technique gave the highest total recognition rate of 91.73% when training to minimize the mean-squared error to 0.01.

Feature Type	Joy	Disgust	Sadness	Fear	Neutral	Total
REE	89.32	93.62	81.56	92.07	88.63	88.87
NRMS	92.21	92.38	88.81	91.13	89.32	90.80
ALREE	95.70	89.23	89.21	89.97	89.03	90.53
ALRMS	94.74	92.62	91.13	90.61	89.58	91.73

In both the regular and the absolute logarithm normalization process, we found that using the RMS value provided 1-2% better recognition over using the energy value. This shows that compressing the data allowed better recognition of the data. In calculating the energy of a signal, the number of samples is not noted, so if all of the signals had the same number of samples, recognition rates for energy and power would be the same because power scales the signal based on the number of samples. Calculating the wavelet energy for each frequency band

Table 4. The coefficient of variation for different frequency bands across all electrode channels. The RMS value gave the lowest coefficient of variation, thus showing the compression of values and allowing higher recognition rates.

Freq. Bands	Power	Energy	RMS	REE	NRMS	ALREE	ALRMS
Gamma (D2)	7.84	7.30	1.17	1.43	0.59	0.29	0.16
Beta (D3)	13.50	7.59	1.01	1.12	0.49	0.34	0.18
Alpha (D4)	14.02	12.26	0.99	1.00	0.42	0.35	0.20
Theta (D5)	18.40	17.58	1.36	0.91	0.39	0.35	0.24
Delta (A5)	25.11	21.06	2.19	0.21	0.21	1.09	0.47

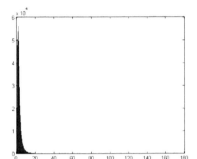 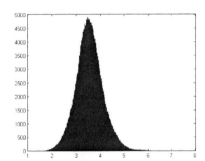

Fig. 1. A histogram of the Gamma frequency band for RMS features (left) and ALRMS features (right). Even though the RMS calculation compresses the data, normalization provides a better distribution for classification.

would have different numbers of samples, so the energy and power calculation would be different. This means that frequency bands with fewer samples will be compressed more, which are specifically the lower frequency bands. Furthermore, the power across frequency bands is higher for lower frequency bands than in higher frequency bands. Therefore, calculating wavelet energy essentially compresses the power calculation. The RMS calculation also compresses the power calculation, but the compression is higher than the wavelet energy calculation, as shown by the coefficient of variation in Table 4. The normalization types gave the best compression of data, showing lower coefficients of variation. ALRMS gave the lowest coefficient of variation across most frequency bands, which produced the best recognition rates. Fig. 1 shows a histogram of the Gamma frequency band compressed by RMS and ALRMS. We can see that a majority of the signal is found in the far left portion of the histogram while higher values are sparsely found elsewhere for RMS. The ALRMS gave a wide normal distribution which is suitable for better classification. To allow a normal distribution of values for RMS, further compression will be needed to compress the higher values, which can be done without decriptor normalization.

7   Conclusions

In this paper, we observed that using normalized frequency spectral descriptors for emotion recognition provided the best classification rates over conventional feature data. These classification rates are due to the wide normal distribution found in all of the features. Our proposed techniques, NRMS and ALRMS, provided the best recognition for normalized frequency spectal descriptors, averaging over 90.8% and 91.7% recognition, respectively. Higher compression of feature types allowed for higher recognition in both normalized and non-normalized spectral descriptors. For future work, we will experiment with further compression to produce a wide normal distribution of values before using normalization and evaluate its effectiveness over previously used features.

References

1. Naqvi, N., Shiv, B., Bechara, A.: The Role of Emotion in Decision Making: A Cognitive Neuroscience Perspective. Current Directions in Psychological Science 15(5), 260–264 (2006)
2. Izard, C.E.: Basic Emotions, Relations Among Emotions, and Emotion-Cognition Relations. Psychological Review 99(3), 561–565 (1992)
3. Cannon, W.B.: The James-Lange Theory of Emotions: A Critical Examination and an Alternative Theory. The American Journal of Psychology 39, 106–124 (1927)
4. Folkman, S., Lazarus, R.S.: The Relationship between Coping and Emotion: Implications for Theory and Research. Social Science and Medicine 26, 309–317 (1988)
5. Essa, I.A., Pentland, A.P.: Coding, Analysis, Interpretation, and Recognition of Facial Expressions. IEEE Transactions on Pattern Analysis and Machine Intelligence 19, 757–763 (1997)
6. Dellaert, F., Polzin, T., Waibel, A.: Recognizing Emotion in Speech. In: 4th International Conference on Spoken Language, vol. 3, pp. 1970–1973 (1996)
7. Mao, X., Zhang, B., Luo, Y.: Speech Emotion Recognition Based on a Hybrid of HMM/ANN. In: Proceedings of the 7th WSEAS International Conference on Applied Informatics and Communications, vol. 7, pp. 367–370 (2007)
8. De Silva, L.C., Miyasato, T., Nakatsu, R.: Facial Emotion Recognition using Multimodal Information. In: Proceedings of 1997 International Conference on Information Communications and Signal Processing, vol. 1, pp. 397–401 (1997)
9. Chen, L.S., Huang, T.S., Miyasato, T., Nakatsu, R.: Multimodal Human Emotion/Expression Recognition. In: Third IEEE International Conference on Automatic Face and Gesture Recognition, pp. 366–371 (1998)
10. Sebe, N., Cohen, I., Gevers, T., Huang, T.: Multimodal Approaches for Emotion Recognition: A Survey. In: Proc. SPIE, vol. 5670, pp. 56–67 (2005)
11. Tran, M.T.T., Asari, V.K.: Brain Signal Analysis for the Classification of Mental States. In: IEEE Workshop on Signal Processing Applications for Public Security and Forensics, pp. 1–4 (2007)
12. Kostyunina, M.B., Kulikov, M.A.: Frequency Characteristics of EEG Spectra in the Emotions. Neuroscience and Behavioral Physiology 26, 340–343 (1996)
13. Ray, W.J., Cole, H.: EEG Alpha Activity Reflects Attentional Demands, and Beta Activity Reflects Emotional and Cognitive Processes. Science 228(4700), 750–752 (1985)

14. Ko, K., Yang, H., Sim, K.: Emotion Recognition using EEG Signals with Relative Power Values and Bayesian Network. International Journal of Control, Automation, and Systems 7(5), 865–870 (2009)

15. Murugappan, M., Rizon, M., Nagarajan, R., Yaacob, S. Hazry, D., Zunaidi, I.: Time-Frequency Analysis of EEG Signals for Human Emotion Detection. In: 4th Kuala Lumpur International Conference on Biomedical Engineering, pp. 262–265 (2008)

16. Salwani, M.D., Jasmy, Y.: Relative Wavelet Energy as a Tool to Select Suitable Wavelet for Artifact Removal in EEG. In: 1st International Conference on Computers, Communications, and Signal Processing with Special Track on Biomedical Engineering, pp. 282–287 (2005)

17. Murugappan, M., Ramachandran, N., Sazali, Y.: Classification of Human Emotion from EEG using Discrete Wavelet Transform. Biomedical Science and Engineering 3, 390–396 (2010)

A Study of the Performance of Motion Estimation in Vector Based Color Image Super-Resolution Analysis for Pure Translational Motion

R.H. Laskar, Utpal Kalita, and Manish Phukan

Department of Electronics and Communication Engineering
National Institute of Technology Silchar, Silchar-788010, Assam, India
rabul18@yahoo.com

Abstract. In this paper, we have used the existing vector-magnitude based super-resolution algorithm and optical flow motion estimation method for super-resolution analysis of color images. In vector-magnitude based approach, all the three color bands are treated as vector instead of processing them separately. Color artifacts are reduced to a great extent when the pixels are treated as vectors and processed. The motion vectors are considered to be unknown and to estimate the motion, the Lucas-Kanade Optical flow method have been used. For over-determined systems, the Lucas-Kanade algorithm can be used in combination with statistical methods to improve the performance in presence of outliers as in noisy images. The advantage of this algorithm is the comparative robustness in presence of noise. The performance of the algorithm is analyzed and compared with the methods that uses known motion vector, by considering Mean Square Error (MSE) and Peak Signal to Noise Ratio (PSNR). The algorithm for deriving the super-resolution color images from a set of low resolution color images is implemented in the MATLAB and simulation results show the effectiveness of this method.

Keywords: Color Artifacts, Diffraction Limit, Motion Estimation, Optical Flow, Outliers, Over Determined Systems, Super-Resolution.

1   Introduction

The super-resolution technique reconstructs a higher resolution image from a noisy and Low Resolution (LR) image sequence. The key to super resolution is that the image sequences have aliasing. Without aliasing, super-resolution becomes merely a denoising, upscaling, and deblurring process. The quality of an image is degraded by many factors and it is necessary to consider these factors to construct the image acquisition model. If a scene is captured by a high-resolution ideal camera and digitized without aliasing, a high-resolution image is acquired. But the relative motion between the object and camera while acquiring the image, sensors used in the image formation system, optical lens

K.R. Venugopal and L.M. Patnaik (Eds.): ICIP 2011, CCIS 157, pp. 582–591, 2011.
© Springer-Verlag Berlin Heidelberg 2011

used in digital camera and the sampling process degrade the quality of an image in practical cameras. Fig. 1, shows the image acquisition model to obtain a low-resolution image from the natural scene. Consider a low-resolution color image

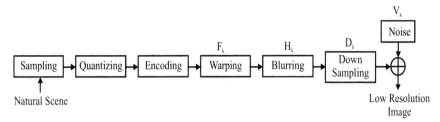

Fig. 1. Image Acquisition Model

Y_k scanned in the raster scan or any other scanning format and rearranged in vector form of size $[M^2 \times 3]$. Let r be the resolution enhancement factor and X_k be the high resolution image rearranged in vector form of size $[r^2M^2 \times 3]$. The three primary things that are necessary to construct a super-resolved image are: image motion, optical blur and the sampling process. If F_k represents geometric warp operation capturing image motion, H_k represents the blurring operation due to point spread function (PSF) of the camera and atmosphere together, A_k represents the effect of sampling by the image sensor and D_k represents downsampling operation, then the relation between high-resolution image X_k, low-resolution image Y_k and the random system noise V_k of size $[M^2 \times 3]$ and is given by

$$Y_k = D_k A_k H_k F_k X_k + V_k \mid k = 1, 2, ..., N. \qquad (1)$$

Here each of the matrices F_k, H_k and A_k are of size $[r^2M^2 \times r^2M^2]$ and D_k is of size $[M^2 \times r^2M^2]$. If all the low-resolution images acquired by a single camera, some of these components vary with time but downsampling, the sampling operation of the sensor and the blurring operation remain constant over time, since these components depend on the construction of the image acquisition system. N represents number of low-resolution images used in the reconstruction process. This equation is called the image formation model or the forward model. There are mainly two approaches to reconstruct such a high quality image. One approach is to operate in some transformed domain. The other approach processes the image samples in the spatial domain directly. The multi-frame super-resolution problem was first addressed in [1], where they proposed a frequency domain approach, extended by others, such as [2]. Although the frequency domain methods are intuitively simple and computationally cheap, they are extremely sensitive to model errors [3], limiting their use. In this paper, the approach based on spatial domain have been used, since it is more convenient to understand intuitively the relationships among neighboring data (measured pixels). A robust super-resolution method was proposed in [4], which was able to remove outliers effectively. For reducing color artifacts, a vector based method was proposed in [5], where each color bands are processed together treating them as vectors. They assumed that motion between the low resolution images was known. If the motion is unknown, image registration can be used to estimate the motion. In this paper we have extended the concept of [4,5,6,7,8] by incorporating motion estimation. This paper is organized as follows. Section 2 explains the main concepts of color image super-resolution. Section 2.1 describes the vector based approach in context of color images. Section 2.2, justifies the optical flow equation for sub-pixel shift. Section 2.3 deals with robust estimation to minimize the data error term. Section 2.4, describes robust regularization and Section 2.5 describes the vector based super resolution implementation. Simulation results on certain images and performance comparison are presented in Section 3 and Section 4 concludes the paper.

2   Color Image Super-Resolution

2.1   Vector Based Approach

This approach is based on the concept that the three color bands are treated as a vector instead of processing them separately which will disturb the correlation that exists between the color bands. Consider a color image scanned in raster scan or any other scanning format and rearranged in vector form. Each vector pixel x_i is represented by a vector as $x_i = [x_r, x_g, x_b]^T$. The color image X is a two-dimensional matrix of three component vectors. Here r, g and b are represent red, green and blue color components respectively. Its magnitude $M_{(x_i)}$ is given by

$$M_{(x_i)} = \|x_i\| = \sqrt{(x_r^2 + x_g^2 + x_b^2)}. \tag{2}$$

and orientation $O_{(x_i)}$ of the vector is defined in terms of the directional cosines and is given by

$$O_{(x_i)} = \frac{x_i}{M_{(x_i)}} = [\frac{x_r}{M_{(x_i)}}, \frac{x_g}{M_{(x_i)}}, \frac{x_b}{M_{(x_i)}}]. \tag{3}$$

In vector based approach we try to estimate just the magnitude part and orientation of the super-resolved image is replaced with orientation of bilinear interpolated image of any one of the low resolution image.

2.2   Optical Flow Motion Estimation

The Lucas-Kanade method is a two-frame differential method for optical flow estimation. It introduces an additional term to the optical flow by assuming the flow to be constant in a local neighborhood around the central pixel under consideration at any given time. The Lucas-Kanade algorithm has been widely used in computer vision for multiple tasks. One of them has been to compute the motion field between a pair of images within an image sequence or video. This technique calculates motion vector estimates $(d_{(l,k)}^{(x,lr)}, d_{(l,k)}^{(y,lr)})$ between LR images l^{th} and k^{th}, where the horizontal and vertical components of the displacement of a pixel (x, y) from the kth LR image into the lth image are represented by $d_{(l,k)}^{(x,lr)}$ and $d_{(l,k)}^{(y,lr)}$ respectively. This satisfies the optical flow equation with the

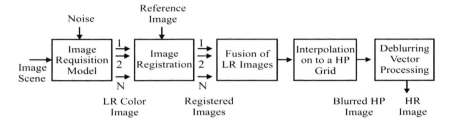

Fig. 2. Super-resolution problem in vector processing context

minimum pixel to pixel variation in the velocity field. The motion vector for each pixel (x, y) is defined by $d_{(l,k)}^{lr(x,y)} = (d_{(l,k)}^{(x,lr)}, d_{(l,k)}^{(y,lr)})$. A window of size m x n is centered on each pixel, thereby the error to be minimized in the optical flow equation will be as follows:

$$LK(d_{(l,k)}^{(x,lr)}, d_{(l,k)}^{(y,lr)}) = \sum_{i=x-\frac{m}{2}}^{x+\frac{m}{2}} \sum_{j=y-\frac{n}{2}}^{y+\frac{n}{2}} \left(M_{(Y_k)}(i, j) \right.$$
$$\left. - M_{(Y_l)}(i + d_{(l,k)}^{(x,lr)}, j + d_{(l,k)}^{(y,lr)}) \right)^2 . \tag{4}$$

where $M_{(Y_k)}$ is the magnitude of kth low resolution image and $M_{(Y_l)}$ is the magnitude of lth low resolution image.

And we have

$$\hat{d}_{(l,k)}^{lr}(x, y) = argmin_d LK(d_{(l,k)}^{lr}) . \tag{5}$$

To obtain more accurate motion vectors, two processes has been added: motion vectors refinement and a hierarchical approximation. The refinement is based on a iterative estimation of the motion vectors (using 5 iterations). Once the initial motion vectors are calculated the image is compensated via this motion field and Eq. (4) is again applied for each pixel. The hierarchical improvement is achieved using a pyramid of three levels to calculate the motion vectors in a coarse to fine approximation. So for N number of low resolution images when compared with k^{th} low resolution image the motion vector is given by

$$F = [\hat{d}_{1,k}^{lr}, \hat{d}_{2,k}^{lr}, ...\hat{d}_{k,k}^{lr}, ...\hat{d}_{(N-1),k}^{lr}, \hat{d}_{N,k}^{lr}]^T . \tag{6}$$

2.3   Robust Estimation (Data Fusion)

An algorithm is said to be robust if it can generate high-resolution image without color artifacts even in the presence of outliers. To estimate high-resolution image from a set of low resolution images we define a cost function $J(X)$ to estimate high-resolution image given as

$$J(X) = \sum_{k=1}^{N} d(Y_k, (DAHF_k X)) \tag{7}$$

where, N represents number of low-resolution images used in estimating the super-resolved image and d represents the distance between the two quantities. Note that in vector based approach it is tried to estimate only the magnitude part and the orientation part is replaced with orientation of bilinear interpolated image of any one of the low resolution image. A popular ML-type estimator is used in this context. Hence the estimated super-resolution reconstruction using the definition of ML estimator is given by

$$M_{\hat{X}} = argmin_X [\sum_{k=1}^{N} d(M_{Y_k}, DAHF_kM_X)]. \tag{8}$$

where $M_{\hat{X}}$ is the magnitude of the vector corresponding to the estimated high resolution image. When L_1-norm is used to find the distance between the magnitude of the color components then the magnitude of the estimated high-resolution image is given by

$$M_{\hat{X}} = argmin_X [\sum_{k=1}^{N} \|M_{Y_k} - DAHF_kM_X\|_1^1]. \tag{9}$$

2.4   Robust Regularization

Super resolution is an ill-posed problem [4]. For the under-determined cases there exist an infinite number of solutions which satisfy Eq. (1). The solution for square and over-determined cases is not stable, which means small amounts of noise will be amplified during matrix inversion. To solve such problems some form of regularization is to be incorporated in Eq. (7). Regularization term added to the above cost function removes the outliers when more than r^2 low-resolution images are present and since super resolution is an ill posed problem this term stabilizes the estimated high-resolution image. It also improves the rate of convergence. For under-determined cases this term compensates the missing information. The minimization function becomes

$$M_{\hat{X}} = argmin_X [\sum_{k=1}^{N} \|M_{Y_k} - DAHF_kM_X\|_1^1 + \lambda\rho(\mu_X)]. \tag{10}$$

where $\rho(X)$ is the regularization cost and λ is the strength with which this penalty is imposed. If the bilateral total variation (BTV) regularization function [8], which preserves edges in color components, is chosen, then

$$\rho_{BTV}(M_X) = \sum_{l=-P}^{P} \sum_{m=0}^{P} \alpha^{|l|+|m|} \|M_X - S_x^l S_x^l M_X\|. \tag{11}$$

where $(l + m) \geq 0$ and S_x^l and S_y^m are matrices which shift M_X by l and m pixels respectively. The scalar weight $|\alpha|$, $0 < \alpha < 1$, is applied to give spatially

decaying effect to the summation. Thus the estimated magnitude of the super'
resolved image is given by

$$M_{\hat{X}} = argmin_X [\sum_{k=1}^{N} \|M_{Y_k} - DAHF_k M_X\|_1^1$$

$$+\lambda \underbrace{\sum_{l=-P}^{P} \sum_{m=0}^{P}} \alpha^{|l|+|m|} \|M_X - S_x^l S_y^m M_X\|]. \tag{12}$$

where $(l + m) > 0$.

2.5   Vector Based Super Resolution Implementation

Applying steepest-descent algorithm for the minimization problem in the Eq.
(12) gives the robust solution to the super-resolution problem.

$$M_{\hat{X}_{n+1}} = M_{\hat{X}_n} - \beta [\sum_{k=1}^{N} F_k^T A^T H^T D^T sign(DAHF_k M_{\hat{X}_n} - M_{Y_k})$$

$$+\lambda \underbrace{\sum_{l=-P}^{P} \sum_{m=0}^{P}} \alpha^{|l|+|m|} [I - S_x^{-l} S_y^{-m}] sign(M_{\hat{X}_n} - S_x^l S_y^m M_{\hat{X}_n}). \tag{13}$$

where $(l + m) \geq 0$ and β is the steepest descent step size in the direction of the
gradient which is scalar. S_x^{-l} and S_y^{-m} are the transposes of the matrices S_x^l and
S_y^m respectively and have a shifting effect in opposite direction to S_x^l and S_y^m.
The matrix F, which represents the geometric warping operator is retrieved from
the Lucas-Kanade Optical Flow Motion Estimation as mentioned in section 2.2.
Though F, H, D and S arerepresented as matrices in mathematical formulation,
they are implemented as image operators like translation for F, blur for H,
decimation for D and shift effect along horizontal and vertical directions for S.
This helps in implementing the algorithm in faster way rather than explicitly
constructing them as matrices.

3   Experimental Results

The test set consists of five images of size 256x256, such as PEPPERS, BA-
BOON, AIRPLANE, LENA and BUTTERFLY. Sixteen low resolution (for
example PEPPERS images as shown in Fig. 3.) images are generated with a
downsampling factor of two along each direction, so that the resulting images
are of size 128x128. We have compare the performance of the proposed super-
resolution algorithm using motion estimation to the performance of the method
using known motion vector. The first experiment is the performance of the proposed method under Gaussian noise condition. For this purpose a high resolution

Fig. 3. Sixteen low resolution images translated, rotated, down sampled by a factor of four and added a Gaussian noise of $10dB$ which are used in super-resolution image reconstruction

color image is taken and given random pixel shift in horizontal and vertical direction. To simulate the effect of camera blur a Gaussian low pass filter of size 5x5 and standard deviation of 1 is chosen as a point spread function. The resultant image is sub-sampled by factor 2 in each direction. The same approach with different motion vectors (shifts) in vertical and horizontal directions was used to produce 16 LR images from the original scene. Gaussian noise of $10dB$ is artificially injected into the resulting LR frames to simulate the effect of V_k . These LR images are shown in Fig. 3. The initial estimate of the super-resolved image is obtained by bilinear interpolation of a single low-resolution image. The magnitude of the bilinear interpolated image is extracted and is used to find out the projected estimate keeping orientation constant. Similarly the magnitude parts of all the LR images are derived. From the obtained magnitude sequence the pixel shift (Motion Vector) of each LR frame relative to the magnitude of corresponding image whose bilinear interpolation was taken, is found out. Steepest descent algorithm is applied only on the magnitude part. The resulted magnitude part along with initial orientation is used to reconstruct the super-resolved image. First the super resolution algorithm is performed by taking known motion vectors. Then for unknown motion vectors, the optical flow algorithm is incorporated to estimate the motion. The performance comparison for both the method is done. The parameters of steepest descent algorithm chosen for this experiment are: steepest descent step size, $b = 0.01$ and regularization step size, $l = 0.04$ for both known and unknown motion vectors. In order to compare the performance, mean square error (MSE) and Peak Signal to Noise Ratio (PSNR) are chosen to be the parameters and are given by

$$MSE = \frac{1}{(M \times N \times 3)}[\sum_{i=1}^{M}\sum_{j=1}^{N}\sum_{k=1}^{3}(I_{original} - I_{super-resolved})^2]. \qquad (14)$$

where M, N and 3 represents number of rows, columns in the super-resolved image. $I_{super-resolved}$ is the super-resolved image which is estimated and $I_{original}$ is the original high resolution image.

$$PSNR = 10log(\frac{I_{max}^2}{MSE}). \qquad (15)$$

where I_{max} is the maximum value of any color in any pixel across the super-resolved image. Fig. 4, shows the performance of the given method for the

| (a) | (b) | (c) | (d) |

Fig. 4. Simulation results of proposed method for the Gaussian noise (a) Original Image, (b) Bilinear Interpolated Image, (c) Super-resolved image with known motion, (d) Super-resolved image with unknown motion

Table 1. Performance Comparison of Peak Signal to Noise Ratio(PSNR) and Mean Square Error (MSE) of the Algorithm for Known Motion and the Estimated Motion for the Gaussian Noise of $10dB$

Image	r	Known Motion		Estimated Motion	
		MSE (min)	PSNR (max)	MSE (min)	PSNR (max)
Peppers	2	73.3775	29.4751	74.3200	29.4197
	4	87.4492	28.7132	89.1911	28.6275
Baboon	2	84.1369	28.8809	84.3495	28.8699
	4	93.7855	28.4094	93.4673	28.4242
Airplane	2	87.8725	28.6923	87.9758	28.6871
	4	99.2349	28.1641	100.0669	28.1278
Lena	2	78.5825	29.1775	79.3545	29.1350
	4	91.4369	28.5196	91.9678	28.4944
Butterfly	2	15.9337	36.1076	16.0519	36.0755
	4	22.8132	34.5489	23.1354	34.4888

"Peppers" image in case Gaussian noise. It is observed that there is no significant visual difference between the super-resolved images using known and estimated motion vectors and this proves the accuracy of the Lucas-Kanade optical flow motion estimation for pure translational motion. Comparison of the algorithms of the known motion with the estimated motion for the test set is done in Table 1, in terms of MSE and PSNR.

From Table 1, it is seen that there is negligible variation in MSE and PSNR for both known and estimated motion technique when Gaussian noise of $10dB$ is used. The second experiment is carried out to test the robustness of the algorithm used. Estimation is said to be robust if it can remove outliers irrespective of noise modeling and data errors. For that purpose, salt and pepper noise of density 2% is added to the Low resolution images. Minimum number of frames used is r^2, where r is the resolution enhancement factor to get the super-resolved image.

| (a) | (b) | (c) | (d) |

Fig. 5. Simulation results of proposed method for the Salt and Pepper noise (a) Original Image, (b) Bilinear Interpolated Image, (c) Super-resolved image with known motion, (d) Super-resolved image with unknown motion

Table 2. Performance Comparison of Peak Signal to Noise Ratio (PSNR) and Mean Square Error (MSE) of the Algorithm for Known Motion and the Estimated Motion for 2% Salt and Pepper Noise

Image	r	Known Motion		Estimated Motion	
		MSE (min)	PSNR (max)	MSE (min)	PSNR (max)
Peppers	2	43.1306	31.7829	45.3991	31.5603
	4	64.8411	30.0123	67.1589	29.8598
Baboon	2	73.4349	29.4718	73.0261	29.4960
	4	83.7292	28.9029	84.3620	28.8693
Airplane	2	42.3717	31.8600	42.2467	31.8728
	4	54.6393	30.7557	54.9007	30.7350
Lena	2	44.1970	31.6769	42.9785	31.7982
	4	58.3508	30.4703	58.7541	30.4404
Butterfly	2	14.4491	36.5324	14.5996	36.4873
	4	21.1356	34.8806	21.6058	34.7851

The parameters for steepest descent algorithm chosen for this experiment are: steepest descent step size $b = 0.01$ and regularization step size $l = 0.04$ for both known and estimated motion vectors. Fig. 5, shows the performance of the given method for the "Peppers" image corrupted with Salt and Pepper noise. It is observed that there is no significant visual difference between the super-resolved images using known and estimated motion vectors when 2% Impulse noise is used. Comparison of the algorithm having known motion along with the estimated motion for the test set is done in Table 2. The comparison is done in terms of both the MSE and PSNR.

4   Conclusions

The performance of motion estimation in vector based color image super resolution approach for pure translational motion have been studied in this paper.

The Lucas-Kanade Optical Flow Motion Estim- ation has been used to calculate the sub-pixel shift of each of the low resolution frame. Quantitative comparisons based on MSE and PSNR measurements have been obtained for both known and estimated motion technique. It is evident that the results obtained by applying Optical flow motion estimation are identical to the results obtained for known motion. The motion estimation have been applied only for translational motion. It has also been considered that the camera blurring function (PSF) is known. Extension of this work includes incorporation of image registration under affine motion and de-convolution operation to estimate camera blur.

References

1. Huang, T.S., Tsai, R.Y.: Multi-frame Image Restoration and Registration. In: Advanced Computer Visual Image Process, vol. 1, pp. 317–339 (1984)
2. Bose, N.K., Kim, H.C., Valenzuela, H.M.: Recurcive Implementation of Total Least Squares Algorithm for Image Reconstruction from, Noisy, Undersampled Multiframes. In: International Conference on Acoustics, Speech, and Signal Processing, Minneapolis, vol. 5, pp. 269–272 (April 1993)
3. Borman, S., Stevenson, R.L.: Super-Resolution from Image Sequences-A Review. In: Proceedings of Midwest Symposium on Circuits and Systems, Notre Dame, vol. 5, pp. 374–378 (April 1999)
4. Farsiu, S., Robinson, M.D., Elad, M., Milanfar, P.: Fast and Robust Multiframe Super Resolution. IEEE Transactions on Image Processing 13(10), 1327–1344 (2004)
5. Kommineni, I.: Vector Based Approach to Color Image Super-Resolution, M.Tech. Thesis, IIT Guwahati (2007)
6. Barreto, P., Alvarez, L.D., Abad, L.D.: Motion Estimation Techniques in Super-Resolution Image Reconstruction, A Performance Evaluation. In: Proceedings of iASTRO MC Meeting and Workshop, Virtual Observatories: Plate Content Digitization, Archive Mining and Image sequence Processing, Sofia, Bulgaria, vol. 1, pp. 254–268 (2005)
7. Farsiu, S., Robinson, D., Elad, M., Milanfar, P.: Advances and Challenges in Super-Resolution. International Journal of Imaging Systems and Technology, Special Issue on High Resolution Image Reconstruction 14(2), 47–57 (2004)
8. Farsiu, S., Robinson, D., Elad, M., Milanfar, P.: Fast and Robust Multiframe super-resolution. IEEE Transactions on Image Processings 13(10), 1327–1344 (2004)

An Innovative Technique for Adaptive Video Summarization

Satyabrata Maity[1], Amlan Chakrabarti[1], and Debotosh Bhattacharjee[2]

[1] A. K. Choudhury School of IT, University of Calcutta, Kolkata-700009, India
[2] Department of Computer Science and Engineering, Jadavpur University,
Kolkata-700032, India
satyabrata.maity@gmail.com

Abstract. Video summarization is a procedure to reduce the size of the original video without affecting vital information presented by the video. This paper presents an innovative video summarization technique based on inter-frame information variation. Similar group of frames are identified based on inter-frame information similarity. Key frames of a group are selected using disturbance ratio (DR), which is derived by measuring the ratio of information changes between consecutive frames of a group. The frames in the summarized video are selected by considering continuation in understanding the message carried out by the video. Higher priority is given to the frames which have higher information changes, and no-repetition to reduce the redundant areas in the summarized video. The higher information changes in the video frames are detected based on the DR measure of the group and this makes our algorithm adaptive in respect to the information content of the source video. The results show the effectiveness of the proposed technique compared to the related research works.

Keywords: Differential Color Histogram, Disturbance-Ratio, Entropy, Information Similarity, Key Frame, Video Summarization.

1 Introduction

Extracting effective information from video data is an important activity for various application areas like surveillance, sports, news, entertainment industry and many more. The raw source video generally contains a huge amount of information which cannot be perceived in a shorter amount of time for decision making purpose or generating the semantic information of the same. At the same time there may be some amount of redundant information in the raw video which leads to greater evaluation time. Video summarization is a process to reduce the enormous size of the raw video by removing the unnecessary information of the video which results to a better understanding as a whole and also results to a considerable reduction in the data size without any kind of redundant information.

Video Summarization is divided into two broad categories (1) Domain Specific [1,2,3,4].(2) Non-Domain Specific [1], [5,6,7,8,9]. Domain specific summarization

K.R. Venugopal and L.M. Patnaik (Eds.): ICIP 2011, CCIS 157, pp. 592–600, 2011.

refers to techniques which specifically cater for a particular domain like sports, music, news, home video, etc.. Focusing on a particular domain helps to reduce levels of ambiguity when analyzing the content of a video stream by applying prior knowledge of the domain during the analysis process. On the other hand in Non-Domain specific techniques solutions are presented for summarizing video content irrespective of any domain.

A survey of related research work in video summarization gives us a good insight to the present research challenges. In [1] a conceptual framework for video summarization is discussed. The framework distinguishes between various video summarization techniques and the results of those techniques. The authors considered the video summarization technique in three broad categories *viz*. internal, external and hybrid. The authors in [5] proposed an approach for the selection of representative (key) frames of a video sequence for video summarization by analyzing the differences between two consecutive frames of a video sequence. The algorithm determines the complexity of the sequence in terms of changes in the visual content expressed by different frame descriptors. In [10] the authors presented a new approach for key frame extraction based on the image entropy and edge matching rate which was proved to be an effective technique.

Our proposed method is a non-domain specific as it is applicable for any type of video information to be summarized. This approach is focused to indentify the similar groups of element and its dynamism (changed occurred within the group) by using DR (Disturbance Ratio) and this differentiates our methodology from the existing related works [5], [10]. The key frames from each group are selected depending upon its importance which is evaluated using the DR of the group; hence our technique is adaptive in terms of the content of the video. To hold the continuity in the summarized video, some frames are added with the selected key frames based on the DR value of a given group. The number of added frames are decided according to the required storage size of the resulting summarized video, this is also a new approach as compared to [5] and [10]. Our approach also aims to fulfill all the three basic requirements as proposed in [10].

The organization of the paper is as follows. Section 2 gives an insight to our proposed technique of video summarization. A detailed analysis of the results is presented in Section 3 and the concluding remarks in Section 4.

2   Present Method

Proposed approach is a Non-Domain specific analysis based on statistical measure model, which utilizes the similarity measurement among consecutive frames for determining the suitable frames of the summarized video. Fig. 1 shows the hierarchical representation of video data, which consists of five levels: video, scene, group, shot, and key frame [11].

We need to reduce the size of video by taking non-repetitive and highly informative frames but there should be a certain amount of similarity among the frames of the same scene, and this is commonly known as continuity in summarized video [5]. In our work we have also tried to maintain the continuity among the resulting frames. Our work is divided into three major steps:

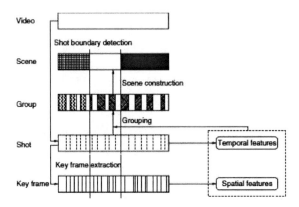

Fig. 1. Hierarchy of a video

1. Similarity group detection: Frames which have a similarity to certain extent are the frames of a similar group.
2. Representative frame selection: Key frame or the representative frame of a certain group is the frame which contains the highest information of the group. Sometimes there may be more than one key frame of a group.
3. Summary generation: Summary is not only the collection of all the representative frames but it also must hold three basic properties as depicted in [5] i.e., continuation to understand the message carried out by video, priority to include the main concern, and no-repetition to reduce the redundant areas of the original video.

We have utilized the DR measure as the key parameter for selecting the required frames for the summarized video. We give a brief insight to the DR measure in the following subsection.

2.1   Disturbance Ratio

Disturbance Ratio (DR) is a way to measure the dynamism of a scene. DR is derived from the information profile of the frames from a video.
Standard Deviation (STD): The standard deviation is the square root of the variance and is given by the following equation

$$STD = \sqrt{\frac{\sum_{i=1}^{N}(X_i - \mu)}{N - 1}}. \tag{1}$$

Where $\mu = \frac{1}{N}\sum_{i=1}^{N} X_i$ and X_i is the information content of the ith frame.

Local δ and Global δ: δ is the difference between the maximum valued element and the minimum valued element. Local is calculated from a block whereas Global MM is calculated from the whole set.

Disturbance Ratio (DR): Measures the dissimilarity between the respective frames of the information profile. It calculates intra-frame dissimilarity of a group so that the amount of changes can be reflected. Standard deviation reflects the disparity of the elements of any group.

$$DR(G_i) = \frac{STD(G_i) \times G_\delta}{\delta_{Gi} \times G_{STD}}. \tag{2}$$

where G_{STD} is the globally calculated Standard Deviation, $\delta_{Gi} = |Max(G_i - Min(G_i)|, G_\delta = (Global(Max) - Global(Min))$ and $STD(G_i)$ is the standard deviation of group G_i.

STD is inversely proportional to the similarity i.e. if standard deviation increases, similarity among the elements must be decreased and *vice − versa*. So standard- deviation is a parameter to measure the DR. Difference between the minimum-valued and maximum-valued element has a big role to measure the DR as it gives the highest deviation in a group. So it is another parameter to calculate DR. Depending on these two parameters four different cases can be drawn *viz.*,

1. Both STD (Standard Deviation) and δ (Difference between Max and Min element in a group) are larger, and then the group has larger varieties as it has a larger STD and a big gap between $max − element$ and $min − element$ in the group. So it can be derived that there must be a huge amount of changes of scene in between frames of the group.
2. Both STD and δ are very smaller, and then the group has negligible varieties as it has a lesser STD and a minor gap between $max − element$ and $min − element$ in the group. Consequently it can be said that the group is static
3. If STD is larger, and δ is smaller, then the group has larger varieties as it has a larger STD but range of the variety is not much as difference between $max − element$ and $min − element$ in the group. So it can be derived that there must be a good amount of changes in between frames of the group.
4. If STD is smaller and δ is larger, then the group has negligible varieties as it has a lesser STD but a major gap between $max−element$ and $min−element$ in the group. That spike represents either noise or a transition.

2.2   Summarization Technique

Pre-Processing. For generating the summarized video, at first we need to analyze the raw frames of the video. In this phase, two operations are performed; first the whole video is divided into frames and in the next step measurement of the information content of each frame is done. We followed two different strategies to measure the information containing in each frame.

Entropy Based Information Measurement: This is the simplest one which follows the traditional entropy measurement procedure to calculate the information of any frame. The information entropy as proposed by Shannon is utilized to evaluate the entropy value of each frame x_i. If we have a frame of size $m \times n$ and 0 to $(L-1)$ are the gray-levels of information, then we have the entropy measure S as follows:

$$s = -\sum_{i=1}^{l} p(x_i) \times (\log p(x_i)).$$ (3)

In the formula,$p(x_i)=num(x_i)m \times n$, $0 \le p(x_i) \le 1$ and $\sum_{i=1}^{l} p(x_i)=1$.

Differential Color-Histogram Based Information Measurement: Color images contain more information than the gray images. On the other hand color histogram is invariant to rotation of the image on the view axis, and changes in small steps when rotated otherwise or scaled [12]. It is also insensitive to changes in image and histogram resolution and occlusion. In this case RGB color-space has been taken. There may be a big difference between the pixels of same location of two consecutive frames because of the moving object, but the actual difference is not that much which is reflected if we do the entropy measure only. To overcome this, we take the entropy of the difference of the histograms of the two consecutive frames.

Group of Similar Frame Detection: Similarity group has been detected with respect to the changing of weight between the frames. If the amount of change between i^{th} and j^{th} frame is less than the calculated threshold ϵ and all the frames between F_i and F_j is in the same group g_k , then F_j must be in g_k.The threshold is calculated by taking the standard deviation of the weight vector. If

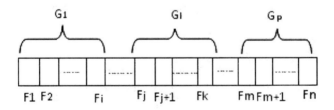

Fig. 2. Similarity groups

$|F_i - F_j|$ and all the frames between $F_i, F_{j-1} \in g_k$ then $F_j \in g_k$, where $i=1$to n numbers of frames and ϵ is the threshold and $k = 1$ to m number of groups.

Representative Frame Selection. The group having larger DR means the variation of the information of consecutive frames is larger. Key frames are selected by using DR and the information measured in preprocessing step. To include the message from each group at least one key frame from each group needs to be extracted. If there is more dissimilarity in the consecutive frames of the same group then we have to take more frames from that group as representation frame, so that the information conveyed by the summary is most appropriate. Representation frames are very crucial to understand the message of that group and it is very effective to make indexing of the original video. In case of shortage of time, one can go through the representation frames instead the whole video, after that one can easily scroll the area of interest which needs more clarification.

Summary Generation: In this phase, we select the frames for summary generation by maintaining three basic properties of video summarization.

Continuation: We take ni number of frames from ith group where ni depends on the disturbance ratio (DR). If any group has greater DR then n_i must be increased to keep the originality of the information as that particular area contains more variation. More variance means the changes between frames of that area is greater.

Suppose, n is the total number of frames required for summary, $DR = \sum_{i=1}^{K} DR_i$ and $n_i = DR_i/DR$, where k is the total numbers of groups and DR_i is the Disturbance ratio of that group. Thus number of frames taken from any group varies upon the DR value of the group. Since the DR ratio depends on the video content, the method is adaptable.

No-Repetition: Frames are taken according to the DR of the group. DR must be decreased when the similarity among the frames is increased. Thus DR helps to reduce the redundancy in summarization.

Priority: DR maintains the priority by taking more frames from the more dynamic area with respect to priority disturbance area so that the originality of information in more dynamic area is taken into account.

Post Processing: Post processing collect the selected frames in the previous phase and construct a video which is very smaller in size but containing all effective information. After getting the summarized video if it is needed to increase or decrease the size of the video, then changing the number of required frames is done by initiating the summary generation phase once again. Number frames to create the summary can be controlled and it can be reduced to the number of selected key frames at most.

3   Result and Discussions

The proposed algorithm has been tested over several videos. Observation results of two videos have been given in the Table 1, which shows a brief description of the videos those we used for our experiment *viz.*, the size of the summarized video and number of frames in the summarized video. Here 1st and 2nd refers to two different strategies described. *viz.*, Entropy Based Information Measurement and Differential Color-Histogram Based Information Measurement.

Fig. 4 shows the extracted key frames form *basketball* [13] and *anni001* video [14].

Table 1. A breif description of tested video

Index No	File name	File type	Size	Frames	Size of SV(in KB)		Frames in SV	
					1st	2nd	1st	2nd
vid1	Anni001	Mpg	5399	913	808	459	90	47
vid2	Basketball	Mov	4332	449	408	324	38	35

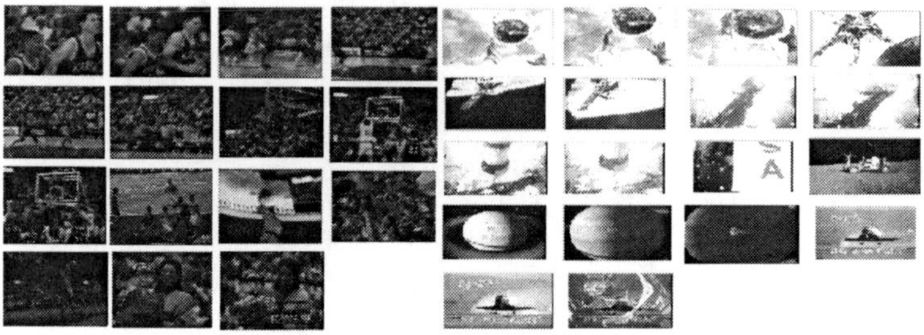

Fig. 3. (a) Key-frames of Basketball (b) Key-frames of Anni001 video

Table 2. Summary of observed result

Vid	NOG	NKF	NSFS	AKFG
Vid1	7	18	90	2.57143
Vid2	5	15	47	3

Table 2 shows a summary of the results which we get after the experiment. Here NOG is the Number of Groups of similar key frames categorized by the approach, NKF refers to the total number of key frames, NSFS is Number of Selected Frames for summary and AKFG stands for Average number of Key Frames per Group. Vid-1 having 913 frames are categorized into 7 different groups containing 18 key frames on an average of 2.57143 key frames per group. On the other hand in Vid-2, 449 frames are categorized into 5 different groups containing 15 key frames on an average of 3 key frames per group. 90 frames and 47 frames have been selected for the summary by the proposed method to maintain the basic properties as mentioned in [5]. Table 3 gives a comparison between our approach and the approach taken by [5] Plots in the Fig. 5 consider the frames of a video along X axis and the corresponding information containing in the Y axis. It has been observed that the changes of information in consecutive frames are not that much but there is a considerable amount of deviation for the transition frames of a scene. To construct the summary, the frames containing the maximum information have been taken in a certain locality i.e., the local maximum frames with respect to the information of the corresponding frames. The frames which have been taken for summary are marked and shown in Fig. 5, and basketball [13] and anni001 [14] video are taken as test videos. It can also be observed that the number of frames to make the summary is greater than number of key frames, this is because to maintain the continuation of the summary.

Table 3. A comparision between [2] and our approach

	MP	CF	Our approach
Automatic key frame selection	Y	Y	Y
Variable number of key frames	N	Y	Y
Similarity group detection	N	N	Y
Can control the no. of frames for summary	N	N	Y
Any priority scheme	N	N	Y
Reference	[2]	[2]	–

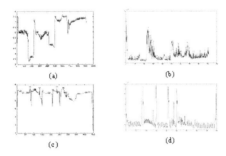

Fig. 4. Marked are the selected frames for summarization (a) Applying procedure-1 on [13], (b) Applying procedure-2 on [13], (c) Applying procedure-1 on [14], Applying procedure-2 on [14]

4   Conclusions and Future Work

This paper explains the proposed methodology of video summarization for non-domain specific video application and hence it can work for any arbitrary video information. Our method tracks most disturbing areas of the video based on DR measure to keep the originality of the information and also to maintain the quality parameters of the summarized video sequences. This method is novel in the sense that most of the existing works are domain specific but our proposed approach is non-domain specific and still generating a good quality of summarized video. In future we would try to establish intelligence rules to incorporate some complex object scenarios like back-ground estimation, knowledge based estimation etc.,

Acknowledgement

This research work is done through the funding provided by the Department of Science and Technology(DST), Government of India under the INSPIRE Fellowship Scheme.

References

1. Money, G., Agius, H.: Video Summarization, A Conceptual Framework and Survey of the State of the Art. ELSEVIER Journal (2007)
2. Benjamas, N., Cooharojananone, N., Jaruskulchai, C.: Flashlight and Player Detection in Fighting Sport for Video Summarization. In: IEEE International Symposium on Communications and Information Technology (ISCIT), Beijing, China, vol. 1, pp. 441–444 (2005)
3. Ekin, A., Tekalp, A.M., Mehrotra, R.: Automatic Soccer Video Analysis and Summarization. IEEE Transactions on Image Processing, 796–807 (2003)
4. Shih, H., Huang, C.: MSN, Statistical Understanding of Broadcasted Baseball Video Using Multi-level Semantic Network. IEEE Transactions on Broadcasting 51, 449–459 (2005)
5. Ciocca, G., Schettini, R.: An Innovative Algorithm for Key Frame Extraction in Video Summarization. Real Time Image Processing, 69–88 (2006)
6. Ferman, A.M., Tekalp, A.M.: Two-Stage Hierarchical Video Summary Extraction to Match Low-Level User Browsing Preferences. IEEE Transactions on Multimedia, 244–256 (2003)
7. Zhu, X., Wu, X.: Sequential Association Mining for Video Summarization. In: IEEE International Conference on Multimedia and Expo (ICME 2003), Baltimore, MD, USA, vol. 3, pp. 333–336 (2003)
8. Cheng, W., Xu, D.: An Approach to Generating Two-Level Video Abstraction. In: 2nd IEEE International Conference on Machine Learning and Cybernetics, Xi-an, China, vol. 5, pp. 2896–2900 (2003)
9. Cernekova, Z., Pitas, I., Nikou, C.: Information Theory-based Shot Cut/ Fade Detection and Video Summarization. IEEE Transactions on Circuits and Systems for Video Technology, 82–91 (2006)
10. Ren, L., Qu, Z., Niu, W., Niu, C., Cao, Y.: Key Frame Extraction Based on Information Entropy and Edge Matching Rate (ICFCC) (2010)
11. Xiong, Z., Radhakrishnan, R., Divakaran, A., Rui, Y., Huang, T.S.: Unified Framework for Video Summarization, Browsing, and Retrieval. Elsevier, Amsterdam (2006)
12. Hu, M.K.: Visual Pattern Recognition by Moment Invariants. IRE Transactions on Information Theory 8, 179–187 (1962)
13. http://www.ivl.disco.unimib.it/temp/video.zip
14. http://www.youtube.com/user/2000turtle

Emotion Recognition from Decision Level Fusion of Visual and Acoustic Features Using Hausdorff Classifier

Vankayalapati H.D.[1], Anne K.R.[2], and Kyamakya K.[1]

[1] Institute of Smart System Technologies, Transportation Informatics Group
University of Klagenfurt, Klagenfurt, Austria
[2] Department of Information Technology, TIFAC-CORE in Telematics
VR Siddhartha Engineering College, Vijayawada, India
raoanne@gmail.com

Abstract. The emotions are generally measured by analyzing either head movement patterns or eyelid movements or face expressions or all the lasts together. Concerning emotion recognition visual sensing of face expressions is helpful but generally not always sufficient. Therefore, one needs additional information that can be collected in a non-intrusive manner in order to increase the robustness. We find acoustic information to be appropriate, provided the human generates some vocal signals by speaking, shouting, crying, etc. In this paper, appropriate visual and acoustic features of the driver are identified based on the experimental analysis. For visual and acoustic features, Linear Discriminant Analysis (LDA) technique is used for dimensionality reduction and Hausdorff distance is used for emotion classification. The performance is evaluated by using the Vera am Mittag (VAM) emotional recognition database. We propose a decision level fusion technique, to fuse the combination of visual sensing of face expressions and pattern recognition from voice. The result of the proposed approach is evaluated over the VAM database with various conditions.

Keywords: Acoustic features, Driver Monitoring System, Hausdorff distance, Visual features.

1 Introduction

In the past years, research related to emotion recognition has been done in psychology and physiology. Here physiological characteristics of the person such as heart rate, brain activity, pupil size, skin conductance and production of stress hormones, and pulse rate are measured and interpreted for inferring the person state or emotion. These characteristics are measured in intrusive way by involving measurement systems such as the Electroencephalogram (EEG) which monitors brain activities [1], [2], the Electrocardiogram (ECG) which measures heart rate variation, the Electrooculogram (EOG) which monitors eye movement, the skin potential level measurement techniques, etc [3,4,5]. These systems need the

K.R. Venugopal and L.M. Patnaik (Eds.): ICIP 2011, CCIS 157, pp. 601–610, 2011.

person's cooperation as the electrodes are attached directly to the person's body. So non-intrusive techniques are introduced. These non-intrusive techniques uses cameras or sensors which are place before the person to measure the head, eye lid movements and face expressions etc. To measure these characteristics, several techniques are available in the literature.

Usually a monitoring system takes the sensor's input sample from the person, extracts features and compares them with the template of the existing emotions to find the best match. This match explains how well the extracted features from the sample match a given template. There has also been a similar increase in use of multimodal techniques to overcome the difficulties of single modal system and for performance improvement [6]. Several real world applications require higher performance than just one single measure to improve road safety. In multimodal techniques, the data collected from different sensors are integrated at different levels are explained in Section. 3. One of the important benefits in multimodal is if one input is highly noisy, then the other input might be helpful to make an overall reliable decision. Most recently, the study concerning the recognizing the emotional state of the person from the visual and acoustic information of the human has been introduced.

In this work also, we considered visual and acoustic information of the person. The visual features (such as global features) and acoustic features (such as pitch, zero crossing rate (ZCR), short time energy (STE) and Mel Frequency Cepstral Coefficients (MFCC) [7,8,9] are selected based on the experimental validation performed) are extracted based on our emotion recognition application.

Each person has many number of emotions. Here emotions like Happy, Anger, Sad, Disgust and Neutral are considered. The Linear Discriminant Analysis (LDA) is used for visual and acoustic feature reduction [10]. The emotions from the visual and acoustic features are classified separately based on the Hausdorff classifier is explained briefly in Section. 2. The emotion for visual information and emotion from acoustic information are recognized separately. Then we fused these two decisions/emotions based on the weighted majority voting rule in decision fusion explained briefly in Section. 4. We recognize the final emotion such as sad, angry, happy, disgust and neutral. The Vera Am Mittag (VAM) emotional database is used to evaluate the performance of the decision level fusing using Hausdorff classifier.

2   Hausdorff Distance Classifier

The Hausdorff Classifier is a non-linear operator, which measures the mismatch of the two sets [11]. The Hausdorff classifier measures the extent to which each point of a 'model' set lies near some point of an 'sample' set and vice versa. Unlike most vector comparison methods, the Hausdorff classifier is not based on finding corresponding mode and speech points. Thus, it is more tolerant of perturbations in the location of points because it measures proximity rather than exact superposition [12], [13]. However, the Hausdorff distance is extremely sensitive to outliers.

The distance between two points a and b is defined as shown in Eq. (1).

$$d(a, b) = ||a - b||. \tag{1}$$

Here, we not only compute the distance between the point a in the finite point set A and the same value b in the finite point set $B = b_1, ..., b_{N_b}$, but also compute the distances between the a_t and its two neighbor values b_{t-1} and b_{t+1} in the finite point set B, respectively, and then minimize these three distances as shown in in Eq. (2) [11].

$$d(a, B) = \min_{b \in B} d(a, b) = \min_{b \in B} ||a - b||. \tag{2}$$

The directed Hausdorff metric h(A,B) between the two finite point set $A = a_1, ..., a_{N_a}$ and $B = b_1, ..., b_{N_b}$ is defined in Eq. (3) and Eq. (4) :

$$h(A, B) = \max_{a \in A} d(a, B) = \max_{a \in A} \min_{b \in B} d(a, b). \tag{3}$$

$$h(A, B) = \left\{ \max_{a \in A} \left\{ \min_{b \in B} ||a - b|| \right\} \right\}. \tag{4}$$

3   Multimodal Fusion

Generally Fusions are of different levels, they are sensor fusion or data fusion, feature fusion, decision fusion. For emotion recognition of the person, we use multimodal system using both visual and acoustic sensors means camera and microphone respectively. In Data fusion, raw data from the multiple sensors are fused to generate the new data from which features are extracted. In visual information, different features are extracted and acoustic information different features are extracted [6]. This is the major limitation which, the fusion at sensor level is not possible in our work. Data fusion is possible only for same types of sensors (either two cameras or two microphone data).

Feature fusion means fusion after feature extraction. In this level we are integrating the feature vectors (extracted from the input sample) from multiple biometric sensors. If two different samples are of the same types (two samples of the same face), then it is possible to combine and create a new and more reliable feature vector from the two vectors. However, if the samples are of different types (face and voice data), the feature vectors can be concatenated into a new and more detailed feature vector.

Fusion at feature level is difficult in practice because of the following reasons [6]: (i) the feature sets of multiple modalities may be incompatible (e.g., eigencoefficients of face and Mel-frequency cepstral coefficients (MFCCs) of voice); (ii) the relationship between the feature vectors of different biometric sensors may not be known; and (iii) concatenating two feature vectors may result in a feature vector with very large dimensionality leading to the 'curse of dimensionality' problem [14].

4   Decision Level Fusion

For decision level fusion, we can use either multiple samples for the same of type of sensors or multiple sample from different types of sensors. Here multiple sensor information namely visual and acoustic are processed independently and their decisions are fused. Fig. 1 shows the fusion at decision level.

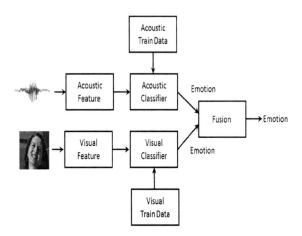

Fig. 1. Schematic description of fusion at decision level

In multimodal verification system, "AND" and "OR" rule is a simplest method to combine the decision output of different multimodal subsystems. The output of "AND" rule is the match when the both subsystems input samples matches with the train data template. By using "AND", the False Acceptance Rate (FAR) is lower than the FAR of individual subsystem [6]. The output of "OR" rule is the match of which one of the subsystem input sample matches the train data template. By using "OR", the False Reject Rate (FRR) is greater than the FRR of individual subsystem [6]. But this "OR" rule is not possible in emotion recognition applications. Because if the two subsystems has different emotions, if we apply "OR" rule, we can't decide which emotion is the final output. And another problem with this "AND" and "OR" rule is, in real world scenario, acoustic information is present in bursts based on the emotion of the person, where as visual information is present throughout the processing. Because of this limitation, we have not considered "AND" and "OR" rule for human emotion recognition.

The most common and simplest rule derived from the sum rule for decision level fusion is majority voting rule. In multimodal verification system, input samples are assigned to the subsystems and identifies the majority of the subsystems agrees the match or not. If the input samples are R, then atleast k are identified as matched then final output of the decision level is "match". k is shown in Eq. (5). Atleast k matchers should agree that identity.

$$k = \{ \begin{array}{l} \frac{R}{2} + 1 \text{ if R is even} \\ \frac{R+1}{2} \quad \text{otherwise.} \end{array} \tag{5}$$

The major drawback in majority voting is all the subsystems are treated or weighted equally. In our emotion recognition, majority of the emotion obtain to either from acoustic subsystem or visual subsystem is the final output. But in real cases, it is not correct. Visual is more reliable than acoustic. To overcome this limitation weighted majority voting rule is used in this work.

In weighted majority voting rule, the weights w_k are assigned based on the reliability (during training process) and k is the number of times the subsystem is matched.

$$s_{j,k} = \begin{cases} 1 \text{ if output of the } j^{th} \text{ matcher is in class } w_k \\ 0 \text{ otherwise.} \end{cases} \quad (6)$$

The discriminant function for class w_k computed using weighted voting is shown in Eq. (7).

$$g_k = \sum_{j=1}^{R} w_j s_{j,k}. \quad (7)$$

Where w_j is the weight assigned to the jth matcher.

Emotions can be classified into different classes like anger, happiness, disgust or sadness. Neutral emotion means no expression/emotion is present. In this work, we classify different expression based on distance from the neutral as shown in Fig. 2.

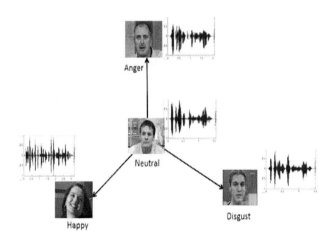

Fig. 2. Illustration of fusion based emotion classification

To validate the performance, the probability for each of the emotions was calculated for the audio and visual features separately and by applying weighted majority voting to get the final result as shown in Fig. 2.

In order to evaluate the recognition algorithm with fused features, we have used the Vera Am Mittag (VAM) emotional database. Performance comparison of different visual-acoustic feature fusion at decision level for emotion recognition application is shown in Fig. 3.

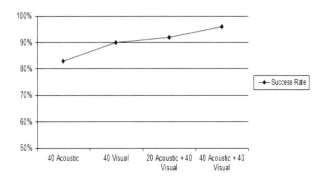

Fig. 3. Performance comparison of different visual-acoustic feature fusion at decision level

5   VAM German Emotional Speech Database

The Vera Am Mittag (VAM) is the audio visual emotional database consists of 12 hours of audio-visual recordings of the German TV talk show named as Vera am Mittag (in English "Vera at noon"), segmented into broadcasts, dialogue acts and utterances. The title of the database is taken from this TV show title. Because there is a reasonable amount of speech from the same speakers available in each session of the TV show [15]. The Sat.1 german tv channel broadcasted these recorded shows between December 2004 to February 2005. Speakers are at the age of 16 to 69 years at the time of recording.

VAM database has 3 different parts. They are VAM-Video database, VAM-Audio database and VAM-Faces Database as shown in Fig. 4 and Fig. 5 respectively. VAM-Video database contains 1421 videos of the 104 speakers. VAM-Faces database is extracted from the VAM-video by taking each frame as one still image. This database classified different emotions as anger (A), happiness (H), fear (F), disgust (D), sadness(Sa), surprise (Su) and neutral (N). VAM-Faces database contains 1867 images by 20 speakers.

Fig. 4. Sample images in Vera Am Mittag (VAM)-Faces database [15]

VAM-Audio database contains 1018 emotional utterances by 47 speakers [15]. It mainly contains the complete sentences but sometime also incomplete sentences. Some examples of the dialogue in this database are

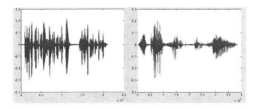

Fig. 5. Sample speech in Vera Am Mittag (VAM)-Audio database [15]

- Melanie: "She said, she would leave him to me, and she would even help me." serious
- Kristin: "Melanie, I do know very well what I told you on the boat!" angry

6 Receiver Operating Characteristic (ROC)

The Receiver Operating Characteristic (ROC) graphs are useful for analyzing the classifier performance. The ROC curve is a plot of the True Positive Fraction (TPF) versus the False Positive Fraction (FPF). It compares the two operating characteristics (TPF, FPF). So ROC is also called as Relative Operating Characteristic curve. These TPF and FPF are calculated by using True Positive (TP), True Negative (TN), False Positive (FP) and False Negative (FN) as shown in Eq. (8)and Eq. (9). Sensitivity is the true positive fraction, expressed as a percentage. Specificity is the true negative fraction, expressed as a percentage.

In Fig. 6 is the example roc curve, Shadow area (ROC space) gives the better classification [16].

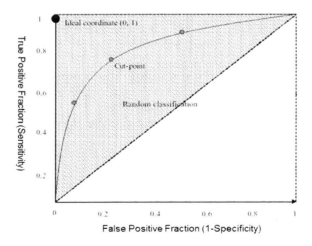

Fig. 6. Receiver Operating Characteristic (ROC) curve [16]

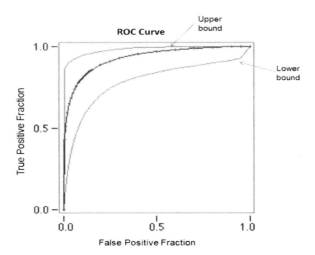

Fig. 7. Receiver Operating Characteristic (ROC) curve for emotion recognition

$$TPF = \frac{TP}{TP+FN}. \tag{8}$$

$$FPF = \frac{FP}{FP+TN}. \tag{9}$$

$$AUC = \frac{TP+TN}{TP+FN+FP+TN}. \tag{10}$$

Fig. 7 demonstrates the recognition performance of LDA based Hausdorff distance classifier on the Vera am Mittag (VAM) audio visual emotional database in which their ROC curves of False Positive Fraction (FPF) and True Positive Fraction (TPF) are shown. VAM Database has emotions like anger (A), happiness (H), disgust (D), sadness (Sa), and neutral (N). In the ordinary data format, each line represents one classifier case and each line has two numbers. In that the first number is either truly negative "0" or truly positive "1" [17]. The second number represents the output level with each case. In our emotion recognition algorithm, we analyze the hausdorff classifier performance by considering the different emotions in the VAM database. For this case, I used 5-point rating scale; the categories would have the following meaning:

- 1 - Definitely negative
- 2 - Probably negative
- 3 - Possibly negative
- 4 - Possibly positive
- 5 - Definitely positive

Each case has a rating from 1 to 5. If the first number in the case "1", a rating of 3 or greater than 3 is considered positive or correct. Remaining are treated as negative or wrong. If the first number is "0" then rating is in reverse order.

7 Conclusions

Multimodal emotion recognition system will be useful to understand the state and emotion of a person. In this work, we came to know that the acoustic information together with the visual information significantly increases the recognition rate. However, in real world scenario acoustic information is available only in burst. A good amount of stress is made in locking the audio burst and in correlating the information at decision level with visual information. Also in this work, we gave weightage to features that predominantly have a role in emotion and omitted other minor features which may have role in recognizing the emotion in order to increase the performance in real time. In this work, we emphasized on performing the evaluation over different databases to check the robustness of the algorithms and to see the scalability of the algorithms.

References

1. Saroj, A.C., Lal, K.L., Boord, P., Kirkup, L., Nguyen, H.: Development of An Algorithm for An EEG-Based Driver Fatigue Countermeasure. Journal of Safety Research 34, 321–328 (2003)
2. Bittner, R., Haná, K., Pousek, L., Smrcka, P., Scheib, P., Vysoký, P.: Detecting of fatigue states of a car driver. In: Brause, R., Hanisch, E. (eds.) ISMDA 2000. LNCS, vol. 1933, pp. 260–273. Springer, Heidelberg (2000)
3. Broggi, A.: Vision-based Driving Assistance. IEEE Intelligent Transport Systems 13, 22–23 (1998)
4. Vankayalapati, H.D., Kyamakya, K.: Nonlinear Feature Extraction Approaches for Scalable Face Recognition Applications. ISAST Transactions on Computers and Intelligent Systems 2 (2010)
5. Vankayalapati, H.D., Anne, K., Kyamakya, K.: Extraction of Visual and Acoustic Fatures of the Driver for Monitoring Driver Ergonomics Applied to Extended Driver Assistance Systems, vol. 81, pp. 83–94. Springer, Heidelberg (2010)
6. Arun, A.R., Nandakumar, K., Anil, K.J.: Handbook of Multibiometrics. Springer, New York (2006)
7. Ververidis, D., Kotropoulos, C.: Emotional Speech Recognition: Resources, Features, and Methods. Speech Communication 48(9), 1162–1181 (2006)
8. Arnott, J., Murray, I.: Toward the Simulation of Emotion in Synthetic Speech: A Review of the Literature on Human Vocal Emotion. Journal of the Acoustical Society of America 93(2), 1097–1108 (1993)
9. Vogt, T., Andr, E., Wagner, J.: Automatic Recognition of Emotions from Speech: A Review of the Literature and Recommendations for Practical Realisation, pp. 75–91 (2008)
10. Hespanha, J.P., Belhumeur, P.N., Kriegman, D.J.: Eigenfaces vs. Fisherfaces: Recognition Using Class Specific Linear Projection. IEEE Transactions on Pattern Analysis and Machine Intelligence 19, 711–720 (1997)
11. Jesorsky, O., Kirchberg, K.J., Frischholz, R.W.: Robust Face Detection Using the Hausdorff Distance. In: Bigun, J., Smeraldi, F. (eds.) AVBPA 2001. LNCS, vol. 2091, pp. 90–95. Springer, Heidelberg (2001)
12. Barbu, T.: Discrete Speech Recognition Using a Hausdorff-Based Metric. In: Proceedings of the 1st Int. Conference of E-Business and Telecommunication Networks, ICETE 2004, Setubal, Portugal, vol. 3, pp. 363–368 (August 2004)

13. Dubuisson, M.P., Jain, A.K.: Modified Hausdorff Distance for Object Matching. In: Proc. of IAPR International Conference on Pattern Recognition (ICPR 1994), Jerusalem, IS, pp. 566–568(1994)
14. Arun, A.R., Govindarajan, R.: Feature Level Fusion in Biometric Systems. In: Proceedings of Biometric Consortium Conference (BCC) (September 2004)
15. Grimm, M., Kroschel, K., Narayanan, S.: The Vera Am Mittag German Audio-Visual Emotional Speech Database. In: Proceedings of the IEEE International Conference on Multimedia and Expo (ICME), Hannover, Germany (2008)
16. Zhu, W., Zeng, N., Wang, N.: Sensitivity, Specificity, Accuracy, Associated Confidence Interval and ROC Analysis with Practical SAS Implementations. Health Care and Life Sciences, NESUG (2010)
17. Eng, J.: ROC analysis: Web-based Calculator for ROC Curves. Johns Hopkins University, Baltimore (updated May 17, 2006), http://www.jrocfit.org

Efficient Feature Extraction Techniques for Palmprint

Badrinath G.S. and Phalguni Gupta

Department of Computer Science and Engineering,
Indian Institute of Technology Kanpur, Kanpur, India - 208016
badri,pg@cse.iitk.ac.in

Abstract. This paper discuses some of the efficient well known feature techniques for palmprint. These feature extraction techniques discussed are based on Gabor filter, Speeded Up Robust Features (SURF), Zernike moments, phase difference information, Stockwell transform, Discrete Cosine Transform (DCT). Performance of the systems with the above mentioned Feature Extraction Techniques has been analysed on IITK, CASIA and PolyU datasets of 549, 5239 and 7,752 hand images.

Keywords: Discrete Cosine Transform, Feature Extraction, Gabor Filter, Palm Print, Stockwell Transform.

1   Introduction

Palmprint based recognition system has received a wide attention from the researchers as a new biometric authentication technology. Palmprint is the region between wrist and fingers and has features like principle lines, wrinkles, ridges, minutiae points, singular points, and texture pattern which can be considered as biometric characteristics. Advantages of using palmprint based biometric system are multi-fold. The features of the human hand are found to be relatively stable and unique. It needs very less co-operation from users for data acquisition. Collection of data is non-intrusive. Low cost devices are sufficient to acquire good quality of data. It is a relatively simple technique that uses low resolution images and provides high efficiency. Furthermore, It can also serve as a reliable human identifier because the print patterns are not found to be duplicated even in mono-zygotic twins.

Like other biometric system, palmprint based system also consists of five major tasks. One of the difficult tasks in palmprint recognition is the feature extraction technique. Feature extraction approaches for palmprint can be classified into structural and statistical features [1]. Some of the efficient techniques to represent palmprint are Palmcode [2], Competitive Code [3], Ordinal Code [4], SURF [5], Zernike moments [6], Phase-Difference information [7], Stockwell transform [8] and DCT [9]. In this paper, some of the well known feature extraction techniques that are used in palmprint based system are discussed.

The rest of the paper is organized as follows. Section 2 discusses the different feature extraction techniques. Next section analyses the experimental results of the system. Conclusions are presented in the last section.

K.R. Venugopal and L.M. Patnaik (Eds.): ICIP 2011, CCIS 157, pp. 611–620, 2011.
© Springer-Verlag Berlin Heidelberg 2011

2   Some Efficient Feature Extraction Techniques

This section discusses different feature extraction techniques which are used to design the palmprint based recognition systems. These techniques include Gabor filter, SURF [5], Zernike moments [6], Stockwell Transform [8], Phase-Difference information [7] and DCT [9].

2.1   Gabor Filter

Gabor filter is one of the best known tunable filters which is appropriate for capturing orientation information from the image. Apart from orientation, it can also give the phase information of the pixel which is invariant to illumination. Further, it is also an effective tool for capturing the texture. 2D Gabor filter can be defined as follows

$$G(x, y, \theta, \mu, \sigma) = \frac{1}{2\pi\sigma^2} exp\left\{-\frac{x^2 + y^2}{2\sigma^2}\right\} exp\{2\pi i(\mu x \cos\theta + \mu y \sin\theta)\}. \qquad (1)$$

where $i = \sqrt{-1}$, μ is the frequency of sinusoidal wave, θ is the orientation and σ is the standard deviation. Using Gabor filter, three well known techniques have been developed. These techniques are Palmcode [2], Compcode [3] and Ordinal code [4].

Palmcode. The palmprint is processed using Gabor filter of particular orientation and the resulting Gabor phase is binarised using zero crossing and it is used as feature. During matching these binary features are matched using distance metric.

Compcode. The palmprint is processed using Gabor using six Gabor filters with different orientation. The filter with the highest response is preserved in the form of three bits. These bits are considered as the feature of palmprint. During matching, binary features are matched using distance metric.

Ordinal Code. The palmprint is processed using three different orthogonal Gabor filters. The difference of orthogonal filter response is coded into bits. These bits are considered as the feature of palmprint. During matching, binary features are matched using distance metric.

2.2   Speeded Up Robust Features

The SURF has been used for extracting highly distinctive invariant features from images. Feature vectors are formed by means of local patterns around key-points detected using scaled up filter size. These extracted feature vectors are found to be distinct, robust to geometric and photometric deformations of image. The major stages to determine the SURF feature vectors of a given image are given below.

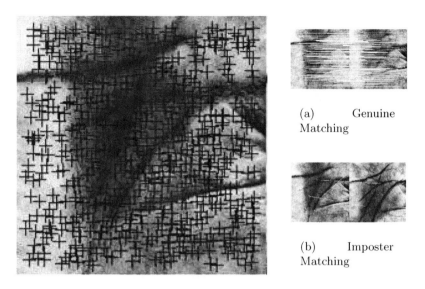

(a)   Genuine
Matching

(b)   Imposter
Matching

Fig. 1. SURF Key-points of Palmprint   **Fig. 2.** Matching SURF Key-points

1. Key-Point Detector: At this stage, SURF key-points are detected using Hessian-matrix approximation. The second order Gaussian derivatives for Hessian matrix are approximated using box filters. Key-points are localized in scale and image space by applying a non-maximum suppression in a $3 \times 3 \times 3$ neighbourhood.
2. Key-point Descriptor: This stage datasets the key-points. The first step consists of fixing a reproducible dominant orientation based on information from a circular region around the interest point. Feature vector of 64 values is computed for the oriented square local image region at keypoint.

The detected SURF key-points for the palmprint image are shown in Fig. 1. During recognition, the SURF features of query palmprint is matched with those of the enrolled palmprints using any distance metric. Based on the number of matching points between the query image and the enrolled image, a decision is done. An example of genuine matching and imposter matching using SURF operator in IITK database has been shown in Fig. 2.

2.3 Zernike Moments

Moments and functions of moments which can provide characteristics of an object that uniquely represent its shape and have been extensively employed as the invariant global features of an image in pattern recognition and image classification. The moments are invariant to translation and rotation. Traditionally, geometric moments have been used. However, the lack of orthogonality of geometric moments introduces certain degree of redundancy. But, Zernike moments can overcome the shortcomings associated with traditional Geometric moments.

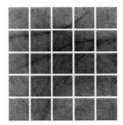

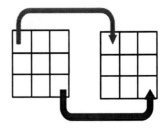

Fig. 3. Palmprint image partitioned into $5 \times 5 = 25$ equal size sub-images

Fig. 4. Schematic Diagram of Corresponding Sub-image Matching

Further, for image recognition, Zernike moments have better performance compared to Legendre moments and Hu moments. Zernike moments of order p and repetition q for an image $I(r,\theta)$ over the polar coordinate space can be defined as:

$$Z_{pq} = \frac{p+1}{\Pi} \int_0^{2\Pi} \int_0^1 V_{pq}(r,\theta)I(r,\theta)rdrd\theta. \tag{2}$$

where $V_{pq}(r,\theta) = R_{pq}(r).e^{\hat{i}q\theta}, \hat{i} = \sqrt{-1}$ and R_{pq} is a real valued radial polynomial defined as

$$R_{pq}(r) = \sum_{n=0}^{(p-|q|)/2} (-1)^n \frac{(p-n)!}{n!(\frac{p+|q|}{2} - n)!(\frac{p-|q|}{2} - n)!} r^{p-2n}. \tag{3}$$

where $0 \leq |q| \leq p$ and $p - |q|$ is even.

For feature extraction, each palmprint is partitioned into non-overlapping equal sized sub-images as described in [6]. Fig. 3 shows an example of palmprint segmented into 5×5 sub-images. Zernike moments are extracted from each sub-image of the palmprint. These moments extracted from all sub-images are concatenated to form the palmprint feature vector. During recognition, features of a sub-image of a query image are matched with the features of corresponding sub-image (as shown in Fig. 4) of a query palmprint using a distance metric.

2.4   Phase-Difference

Phase information, rather than amplitude information, can provide the most significant information of an image. Further, it is found to be inherently stable over amplitude and is independent to intensity levels of the image and hence, the measurements are invariant to smooth shading and lighting variations. Thus, one can use phase based features to design an efficient technique for feature extraction. The phase of 1D-signal x can be obtained using Fourier transform.

The Fourier transform X of time varying 1D-signal x of length M is given by

$$X_j = \sum_{m=0}^{M-1} x_m e^{-\frac{2\pi i}{M}jm} \qquad j = 0, \ldots, M-1. \tag{4}$$

The Fourier transform X of the signal x can be represented in amplitude and phase form as $X_j = \rho_j^x e^{i\Phi_j^x}$ where the magnitude ρ_j^x and the phase of signal x, Φ_j^x, are given by

$$\rho_j^x = \sqrt{Real(X_j)^2 + Imaginary(X_j)^2}. \tag{5}$$

$$\Phi_j^x = \tan^{-1}\left(Imaginary(X_j), Real(X_j)\right). \tag{6}$$

If X and Y are the Fourier transforms of 1D signals x and y respectively, then the phase-difference Θ_j of signals x and y is obtained as $\Theta_j = \Phi_j^x - \Phi_j^y$.

For feature extraction, the palmprint is divided into overlapping square blocks of size $W \times W$. The square block shown in Fig. 5(a) is the basic structure used to extract features of the palmprint in this paradigm. Fig. 5(b) shows the schematic diagram for segmentation of the palmprint. The palmprint which is partitioned into square blocks is shown in Fig. 5(c). Each segmented block, is averaged across horizontal and vertical direction to obtain 1D intensity signals of length W. This average reduces the noise and other image artifacts. The 1D intensity signals are windowed using Hanning window and then are subjected to Fourier Transform to reduce the spectral leakage and 1D phase is obtained. The Phase-difference between the vertical and the horizontal phases of the corresponding 1D intensity signals is computed and results are binarised using zero crossing. The resulted W bit binary vector is considered as features of a square block and these features from all square blocks are concatenated. The concatenated binary vector is considered as the feature vector of palmprint. During recognition, sub-feature vectors of corresponding blocks of query and enrolled palmprint are matched using a distance metric and then the scores from all the blocks are weighted fused to generate the matching score. This process has been discussed in [7].

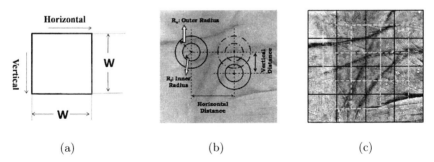

| (a) | (b) | (c) |

Fig. 5. (a) Basic Block of Proposed System (b) Overlapping Square Blocks and Other Parameters (c) Schematic Representation of Segmented Palmprint

2.5   Stockwell Transform

Traditionally, amplitude and phase information are used to represent the palmprint image for biometric systems. However, palmprint image signals have strong time dependent for their frequency and phase information. So, the signal amplitude and phase described as time-frequency representation (TFR) are more informative because TFR provides same information with resolution in both time and frequency. The Stockwell transform can represent the image amplitude and phase as TFR. The generalised Stockwell transform, $S(\tau, f)$, of time varying 1D-signal $x(t)$ is defined as

$$S(\tau, f) = \int_{-\infty}^{\infty} x(t) \frac{|f|}{\sqrt{2\pi}} e^{-\frac{(\tau-t)^2 f^2}{2}} e^{-i2\pi ft} dt. \tag{7}$$

where both t and τ represent time, f is the frequency. $S(\tau, f)$ of the signal $x(t)$ can be represented in amplitude and phase form as $S(\tau, f) = A_x(\tau, f)e^{i\phi_x(\tau,f)}$ where $A_x(\tau, f)$ is the amplitude at time step τ for frequency f defined as $A_x(\tau, f) = abs(S(\tau, f))$ and $\phi_x(\tau, f)$ which is the phase at time step τ for the frequency f is given by

$$\phi_x(\tau, f) = atan(real(S(\tau, f)), imaginary(S(\tau, f))). \tag{8}$$

The phase $\phi_x(\tau, f)$ at each time step τ for f is the *instantaneous-phase* which is used to represent the palmprint features because phase does not depend on intensity levels of the image. Hence, phase of image is robust to lighting conditions.

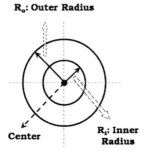

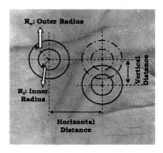

Fig. 6. Basic Structure of the Proposed Feature Extraction using Stockwell transform

Fig. 7. Overlapping Circular Strips and Other Parameters

The palmprint is segmented into overlapping circular-strips as descried in [8] for feature extraction where circular-strip is the circular region of inner radius R_i and outer radius R_o as shown in Fig. 6 and is the basic structure used to extract features of the palmprint. Fig. 7 shows the schematic diagram for segmenting the palmprint and other parameters of the proposed palmprint feature extraction. The segmented circular-strip is averaged across its radial direction to obtain 1D-intensity signal Avg. The obtained 1D intensity signal $Avg(P)$ is subjected to Stockwell transform defined in Eq.7 and *instantaneous-phase* $\phi(\tau, f)$ is obtained from Stockwell transform as defined in Eq. 8. The *instantaneous-phase* differences along the corresponding time resolutions of vertically adjacent circular-strips are computed and the obtained results are then binarised using zero crossing. The resulted $| \tau | \times | f |$ bits binary matrix is considered as sub-feature matrix and combining sub-feature matrices from all the vertically adjacent strips forms a feature vector of palmprint. These $| \tau | \times | f |$ bits sub-feature matrices form a basis of feature vector for the matching process. During recognition, the feature vectors of the query and enrolled palmprints are matched using a distance metric.

2.6   The Discrete Cosine Transform

The DCT is a real valued transform with very low computation complexity and has variance distribution closely resembling to that of the Karhunen-Loeve transform. Further, there exists fast computation techniques. There are several variants, but most commonly used operates on a real sequence A_n of length W to generate co-efficient as

$$CT_k = \frac{2}{N} s(k) \sum_{n=0}^{W-1} A_n \cos \left[\frac{\pi}{W} \left(n + \frac{1}{2} \right) k \right], \quad k = 0, \ldots, W-1 . \tag{9}$$

where $s(k) = 1/\sqrt{2}$, $k = 0$ and $s(k) = 1$, $1 \le k \le W - 1$.

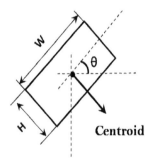
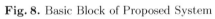

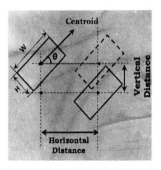

Fig. 8. Basic Block of Proposed System

Fig. 9. Overlapping Rectangular Blocks Oriented at Particular Direction θ and Other Parameters

The palmprint is segmented into overlapped rectangular blocks oriented at particular direction θ for feature extraction as described in [9]. The oriented rectangular block is of size $W \times H$, where W is the width and H is the height of the block. The rectangular block as shown in Fig. 8 is the basic structure used to extract features of the palmprint. Fig. 9 shows the schematic diagram for segmenting the palmprint and other parameters that can be used for feature extraction. The segmented block is averaged across its height to obtain 1D-intensity signal of width W. The obtained 1D intensity signal is windowed using Hanning window and then subjected to one dimensional DCT. The 1D average signal is windowed using Hanning window prior to subjecting for the DCT to reduce the spectral leakage. The difference of DCT coefficients from each vertically adjacent blocks are computed and results are binarised using zero crossing. The resulted W bit binary vector is considered as sub-feature vector and combining sub-feature vectors from all adjacent blocks forms feature vector of palmprint. The W bit sub-feature vector forms a basis of feature vector and is used in matching process. During recognition, the feature vectors of the query and enrolled palmprints are matched using distance metric.

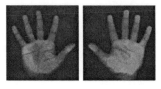

Fig. 10. Sample of hand image from IITK database

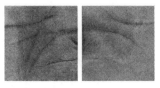

Fig. 11. Sample of extracted palmprint images from IITK database

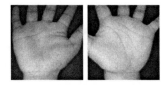

Fig. 12. Sample of hand image from CASIA database

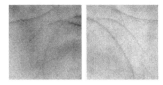

Fig. 13. Sample of extracted palmprint images from CASIA database

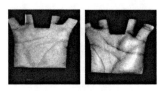

Fig. 14. Sample of hand image from PolyU database

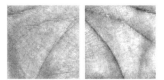

Fig. 15. Sample of extracted palmprint images from PolyU database

3   Experiments and Results

Systems based on these feature extraction techniques are evaluated against three different sets of hand image databases. These databases are obtained from The Indian Institute of Technology Kanpur (IITK), The Hong Kong Polytechnic University (PolyU) and The Chinese Academy of Sciences Institute of Automation (CASIA). These images form diverse representation of palmprint in terms of regions (ethnicity), device used to capture the images, resolution, lightning conditions and constraints (with or without pegs) used of placing hand. The region of interest (ROI) or palmprint from the hand images are extracted with respective to stable points between the fingers as described in [8]. Further, the extracted palmprint images are enhanced to improve the texture of the palmprint as described in [6].

IITK Database: It consists of 549 hand images obtained from 150 users corresponding to 183 different palms. Three images against each palm are collected using flat bed scanner at the resolution of 200 dpi with 256 gray-levels. Samples of hand images are shown in Fig. 10 while samples of extracted palmprint images are shown in Fig. 11. One image per palm is considered for training while remaining two images are used for the testing.

CASIA Database: It contains 5, 239 hand images captured from 301 subjects corresponding to 602 palms [10]. For each subject, around 8 images from left hand and 8 images from right hand are collected. All images are collected using CMOS and 256 gray-levels. Samples of hand images are shown in Fig. 12 while samples of extracted palmprint images are shown in Fig. 13. Two images per palm are considered for training while remaining six images are used for testing.

PolyU Database: It consists of 7752 grayscale images from 193 users corresponding to 386 different palms [11]. Around 17 images per palm are collected in two sessions. The images are collected using CCD [2] at spatial resolution of 75 dots per inch and 256 gray-levels. Sample of PolyU hand images are shown in Fig. 14 while Fig 15 shows sample of PolyU extracted palmprint images. Six images of each palm are considered for training while remaining ten images are used for the testing.

Performance of these systems are measured with the help of Correct Recognition Rate (CRR) and Equal Error Rate (EER) for identification and recognition respectively. The CRR of the system is defined as $CRR = N1/N2 * 100$, where $N1$ denotes the number of correct (Non-False) recognition of palmprint images and $N2$ is the total number of palmprint images in the testing set. At a given threshold, the probability of accepting the imposter, known as False Acceptance Rate (FAR) and probability of rejecting the genuine user known as False Rejection Rate (FRR) is obtained. Equal Error Rate (EER) which is the defined as $FAR = FRR$ is considered as the important measure for verification. The CRR and EER of various well known systems are given in Table 1.

Table 1. Performance of Well Known Systems

Feature	IITK CRR (%)	IITK EER (%)	CASIA CRR (%)	CASIA EER (%)	PolyU CRR (%)	PolyU EER (%)
Palmcode [2]	100.00	5.2108	99.619	3.6730	99.916	0.5338
Compcode [3]	100.00	2.9587	99.716	2.0130	99.964	0.3082
Ordinalcode [4]	100.00	1.1882	99.843	1.7540	100.00	0.0709
SURF [5]	89.474	11.973	95.524	5.4337	95.925	4.3689
Zernike [6]	100.00	2.6187	99.750	2.0033	100.00	0.2939
Phase [7]	100.00	0.0095	100.00	0.1575	100.00	0.0020
S Transform [8]	100.00	0.9673	100.00	1.1606	100.00	0.0055
DCT [9]	100.00	0.0001	100.00	1.0040	100.00	0.0033

4   Conclusions

In this paper, some efficient feature extraction techniques to represent palmprint have been discussed. These techniques are Palmcode [2], Competitive Code [3], Ordinal Code [4], SURF [5], Zernike moments [6], Phase-Difference information [7], Stockwell transform [8] and DCT [9]. The performance of these techniques are evaluated for both identification and verification mode using CRR and ERR respectively. Further, these systems are tested on three different datasets from IITK, CASIA and PolyU.

References

1. Kong, A., Zhang, D., Kamel, M.: A Survey of Palmprint Recognition. Pattern Recognition (42), 1408–1418 (2009)
2. Zhang, D., Kong, A.W., You, J., Wong, M.: Online Palmprint Identification. IEEE Transactions on Pattern Analysis and Machine Intelligence (25), 1041–1050 (2003)
3. Kong, A., Zhang, D.: Competitive Coding Scheme for Palmprint Verification. In: International Conference on Pattern Recognition, pp. 520–523 (2004)
4. Sun, Z., Tan, T., Wang, Y., Li, S.: Ordinal Palmprint Representation for Personal Identification. In: International Conference on Computer Vision and Pattern Recognition, pp. 279–284 (2005)
5. Badrinath, G.S., Gupta, P.: Robust Biometric System using Palmprint for Personal Verification. In: International Conference on Biometrics, pp. 554–565 (2009)
6. Badrinath, G.S., Kachhi, N., Gupta, P.: Verification System Robust to Occlusion using Low-Order Zernike Moments of Palmprint Sub-Images. Telecommunication Systems, 1–16 (2010)
7. Badrinath, G.S., Gupta, P.: Palm-Print Based Recognition System using Phase-Difference Information. Future Generation Computer Systems (in press, 2011)
8. Badrinath, G.S., Gupta, P.: Stockwell Transform Based Palm-Print Recognition. Applied Soft Computing (in Press)
9. Badrinath, G.S., Gupta, P.: Palm-Print Based Recognition System using DCT. Pattern Recognition Letters (Revised and Communicated)
10. The Casia Palmprint Database, http://www.cbsr.ia.ac.cn/
11. The Polyu Palmprint Database, http://www.comp.polyu.edu.hk/~biometrics

Studying the Elemental Resistivity Profile of Electrical Impedance Tomography (EIT) Images to Assess the Reconstructed Image Quality

Tushar Kanti Bera and Nagaraju J.

Department of Instrumentation and Applied Physics,
Indian Institute of Science, Bangalore-560012, India
solarjnr@isu.iisc.ernet.in

Abstract. Studying of elemental resistivity profile of reconstructed images in Electrical Impedance Tomography (EIT) is essential to assess its image quality, reconstruction process and the systems performance. Visual assessment of the impedance images must not be accepted as the ultimate and sufficient judgment criteria for reconstruction efficiency of the tomograph. To identify the best image quality in EIT reconstruction, resistivity images are reconstructed from the simulated data using Electrical Impedance Diffuse Optical Reconstruction Software (EIDORS) and their elemental resistivity profiles are analyzed with image analyzing parameters. Results show that the image analyzing parameters are essential to assess the reconstructed images more technically, qualitatively and quantitatively.

Keywords: Electrical Impedance Tomography (EIT), EIDORS, Image Analysis, Image Analyzing Parameters, Impedance Images, Phantom, Resistivity Images.

1 Introduction

Studying of impedance reconstruction in Electrical Impedance Tomography (EIT) [1] using boundary data of phantoms [2] is essential to assess the performance of EIT systems (Fig. 1) for its validation, calibration and comparison purposes. Boundary data errors and the errors produced by reconstruction algorithm in practical EIT-systems make the reconstruction study difficult and complex in real case. Reconstruction accuracy is mainly reduced due to the poor boundary data containing a numbers errors [3], [4] contributed by phantom, surface electrodes [5], instrumentation and the data acquisition system [6]. Boundary data errors are responsible for poor image quality and incorrect reconstruction which may mislead our EIT study producing a lot of wrong information.

Insufficient image analysis method leads to incorrect information which may make our image interpretation more difficult in EIT study. Visual assessment of the impedance images must not be accepted as the ultimate and sufficient judgment criterion for image analysis in EIT reconstruction. Image blurring is

K.R. Venugopal and L.M. Patnaik (Eds.): ICIP 2011, CCIS 157, pp. 621–630, 2011.
© Springer-Verlag Berlin Heidelberg 2011

a visual and relative characteristics of reconstructed image and is required to interpret an EIT image in some aspects but it is not sufficient for proper assessment of reconstructed images. In this context some image analysing techniques essential for assessing the reconstructed images in 2D-EIT are proposed and the corresponding image analyzing parameters are studied. Impedance images are reconstructed from simulated boundary data and the reconstructed images are analysed by image analyzing parameters. Mean Inhomogeneity Resistivity (IR_{Mean}), Mean Background Resistivity (BR_{Mean}), Contrast to Noise Ratio (CNR), Percentage of Contrast Recovery (PCR) and Diametric Resistivity Profile (DRP) are calculated from the elemental resistivity profile and the images are analyzed.

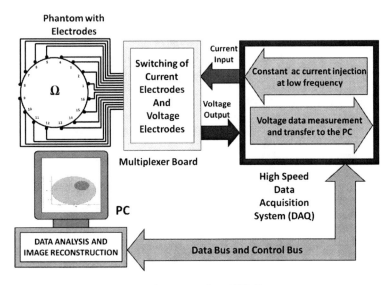

Fig. 1. Schematic of an EIT System

2 Materials and Methods

2.1 Boundary Data Simulation

Simulated boundary data are generated for two different phantom geometries. Phantom 1 is designed with a circular domain (150 mm diameter) containing a circular inhomogeneity (40 mm diameter) near electrode number 1. Phantom 2 is designed with a circular domain of 150 mm diameter and contains a circular inhomogeneity (60 mm diameter) near electrode number 3. For both the phantoms, the resistivity of the inhomogeneity is taken as 33Ωm where as the homogeneous background resistivity is set at 2.5Ωm. Boundary data generated for circular inhomogeneity by simulating a constant current (1 mA r.m.s.) using opposite current injection protocol [7] and the resistivity images are reconstructed using Electrical Impedance Diffuse Optical Reconstruction Software (EIDORS) [8].

2.2   Image Reconstruction in EIDORS

EIDORS is an open course software that aims to reconstruct the 2D-images from electrical or diffuse optical data. EIDORS is a $MATLAB$ based high speed reconstruction algorithm and it is developed using Gauss Newton method of approximation method. It is developed as a rapid prototyping, graphical user interface construction software and image displaying algorithm which can be easily modified and used for different phantom configurations according to the required specifications. It can be used for two-dimensional mesh generation, solving the forward problem and reconstructing and display the reconstructed images of the resistivity or admittivity distribution.

In the present study, EIDORS is modified with the geometry of the domain under test with proper dimension and coordinates. The forward and inverse solution are conducted with a FEM mesh of 1968 triangular elements and 1049 nodes (Fig. 2) for the resistivity imaging using the boundary data simulated with two different phantoms.

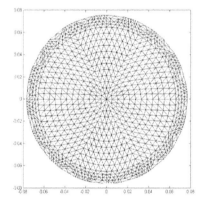

Fig. 2. FEM mesh (containing 512 elements and 289 nodes) used in EIDORS

2.3   Image Analysis with Image Parameters

Resistivity images are reconstructed from simulated boundary data and the reconstructed images are analysed by image analyzing parameters. IR_{Mean}, BR_{Mean}, CNR, PCR and DRP are calculated from the elemental resistivity profile and the images are analyzed.

IR_{Mean} is calculated by the dividing the sum of the resistivities of all elements in inhomogeneity region (A_i) by the number of elements in A_i. If the number of elements (n) in the FEM mesh within A_i and its elemental resistivity are denoted by N_i and IR_e respectively, then IR_{Mean} is given by:

$$IR_{Mean} = \frac{\sum_{n=1}^{N_i} IR_e}{N_i}. \tag{1}$$

Similarly, if the number of elements (n) in within background region (B_i) and its elemental resistivity are denoted by N_b and BR_e respectively, then BR_{Mean} is given by:

$$BR_{Mean} = \frac{\sum_{n=1}^{N_b} BR_e}{N_b}. \qquad (2)$$

CNR [9] is defined as the ratio of the difference between the mean inhomogeneity resistivity (IR_{Mean}) and the mean background resistivity (BR_{Mean}) to the weighted average of the standard deviations in the IR (SD_{IR}) and BR (SD_{BR}):

$$CNR_R = \frac{IR_{Mean} - BR_{Mean}}{\sqrt{\omega_I (SD_{IR})^2 + \omega_B (SD_{BR})^2}}. \qquad (3)$$

Where ω_I is the fraction of the area of the region of interest with respect to the area of the whole image; ω_B is defined as $\omega_B = 1 - \omega_I$; IR_{Mean} and BR_{Mean} are the mean values of the inhomogeneity resistivity and the background resistivity in the reconstructed images. Greater CNR values are considered to imply a better image quality.

Similarly for conductivity imaging and permittivity imaging the CNRs are defined as:

$$CNR_C = \frac{IC_{Mean} - BC_{Mean}}{\sqrt{\omega_I (SD_{IC})^2 + \omega_B (SD_{BC})^2}}. \qquad (4)$$

$$CNR_P = \frac{IP_{Mean} - BP_{Mean}}{\sqrt{\omega_I (SD_{IP})^2 + \omega_B (SD_{BP})^2}}. \qquad (5)$$

Where IC_{Mean} and BC_{Mean} are the mean values of the inhomogeneity conductivity and the background conductivity; SD_{IC} and SD_{BC} are the corresponding standard deviations. IP_{Mean} and BP_{Mean} are the mean values of the inhomogeneity permittivity and the background permittivity; and SD_{IP} and SD_{BP} are the corresponding standard deviations.

PCR [10] in EIT is defined as the difference between the averaged resistivity within the reconstructed image ($IR_{reconstructed}$) and the reconstructed background ($BR_{reconstructed}$) divided by the difference between the averaged resistivity within the reconstructed image ($IR_{original}$) and the reconstructed background ($BR_{original}$):

$$PCR = \frac{IR_{Mean\ reconstructed} - BR_{Mean\ reconstructed}}{IR_{original} - BR_{original}} \times 100. \qquad (6)$$

Resistivity images are reconstructed from the simulated boundary data in EIDORS and the image parameters (IR_{Mean}, BR_{Mean}, CNR, PCR and COC) are calculated and the reconstructed images are analyzed and studied to assess the reconstruction process.

DRP is defined as the resistivity profile (ρ) along the phantom diameter (D) connecting the centre of the reconstructed object and the centre of the phantom. The elemental resistivity along the phantom diameter (D) connecting the centre of the reconstructed object and the centre of the phantom is plotted against the length of the phantom diameter as shown in Fig. 3. This resistivity plot is termed as the diametric resistivity plot (DRP). In Fig. 3, if the phantom is simulated with a circular background (resistivity $= \rho_1$) containing a circular inhomogeneity (resistivity $= \rho_2$), the DRP is defined as the resistivities of the finite elements positioned along the phantom diameter $A_1 B_1$ plotted against D.

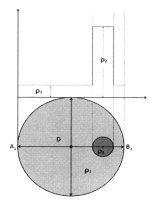

Fig. 3. DRP for the Image with Inhomogeneity near Electrode 1 (Background Resistivity is ρ_1 and Inhomogeneity Resistivity is ρ_2)

3   Results and Discussion

3.1   Resistivity Imaging with Simulated Phantom-1

Resistivity imaging of phantom-1 (Fig. 4(a)) shows that the reconstructed images (Fig. 4(b)-4(u)) are varied in quality from iteration to iterations.

Results (Fig. 5(b)-5(u)) show that the reconstruction starts with a relatively poor quality image at the first iteration and then the image quality gradually improves as the iteration goes on.

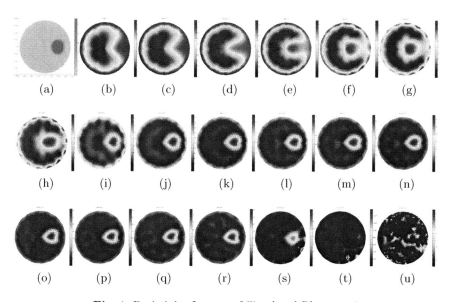

Fig. 4. Resistivity Images of Simulated Phantom-1

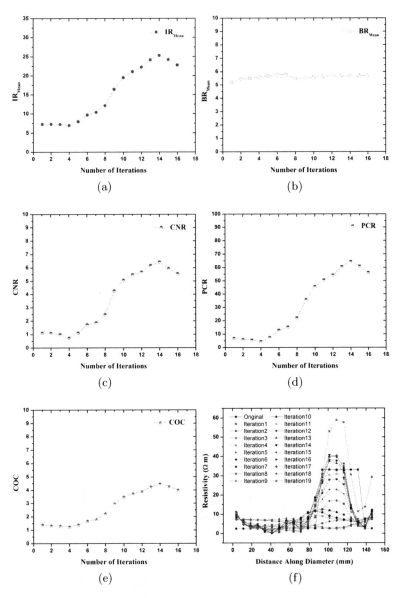

Fig. 5. Image parameters (a) IR_{Mean}, (b) BR_{Mean}, (c) CNR, (d) PCR, (e) COC, (f) DRP

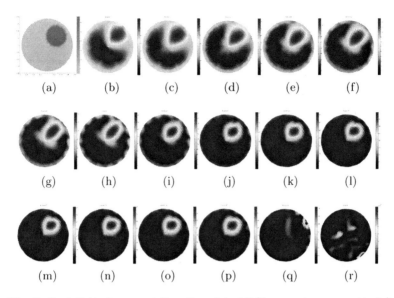

Fig. 6. Resistivity Images at iterations 1 to 17 (figure a to r respectively)

It is observed that the IR_{Mean} reaches a moderated value after 10th iteration and it reaches to its maximum (25.28 Ωm) value at 14th iteration (Fig. 4(o)). IR_{Mean} (Fig.5(a)) is found more variable than the BR_{Mean} (Fig. 5(b)). BR_{Mean} varies from 5.19 Ωm to 5.78 Ωm up to 18th iteration and at 19th and 20th iteration the image is lost (Fig. 4(t)-4(u)).

Results show that CNR (Fig. 5(c)) is comparatively poor at the first eight iterations and gradually it is improved with a consequent improvement in image quality. From 9th to 14th iteration it increases gradually and at 14th iteration it becomes maximum (6.42). PCR (Fig. 5(d)) and COC (Fig. 5(e)) are also increased from iteration to iteration and they become maximum (64.33 % and 4.47 respectively) at the 14th iteration (Fig. 5(c)-5(d)).

It is observed that the $DRPs$ (Fig. 5(f)) of all the images at 10th to 16th iterations follow the original resistivity profile. Hence the resistivity imaging study with phantom-2 show that the resistivity image reconstructed at the 14th iteration is the image with better contrast and better quality.

3.2   Resistivity Imaging with Simulated Phantom-2

Resistivity imaging of the simulated phantom-2 (Fig. 6(a)) that the reconstructed images (Fig. 6(b)-6(r)) are varied in quality from iteration to iterations. Results show that the image reconstruction starts with a poor quality images and they get modified gradually as the iteration goes on.

Result show that the IR_{Mean} (Fig. 7(a)) reaches a moderated value after 11th iteration and it remains almost constant up to 14th iteration. At the 12th iteration IR_{Mean} becomes maximum (29.96). BR_{Mean} (Fig. 7(b)) is found less

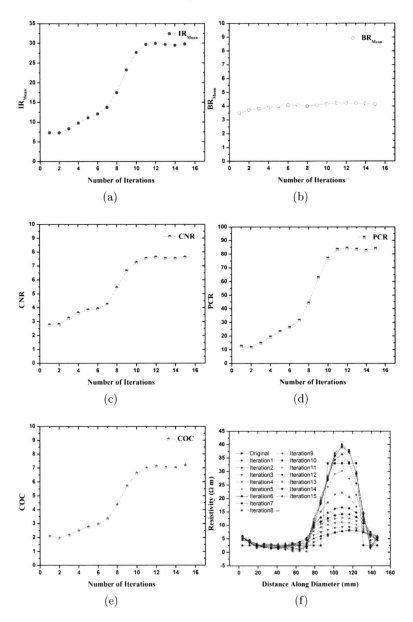

Fig. 7. Image parameters (a) IR_{Mean}, (b) BR_{Mean}, (c) CNR, (d) PCR, (e) COC, (f) DRP

variable than the IR_{Mean}. BR_{Mean} varies from 3.49 Ωm to 7.48 Ωm up to 15th iteration (Fig. 7(b)) and at 16th and 17th iteration the image is lost (Fig. 6(q)-6(r)). From 6th to 16th iterations it remains almost constant.

It is observed that the CNR (Fig. 7(c)) is comparatively poor in value at the first iteration and gradually they all are improved with a consequent improvement in image quality (Fig. 7(c)). From 11th to 14th iteration it gets larger values and at the 12th iteration CNR becomes maximum (7.62). PCR (Fig. 7(d)) is also increased from iteration to iteration and it becomes much larger during 11th to 14th iteration. At the 12th iteration PCR becomes maximum (84.43%). It is observed that the COC (Fig. 7(e)) is comparatively poor in value at the first iteration and gradually it is improved with a consequent improvement in image quality (Fig. 7(e)). Result show that at 12th iteration COC becomes maximum (7.12). For the resistivity imaging of phantom-2, it is also observed that the $DRPs$ (Fig. 7(f)) of all the images at 9th to 15th iterations follow the original resistivity profile. Hence the resistivity imaging study with phantom-2 show that the resistivity image reconstructed at the 12th iteration is the image with better contrast and better quality. The images reconstructed at the 11th and 13th iteration can also be considered as the suitable reconstruction as they also have approximately same image quality as the image of 12th iteration.

4 Conclusions

Reconstructed images are suitably analyzed with the parameters and the reconstruction process and reconstruction performance are technically understood. Resistivity images are assessed more suitably and technically than a visual assessment carried out in terms of resistivity profile and image contrast. Minimal visual dissimilarities are also distinguished by the image analysis calculating the image parameters. Image analyzing parameters facilitates the assessment of reconstruction process and hence they are essential for accurate assessment of the reconstruction performance.

References

1. Webster, J.G.: Electrical Impedance Tomography. Adam Hilger Series of Biomedical Engineering. Adam Hilger, New York, USA (1990)
2. Holder, D.S., Hanquan, Y., Rao, A.: Some Practical Biological Phantoms for Calibrating Multifrequency Electrical Impedance Tomography. Physiol. Meas. 17, A167A (1996)
3. Kolehmainen, V., Vauhkoneny, M., Karjalainen, P.A., Kaipio, J.P.: Assessment of Errors in Static Electrical Impedance Tomography with Adjacent and Trigonometric Current Patterns. Physiol. Meas. 18, 289–303 (1997)
4. Breckon, W.R., Pidcock, M.K.: Data Errors and Reconstruction Algorithms in Electrical Impedance Tomography. Clin. Phys. Physiol. Meas. 9(suppl. A), 105–109 (1988)
5. Webster, J.G.: Medical Instrumentation: Principle and Design. John Wiley and Sons, Hoboken (1995)

6. Rosell, J., Murphy, D., Pallas, R., Rolfe, P.: Analysis and Assessment of Errors in a Parallel Data Acquisition System for Electrical Impedance Tomography. Clin. Phys. Physiol. Meas. 9(suppl. A), 93–99 (1988)

7. Bera, T.K., Nagaraju, J.: A Multifrequency Constant Current Source for Medical Electrical Impedance Tomography, In: Proceedings of IEEE International Conference on Systems in Medicine and Biology, IIT Kharagpur, India, pp. 278–283 (2010)

8. Vauhkonen, M., Lionheart, W.R.B., Heikkinen, L.M., Vauhkonen, P.J., Kaipio, J.P.: A MATLAB Package for the EIDORS Project to Reconstruct two Dimensional EIT images. Physiol. Meas. 22, 107–111 (2001)

9. Bera, T.K., Nagaraju, J.: Resistivity Imaging of a Reconfigurable Phantom with Circular Inhomogeneities in 2D-Electrical Impedance Tomography. Measurement 44, 518–526 (2011)

10. Bera, T.K., Biswas, T.K., Rajan, K., Nagaraju, J.: Improving Image Quality in Electrical Impedance Tomography (EIT) using Projection Error Propagation-Based Regularization (PEPR) Technique: A Simulation Study. Journal of Electrical Bioimpedance 2, 2–12 (2011)

Stereo Correspondence Using Census Based Dynamic Programming and Segmentation

Arjun P.R. and Govindan V.K.

Department of Computer Science and Engineering,
National Institute of Technology Calicut, India
arjunpkd@gmail.com, vkg@nitc.ac.in

Abstract. The paper describes a novel algorithm for stereo correspondence combining an improved dynamic programming method and segmentation. Dynamic programming is one of the widely used techniques for obtaining a dense stereo. The standard dynamic programming approach processes each pair of epipolar lines independently disregarding inter scanline dependency. This results in horizontal streaks in the computed disparity map. This problem is eliminated by segmenting the reference image to refine the disparities globally. The segmentation implicitly models the inter scanline dependency and also acts a global technique to refine the disparities. Further, the dynamic programming step performed on census transformed image improves the accuracy of its output. The algorithm is evaluated with standard datasets and found to have accuracy and efficiency comparable with top ranking algorithms.

Keywords: Census Measure, Correspondence Problem, Disparity Map, Dynamic Programming, Segmentation, Stereo Vision.

1 Introduction

Human beings have the ability to view the world in 3-D. This fascinating skill allows us to move around, interact with surrounding objects, avoid obstacles, and identify hazards. Nevertheless, the human visual system is very spontaneous and accurate in its functioning. Building a stereo vision system that can mimic its operations with a comparable speed and accuracy is still a difficult goal to achieve. A main reason for this is due to optical distortions, shape changes, object occlusion and changes in viewpoint. As a result, different views of the same object can give rise to widely different images.

Stereo correspondence is a widely addressed problem in computer vision. Numerous approaches have been put forward to tackle the problem. One of the most popular global optimization used for obtaining a dense disparity map is dynamic programming. The high efficiency offered by standard dynamic programming however comes with a disadvantage that it neglects inter scanline dependency. Objects in the image span multiple scanlines and hence there exists strong inter scanline dependency. In dynamic programming each pair of epipolar lines is processed independently. This leads to a streaky effect in the resultant disparity map.

K.R. Venugopal and L.M. Patnaik (Eds.): ICIP 2011, CCIS 157, pp. 631–638, 2011.
© Springer-Verlag Berlin Heidelberg 2011

The paper describes an elegant approach incorporating two refinements in the standard dynamic programming method for stereo correspondence. Firstly, the parametric measure generally used in dynamic programming like sum of absolute distances (SAD), sum of squared distances (SSD) is replaced by a much stronger non-parametric measure called census transform [1]. Secondly, the elimination of the undesirable streaking effect in the disparity map produced by the dynamic programming and the disparity refinement are performed with the help of segmentation. The segmentation implicitly models the inter scanline dependency ignored by dynamic programming. Thus the algorithm, modified with the above mentioned refinements, produces a dense and accurate disparity map.

2   Literature Survey

Stereo vision algorithms can be broadly classified as local algorithms and global algorithms. In local algorithms, the disparity computation at a point depends on the neighbourhood pixels of that point implicitly taking care of the smoothness constraints. In global algorithms however, the stereo correspondence problem is formulated as a global optimization problem, along with explicit smoothness constraints. The optimization problem can then be solved using any of the available techniques like simulated annealing [1], dynamic programming [2], [3], Graph Cuts [4], cooperative optimization [5]. The rest of the literature survey is focused on optimization through dynamic programming techniques. A detailed survey of stereo vision algorithms can be found in [6].

Yuichi and Kannade [2] have proposed a method of stereo correspondence by two level dynamic programming method. Apart from the inter scanline search, which basically is the correspondence between rows, the paper proposed an intra scanline search. Vertical lines from images are matched to improve the accuracy of intra scanline search. In a similar approach by J.C Kim *et al.*, [3], ground control points obtained from images using oriented spatial filters are used to improve matching accuracy. An improved method of dynamic programming using information obtained from edges and corners has been suggested by Torr *et al.*, [7]. The three methods described above basically have a characteristic in common. They tried to incorporate edge and corner information in the dynamic programming computation framework.

This paper however addresses the problem in a slightly different manner. One difference is that a non-parametric measure called census transform [8] is used in the dynamic programming stage to improve accuracy. Working on census transformed images is highly beneficial as it is immune to image gain and bias. Hamming distance is the measure used to compare pixel similarity. Also segmentation of reference image is used to increase the accuracy of disparity map and to enforce smoothness constraint. It also handles the occlusion problem as the segmentation groups the occluded pixels to any segment consisting of non-occluded pixels. The method is much simpler as it does not require any edge or corner matching step mandatory in currently existing works eliminating much of the computational overhead.

Fig. 1. Tsukuba stereo pair images

3   Stereo Vision System

3.1   Census Transformation

Correspondence algorithms generally make use of parametric measures like absolute intensity difference (AD), squared intensity difference (SD) for pixel matching. Parametric measures are affected by camera gain or bias. Hence, more robust non-parametric measures are required for a good correspondence matching. Census transform is a non-parametric transform that relies on the relative ordering of local intensity values. The centre pixel's intensity value is replaced by a bit string composed of a set of boolean comparisons performed on the local neighbourhood.

Let P be a pixel with intensity $I(P)$ and $N(P)$ be the set of pixels in the neighbourhood of P. Define $\psi(P, P')$ as

$$\psi(P, P') = \begin{cases} 1 \text{ if } I(P) > I(P') \\ 0 \text{ if } otherwise \end{cases}$$

The census transform can then be specified as,

$$C_t(P) = \bigoplus_{p \in N(P)} \psi(P, p)$$

where $\bigoplus$ is the concatenation operator.

A 5×5 window is used as neighbourhood in this algorithm and scanned from left to right from top to bottom. If the current pixel intensity is greater than the center pixel intensity, the bit is set otherwise it is unset. For each comparison the bit is shifted left to form a 24 bit string. The center pixel intensity value is then replaced with this bit string. Since the census transform is based on the relative intensity value of neighbouring pixels, it captures the image structure and is much robust for matching purposes. Fig. 1 shows the left and right Tsukuba stereo images from Middlebury dataset and Fig. 2 shows the result of census transformation on the reference (left) image.

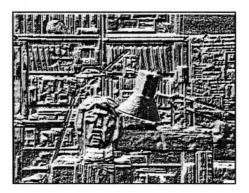

Fig. 2. Census transformed reference image

3.2 Stereo by Dynamic Programming

Stereo correspondence basically requires finding the maximum matches between a pair of rows from the left and right stereo image. The attempt is to obtain the optimal alignment between the epipolar pairs. This can be accomplished using dynamic programming which essentially minimizes the matching cost between the pair of epipolar lines to find the optimal alignment.

Consider the Fig. 3 which shows the matching of a pair of left and right epipolar lines from an image. The points a_1 of left image match with a_2 of right image. Similarly, the points b_1 and b_2 are matched. For any general image the task is to find a match between every pair of pixels on left and right image. These matches lie on a line that starts from bottom left corner to top right side. The task of dynamic programming is to find this optimal path.

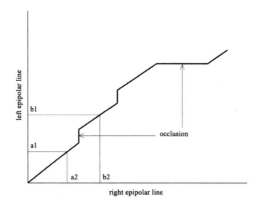

Fig. 3. Visualization of matching using dynamic programming

Now, consider two rows $I_l(i)$ and $I_r(j), 1 \leq i, j \leq N$, where N is the number of pixels in each line. Pixels in each row may be matched or skipped (considered to be occluded in either the left or right image). Let d_{ij} be the cost associated with matching pixel $I_l(i)$ with pixel $I_r(j)$. Here d_{ij} is the Hamming distance measure since census transformed image is used. The cost of skipping a pixel is given by a constant c_0. Given these costs, the optimal (minimal cost) alignment of two scanlines is computed recursively as follows:

$$D(1,1) = d_{11},$$
$$D(i,j) = min(D(i-1,j-1) + d_{ij}, D(i-1,j) + c_0, D(i,j-1) + c_0)$$

The intermediate values are stored in an N-by-N matrix, D. The total cost of matching two scanlines is $D(N,N)$. Given D the optimal alignment is obtained by backtracking. In particular, starting at $(i,j) = (N,N)$, choose the minimum value of D from $(i-1,j-1),(i-1,j),(i,j-1)$. Selecting $(i-1,j)$ corresponds to skipping a pixel in I_l (a unit increase in disparity), while selecting $(i,j-1)$ corresponds to skipping a pixel in I_r (a unit decrease in disparity). Selecting $(i-1,j-1)$ matches pixels (i,j), and therefore leaves disparity unchanged. Beginning with zero disparity, one can work backwards from (N,N), tallying the disparity until $(1,1)$ is reached. The process is repeated for each row of the image to obtain the disparity map. Fig. 4 shows the result of dynamic programming and the subsequent application of median filter on it.

Fig. 4. Results of stereo by DP. (a) disparity obtained by dynamic programming (b) disparity refinement using median filter.

3.3 Disparity Refinement by Segmentation

Dynamic programming method computes disparity map taking one row at a time. The picture of an object in an image may however span many rows. This disregard for inter scanline dependency causes a streaky effect in the obtained disparity map. Segmenting an image causes grouping of homogeneous regions. It can be used to enforce the smoothness constraints required for obtaining accurate disparity map. Hill climbing algorithm for segmentation proposed by Ohashi *et al.*, [9] is used in this paper for segmenting the reference image. The disparity obtained by dynamic programming is refined with the help of this segmented image (Fig. 5).

Let S denotes an $m \times n$ label matrix corresponding to the segmented image. Define T_k be the set of pixel intensity values such that $S_{ij} = k$. Define M such that $M_{ij} = mode(T_k)$, where $S_{ij} = k$ and *mode* function returns the most frequently occuring value in the set. M represents the final disparity map.

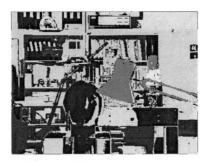

Fig. 5. Result of segmentation on reference image

For each segment in segmented image, the disparities of its points are noted. Then the mode of the disparity values is calculated. This value becomes the actual disparity of that particular segment and the existing disparity values in that segment is replaced the mode value in the disparity map. Since disparity can vary over an object surface, over segmentation of an object is preferred so that disparity values at those regions are not lost. As the segmentation can identify object boundaries, it can remove the streaky lines in disparity map obtained from dynamic programming stage. Certain pixels in the one of the stereo pair may be absent in the other due to occlusion of objects in the scene. These pixels in reference image are known as occluded pixels. Disparity values cannot be calculated for such pixels. However, during segmentation the occluded pixels become a part of some segment. Hence, the occluded pixels receive the disparity value calculated as the mode value of the segment. As a result this becomes a simple method for calculating disparity of occluded pixels. Dynamic programming and segmentation techniques are combined to obtain a simple algorithm that provides an accurate disparity map Fig. 6.

Fig. 6. Output disparity image, ground truth image and bad pixels map

4   Experimental Results

The proposed algorithm is evaluated with Middlebury stereo benchmarking datasets. Tsukuba and Venus datasets were chosen from the Middlebury sets for evaluation. Quality of the disparity map is represented as bad pixels which is the percentage of pixels with disparity errors (differences between evaluated and ground-truth disparity maps) exceeding given threshold. Additionally, similarity scores Normalized Bad Pixel - SAD (NBP-SAD) and Normalized Bad Pixel - SSD (NBP-SSD) are also used that provide information about magnitude and energy of errors [10].

$$NBP\text{-}SAD = \frac{1}{count\ of\ bad\ pixels} \sum_{x,y \in bad\ pixels} |G(x,y) - d(x,y)| \ .$$

where G(x,y) is ground-truth disparity map, d(x,y) is evaluated disparity map.

NBP-SSD is similar to NBP-SAD but measures energy instead of magnitude.

$$NBP\text{-}SSD = \frac{1}{count\ of\ bad\ pixels} \sum_{x,y \in bad\ pixels} |G(x,y) - d(x,y)|^2 \ .$$

where G(x,y) is ground-truth disparity map, d(x,y) is evaluated disparity map.

The results are provided in Table 1. The algorithm was also evaluated at Middlebury online stereo evaluation site for errors. The site computes error measure scores non-occ, occ, overall. non-occ computes error only at non occluded parts, occ at only occluded regions and overall gives an overall error measure score (Table 2).

Table 1. Error results for Tsukuba and Venus datasets

Dataset	Bad Pixels	NBP-SAD	NBP-SSD
Tsukuba	1.4345	4.4404	24.4722
Venus	5.2707	2.8732	9.3779

Table 2. Middlebury evaluation results for Tsukuba and Venus datasets [11]

Dataset	non-occ	occ	overall
Tsukuba	3.77	18.9	5.33
Venus	13.7	35.4	14.4

5   Conclusions

This paper proposes a new stereo matching algorithm which integrates the strengths of an improved dynamic programming approach and segmentation. The algorithm stands as an improvement to stereo using traditional dynamic programming. The use of census measure has greatly boosted the accuracy of depth map. Segmentation is used to enforce smoothness constraints and improve the result from dynamic programming. The algorithm is very simple and yet is capable of producing accurate disparity maps. Online evaluation at Middlebury vision page placed the algorithm along with other top listed stereo algorithms.

References

1. Barnard, S.T.: Stochastic Stereo Matching Over Scale. International Journal of Computer Vision 3(1), 17–32 (1989)
2. Ohta, Y., Kanade, T.: Stereo by Two-Level Dynamic Programming. IEEE TPAMI 7(2), 139–154 (1985)
3. Kim, J.C., Lee, K.M., Choi, B.T., Lee, S.U.: A Dense Stereo Matching using Two-Pass Dynamic Programming with Generalized Ground Control Points. In: IEEE Computer Society Conference on Computer Vision and Pattern Recognition, CVPR 2005, vol. 2, pp. 1075–1082 (2005)
4. Boykov, Y., Veksler, O., Zabih, R.: Fast Approximate Energy Minimization *via* Graph cuts. IEEE Transactions on Pattern Analysis and Machine Intelligence, 1222–1239 (2001)
5. Wang, Z.F., Zheng, Z.G.: A Region Based Stereo Matching Algorithm using Co-operative Optimization. In: IEEE Conference on Computer Vision and Pattern Recognition (2008)
6. Scharstein, D., Szeliski, R.: A Taxonomy and Evaluation of Dense Two-Frame Stereo Correspondence Algorithms. International Journal of Computer Vision 47(1), 7–42 (2002)
7. Torr, P.H.S., Criminisi, A.: Dense Stereo using Pivoted Dynamic Programming. Image and Vision Computing 22(10), 795–806 (2004)
8. Zabih, R., Woodfill, J.: Non-Parametric Local Transforms for Computing Visual Correspondence. In: Eklundh, J.-O. (ed.) ECCV 1994. LNCS, vol. 801, pp. 151–158. Springer, Heidelberg (1994)
9. Ohashi, T., Aghbari, Z., Makinouchi, A.: Hill-Climbing Algorithm for Efficient Color-Based Image Segmentation. In: IASTED International Conference on Signal Processing, Pattern Recognition, and Applications, pp. 17–22 (2003)
10. Stankiewicz, O., Wegner, K.: Depth Map Estimation Software version 3, ISO. Technical Report, IEC JTC1/SC29/WG11 (MPEG) Doc. M15540
11. Middlebury Stereo Vision, `http://vision.middlebury.edu/stereo/` (accessed April 28, 2010)

Unsupervised Color Image Segmentation by Clustering into Multivariate Gaussians

Jobin Raj and Govindan V.K.

Department of Computer Science and Engineering
National Institute of Technology Calicut, India
jobinr@gmail.com, vkg@nitc.ac.in

Abstract. An Unsupervised Color Image Segmentation Algorithm by using Finite Gaussian Mixture Model (GMM) is proposed in this paper. The parameters of GMM are estimated using Expectation Maximization (EM) Algorithm. A novel technique for initializing the EM Algorithm is presented. The algorithm runs in two stages. The first stage performs an initial segmentation which initializes the EM Algorithm. The second stage is the parameter estimation phase using EM Algorithm. The scheme is computationally efficient in terms of space and time complexity.

Keywords: Expectation Maximization Algorithm, Gaussian Mixture Model, Image Segmentation, Model-based Segmentation, Multivariate Gaussian Distribution.

1 Introduction

Image segmentation is the process of dividing an image into non overlapping regions which are homogeneous in some sense. This is a crucial task in image analysis and understanding. Segmentation techniques for intensity images are broadly classified into three categories: continuity-based schemes or region-based schemes, discontinuity-based or edge-based schemes and clustering schemes. In edge-based schemes, an edge operator is applied on the image to detect edges which are identified by a rapid change in image feature. Segments are identified by tracing the closed boundaries formed by linking edge elements. Region-based approaches assign contiguous image points that do not differ in image characteristic by more than a threshold, to the same region. Hybrid schemes, exploiting the complementary strengths of region-based and edge-based schemes, can also be found in literature. Clustering schemes use supervised or unsupervised techniques to classify the pixels into different clusters [1]. Graph theoretic approaches [2] and fuzzy connectivity based approaches [3] also have been proved effective in segmentation problem.

There has been considerable interest in stochastic model-based image segmentation techniques since the past decade [4]. In such techniques, an image is separated into a set of disjoint regions with each region associated with one of a

K.R. Venugopal and L.M. Patnaik (Eds.): ICIP 2011, CCIS 157, pp. 639–645, 2011.
© Springer-Verlag Berlin Heidelberg 2011

finite number of classes. Unsupervised techniques for model parameter estimation have also been developed since then. Lalit Gupta and Thotsapon Sortrakul [5] formulated and developed an autonomous gaussian-mixture based segmentation algorithm which could accurately segment a wide class of degraded images. Their goal was to develop a segmentation algorithm which is invariant to target environmental changes. Caillol et al., [6] introduced a procedure for estimation of fuzzy Gaussian distribution mixtures, which was an adaptation of the iterative conditional estimation (ICE) algorithm to the fuzzy framework. A color image segmentation method based on finite Gaussian mixture model was proposed by Yiming Wu et al., [7]. The number of mixture components was automatically determined by implementing the Minimum Message Length(MML) criterion. Segmentation was carried out by clustering each pixel into appropriate component according to maximum likelihood (ML) criterion. Haim Permuter et al., [8] defined Gaussian mixture models (GMM) of colored texture on several feature spaces and compared the performance of these models in various classification tasks. Peñalver et al., [9] presented a method for finding the optimal number of kernels in a Gaussian Mixture, based on maximum entropy and used this technique in unsupervised color image segmentation. Attempts have been made in segmenting images by fitting Gaussians in image histograms [10], [11].

Gaussian mixture model has evidently received considerable attention in the development of algorithms for image segmentation. Considering the fact that the intensity values of pixels in each object region of an image approximates a Gaussian distribution, an image can be considered as a mixture of Gaussians. Consequently, image segmentation can be formulated as a problem of clustering the pixels into Gaussians. Multispectral/Color image segmentation can be addressed by a d-variate GMM where d is the dimension of the color model used. The common and efficient method to estimate the parameters of a GMM is the EM algorithm which is based on likelihood maximization. However, EM Algorithm converges to local minima and is sensitive to initialization. Determining the initial values for parameters is therefore quite a significant task. In this paper, we propose a novel method to get an initial segmentation, which aids in estimating the initial parameter values. Section 2 describes the theory and the proposed segmentation scheme. Experimental results are summarized in section 3. Section 4 gives the summary of the paper and the scope for future work.

2   The Proposed Method

The proposed method comprises of two key phases, *viz.*, the initial segmentation phase and the GMM parameter estimation phase.

2.1   Initial Segmentation

A coarse clustering of the image pixels is performed in this phase. The strategy is to identify homogenous regions of the image (seed regions) and to grow these regions iteratively until the required number of segments is obtained. The number of segments is estimated from the image histogram, under the assumption that each local maxima in the histogram corresponds to a segment/object region.

An image can be represented as an $m \times n$ matrix I of intensity values. A binary edge image E is generated from I by applying an edge operator (say Sobel) on I, followed by thresholding it. The next step is to estimate the value of (x, y) which maximizes a, subject to the condition that

$$\sum_{i=0}^{a-1}\sum_{j=0}^{a-1} E_{(x+i),(y+j)} = 0 .$$

The values x, y & a define a square region in the image with top left corner at (x, y) and side length a. The sub image region corresponding to this square is homogenous and provides a cue about the statistical properties of the object. The square region is assumed to be within an object region though there is a chance that some pixels in the corner regions of the square could be from other object regions. Error pixels creep in due to the fact that noise and degradation in image cause discontinuities in the detected edges after thresholding. Let d be the length of the largest possible break in terms of number of pixels. The value of d depends on the extent of degradation and the threshold used in the binary edge image generation. Consequently, the value of d can be minimized by choosing an appropriate value for the threshold and by applying noise cleaning measures in the preprocessing phase. A break of d pixels in the edge can result in maximum of $d^2/4$ error pixels at a corner. Even if we assume that error pixels crept in at all the four corners though the probability is meager, the maximum error pixels that can creep in the square region are d^2. Since $d \ll a$, the fraction of error pixels $(= (d/a)^2)$ is negligibly small.

Let S be the $a \times a$ matrix of pixel intensity values corresponding to the sub image region defined by x, y & a. It is assumed that $S \sim \mathcal{N}_d(\mu, \Sigma)$ where $\mathcal{N}_d$ is a d-variate Gaussian with mean vector μ and covariance matrix Σ.

$$\mu_k = \frac{1}{a^2}\sum_{i=1}^{a}\sum_{j=1}^{a} S_{ij}^k \qquad 1 \le k \le d. \tag{1}$$

$$\Sigma_{ij} = E[(S^i - \mu_i)(S^j - \mu_j)] \qquad 1 \le i, j \le d. \tag{2}$$

where $E[X]$ denotes the expected value of X.

The probability density function of $\mathcal{N}_d(\mu, \Sigma)$ is given by

$$f(x) = \frac{1}{\sqrt{(2\pi)^d|\Sigma|}}e^{-\frac{1}{2}(x-\mu)\Sigma^{-1}(x-\mu)^T}. \tag{3}$$

For every pixel $I_{ij} \in I$, $f(I_{ij})$ is estimated. Let P^k be an mn matrix such that $P_{ij}^k = f(I_{ij})$. Let B^k be a bitmap such that

$$B_{ij}^k = \begin{cases} 1 \text{ if } P_{ij}^k \ge \theta \\ 0 \text{ otherwise.} \end{cases} \tag{4}$$

where θ is the threshold value.

Let $E^{'} = E|B^k$ where $|$ represents the binary OR operation. The aforementioned steps, starting from the estimation of values of x, y & a, are repeated with $E^{'}$ as the new edge image, until the required number of segments is obtained.

Choosing a value of the threshold θ is quite critical since a high value of θ will result in a failure to label a large fraction of pixels and a low value of θ may result in under segmentation or larger overlap between segments. There could even be situations where a large fraction of pixels may remain unlabelled even at low values of θ. This can be rectified by choosing a different value for (x, y) by relaxing the criterion of maximizing a. The initial segments are obtained from the bitmap array B. Let L be the label matrix of initial segmentation.

$$L_{ij} = k \text{ if } B_{ij}^k = 1 \text{ and } B_{ij}^l = 0 \ \forall l : 1 \leq l \leq k. \tag{5}$$

If there are unlabelled pixels in L, label them as follows

$$L_{ij} = k \text{ if } max(P_{ij}) = P_{ij}^k. \tag{6}$$

2.2   Gaussian Mixture Model and EM Algorithm

A Gaussian Mixture Model is a weighted sum of k Gaussian densities as given by the equation

$$p(x|\lambda) = \sum_{i=1}^{k} \phi_i g(x|\mu_i, \Sigma_i). \tag{7}$$

$g(x|\mu_i, \Sigma_i)$ is the probability density function of the ith Gaussian component with mean vector μ_i and covariance matrix Σ_i. The GMM is parameterized by the mean vectors, covariance matrices and the mixture weights.

$$\lambda = \{\phi_i, \mu_i, \Sigma_i\} \quad 1 \leq i \leq k. \tag{8}$$

A color image can be considered as a mixture of d-variate Gaussian distributions where d is the dimension of the color model used. Segmentation can be considered as a task of estimating the underlying model, the GMM parameters. Our method uses EM Algorithm to estimate the mixture parameters λ. The basic idea of EM Algorithm is, starting with an initial model λ, to estimate $\bar{\lambda}$ such that $p(x|\bar{\lambda}) \geq p(x|\lambda)$.

Define a bitmap array T such that

$$T_{ij}^l = \begin{cases} 1 \text{ if } L_{ij} = l \\ 0 \text{ otherwise.} \end{cases} \tag{9}$$

The initial parameters $\lambda(t_0)$ are estimated as follows:

$$\phi_l(t_0) = \frac{1}{mn} \sum_{i=1}^{m} \sum_{j=1}^{n} T_{ij}^l. \tag{10}$$

$$\mu_l(t_0) = \frac{\sum_{i=1}^{m} \sum_{j=1}^{n} T_{ij}^l . I_{ij}}{\sum_{i=1}^{m} \sum_{j=1}^{n} T_{ij}}. \tag{11}$$

$$\Sigma_l(t_0) = \frac{\sum_{i=1}^{m} \sum_{j=1}^{n} T_{ij}^l (I_{ij} - \mu_l(t_0))(I_{ij} - \mu_l(t_0))^T}{\sum_{i=1}^{m} \sum_{j=1}^{n} T_{ij}^l}. \tag{12}$$

where $1 \leq l \leq k$.

Let Z be a set of latent random variables such that I_{ij}, Z_{ij} form a joint distribution.

$$P(I_{ij}, Z_{ij}) = P(I_{ij}|Z_{ij})P(Z_{ij}). \tag{13}$$

Z_{ij} follows a multinomial distribution parameterized by ϕ.

$$\phi_l \geq 0, \quad \sum_{l=1}^{k} \phi_l = 1. \tag{14}$$

Z_{ij} can be considered as a variable indicating the mixture component to which I_{ij} belongs to. The conditional distribution of I_{ij} given $Z_{ij} = l$ follows a Gaussian as per our GMM assumption.

The log likelihood of parameters λ is given by

$$l(\lambda|I) = \sum_{i=1}^{m} \sum_{j=1}^{n} \log p(I_{ij}, Z_{ij}|\lambda) . \tag{15}$$

The EM algorithm runs in two steps: the E-step and the M-step. E-step involves estimation of the expected value of the log likelihood function, with respect to the conditional distribution of Z given I, under the current estimate of parameters λ. The M-step re-estimates the parameters so as to maximize the log likelihood. Each iteration re-calculates the parameter values as follows which ensures monotonic increase in the likelihood of model parameters.

$$\begin{aligned} w_{ij}^l(t_n) &= P(Z_{ij} = l|I_{ij}, \lambda) \\ &= \frac{P(I_{ij}|Z_{ij} = l)P(Z_{ij} = l)}{\sum_{x=1}^{k} P(I_{ij}|Z_{ij} = x)P(Z_{ij} = x)}. \end{aligned} \tag{16}$$

where $P(Z_{ij} = l) = \phi_l(t_{n-1})$ and $P(I_{ij}|Z_{ij} = l)$ is given by the pdf of $\mathcal{N}(\mu_l(t_{n-1}), \Sigma_l(t_{n-1}))$.

$$\phi_l(t_n) = \frac{1}{mn} \sum_{i=1}^{m} \sum_{j=1}^{n} w_{ij}^l(t_n). \tag{17}$$

$$\mu_l(t_n) = \frac{\sum_{i=1}^{m} \sum_{j=1}^{n} w_{ij}^l(t_n).I_{ij}}{\sum_{i=1}^{m} \sum_{j=1}^{n} w_{ij}^l(t_n)}. \tag{18}$$

$$\Sigma_l(t_n) = \frac{\sum_{i=1}^{m} \sum_{j=1}^{n} w_{ij}^l(t_n)(I_{ij} - \mu_l(t_n))(I_{ij} - \mu_l(t_n))^T}{\sum_{i=1}^{m} \sum_{j=1}^{n} w_{ij}^l(t_n)}. \tag{19}$$

The parameters are re-estimated iteratively until the convergence criterion is met. The parameter estimation phase is followed by pixel labeling. A pixel I_{ij} is labeled m if the value of w_{ij}^l is maximum for $l = m$.

3   Experimental Results

The proposed algorithm has been tested with color images from Berkeley Segmentation Benchmark database [12]. Fig. 1 shows the results of segmentation by the proposed algorithm. Testing was performed using RGB and Lab Color models. Lab Color model was found to give better results than RGB model. The Segmentation algorithm has been evaluated using the Segmentation evaluation database [13] of Department of Computer Science and Applied Mathematics, Weizmann Institute of Science. Table 1 summarizes the results of evaluation. The proposed algorithm took on an average 1.7485 seconds to segment an image of the evaluation database on an AMD Turion 64 Dual-Core 1.80GHz machine.

Table 1. Segmentation Evaluation Results

	F-score	Recall	Precision
Min Value	0.4407	0.3198	0.7090
Mean Value	0.7433	0.7877	0.8466
Max Value	0.9925	0.9992	0.9859

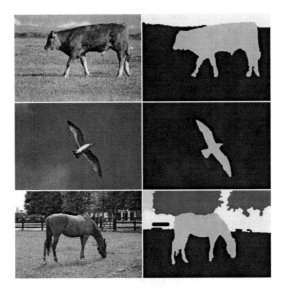

Fig. 1. Image Segmentation Results of Proposed Algorithm

4   Conclusions

Image Segmentation algorithms based on GMM uses EM algorithm for parameter estimation. However, EM algorithm is sensitive to initialization. Here we propose a GMM based segmentation algorithm which uses a novel technique to initialize the EM algorithm. The initialization step has a time and space complexity of $O(n)$ where n is the number of pixels. The initialization phase performs a coarse segmentation and hence the EM algorithm which follows, converges in lesser number of iterations. Hence the algorithm is efficient in terms of time and space complexity.

The second phase of the proposed scheme does not take into account spatial information, even though it is taken care in the initialization stage. The EM algorithm can be fine tuned by taking into account, the spatial information.

References

1. Ohashi, T., Aghbari, Z., Makinouchi, A.: Hill-Climbing Algorithm for Efficient Color-Based Image Segmentation. In: IASTED International Conference on Signal Processing, Pattern Recognition, and Applications, pp. 17–22 (2003)
2. Shi, J., Malik, J.: Normalized Cuts and Image Segmentation. IEEE Transactions on Pattern Analysis and Machine Intelligence 22(8), 888–905 (2002)
3. Udupa, J., Samarasekera, S.: Fuzzy Connectedness and Object Definition: Theory, Algorithms, and Applications in Image Segmentation. Graphical Models and Image Processing 58, 246–261 (1996)
4. Zhang, J., Modestino, J., Langan, D.: Maximum-Likelihood Parameter Estimation for Unsupervised Stochastic Model-Based Image Segmentation. IEEE Transactions on Image Processing 3(4), 404–420 (1994)
5. Gupta, L., Sortrakul, T.: A Gaussian-Mixture-Based Image Segmentation Algorithm. Pattern Recognition 31(3), 315–325 (1998)
6. Caillol, H., Pieczynski, W., Hillion, A.: Estimation of Fuzzy Gaussian Mixture and Unsupervised Statistical Image Segmentation. IEEE Transactions on Image Processing 6(3), 425–440 (1997)
7. Wu, Y., Yang, X., Chan, K.: Unsupervised Color Image Segmentation Based on Gaussian Mixture Model. In: Proceedings of the Fourth International Joint Conference and the Fourth Pacific Rim Conference on Multimedia Information, Communications and Signal Processing, 2003, vol. 1, pp. 541–544. IEEE, Los Alamitos (2003)
8. Permuter, H., Francos, J., Jermyn, I.: A study of Gaussian Mixture Models of Color and Texture Features for Image Classification and Segmentation. Pattern Recognition 39(4), 695–706 (2006)
9. Peñalver, A., Escolano, F., Sáez, J.M.: Color Image Segmentation Through Unsupervised Gaussian Mixture Models. In: Sichman, J.S., Coelho, H., Rezende, S.O. (eds.) IBERAMIA 2006 and SBIA 2006. LNCS (LNAI), vol. 4140, pp. 149–158. Springer, Heidelberg (2006)
10. Harimi, A., Ahmadyfard, A.: Image Segmentation Using Correlative Histogram Modeled by Gaussian Mixture. In: International Conference on Digital Image Processing, pp. 397–401. IEEE, Los Alamitos (2009)
11. Huang, Z., Chau, K.: A New Image Thresholding Method Based on Gaussian Mixture model. Applied Mathematics and Computation 205(2), 899–907 (2008)
12. Martin, D., Fowlkes, C., Tal, D., Malik, J.: A Database of Human Segmented Natural Images and Its Application to Evaluating Segmentation Algorithms and Measuring Ecological Statistics. In: Proc. 8th International Conference on Computer Vision, vol. 2, pp. 416–423 (2001)
13. Alpert, S., Galun, M., Basri, R., Brandt, A.: Image Segmentation by Probabilistic Bottom-up Aggregation and Cue Integration. In: Proceedings of the IEEE Conference on Computer Vision and Pattern Recognition (2007)

A Novel Approach to Writer Identification in Malayalam Using Graphemes

Sreeraj M. and Sumam Mary Idicula

Department of Computer Science,
Cochin University of Science and Technology, Cochin, India
{msreeraj,Sumam}@cusat.ac.in

Abstract. This paper proposes a Writer Identification scheme for Malayalam handwritten documents. The novelty of the scheme lies in the fact that the graphemes were used in the training and identification phase of the system. Graphemes are small writing fragments extracted from the handwritten documents which contain meaningful patterns and possess individuality of each writer. The scheme has been tested on a test bed of 280 writers of which 50 writers having only one page, 215 writers with at least 2 pages and 15 writers with at least 4 pages. A recognition rate of 89.28% was achieved.

Keywords: Codebook, Feature Extraction, Grapheme, Malayalam, Writer Identification.

1 Introduction

The importance of the technique "writer identification" is ever increasing as it is significant in digital rights administration, forensic expert decision-making systems, document analysis and also as a strong tool for physiological identification purposes. Although many of the world languages including Chinese, Arabic, and Persian have put consider growth in this area of studies, Malayalam- a regional language in India is leaving no trace of notable works on writer identification scheme. A distinguished work in this course is [1] by Srihari et al., which proposes the features necessary for the writer identification scheme at different levels.

The motivation for Malayalam writer identification scheme stems out from the challenges like

(i) *Meager Allographic Variation of writers in Malayalam language* (ii) *Insufficient discriminating capacity of a single character in Malayalam language* (iii) *Non-existence of uppercase and lowercase in Malayalam language* (iv) *Absence of dataset.*

In this paper, Section 2 details a design of the writer identifications scheme for Malayalam language using graphemes. Section 3 outlines the implementation details. Section 4 analyses the results obtained and provide valid conclusions. The paper is concluded in Section 5.

K.R. Venugopal and L.M. Patnaik (Eds.): ICIP 2011, CCIS 157, pp. 646–651, 2011.

2   System Architecture

The system architecture in Fig. 1 shows the training and identification phases of the writer identification scheme.

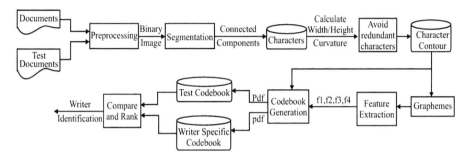

Fig. 1. System Architecture

The images of the documents were processed in order to obtain the fragmented connected components representing each character in Malayalam. If the images were are all scanned at the same resolution the size of characters in the writing is a writer-dependent attribute and should not be normalized. Also, some writer-specific information could be lost while using thinning algorithm. The nave image of documents should be pre-processed at first hand through the following steps.

1. Calculate the threshold value by selecting the image mean and the standard deviation and normalize.
2. Convert the grey-scale of the documents to binary image using the above threshold.
3. Image de-noising is practiced to attain the perfect binary image of the documents [2].

Because of its peculiar nature, each connected components of Malayalam has to be considered as a character. Using the segmentation phase each character is separated for avoiding redundant characters. The necessary characters of each writer will be on the account of individuality identification in order to classify the writers. Omitting the unnecessary, repeated characters, we are taking into consideration of similarity measurement of the width/height ratio and the curvature of each character. The splitting of the connected components into meaningful units called graphemes and is done by using square windows of size n. The value of n should be large enough to contain plentiful information about the style of the writer and small enough to guarantee a good identification performance. For our system, the window size was fixed to 11x11. The splitting is carried out according to the sliding window positioning algorithm as mentioned in [3].

2.1   Feature Extraction

This phase is used for both the training and the identification. The following features are considered for Malayalam handwritten documents.

Directional features (f1, f2). Directional features and their variants have been applied to character/word recognition [4,5,6] as well as classification of writing styles in handwritten document images [7]. In order to confine the overall orientation information globally, the eight bins of the histogram represents the eight principal directions contributions in an individual's writing. We have to count the chain code pairs, in a histogram *f1* to confine the finer details. The local direction *f2* is calculating by building an accumulator which is been initialized with all bins set to zero. For each window w, containing the chain code sequence CS^w, the $bin(i,j)$ of the histogram (accumulator)is incremented by 1 if the frequency of direction i is represented in the jth interval, where

$$j = ceil\left(\frac{cardinality(CS_i^w)}{cardinality(CS^w) \times p} \times 100\right) With(CS_i^w) = \{CS_k \in CS^w | Cs_k = i\}. \tag{1}$$

and *i=0, 1., 7* . The number of intervals p should be large enough to capture the distribution differences of direction and small enough to allow marginal different distributions which has been contributed to the same intervals of *f2*. Value of p is chosen as 10 for our system.

Curvature (f3). The contour of the fragments is convolved with the Gaussian smoothing kernel. The curvature value of each pixel of the contour is computed using

$$K_i^j = \frac{\Delta x_i^j \Delta^2 y_i^j - \Delta^2 x_i^j \Delta y_i^j}{\left[\left(\Delta x_i^j\right)^2 + \left(\Delta y_i^j\right)^2\right]^{3/2}} \quad for \quad i = 1, 2, \ldots\ldots, N, \tag{2}$$

$$Where \ \Delta x_i^j = \left(x_{i+1}^j - x_{i-1}^j\right)\Big/2, \quad and \quad \Delta y_i^j = \left(y_{i+1}^j - y_{i-1}^j\right)\Big/2. \tag{3}$$

$$\Delta^2 x_i^j = \left(\Delta x_{i+1}^j - \Delta x_{i-1}^j\right)\Big/2, \quad and \quad \Delta^2 y_i^j = \left(\Delta y_{i+1}^j - \Delta y_{i-1}^j\right)\Big/2. \tag{4}$$

Angle pair. Edge-hinge distribution is a feature that characterizes the changes in direction of a writing stroke in handwritten text and is extracted by means of a window that is slid over an edge-detected binary handwriting image [8]. Whenever the central pixel of the window is on, the two edge fragments (i.e., connected sequences of pixels) emerging from this central pixel are considered. Their directions are computed and stored as pairs. We consider a complete 2D probability distribution that takes into account all possible combinations of angles pairs as the feature *f4*.

2.2   Codebook Generation

In order to generate a codebook of the characteristic writing fragments this is represented by a set of features. We group similar fragments into different classes in a variety of ways. Methods like k-means, fuzzy c-means, learning vector quantization and the closely related self organizing maps have been successfully applied to similar problems of clustering allographs or graphemes [9], [10]. The Kohonen self-organizing feature map (SOM 2D) is used for the clustering the graphemes in our scheme and the network size was varied from 2x2 to 60x60.

3   Implementation

A total of 280 writers contributed to the data set with 50 writers having only one page, 215 writers with at least 2 and 15 writers with at least 4 pages. Each page consists of 21 lines of words with a minimum 30 characters in each line. We kept only the first two images for the writers having more than two pages and divided the image into two parts for writers who contributed a single page thus ensuring two images per writer, one used in training while the other in testing.

Firstly, the dataset is fed to the preprocessing and extract the characters by the segmentation phase and make the character database of each writer for avoiding the redundant characters as explained earlier.

Phase1 (Training):

1. Compute contour of each character using Moor's algorithm.
2. Resample the contour sequence to contain 100 coordinate pairs.
3. Obtain the fragments of the character called graphemes.
4. Obtain the features of each grapheme.
5. Present the set of features to a kohonen SOM. The result will be a set of probability value corresponding to each pattern in the nodes of the kohonen SOM.

It is assumed that a writer generates a finite number of basic patterns, each of which consisting of directional features, curvature and angle pair. Each writer may be assumed to have a pdf (probability density function) for producing each grapheme.

Phase2 (Generating the writer code book):

1. Extract the graphemes for every sample of handwriting.
2. For every grapheme g in the sample, the nearest codebook prototype w(the winner) is found using the Euclidean distance i.e.,

$$w = \arg \min_n \left[dist \left(g, C_n \right) \right], h_{iw} \leftarrow h_{iw} + 1. \tag{5}$$

Where n is an index that runs over the shapes in the patterns obtained after the result of kohonen SOM.

3. The histogram h_i is normalized to a probability distribution function (p_i) that sums to 1. This pdf is the writer descriptor used for identification called writer specific codebook.

Phase3 (Identification):

1. Perform the nearest-neighbor classification in a "leave-one-out" strategy between the writer descriptor of test document (query descriptor) and writer specific codebook of trained documents.
2. Prepare a sorted hit list with increasing distance value between the query descriptor and writer specific codebook.
3. Select the first ranked sample which will ideally identify the writer.

4   Experimental Results

According to [11], they improved the writer identification by random selection. Due to low allographic variation in Malayalam this scheme didn't provide much accuracy. So we employed new scheme to choose the appropriate characters providing the individuality of each writer as mentioned earlier. The Fig. 2 shows the comparison results of both schemes. The redundant characters are selected according to the different distance measurement such as Euclidean, chi-square and Manhattan. Among these the Chi-square makes good achievements. Fig. 3

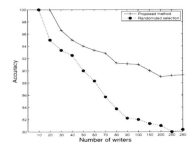
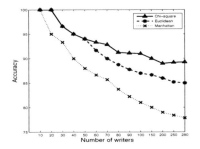

Fig. 2. Comparative results of random selection and Avoid redundant character scheme

Fig. 3. Accuracies of various distance measurement in Avoid redundant character scheme

Table 1. Comparative evaluation of features

Number of writers	F1	F2	F3	F4	Combined feature (f1+f2+f3+f4)
10	70	80	90	100	100
25	64	72	88	96	96
50	62	70	86	94	94
75	61.33	68	85.33	90.66	92.33
100	60	67	85	88	91
150	59.33	66	84	86	90
200	59	65.5	83	84	89
250	58.8	64	82.4	83.2	89.2
280	58.2	63.2	82.14	82.85	89.28

shows the different accuracies of each writers and distance measurements. Also the experiments yielded us with the performance of each feature in the system of writer identification of Malayalam documents as shown in the following Table 1 (numbers represent percentage).

5   Conclusions

This paper implements a writer identification scheme for Malayalam language using graphemes. The customized feature vector for Malayalam characters designed here is a fusion of four features, and is further used in the training and identification phase. The accuracy obtained through usage of graphemes was compared with that of the randomized selection method and was noted that our scheme outperforms the same. The entire scheme was tested on handwritten documents of 280 writers and an accuracy of 89.28% has obtained.

References

1. Srihari, S., Cha, S., Arora, H., Lee, S.: Individuality of Handwriting. Forensic Sciences 47(4), 1–17 (2002)
2. Al-Dmour, A., Zitar, R.A.: Arabic Writer Identification based on Hybrid Spectral-Statistical Measures. Experimental and Theoretical Artificial Intelligence 19(4), 307–332 (2007)
3. Siddiqi, I., Vincent, N.: Writer Identification in Handwritten Documents. In: ICDAR 2007: Proceedings of the Ninth International Conference on Document Analysis and Recognition, vol. 1, pp. 108–112 (2007)
4. Blumenstein, M., Liu, X.Y., Verma, B.: An Investigation of the Modified Direction Feature for Cursive Character Recognition. Pattern Recognition 40(2), 376–388 (2007)
5. Yamada, H., Nakano, Y.: Cursive Handwritten Word Recognition using Multiple Segmentation Determined by Contour Analysis. IEICE Transactions on Information and Systems E79-D, 464–470 (1996)
6. Blumenstein, M., Verma, B., Basli, H.: A Novel Feature Extraction Technique for the Recognition of Segmented Handwritten Characters. In: ICDAR 2003: Proceedings of the Seventh International Conference on Document Analysis and Recognition, pp. 137–141 (2003)
7. Dehkordi, M.E., Sherkat, N., Allen, T.: Handwriting Style Classification. Int. J. on Document Analysis and Recognition 6, 55–74 (2003)
8. Bulacu, M., Schomaker, L., Vuurpijl, L.: Writer Identification using Edge-based Directional Features. In: Proceedings of ICDAR 2003, Edinburgh, UK, pp. 937–941 (2003)
9. Tan, G.X., Viard-Gaudin, C., Kot, A.C.: Automatic Writer Identification Framework for Online Hand Written Documents using Character Prototypes. Pattern Recognition 42, 3313–3323 (2009)
10. Chang, F., Chou, C.H., Lin, C.C., Chen, C.J.: A Prototype Classification Method and its Application to Handwritten Character Recognition. In: Proceedings of IEEE International Conference on Systems, Man and Cybernetics (2004)
11. Van der Maaten, L., Postma, E.: Improving Automatic Writer Identification. In: Proceedings of 17th Belgium-Netherlands Conference on Artificial Intelligence (BNAIC 2005), Brussels, Belgium, pp. 260–266 (2005)

A Linear Manifold Representation for Color Correction in Digital Images

Alex Mathew, Ann Theja Alex, and Vijayan K. Asari

Computer Vision and Wide Area Surveillance Laboratory,
Department of Electrical and Computer Engineering,
University of Dayton, Dayton, Ohio
{mathewa3,alexa1,vijayan.asari}@notes.udayton.edu

Abstract. Images captured using a camera loses its dynamic range of colors as they are digitized. This problem is not encountered by the human visual system as it supports a wider dynamic range. Our enhancement model is based on the human visual system involving three processing steps-color characterization, color enhancement and color correction. Each pixel in an image, along with its neighborhood forms color manifolds in RGB space. In the proposed color characterization method, these manifolds are modeled as lines. In the color enhancement step, a hyperbolic tangent function compresses the dynamic range of the image. This nonlinear function enhances the image preserving its details, but not the color relationships. Each enhanced pixel is projected to a point on the best fit line corresponding to its manifold to restore the original color relationships. Being a single-step convergence algorithm, it is faster than other iterative methods.

Keywords: Color Correction, Image Enhancement, Linear Manifold, Manifold Learning, Skin Segmentation.

1   Introduction

Human visual system can process and perceive a wide range of colors. This makes it easy for eyes to view objects in dark and well lit conditions. Images captured using a camera loses the dynamic range of colors in a scene. Due to this problem, images of real scenes with shadows and low contrast lose some information. Very often such images make it hard even for human eyes to identify and detect objects in the scene. It is even harder for computer vision algorithms to process these low contrast images for applications such as face recognition, object recognition and object tracking. This necessitates a preprocessing step. The aim of such a preprocessing step is to compress the dynamic range of the input image and stretch the contrast of the output image. There are several functions such as power transform, logarithmic functions and hyperbolic tangent functions that can reduce the dynamic range. But such range compression schemes result in loss of original color characteristics in the scene. Many researchers have proposed several algorithms for image enhancement. J. von Kries proposed an approach

K.R. Venugopal and L.M. Patnaik (Eds.): ICIP 2011, CCIS 157, pp. 652–658, 2011.

based on linear scaling applied to independent receptor channels [1]. Land (1964) proposed that three lightness values determine the color of an object. It assumes that the average reflectance is the same in all the three channels [2-4]. Funt, Cardei and Barnard, in 1996, proposed a neural network based methodology. The network is trained with chromaticity information for color constancy [5]. Based on the fact that the color relationships and relative contrast between regions help humans perceive color, Seow and Asari (2009) proposed an associative memory based approach for color constancy and color correction [6]. The associative memory models a color manifold in RGB space as a bounded region around a line or curve. Reducing the dynamic range and retaining the color characteristics simultaneously is a hard task. Though a neural network based approach may yield good results, neural network implementations are iterative and slow. The proposed algorithm offers a three step procedure for effectively compressing the dynamic range while retaining the color relationships.

2   Theoretical Background

The algorithm uses a three step procedure for enhancing images. The steps involved are color characterization, color enhancement and color correction. The processing is done in RGB space.

2.1   Color Characterization

In color characterization, each pixel and its neighborhood is taken into consideration. The color component relationships of each pixel and its neighborhood form a manifold in color space. The manifold encapsulates the range of values of that particular pixel and its neighborhood. A best fit line passing through each manifold characterizes the relationships of the pixels in that manifold. Fig. 1 shows a manifold formed by pixels in a neighborhood. The neighborhood size is determined based on the variance of intensity values in a neighborhood. Thus corresponding to each pixel in the original image, the color relationships are learnt as lines in color space. Manifolds can be modeled more accurately using higher order polynomials. The direction vectors of the line are computed as the principal components of color variation. In vector form, principal components can be represented as

$$\boldsymbol{v} = v_r \hat{r} + v_g \hat{g} + v_b \hat{b}. \tag{1}$$

where $\hat{r}$, $\hat{g}$ and $\hat{b}$ are the unit vectors in the direction of the R, G and B components. Thus the geometric model is

$$r = r_0 + t v_r. \qquad g = g_0 + t v_g. \qquad b = b_0 + t v_b. \tag{2}$$

where t is a parameter and r_0, g_0, b_0 is the centroid of the data in the respective manifolds.

(a)

(b)

(c)

Fig. 1. (a) Input image. (b) A representative neighborhood. (c) Manifold formed by the neighborhood.

2.2 Color Enhancement

We use a hyperbolic tangent function for color enhancement. The function compresses the dynamic range without over saturating bright regions. The output of the function is computed for each pixel along with its neighborhood. It takes into account, the local mean of the neighborhood and the global mean of the image. To compute the local mean, the method uses a wide Gaussian. The values of these parameters are experimentally computed. Equations. 3, 4 and 5 show the hyperbolic tangent functions as applied on each color channel.

$$R^{+}_{(x,y)} = max\{255[\frac{2}{1+\exp\left(\frac{-2R_{(x,y)}}{\phi\mu_{red}+\gamma\beta^{red}_{(x,y)}}\right)}], R_{(x,y)}\}. \tag{3}$$

$$G^{+}_{(x,y)} = max\{255[\frac{2}{1+\exp\left(\frac{-2G_{(x,y)}}{\phi\mu_{green}+\gamma\beta^{green}_{(x,y)}}\right)}], G_{(x,y)}\}. \tag{4}$$

$$B^{+}_{(x,y)} = max\{255[\frac{2}{1+\exp\left(\frac{-2B_{(x,y)}}{\phi\mu_{blue}+\gamma\beta^{blue}_{(x,y)}}\right)}], B_{(x,y)}\}. \tag{5}$$

where β is the local mean, μ the global mean, $R_{(x,y)}$, $G_{(x,y)}$, $B_{(x,y)}$ the red, green and blue channels and $R^{+}_{(x,y)}$, $G^{+}_{(x,y)}$ and $B^{+}_{(x,y)}$, the corresponding outputs. ϕ and γ are two parameters for controlling the slope of the function. Fig. 2 shows the effect of applying the hyperbolic tangent function on an input image. The hyperbolic tangent function enhances the image, but the image loses its original color characteristics. The loss of color characteristics when compressing the range is referred to as the dynamic range problem.

(a)   (b)

Fig. 2. (a) Input image. (b) Image obtained after the application of hyperbolic tangent function.

2.3 Color Correction

Every pixel in the enhanced image is projected to the geometric model obtained in the color characterization step. Since the output image is produced by re-tuning the pixels to the original color characteristics, the dynamic range problem is eliminated. The output of this step is shown in Fig. 3. The corrected RGB values are obtained using the following equations.

$$t = \frac{(v_r(R^+_{(x,y)} - r_0) + v_g(G^+_{(x,y)} - g_0) + v_b(B^+_{(x,y)} - b_0))}{(v_r^2 + v_g^2 + v_b^2)}. \tag{6}$$

$$R^c_{(x,y)} = r_0 + v_r t. \qquad G^c_{(x,y)} = g_0 + v_g t. \qquad B^c_{(x,y)} = b_0 + v_b t. \tag{7}$$

where $R^c_{(x,y)}, G^c_{(x,y)}$ and $B^c_{(x,y)}$ are the corrected pixel values.

(a)   (b)

Fig. 3. (a) Color enhancement output image. (b) Final output after color restoration. It can be seen that the image on the right has a more natural appearance than the image on the left.

3   Experimental Results

A qualitative evaluation of the algorithm is done by applying the algorithm on several images. Fig. 4 shows a sample test image and the enhancement output. The histograms of the input and the output images are shown in Fig. 5. It is observed that the low contrast image is converted to a high contrast image using our technique while preserving the color characteristics. The effectiveness of our approach is demonstrated quantitatively using an algorithm for skin segmentation applied on face images. This algorithm is based on the Sparse Network of Winnows [7]. The output image obtained after the color correction step produces a better segmentation output. The results are shown in Fig. 6 and Fig. 7. The output obtained using the proposed method is compared with the output of Luminance Based Multiscale Retinex (LBMSR) [8].

(a)   (b)   (c)

Fig. 4. (a) Original image. (b) Enhanced image. (c) Color restored output.

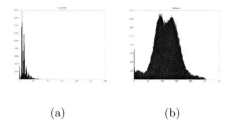

(a) (b)

Fig. 5. (a) Histogram of image in Fig. 4(a). (b) Histogram of image in Fig. 4(c).

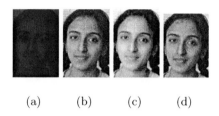

(a)   (b)   (c)   (d)

Fig. 6. (a) Input image (b) Enhanced image (c) Restored image using LB MSR (d) Restored image using the proposed method

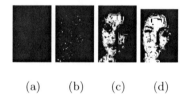

(a)   (b)   (c)   (d)

Fig. 7. Results of skin segmentation applied on the test image, enhanced image, color corrected output of LB MSR and color corrected image using the proposed method

4   Conclusions

We have proposed a robust mathematical model for restoring the color relationships in enhanced images. The method is a preprocessing step for enhancing and color correcting real life images. The procedure restores natural color characteristics that are lost when enhancement functions are applied on images. We have shown the qualitative effectiveness of our method with several images. The effectiveness of the algorithm is shown quantitatively using skin segmentation performed on face images. We have also compared our results with the results of luminance based multiscale retinex (LBMSR).

References

1. Lightness Algorithms, http://web.media.mit.edu/~wad/color/node1.html
2. Land, E.H.: The Retinex. American Scientist 52, 247–264 (1964)

3. Brainard, D.H., Wandell, B.A.: Analysis of the Retinex Theory of Color Vision. Journal of the Optical Society of America, 1651–1661 (1986)
4. Land, E.H.: Recent Advances in Retinex Theory. Vision Research, 7–21 (1986)
5. Funt, B., Cardei, V., Barnard, K.: Learning Color Constancy. In: Proc. of the Fourth IS&T/SID Color Imaging Conference, pp. 58–60 (1996)
6. Seow, M.J., Asari, V.K.: Towards Representation of a Perceptual Color Manifold using Associative Memory for Color Constancy. Neural Networks 22, 91–99 (2009)
7. Gottumukkal, R., Asari, V.K.: Learning Skin Distribution using a Sparse Map. In: Proc. IEEE International Conference on Image Processing, ICIP 2004, pp. 199–202 (2004)
8. Tao, L., Asari, V.K.: Modified Luminance Based MSR for Fast and Efficient Image Enhancement. In: Proc. IEEE of 32nd Applied Imagery Pattern Recognition Workshop, p. 174 (2003)

Combining a Content Filtering Heuristic and Sentiment Analysis for Movie Recommendations

Vivek Kumar Singh, Mousumi Mukherjee, and Ghanshyam Kumar Mehta

Department of Computer Science,
Banaras Hindu University, Varanasi, India
vivek@bhu.ac.in, {mou.sonai,ghanshyam4u2000}@gmail.com

Abstract. This paper presents our experimental work on a new approach to hybrid recommender systems. Traditionally recommender systems are categorized into three classes: content-based, collaborative filtering and hybrid approaches. The hybrid approach to recommender systems combines both content-based and collaborative filtering schemes to obtain better recommendations to harness advantages of both the approaches. We have experimented with an alternative formulation, where we combined the content-based approach with a sentiment analysis task to improve the recommendation results. The final recommended list contains only those items that are both similar in content to the items liked by the user in the past, and also labeled as 'positive' on sentiment classification. The paper concludes with a discussion of experimental results on Movie review domain and usefulness of this work.

Keywords: Content-based Recommendations, Movie Reviews, Opinion Mining, Recommender Systems, Sentiment Classification.

1 Introduction

A recommender system is a program that automatically filters and presents items of interest to users. The increased penetration of the Internet and the new participative *Web 2.0* has facilitated a large number of users to use and interact with web applications. The users are now interacting with web applications in a more participative way by contributing in a variety of forms, such as rating, tagging, writing blogs, social networking and sharing items with friends. This increased interaction is generating huge amount of information. This information overload often becomes problematic for users when they try to search and find a desired item on the *Web*. Recommender systems address this problem and provide personalized recommendation to users. *Amazon, Netflix, Google News personalization* and *MovieLens* are some of the popular industry scale recommender systems. There are three kinds of recommender systems: content-based, collaborative filtering and hybrid approaches. Content-based methods memorize a user's preferences and recommend him those items that are similar in content to the ones liked by him in the past. Collaborative filtering also recommends items to a user based on his past transaction history, however, it does not take

K.R. Venugopal and L.M. Patnaik (Eds.): ICIP 2011, CCIS 157, pp. 659–664, 2011.
© Springer-Verlag Berlin Heidelberg 2011

into account the content of the items for recommendation decision. It treats items as black box and generates recommendations on the basis of either item-to-item similarity or user-to-user similarity. In item-to-item similarity a user is recommended those items that are similarly rated (by other users) to the items liked by the user in the past; whereas in user-to-user similarity a user is recommended those items that are liked by the other users who are similar (in terms of their rating preferences) to the user. Collaborative filtering requires data about user transaction history (browsing, rating, tagging etc.,), which however may not be readily available.

Both content-based and collaborative filtering have some disadvantages. A hybrid method (the third approach) combines content-based and collaborative approaches to minimize the disadvantages and produce better results. In this paper, we present an alternative kind of hybrid recommender system which combines content-based method with sentiment analysis to improve the recommendations in movie recommendation domain. Sentiment analysis labels each item as 'positive' or 'negative'. We collected data about a large number of movies including their name, description, genre and 10 user reviews each from IMDB [1] and then applied both, a content-based filtering to obtain a first level list of movies of interest to a user and then the sentiment analysis to label every movie in the first level result as 'positive' or 'negative', based on their user reviews. The final recommended list contains only those movies which match with user's interests and are also labeled as 'positive'.

2   Content-Based Recommendation

Recommender systems aim to show items of interest to a user. In order to do so a recommender system may exploit the following inputs: (a) user's profile - attributes like age, gender, geographical location, net worth etc., (b) information about various items available - content associated with item, (c) interactions of users - such as ratings, tagging, bookmarking, saving, emailing, browsing history etc., and (d) the context of where the items will be shown. These inputs may be used by a recommender system to produce following kinds of results: (a) users who watched this video watched these other videos, (b) new items related to a particular item, (c) users similar to a particular user, and (d) the products a user may be interested in. The recommendation problem can be formally defined as follows: Let U be the set of all users and I be the set of all possible items that can be recommended. The set I of items can be very large, with possibly millions of items. And similarly the set U of users can also be very large with millions of users in some cases. Let r be a recommender utility function that measures the usefulness of an item i to a user u, i.e., r : U X I $\longrightarrow$ R, where R is a totally ordered set of non-negative integers or real numbers. Then the recommendation problem is to choose for each user $u \in U$, such items $i \in I$ that maximizes the users utility, i.e., $i_u = \arg max_{i \in I}$ r (u, i). The utility usually refers to some rating value associated with different items [2]. However, the central problem is that the recommender utility r is usually not defined on the whole of U X I space, but only on some subset of it. Therefore, the recommender system needs to extrapolate from known to unknown ratings. This extrapolation can be done in a number of ways using machine learning, approximation theory and heuristics.

In content-based approach a user is recommended those items that are similar in content to the items liked by him in the past. The items in the set I are compared with the items liked by the user in the past and only the best matching items are recommended. The items in content-based recommendation approach are textual in nature, which need to be represented using appropriate data structure. A commonly used scheme is the vector space model [3],[4], in which every text document is represented as a term vector. A term vector consists of the distinct terms appearing in the document and their relative weights. The weight associated with each term could be either a *tf* measure or a *tf-idf* measure. The vector *V(d)* derived from the document *d* thus contain one component for each distinct term in the entire vocabulary of the text space. Once we have all texts represented as document vectors, their similarity can be computed using cosine similarity measure (Eq. 1) as follows:

$$CosineSimilarity(d_1, d_2) = [V(d_1).V(d_2)] / [\|V(d_1)\|\|V(d_2)\|] . \qquad (1)$$

The content-based recommendation problem is thus to obtain $r(u,i)$ = score [content-based profile (u), content(i)]. This is done for all items $i \in I$ and the best matching items are recommended. We have performed content matching in two ways: (a) through a heuristic vector for new users, and (b) through cosine-based similarity computation for a known user whose rating profile is known.

3   Sentiment Analysis

The sentiment analysis problem can be formally defined as follows: Given a set of documents D, a sentiment classifier classifies each document d $\in$ D into one of the two classes, *positive* and *negative*. Positive means that d expresses a positive opinion and negative means that d expresses a negative opinion. The sentiment analysis task usually employs one of the two approaches: (a) using a text classifier - such as Naive Bayes, SVM or kNN- that takes a machine learning approach to categorize the documents in positive and negative groups; and (b) using an unsupervised semantic orientation approach that computes sentiment of documents based on aggregated semantic orientation values of selected opinionated POS tags in it. Some of the prominent research works on sentiment analysis can be found in [5-9]. We have used the unsupervised semantic orientation approach for classifying texts as 'positive' and 'negative'.

In semantic orientation approach we first extract selected POS tags that conform to a specified pattern [10]. Thereafter the semantic orientation of extracted phrase is computed using the Pointwise Mutual Information (PMI) measure as in Eq. 2,

$$PMI(term_1, term_2) = log_2 [Pr(term_1 \triangle term_2)/Pr(term_1).Pr(term_2)] . \quad (2)$$

where, $Pr(term_1 \triangle term_2)$ is the co-occurrence probability of term1 and term2 and $Pr(term_1)$. $Pr(term_2)$ gives the probability that two terms co-occur if they are statistically independent. The ratio between $Pr(term_1 \triangle term_2)$ and $Pr(term_2).Pr(term_2)$ measures the degree of statistical independence between them. The log of this ratio is the amount of information that we acquire about the presence of one word when we observe the other. The Semantic Orientation (SO) of a phrase can thus be computed by using Eq. 3 below,

$$SO(phrase) = PMI(phrase,"excellent") - PMI(phrase,"poor"). \quad (3)$$

where, PMI (phrase, "excellent") measures the association of the phrase with positive reference word "excellent" and PMI (phrase, "poor") measures the association of phrase with negative reference word "poor". These probabilities are calculated by issuing search query of the form "phrase * excellent" and "phrase * poor" to search engine. The number of hits obtained is used as a measure of probability value. To determine the semantic orientation of the entire document, the SO values of the opinionated phrases in it is aggregated, and if the average SO is above a threshold value the document is labeled as 'positive', and 'negative' otherwise.

4   Experimental Setup and Results

We have designed our hybrid recommender system for use in Movie review domain. We collected a total of 2000 movie reviews (10 reviews each for 200 movies) and applied our hybrid design to obtain relevant recommendations for users. For every movie, we collected its name, genre, year of release, its rating, and 10 user reviews. The genre of a movie is an indicator of its type such as action, comedy, drama etc. For every review written by a user we also recorded the name (id) of the reviewer. Movie recommendation involved a two level filtering process using content-based similarity at first level and sentiment analysis at second level. Since the collected review data was textual, we transformed it into vector space model. First we preprocessed the data to remove stop words (words like 'is', 'am', 'are', 'to', 'from' etc.). Then every review was transformed into a term vector. For new users we used the term values rather than their frequency.

4.1   Computing Content Similarity

We used content-based approach as our first level of filtering. In case the recommendation is to be generated for an existing user who has already reviewed some movie in the dataset, we compute cosine-based similarity between user's reviews with the review sets of all the movies. All the movies having cosine similarity value above a threshold are included in first level filtered results. We kept the threshold low (around 0.3) to obtain a good number of movies. When the recommendation is to be made for a new user, we ask the user about what kind (genre) of movies he is interested in. The genre information entered by the user is used to employ a predefined query vector as a heuristic and compare it with the review vectors of all the movies. The query vector for a genre contains its synonyms and such other terms that are frequently used by reviewers in positively reviewing that kind of movies. All the movies having terms in the query vector present in their review are included in the first level filtered result.

4.2   Sentiment Analysis

We used SO-PMI-IR algorithm as described in section 3 to compute the sentiment of a user review. The overall sentiment of a movie was aggregate of the sentiment labels of the 10 reviews of that movie, i.e., a movie was labeled as 'positive' only if at least 6 (or say 7) of the 10 reviews for that movie was labeled as 'positive'. Every review is labeled as positive or negative based on the aggregate SO value of the selected POS tags in that review. Every term having SO value greater than a threshold (say 1) adds '+1' to aggregate score of the review and every term having SO value below that adds '-1' to the aggregate score. These values are then added and if the aggregate score for a review is greater than a given threshold value, we label that review as 'positive'. This is done for all review vectors and every movie is then accordingly labeled. The final list of recommended movies, from among the first level filtered result, then contain only those movies which are labeled as 'positive'. This is logically equivalent to recommending those movies which have been appreciated by a good number of users. We have verified the accuracy of sentiment labeling of movie reviews by SO-PMI-IR algorithm through a Naive Bayes machine learning classifier, trained on another popular movie review dataset [11].

4.3   Results

We obtained interesting results. While the first level filtering produced a list of interest; the second level of filtering (using sentiment analysis) produced final list of recommended movies. The recommended movies were also rated sufficiently high on overall rating. A snapshot a sample run is given in Fig. 1. The final recommended list in virtually all the cases contains movies that have been appreciated by reviewers. The method also has the advantage that it can produce relatively good recommendations for new users as well. The hybrid that we designed thus not simply recommends all the movies that match a user's taste, but only those movies that are also rated high.

5   Conclusions

We designed a new kind of hybrid recommender system that combined content-based recommendation system with sentiment analysis to produce high quality recommendations. We experimented with movie review domain and the results obtained were quite accurate and of high quality. The first level filtering was based on content similarity and the second level filtering labeled a review as 'positive' or 'negative'. The final recommendation list comprised of those results

```
Run
Enter the Genre : Action
Processing. . .
First Level Filtering high query Vector similarity:
mb005 mb011 mb013 mb014 mb023 mb026
mb028 mb032 mb036 mb045 mb052 mb053
mb076 mb091 mb099

Recommended List of Movies - positive reviews
Movie id    Movie Name           Ratings
mb032       Jodha Akbar          7.2/10
mb062       kabhi Hum Jee Jaan Se 6.1/10
mb063       Don                  6.3/10
mb065       Main Hoon Naa        6.2/10
mb073       Krish                6.1/10
```

Fig. 1. A sample run of the system for a new user

which rated favourable in both levels of filtering. Further, the number of recommendations can be preset by using suitable threshold values. This new kind of hybrid approach to recommender system can be successfully applied in many other domains which use textual review data, more particularly opinionated texts.

References

1. Internet Movie Database, http://www.imdb.com
2. Adomavicius, G., Tuzhilin, A.: Towards the Next Generation of Recommender Systems: A Survey of the State-of-the-Art and Possible Extensions. IEEE Transactions on Knowledge and Data Engineering 17(6), 734–749 (2006)
3. Alag, S.: Collective Intelligence in Action, pp. 41–48. Manning, New York (2009)
4. Manning, C.D., Raghavan, P., Schutze, H.: Introduction to Information Retrieval, pp. 107–116. Cambridge University Press, New York (2008)
5. Turney, P.: Thumbs Up or Thumbs Down? Semantic Orientation Applied to Unsupervised Classification of Reviews. In: 40th Annual Meeting of the Association for Computational Linguistics, Philadelphia, US, pp. 417–424 (2002)
6. Esuli, A., Sebastiani, F.: Determining the Semantic Orientation of Terms through Gloss Analysis. In: 14th ACM International Conference on Information and Knowledge Management, CIKM 2005, Bremen, DE, pp. 617–624 (2005)
7. Pang, B., Lee, L., Vaithyanathan, S.: Thumbs Up? Sentiment Classification Using Machine Learning Techniques. In: Conference on Empirical Methods in Natural Language Processing, Philadelphia, US, pp. 79–86 (2002)
8. Kim, S.M., Hovy, E.: Determining Sentiment of Opinions. In: Proceedings of the COLING Conference, Geneva (2004)
9. Durant, K.T., Smith, M.D.: Mining Sentiment Classification from Political Web Logs. In: Proceedings of WEBKDD 2006. ACM, New York (2006)
10. Liu, B.: Web Data Mining: Exploring Hyperlinks, Contents and Usage Data, pp. 411–416. Springer, Heidelberg (2002)
11. Movie Review Dataset,
    http://www.cs.cornell.edu/people/pabo/movie-review-data/

Real Time Image Representation
for Weather Forecast over Launch Pad

Satish R. Kulkarni[1], C.G. Patil[1], and A.M. Khan[2]

[1] Master Control Facility, ISRO, Hassan, Karnataka State, India
[2] Electronics Department, Mangalore University, Mangalore, Karnataka State, India
satish_mcf@rediffmail.com

Abstract. Weather condition over the launch pad is one of the deciding factors for launch activities. Synoptic observations from weather satellites being vital source of data, it is essential to preprocess this data for various error corrections, derive meteorological parameters and construct the processed imageries at the earliest to make them available for use by the meteorologist. A system has been developed and operational at Master Control Facility-Hassan, India to generate near real-time, ready to use image products embedded with processed information. This paper describes the methodology, calibration technique and the implementation details of the system.

Keywords: Brightness Temperature, False Color Composite, Image Representation, Palette Encoding, VHRR, Weather Prediction

1 Introduction

Satellite imageries are the indispensable source of information for weather prediction. The synoptic coverage on a repetitive basis as provided by satellites is ideally suited to study weather-related, dynamic atmospheric processes on different scales. The meteorological parameters derived from satellite imagery [1], [2] play a critical role in improved definition of initial and boundary conditions for weather prediction models. The impact of satellite data is phenomenal in certain areas of meteorological applications such as cyclone monitoring [3], [4] short-range forecasts, aviation forecasts, and forecasts for rocket launch, especially in the tropics.

Weather being one of the Go/No-Go conditions for the rocket launch and pre launch activities; its prediction over launch pad is very crucial. An update on the current weather condition in the form of processed satellite image just before launch plays an important role. It is desirable for the meteorologist to have a processed image from which the meteorological parameters can be readily referred to.

In Indian scenario, INSAT spacecrafts with meteorological payloads [5] being operated at geo-stationary orbit offer a vantage platform to monitor and study the process of genesis, growth and decay of weather systems. The Met-Payload Data Processing System (MPDPS) at Master Control Facility (MCF),

K.R. Venugopal and L.M. Patnaik (Eds.): ICIP 2011, CCIS 157, pp. 665–670, 2011.

Hassan has been enhanced to generate the processed imageries in near real-time and make them available at Satish Dhavan Space Center (SDSC), Shriharikota through the direct satellite link between MCF and SDSC established exclusively for this purpose. These imageries need to contain the processed information, at the same time they need to be generated on the fly so that they are immediately available for use by the meteorologists at the rocket launch facility. The method employed to generate these image products in general and the Palette Encoding Technique in particular are discussed here.

2   Methodology

The Imaging Instrument - VHRR (Very High Resolution Radiometer) onboard-INSAT spacecrafts [6] images the earth in three spectral bands (channels) namely VIS-Visible, TIR-Thermal Infrared and WVP-Water Vapor. To start with we considered to generate processed images covering the Indian sub continental region spread approximately from 65^0E to 95^0E longitude in east-west direction and 8^0N to 38^0N latitude in north-south direction. This portion of the image forms the sub set of VHRR image as shown in the Fig. 1(a). and Fig. 1(b).

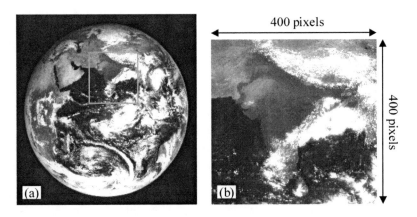

Fig. 1. Shows (a) Full mode VHRR image (Visible band), (b) Required subset of VHRR image

2.1   Conventional Imageries

Conventionally the images in each spectral band, namely Visible, Thermal Infrared and Water Vapor are generated by mapping the corresponding digital counts to image pixel gray values through defined mapping functions.

$$G_v = f_v(DN_v). \tag{1}$$

$$G_t = f_t(DN_t). \tag{2}$$

$$G_w = f_w(DN_w). \tag{3}$$

Where, G_v, G_t, G_w are the gray values corresponding to the digital counts DN_v, DN_t, DN_w, mapped by the mapping functions f_v, f_t, f_w respectively. The subscripts v, t and w indicate the spectral bands Visible, Thermal Infrared and Water Vapor respectively.

2.2   False Color Composite Image

Visible and Thermal Infrared data imaged simultaneously are used by the meteorologists for discrimination analysis [7]. False Color Composition (FCC) is an attempt to amalgamate the data from both these channels to form a single composite image, which is generated by mapping normalized digital counts from Visible and Thermal Infrared channels to the RGB components of the pixel through the following mapping functions.

$$FCC_r = f_v(DN_v). \tag{4}$$

$$FCC_g = f_v(DN_v). \tag{5}$$

$$FCC_b = f_t(DN_t). \tag{6}$$

Where, FCC_r, FCC_g, FCC_b are the intensity values of the image pixel corresponding to red, green and blue components respectively.

2.3   Enhanced IR Image - Palette Encoding

The meteorologist will be interested in knowing the precise temperature range of features like sea surface, cloud top as derived from TIR channel [8] and humidity thresholds as derived from WVP channel [9], [10]. The processed information from Thermal Infrared and Water Vapor channels has been embedded into single image to form an Enhanced IR image.

In an approach to indicate the temperature ranges of the features, colors from the predefined palette are encoded. The color palette is created by assigning shades of selected colors to the convenient temperature ranges covering the total dynamic range of TIR channel. The temperature value for every pixel in the image is obtained using corresponding TIR digital count as an index to the look-up-table, which is generated during calibration process as explained in the next section.

In order to encode the abundance of water vapor, two humidity thresholds from the WVP channel have been identified. These two thresholds are marked on the EIR image as + and # symbols.

3   Calibration of Data for Brightness Temperature

The digitized raw counts corresponding to the internal black body view and its temperature recordings by four sensors are used for calibration of thermal channels. The average of these four values gives T_r the black body reference temperature. The digital counts for each band are also averaged to get mean counts DN_λ.

The emitted radiance from the black body reference as detected by the sensor at wavelength band λ, is then calculated using Plank's radiation law as

$$L_{\lambda,r} = \frac{C_1}{\lambda^5 [e^{\frac{C_2}{\lambda T_r}} - 1]\pi}. \tag{7}$$

For various reference temperatures T_r, the corresponding emitted radiance $L_{\lambda,r}$ is computed. With these values, the calibration is constructed, with gradient G_λ

$$G_\lambda = \frac{\sum (DN_\lambda L_{\lambda,r}) - n\mu(DN_\lambda)\mu(L_{\lambda,r})}{(DN_\lambda DN_\lambda) - n\mu(DN_\lambda)\mu(DN_\lambda)}. \tag{8}$$

and intercept I_λ

$$I_\lambda = \mu(L_{\lambda,r}) - G_\lambda\mu(DN_\lambda). \tag{9}$$

Where $\mu(DN_\lambda)$ and $\mu(L_{\lambda,r})$ are the mean values of digital counts and the radiance respectively, n is the number of samples collected.

With these, the measured radiance $L_{\lambda,m}$ in each pixel of the image for wavelength band λ can be obtained from

$$L_{\lambda,m} = G_\lambda DN_\lambda + I_\lambda. \tag{10}$$

The value of $L_{\lambda,m}$ for each pixel can be interpreted in terms of brightness temperature T_b, the temperature of the perfect emitter which would produce that radiance if there were no intervening atmosphere. This is related to $L_{\lambda,m}$ by

$$L_{\lambda,m} = \frac{C_1}{\lambda^5 [e^{\frac{C_2}{\lambda T_b}} - 1]\pi}. \tag{11}$$

Which is not readily inverted to obtain T_b from $L_{\lambda,m}$ instead Eq. 11 is used to construct a curve of the form

$$T_b = A + Bln(L_{\lambda,m}). \tag{12}$$

A and B being obtained by a least square fit. Thence look-up-table to relate every value of DN_λ to a value of T_b can be constructed from Eq. 10 and Eq. 12, and the image data set for wavelength band λ is now calibrated in terms of T_b.

Computationally this is far more efficient than seeking to invert Eq. 11, since Eq. 12 need be evaluated over only a limited range of temperatures corresponding to a limited range of DN_λ appropriate to the features in the scene. The T_b image can then be used as a rough indication of temperature of the features of meteorological interest, or can even form the input to an atmospheric-correction algorithm.

4   Implementation

The MPDPS system runs a separate thread for image display task. This thread being an ideal host for additional processing requirements on the image data, creates two more threads namely 1) Data Collection Thread and 2) Products Generation Thread. This design of splitting the processing functionality into separate threads gives the following advantages.

- The Image Display Thread is not loaded/complicated further with additional processing requirements, except for sending a signal to Data Collection Thread.
- Soon after the collection of required data, the image products are independently and immediately generated and are made available for the user, even though the Image Display Thread continues displaying image while the VHRR continues to scan the remaining portion of the earth disk. The time diagram for these threads is shown in the Fig. 2.

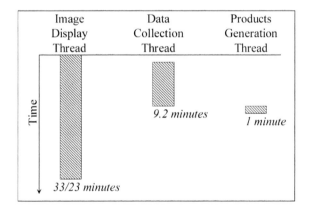

Fig. 2. Time diagram of three threads, showing generation of image products well before scan completion

5   Results and Conclusions

As a test case, the Enhanced IR image thus created was compared with the Indian region of the similarly encoded Meteosat-5 image for the same day and same time. Though the processing details of Meteosat-5 imagery are unknown, there is a good agreement in the representation of temperature ranges. The only visual difference was due to the different look angles of both the satellites and interchange of the red and yellow color positions in the palette. After trial operations, the coverage area of the images products has been enhanced to 600 x 600 pixels.

Ever since its implementation, this system has been supporting the weather prediction activities of the GSLV (Geostationary Satellite Launch Vehicle) and PSLV (Polar Satellite Launch Vehicle) launches from SDSC Shriharikota.

Acknowledgments. The authors would like to express their sincere thanks to Dr. M.Y.S. Prasad for his inspiration and encouragement, Dr. G.V. Rama & Dr. Appa Rao for suggestions and feedback, the VHRR design team at SAC, ISRO for providing exhaustive information on INSAT-VHRR.

References

1. Singh, D., Bhatia, R.C., Srivastav, S.K., Singh, B.: Retrieval of Atmospheric Parameters from NOAA-16 AMSU Data over Indian Region - Preliminary Results. Mausam 54, 107–110 (2003)
2. Joshi, P.C., Pal, P.K.: Geophysical Parameter Retrieval and Applications Using KALPANA1 Data. In: Seminar on KALPANA1 Satellite and Utilisation, ISRO, pp. 101–110 (2007)
3. Kalsi, S.R.: Use of Satellite Imagery In Tropical Cyclone Intensity Analysis and Forecasting. In: Met. Monograph, Cyclone Warning Division, IMD, India, 83 pages (2002)
4. Kelkar, R.R.: Satellite-based Monitoring and Prediction of Tropical Cyclone Intensity and Movement. Mausam 48, 157–168 (1997)
5. Joshi, P.C., Narayanan, M.S., Bhatia, R.C., Manikiam, B., Kirankumar, A.S., Jayaraman, V.: Evolution of Indian Satellite Meteorological Programme. Mausam 54, 1–12 (2003)
6. George, J., Iyengar, V.S., Nagachenchaiah, K., Kiran Kumar, A.S., Aradhye, B.V., Kaduskar, V.N., Dave, R.K., Nagarani, C.M.: Very High Resolution Radiometers for INSAT2. Current Science 66, 42–66 (1994)
7. Visible and Infrared Images - A Physical Explanation: The Use of Satellite Data in Rainfall Monitoring, pp. 82–123. Academic Press, London (1981)
8. Arkin, P.A., Meisner, B.N.: The Relationship Between large-scale Convective Rainfall and Cloud Top Temperature over the Western Hemisphere during 1982-84. Mon. Wea. Rev. 115, 51–74 (1987)
9. Weldon, R.B., Holmes, S.J.: Water Vapor Imagery Interpretation and Application to Weather Analysis and Forecasting. NOAA Technical Rep., NESDIS, US Department of Commerce, Washington DC, 57, 213 pages (1991)
10. Bhatia, R.C., Bhushan, B., Rajeswara Rao, V.: Application of Water Vapor Imagery Received from INSAT-2E. Current Science 76, 1448–1450 (1999)

Development of Edge Detection Technique for Images Using Adaptive Thresholding

Debabrata Samanta and Goutam Sanyal

Department of Computer Science and Engineering,
National Institute of Technology, Durgapur,
Mahatma Gandhi Avenue, West Bengal, India - 713209
debabrata.samanta369@gmail.com

Abstract. Edge detection is a terminology in image processing and computer vision, particularly in the areas of feature detection and feature extraction, to refer to algorithms which aim at identifying points in a digital image at which the image brightness changes sharply or more formally has discontinuities. In this paper a simple edge detection technique is performed by convoluting the image using a five order mask and then Selecting a threshold from taking the sum of mean value and the standard deviation of the gradient image within a 3 X 3 window. In Canny edge detection a gauss kernel is used for smoothing the image in order to eliminate the noise. But in our algorithm a single mask perform the noise smoothing as well as finding the edge strength.

Keywords: Adaptive Threshold, Background Pixel, Gradient.

1 Introduction

An adaptive edge-detection algorithm is necessary to provide a robust solution that is adaptable to the varying noise levels of these images to help distinguish valid image contents from visual artifacts introduced by noise. The performance of the Canny algorithm depends heavily on the adjustable parameters, which is the standard deviation for the Gaussian filter, and the threshold values, T_1 and T_2 also controls the size of the Gaussian filter [1-11].

In this paper the methodology will be proposed a very simple and less complexive where we also have followed the gradient approach for edge detection and proposed a five order mask to convolute the image which not only find the gradient of the image but also reduced the noises by giving the maximum values at the center of the original signal. After obtaining the gradient of each pixel we have generated the threshold value dynamically region wise. Then the points whose gradient value is greater than the threshold those points are considered as edges.

2 Proposed Method

In our methodology first we have to convolute the image with a five order mask according to the X and Y direction respectively to obtain the gradient of each

K.R. Venugopal and L.M. Patnaik (Eds.): ICIP 2011, CCIS 157, pp. 671–676, 2011.

points. Then the ultimate gradient is obtained by the following formula:

$$\delta f(x, y) \; = \; [G_X G_Y] \; = \; |\,\delta f / \delta x \delta f / \delta y\,|\,. \tag{1}$$

The weight of the vector is :

$$\Delta f(x, y) \; = \; mag(\Delta f(x, y)) \; = \; \sqrt{(G_X^2 + G_Y^2)}\,|\,. \tag{2}$$

Gradients of points give the maximum location at the center of the original signal thus removing the noises. After that threshold value is generated dynamically and region wise means in a image where some portion is brighter and some portion is darker. Then the threshold generated dynamically in the brighter area is higher than the darker portion.

2.1   Convolution with Five Order Mask

We have proposed a 5 X 5 convolution mask Fig. 1. One estimating the gradient in the X direction and the other estimating the gradient in the Y direction. The two components of the gradient are conveniently computed and added in a single pass over the input image using the pseudo-convolution operator shown in the following table:

The mathematical function of mask according to the X and Y direction given below:

$$d_x = 1 \setminus 15\{(P_4 + P_5 + 2P_9 + P_{10} + 3P_{14} + 2P_{15} + 2P_{19} + P_{20} + P_{24} + P_{25}) -$$

$$(P_1 + P_2 + P_6 + 2P_7 + 2P_{11} + 3P_{12} + P_{16} + 2P_{17} + P_{21} + P_{22})\}. \tag{3}$$

$$d_y = 1 \setminus 15\{(P_{16} + 2P_{17} + 3P_{18} + 2P_{19} + P_{20} + 2P_{21} + P_{22} + 2P_{23} + P_{24} + P_{25})$$

$$- (P_1 + P_2 + 2P_3 + P_4 + P_5 + P_6 + 2P_7 + 3P_8 + 2P_9 + P_{10})\}. \tag{4}$$

We can define the 5 X 5 mask according to the X and Y direction as follows:

P_1	P_2	P_3	P_4	P_5
P_6	P_7	P_8	P_9	P_{10}
P_{11}	P_{12}	P_{13}	P_{14}	P_{15}
P_{16}	P_{17}	P_{18}	P_{19}	P_{20}
P_{21}	P_{22}	P_{23}	P_{24}	P_{25}

Fig. 1. Pseudo-Convolution masks for computing approximate gradient magnitude

-1	-1	0	1	1
-1	-2	0	2	1
-2	-3	0	3	2
-1	-2	0	2	1
-1	-1	0	1	1

-1	-1	-2	-1	-1
-1	-2	-3	-2	-1
0	0	0	0	0
1	2	3	2	1
1	1	2	1	1

Fig. 2. Convolution masks (M_X) and Convolution Masks (M_Y)

So the gradient of the pixels is calculated as :

$$G_X(i,j) = I(i,j) * M_X = \frac{1}{15} \sum_{K=\frac{-5}{2}}^{\frac{5}{2}} \sum_{K=\frac{-5}{2}}^{\frac{5}{2}} M_X(i,j)I(i-H,j-K). \quad (5)$$

And other hand,

$$G_Y(i,j) = I(i,j) * M_Y = \frac{1}{15} \sum_{K=\frac{-5}{2}}^{\frac{5}{2}} \sum_{K=\frac{-5}{2}}^{\frac{5}{2}} M_Y(i,j)I(i-H,j-K). \quad (6)$$

where $*$ indicates a discrete convolution,M_X and M_Y are the 5X5 mask,and $I(i,j)$ is a h X w image Fig. 2. Compute the gradient magnitude approximation at each pixel (i,j) as :

$$G(i,j) = \sqrt{((G_X(i,j))^2 + (G_Y(i,j))^2)}. \quad (7)$$

2.2 Adaptive Thresholding

Image thresholding is a segmentation technique because it classifies pixels into two categories. Category1: Pixels whose gray level values fall below the threshold and Category2: Pixels whose gray level values are equal or exceed the threshold. Thus, thresholding creates a binary image. If T is a threshold value, then any pixel (x,y) for which $f(x,y) \geq T$ is called an object point; otherwise the pixel is called a background pixel.

For thresholding we compute adaptive threshold of local intensity variations as:

1. First the overall mean value of the gradient image is calculated. So the pixels having lower edge strength than this mean value are already discarded. Threshold1 = mean (G).
2. Then a 3 X 3 window is splits over the gradient image where the mean and variance of the gradient image within this window are calculated. Then taking the sum of this mean value and standard deviation and this is considered as the threshold value of that pixel. Now if the gradient of this image exceeds this threshold then the pixel is treated as edge.

2.3   Non-Maximal Suppression (NMS)

We calculate the gradient direction at each location in the image Fig. 3 under consideration using the following expression:

$$\theta = arctan(G_Y/G_X). \tag{8}$$

For simplicity, the values of the directions obtained are then approximated $\theta_{x,y}$ to the closest among the following set, $[0, 45, 90, 135]$. We then retain only those $G_{x,y}$ which are greater than the other gradient values in local surrounding and in the corresponding gradient directions $\theta_{x,y}$.

Now we get:

Fig. 3. Edges in Lena image obtained using Sobel method with 0.6 threshold value and Edges in Lena image obtained using adaptive threshold

2.4   Proposed Algorithm

1. Start.
2. Read the image.
3. Obtain gradient of each pixel by convolution using 5X5 mask.
4. Generating threshold adaptively as follows: If $G(x,y) \geq Threshold1$ then

$$mean(x,y) = \frac{1}{9}\sum_{i=0}^{n} G_{(x+n,y+n)}. \tag{9}$$

$$variance(x,y) = \frac{1}{9}\sum_{i=0}^{n} G_{(x+n,y+n)} - mean(x,y). \tag{10}$$

σ (x,y) = $\sqrt{}$ variance (x,y).
Threshold (x,y) = mean$(x,y) + \sigma(x,y)$.
Else the pixels are treated as non edge.

$$Edge(x,y) = 1 \quad if\ G(x,y) \geq Threshold(x,y) = 0\ otherwise. \tag{11}$$

5. Suppressing the binary image using canny non maximal suppression.
6. Edge image is obtained.
7. Stop.

3 Experimental Results

Input image and the final edge image of given image (Fig. 4):

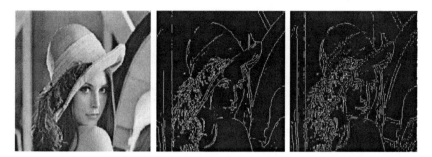

Fig. 4. Original image and Edges in Lena image obtained using Sobel method with 0.6 threshold value and Edges in Lena image obtained using adaptive threshold

4 Conclusions

In case of detecting the edges in an image using a static one or two global threshold value may not be the best solution for all type of images specially for those images where there exists non uniform illumination.

To overcome this non-uniform illumination a robust edge detection approach is presented. The approach consists of two main steps:

1. Obtaining the gradient of each pixel so that higher intensity pixels are getting maximum priority and the others points are flattened out.
   $Threshold1 = mean(G)$.
2. Detecting the edges by generating the threshold adaptively by summing the mean and standard deviation of the local neighbours.

Results in the binary images produced by the combination of the mask and the adaptive thresholding show that the edges of Lena image is robustly detected. In addition, the presented edge detection approach is quite robust towards varying illumination conditions.

It has been observed, that the complexity of the given method is very less than the other existing method. The mask not only find the edge strength but also reduce the noise in a very efficient way where the most popular canny algorithm uses two convolution first for smoothing the image by the very completive Gaussian kernel and then with any other mask in order to find the edge gradient, thus complexity is very high. Moreover, the proposed methodology has been seen to score over the few existing techniques of using adaptive threshold but still the result needs more accuracy.

References

1. Maini, R., Aggarwal, H.: Study and Comparison of Various Image Edge Detection Techniques, International Journal of Image Processing (IJIP) 3(1) (July 2003)

2. Qian, R.J., Huang, T.S.: Optimal Edge Detection in Two-Dimensional Images. IEEE Trans. on Image Processing 5(7) (July 1996)
3. Paplinski, A.P.: Directional Filtering in Edge Detection. IEEE Trans. on Image Processing 7(4) (April 1998)
4. Wong, H.-S., Guan, L.: A Neural Learning Approach for Adaptive Image Restoration using a Fuzzy Model-based Network Architecture. IEEE Trans. on Neural Networks 12(3), 516–531 (2001)
5. Venkatesh, S., Rosin, P.L.: Dynamic-Threshold determination by Local and Global Edge Evaluation. Applications of Artificial Intelligence 1964, 40–50 (1993)
6. Lindeberg, T.: Edge Detection and Ridge Detection with Automatic Scale Selection. International Journal of Computer Vision 30(2), 117–154 (1998)
7. Ahuja, N.: A Transform for Multiscale Image Segmentation by Integrated Edge and Region Detection, vol. 18(12). IEEE Computer Society, Los Alamitos (1996)
8. Marimont, D.H., Rubner, Y.: A Probabilistic Framework for Edge Detection and Scale Selection. In: Sixth International Conference on Computer Vision, January 4-7, pp. 207–214 (1998)
9. Jarvis, J., Roberts, C.: A New Technique for Displaying Continuous Tone Images on a Bilevel Display. IEEE Trans. Commun., 891–898 (August 1976)
10. Widrow, B., Stearns, S.: Adaptive Signal Processing. Prentice-Hall, Englewood Cliffs (July 1985)
11. Wong, H., Guan, L.: A Neural Learning Approach for Adaptive Image Restoration Using a Fuzzy Model-based Network Architecture. IEEE Trans. Neural Network 12(3), 516–531 (2001)

Speeded-Up Robust Features Based Moving Object Detection on Shaky Video

Minqi Zhou[1] and Vijayan K. Asari[2]

[1] Old Dominion University, Norfolk, Virginia, USA
`mzhou001@odu.edu`
[2] University of Dayton, Dayton, Ohio, USA
`Vijayan.Asari@notes.udayton.edu`

Abstract. In this paper we propose a novel moving object detection method on shaky video employing speeded-up robust features (SURF). SURF features are extracted and tracked in each frame to estimate projective transformation parameters. We adopt RANdom SAmple Consensus (RANSAC) to improve the estimation accuracy. We use an efficient background subtraction method to detect moving objects in the scene. The background template is registered and updated in each frame to ensure the stability of the system. Experimental results performed on various video sequences demonstrate that our method can detect moving objects accurately and quickly. The proposed algorithm has the potential to achieve real-time performance.

Keywords: Background Subtraction, Motion Detection, RANSAC, SURF.

1 Introduction

Moving object detection is very important in many applications such as road surveillance and traffic flow statistics assessments. Several main-stream motion detection methods such as temporal difference [1-3], optical flow approach [4-5], and background subtraction method [6-7] are available in the literature. Temporal difference is efficient if the moving objects move relatively fast. This method is simple and has low computational complexity. However, it yields poor performance if both the background and the foreground are complex [3]. In addition, the holes always appear with the detected moving objects [2], which influence the integrality of detected objects.

Optical flow method provides the entire motion information. However, it is computationally intensive, and the noise components would directly influence its performance. Background subtraction method is the most popular and effective one, since it is relatively simple in computing in a static scene. However, this method is sensitive to camera motion, which would probably cause unexpected error. To solve this problem, a Spatial Distribution of Gaussians

K.R. Venugopal and L.M. Patnaik (Eds.): ICIP 2011, CCIS 157, pp. 677–682, 2011.

(SDG) model was proposed in [8]. It classifies each pixel based on SDG model to achieve motion detection with approximate motion compensation. To compensate the motion completely, Zhou et al., [9] proposed a SIFT based moving object detection method. This method accurately compensates the camera motion through SIFT feature descriptors and then extracts the moving objects through background extraction. However, due to its high dimensionality and computational complexity, SIFT feature descriptor is not suitable for real-time applications.

In this paper, we present a fast moving object extraction method based on speeded-up robust features (SURF). It extracts and tracks all the significant features from each frame in the video. The features are matched and then used to estimate and compensate camera motion. We use RANdom SAmple Consensus (RANSAC) to further refine the matching features. The background is registered and updated in each frame, which greatly improve the reliability of our method. In addition, SURF combines fast Hessian matrix and integral image, which greatly reduces the computational time consumption.

The forthcoming sections of the paper are organized as follows: Section 2 introduces the frame work of our method. SURF implementation details including feature extraction and feature matching are presented in Section 3. Section 4 introduces RANSAC, motion estimation and the dynamic background subtraction method. Experimental results and discussion are presented in Section 5, and the conclusions are summarized in Section 6.

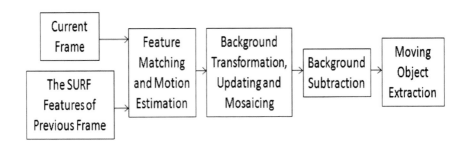

Fig. 1. Flow Diagram of Motion Detection from Shaky Video

Fig. 1 shows the flow diagram of the proposed method. First, we extract the features from current frame through SURF. Those features are matched with the ones extracted from the previous frame. RANSAC is used to eliminate the outliers. Subsequently, we estimate the inter-frame motion through least squares method. We adopt projective model to transform the background using the pre-computed parameters. After that, the background is subtracted from the current frame. The remaining pixels which are greater than the threshold are marked as moving objects. Finally, the background template is updated by mosaicing the trivial areas with the current frame.

2   SURF Implementation Details

Speeded-up Robust Feature (SURF) was proposed in 2006 [10], which has been proved to be equivalent or even better than other feature descriptors with respect to repeatability, distinctiveness, and robustness [10-12]. SURF detector is based on Hessian matrix which contributes to its good performance in accuracy. It uses the determinant of fast Hessian to locate the feature points. SURF approximates Laplacian of Gaussian by using box filter representation of corresponding kernels to bulid the image pyramid. The kernel approximation is efficient in computation by using the integral images.

SURF adopts Haar wavelet in x and y directions to compute a reproducible orientation from a circular region of radius 6s around the keypoint, where s is the scale of a detected feature. The responses are weighed with keypoint centered Gaussian filter (2s). The dominant orienation is calculated by summing the responses in x and y directions within a sliding window of size $pi/3$, and the orientation with the biggest amplitude is selected as dominant orientation. To achieve rotation invariance, SURF builds up a square region aligned to the dominant orientation with the size of the suquare as 20s. The square region is further divided in to 4x4 blocks. In each sub-window, it has 55 space sample points and totally 25 Haar wavelet responses are calculated. To take the polarity of intensity changes into account, the absolute value of the responses are computed. The responses can be written as:

$$V = (\sum d_x, \sum d_y, \sum |d_x|, \sum |d_y|)$$

. (1)

The responses are weighed with a Gaussian filter centered at the keypoint which has 3.3s standard deviation. Finally we can get the SURF descriptors by chaining the four-dimensional descriptors in each block. Computing the Harr wavelet through integral images decreases computation time as each wavelet requires only six operations.

We drop the unreliable matching through comparing the Euclidean distance. The measurement actually compares the ratio of distance from the closest neighbor to the distance of the next closest neighbor with a predetermined threshold. The threshold is set as 0.6 in our experiment.

3   Motion Estimation and Dynamic Background Subtraction

Since the motion between frames is three dimensional, it is observed that projective transformation is the best model to describe the real camera motion. We use least squares method to estimate the motion parameters to with the matched features. Though we have roughly eliminated those unreliable features, the local motion vectors still contain some wrong matched features, or the matched features belong to moving object, which cannot reflect the camera motion. Since least squares method is sensitive to outliers, it would introduce estimation error if we directly estimate the motion parameters with those features. To solve this problem and get the accurate motion parameters, we adopt RANdom SAmple Consensus (RANSAC) to refine the matching features [13]. This procedure is to repeatedly guess the model parameters with minimal subsets of data drawn randomly from the input matching features until we get the best result. We can transform the background with the pre-computed motion parameters. The background template is directly subtracted from the current frame. If the pixel difference is smaller than certain preset threshold, it is set to 0 and is classified as the background, otherwise it is set to 255 and is classified as the foreground. To get the new background template at frame n, we update and mosaic the previous background template.

4   Experimental Results

To boost the processing speed and ensure the number of extracted features per frame; the size of all input sequences is fixed to 240x320. The experiment is carried out with Visual Studio 2008 and Windows Vista Operating System on Intel Core 2 Duo 2.4GHz CPU system.

We compare our moving object detection method with the direct background substraction method and the method presented in [1] which is based on temporal difference. We adopt false positive (FP) rate (background pixel being classfied to foreground) and false negative (FN) rate (missing foreground pixel) to evaluate the performance of different methods. We use the manual segetmentaion to get the ground truth moving object. The experimental results are given in Table 1. The proposed method has the minimun FN and FP on average, which means our method can extract relatively moving objects yielding minimum noise among all the other methods. Fig. 2 shows the pictorial illustration of the experimental results. As we can see from Fig. 2, direct background subtraction has poor performance. Since the moving object is covered by noise, it is almost impossible to directly extract the forground from the background. The method based on temporal difference produces much less noise. However, it cannot detect the moving object correctly if the object moves slowly. In contrast with the aforementioned algorithms, our method has better performance. Though it still present some noise in the resulting image, these noise can be filtered out through morphological operations. In addition, our method costs much less time than SIFT based motion detection. SURF based motion detection only costs about 150ms on average compared with SIFT which costs about 2s to process each frame.

5   Conclusions

A fast motion detection method based on the speeded-up robust feature extraction and tracking phenomena has been presented in this paper. We compared the performance of the proposed method with direct background substraction,

Table 1. Performance comparison of different moving object detection methods

Image	FP(a)	FN(a)	FP(b)	FN(b)	FP(c)	FN(c)
Direct-Substraction	26.07%	1.03%	33.29%	0.54%	42.48%	0.14%
Method in [1]	1.38%	5.37%	1.01%	2.33%	1.25%	0.65%
Proposed method	0.51%	1.21%	0.34%	0.51%	0.27%	0.12%

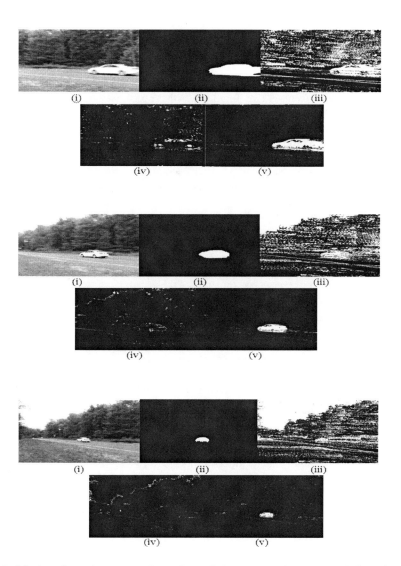

Fig. 2. Motion detection comparison. In each image set, from upper left to bottom right: (i). Original image, (ii). Ground truth, (iii). Direct background subtraction, (iv). Method in [1], (v). Our proposed method

temporal difference based method and SIFT based motion detection. The experimental results show that the SURF based technique outperforms all other state of the art methods in detecting moving objects and also yields minimum noise in the detection results. Since we can directly apply the box filter of any size on the image, the convolution process can be finished in parallel. This would help the application of additional hardware to exploit more parallel execution which boosts the speed of the system and makes real-time implementation possible for moving object detection in larger video frames.

References

1. Yu, Z., Chen, Y.: A Real-Time Motion Detection Algorithm for Traffic Monitoring Systems based on Consecutive Temporal Difference. In: 7th Asian Control Conference, ASCC, pp. 1594–1599 (2009)
2. Choi, Y.-s., Zaijun, P., Kim, S.-w., Kim, T.-h., Park, C.-b.: Salient Motion Information Detection Technique Using Weighted Subtraction Image and Motion Vector. In: ICHIT International Conference, vol. 1, pp. 263–269 (2006)
3. Hu, F.-Y., Zhang, Y.-N., Yao, L.: An Effective Detection Algorithm for Moving Object with Complex Background. Machine Learning and Cybernetics 8, 5011–5015 (2005)
4. Denman, S., Fookes, C., Sridharan, S.: Improved Simultaneous Computation of Motion Detection and Optical Flow for Object Tracking. In: Digital Image Computing: Techniques and Applications, pp. 175–182 (2009)
5. Baier, V., Sahin, F.: Detection and Tracking of High Motion Objects in Arm Robotics. In: Fifth International Conference on ICSCCW, pp. 1–4 (2009)
6. Kurylyak, Y.: A Real-Time Motion Detection for Video Surveillance System. In: Intelligent Data Acquisition and Advanced Computing Systems: Technology and Applications, pp. 386–389 (2009)
7. Cucchiara, R., Grana, C., Piccardi, M., Prati, A.: Detecting Moving Objects, Ghosts, and Shadows in Video Streams. IEEE Transactions on Pattern Analysis and Machine Intelligence 25(10), 1337–1342 (2003)
8. Ren, Y., Chua, C.-S., Ho, Y.-K.: Motion Detection with Non-Stationary Background. Image Analysis and Processing, 78–83 (2001)
9. Zhou, D., Wang, L., Cai, X., Liu, Y.: Detection of Moving Targets with a Moving Camera. In: IEEE International Conference on Robotics and Biomimetics (ROBIO), pp. 677–681 (2009)
10. Bay, H., Ess, A., Tuytelaars, T., Van Gool, L.: SURF: Speeded Up Robust Features. Computer Vision and Image Understanding (CVIU) 110(3), 346–359 (2008)
11. Ramisa, A., Vasudevan, S., Aldavert, D.: Evaluation of the SIFT Object Recognition Method in Mobile Robots. In: Proceedings of the 12th International Conference of the Catalan Artificial Intelligence Research and Development, pp. 9–18 (2009)
12. Juan, L., Gwun, O.: A Comparison of SIFT, PCA-SIFT and SURF. International Journal of Image Processing (IJIP) 3(4), 143–152 (2009)
13. Fischler, M.A., Bolles, R.C.: Random Sample Consensus: A Paradigm for Model Fitting with Applications to Image Analysis and Automated Cartography. Communication of ACM 4(6), 381–395 (1981)

Author Index